JOE FULKS
26
JOHNNY FEAGAN
20
BENNIE PURCELL
21
GARRETT BESHEAR
16
HOWIE CRITTENDEN
19
JEFF MARTIN
15
PAUL KING
30
54
5
24
Restrooms
MURRAY

Banner Years

Murray State Basketball

RACERS™

1925-2013

Acclaim Press
— Your Next Great Book —
P.O. Box 238
Morley, MO 63767
(573) 472-9800
www.acclaimpress.com

Banner Years
Murray State Basketball
1925-2013

Authors:
Will Aubrey, Sid Easley, Steve Parker, Kim Trevathan, Jimmy Wilder

Published By:
Acclaim Press

Presented By:
Proud To Be A Racer Publications, Inc.

Compiled and Edited By:
Jimmy Wilder and Will Aubrey

Assisted By:
Duane Bolin, Tim Tucker and Kim Trevathan

Layout and Design By:
M. Frene Melton, Acclaim Press

Contributing Writers:
Duane Bolin, Justice Bill Cunningham, Ricky Martin, Eddie Sheridan, Dusty Luthy Shull, Kevin Stewart, Gary P. West, Dave Winder

Photo/Memorabilia Credits:
Scott Adams, Lance Allison, Marilyn Aubrey, Tab Brockman, Billy Chumbler, Howie Crittenden, Nancy Hodges Darnell, Johnny Gingles, Jim Jennings, Barry Johnson, Cal Luther, Shirley Martin, Herb McPherson, Don McQuistion, Julie McQuistion, Fred Mullane (Murray State Athletics), Murray State Athletics Media Relations, Murray State Pogue Special Collections Library, Steve Newton, Ohio Valley Conference, Bennie Purcell, Bill Rayburn, Johnny Reagan, Lindy Suiter, Dr. Randy Taylor, Kevin Weaks

Library of Congress Cataloging-in-Publication Data

Aubrey, Will.
Banner Years: Murray State Basketball / by Will Aubrey, Sid Easley, Jimmy Wilder, Steve Parker, Kim Trevathan.
pages cm
ISBN 978-1-938905-35-3 (alk. paper) -- ISBN 1-938905-35-0 (alk. paper) 1. Murray State University--Basketball--History. 2. Murray State Raccers (Basketball team)--History. I. Title.
GV885.43.M87A84 2013
796.323'630976992--dc23
2013038750

First Printing: 2013
Printed in the United States of America
10 9 8 7 6 5 4 3 2 1

This publication was produced using available information. The publisher regrets it cannot assume responsibility for errors or omissions.

Contents

Racer Basketball by the Numbers

1,500 ALL-TIME WINS

.642 WON-LOST PERCENTAGE

26 CONSECUTIVE WINNING SEASONS

610 OHIO VALLEY CONFERENCE WINS

.658 OVC WON-LOST PERCENTAGE

23 OVC REGULAR-SEASON CHAMPIONSHIPS

1950-51	1982-83	1993-94	1999-00
1963-64	1987-88	1994-95	2005-06
1967-68	1988-89	1995-96	2009-10
1968-69	1989-90	1996-97	2010-11
1979-80	1990-91	1997-98	2011-12
1981-82	1991-92	1998-99	

15 OVC TOURNAMENT CHAMPIONSHIPS

1951	1991	1998	2006
1964	1992	1999	2010
1988	1995	2002	2012
1990	1997	2004	

15 NCAA TOURNAMENT APPEARANCES

1964	1991	1998	2006
1969	1992	1999	2010
1988	1995	2002	2012
1990	1997	2004	

7 NATIONAL INVITATION TOURNAMENT APPEARANCES

1980	1983	1994	2011
1982	1989	1996	

6 NAIA TOURNAMENT APPEARANCES

1938	1941	1943	1952
1939	1942		

3 NAIA TOURNAMENT FINAL FOURS

1941	1943	1952

Foreword

by Bennie Purcell

The 2011-12 Murray State season was special, but it would be inappropriate for anyone to separate it from the university's long-standing winning tradition in men's basketball.

Going all the way back to MSU's first game in January 1926, Murray State has had outstanding teams, players and coaches.

This was never more apparent than in March 2012, when former Racer coaches Mark Gottfried and Mick Cronin saw their North Carolina State and University of Cincinnati teams advance to the Round of 32 in the NCAA Tournament, where they were joined by coach Steve Prohm's first Murray State team, which featured three outstanding seniors (Ivan Aska, Donte Poole and Jewuan Long), an All-American guard (Isaiah Canaan) and an imposing shot blocker (Ed Daniel).

Eighty-eight years of Racer basketball have produced these enviable results: 1,500 victories, 26 consecutive winning seasons and an Ohio Valley Conference-best 39 championships. Murray State has participated 15 times in the NCAA Tournament, seven times in the National Invitation Tournament and six times in the NAIA Tournament, making it to the title game in 1941 and 1952.

There is great optimism about the future of Murray State basketball. If one knows the history of the program or has followed the Racers for even a short period of time, why wouldn't there be?

The remarkable 31-2 season of 2011-12 and No. 12 ranking in the final Associated Press Top-25 poll are reasons enough for Racer fans to be on fire.

Another is the university's commitment to provide MSU basketball with the financial resources and amenities needed to continue its winning tradition – and ultimately move the Racers beyond the NCAA Tournament's Round of 32.

The CFSB Center, Murray State's home basketball arena, leaves little to be desired, now that an adjoining $3.5 million practice facility has opened. The practice facility includes the first MSU Hall of Champions, a section of which is devoted to honoring past Racer basketball teams, players and coaches.

As a former player and coach, I understand the challenges faced by Racer basketball and the rewards that come from being a Murray State student-athlete. I feel it is unrealistic to expect another 31-win season anytime soon, but I'm confident Murray State will win a lot of games every year, contend for OVC championships and be recognized nationally for its excellence. Sometime in the not-to-distant future I expect to see Isaiah Cannan's jersey retired and displayed above the CFSB Center court, hanging there with the other retired jerseys and OVC championship banners.

I'm proud to call myself a Racer and be a part of *BANNER YEARS* and the legacy of Murray State basketball. Those who read this book will know why and hopefully share my passion for Racer basketball.

Bennie Purcell

Preface

by Jimmy Wilder

BANNER YEARS: Murray State Basketball 1925-2013 is a testimony to the determination of Bennie Purcell, whose defining attribute might be his drive to persevere even when doors sometimes close.

For most of the past decade, Purcell talked the talk, trying to interest someone in writing a book about the history of Murray State Racer basketball. But MSU's first 1,000-point career scorer had no takers until the summer of 2009, when he and yours truly sat together at a gathering of memorabilia collectors. We discussed his desire to see something in print devoted specifically to Racer basketball other than media guides or special newspaper sections.

Later that day, I made a commitment to help Bennie walk the walk, outlining a plan that I felt could eventually lead to a coffee table-style book telling the story of Racer basketball in words and pictures. And now, after countless interviews and phone calls, considerable research, untold hours at the computer, and an extended fund-raising campaign, Bennie's wish has come to fruition.

BANNER YEARS covers the first 88 years of Racer basketball, including the magical 31-5 season of 2009-10 which included a stirring 66-65 win over Vanderbilt in the NCAA tournament, and an almost surreal 2011-12 season that saw the Racers ranked as high as 7th in the nation and produced another victory in the NCAA tournament, this time over Colorado State. Still, the book – produced my Proud To Be A Racer Publications of Murray, Ky., and published by Acclaim Press of Morley, Mo. – should not be viewed simply from a historical perspective. My intent as editor and one of its authors is to provide readers stories of Murray State's most acclaimed players and coaches, and to acknowledge others whose stories merit inclusion.

BANNER YEARS also documents the impact fans, staff and support personnel have had in making Racer basketball nationally prominent. It includes a number of interesting anecdotes. Memories of days gone by will also be rekindled. Perhaps the book might even encourage former Racers to reconnect.

While some things must be shared in private, *BANNER YEARS* offers even the most informed supporter insights into Racer basketball. Every effort has been made to verify all the facts in this book, but a few may be stated a little differently than they were when they transpired – memories change over time, and some sources are known to embellish their tales.

Here's one *BANNER YEARS* tidbit from Murray realtor Bill Kopperud that partially checks out. "I was listening on the radio to the game when Bennie

Purcell scored 21 points on his 21st birthday and Murray State won by 21 points," Kopperud said. "It was really neat because Bennie's jersey number was 21." Kopperud shared this information with Bennie and me at lunch at the social.

One problem. On Bennie's 21st birthday (Dec. 10, 1950), Murray State didn't have a game. But on Bennie's 22nd birthday, he did score 22 points and the Racers won at home by 22 points, beating Evansville, 82-60. Afterward he was given the game ball.

Kopperud gets a pass for his faux pas – he was eight-years of age when Purcell turned 21, an elementary school kid infatuated with Murray State basketball and Bennie Purcell.

"Bennie was an idol of mine," he explained. "It was amazing how he could dribble the ball and get up and down the floor. I pretended I could handle the ball like him, but that was only in my dreams. I loved watching Murray State games when Bennie was on the team, and when I wasn't at the games I was by the radio, listening to every word."

Before moving beyond birthdays, I want to mention this unusual happening involving a Racer that you can take to the bank.

I was the Murray State sports information director when an MSU road game against Arkansas State started in one year (Dec. 31, 1991) and ended another (Jan. 1, 1992). Maurice Cannon, who wore uniform No. 24, had his 22nd birthday on that New Years Day, but there was no celebrating in the Racer locker room even though Cannon scored 26 points.

Why no game ball for Cannon as a birthday present? Arkansas State beat the Racers, 63-59. Why was this MSU-ASU game played over two calendar days? Tipoff was 11 p.m. because the game was part of an Ohio Valley Conference-ESPN television package that allowed mid-major conferences slotted times when select games were carried by the national cable network. Naturally, this one ended well past midnight, around 1:30 a.m.

Now, back to Bennie Purcell and my involvement with *BANNER YEARS*, which represents a labor of love for Bennie and me, Will Aubrey, Steve Parker, Lindy Suiter, Sid Easley, Kim Trevathan and Dave Winder.

Purcell's association with Murray State goes all the way back to 1948, when he was a freshman guard on coach Harlan Hodges' first team. It resumed in 1963, when he was hired by Cal Luther to be one of his assistants. And it continues today, as he lives near campus, seldom misses a Racer basketball game, and is a great ambassador for the university. For an in-depth look at Bennie, read the *BANNER YEARS* chapter written by Will Aubrey.

My association with Murray State pales in comparison to Purcell's, but I was twice employed by the MSU athletic department (from 1980-83 as the first Racer Club/promotions director and from 1991-93 as sports information director). "Retired" and living in Murray since 2004, after working for six years as director of athletic development at UNC Asheville, my love and respect for MSU and Racer hoops seems to grow yearly.

I hope that is reflected in my effort to help write a book about Murray State basketball for public enjoyment. I know for certain the timing for *BANNER YEARS* couldn't be better.

This book is dedicated to my wife, Joanna Sykes Wilder, who was always in my corner during the long journey to get BANNER YEARS *to press.*
– Jimmy Wilder

MURRAY
STATE UNIVERSITY

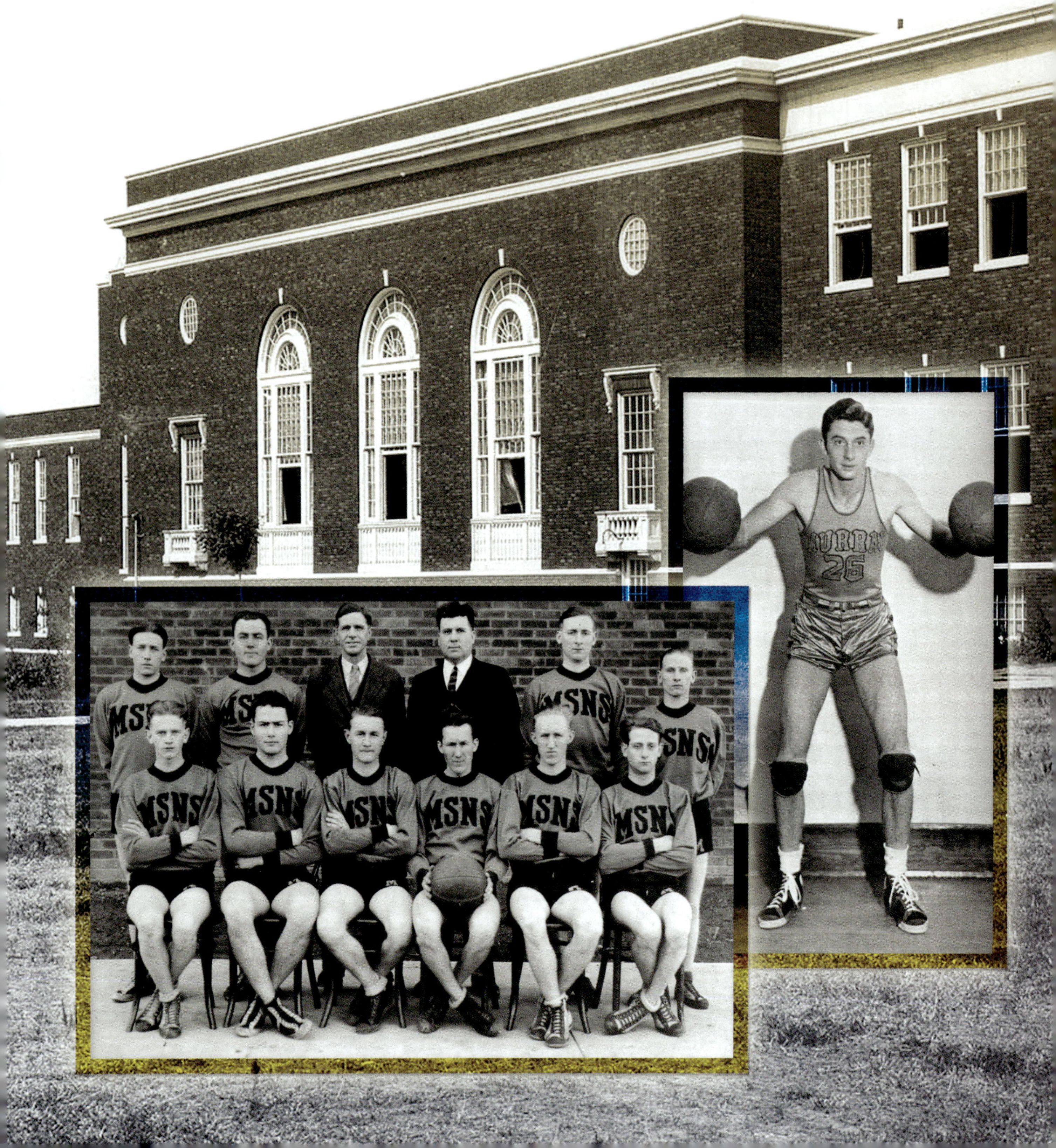

The Early Years

THE EARLY YEARS

by Sid Easley

At the base of the statue of Rainey T. Wells, the founder of Murray State University, is a proclamation written by Dr. C.S. Lowry, a renowned scholar and faculty member. He wrote of the influence Wells had on the University, "His dedicated service as its second President (1926-1932) endowed it with its fierce pride and undaunted spirit."

Rainey T. Wells

John Wesley Carr

The history of Murray State basketball is inseparable from the history of the university itself. Both are the result of the determination of people, despite the odds against them, to do their best and to become the best they are capable of becoming. Coach John Wooden referred to it as "Achieving Competitive Greatness."

The university's history began with a story that has become legendary. Rainey T. Wells, Murray lawyer, state legislator, and chairman of the powerful Kentucky State Tax Commission led a spirited group of Calloway County citizens in 1922 in raising $100,000 to assure that the new Normal School was located in the then small town of Murray, Kentucky. The commission determining the college site had announced that the town receiving the Normal School would be required to raise $100,000 which would be used to construct the first building on the campus. This was a large sum of money in 1922. Rainey T. Wells presented Murray's case before the commission and in an impressive ending said to the members, "others have told you what they intend to do; but Murray and Calloway County have already done it." Then he dramatically laid two certified checks on the table before the Commission totaling $100,000.00.

Wells' dogged determination to bring the Normal School to Murray did not end with the commission's decision. He later told his grandson Wells Lovett, "I didn't want Murray to be just any teachers college. I wanted it to be equal to the great colleges of the country." He continued his mission by seeking the best educational leader he could find for the school's first president. In the end he chose Dr. John Wesley Carr, a nationally recognized scholar who was a native of Indiana and a graduate of Columbia University, to become the first leader of the Normal School.

The two men worked together with incredible efficiency to make the college what it is today. Dr. Carr said, "Rainey and I agreed that I would take care of the college and he would take care of the funding and the politics."

Knowing that institutions are only as good as the people who lead them, both Carr and Wells searched diligently for the best faculty and the best coaches they could find. Politics was not a part of the selection process. They wanted the very best they could get.

In the 1930's, speech and debate were extremely competitive endeavors, and young men coming out of high school were often skilled debaters. A debate team was soon established at Murray, and Rainey Wells later told Lovett, "I did not want Murray to have a second rate debate team. I wanted them to have the best and to compete against the best."

Location of Murray, Kentucky

According to the Murray State yearbook, *The Shield*, the Murray team debated a squad from Cambridge in 1931, "Before the largest debate audience (2000) ever, the Murray Debaters met Cambridge, England in the most interesting debate of the year. At the request of the English speakers, no decision was given."

In 1932 the Murray debaters defeated Oxford College of England, the University of Kentucky, the University of North Carolina, and the University of South Carolina. They were one of the top four teams in the 32 team Southern Debate Tournament.

Murray State had only been in existence nine years, and they were competing and winning against the best in the country.

In 1933 the country was mired in the Great Depression. Murray State and Western Kentucky were natural rivals. Before Murray was founded most people from far western Kentucky seeking a college education went to Western. It had been founded in 1906 and was an established institution when Murray began offering classes in 1923.

The two schools quickly developed a heated rivalry in basketball, football, and baseball. In 1932 Western came to Murray and won the football game 6-0 before 4,000 fans. At the time the football field was immediately north of the auditorium. Murray had just beaten Louisville 105-0, and the loss hurt.

Murray had most of its players back in 1933, and it was undefeated going into the game at Western. Newspapers, including the *Louisville Courier Journal*, chronicled the game as one of the great rivalries of the decade. Governor of Kentucky Ruby Laffoon was in attendance, joining 6,000 fans for Western's homecoming.

Rainey Wells had retired as President, but he still had a fiery determination to make Murray the best. He arranged for a special train to carry the team, cheerleaders, and fans to Western from Murray. It was a festive day, and the Murray fan base was hungry for a victory. So was Rainey Wells.

During the first half of the game Wells sat in the stands in a prominent seat by his friend, the governor. At halftime he decided he could take it no longer. He had to go to the sidelines and do anything he could to help Murray win the game. The story of Rainey Wells walking the sidelines and exhorting his Thoroughbreds during the second half has been told countless times.

Wells Lovett remembers the *Louisville Courier Journal* report, "Murray's goal line stand has never before been equaled in the history of the state. Some of the Murray players would have died in their tracks if necessary to stop Western."

"Granddaddy always spoke of that day with great pride." Lovett said. Murray came away with a hard fought 20-6 victory.

EXPLANATION OF THE TERM "NORMAL SCHOOL"

An article written by Don Pepper of the *Paducah Sun-Democrat* for a September 24, 1973 Murray State University 50th Anniversary special edition insert that appeared in the *Murray Ledger & Times* offers an explanation for the term "normal school." According to Pepper, at the time of the university's founding in 1922 as Murray State Normal School, normal schools were schools in Kentucky that taught the four high school grades and the first two years of college. When Murray State first began classes in 1923 at Murray High School, its student body consisted of 87 students of college rank. All others were of high school standing. One year later, Murray State students of sophomore rank were gaining classroom experience by doing practice teaching at the recently organized Murray Training School, which consisted of elementary school students, grades one through eight.

Basketball in Far Western Kentucky

Far western Kentucky was basketball country; and farm boys from small rural high schools loved the sport. In a day when recreation other than hard farm work was limited, young men spent hours on make-shift dirt courts, dribbling, shooting, playing horse, or rough house one-on-one. Out of that hardscrabble competition there emerged some outstanding athletes. Many of these young competitors, who would not otherwise have had the opportunity, matriculated to nearby Murray to play "college" ball. It was their opportunity to succeed in life.

In the years from 1929 to 1959 five small schools in the eight county Jackson Purchase won the Kentucky state basketball tournament – Heath, Sharpe, Brewers, Cuba and North Marshall – an amazing feat when compared with larger towns and more populated sections of the state. The love people had for basketball and the excitement of having a team nearby created an avid fan base for Murray State. Basketball was king in the Purchase area of Kentucky and has remained so to this day. It is this passion that has sustained Murray's winning tradition through the years.

A New College and a New Gym

The law establishing Murray State Normal School was passed in 1922; but the first classes were held in what is now Murray Middle School in September 1923.The first building on Murray State's campus was built with the $100,000 that Murray residents had raised to assure the school was built in Murray.

That first building was called The Administration Building (now Wrather Hall). It contained classrooms, an auditorium, stage, orchestra pit, and a temporary gymnasium. Classes were first held in that building in 1924.

By 1925, with a substantial state appropriation, a new administration building (now Wilson Hall) was built. This building contained more classrooms, a library, a bookstore, a gymnasium for boys' basketball, and a gymnasium for girls' basketball. This enabled Murray State to field its first boys' basketball team.

The university catalog from that year described the gym thusly, "The new gymnasium is 50 feet by 70 feet and has seating capacity for 800 spectators."

Murray resident Popeye Ross attended the college training school and recalled playing basketball there, "I recall there was a good hardwood floor in the boys' gym, and the spectators would sit in a balcony on the west end of the gym. The boys' gym was on the ground floor on the north side of the building, and the girls' gym was right above it on another floor."

"The cheerleaders led cheers in the balcony with the fans," Thelma Bailey of Murray remembered.

Basketball in the Twenties and a Coach is Hired

Ross described the style of basketball at the time. "There wasn't much fast breaking in that day," he said. "No one shot a jump shot, and everyone shot their free throws from between their legs. All shots were two handed and shots from outside were always what we call set-shots. The real difference in the game was that the teams jumped at center court after every basket. Many games were low scoring, and in the early years there was no time limit in getting the ball across the center line."

Carr and Wells knew there was no substitute for a good coach. They spent a lot of time investigating prospects and concluded that Carlisle Cutchin, a coach and teacher from Mayfield was the best leader they could find. He was a scholar, a great teacher and loved athletics. On May 12, 1925 Cutchin was hired and soon was assigned a plethora of responsibilities. He was to teach mathematics and history, organize the physical education department, and coach the football, basketball, and baseball teams. He was a perfect selection, and was an example of the multi-talent-

Carlisle Cutchin

ed people Carr and Wells hired in those early days of the college.

THE FIRST TEAM AND THE YEARS 1926, 27, AND 28

In the fall of 1925, the first year of basketball at Murray, 40 young men went out for the team. After several weeks of what *The Shield* described as "strenuous practice," Coach Cutchin divided the men into four intramural teams which competed against each other. Out of those teams he selected the squad that would represent the new Murray Normal School.

The first intercollegiate game at Murray was played in the Wilson Hall gym on January 17, 1926 against a team called Will Mayfield. Murray lost that first game 31-14. Will Mayfield was a Baptist college then located across the Mississippi River in Marble Hill, Missouri. It closed in 1934. They lost to

Above: *A girls physical education class in the Wilson Hall gymnasium, circa 1926.*
Left: *1925-26 Murray State men's basketball team.*
Below: *Outside view of Wilson Hall, which had the first basketball home court.*

Will Mayfield again in the second game of the season 40-19.

After only two games the winning tradition began. In the third game of the season the young Murray cagers experienced victory for the first time as they defeated Hall-Moody, another Baptist school located in Martin, Tenn. 27-25.

The team went on to a winning season that year as they won their final game in February against Bethel College (from Russellville, Kentucky) 31-14. Their record for the first year was 9-5.

The leading scorer for Murray Normal that first season was Preston Ty Holland who would later become a legendary high school football coach at Murray High and have the school's football stadium named for him. Holland led the team in scoring in 1926, 1927, and 1928, averaging 11, 11, and 9.2 points. The 1927 *Shield* said of him, "'Ty' played the position of forward in fine style. He was a little slow on the floor, but made up for this with his keen eye for the basket."

Joining Holland on the '26, '27, and '28 teams was Auburn Wells, a local boy known for his strength and

Ty Holland

Outside view of Lovett Auditorium, which had the second basketball home court.

Murray State's Teams Become Thoroughbreds

In their first four years of competition, Murray State's teams did not have an official nickname, although they were sometimes called the Cutchinmen. That changed in June of 1928 when school president Rainey T. Wells announced the teams would be called Thoroughbreds. He also said an image of the head of Man O' War, perhaps the greatest racehorse of all time, would be the college's athletics logo.

The nickname Wells gave the teams and the logo he chose for them were popular. And in January of 1929 the *Murray State College News* showed its support for the nickname by publishing an editorial titled *A Thoroughbred Code.*

Man O' War

The text of the editorial:

"Athletes of Murray State Teachers College have a name that should inspire them to become outstanding, not only in physical vigor but in moral and mental fiber. To be a Thoroughbred is to be well-bred, to be a gentleman.

"A Thoroughbred will not:

"Break training by smoking, drinking or keeping late hours; disobey the instruction of the coach whether on the field or on the campus; be guilty of foul play in any game; use profanity in public or private; complain if he is taken out of the game; or underrate his teammates' ability.

"A Thoroughbred will:

"Always practice at specified times; play for the love of the game and the honor of Murray State Teachers College; be modest in victory and honest in defeat; accept gratefully the decisions of the officials; and play for the team, not for the grandstand.

"Players who break training are not Thoroughbreds."

defensive ability. An outstanding athlete, Wells also starred on the football and baseball teams.

After graduation and graduate school he returned to Murray State where he became a respected political science professor, and a noted terror on the handball court.

The 1927 team also played in the Wilson Hall gym, and Murray again ended that year with a winning record, 11-9. 1928 was the last year games were played in the Wilson Hall and was also one of the rare years Murray State posted a losing record as they finished 8-9.

Basketball is Played "On the Stage"

The 1928 season was special in another way. The Thoroughbreds were given a new place to play basketball. For the players and fans it was truly a luxurious facility that doubled as an auditorium for music, drama, speech, and all types of public presentations, together with a full sized basketball court.

Dr. Carr described the new auditorium that was opened in January of 1928, "The auditorium is one of the largest in Kentucky with a seating capacity of 4,000," he said. For a basketball game it held up to 3,500. The building also contained classrooms, offices, and dressing rooms, and comfortable seating. Its cost was $176,549.37.

J.D. Rayburn who played on that court for four years described it this way, "It was a regulation sized court. The scorekeeper sat in an elevated platform on the north wall. The teams' benches were also on the north side of the floor facing the fans. The scorekeeper used a bell he rang by hand rather than an electric buzzer. Often the ball would go out into the crowd and would be thrown back by a fan. The cheerleaders would come up on the stage during timeouts and at halftime, and lead cheers. Since the stage was recessed fans had to seat themselves in areas where they could see the entire court. If you sat too far to either side you could only see one goal. You had to get there early to get good seats. We had good crowds, and when we played Western we filled it up."

1928-29 • 12-8

The 1929 season brought brighter days to Thoroughbred basketball. Murray State began to play larger schools such as Delta State from Cleveland, Mississippi and Southern Illinois College at Carbondale, Ill. They swept Delta State in two games that year, but lost to Southern Illinois twice – the last game by two points. Still, they finished 12-8 and outscored their opponents 785 to 602. A tall center from Missouri began

John Miller

Ladies Come First for Murray State and Western Kentucky

The Murray State-Western Kentucky athletics rivalry didn't start in the 1931-32 school year when the school's football, men's basketball and baseball teams played for the first time. Mark down the 1928-29 school year for when Murray and Western first competed head-to-head in athletics, because that is when the MSU and WKU women's basketball teams played twice. Western won both games. Western also beat Murray twice in the '29-30 season. The schools didn't play again in women's basketball until the 1973-74 season, when Murray beat Western three times. Murray State discontinued its women's basketball program for 39 years after the 1931-32 season, which ended prematurely with the school declining an invitation for its team to participate in the AAU National Tournament.

1928-29 Murray State women't basketball team

to make a difference in the team. John Miller became a stalwart in the all-important center jump averaging 10.5 points a game in 1929. He later coached the freshman team when J.D. Rayburn played.

1930's Produce 175 Wins, 51 Losses and Three Championships

The 1930's should be remembered for the success Murray State basketball enjoyed with Carlisle Cutchin as its coach: 175 wins, only 51 losses, a Mississippi Valley Conference tournament championship, two Southern Intercollegiate Athletic Association titles and two appearances in the NAIB tournament in Kansas City, Mo.

The NAIB tournament determined the national small college champion. It is now called the NAIA tournament and is still played annually in Kansas City.

The decade of the 1930's is also when the Murray State-Western Kentucky rivalry began (1931-32) in football, men's basketball and baseball. And it's when Thoroughbred basketball moved to the Carr Health Building, a facility that had three basketball courts and a pool. It also served as the classroom building for Murray State's physical education department.

Following the 1930 football season, basketball became more of a focus for Cutchin because he gave up his football coaching duties. Initially, a few football players continued to have prominent roles on the basketball team, but that trend ended by the middle of the decade.

Murray State's recruitment of Willard Bagwell, who became a four-year starter and a double-figure scorer, created a lot of buzz at the beginning of the decade as the Thoroughbreds posted a 19-2 record and won the MVC tournament in the '29-30 season. It reached its pinnacle when Murray State won 27 of 30 games and finished third in the NAIB tournament in the '37-38 season.

Willard Bagwell

Why Are Murray State's School Colors Blue and Gold?

A replica of a shield has always been the seal of Murray State University and the school colors have always been blue and gold. Here's an explanation: The seal is taken from the heraldic coat-of-arms of the family of William Murray, the Earl of Mansfield and Lord Chief Justice of Great Britain in 1756. The shield is blue with a double gold border and has three stars, which represent hope, endeavor and achievement. William Murray was an ancestor of United States congressman John L. Murray, from whom the city of Murray and Murray State University take their names.

The decade ended with the Thoroughbreds making their second consecutive appearance in the NAIB tournament.

1929-30 • 19-2

• MVC Tournament Champion

The 1929-30 season was a banner year for Murray State basketball as the 19-2 Thoroughbreds won the Mississippi Valley Conference Tournament in a dominating fashion.

They opened the season by winning their first four games handily.

Willard Bagwell, the "flashy star" from Heath's state championship team, led Murray State in scoring and was followed closely by William Smith, another star player from Heath. Jim Miller who had been the previous year's captain was third in scoring.

Hal Houston Sr., the father of Dr. Hal E. Houston, long time team physician and Racer fan extraordinaire, was the team's play-maker at guard.

With Murray State 4-0, the *Paducah Sun-Democrat* said of him, "Hal Houston, the outstanding guard for the Murray aggregation, has played 117 minutes, that being more than any other person."

The entire region raged with excitement before the January 18 game against West Tennessee, now the University of Memphis, on the stage in the brand new auditorium.

The *Sun-Democrat* previewed the game, saying, "It is generally agreed that one of the two teams will be the

1929-30 Murray State men's basketball team

probable winner of the conference tournament to be held in Memphis on March 3-6."

On Friday morning before the Saturday game the student body assembled in the auditorium as the band, cheerleaders, students, basketball players, and faculty joined in a pep rally during the chapel hour.

Murray State beat the visitors 42-26 as Bagwell led the way with 12 points. Smith had eight and Houston, who was credited with playing outstanding defense by reporters, chipped in with four points. The victory snapped West Tennessee's 22 game winning streak.

On February 18 of that year Murray swamped Delta State 57 to 26 and the *Sun-Democrat* noted, "Bill Smith, the former Heath star, and Howard Harris, a luminary at LaCenter High School at the same time, were the outstanding stars in Murray's runaway victory tonight. Hal Houston and Jimmie Brookshire did sparkling work at the guards."

Murray was 16-2 heading into the conference tournament with their only losses coming on the road at West Tennessee and Middle Tennessee.

Excitement reigned as the tournament approached. Several teams had matured as the season came to an end, and the games to be played on West Tennessee's home floor were expected to be competitive. But Murray was one of the favorites, and the Heath boys who led them were no strangers to big time competition.

Even so, Murray struggled against Delta State in their first game failing to get their offense untracked. But the Thoroughbreds' defense saved the day as Houston scored nine points in the 34-22 victory.

Murray walloped Tennessee Tech in the semifinals 61 to 21 and prepared for the final against West Tennessee, a team they had split with during the regular season.

The *Sun-Democrat* described what was termed Murray's finest hour in their four years of basketball, "Murray, Ky. State Teachers College, whose record outshone all other Mississippi Valley quintets, reigns supreme as the best basketball team in the Valley...."

They beat mighty West Tennessee for the championship on their home court 36-31.

Willard Bagwell and Jim Miller were named to what was called the "mythical five" or the all-tournament team.

The excitement of Murray State fans and the College could not be contained. The *Sun-Democrat* said, "The band was playing, the students cheering, and the speakers orating at Murray State Teachers College Wednesday when the Thoroughbreds, champions of the Mississippi Valley Conference came back from Memphis, Tennessee. The champions were escorted to the steps of the administration building where President (Rainey T.) Wells welcomed the men...."

1930-31 • 12-6

1931 was a difficult year for America and also for Kentucky. The students and their families were experiencing the overwhelming heartbreak of the Great Depression. There was little money in circulation and students, who relied primarily on their parents for money, were suffering. The college itself was strapped for funds and looked in every corner to find money to pay the faculty.

The Thoroughbreds had changed conferences. They were now in the SIAA, preparing to play Kentucky teams for the first time. Perhaps because of the change, the schedule appears to have been hastily put together.

Murray State played Vanderbilt early in the year, and lost by the one-sided score of 48 to 29. They played both Southern Illinois and Southeast Missouri for the first time that year and scheduled games against UT Jr. College (now UT-Martin) for the first time. Led again by Jim Miller and Willard Bagwell the team beat UT Jr. College handily, and also beat Southern Illinois twice.

They split with Southeast Missouri and ended the regular season with a very respectable 11-5 record. Miller led the team in scoring.

Bagwell scored 20 points against Oakland City in the second game of the season but was soon thereafter diagnosed with the "mumps," a childhood disease common at the time. It was more serious for Bagwell because of his age, and he was held out until late January.

T.R. Graham from LaCenter had a very respectable year while Peg Mahew and Foster replaced guards Houston and Brookshire who had graduated in 1930.

Proud that they had been accepted as a member of the SIAA the 1931 Thoroughbred basketball team prepared to go to Winchester, Kentucky in February to participate in the Kentucky division of the SIAA basketball tournament. The University of Kentucky, University of Louisville, Centre, Kentucky Wesleyan, Transylvania, Berea, Eastern Kentucky and Western Kentucky also played in the Kentucky division.

Then the Thoroughbreds received a telegram from tournament officials saying that Murray State would not play in the event. They offered the lame excuse that Murray was too far away, and it would cost too much for them to attend.

This telegram infuriated Rainey Wells. He was going to personally see to it that Murray was not treated as second class in anything. He immediately began making phone calls and sending telegrams to all of his Kentucky contacts. It was soon clarified that the reason for Murray's exclusion was the fact that they had not played the minimum of six games against conference members.

However with Wells influence, most of the conference members reversed their vote the next day and Murray was invited to play in the tournament. Wells, a political powerhouse in the state, in a zinging one liner told reporters, "Murray may be eliminated in the tournament, but not before the tournament."

The fight was not over. Just before the tournament began the tournament committee declared two Murray starters ineligible because they had transferred from other schools. Starting guard Peg Mahew was one of those disqualified.

Wells was incensed. He ordered Cutchin to play the two in the first game against Berea. He said, "If we win the tournament and the SIAA says we are playing with ineligible players we will simply forfeit the games." Again, he was determined that Murray would be treated fairly.

Murray faced tournament favorite Berea in the first game. which went down to the wire with Berea edging the Thoroughbreds 32 to 31. The question over the eligibility of the two players became moot. Berea went on to win the tournament, but Murray let it be known that they would never be treated in a cavalier manner by other teams in Kentucky.

J.D. Rayburn said of Wells, "He was our main cheerleader. Many times he would come to chapel and speak and lead cheers for our basketball and football teams. He was a great man and a visionary."

New Affiliation For Murray State Athletics

The 1930 tournament championship was Murray State's only one as a member of the Mississippi Valley Conference because Murray left the league following the 1929-30 season to join the more prestigious Southern Intercollegiate Athletic Association.

Here are some details of the move from the MVC to the SIAA, the largest college athletics entity in the south at the time:

While attending an MVC meeting in Memphis in December of 1929, John Wesley Carr was called by Murray State president Rainey T. Wells, who instructed him to go immediately to Mobile, Ala., and make an application for Murray State to be admitted to the SIAA.

Trip taken. Words spoken. Mission accomplished. Murray State was given provisional membership in the SIAA.

One year later, Murray State was voted full membership in the SIAA, and the Thoroughbreds participated in their first SIAA Tournament in February of 1931. When formed in 1894, the SIAA included many of the schools that are now members of the Southeastern, Big 12 and Atlantic Coast conferences. The association was comprised of institutions identified athletically as small colleges and universities when Murray State joined the SIAA.

1931-32 • 17-3

The 1931-32 season would prove to be one of the best in the history of Murray State basketball. The

Members of the 1931-32 men's basketball team, top row, left to right: King, Stalls, Hays, K. Bagwell, Laster, Hall, Twitchell. Bottom row: Coach Cutchin, Foster, Caldwell, Captain Bagwell, Crider, Smith, Shaw.

team had lost leading scorer Jim Miller, but retained the outstanding duo from Heath High School's state championship team, Willard Bagwell and Bill Smith. 6-foot-4 inch Basil Crider gave them a big man in the middle. And the *Sun-Democrat* called guards W.H. Foster and Herman Shaw, "two of the fastest little men in Kentucky basketball."

The Thoroughbreds won their first two games and then lost at Southern Illinois 38-34, with Bagwell out sick, on January 9. Then they reeled off 15 straight victories, most by convincing margins.

On January 18 they avenged the earlier loss to Southern Illinois by beating them in Murray 51-27. Middle Tennessee came to town for the next game on January 23, and they were overwhelmed by the Thoroughbreds 63-18.

Two days later Western Kentucky came to Murray to play on the auditorium stage and Murray stunned the experienced Hilltoppers 26 to 24. In only their fifth year of basketball, they served notice that they were a force to be reckoned with.

Jim Miller

On February 1 Murray traveled by car to Bowling Green where they played the Hilltoppers on successive nights. The Murray Ledger noted that the game was attended by over 2,000 fans. Murray won the first game 38 to 26 and the next night they beat the Hilltoppers again 34-21.

Murray State president Dr. Rainey T. Wells could not have been prouder. It was another example of David beating Goliath and it furnished Dr. Wells with a living example for use in countless chapel speeches.

"You are as good as you think you are," he would say. "It doesn't matter where you live, how much money you have, or how little other people may think of you. You can do whatever you set your mind to doing."

He believed that, and he was able to communicate it to others. Everyone at Murray State, especially the students, began to believe it too.

The team continued its winning ways and finished the regular season with a 17-1 record.

The SIAA tournament was held in Jackson, Tenn. and Murray was given the top seed. The Thoroughbreds walloped Western again 40-27. But they were upset in the second game, 47-37 in overtime, by a very good Millsaps team. Then they lost the consolation game to Louisiana Normal 61-37.

Still, it was an incredibly successful year with a sole loss to Southern Illinois on the road in early January and a near perfect record until the tournament.

A *Sun-Democrat* writer using the pen name Scribbles made an interesting observation about the 1931-32 Thoroughbreds, "And again we claim that Murray has one of the best basketball teams in the country, and that's not barring the University of Kentucky, who despite two decisive defeats is rated above the Thoroughbreds on that old time gag of meeting a better grade of competition."

1932-33 • 14-6

Willard Bagwell's senior year at Murray State didn't result in another KIAC championship or a SIAA title, but it did lend credence to what was already proclaimed by many: Bagwell was the best player in both conferences, and one of the best in the south.

Bagwell's offensive contributions in Murray's 14-6 season of 1932-33 are reflected in the numbers he put

MURRAY STATE GETS THE LAST LAUGH... AND A FIGHT SONG

The adoption of *The Old Gray Mare* as Murray State's fight song can be traced to halftime of the second-ever Murray State-Western Kentucky football game, the Oct. 22, 1933 Hilltoppers' homecoming game.

Western led Murray 6-0 at halftime of that game, and a partisan crowd was confident the Toppers would win, so much so that Western derided Murray State by dressing a student in a decrepit "old gray mare" costume and parading him around the field as the band played *The Old Gray Mare.*

The pace of the "old gray mare" slowed as the band played on, and at the end of the song the student fell prostrate on the ground, to the delight of many of the spectators.

But Murray State's fans – and team – didn't take kindly to the parody. The Thoroughbreds recovered from the halftime deficit to win convincingly, 21-6. And at game's end, the Murray State band played its own version of *The Old Gray Mare.*

Murray State's version ended that October day with these words:

The Old Gray Mare,
She ain't what she used to be
She's a Thoroughbred now!

The Old Gray Mare has been Murray State's fight song ever since.

up: a school-record 345 points, a school-record 17.3 per-game scoring average, and a school-record 33 points against Lambuth in a 76-41 Thoroughbred win.

The Breds were fast out of the gate for the second straight year, winning their first five games. They took a 11-2 record into a February road trip to Tennessee Tech and Middle Tennessee State, but lost both games, 36-35 to Tech and 23-22 to Middle. The Breds then won three consecutive games, beating Western Kentucky 57-41 at Bowling Green in their regular-season finale and beating Centre College 34-31 and the University of Louisville 57-40 in the KIAC Tournament at Winchester.

But Western came up big defensively and beat Murray in the KIAC title game, 30-17. Three days later, Tennessee Tech beat the Breds in the SIAA Tournament, 53-48 at Jackson, Tenn., bringing an end to Bagwell's decorated college career (he was twice selected All-KIAC and All-SIAA and was an All-MVC pick in 1930.)

Bagwell's impact on Murray State's career scoring chart was evident for years.

His 936 points – accumulated in 69 games – stood as the school record until Johnny Reagan totaled 973 points – accumulated in 92 games – in a four-year career that ended in 1948. And Bagwell's 13.6 points per-game career average ranked No. 1 at Murray State until 1953, when Garrett Beshear closed out his four-year Thoroughbred career with a 15.3 points per-game average.

Willard Bagwell

Bagwell and former teammate Hugh May were inducted in the second class of the Murray State Athletics Hall of Fame in 1967, joining Floyd Burdette, another former Breds basketball player, in the class.

Asked in early 2011 about Bagwell's basketball abilities, J.D. Rayburn had this to say about his one-tune Murray State teammate: "He was a great player., He was a natural. He could shoot with the best of them, and when he missed he was a master at following his shot. I've never seen anyone with a better nose for the ball."

Bagwell coached basketball at Heath High School after graduating from Murray State.

1933-34 • 11-6

The 1933-34 Thoroughbreds struggled after losing three starters from the previous year. However, they were laying a foundation for the future. They were led in scoring by a young man named Cecil Kent. Kent was a multi-sport athlete and a star halfback on the football team, which in 1934 had a perfect season, 9-0, and won the SIAA championship. Kent was the second highest scoring football player in the nation, and the 6 ft. 2 in. speedster halfback was an honorable mention All-American.

The basketball team continued to play all their home games on the auditorium stage. Obviously strapped for money, the college limited the number of games the team played to 17 that year. They were 5-1 by mid-January despite being upset by Lambuth.

The eighth game of the season was against Western Kentucky, and the Hilltoppers' star player Harry Hardin, posed a real problem for the young Murray team. The player expected to guard him was ill, and Cutchin turned to little J.D. "Stumpy" Rayburn. The *Sun Democrat* had this to say about the legendary Rayburn, "Rayburn is short and fast and can keep up with Western's Hardin."

Stumpy did a good job on Hardin that night, but the big Murray crowd left the auditorium smarting from a 25-20 Western victory.

Murray beat Eastern and Morehead on the road, but Western beat them a second time in Bowling Green on February 6. The Thoroughbreds finished the season with four straight victories and were eagerly anticipating the KIAC tournament, held in Louisville that year. Unfortunately they lost in the first round to a very good Louisville team, 28 to 18.

Murray State finished the season with an 11-6 record.

1934-35 • 18-6

The 1934-35 Thoroughbreds won their first four games in convincing fashion. Among those victories was a 63-18 drubbing of West Tennessee.

J.D. "Stumpy" Rayburn was a senior, and he was joined by captain James Phillips from Tolu, Ky. and Ross Magruder.

Basil Crider

Before 3,500 people in the auditorium, the largest crowd of the season, the Murray five lost by a narrow margin to Western Kentucky 32-29.

Judge Bob Miller, a basketball fan, a popular political figure, and Hazel native, often related a humorous story about that game. He loved telling it to anyone who would listen.

"Everybody in Hazel came to see Murray beat Western," he said "While we were there it came the biggest rain you ever saw. The creeks between Murray and Hazel overflowed, and there was no way we could get home. So the whole town of Hazel ended up spending two nights in Murray waiting for the creeks to go down."

The Thoroughbreds, referred to by local journalists, as the Murray "Men-o'-War" won three straight games in the KIAC tournament held in Bowling Green, but again were edged by Western in the final 23-20.

Phillips and Magruder were named to the all KIAC team. Murray State outscored their opponents 925 to 657 and swept Tennessee Tech, Middle Tennessee, and Eastern Kentucky, finishing the season 18-6.

CECIL KENT WAS THE BEST IN FOOTBALL... AND A GOOD ONE IN BASKETBALL

During the first decade of Murray State athletics, coach Carlisle Cutchin benefited from more than a dozen football players who exchanged their cleats for sneakers each December and acquitted themselves quite well on the hardwood. Ty Holland, Auburn Wells, John and Jim Miller, Hugh May and Cecil Kent were the best of the group of two-sport lettermen.

It is pure conjecture to say who the best dual-sport star was and who the best basketball player was. But when it comes to picking the best football player among the group, there is no debate. That was Cecil "Slim" Kent of Henderson, Tenn.

Cecil Kent, football player (left) and basketball player (right).

Kent started at left halfback on four Murray State football teams that collectively won 24 games and lost only five. And he was the college's first football All-American, being recognized as an honorable mention selection on the 1933 Associated Press All America team. In 1933, the 6-2, 180-pounder was the nation's No. 2 scorer, accumulating 90 points, and the Thoroughbreds won all nine of their games. They were champions of the Southern Intercollegiate Athletic Association. In the 1933-34 basketball season, Kent was Murray State's' No. 2 scorer, totaling a whopping 106 points in 15 games. Murray's record that season was 11-6.

Kent was captured by the Japanese in the Philippines in World War II and subjected to the Bataan Death March. He weighed about 120 pounds when he was rescued by United States troops. In 1967, he was posthumously inducted in the second class of the Murray State Athletics Hall of Fame.

J.D. RAYBURN WAS THE "GRAND OLD MAN" OF MURRAY STATE ATHLETICS

by Jimmy Wilder

J.D. Rayburn was a two-sport athlete at Murray State when both basketball and football were in their infancy. And for a time, leading up to his death in 2012, he was the oldest living player to earn a letter in both sports.

"I never considered myself a special athlete in college," Rayburn said, a couple of years before his passing. "But I started several games on some very good teams. I have great memories as a Murray State student and athlete, and I've had a lot of fun being a fan of Murray State athletics. Obviously, I love Racer football and basketball. I do everything I can to support the teams and the university."

Rayburn never would have gotten to Murray State had he not changed his career aspirations. Or had them changed for him.

After graduating from Providence (Kentucky) High School in 1930, Rayburn thought he was going to play professional baseball. That changed when his dad, Allen Rayburn, told him he was going to have to find himself a job if he didn't go to college or sign a pro baseball contract.

No professional offer was forthcoming for the speedy outfielder who began playing in an independent league during the summer when he was 15. So for one year, Rayburn greased cars that went into the coal mines near Wheatcroft and also worked part-time for the Illinois Central Railroad.

He first considered attending college after accompanying his older brother, William, on the 80-mile trip from Wheatcroft to Murray State, where William's girlfriend was enrolled. The journey changed Rayburn's life.

"Baseball was my sport as a kid and it drew me to Murray State," he said. "I was told Murray had a good baseball program, and I figured if I played for Murray State and did well, I'd get a pro contract. And if that didn't happen, I'd still get a degree and be a teacher and a coach."

More than a year out of high school, Rayburn headed back to Murray State in September of 1931, bringing with him $200, a few clothes and the expectation that he would play football, basketball and baseball for the Thoroughbreds, even though he had never played organized football.

"I transferred from Wheatcroft to Providence for my senior year in high school because Providence had a football team and Wheatcroft didn't," Rayburn said. "But I never got on the field. Dad wouldn't let me play football. He was afraid I'd get hurt."

J.D. Rayburn at his 100th birthday celebration, with Bennie Purcell..

His father had no problem with J.D. playing basketball for Providence, and he was a key contributor on a team that won 25 straight games before losing in the regional final.

Why did the 5-foot-6, 167-pound Rayburn think his dad would allow him to play football for Murray State? "Dad wouldn't be around," he said. "He wouldn't know I had gone out for football until after I had made the team."

Rayburn's desire to play football in college was two-fold. "I had it in my mind that I was going to be a coach and I needed to play football if I were going to coach football. I'd get paid more coaching football and basketball than just coaching basketball."

Being chosen for the Murray State freshman football team was initially a losing proposition for Rayburn. Making the freshman basketball team was somewhat easier.

"Once school began, they had football tryouts," Rayburn said. "I didn't make the team, but I'd go to practice every day. I wanted to learn all I could. One day a player quit and I told a manager to give me the player's uniform. I got the uniform and soon I was even given one that fit. I guess I showed them something. I could run with the backs. I learned to block and knew my assignments. I had a knack for making tackles behind the line of scrimmage."

Members of the Murray State freshman football team.

Rayburn started at guard on coach John Miller's 5-0-1 freshman football team that outscored the opposition 217-0. A scoreless tie with Middle Tennessee State was the only blemish.

A knee injury limited Rayburn's playing time on the varsity as a sophomore, but he lettered the next two years as a guard on squads that had records of 9-0 and 6-3. The undefeated squad of 1933 had five shutouts and won the Southern Intercollegiate Athletic Association championship.

Rayburn lettered three years in basketball on teams with records of 14-6, 11-6 and 18-6, and he started at guard on Miller's freshman team. That team lost just one game, at home to Western Kentucky. But they beat Western in Bowling Green.

Rayburn unwittingly jump-started his chances for a spot on the freshman basketball team by playing pickup games on Saturday mornings in the fall of 1931 in the gym at Murray State's Wilson Hall. On those occasions, he and four friends from Henderson, Tenn., brothers Keith and John King, Winfred DeShazio and Cecil Kent took on all comers, including returning varsity players who weren't members of the football squad.

Miller had an office in Wilson Hall and sometimes observed the pick-up basketball games. Rayburn caught Miller's eye and when basketball tryouts were held in December, he was called out by the coach.

Freshmen tryouts were held on the stage in Lovett Auditorium, Murray State's home court, and attracted a significant portion of the student body. "We had over 100 boys show up," Rayburn said. "Coach Miller threw three or four balls out on the court and told us to take some shots. Then he blew a whistle, told us to sit down, and started talking.

"He said he wanted to divide us into teams and watch us play. Then he said, 'Stumpy come here.' He told me to pick my team. I chose the King brothers, DeShazio and Kent, and nobody beat us. Coach soon cut the squad down to around 40 and we played intramural ball. Eventually, he picked all five guys on my team for the freshman team. We all started."

Keith and Kent King earned three Murray State varsity letters in basketball and football and many more accolades than Stumpy.

Scoring was not Rayburn's forte´ in basketball in college because most of the points came around the basket, and he was usually the smallest player on the court. "Coach (Carlisle Cutchin) worked with me on my shot but my role was to handle the ball, make a pass, go set a screen and get back to the middle of the court, ready to guard against a fast break," Rayburn said.

His highest scoring game on the varsity (12 points) came in his junior season. As a senior in back-to-back road games, he and Jim Phillips tied for scoring honors with seven points in a 29-23 win over Tennessee Tech, and he and Kent King combined for 23 points in a 47-25 Breds win over Eastern Kentucky (King had 14 of the points).

Basketball was a far different game in the 1930s and Murray State Teachers College bore little resemblance to the Murray State University of today.

Can you imagine a Murray State campus surrounded by woods that had seven buildings, a training school for teachers, no football stadium and a few hundred students, none of whom drove cars to class? How would you like to attend a college where no tuition was paid by in-state students, room and board was $5 a week, textbooks could be purchased for $4 and the registration fee was $27?

This is what awaited Rayburn when he enrolled at Murray State.

Timeouts Were for Resting and Subbing; Games Were Low Scoring

College basketball today bears little resemblance to the game J.D. Rayburn played in the 1930's.

"During timeouts, the guys in the game had to stay on the court. Coaches couldn't talk to them. Timeouts were for resting and getting subs into the game. There was a jump ball to start each half and after every made basket, and you didn't have to advance the ball past center court. You wanted to get every jump ball and score and get the ball back again. If you had a lead in the second half, you could just hold the ball."

Often in the 1930s, teams could score less than 30 points and win a game. And double figure scorers weren't always necessary.

Western Kentucky employed a tactic know as "stall ball" in the second Murray State-Western freshman game in the 1931-32 season.

"Western scored first and held the ball the rest of the half on their end of the court," Rayburn said. "Coach (John) Miller told us to stay back and guard the basket. At halftime he drew up a play for us to get the jump ball and score, and we did. I got the basket on a layup. After playing with the ball a little bit, we got another basket and went ahead 4-2. We kept on holding the ball as long as we could and won the game, 11-9."

A 28-win Western Kentucky squad beat the University of Louisville 13-12 for the 1934 KIAC Tournament championship. The Hilltoppers split their two regular-season meetings against Murray State in the 1933-34 season.

Averaging 9.2 points per game, Fred Curtis led the University of Kentucky in scoring in the 1938-39 season when the Wildcats won their fourth Southeastern Conference championship.

Finances were challenging for Rayburn then just as they are now for many college students. The $200 he brought with him as a freshman had to last the school year until he could supplement his finances.

The Great Depression of the late 1920s lingered into the 1930s. Jobs were no sure thing. Murray State faculty and staff were being laid off, taking pay cuts and sometimes going months without receiving checks. There was talk of the college having only intramural sports.

"But there was a lot of school spirit," Rayburn said. "We had a weekly 10 a.m. chapel service in Lovett Auditorium that everyone had to attend. They had good programs at chapel and sometimes they turned into pep rallies with President Wells (Rainey T. Wells) leading the yells. The students bonded and stayed on campus most of the time. They looked forward to the football and basketball games. And so would the faculty and staff. There wasn't much else to do."

Some financial relief came Rayburn's way after his first semester when he got a campus job sweeping floors and cleaning rooms at the training school. Later, he was moved to the president's office and during his senior year, he was up at 4 a.m. in the winter, lighting six stoves in Wells Hall, the women's dorm.

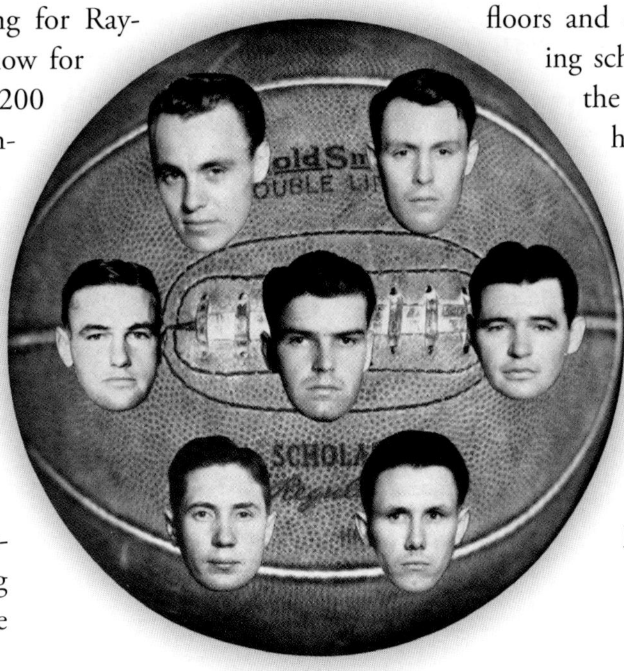

Members of the Murray State basketball squad: J.D. Rayburn, Guard; Wilford Baker, Guard; Bennie Muse, Manager; James Phillips, Guard; Lewis Graham, Forward; Clarence Butler, Center; and Robert Goheen, Forward.

"I had a key to Wells Hall," Rayburn said, "but I didn't let anyone have it. I wasn't going to get kicked out of school and I didn't want to see anyone else get kicked out either."

And what became of Rayburn's baseball career at Murray State?

After his freshman year, the college dropped baseball for financial reasons and didn't re-start the program until the spring of 1942.

However, Stumpy parlayed a Murray State bachelor's degree in physical education into high school teaching and coaching jobs at Wheatcroft, Clay and Providence, where he became school superintendent. From 1966 until his retirement in 1977, Rayburn was coordinator of the student teaching program at Murray State. For the next 35 years he lived in his home on Olive Boulevard, less than two blocks from Ordway Hall, the dorm he lived in as a student.

The 'Breds Excelled With Jim Phillips in Uniform

by Will Aubrey

In the 1930's there was no television. People listened to the radio for entertainment. There were no personal computers – no computers of any kind for that matter. Much of Kentucky was connected by dirt roads, women bought dresses for five dollars, and it cost a quarter to go to the movies.

Even the game of basketball was much different than it is today. There was a jump ball at midcourt after every made basket, no one had even dreamed of a jump shot and the NCAA basketball tournament would not be contested for the first time until the close of the decade.

Jim Phillips

It was against this backdrop of dirt roads, radio and set shots that Jim Phillips played out a career that made him one of Murray State's first star athletes.

Phillips grew up in Tolu, Ky., a small Crittenden County community on the banks of the Ohio River, where he attended Tolu High School.

"It was a small school," he said. "We only had about 30 some odd kids in the high school. But, we went to the state tournament twice. We won the regional in Murray two straight years. The first year we were eliminated by the state champions, Corinth, in the semifinals. They beat us by one point. The next year we went to the finals and Manual beat us."

That Phillips and Tolu were able to make a run deep into the state tournament is amazing, like the story told in the movie Hoosiers. But, when you consider that they didn't even have a floor to practice on, the accomplishment is probably too astonishing even for Hollywood.

"We didn't have a gymnasium," Phillips recalled. "We just had an outdoor court. We practiced with gloves on, we practiced in the mud and snow. The court wasn't even paved, it was a dirt court. All the games we played had to be in someone else's gymnasium. We played all of our games away."

If that wasn't bad enough, there was no paved highway into Tolu. To get out of town you had to negotiate nine miles of dirt road.

And in those days the homecourt advantage was even greater than it is today. Gym floors weren't all the same size then. Some were short; some were narrow; some were long. And, some had posts to support the ceiling. The home team had an advantage because they were familiar with the floor.

Adolph Rupp, the legendary Kentucky coach, once recalled a particularly unusual gym at Vanderbilt.

"It was L shaped," Rupp said. "From our bench we could only see one goal. When Vandy got the opening tip I turned to Harry Lancaster, my assistant, and said, 'Harry, where the hell did everybody go?' A few seconds later I saw one of our boys come steaming around the corner on the dribble and I said, 'Never mind Harry. They're coming our way and we've got the ball.'"

Phillips played in his share of unusual facilities. In high school he played in a tobacco warehouse in Kuttawa. And, after he got to Murray State he played on an indoor asphalt floor at Arkansas State.

But, the highlight of his high school career was, of course, those two trips to the state tournament.

"Going to the state tournament was great for us," Phillips said. "We were just country boys. We hadn't been very many places. So, we really enjoyed it."

In 1931 his Tolu team made it all the way to the state final before losing to Manual 34-23. Along the way they beat Blackford, another team that did not have a gymnasium. Phillips scored nine points in the 32-13 rout and legendary Courier Journal columnist Earl Ruby described it thusly...

"The gymless ones played better basketball than a lot of teams that have polished hardwood floors for practice," he wrote. "But, as was the case with Carr Creek two and three years ago, both Tolu and Blackford gained most of their ground with well executed passes rather than dribbles."

You might think, like most boys who grew up in the '30's, that Phillips would have followed the Kentucky Wildcats on the radio and dreamed of playing for Rupp. But, you would be wrong.

"I wasn't a fan of any college when I was growing up," he said. "You could listen to games on the radio but I rarely did. In fact, I had no idea that I would ever go to college. I liked to hunt and fish. Any chance I got I was hunting or fishing. During the summer time I'd hire out and work on a farm for 50 cents a day. I chopped corn and put up hay, that sort of thing."

Indeed, college was so far from Phillips' mind that he didn't even consider it after helping lead Tolu to a second place finish at the state tournament. But, at least one college coach had the Tolu star on his mind.

"I was swimming in the Ohio River, there were five or six of us just as naked as jaybirds," Phillips recalled. "And, a car pulled up on the bank and a fellow got out and said, 'Is Jim Phillips down there?' I said, 'Yeah.' And he said, 'I want to talk to you.' It was John Miller, the freshman basketball coach at Murray and he offered me a scholarship with me standing there on the riverbank, naked as a jaybird. My parents said I was going to take it, so I did. Really, I had no desire to go college."

As a freshman at Murray State, Phillips, who had played forward in high school and would play guard as an upperclassman, wound up as the starting center despite standing just a shade over six feet tall.

"Freshmen weren't allowed to play varsity back then," he said. "We had a freshman team and I was supposed to play forward on that team. But, our center dropped out of school and I ended up playing center. I played guard the other three years."

Still, that freshman squad managed a 9-2 record with their only losses coming to Western Kentucky.

In 1934 Phillips stepped up to the varsity and started at guard for a team that finished 11-6. He was the team's third leading scorer, averaging five points per game and he scored 15 in a 51-34 win over Middle Tennessee.

The following year Phillips was selected to be the team's captain and at season's end he was an All-Kentucky Intercollegiate Athletic Association honoree. Murray State finished second in the KIAC tournament, losing in the finals to Western as the Hilltoppers beat them for the third time that year.

Phillips downplayed his offensive prowess. Asked how many points he averaged, he said, "I never scored much." But, as a junior, he regularly reached double figures and led the team in scoring on several occasions, netting 18 in a 63-18 drubbing of the University of Memphis then called West Tennessee Teacher's College.

Today, most MSU fans revere Racer Arena as though it were an ancient cathedral. But, it hadn't even been built when Phillips played. Basketball games were played on the stage at Lovett Auditorium. Still, the crowds were large and enthusiastic. In 1935, 5,500 turned out for a game against Western. And, at the time the school only had about 500 students.

"Some of the fellows were afraid they might run off the stage," Phillips recalled. "But, I didn't mind. There was quite a distance between the court and the edge of the stage. It was a good place to play basketball. And, it was a wonderful place to watch a ballgame because you had cushioned seats."

In the mid '30's the team was called by a variety of names, Cutchinmen, Thoroughbreds, and Horses. But, the most popular seems to have been Racehorses.

Campus life was different for the players then too. Today, players aren't allowed to work. But, back then it was required.

"All the players worked," Phillips said. "At the time we had a coal burning furnace that provided heat for all the buildings. Some of the guys tended that. Others worked in the kitchen. Some of us mowed grass. We did everything. I was fortunate though, my senior year once the basketball season started they didn't assign me another job."

The 1936 season started on a sour note as two regulars from the previous year withdrew from school, the high scoring Ross Magruder and Curran Howle. But, coach Carlisle Cutchin's squad reeled off 16 victories to start the season and they were widely hailed as a "wonder team" and ranked among the best in the South.

"He was a great person," Phillips said of Cutchin. "I wouldn't say that he knew more basketball than anybody because I don't think he did. But, he got along real well with his players."

Among the 16 victories at the beginning of the season was a 31-15 pasting of arch-rival Western Kentucky coached by Ed Diddle.

Diddle, one of the real characters in coaching at the time was famous for torturing the English language. He once marveled at a players' size saying, "He must be 6-feet-13 or 14 at least."

And, he always had a red towel on the bench. He threw it, chewed on it, and waved it. By the end of Phillips' senior year Murray would have him crying in it.

"I think the team we had in '36 was one of the better ball-teams Murray's ever had,' Phillips said. "We had two boys that had played with us the year before that didn't come back that year. If we'd had them we would've been unstoppable."

With the NIT and NCAA tournaments not starting until 1938 and '39 respectively, there was no national championship of any kind in the mid '30's. Teams belonged to loosely configured conferences or athletic associations which held tournaments at the end of the year. Murray State belonged to both the KIAC and the Southern Intercollegiate Athletic Association.

Throughout the 1936 season Murray and Western were clearly the top two teams in both leagues. And, when the 'Toppers beat MSU in the KIAC final most people assumed they'd go on to win the more prestigious SIAA title as well.

In the first round of the tournament Murray State crushed Louisville 46-26 and they beat Louisiana Normal 40-32 in the second round to set up a fourth game with Western in the final.

Sixty fans followed the team to Jackson, Miss. for the tournament and both the semifinal and final games were broadcast via telephone over the loudspeakers in Lovett Auditorium. Over 1,000 people listened to the phonecast of the final, filling Lovett with their raucous cheers as Murray beat Western 28-26 for the championship.

"Murray's towering center (Ethridge) McKeel was the lad who sent a spin shot through the draperies as the timer's clock showed 50 seconds left to play," wrote the Courier Journal's Kelly Thompson.

That proved to be the winning shot as Western was unable to score and Murray State came home with the championship trophy and a 23-2 record.

Phillips earned first team All-KIAC and SIAA honors at the end of the year. And the 1936 yearbook shows the high regard his fellow students held him in, calling him "as fine a leader as ever stepped on a basketball floor."

Jim Phillips when he was inducted into the Hall of Fame in 1988. Courtesy Murray State Athletics Media Relations.

1936-1948

by Sid Easley

1935-36 • 23-2

• *SIAA Tournament Champion*

The 1935-36 season was the last in which Murray State played on the auditorium stage. They won their first 16 games, setting a record that would stand until 2012. And they ended the season with an SIAA championship.

Big Red Burdette led Murray as they waltzed through opponent after opponent both on the road and at home, winning most games in convincing fashion by 10 points or more.

During this string they beat both Middle Tennessee and Tennessee Tech at home and on the road. They overwhelmed Western at home on January 15 by a score of 31 to 15.

They won 16 games in a row as newspapers and fans all over the state were singing the praises of the team often referred to as the Racehorses.

Finally on February 6, they faced Ed Diddle and his Western five in Bowling Green and suffered their first loss, 29-23.

1936 SIAA Tournament Champs

Murray resumed its winning ways with three straight victories, including an impressive 46-26 drubbing of Louisville in the KIAC tournament. Sadly, they lost in the finals of that tournament to Western by a one-sided score of 55-31.

Knowing they had a great team, Murray fans looked forward to the prestigious SIAA tournament to be held in Jackson, Mississippi. "They can't beat us three times," the wise fans opined.

Members of the Murray State 1935-36 basketball squad: Joe Herndon, Guard; Ross Magruder, Forward; Willard Carroll, Forward; Cecil Kent, Guard; Curran Howle, Center; Riley Dennington, Center; and Virgil Stewart, Guard.

The 1936 *Shield* describes the end of the successful season best, "Climaxing a record-breaking season with a 28-26 win over their arch-rivals, the Western Kentucky Hilltoppers, in the final game of the conference tournament held in Jackson, Miss., the Thoroughbreds brought back to Murray its first SIAA Championship. Over 1,000 fans sat in the Murray College Auditorium to listen to a play-by-play phonecast of the contest."

Even in 1936 with poor roads and cars that were often unreliable, the Murray fans followed their team. The *Shield* continued, "A happy group of 60 Thoroughbred followers who went to Jackson for the tournament, carried the 'five aces' and 'four jacks' off the floor, while back in Murray the biggest parade in the history of the college was being prepared to celebrate the victory."

The Racehorses were led by 6-foot-4 inch sophomore Floyd "Red" Burdette who scored 225 points that year. Team captain James "Sunny" Phillips helped Burdette lead them to a 23-2 record. They beat the University of Louisville twice, and also swept Middle Tennessee, Tennessee Tech, and Arkansas State. They were 18-1 during the regular season. And they became the first Murray team to score over 1,000 points in a season.

This was the first year of the three second rule which said no offensive player could remain in the free throw lane either with or without the ball for more than three seconds. That may have played some role in the increase in scoring.

> *"Murray is a rising, and not a setting sun."*
> – John Wesley Carr, 1935 *Shield*

1936-37 • 22-3

The 1936-37 team had another amazing season. Referring to this outstanding team as the "bluebloods," the *Shield* reveled in the feats of the team that finished the regular season with only one loss. The Thoroughbreds finished 17-1, losing only to rival Western Kentucky on the road. They had beaten Western at home 31-26. They added Delta State and Louisiana Normal to their schedule that year and beat them both. They swept Morehead, Tennessee Tech, Middle Tennessee and West Tennessee.

Burdette, who stood almost 6-4, led the team in scoring. For the first time, Murray enjoyed the services of "twin towers" in the lineup. Head Coach Carlisle Cutchin had recruited a young man from Rector, Ark., who was to make quite a splash in the SIAA. Ethridge "Big Mac" McKeel stood 6-5-plus, and his photo indicates he weighed over 200 pounds. These two big men led the way in 1937.

The SIAA tournament was again held at Bowling Green, as Western coach Ed Diddle seemed to have a way of securing the tournament on his home turf. Murray won the first three games and again met

A NEW GYMNASIUM FOR THE 1937 SEASON

The Thoroughbred basketball team played its first two seasons in what is now known as Wilson Hall and then for nine years made its home on the auditorium stage. It was a unique setting, and no doubt became a special place where memories were made and cherished.

The '30s were a difficult time in America. The stock market had crashed in 1929, unemployment was high and, most importantly to these young rural college men, the tobacco market had tumbled. Times were hard. Their struggling families had sacrificed mightily to permit them to attend college when their labor was so badly needed at home on the farms where most of them lived.

To recover from the Great Depression, government programs with familiar acronyms like the WPA, CCC and PWA were instituted to provide work for the unemployed and put money in circulation. John Carr, ever attentive to the needs of his college, sought funds from the Public Works Administration to construct a building for physical education. Carr had originally come to Kentucky to advance physical education in the curriculum of all schools. He believed that a student should educate and improve both the mind and body. He was a pioneer in physical education. Athletics were important to the character, as he put it.

James Richmond became president of the university in 1936 and joined Carr in making every effort to build what they referred to as a "health building." Ground was broken for the building in March 1936 and by June 14, 1937, it was ready for occupancy. It was officially dedicated in December 1939 by a man who would later become vice president of the United States, Sen. Alben Barkley. It was appropriately named for Murray's first president and gifted leader and from that day forward was called the Carr Health Building.

This new building contained a modern gymnasium that was to be the home of the basketball Thoroughbreds for 18 seasons. The then spacious gymnasium, still used today for intramurals, had movable bleachers that permitted the seating of over 2,000 spectators. These bleachers could be folded against the wall providing room for more than one practice court. The building also contained a swimming pool, classrooms for health and physical education, offices, boxing rooms, wrestling rooms, and weight rooms as well as handball and racquetball courts. The building cost $247,000 and Carr was fond of saying, "It didn't cost Murray State a cent."

Bennie Purcell, played in the Carr Health Building gymnasium for four years, said this about the place: "The atmosphere was unbelievable. Just picture 2,000 screaming fans sitting right on top of you. It was Racer Arena and more. It was a day of no television and Murray State basketball was the only game in town. Everybody wanted a ticket and many times disappointed fans were turned away by the local fire marshal."

Western in the finals. The rivalry by now had grown, and statewide news coverage hyped the big game. Here is the account of the game as it appeared in the *Shield*:

"Flash; SIAA FINALS SCORE: Western 37, Murray 32. Fouls: Murray 15, Western 5. This itself tells the story of the most gallant fight that any Thoroughbred waged against the greatest odds that Murray was ever called to face." The Philistines had won again.

1937-38 • 27-4

The 1937-38 Thoroughbreds were given the nickname "Racehorses" by the 1938 *Shield*. The team's regular-season record was almost perfect, losing only once to Western Kentucky at Bowling Green by three points.

The home game against Western in the Carr Health Building was excitedly described by a College News writer. "Whatta game! What a night! Whatta game! Need we say more? Everybody was there – even Mr. Lowry (referring to C.S. Lowry, the renowned economics professor). The Racehorses were never more brilliant … Murray was never behind."

In addition to sweeping Morehead, Tennessee Tech, Eastern Kentucky, Middle Tennessee and Delta State, Murray beat Arkansas, 43-40. The Razorbacks were described as being "one of the nation's leading quints."

Murray lost to Western in the SIAA tournament finals held at Bowling Green. But because of their stellar record, they were invited to the National Association of Intercollegiate Basketball tournament held in Kansas City, Mo., in March. This tournament, which led to the formation of the National Association of Intercollegiate Athletics (NAIA), was in its second year showcasing the nation's best small-college teams with the goal of crowning a national champion.

This historic Murray team opened national tournament play by defeating Drake 47-40. In the second game, the Thoroughbreds beat Maryville College of Missouri 38-30. Advancing in the tournament and thrilling the growing west Kentucky fan base, the Thoroughbreds came from behind and defeated New Mexico, a team that had been favored to win the tournament, 30-29.

Cutchin's men finally faltered in the semifinal game, losing to Roanoke College of Virginia 35-29. But they recovered in the consolation game to beat Washburn College of Kansas for third place in the tournament. This was one of Murray's great teams, and it was often said that if some of the players had not been suffering from the flu, they would have won the tournament. It was reported that Burdette had a temperature of 101 during the week.

Floyd "Red" Burdette

This was Burdette's senior season. He was both an outstanding student and an outstanding basketball player, finishing his three-year varsity career with 833 points. As of 1947, he was second only to Willard Bagwell in all-time Thoroughbred scoring. Burdette hit 63 percent of his free throws and 325 field goals in his career.

Three players on the 1938 team, Ross Magruder, Ethridge McKeel and Burdette were named to the all-KIAC and SIAA teams. McKeel became the first Murray player to be named an All-American by the NAIA.

Meanwhile in a nearby Marshall County high school, the team from Sharpe led by Durward "Red" Culp and James King stunned the Kentucky basketball world by beating Maysville to win the state tournament by a score of 36-27. Culp would later bring his basketball talents to Murray.

1938-39 • 13-8

Cutchin continued his successful tenure as the Thoroughbred basketball coach, having held the job since 1926. His 1936, 1937 and 1938 teams compiled a 72-9 record. The *Shield* editor described him in the 1940 annual, "This genial coach came to Murray in 1925. Since then he has achieved one of the outstanding records in the South."

1939 was a rebuilding year for the Thoroughbreds. Returning from the great team of 1938 were captain Gene Bland, an all-SIAA guard; Ross Magruder; James Hurley of Calvert City, Ky., who starred in the game against Arkansas; and junior Bill Carneal of Heath, Ky. Without the twin towers of McKeel and Burdette, who graduated the previous year, they posted a 13-8 record.

Often referred to as the Bluebloods, the 1939 team wore kneepads and knee socks in their photographs for the *Shield* that year. It was a testament to the roughness and intensity of the game. In addition to the number on the front of the uniform tops, there was the silhouette of the head of a Thoroughbred neatly surrounded by a circle.

1938 team

The high points of the year included victories over Delta State, Middle Tennessee, Tennessee Tech and Louisiana Normal. It was the senior year for Magruder, who ended his two-year career as a Thoroughbred with 505 points.

The leading scorer was 6-5 giant Ned Washer of Kirksey, Ky., who averaged 13.1 points in the team's 21 games. Washer had led Kirksey to two state tournament appearances as a high schooler. He set a Murray State individual scoring record on two occasions in 1939 by scoring 32 against Union early in the year, and then breaking his own record by ripping the nets with 35 points against Middle Tennessee.

1939-40 • 14-9

1940 was the first year fan-shaped backboards were permitted, and the Carr Health building was soon outfitted with this fashionable change. The 1940 Thoroughbreds hit their peak with a 36-30 win over Western Kentucky. The *Shield* editor remarked: "The Race Horses played the hardest schedule ever attempted by a Murray team, winning thirteen and losing seven." It was the first year they added Southeast Missouri, Culver Stockton and Jacksonville, Ala., to the schedule. They also played Vanderbilt during the regular season. They lost that game, 46-37, but thrilled local supporters who had great admiration and respect for what was commonly known as "The Harvard of the South."

Murray State dropped two very close heartbreaking tournament games – a 41-39 KIAC game to Morehead and a 25-23 loss to Western in the SIAA tournament.

They were led by "high scoring and aggressive" captain Bill Carneal of Heath, who was named all-conference and finished his career with 431 points. Carneal would go on to a very successful business career with Texas Gas and serve on the Murray State Board of Regents and Foundation for many years.

The fans looked forward to a good year in 1941 with local boys "Red" Culp, described as "a natural," and Carl Steffin, a transfer from Jordan College in Wisconsin.

None of the fans, the students or these young men could foresee what would happen to their world in the upcoming year. The Japanese invasion of Pearl Harbor in Hawaii on Dec. 7, 1941, would change their lives forever.

Duward "Red" Culp

Carl Steffin

1940-41 • 26-5

• *KIAC Tournament Champion*

The year began with Carlisle Cutchin, teacher, basketball coach, football coach and baseball coach, announcing that he would retire at the end of the season. A fitting tribute to this revered and most successful coach appeared in the *Shield.* The writer said, "Coach Cutchin not only makes athletes of his men, but he instilled in them some of the character that is so deeply rooted in himself."

Carlisle Cutchin

His retirement announcement must have been a factor in spurring the Thoroughbreds to a sensational season. The season began with a victory over nearby Southeast Missouri and then a defeat at the hands of Arkansas, who was the reigning Southwest Conference champion. Murray went on to win six straight and then lost to Western Kentucky, 38-34, in Murray before a "screaming house."

Undaunted by the loss, the Thoroughbreds soon defeated Mississippi State, 56-36, and continued their winning ways with four straight victories. The stage was set for the annual trek to the Red Barn in Bowling Green for a shot at revenge. In an upset, Murray came out on top 38-34. The *Shield* editor, using colorful language, said, "Bob Salmon jumped so high he hung his ______ on the hoop and his shoestring got caught in the net."

Winning their last 10 games in succession, they compiled a regular-season record of 17-2.

Then, they won the KIAC Tournament by beating Eastern, Western and Union College.

The headline in the *Murray Ledger and Times* on Thursday afternoon, March 6, 1941, read: "Murray Celebrates First KIAC Net Championship." The students were ecstatic.

Murray State president James Richmond said, "Murray and Western are the two best teams in the South… the main reason is that Ed Diddle and Carlisle Cutchin are the two best coaches in the South. Diddle says this is the best Western team he has ever coached."

The local paper continued, "Immediately following the auditorium session a parade was staged downtown with Murray's 96 piece band in front."

The students chartered buses for the SIAA tourney to be held in Bowling Green the next week. Excitement reigned. Breezing to the finals of the SIAA tournament, the Thoroughbreds ran up against the home team, Western again. Diddle's men edged Murray for the championship, but undaunted, the Breds prepared for a trip to Kansas City for the national tournament.

This was their second invitation to the tournament in Kansas City. The significance of the National Association of Intercollegiate Basketball (NAIB) tournament must be seen in relation to other national basketball tournaments then in existence. In 1941, the NCAA Tournament had only eight teams participating and the NIT had eight teams. The NAIB was formed in 1937, when Dr. James Naismith and local leaders formed the national tournament staged at Municipal Auditorium in Kansas City. The goal of the tournament was to establish a forum for small colleges and universities to determine a national basketball champion. The original eight-team NAIB tournament expanded to 32 teams in 1938.

The Thoroughbreds began their play in this most prestigious event with a stunning 68-46 drubbing of Oregon State. The AP story read, "The Kentuckians gave tournament spectators a flashing demonstration of expert ball handling in their contest with the Oregon school."

Next they eliminated Alma College of Michigan, 51-33, and in the quarterfinals edged out Maryville College of Missouri, a perennial basketball powerhouse, 46-43. In the fourth game of the 32-team tournament before a sellout crowd of 7,000, Murray was victorious over the Santa Barbara (Calif.) Gauchos, 35-33. The Murray Thoroughbreds, who had been playing basketball for only 15 years, were now in the finals of the NAIB Tournament against San Diego.

The game was tied 28-28 with a few minutes remaining. San Diego then began to pull away. Not to be denied, the Breds went on a tear in the final minutes of the game only to fall two points short, 36-34.

COACH CARLISLE CUTCHIN AND "RED" CULP

"I used to think that games were won and lost because of the players until I became a coach and became a real student of the game," remembered the 90-year-old Glen D. "Red" Culp.

"I know you have to have players, but the coach has a lot to do with winning or losing. Coach Cutchin knew how to use his players. He had a way of getting the most out of them. I still recall how he utilized the two big men, Ethridge McKeel and Red Burdette. He knew he had two good big men; so he designed a double-pivot offense that took advantage of their natural strengths.

"He believed in defense and for him there was no zone. It was always man to man with coach Cutchin.

"Yes, the coach is crucial," Culp continued. "My last year at Murray is an example of the misuse of a player. I was a natural forward, and at the very end of my junior year I hurt my knee. We got a new coach and for some reason he wanted me to play guard. I had never played guard, and with a bum knee I had a lot of trouble there."

Culp describes Cutchin: "He was just a top-notch guy. He was quiet, smart, and he knew his players and what they could do." The *Shield* called Cutchin "Western Kentucky's Father of Basketball."

Cutchin was a great teacher, and Culp became a living example of the character traits Cutchin wanted to instill in his players. Culp had been a star basketball player in tiny Sharpe in Marshall County joining with James King, who later played for Adolf Rupp at Kentucky, to lead Sharpe to a Kentucky state tournament title. "We were poor," he said. "Everybody was poor."

"I came to Murray because they agreed to buy my books," he said with a laugh. "Ed Diddle at Western introduced me to a pretty girl when I visited Bowling Green," he grinned.

Culp, who was No. 5 on Murray's all-time scorers list in the 1947 statistics, graduated from Murray with his bachelor's degree in hand. He served in the Army during World War II and, using the benefits of the GI Bill, was later awarded a master's degree from the University of Kentucky. He taught high school agriculture and coached for several years before becoming an executive with Farm Bureau Insurance Company. He had an outstanding career with that company in Kentucky, then became general manager and executive vice president of North Carolina Farm Bureau Insurance Company in Raleigh, N.C., where he and his wife live today.

The *Paducah Sun-Democrat* quoted the AP writer: "The strain of three tournaments in three weeks proved too much and it was a weary band of Kentuckians which fell behind in those closing moments."

"Red" Culp rremembered the game well: "It was an honor to have been invited to compete in that tournament. We should have won that final game; we were the best team. I recall that all their players shot one-hand shots, played hard and were smart. We had a good team. I played forward and we had two great guards who were tall for guards in that day 6 feet 3 inches or so – Leslie McKeel (Ethridge's brother) and Jack Haines from South Bend, Ind. Salmon and Steffin were transfers from Michigan and Wisconsin – Salmon from Jordan in Michigan and Steffin from Beloit College in Wisconsin. Salmon was 6 foot 4 or so, played center, and was a great player. He was also outstanding off the court, too. He was president of the student body at Murray, continued his education, and became a university professor."

The team returned to Murray after the tournament for a hero's welcome. They had been to the big time and were the talk of the basketball world.

They were led in scoring by Culp of Sharpe, who finished the year with 321 points. Salmon added 269 and Steffin, the transfer, chipped in 243. It was said of Culp, "that there was no better forward in the state." Salmon was Mr. Everything being named All-KIAC, NIBT All-American, and All-SIAA. Steffin also was named All-KIAC and All-SIAA. Leslie McKeel likewise was honored by being named to both the KIAC and SIAA first teams. A young man from Murray, Haron West, was considered a promising prospect.

The *Shield* writer said it well: "To this team goes the admiration from all the student body for…having established themselves as one of the best, if not the best, basketball team Murray has ever had."

While the Thoroughbreds were being lauded for their performance in a national tournament, the nearby community of Hardin was euphoric over the performance of their team in the Kentucky state basketball tournament. Hardin made it all the way to the semifinals, losing finally to Inez, the eventual state champion, 32-31, on March 23, 1941.

1941-42 • 18-4

The Great War was underway in Europe and the Pacific, but basketball at Murray continued to be played. Some of the players would later be called upon to serve and some, like Paul Johnson, made the supreme sacrifice. With a new coach, Rice Mountjoy of Danville, Ky., at the helm, the Racehorses started the year with great promise.

Salmon and Culp returned from the great '41 team and were named co-captains. A rangy 6-foot5 player from Birmingham in Marshall County named Joe Fulks, who would go on to become a great NBA player, made his debut. He was young and had trouble with his temper some would later say. But he could play with the best of them. With Fulks joining Culp and Herb Hurley of Calvert City, Ky., the 1942 team had three outstanding players from Marshall County.

Bob Salmon and Duward "Red" Culp

They began the season with a disappointing loss to Southeast Missouri but Murray State followed that loss with five straight wins. Then they made the trip to the "Red Barn" on the "hill" at Bowling Green and suffered a disappointing two-point loss to Western Kentucky, 29-27.

They won the next six games and prepared for a return game with Western to be played in the Carr Health Building. Culp described the game: "We were behind Western with about three minutes to go, and I was on the bench. Coach put me in, and things began to click. I hate to say it, but I just took the game over. I scored seven points, made several assists to Salmon and Fulks, and we beat them." The final score was Murray 43, Western 37.

The *Shield* writer also describes the game Culp played with colorful language: "Murray beat Western with the spectacular game-saving antics of 'Under Pressure Red Culp;' rangy Joe Fulks, his rebounding and shot making; Bob Salmon, whose ball handling and team play helped keep the team together; a spot game breaker by the name of Herb Hurley; the consistency of Bones Grimmer and several unsung substitutes." The Western victory was the game all would remember that year.

Murray won the last five games to end the regular season with an 18-2 record.

Despite a great regular season, the Thoroughbreds didn't fare well in the tournaments and "the local boosters weren't happy," recalled Culp. The team that had done so well in the both conference and national tournaments the previous year lost to Western by two points in the first game of the KIAC Tournament, 46-44. Despite that loss, because of their record and previous year's performance, they received another invitation to the NAIB Tournament in Kansas City. Again, by the narrowest of margins, they lost the first game of that tournament to East Central State of Ada, Okla., by a score of 46-45.

Though it was not a losing season, it was an unsatisfactory one for a team from whom so much was expected. Interestingly, this was the last season for Mountjoy, who after only one year as coach moved to Paducah and became Tilghman High School's football coach. It was difficult to follow the Cutchin legend. Mountjoy was replaced by longtime freshman coach and former Murray player John Miller.

1942-43 • 21-5

The 1942-43 season began with a new coach for the second year in a row. But this coach was not new to the players or the fans. John Miller had been a good basketball player and an outstanding football player for the Thoroughbreds and was named the "best all-around man" when he was a senior.

Many new coaches come into a program with an "empty stall" of players, but Miller came on the scene inheriting one of the great legends of Murray State basketball, Joe Fulks.

"Fulks was a great player," Culp remembered. "I played against him in high school and everyone knew even then he was going to be some kind of player.

What made him such a good player? "It was his determination," Culp said. "I have never met a more determined person. Oh, he was strong and he had both size and talent, but when he wanted to score it was hard to keep him from it."

He shot a beautiful jump shot. His NBA coach, Eddie Gottlieb of the Philadelphia Warriors, would always say to his players, "Get the ball to Fulks and let him shoot. The people come to these games to see Joe Fulks shoot."

"Jumpin' Joe" Fulks, as he came to be known, and his supporting cast of captain Hyland Grimmer, center John Padgett of Hardin, and Herb Hurley opened the season by beating Southeast Missouri, Austin Peay and Southern Illinois in succession. Then after a loss to Southeast Missouri in a second meeting, they beat Tennessee Tech twice, then Evansville, but lost at Western Kentucky.

Joe Fulks

Circa 1943

They then won out, avenging their loss to Western by a 41-28 score in Murray, and ended their regular season with a 17-2 record. Ending seasons with an overwhelming won-lost record was becoming commonplace for what The *Shield* referred to as the "galloping Thoroughbreds."

Miller was a no nonsense guy, and The *Shield* reported that all will "long remember Miller's 'dressing down session' during the Howard (of Birmingham, Ala.) game. The Breds were behind midway in the first period when coach removed the entire first five and very calmly and deliberately led them to the dressing room. Five minutes later they returned to the game and quickly regained the lead, finally winning the game decisively."

The team was once again invited to the NAIB Tournament in Kansas City in March. In the first game of that tournament, they defeated Springfield Teachers College (now Missouri State) 72-44. The *Murray Ledger & Times* reporter graphically described the game: "The Missouri teachers were completely handcuffed by the close guarding Kentuckians and buried from

John Padgett

the start under the score that piled up with machine-gun rapidity."

In its second game, Murray beat Central Collegiate Conference champion Southwestern Kansas, said to be one of the strongest teams in the Midwest, by a score of 44-42. Fulks scored 22 points in that game. In the third game of the tournament, the Thoroughbreds continued their winning ways by beating Pepperdine 44-38. Finally in the semifinals, they met their match and lost to Southeast Missouri in the final 30 seconds, 38-36. Murray finished with 22 wins and 4 losses.

Though Fulks was reputed to be the star of the 1943 team, it was a balanced lineup with Elvin Phillips and Billy Joe Saunders being named to the All-Regional team. Hurley was also a mainstay on the team.

Fulks was drafted into the Army after his junior year and ended his career at Murray by leading the 1943 team in scoring with 337 points. Grimmer had 251 and Padgett 195. After two brilliant years, the unstoppable Fulks brought his two-year scoring average to 310 points a year and sank 63 percent of his career 173 foul shots. Fulks became the third Thoroughbred in history to be named an All-American by the NAIA.

Six-foot-six inch John Padgett, from nearby Hardin, was also drafted into the Army that year. He was a part of the 45th Infantry Division and served in five separate theaters of operation. He was awarded the Bronze Star for gallantry during the Italian campaign, and would return after the war to play for the Thoroughbreds.

1943-44 • 5-9

With Joe Fulks and others in the U.S. Army, the only member of the 1942-43 team remaining was Herb Hurley.

It was a most inexperienced team with Hurley being the only member the armed services did not take into the fold. Murray had a Navy Pre-Flight program with the men stationed on campus. Eight of them were part of the basketball team that played an abbreviated schedule that year.

Murray had quality wins over Tennessee Tech and Marshall and beat previously undefeated Morehead, 34-30. However, it would go down in the record books as the second losing season in school history, posting a 5-9 record. Because of the war, it was a most atypical season.

Hurley led the team in scoring with 168 points. He was described as a "rough little guard" and was lauded for his play.

These young men practicing, playing and studying with a World War surrounding them, their families, and their fellow students, bravely went on with their lives as best they could. Many had brothers and close family members "overseas" and they no doubt were in

1944 team

constant fear that their names would be drawn and they would be called to join their comrades in war. For them, D-Day was no history lesson. They listened by the radio in their dormitory rooms and anxiously read letters from their families and friends. They were a part of what Tom Brokaw has popularly labeled "The Greatest Generation," and the war was real to them.

Circa 1945

1944-45 • 12-10

• ***Mid-West Tournament Champion***

The team was devastated by the draft. All the upper classmen were serving their country. So, head coach John Miller took captain Kenny Cain and Scott Smith and combined them with a talented crew of freshmen to re-establish Murray's winning tradition. Newspapers followed every step of the team they called the team the "Hosses."

One of the freshmen was 5-foot-11, 128-pound forward from Bismark, Mo., Johnny "Red" Reagan. The future Murray Hall of Famer came to Murray following a heralded high school career where he led tiny Bismark to a victory in the Missouri State Basketball Tournament. The *Shield* of 1945 described him as "Murray's most spectacular player" and noted that he had been named captain of the Missouri All-State team in 1944.

Because of the continuation of World War II, this was again a year of uncertainty for the Thoroughbreds. They played a demanding schedule, but persevered and finished with a 12-10 record. They had quality wins over Arkansas State, Southern Illinois, Eastern Illinois, Indiana State, Marshall, Evansville and Morehead before losing the final game of the regular season to Tennessee, 57-38. The only tournament the team entered that year was the Mid-West Invitational in Terre Haute, and they won it.

Johnny "Red" Reagan

In the big game of the year, and any year for that matter, the Thoroughbreds experienced a disappointing loss to Western Kentucky at home in February. *The Ledger and Times* excitedly described the game: "In a game that kept the fans off and under their seats from the opening play until the sound of the final horn died away, again the Diddlemen staged a last half rally to top the Murray Thoroughbreds 37-33 in Carr Hall Saturday night."

Reagan made it clear that he would be a player to be reckoned with in the seasons to come. He led the team in scoring with 255 points. He scored a high 22 points in the team's 39-38 win against Morehead State in the final game of the season and led the team in scoring against Western with 17.

It is difficult to comprehend the emotional drain these young men were experiencing from the war in 1945 as well as in the preceding years. The local papers were filled with the names of draftees, photos of local servicemen fighting all over the world, and obituaries of those who made the ultimate sacrifice in service to their country. Shortly after the 1945 season ended, the players and the Murray State family was encouraged by a headline in May 3 *Ledger and Times* that reported Adolph Hitler's death as a result of suicide in Berlin on May 2, 1945.

1945-46 • 10-13

The *Shield* began its description of the 1945-46 season by saying Murray State would play one "of the most difficult schedules ever undertaken by a Murray team."

The ambitious schedule included two games against Louisville, and two with Southern Illinois, as well as games against DePaul, Marshall and Vanderbilt. Although the team finished the season with a losing record at 10-13, there were significant wins over Louisville (54-43), Western Kentucky (55-27) and Marshall (63-40).

Circa 1945

Murray State ended the season with a stunning victory in Carr Hall against mighty Vanderbilt, 53-34. The *Ledger and Times* reporter said the game was played before a large crowd and also noted that, "The tilt Saturday night was Murray's first win over a Vanderbilt team, the Bluebloods falling in 1934 and again in 1940 to Vanderbilt fives." Junior Kenny Cain led the team in scoring that night with 17 points.

A young freshman from Heath High School, Zadia Herrold Jr., scored 251 points including 61 free throws to lead the team in scoring. Big John Padgett, the 6-foot-6 sophomore center from Hardin, returned from the Army and filled the nets with 203 points.

Continuing his sterling contributions to the team with 195 points was Johnny Reagan, who was described by *The Shield* editor as one "who showed the fans some more of that flashy floor work and ball handling that makes him a truly great player." Rounding out the scoring for the year was guard Dale McDaniel with 172 points, Cain with 79, Carol Grammar with 66 points, Jack Haines with 48 points, Dale Riggins from Murray with 37 and Allen Russell also from Murray with 32.

Miller's team ended the season in the KIAC Tournament by walloping Union 62-26 in the first game. The return match against Louisville resulted in a four point loss, 60-56, and the season ended with great hopes for the coming year.

A *St. Louis Star Times* reporter said Reagan was "not a one man show, but an extremely modest, shy and cooperative player whose coach complains because he won't shoot more. However, those who have seen him in action, rate him in the class of Jumpin' Joe Fulks, who is the current sensation in professional basketball."

1946-47 • 14-11

The Second World War was over and the boys returned home. 1946-47 was a rebuilding year and Miller assembled a very difficult schedule for this "new" team. Murray fans speculated about which war veterans would return and play for the team. In January 1946, *The College News* reported that "all-time great" Joe Fulks would be back. He had been playing with the All-Star Service League with some of the best players in America. The rumor turned out to be untrue as Fulks went on to play in the Basketball Association of America, the forerunner to the NBA.

This was the first year for young Jim Frank from Barlow, Ky. Frank would end up playing for three coaches in three years at Murray. When asked about coach Miller, Frank said, "Coach Miller worked us hard and ran us to death."

Amazingly, the team had 13 players who were returning veterans and the rest were either freshmen or a few returning upperclassmen. This season started off with a record-breaking win against soldiers from nearby Camp Campbell (now Fort Campbell) by a score of 86-18. This margin of victory still stands as the largest in school history.

In the fifth game of the season, on Dec. 11, the Thoroughbreds defeated a prestigious Texas A&M team 49-46 with Rex Alexander and Charles Snow leading the way. Two games later, the giant killers upset Louisville, 56-45. Beating Peck Hickman's Cardinals team was indeed a spectacular victory. "The Cards had previously conquered Western and Indiana but they proved no match for the Thoroughbreds," reported

The College News. Reagan led Murray in scoring with 19 points.

The season ended with the KIAC tournament that seemed always to be held at Bowling Green. Murray defeated Union 39-31, but lost in the second round to Eastern Kentucky, 59-50. The team improved on their 1945-46 post-war record, finishing with 13 win and 10 defeats.

1947-48 • 12-12

The Carr Health Building gymnasium with its fan-shaped backboards and screaming crowds remained the home of the Thoroughbreds and the news media called them the "Men of War." The exploits of the great Carlisle Cutchin teams before the war were fondly remembered by Murray fans, and in this John Miller team fans saw a "strong aggressive team" that reminded them of the Thoroughbred squads of the past.

One must read between the lines to understand what happened in a coaching change that occurred only three games into the season. Longtime Murray teacher, football and basketball coach Miller had taken over from Cutchin as head basketball coach in 1943. He pieced together teams during that war-torn era, but now he faced a different challenge. Men like Padgett, who had fought in the war, were returning to play basketball and had their own ideas about how the game should be played. Miller was apparently a headstrong coach, and rumors abounded that there was a team insurrection against him early in the year. The team won its first game against Evansville, 62-60, but quickly lost games to Southern Illinois and Delta State. After the Delta State game on Dec. 15, Miller resigned as coach and was quickly replaced by Cutchin.

The *Louisville Times* would later report that "John Padgett, the 6' 5" starting center...only reported for basketball following the resignation of Coach John Miller and the appointment of Carlisle Cutchin as mentor."

The *Louisville Courier-Journal* reported later, "When Murray lost Miller as coach it regained a former star player Johnny Padgett.... After playing with Murray for three seasons, Padgett, at odds with Miller, dropped out of the sport (a part of) last season."

Two names that would live on in the lives of the Thoroughbreds, and later the Racers, played on that team. Rex Alexander, a 6-2 sophomore from Ilsley, Ky., was described in the *Shield* as a "fine clutch player." The second was Jim Frank, who was described as "a big, fast boy with a good eye for the basket."

Padgett, the war hero, earned a master's degree and moved to Frankfort, Ky., where he worked for the state Department of Education, taught, and coached basketball. Later he returned to west Kentucky and worked for the Atomic Energy Commission.

Reagan was the star in 1947-48, and was lauded in the *Shield* as "the redhead that sparked the Thoroughbreds to a successful season."

Of all Reagan's records, the most notable was his becoming the greatest point-getter in Murray's history, scoring 973 career points, surpassing a record Willard Bagwell set in 1933.

The *Courier-Journal* described Reagan as an "aggressive player." He held Murray's record for most personal fouls but the reporter said, "Reagan's aggressive play has given the Breds a great many more points on stolen balls that they have lost by fouls called on him." He also held the record for games played, foul shots tried and foul shots made. L.J. Hortin, famed Murray State journalist and historian, said of him, "At ball-hawking he has few superiors, at passing he is superb, and at shooting he has few equals."

Reagan was selected by a vote of his fellow students as student body president and was also named to "Who's Who in American Colleges and Universities."

Famed St. Louis sports broadcaster Harry Caray in 1944 said it best when he described Reagan in glowing terms.

"To put it simply, Bismark's fabulous Johnny Reagan is a great competitor, good at his worst, and one of those athletes who is greater than his best when the chips are down. At a time in our history when supreme competitive spirit is of greater interest than ever, Reagan gave an excellent example of what remarkable individual leadership and inspiration coupled with unselfish cooperation and team play can do."

While in college, he played all three positions – center, forward and guard. If there was a need, he was there to fill it. Famed coach Ray Meyer of DePaul said of him, "He is one of the best players my team has ever faced on the hardwood."

JOE FULKS... THE BEST BASKETBALL PLAYER IN THE WORLD

by Judge Bill Cunningham

Kentucky winters are brightened by the game of basketball. The full force of fan hysteria arrives at its annual crescendo in early spring of each year.

March Madness.

It's then that basketball comes crashing down the stretch through the rushing flume of tournament action. In Kentucky, at least, it becomes larger than life. While college and high school teams battle on the hardwood, fans talk of the game at country stores, coffee shops and church socials.

Ultimately, great names of basketball lore are cast about. Hagan and Ramsey. Unseld and Givens. Rupp and Diddle. "King" Kelly Coleman and Clem Haskins. Cotton Nash and Kenny Walker. On and on the names are legendary and endless. From the glittering roster of winters past, stars will be compared and enlarged. Most likely, and inexplicably, one basketball giant will never be mentioned.

In his day, he was the best. Joe Fulks, the Kuttawa Clipper.

Maybe it's the passage of time or the drastic change in the nature of the game since he played. But for some reason, "Jumping Joe" – the lanky, good-natured star from the Tennessee River bottom – has faded into the gray, forgotten wasteland of yesteryear. Even his hometown has been erased from the face of the earth. Like the legendary continent of Atlantis, little Birmingham, Kentucky has sunken beneath the waters. Only "Birmingham Island" can be seen today arising out of Kentucky Lake. Most of the dead, who once slumbered there, have been removed from their resting places to Birmingham Cemetery several miles away.

Birmingham was in Marshall County on the Tennessee River some twelve miles from the county seat of Benton. A ferry ran back and forth, connecting the community with Lyon County and the towns of Eddyville and Kuttawa. It was there that Joe was born to Leonard and Mattie Fulks on October 26, 1921. The small river town of less than 400 residents did have a high school – a substantial brick building in the middle of town. And the high school had a basketball team.

Joseph Franklin Fulks fell in love with basketball early in his life. On cold winter nights, this dreary little shanty town would brighten as the lights at the high school gym, generated by the school's own gasoline dynamo generator, glowed through the darkness. Old cars, pickup trucks, and even a few mule drawn wagons from up and down the valley surrounded the school on ball game nights as crowds packed the cozy gymnasium.

Joe gazed upon it all through wide, young eyes of wonderment. He went to the games and silently admired the older boys who performed under the bright lights on the shiny hardwood floor. It was a fantasy land where young, strong athletes – mere mortals by day – transformed into something heroic at night under the thunderous approval of the friendly crowd and the adoration of pretty girls.

Joe Fulks

But in the early impoverished years of Joe Fulks, a basketball was a rare luxury – one which he had to do without. So he improvised. The high school varsity team practiced on an outside court when the weather allowed. But every morning they would find the nets on the goals riddled to pieces. The coach of the little school, Robert Goheen, was baffled by the mystery of the disappearing nets. So after practice one evening, Goheen decided to solve the mystery.

He hid in the weeds beside the ball court and waited. Around dark, a tall, ambling youngster came upon the scene, playfully tossing half of a brick up in the air and catching it with the greatest of ease when it came back down. The trespasser then walked onto the court and began shooting the brick through the basketball goal with uncanny accuracy. The coach watched in amazement as one net was demolished and the hoopster moved on to finish off the other one. With both nets in shreds, he nonchalantly walked off the court, still tossing the brick in the air.

It was Joe. The next day Coach Goheen gave Joe a basketball and told him to keep it up. And so he did. Joe became a star at Birmingham High School. But drastic change and upheaval were enveloping the town and the entire lower Tennessee River Valley. In 1938, the construction of Kentucky Dam began just a few miles downstream. The village of Birmingham was doomed to be torn down and flooded by Kentucky Lake. With the town going down the tubes around him, Joe became a star on the Birmingham Five.

Then, just before his senior year, he moved with his parents to Kuttawa. For the Lyon County team, it was manna from heaven. But it led to allegations against the school for illegal recruiting. A full-blown investigation was conducted by the Kentucky High School Association Board of Control. The school was charged with securing employment in Kuttawa for Joe's father in order to lure the high school star away from Birmingham. The evidence was deemed insufficient to suspend the school, but the final report "deplored a tendency of schools to build up winning teams through use of imported athletes," a concern that is still with us today.

Joe Fulks

Fulks led the Kuttawa Lions to a brilliant 22-2 record that included a trip to the state tournament. The Lions were beaten there by Morganfield in overtime. The slender youngster was a pure shooter – inside, outside, right hand, left hand. A terrific rebounder, the 6-foot-3 center could do it all. In the little river towns of Birmingham and Kuttawa, Joe Fulks developed a shooting technique that would revolutionize the game of basketball. He explained it later: "People were shooting on the run during those days. But I discovered that by stopping and jumping, I was much more accurate and able to get open more for better shots." The World Book Encyclopedia reported years later that "the one-handed shot was the most popular shot in basketball until Joe Fulks popularized the jump shot… it became the most popular shot in basketball and greatly increased scoring."

Legendary Coach Ed Diddle of Western Kentucky University practically spent the summer of 1940 with Joe Fulks. Diddle was competing with Kentucky's Adolph Rupp and Indiana coach Branch McCracken in the recruiting war for the Kuttawa Clipper, as Fulks was now being called. He fooled them all and went to Murray State. At Murray, Joe played varsity ball for two years and was named an All-American. While there he acquired the label that would follow him the rest of his days – "Jumping Joe."

As good as he was, Joe Fulks was about to enter a phase of his life that would propel him into the superstar range. World War II came along and he was drafted out of college and went into the Marine Corps. He had grown to six-feet-five-inches without losing any of his grace and agility. He was assigned to a Fleet Marine Force basketball team which toured the South Pacific entertaining the troops. The military rosters were filled with some of the top basketball players of war-time America.

It was a great recruiting arena for professional teams back home. Eddie Gottlieb, coach and owner of the Philadelphia Warriors, headed out that way on a scouting trip. Gottlieb – the premier basketball guru of his day – was primarily interested in All-American Andy Phillip of the University of Illinois. But he quickly learned that across the broad South Pacific, the basketball player everyone was talking about was a skinny kid from Kentucky with wavy hair. Joe was playing circles around them all. Gottlieb was impressed and signed Fulks to the tune of a $10,000 bonus – a gargantuan sum in those days.

The slender and likable country boy from Kentucky exploded upon the professional scene. In his rookie year of 1946-47, he led the league in scoring with a 23.2 point average. These were the fledgling years of the National Basketball Association when there was no shot clock or three-point line and the game was played at a much slower pace. Consequently, teams scored far fewer points. During his initial year, for instance, the Warriors averaged only 68.6 points with Joe scoring a third of them. The New York Knicks had no player to average in double figures. Four of the league's teams couldn't match Fulks' output with their top two scorers. It all makes his performance that much more remarkable.

In short, the shy and soft-spoken cager with the southern drawl was an overnight sensation. He almost single-handedly propelled professional basketball into national prominence. His Warrior team was the first to utilize air travel for road games. "If it hadn't been for Joe," Hall of Famer and former Warrior Paul Arizin put it, "I don't think pro basketball would have made it those first few years." Just as he was at Birmingham, Kuttawa, Murray State, and in the wide Pacific, Jumping Joe was a winner. In that first year, he led the Warriors to the championship. In the first game of the playoffs against Chicago, Joe scored 21 points in the final quarter. Five men guarding him throughout the game accumulated a total of 20 fouls. The single quarter scoring record stood until Isaiah Thomas broke it forty-one years later.

During his first season in the pros, Fulks hit 49 free throws in a row. He missed and then hit 49 more in a row. The Warriors gave Joe a brand new Buick as a bonus for leading the league in scoring. That summer, he

Joe Fulks

Joe Fulks (No. 10) and his teammates of the Philadelphia Warriors, 1947

Fulks in action while a member of the Philadelphia Warriors.

large part to Joe's popularity and his draw at the gate, the city began construction of a new basketball arena. A cartoon in the local newspaper showed a caricature of Joe shooting basketballs into a concrete mixer.

The Kuttawa Clipper was hailed as the "Babe Ruth of basketball." In 1948, the prestigious *Sporting News* acclaimed him as "Athlete of the Year." To place this honor in proper perspective, it should be noted that Joe beat out some heavy timber. Such names as Ted Williams, Joe DiMaggio, Doak Walker, Ben Hogan, Pancho Gonzales, and Joe Louis were at their peaks. Stan Musial of the St. Louis Cardinals, who performed just a few blocks away from the Sporting News office, batted .376, stroked 39 home runs, drove in 131 runs, and was selected the National League's Most Valuable Player in 1948.

Joe played in the NBA for eight years. But personal problems – basically alcoholism – cut his career short and narrowed his heroics to a five-year span. Joe closed out his playing days in 1954 – a time of positive transition in professional basketball for which he was largely responsible. He amassed a total of 8,003 points – an average of 1,000 per year. His career average of 16 points a game is deceptive since his playing time was severely limited during his final two years. "He was a great, great player," says Hall of Fame coach Red Auerbach. "He could shoot them any way, from any place."

As much fanfare as Joe received in the "City of Brotherly Love" and elsewhere, he never lost his love for his native West Kentucky. He would return to the land of his birth in the off season. Once, some of his old high school friends traveled to St. Louis to watch him play. After the game, he threatened to go home with them. That was Joe. Sensational and yet simple, with his heart always close to home.

proudly drove it home to Kuttawa to show it off to his friends. But Joe was the same old Joe – quiet, friendly, and unassuming. Success did not go to his head. For three straight years, Joe was the leading scorer in the NBA. On the cold winter night of February 10, 1949, in Philadelphia, the few fans who had braved the raging blizzard were rewarded with an epoch-making performance. From the same hands that had shredded nets with a half brick in tiny Birmingham came an incredible barrage of baskets. Before the night was over, Joe had scored a whopping 63 points – a record held in the NBA until broken by Elgin Baylor in 1959 after the advent of the shot clock. Joe left the game with two minutes to play. This modest boy from Kentucky with his winning ways took Philadelphia by storm. Fans adored him and he was the toast of the town. Due in

The name of Joseph Franklin Fulks has now been enshrined in the Basketball Hall of Fame in Springfield, Massachusetts. At the 1971 NBA All Star game in San Diego, Joe was recognized for being selected as one of the ten members of the Silver Anniversary Team of the National Basketball Association. The others were Paul Arizin, Bob Davies, Bob Cousy, Bill Sharman, Bill Russell, George Mikan, Dolph Schayes, Bob Pettit, and Sam Jones.

During the early morning hours of March 21, 1976, Joe Fulks died in Eddyville, just two miles from the site of the old Kuttawa gym. How would Joe have fared in today's game of muscled titans, three-point lines, and shot clocks? Probably not as well. Too thin, too slow, and too polite. But the giants of today may also not have fared as well in Joe's day. Too powerful, too undisciplined, and too erratic.

Greatness must be judged in the context of the times. Lincoln may not have made a great television president. Television made John F. Kennedy. Suffice it to say, there was a time when Joe Fulks was the best basketball player in the world.

NBA Silver Anniversary Team, 1971.

JOHNNY REAGAN IS A HARD MAN TO PIN DOWN AND BEAT

by Ricky Martin

For a man with longer ties to the university than most, Johnny "Red" Reagan (class of 1948) has trouble narrowing down his favorite Murray State moment. That is understandable to those who know the former Thoroughbred and Racer.

Reagan's association with Murray State University goes back to 1944 when he enrolled at Murray State Teachers College on a basketball scholarship. Since then, he has worn many hats for the institution, distinguishing himself as a student-athlete, coach, classroom teacher and athletic director.

Even today he keeps giving his talents and time to Murray State, attending many of its athletic events and making contact by letter or telephone with university alumni, imploring them to stay connected to their alma mater. He takes pride in the fall when former Thoroughbred baseball players return to campus for the Racers' football homecoming weekend and participate in an annual baseball alumni game that he started.

Asked in the summer of 2012 what his favorite Murray State moment or accomplishment was, the Bismarck, Mo., High School legend didn't give a definitive answer.

"Maybe the highlights would be the championships our teams won when I was A.D. for almost a decade (1978-1986)," Reagan said. "But there have been so many great athletes and so many great teams, especially in men's basketball. I just don't know how I can pinpoint one thing."

A student-athlete in the truest sense, Reagan was a two-sport letterman at Murray State, the shining star on four Murray State basketball teams that had to pull themselves together and build back up a program that had lost a great deal of its sizzle. His hoops career ended on Feb. 28, 1948 when the 'Breds beat Eastern Kentucky, 78-77, in the consolation game of the Kentucky Intercollegiate Athletics Conference Tournament in Louisville.

Johnny Reagan

The win gave the '47-48 'Breds a 12-12 record in a season that can best be described as unsettling. Reportedly there was unrest on the team triggered by some rather harsh practice and dining decisions made by sixth-year coach John Miller. Four games into the season, he was replaced by former coach Carlisle Cutchin, who was coach of the 'Breds baseball team. He took over the basketball job on a temporary basis only.

For the normally unflappable and soft-spoken Reagan, college life was still good. There was a season of 'Breds baseball to play. Graduation wasn't that far off. Then once someone hired him, he could get on to coaching and being an educator. And according to more than one person, he was married to the most attractive Murray State hometown coed, the former Carolyn Carter.

Murray State has retired Reagan's basketball and baseball jersey numbers.

He's the only Murray State alumnus who has had two campus venues named after him: the current Reagan Field that is located just north of Roy Stewart Stadium and the long gone Reagan Field whose location near the Curris Center was a gathering place on spring afternoons for Murray State students wanting to see college baseball or see what the girls were wearing on warm afternoons.

He has been inducted into five halls of fame: the Ohio Valley Conference Hall of Fame, the Murray State Hall of Fame, the American Baseball Coaches Association Hall of Fame, the Missouri High School Hall of Fame, and the Bismarck High School Hall of Fame.

Reagan with the 1979-80 OVC men's all-sports trophy and the 1980-81 OVC women's all-sports trophy.

And in 1944, after leading tiny Bismarck to the Missouri State Basketball Tournament championship, Reagan was proclaimed the mayor of Bismarck. Having also played and coached baseball at Bismarck High, the school's baseball venue is called Reagan Field.

Oh yes, Reagan's first employment opportunity – after a brief stint playing professional baseball – took him back to Bismarck High, where he was the boys' basketball coach and the baseball coach.

Coming out of high school, Reagan thought he would be drafted into the military to fight in World War II, meaning he wouldn't be going to college for awhile. But he wasn't drafted and the conflict would soon be winding down, so in the summer of 1944 he looked into two college options: Western Kentucky and Murray State.

He first visited Western, but a joy ride over the hills of Bowling Green with some Hilltopper athletes left him queasy and wanting to be on flatland like he was used to at Bismarck. Next came a stop at Murray State, where things were a little more to Reagan's liking, entertainment-wise. Robert Johnson, a former high school teammate, was a rising sophomore at Murray State and doing his best to convince Reagan that Murray, Ky., was the place for him.

Presto, the 1944-45 Murray State Thoroughbred basketball team soon had a commitment from Reagan, the most acclaimed high school player in the state of Missouri the season before. The 'Breds roster was ever changing during the '44-45 season, but Murray State won 12 of 22 games, a vast improvement over the 5-9 record in the '43-44 season.

And in Reagan, a guard/forward, Murray State had a gem, as he became the first 'Bred to lead the team in these noteworthy offensive categories: most field goals made in a season (102), most free throws made in a season (51), most points scored in a season (255) and best scoring average (11.6). The 'Breds won their first six games, with three of the wins coming in the Mid West Tournament at Terre Haute, Ind. Reagan was the tourney MVP and his top scoring game during the season (22 points) came in the tournament against Murray State.

Newcomer Zadia Herrold led a 10-13 Murray State team in scoring (10.9 ppg) in the 1945-46 season, followed by John Padgett, who was back from the war, and Reagan. In his final two seasons, Reagan was Murray's top scorer, averaging 12.0 and 9.0 points a game. In his junior year the 'Breds won 14 of 25 games, beating

the University of Louisville, 56-45, in Louisville and sweeping Arkansas State, Evansville and Morehead State. His 973 career points were a new school record, eclipsing the previous record of 936, set in the early 1930's by Willard Bagwell.

Johnny Reagan

Here's how Reagan describes himself as a Murray State basketball player. "I could jump and handle the ball," he said. "I had good peripheral vision and see the floor. I was pretty well rounded on offense. Defensively, I had good hands and could anticipate things."

While his contributions to Thoroughbreds basketball are paramount, Reagan was also a hard throwing right-handed pitcher on the 'Breds baseball team, once tossing a no-hitter against Western Kentucky. Years later, he built Murray State baseball into a program that many rivals envied.

First, Reagan had to give pro baseball a try, pitching two years in the St. Louis Cardinals minor-league system. "I could throw it hard," he said, "but my control wasn't very good. I knew I didn't have a future in the big leagues."

In 1955, Reagan was hired as

Johnny Reagan

an assistant basketball coach at Northeastern Louisiana State College, where he stayed two years. He then returned to Murray State in 1957 to take over the 'Breds baseball coaching duties and be an assistant basketball coach.

"I didn't know there was a vacancy in the beginning," Reagan said "I didn't know until someone contacted me. In that period of time, being hired was a completely different story than it is now. There wasn't a committee in Murray's search for a baseball coach. The school president (Dr. Ralph H. Woods), the athletic director (Roy Stewart) and the basketball coach (Rex Alexander) were 'the committee.'

"Dr. Woods was the president when I was a student at Murray State, so he knew of me. He knew that I was a two-sport guy, and this was a two-sport job at that time."

B 8 The Courier-Journal, Tuesday morning, July 6, 1982

SPORTS

Murray earns No. 1 sports rating among Kentucky colleges

Kentucky, Louisville do poorly

Murray programs rated Kentucky's best

"We feel like we've got an exceptionally good, and stable, coaching staff. Another factor is that we have a strong commitment from our board of regents and administrators." Johnny Reagan.

The Murray Ledger & Times

Murray State rates best sports program in state

WE'RE STILL THE ONE!

The spring of 1958 was Reagan's first as Murray State's baseball coach and he held the job until the summer of 1993, when he retired and was replaced by long-time assistant Mike Thieke.

Reagan directed the 'Breds to 27 consecutive winning seasons,

Reagan's retirement. Murray State has retired his basketball and baseball jersey numbers.

11 Ohio Valley Conference championships (the last in 1991) and two appearances in the NCAA Division I College World Series (1975 and 1979). Three of his Murray State standouts (pitchers Pat Jarvis and Kirk Rueter and infielder Jack Perconte) went on to play in the major leagues.

Current Murray State athletics media relations director and former 'Breds first baseman Dave Winder, says some of the best memories of his life came under Reagan's watch.

"I just felt a sense of pride that he was my coach," Winder said. "There was just something about the guy, and he played the game a certain way. He taught us to have respect for the game and for our opponents, and it was great being a part of that. To this day, I carry what I learned from him with me to work every day. He's a big reason why I have so much pride in Murray State."

"The halls of Fame certainly give me a great feeling of satisfaction," Reagan said. "It makes me feel that I did my job at least reasonably well, and that I did it with a degree of class. Those are the things that are most important to me."

MURRAY
STATE UNIVERSITY

OHIO VALLEY
OVC
CONFERENCE

The OVC Years

Murray State is a Trailblazer in the Ohio Valley Conference

by Jimmy Wilder

The Ohio Valley Conference traces its roots to 1941, when athletic directors Roy Stewart of Murray State and Charles Hughes of Eastern Kentucky met with Western Kentucky public relations director Kelly Thompson and discussed plans for an athletics conference that would be comprised mostly of the state-supported schools from the Kentucky Intercollegiate Athletics Conference and place a strong emphasis on football and basketball.

World War II put their idea on hold, but at war's end, they resumed talking about a league for their own. And at a February 1948 meeting in Louisville, the University of Louisville, Evansville and Morehead State joined Murray State, Eastern Kentucky and Western Kentucky to form the OVC, which soon afterwards added Marshall and Tennessee Tech to its ranks.

The OVC is now the eighth-oldest NCAA Division I conference and has seen its membership change – and grow – considerably over the years. But not the benchmark that Stewart, Hughes and Thompson envisioned for the league in basketball.

From its onset, the Ohio Valley Conference has been blessed with institutions which have enjoyed many great moments on the hardwood. The most obvious of these – from the mid-1980s on – has been Murray State University.

Since joining the OVC, Murray State has received more accolades than ever envisioned by Stewart or Ralph Woods, MSU's president from 1945 to 1968. The Racer basketball media guide shows the university with an OVC-best 38 league championships and an OVC-best 15 NCAA Tournament appearances, and notes that Murray State's 31 wins in the 2009-10 and 2011-12 seasons are the most ever by an Ohio Valley Conference school. It also points out that MSU's current streak of 25 winning seasons in a row ties the University of Connecticut for the nation's fourth longest streak of consecutive winning seasons.

What the guide doesn't mention is Murray State's most laudable achievement in men's basketball. It occurred in the 1963-64 season, when MSU was once again an OVC trailblazer, this time for breaking the color barrier by having a highly recruited African-American, sophomore forward Stewart Johnson of Clairton, Pa., on its varsity roster...in a starring role.

Murray State won the '63-64 OVC regular-season and tournament titles, and more than held its own in the NCAA Tournament against defending national champion Loyola Chicago, whose roster was filled with players of color, some from the South.

Up until Johnson's Racer debut, only one African-American – Marshall Banks of Morehead State – had

Stewart Johnson

suited up on the varsity for an OVC basketball team. But after Johnson's impactville season, every school in the conference began recruiting African-America basketball players. With an expanded talent pool to choose from, Ohio Valley Conference basketball got even better.

Beginning in the 1964-65 season, forward Clem Haskins of Campbellsville, Ky., was a three-time OVC Player of the Year for Western Kentucky. In 1970, Western advanced to the NCAA Tournament's Final Four, starting five blacks – all from the state of Kentucky. Murray State had five black starters in the 1987-88 season when the Racers upset North Carolina State in the NCAA Tournament. Each starter on Murray State's record-setting teams of 2009-10 and 2011-12 was an African-American.

Though it was a game-changer, those who read the stories that follow will understand that the end of segregation is but one defining aspect of Racer basketball and the Ohio Valley Conference.

A game action shot of Murray State's Herb McPherson scoring against Western Kentucky's Clem Haskins.

A Look at the Ohio Valley Conference

Year the OVC was Founded
1948

First OVC Member Schools
Eastern Kentucky, Evansville, Louisville, Morehead State, Murray State, Western Kentucky

Present OVC member schools
Austin Peay, Belmont, Eastern Illinois, Eastern Kentucky, Jacksonville State, Morehead State, Murray State, Southern Illinois Edwardsville, Southeast Missouri, Tennessee State, Tennessee Tech, UT Martin

All-Time OVC Membership List
Akron (1981-1987)
Austin Peay (1962-present)
Belmont (2012-present)
Eastern Illinois (1996-present)
Eastern Kentucky (1948-present)
East Tennessee State (1957-1978)
Evansville (1948-1952)
Jacksonville State (2003-present)
Louisville (1948-1949)
Marshall (1948-1952)
Middle Tennessee State (1952-2000)
Morehead State (1948-present)
Murray State (1948-present)
Samford (2003-2008)
Southern Illinois Edwardsville (2008-present)
Southeast Missouri (1991-present)
Tennessee State (1986-present)
Tennessee Tech (1949-present)
UT Martin (1992-present)
Youngstown State (1981-1988)
Western Kentucky (1948-1982)

Winners of OVC Regular Season Championships
Murray State (23 times) – 1950-51, '63-64, '67-68, '68-69, '79-80, '81-82, '82-83, '87-88, '88-89, '89-90, '90-91, '91-92, '93-94, '94-95, '95-96, '96-97, '97-98, '98-99, '99-00, 2005-06, '09-10, '10-11, '11-12
Western Kentucky (19 times) – '48-49, '49-50, '51-52, '53-54, '54-55, '55-56, '56-57, '59-60, '60-61, '61-62, '65-66, '66-67, '69-70, '70-71, '71-72, '75-76, '79-80, '80-81, '81-82
Morehead State (9 times) – '55-56, '56-57, '60-61, '62-63, '68-69, '71-72, '73-74, '83-84, '02-03
Austin Peay (8 times) – '72-73, '73-74, '76-77, '96-97, '02-03, '03-04, '06-07, '07-08
Tennessee Tech (7 times) – '55-56, '57-58, '62-63, '84-85, '00-01, '01-02, '04-05
Eastern Kentucky (6 times) – '52-53, '58-59, '60-61, '64-65, '71-72, '78-79
Middle Tennessee State (5 times) – '74-75, '77-78, '85-86, '86-87, '88-89
East Tennessee State (2 times) – '67-68, '77-78
Tennessee State (2 times) – '92-93, '94-95
Akron (1 time) – '85-86
Belmont (1 time) – '12-13
Southeast Missouri (1 time) – '99-00
UT Martin (1 time) – '08-09

Winners of OVC Tournament Championships
Murray State (15 times) – '50-51, '63-64, '87-88, '89-90, '90-91, '91-92, '94-95, '96-97, '97-98, '98-99, '01-02, '03-04, '05-06, '09-10, '11-12
Western Kentucky (10 times) – '48-49, '51-52, '52-53, '53-54, '64-65, '65-66, '75-76, '77-78, '79-80, '80-81
Eastern Kentucky (5 times) – '49-50, '54-55, '78-79, '04-05, '06-07
Middle Tennessee State (5 times) – '74-75, '76-77, '81-82, '84-85, '88-89
Austin Peay (4 times) – '86-87, '95-96, '02-03, '07-08
Morehead State (4 times) – '82-83, '83-84, '08-09, '10-11
Tennessee State (2 times) – '92-93, '93-94
Akron (1 time) – '85-86
Belmont (1 time) – '12-13
Eastern Illinois (1 time) – '00-01
Southeast Missouri (1 time) – '99-00
Tennessee Tech (1 time) – '66-67

Participants in the NCAA Tournament
Murray State (15 times) – 1964, 1969, 1988, 1990, 1991, 1992, 1995, 1997, 1998, 1999, 2002, 2004, 2006, 2010, 2012
Western Kentucky (10 times) – 1960, 1962, 1966, 1967, 1970, 1971, 1976, 1978, 1980, 1981
Eastern Kentucky (7) – 1953, 1959, 1965, 1972, 1979, 2005, 2007
Morehead State (7 times) – 1956, 1957, 1961, 1983, 1984, 2009, 2011
Austin Peay (6 times) – 1973, 1974, 1987, 1996, 2003, 2008

Middle Tennessee State (5 times) – 1975, 1977, 1982, 1987, 1989
Tennessee State (2 times) – 1993, 1994
Tennessee Tech (2 times) – 1958, 1963
Akron (1 time) – 1986
Belmont (1 time) – 2013
Eastern Illinois (1 time) – 2001
East Tennessee State (1 time) – 1968
Southeast Missouri (1 time) – 2000

Games Won in the NCAA Tournament

Western Kentucky (9) – beat Miami (Fla.) and Ohio in 1960, beat Dayton in 1962, beat Loyola Chicago and Dayton in 1968, beat Jacksonville, Kentucky and Kansas in 1971, beat Syracuse in 1971
Morehead State (6) – beat Marshall and Wayne State in 1956, beat Xavier (Ohio) in 1961, beat North Carolina A&T in 1984, beat Alabama State in 2009, beat Louisville in 2011
Murray State (3) – beat North Carolina State in 1988, beat Vanderbilt in 2010, beat Colorado State in 2012
Austin Peay (2) – beat Jacksonville in 1973, beat Illinois in 1987
Middle Tennessee State (2) – beat Kentucky in 1982, beat Florida State in 1989
East Tennessee State (1) – beat Florida in 1968

Editors' note: Beginning in the 1955-56 season, the Ohio Valley Conference has had an automatic qualifier in the NCAA Tournament, and for the past 49 years, the OVC Tournament champion has represented the league in the annual NCAA tourney.

Participants in the National Invitation Tournament

Murray State (7 times) – 1980, 1982, 1983, 1989, 1994, 1996, 2011
Western Kentucky (7 times) – 1949, 1950, 1952, 1953, 1954, 1965, 1982
Austin Peay (2 times) – 2004, 2007
Middle Tennessee State)2 times) – 1986, 1988
Tennessee Tech (2 times) – 1985, 2002
Akron (1 time) – 1987
UT Martin (1 time) – 2009

Games Won in the National Invitation Tournament

Western Kentucky (4) – beat Niagara in 1950, beat Louisville in 1952, beat Bowling Green in 1954, beat Fordham in 1965
Tennessee Tech (3) – beat Georgia State, Dayton and Yale in 2002
Middle Tennessee State (2) – beat Tennessee and Georgia in 1988
Murray State (2) – beat Jacksonville and Alabama in 1980
Austin Peay (1) – beat Belmont in 2004

OVC Commissioners

Art Guepe (1963-1975)
Paul Dietzel (1975-1976)
Bob Vanatta (1976-1979)
Jim Delany (1979-1989)
Dan Beebe (1989-2003)
Jon Steinbrecher (2003-2009)
Beth DeBauche (2009-present)

Editors' note: When the OVC was established in 1948, the presidents of each school was the governing body of the conference. In 1963, former Vanderbilt football coach and athletic director Art Guepe was hired as the league's first full-time commissioner. Altogether seven different people have held the position, including Jim Delany, who served the conference for 10 years before becoming commissioner of the Big Ten Conference in 1989. Today he is one of the most influential administrators in college athletics as he continues his duties at the Big Ten.

MSU BASKETBALL – 1948-59

by Sid Easley

Months before Murray State played its first game as a member of the Ohio Valley Conference, Roy Stewart pushed all of the right buttons in convincing Southern Illinois Carbondale assistant basketball coach Harlan Hodges to sign on as Murray State's head coach. Hodges, a native Illinoisan, viewed himself as SIU's head-coach-in-waiting, but Stewart saw him as Murray State's head-coach-to-be. It didn't take long for Hodges to show the Racer faithful why Stewart wanted him to be Murray State's head coach.

1948-49 • 13-12

The 1948-49 season began with Murray's fourth basketball coach at the helm. The hiring of coaches is always a "story" for basketball fans. Avid cage fans love to speculate on recruiting and coaching changes during the off season. The coaching change rumor mill had worked overtime following the "resignation" of Miller in December and Cutchin's temporary return.

Most rumors swirled around one of Murray's great players from the past – big Floyd "Red" Burdette. Burdette, from nearby Martin, Tennessee, was the second leading scorer in Thoroughbred history before Reagan's exploits had lowered him to the third position behind Willard Bagwell and Reagan. After college and military service Burdette had begun coaching, and had advanced quickly in the ranks to become the head coach at the University of Alabama.

The *Courier Journal* staff writer when writing about Reagan in early 1948 had speculated on the coaching change and reported, "Another auburn-haired tosser, Red Burdette, now cage coach at Alabama is first choice if he can be lured away to pilot the Murray cagers next season."

Don Brumbaugh who was described as a demon statistician for the *Murray Ledger and Times* said, "Burdette's the fellow Murray would like to get, but the school doesn't think it can entice him to leave Alabama." Brumbaugh was correct, and Burdette elected to stay at Alabama.

The Thoroughbred brain trust, which no doubt was headed by Athletic Director Roy Stewart and President Ralph Woods (a hands-on President), selected a man who directed the team for the following six seasons – Harlan Hodges. President Woods had coached high school basketball and players during the era said that he would come to practice often twice a week. Jim Frank recalled that Dr. Woods would see the team off on road trips and be there to welcome them home. Both Woods and Stewart were winners and neither would settle for second best.

There were of course local favorites, but Woods and Stewart liked what they saw in Harlan Hodges from Illinois. Woods had great connections at the University of Kentucky and was friends with Adolph Rupp. Rupp recommended Hodges and that was good enough for Woods.

Hodges' first team began the year by winning seven straight over Ky. Wesleyan, two at Austin Peay, Southeast Missouri, Middle Tennessee, Tennessee Tech, and Delta State. The team was led in scoring by senior forward Junior Herrold who scored 259 points in the 23 games. Charlie Snow from Flat River, Missouri was close behind with 228, and scrappy guard Harold Loughary thrilled the fans with his ball-hawking and defensive prowess. Don Stephenson from Valley High School in Louisville also was a great contributor, and *The Shield* editor reported, "He never rested a minute through a game and generally poured in a large share of points."

Future Murray coaches and teachers Rex Alexander and Jim Frank were major contributors to this team as was Melvin DeWeese who was said to have put on a great defensive show against rival Western Kentucky. Alexander graduated that year and was named in Who's Who in American Colleges and Universities.

In his first season as a Thoroughbred young Bennie Purcell from Mt. Vernon, Illinois thrilled the fans any time he came on the floor. The *Shield* reported, "The crowd always cheered and knew what would happen when Bennie Purcell came onto the floor. Complete attention was commanded from the spectators by Bennie's zig-zag dribbling."

A photo in the Shield of 1949 shows Bennie shooting one of his famed jumpers toward the fan shaped backboard before a full house in the Carr gymn. A thick pad protecting the player from crashing into the wall is visible under the basket, as well as a "No Smoking" sign, and another sign admonishing all who would listen that "Street Shoes are Not Permitted on this Floor."

Murray ended the season with 13 wins and 10 losses. Though the record was not spectacular, Hodges had done a wonderful job with a team that had few experienced players. His team had beaten Middle twice, split with Evansville, and had taken Louisville and Memphis State to the wire in games at the end of the season.

The President of the Alumni Association that year was a popular local surgeon Dr. Hal Houston of Murray. Dr. Houston, father of recent team doctor Hal E. Houston M.D., was team physician for many years for the Breds. He became a noted surgeon, and was decorated for his innovative brain surgery techniques in Europe on the battlefront during the Second World War.

Pregame Meals and Rules of the Game

Jim Frank who later was a full Professor at Murray and served as athletic director for a time played on three of the teams from 1946 through 1949. His wife Norma was a cheerleader. He recalled that he played under three different coaches in his three years and his memories of those times are fascinating. He said that the team always traveled in cars until Coach Hodges arrived and then began traveling by bus most of the time.

Pregame meals are always an integral part of the team's away games and having played under all three coaches Jim Frank remembered each of them.

1. Coach Miller required a 5 o'clock meal of dry beef on toast with hot tea without sugar.
2. Coach Cutchin's pregame menu consisted of poached eggs on toast and hot tea with no sugar.
3. Hodges' meals included a bowl of fruit cocktail, tea without sugar, and dry toast.

This was a period of the college game when players began converting their style of free throw shooting from a between the legs swing shot to the modern one hand method.

Basketball rules are always evolving. Bennie Purcell recalled the prevailing rules during the time he played: "You could dribble forever," he said. "There was no counting seconds on the dribbler." There were four 10-minute quarters as opposed to 20-minute halves today. Although a few televisions began to appear in the early 50's no Murray games were televised. TV timeouts were a late invention. You could not dunk the basketball, and there was a jump ball at the beginning of each quarter and after every tie ball. In the 50's the rule changes permitted teams awarded a free throw in the waning minutes of the game to elect to take the ball out in lieu of taking the free throw.

There were only two referees, but Jim Frank does recall an experimental game in Louisville with three referees. One ran up and down with the teams and the other two sat on each of the two frames that held the backboards and baskets. That was one experiment that never came to fruition. But all players and fans from that era agreed that the game was called much closer in those days, and there was a minimal amount of contact allowed. The shooter was much better protected, and there was little contact in the areas away from the goal.

1949-50 • 18-13

The 1949-50 season was considered a rebuilding year for the Thoroughbreds. But the visionary and challenging schedule patiently put together by Athletic Director Roy Stewart and Harlan Hodges was destined to thrust the team into the national limelight in the following years. In addition to a rugged OVC schedule this team traveled extensively.

The team featured Madison Stanford, a native of Mississippi, Harold Loughary from Caldonia, Missouri (now a Hall of Fame member) and Charles Snow from Flat River, Missouri, as well as future greats Garrett Beshear and Bennie Purcell, Brewers' high school star Mason Cope, Gene Dick, and Charles Lampley from Sharpe. In fact it was a team so deep and talented that Hodges introduced a two-platoon system that left opponents gasping for breath.

At that time there were four 10-minute quarters. Hodges would send in five of his taller players for the first 10 minutes and replace them with his shorter players who would press and fast break for the next ten minutes. Sport writers tagged them the "jumpers" and the "runners," said the *Shield* editor.

When the team was playing at home the "second five" would conveniently excuse themselves and practice in the small gym in Carr Health during the quarter the other team was playing so they would be warmed up when they went in. "I always wondered if that was legal," said Jim Frank, "but Hodges got by with it."

Mason Cope had been the only player at the time to come to Murray from the storied and historic Brewers High School team in Marshall County coached by McCoy Tarry that won the Kentucky State Basketball Tournament in 1948. Incredibly this team ended their historic season with a perfect 36-0 record. Later a second member of the Redmen, Barney Thweatt, would enroll at Murray and become an outstanding guard for the Thoroughbreds.

This Murray team traveled extensively. They went to Cleveland, Mississippi to play Delta State, Huntington, W. Va. to play Marshall, Beloit, Wisconsin to play Beloit College, and to New Orleans and Mobile to play Loyola and Springhill colleges. The most ambitious trip, obviously designed to attract the attention of the eastern press corps, was a February journey to play Seton Hall in East Orange, N. J., Brooklyn College in Brooklyn, New York, and Connecticut State in New Britain, Connecticut.

That historic and visionary trip turned out to be more successful than expected. The Breds won two of three games and the sportswriters of the country moved them up to 21st in the country. They remained there for much of the latter part of the season.

The Thoroughbreds set a Murray record on February 4 when they scored 100 points in a game against Middle Tennessee held at the Carr Building in Murray. In a day when no one had dreamed of a three point shot this was quite a feat. A remarkable individual scoring performance was turned in by center Madison Stanford when he thrilled the fans with a 38-point outburst in the Breds' December 7 drubbing of Tennessee Tech 96-71. Fans said he simply couldn't miss that night and that he was hitting hook shots without looking at the basket.

Murray returned home from their Eastern trip to beat a good Memphis State team in Murray 64 to 57. The OVC tournament followed on the heels of these heady accomplishments. The tournament began with a strong victory over Morehead, 75-60, but Western Kentucky edged them in the second game of the tournament 58-54.

Despite that, the Breds were invited to The NAIB tournament in Kansas City, but regrettably lost the first game to Central Washington.

This team had balanced scoring and was led by Stanford's average of 9.9 points per game, Loughary checked in at 9.2, and Beshear at 8.3. They had scored a thrilling 2,008 points for the year and finished with an 18-13 record. It had been a great year with local fans experiencing the pride and euphoria that goes with a national ranking. And the future was bright with Purcell and Beshear returning.

This was the first year for 26-year-old Garrett Beshear to play for the Breds. He was unique, both because of his age, and his uncanny ability to put the ball in the basket. The Dawson Springs native had entered the Army after high school. Western had recruited him when he was in high school. But after he came back from the Army he remained in Dawson Springs for a couple of years and then Murray found him.

Bennie Purcell played with Beshear for three years and described thusly, "He had an amazingly deceptive fake. He would sometimes fake with his head and arms two or three times. While everyone, including the referees, was following the fake he was beginning his move. He had an unusually quick first step that often involved movement of his pivot foot, which gave him great advantage. Frankly, he probably walked a lot, but with only two referees he seldom got caught. He also had an unbelievable knack for getting open in the pivot and was a fantastic rebounder too. He seemed always to have the ability to know where that ball was going when it came off the basket. Through the years there have been very few players with that ability."

1950-51 • 21-6

• *OVC Regular Season Champion*
• *OVC Tournament Champion*

This was to be Harlan Hodges' third year as coach. He had recruited well. He was presiding over what knowledgeable fans realized was a revolution in the way basketball was played. The jump shot had been around for several years. Joe Fulks shot it, and other Murray players had shot it, but it was by no means universally accepted. Many coaches did not grasp how important it was for a player to be able to run down the court at full speed and suddenly rise straight up, and shoot the ball at the height of his jump. Bennie Purcell had been taught the shot between his junior and senior year in high school, and he brought that skill with him to Murray.

The second revolutionary part of the game as Hodges taught it was the fast break. Little Brewers in Marshall County had gone through the 1948 season without losing a game and finished a perfect season by winning the Kentucky State Tournament. They did it with a torrid fast break. Several high schools in Illinois and Indiana had also used it. And Western was a running team with Coach Ed Diddle at the helm.

Hodges was not afraid to try something new, and in the 1949-50 season he had created a "two platoon" system. One team composed of his bigger players played conventionally. But a second five specialized in the full-court press and fast-breaking.

To the sophisticated Murray fans, most of whom had watched local high school teams run and press, this was their kind of basketball. Additionally the fans had already fallen in love with the dribbling, jump shooting, and driving of Bennie Purcell. They also loved the one they called "the old man" Garrett Beshear who could fake and shoot with the best of them.

The supporting cast for these two heroes included 6-9 Madison Stanford from Cotton Patch, Mississippi. Stanford was skinny as a rail when he arrived on the campus. But basketball fans Lubie Veal and George Steele owned The Hub restaurant and they quickly began feeding him all the milk shakes he could drink. In no time he gained 20 pounds and soon tipped the scales at 190. Melvin Deweese was 6-7, and Hodges often used them in a double post. Gene Garrett from LaCenter was a very good player, as was Don Stephenson from Valley High in Louisville, and Charlie Lampley from Sharpe. Gene Dick, the old vet, Mason Cope from Brewers, and J.M. Gipe rounded out the best overall talent Murray had seen in several years.

The season started with a bang as the team "opened the schedule like a house afire," according to *The Shield* editor. The Breds won lopsided decisions from Southeast Louisiana, Tennessee Tech, and Memphis State. Memphis State was coached by former Brewers coach McCoy Tarry, who had taken his state tournament winning team en masse to Memphis with him. Murray beat them by 20 points.

The Breds continued their winning streak by beating New Mexico A&M and then traveled to Marshall where they won the Marshall Invitational by whipping Marshall and West Texas State. Purcell and Beshear made the all-tournament team. They returned home to drub High Point by 42, squeaked by highly regarded Beloit, Wisconsin, and ended their pre-Christmas schedule by beating Texas Tech 66 to 52.

They knew the conference season would be a tough one though. Diddle's finesse teams at Western always featured talented players who could fast break. Eastern was different. Coach Paul McBrayer could always find some big rough mountain boys who really enjoyed beating up on you. "If the referees let them get by with it, they were tough to beat," Bennie Purcell said with a grin.

After beating SIU, Evansville, and Memphis State for the second time, they lost their first game of the season to Eastern by one. Then came Western, and the Toppers won by nine. After wins at Tennessee Tech, Morehead, and Marshall they met Eastern again and were beaten by nine.

Bennie Purcell told the story about Eastern. "Hodges believed strongly in a man to man defense and he didn't want us to switch either. In the first two games against Eastern those big rugged guys screened us time after time, blocked out well, and simply used their size and strength to manhandle us. With a non-switching man to man we just couldn't fight through their screens, but the coach learned his lesson, and in the OVC Tournament our strategy changed."

Scheduling is always difficult regardless of where you are. That year Murray and SIU reached a deadlock over where the game would be played. SIU wanted it at their place and Murray wanted it at theirs. The argument raged on and some modern day "Henry Clay" came up with the bright idea that they would meet half way. They did and agreed to play at the Metropolis, Ill. High School gymnasium. Murray won the game 76-61.

Murray continued the season, rolling over Morehead, Marshall and Evansville and was excited to play Western again. Diddle had made the red towel famous at Western and the two schools intensified the rivalry by giving a red towel to the winner after each game. So this was the "battle for the towel." The game was a barn burner and the fast-breaking Breds led by Purcell and Beshear led Western by as much as 18 points in the second half. Western staged a comeback, but Murray held on to win by seven.

There is a photo in the *Shield* of Western Coach Ed Diddle giving the big red towel to Bennie Purcell who is decked out with his warm-ups and white Converse shoes. He is surrounded by several beautiful admiring cheerleaders and co-eds.

The team prepared for their second trip "up east" where they would take on three of the nation's best teams on their home court. A most interesting story would much later be told about this trip.

Long Island was the number one team in the country at the time and had the number one player in the country, 6' 7" Sherman White. They were coached by legendary coach and writer Claire Bee. Coach Hodges sent his assistant Tim O'Brien to St. Louis to scout Long Island's game against the Billikens. He returned home with an encouraging report. "I watched Long Island closely and you guys can play with them," O'Brien confidently told Hodges and the team.

The team flew to New York, and was excited that the game was scheduled to be played in world famous Madison Square Garden. For some reason Madison Square Garden was unavailable, and they ended up playing in Long Island's gym. It was a tiny place, only 65 feet in length, and located in an upstairs building. They whipped Murray 90-67, and the floor size didn't help matters.

Amazingly only 10 days later the huge 1951 gambling scandal charging basketball players with shaving points broke. Six of those charged were from Long Island University, and one of the games they were accused of "fixing" was the St Louis game that the Murray assistant had scouted.

ESPN Classic describes the relevant parts of the scandal. "On Feb. 20 Sherman White, LeRoy Smith and Adolph Bigos of Long Island University were arrested for taking bribes from Sollazzo via Gard 'to throw' games. The previous day, White had been named Player of the Year by *The Sporting News*. White had averaged 27.7 points per game and needed 77 points to set an all-time collegiate scoring record."

White was perhaps New York college basketball's best player ever. Bigos was a 25-year-old senior who had served 2½ years in the Army and earned a Bronze Star. He enrolled at Long Island under the GI Bill. He tried out for Coach Clair Bee and earned a basketball scholarship. Smith, from the streets of Newark, was a former Marine."

Three University of Kentucky players were also implicated in the scandal. Alex Groza, Dale Barnstable and Ralph Beard were all three convicted and received suspended sentences. Sherman White from Long Island was sentenced to a year in jail and served nine months.

The last two games on Murray's road trip were against Seton Hall and St. Bonaventure. Both were ranked in the top 20 in the country. Murray lost to Seton Hall by six and to St. Bonaventure by four.

Though they lost all three games on this ambitious road trip they returned home to find that they were ranked #16 in the nation in the Associated Press poll. Additionally they had won the Ohio Valley Conference outright.

The OVC Tournament was then held in the Louisville Armory with a seating capacity of over 5,000 people. A large contingent of Murray students and fans made the long trip to Louisville by car traveling east to Bowling Green, north via U.S. 31-W. through Fort Knox and then to Louisville – a seven hour trip.

They were not disappointed. Murray eliminated Tennessee Tech by 10 in the first game. The tournament officials set both the semi-final and final game on Saturday afternoon and Saturday night. For Murray it was a legendary day.

In the first game on Saturday afternoon Murray faced off against powerful Western. The Shield described it as a "heart-stopper" and Murray beat the Hilltoppers by one, 78 to 77.

The second game was that same night against Eastern, the big and rough team that had beaten Murray twice in the regular season. This time Hodges was prepared for the Maroons. Though he had always adamantly opposed switching in his sticky man to man defense, this time he learned from his mistakes and changed his strategy.

"Hodges told us that when we were 'picked' or 'blocked' we needed to switch. We had practiced it, and it worked," remembered Bennie Purcell. The revised defense was successful, and Murray's offense was unstoppable. The *Shield* describes the game.

"In this pay-off struggle Murray's 92 points set a new tournament single-game record, and the two-team mark of 175 shattered another. A new individual tournament record was set by Garrett Beshear, Murray's amazing 28 year old sophomore, who poured in 37 points in the final game." Murray won it 92-83."

On a historic day in 1951, Murray, with perhaps their best team in history to that time, had beaten both Eastern and Western on the same day. They were the undisputed OVC Champs – the first Murray team ever to win that honor.

Thinking the OVC winner would receive a bid to the NIT, the team returned home awaiting the phone call. They turned down an invitation to the NAIB Tournament in Kansas City believing the NIT was a sure thing. It was not. The NIT bid never came, and sadly there was no postseason tournament for this truly great team.

Nevertheless it was a record setting year. They had ended the season with Murray's highest national ranking in history and a team scoring average of 71.4 points a game. Beshear set the all-time scoring record with 366, and the team scored 1,927 points for the season. Beshear, Purcell and Garrett were on the All OVC tournament team and Bennie Purcell received honorable mention on the United Press All-American team.

1951-52 • 24-10

With Bennie Purcell, Garrett Beshear, Gene Garrett, Melvin Deweese, Charlie Lampley, J.M. Gipe and Mason Cope returning and the memories of a legendary season just past, the students and fans could not wait for the season to begin. The Associated Press ranked them #10 in the nation at the beginning of the year.

Purcell commented on what practice was like with Hodges in charge, "We scrimmaged almost every practice, and believe me we were in shape."

Once again, Murray started the season with a bang. They won the first seven games and then flew out of Paducah by charter on a Texas tour. They won the first game against Houston 67 to 65, then flying to Austin they took on the mighty University of Texas Longhorns and beat them 64 to 63. For the third game of the road trip the team played Baylor at Waco. With a second half surge they handily beat the Bears by 18. It was a fantastic road trip.

They returned home to beat Kentucky Wesleyan but suffered their first loss of the year, 69-55, against a Dayton team that had been an NIT finalist the previous year. Then they encountered two disappointing losses dropping an away game against Eastern Kentucky, and then losing to Western Kentucky at home. The team was struggling.

Then they suffered a devastating loss. Gene Garrett, a 6-2 hard driving forward from LaCenter was a good player. He started and averaged 10.6 points a game for the first 14 games of the season. Suddenly he was notified that he had been drafted into the Army. He was replaced by Bobby Clark, who played just two games and then he also was drafted.

The United States had entered the Korean War in June of 1950 and the draft was reinstituted. Each local draft board had quotas and both Garrett and Clark's names were called.

Their position then had to be filled by a freshman, Joe Mikez. Mikez would go on to be a good player, but his inexperience showed and the team suffered.

On January 15 Murray lost to Memphis State by four, registering their fourth straight loss. In the following game they rebounded against Marshall with a 26 point win.

The next game was played in Owensboro against a very strong Kentucky Wesleyan team and Murray lost it 102-101. Purcell scorched the nets for 41 points. "Beshear was sick that night," Purcell remembered.

"They always kidded me about taking 45 shots in that game. They are right, but there were reasons for it," he grinned. "First in those days they counted it a shot even if you were fouled while shooting. Near the end of the game with Beshear not playing and several others fouling out Hodges told the team, 'nobody shoots but Bennie.' I did what he said."

Bennie continued. "So many fouled out that night we ran out of players. Dean Akridge and Carlos Bailey were freshmen, and didn't travel with the varsity. They simply drove up to watch the game, and when Hodges saw he wasn't going to have five left to play, he yelled for Akridge and Bailey to get dressed. They did, and played several minutes."

"The funniest thing that happened was the story about Akridge's shoes. He was dressing quickly and looked all over the dressing room for shoes to wear. When he came on the floor he noticed he had on two shoes of different sizes – one size 11 and one size 9. He played that way. We laughed about that game a lot in later years," recounted Purcell.

Murray then began another winning streak beating Eastern by 14, Austin Peay by 31 and Evansville by 25. They avenged their earlier loss to Memphis State

1951-52 Thoroughbreds. Kneeling, left to right: Carlos Bailey, Charlie Lampley, Robert Glin Jeffrey, Bennie Purcell, Karl Hussung, Bunt Anders. Standing, middle row: Coach Harlan Hodges, Assistant Coach Tim O'Brien. Standing, back row: Gene Garrett, Bob Best, J.M. Gipe, Melvin Deweese, Richard Gott, Garrett Beshear, Dean Akridge, Joe Mikez, Bobby Clark. Not pictured: Jean Coke, Paul Doss, Ted Koenigsmark, Charles Sermons, Fred Smith and Ray Solomon.

beating them 72 to 70 and then easily walked over Union by 22.

Then they went on Hodges' northeastern trip again. This time they played St Bonaventure in Buffalo, and LaSalle in Philadelphia. Kentucky was ranked number one in the country at the time and St. Bonaventure was unbeaten and ranked fourth.

Mikez was left in Murray with the flu. The *Paducah Sun Democrat* said, "The Bonnies found their difficulties in the third period as Beshear sparked a scoring drive that cut the margin to four points." Both Purcell and Deweese fouled out and St Bonnie won by 11. Beshear scored 21 to lead the Racers and Purcell ended the game with 18.

With the nickname Racers being used by Ed Kellow in the *Paducah Sun Democrat* for the first time, he raved about the play of Bennie Purcell from Murray. Though Murray went on to lose to LaSalle by a big margin it was notable that Purcell guarded All American and later All-Pro Tom Gola, and outscored him 33 to 20. Kellow said in his column, "The eastern press was singing the praises of Bennie Purcell in Philadelphia this week. They said that Bennie Purcell was the best little man in basketball." "Bennie would have broken the Philadelphia Convention Hall individual scoring record had he or Coach Harlan Hodges known about the mark. The mark is 34 and Bennie had 33."

Just prior to the eastern trip Kellow had again praised Purcell in his column, "Timeout." He wrote. "Bennie Purcell's seven game scoring spree is something to write home about. Here are his totals and the teams he has scored against. Marshall 26, Kentucky Wesleyan 41, Eastern Kentucky 27, Austin Peay 27, Evansville 30, Memphis State 23 and Union 28…"

Other newspapers were now using the nickname Racers to describe the team, together with other nicknames like the Bluebloods and Racehorses. Murray returned home after the eastern trip and beat Tennessee Tech, only to lose to Western Kentucky in the final regular season game.

Western had become Murray's number one rival, and the stories people tell about games in the Little Red Barn in Bowling Green are classic. "They always said that Western paid the referees $35 a game, but if Western won the referees got $50," Purcell said. "They had two referees out of Nashville that called what seemed like every game up there, and Murray fans always said both of them wore Western letter jackets." Seriously though, Bennie recalled that Murray always had an excellent relationship with Ed Diddle, the famous Western coach. "Diddle spoke at our basketball banquet in Murray more than once," he said.

Murray won the first two games in the Ohio Valley Conference tournament in Louisville beating Tennessee Tech in the first game by 11 and then besting Eastern Kentucky by 10. The finals were to be played against a highly favored Western team.

Hodges decided to change Murray's fast breaking style and slow down the game. He also installed a double post offense with DeWeese and Beshear down low. The game was close all the way, but Western won on what the *Shield* editor called a "fluky shot." The final was Western 47 Murray 45.

Murray was quickly invited to participate in the NAIB Tournament in Kansas City. They beat Centenary, West Texas State, Whitworth of Washington, and Portland, Oregon before losing to Southwest Missouri in the final game. "Garrett Beshear's father passed away during the tournament and it was a most difficult time for him and for us," Purcell said.

Purcell was named the MVP of the tournament and both he and Beshear were named to the All-Tournament team. It was a grand showing for a great Murray team.

The Racers finished the season with a 24-10 record and they averaged 71.9 points a game. The *Shield* editor couldn't say enough about the play of Bennie Purcell. He set scoring records for an all-time high in a season with 600 points scored, all-time high points in a game 41, all-time high for scoring in a college career with 1,108. He was an All-OVC Tournament selection, UPI All-America honorable mention, and NAIB All-American.

The now 29-year-old Beshear had another great year with 541 points topping his 366 points the previous year. Charlie Lampley ended the year with 360 points, Melvin Deweese with 320 and Joe Mikez with 195. Gene Garrett scored 148 in his 14 games.

Two men who were reserves on that team should be mentioned. First was Robert Glin Jeffery from Murray who went on the become Superintendent of Schools of the Murray Independent District. The second is Karl

Hussing. Hussing became a Distinguished Chemistry Professor at Murray State University and for many years was an exceptional academic adviser to the basketball team. He is indeed a Murray great whose contributions to Murray basketball rank him at the very top of the class.

It was very unusual to have two Racer legends on the same team – two of the first players to ever have their jerseys retired at Murray. Both were great competitors and both great shooters. One might think that with two such record setting players and scorers on the same team, there would be some dissension along the way. Purcell was asked about his relationship with Beshear in the years they played together. "We respected each other, and we never had a cross word."

1952-53 • 18-9

All teams have different personalities depending on the mix, and the season that began in the fall of 1952 was no different. The great Bennie Purcell, who was destined to have his number permanently hung in the rafters was gone. He would be most difficult to replace, so Hodges badly needed a guard.

Just 18 miles down the road in Graves County one of the most gifted basketball players the Commonwealth had ever produced had delighted the high school basketball world in 1951 and 1952 with his speed, his dribbling, his shooting, and his incredible competitive spirit. Howard Crittenden, known as "Howie," had led tiny Cuba to high school stardom and legendary status in Kentucky with a team that won the state tournament in 1952 by beating powerful Louisville Manual in the final game. The team was coached by a Murray State graduate, Jack Story, and Crittenden gives him all the credit for this storied team. Also on that team were two other players that came to Murray to play – Charles "Doodle" Floyd and Joe Buddy Warren.

The recruiting of Crittenden by Murray could fill an entire chapter, but suffice to say the great Adolph Rupp visited him three times in Cuba and Ed Diddle was constantly scheming to lure him to Western Kentucky – even after he agreed to come to Murray. Crittenden enrolled at Murray State in the fall of 1953, and became the first and perhaps the last High School All-American to wear the blue and gold.

Like all of Hodges' teams, this one faced a very challenging schedule in what most termed a rebuilding year despite the presence of 30 year old Garrett Beshear. Affectionately called "Daddy" he practically rewrote the record book as he completed a brilliant career at MSU. Scoring 643 points he set the Murray record for the most points scored in a season. He also set the Carr Health building scoring record with 40 points in a December 22 game leading the team to an 84 to 70 victory over powerful Dayton.

The season began with an impressive winning streak including two wins over Evansville, a win over Tennessee Tech, and an impressive road victory over Middle Tennessee. They lost their first game of the season in what was termed a "thriller" to the Houston Cougars in Murray in mid-December.

Players become fan favorites for many reasons and the place they call home usually makes little difference once the player's familiarity is established. But this team had an unusual crop of "local" players. Barney Thweatt who had starred on the state champion Brewers team started much of the year at guard. Steady Dean Akridge, a man of stellar character, who would later become a member of the Murray State Board of Regents played on this team. Not to be forgotten was the popular and gifted Charles "Doodle" Floyd from Cuba who thrilled the crowds with his patented "windmill" hook shot. In a day with no television, local fans developed an unusual pride in this group of players.

Playing a torrid schedule, they lost games on the road to Marshall, Western Kentucky, and Eastern Kentucky in late December and early January. Again in the Marshall game "Daddy" Beshear led the Breds with another 40-point effort. Also in late December and early January the team traveled to Philadelphia where they took on highly rated St. Joseph's and came away with a 76-63 victory, thrilling Murray fans glued to their radios in practically every west Kentucky farm house.

The *Paducah Sun Democrat* reporter graphically described young Crittenden and the reaction of the Philadelphia fans. "Freshman Howie Crittenden proved to be the darling of the crowd though. The clever playmaker was booed early in the game for his fancy dribbling, but soon drew cheers galore from the huge crowd which remembered Bennie Purcell."

After losing to a good Lawrence Tech team in Detroit, Murray returned to play Kentucky Wesleyan in Owensboro in a game they won 89-83. The combination of 30-year-old senior Beshear and the spectacular 19 year old freshman Howie Crittenden provided the news media and fans with unique excitement.

Crittenden laughingly describes the night. "In the Wesleyan game I had one of those nights when everything you shoot goes in the basket. I thought I would score 40, but as we went back on the floor after the half Beshear called me over and said, 'Hey freshman, I've been open inside all night – you need to get the ball inside to me this half.'"

The OVC was exceptionally strong that year. Western led by Tom Marshall had a great team, and was ranked in the top 10 of the country most of the season. Eastern also had one of their strongest teams and proved to be a formidable adversary both to Western and Murray.

Ever the tactician, Hodges began to analyze his team as the season progressed. Western was a running team as were some of the teams that had been giving Murray trouble through the year. Though Hodges always favored a man-to-man defense he knew there was no way to stop Western's speed without a zone. So before the first Western game in January he installed what he called a T-zone offense. Though he lost to powerful Western anyway 62-57, he found the zone worked so well he stuck with it the rest of the season.

After the Western game the conference season was under way in earnest and the team beat both Middle and Morehead at home. They suffered a nine point loss at Eastern. The team then traveled to Florida, and won both at Rollins College in Orlando and at Miami University. Returning home they beat a good University of Tampa team.

The big game of the year approached. On February 14th it was Western at Murray in the Carr Health building with all of the drama of great theatre. While the local fire marshal looked the other way they packed the house.

Western was ranked 8th in the country, and in warm ups they could not conceal their cocky attitude. They were buoyed by the reappearance of their storied coach Ed Diddle. Diddle had been sidelined with a heart ailment for much of the season and had recently returned from rehab in Florida to coach this game.

What happened that night in Murray's Carr Health building before the game is a testament to the sportsmanship of the basketball fans of Murray and the respect each of these great basketball programs had for each other. Diddle strode in with the team that night and the *Paducah Sun Democrat* reporter describes what occurred when he was introduced, "…he received a standing ovation and the capacity crowd stood as one and cheered for more than two full minutes. Diddle wept as he waived his red towel to the fans."

The crowd stirred with emotion prepared for the game of the year. Hodges was convinced he had to slow the game down, and use the zone defense he had designed earlier in the year. Western was not going to let "Daddy" Beshear beat them, and often when the ball went into him as many as three defenders collapsed on him.

With Beshear covered, Crittenden began to drive to the basket and dish it off. Amazingly he finished the game with just four field goals but drew 23 personal fouls. With Crittenden's stellar floor game and his ability to feed Beshear, the "old man" and the "kid" engineered a stunning upset. When the final buzzer sounded and the emotionally drained crowd looked at the scoreboard, it read Murray 77 Western 67. The scorebook showed Beshear with 26 and Crittenden with 22.

The *Paducah Sun Democrat* said of Crittenden in its Sunday edition, "He completely demoralized Western with his clever ball handling and dribbling."

An ecstatic Hodges said after the game. "It was the greatest game a team ever played for me. We can beat anybody when they play like that."

Though Murray played other good games that year the victory over Western turned out to be the highlight of the season. Murray lost both games on a road trip to Oklahoma City and Wichita State. In the Wichita game Crittenden broke his hand and Floyd broke his wrist. They were out for the rest of the year. Floyd had begun to score some points at the time and of course Crittenden's play outside was indispensable to the team. Murray continued its string of bad luck when starting forward Leo Understall suffered a badly sprained ankle against Eastern in the final game of the season.

They entered the OVC tournament at Louisville hoping to upset either Western or Eastern. They won the first game of the tournament over Middle 79-70 with Rich Gott and Thweatt starting at guard. Beshear scored 26. In the semifinal Eastern proved too much for the crippled Racers winning by a score of 52-43. Eastern won the regular season crown and went to the NCAA tournament. Western was a #3 seed in the NIT that year.

It was the last year for the great Garrett Beshear. The beloved 30 year old, holder of several Racer records, was fondly remembered and became a legend in Murray State Athletics.

An excellent description of Beshear was furnished the news media by Earl Sensing, the Sports Information Director for Murray State.

"First of all he is in top physical condition. There isn't an ounce of fat on his lean, muscular six-foot four frame. But most important of all is his court savvy. He does just exactly what is necessary – and no more, conserving his energy for the all-important split-seconds that count.

"Beshear is deadly accurate at about six feet from the basket. When his teammates get the ball he slowly moves into position, with little or no effort to avoid his guard. Usually when he gets his pass his back is to the basket with his guard behind him. One of two things is about to happen. Beshear will either jump straight up and whirl and shoot or take one step to the other side and shoot.

"The secret of his success is his faking. So far he hasn't found a guard who can tell whether he's going to jump and shoot or step aside and shoot. Frequently before the guard can make his mind what is going to happen he finds himself a-straddle Beshear and Beshear at the free throw line."

Murray State ended the season with an 18 and 9 record and Beshear's days as a player were over. He would return to Murray State as a coach and teacher until his untimely death at the age of 46 from an inherited heart ailment.

1953-54 • 15-16

When you study the Harlan Hodges era you become increasingly impressed with his vision for Murray State Basketball. But Hodges alone would have amounted to nothing without the brilliant Director of Athletics Roy Stewart and university President Ralph Woods who knew that a great basketball team was an integral part of a great university. Jim Frank said, "when we played Dr. Woods would see the team off on a road trip and meet them when they came home."

The vision these men had was not apparent in what they said but in what they did. Pete Waldrop who grew up on the Murray campus said of them, "They got the job done but they did it quietly and effectively. They were all highly respected."

That vision was most apparent in the schedule the team played and the facilities they planned. By the spring of 1953 these men quietly sought a new place for Murray to play basketball. The program had outgrown Carr Health and it was obvious to all that a new facility was needed.

In his column in the *Paducah Sun Democrat* in February of 1953 Bill Carter discussed the plans. He pointed out that there was a great deal of discussion about simply increasing the size of the Carr Health Building by knocking out the north wall. Professional estimates for that renovation indicated that it would cost more than $400,000. Athletic Director Roy Stewart had studied the topography of the land east of Carr Health and like a good coach who designs his offense according to the ability of his players, Roy Stewart came up with the idea of a "sunken" gymnasium. The wooded area immediately east of Carr Health contained a small valley or swale with gentle slopes that seemed to be ideally suited for a bowl shaped gymnasium. The most appealing part of the idea was the money that would be saved in the construction making the idea acceptable to state finance officials who had to approve it.

By mid-March 1953 the state finance authorities had approved Stewart's plan for a gymnasium that would seat 6,000. Though the cost was initially projected at $250,000 by the time the arena was completed in 1955 that sum had grown to $372,000. Even with the increased cost the entire bowl was not completed until 1962 when an additional $181,000 was spent to round out the bowl by constructing seats on the north end. The arena was initially called the field house.

Hodges' and Stewart's vision did not end with facilities. It extended to scheduling. These were men who did not have excuses in their vocabulary. Coaches of that generation were famous for the principle they constantly preached to their players, "Alibis will get you nowhere." They refused to accept the oft repeated phrase reputed to be "wisdom" that "teams won't come to Murray." Neither were they afraid to travel to play teams with great traditions, knowing that you had to play the big name schools if you were going to advance as a program. It was another way of saying that you had to "dare to be great" coupled with the thought that you can do anything you want to do so long as you work hard enough.

The 1953-54 schedule is a perfect illustration of the fearless vision of Hodges and Stewart. Murray State was still playing in the 2,300 seat Carr Health Building. The season began with a road trip to Albany, New York to play a good Siena team, and on the second night to play St. Bonaventure in western New York. Both were Franciscan Catholic Universities with great basketball traditions and often ranked nationally. As the season progressed Murray played Brigham Young twice, Xavier twice, Villanova, Dayton, Memphis State twice, Oklahoma City, Tulsa, Georgia Tech, and Houston. Xavier, Villanova, Memphis State, and Georgia Tech came to Murray and played in Carr Health.

This awesome schedule was coupled with an OVC slate that included powerful teams from Western Kentucky, Marshall, Evansville and Middle Tennessee. There were no "cupcakes" on Hodges' schedule. His philosophy was always, "if you want to be the best you have to play the best."

With only five members of the previous year's squad returning and the loss of the legendary Garrett Beshear, Hodges and his new assistant Rex Alexander had their work cut out for them. They lost their big center Rich Starkey because of an irregular heartbeat early in the season, but fortunately picked up Gene Garrett from LaCenter, Ky. who returned from a stint with the Marines.

Murray State had some signature victories that year and finished second in the Ohio Valley Conference race. They split with Memphis State and beat Georgia Tech.

Howie Crittenden established himself as one of college basketball's truly outstanding players by his play during this season. He played in all 31 games and averaged 21 points. By scoring 638 points he surpassed Beshear's single season record for a Murray State player set the previous year. For his play he was named to the All-OVC team as a sophomore. Joining him on the team was Gene Garrett who averaged 15.3 points after returning from the military. Ted Koenigsmark from Murphysboro, Ill. averaged 9.6 points that year, Bobby McLemore from Calvert City nine, Fran Watrous from Hamburg N.Y. 7.5, John Powless from Flora, Illinois 7.1, Dean Akridge 6.4, and Richard Starkey who played in only four games averaged six points a game. Crittenden, Koenigsmark, McLemore, and Watrous played in all 31 games and were joined by Akridge and Powless who played in 28.

The season ended with a overall record of 15-15. The Racers were upset by Middle Tennessee in an overtime game 86 to 84 in the first round of the OVC tournament in Louisville. They had beaten Middle twice during the year but the Blue Raiders handed Murray a disappointing loss to end their season. With the schedule they played the team's 500 record was more impressive than many with winning records who played much weaker schedules.

They beat an outstanding Western Kentucky team 77-72 in the first round of the OVC tournament in Louisville.

Though Murray lost to Eastern Kentucky in an overtime game, Howie Crittenden broke a Murray State record in the game. Despite fouling out with 8:30 left, his 18 points broke Beshear's single season scoring record and the sophomore finished the year with an incredible 652 points.

Gene Garrett joined Crittenden on the All-OVC team but this was his final year. Joining him in graduation was steady and reliable Dean Akridge. It is interesting to note that sports writers continued to refer to the team in most articles as the Thoroughbreds or the Breds. The term Racers wasn't used exclusively until the Cal Luther era.

At the end of the season Coach Hodges was offered the coaching position at the University of Idaho in the Pacific Coast Conference. He left a good nucleus of players for the coming season and many accomplishments at Murray.

During his last year at Murray, Hodges occasionally wrote a column in the *Paducah Sun* and in some fascinating remarks on January 14, 1954 he described the state of basketball at the time.

He said he had heard much criticism of coaches who were described as, "too lazy to teach defense."He admitted that there had been a great emphasis on teaching offense in the past few years but he said there were many other factors at work that had contributed to the increase in points scored in games. He mentioned changes in the rules, better lighting, larger courts and the use of two officials rather than one. He also discussed the "new coaching techniques especially related to the fast break, the double and triple pivots, blocking, and screening."

Most notable he said were the rule changes such as the elimination of the center jump and the one plus one free throw. He opined that those two rule changes alone had added 33 points to the game and calculated that if "we combine this sum with the 25 points which composed the average score in the early thirties we have 58." He concluded, "And so it is evident that those two changes plus the fast break have done much toward making the game what it is today."

1954-55 • 11-15

This season inaugurated the sparkling new fieldhouse with a team that was still often referred to as the Thoroughbreds destined to play in n a sparkling new facility that was the gem of the Ohio Valley Conference. The local press may have been slightly liberal with their numbers when they announced it had a capacity of 6,000, but regardless it was the largest in the OVC and exceeded Western's Red Barn capacity of 4,500 at the time. All thought that the new gym would boost Murray's chances to reach the "big time" in basketball. Oklahoma City had already agreed to a home and home with Murray and fans were sure more great teams would be visiting Murray in the future.

This was also the first season under new coach Rex Alexander. This mild mannered and gentlemanly former Thoroughbred team captain and assistant coach took over the reins from Hodges. He hired one of Murray's greats, Garrett Beshear, and Waldo Sauter as his assistants.

Beginning the season, the fans were excited over two transfers who were expected to improve the Bred's fortunes. Giant Jim Gainey measured 6 ft. 8 inches and tipped the scales at 225. He was joined by transfer Dick Kinder, a guard from Indiana. With Kinder and Crittenden at guard Murray was thought to have one of the best backcourts in the country.

Murray began the young season with two victories and one loss and prepared to open the new Fieldhouse against Middle Tennessee on December 11, 1955. Excitement reigned and Racer fans crowded into the brand spanking new gymnasium that had yet to be named. The opponent was Middle Tennessee. The attendance was recorded at 3,800, which, at the time, was probably the largest crowd ever to witness an athletic event in the history of far western Kentucky. A photo in the local paper showed Rex Alexander, Athletic Director Roy Stewart and asst. to the President M.O. Wrather doing a quick clean up job to get the gym ready on the afternoon of the game.

Though big Jim Gainey scored the first field goal and free throw in the new arena, it was up to the sensational guard Howie Crittendon to thrill the fans. Dix Winston, *Sun Democrat* Staff writer said it best.

"Howie Crittenden, sensational guard from Cuba, baptized Murray State College's new gym tonight with a scorching 41 points as he led the Thoroughbreds to a 104-80 victory over Middle Tennessee. Crittenden's tremendous performance eclipsed the home scoring record of 40 points set by Garrett Beshear and tied Bennie Purcell's all-time mark."

An interesting sidelight of the blistering performance occurred when the public address announcer announced that Crittenden had scored 42 points and had set the record with five minutes to go in the game. The scorekeeper then quickly checked his figures and found that Crittenden had only 40. Alexander quickly put Crittenden back into the game and the team began to feed him the ball permitting him to set the record. Crittenden tells it best. "I had hit everything I shot that night but when he put me back in I was stone cold. Nothing would go in." Finally with 3 seconds to go Crittenden was fouled. The first shot rimmed out, but the second popped right through and Crittenden had set the school record with 41 points. What a night for Murray State basketball and for Howie Crittenden. According to news accounts, with that performance following his incredible high school career at nearby Cuba many fans were urging the Board of Regents to name the new field house after Crittenden.

Playing Morehead, Memphis State, Texas Western, Louisville, and Western Kentucky in a 15 day stretch beginning December 15th that included the Kentucky Invitational tournament, these fearless Thoroughbreds won two of the games and played close in the rest.

It began the New Year in the new field house by entertaining Brigham Young on January 1, 1955. Before a partisan screaming crowd of 5,000 fans they beat a good team in an 86-85 thriller. Murray fans reveled in the big time atmosphere.

After beating Middle Tennessee in the next game the young team hit the February doldrums. But when your losses come at the hands of teams like Memphis State, Oklahoma City, Xavier, Villanova, Houston and Dayton you do not hang your head in shame.

On February 19 Governor Lawrence Wetherby and other state dignitaries came to town to formally dedicate the new fieldhouse with Eastern Kentucky as the opponent. The game went into overtime but Eastern prevailed 83-77.

The *Sun Democrat* writer Bill Carter opined after the game that the new Gym would be named after the then President of the College Dr. Ralph Woods. For some reason that was never done and the women's residence hall built later would bear the name of "Ralph Wood's Hall." He further described the gym, "The fieldhouse may not be the largest in the country but it has few equals otherwise. The lighting system certainly is one of the best, there isn't a blind spot among the 5,000 permanent seats and no other hall offers more space per seat."

An interesting event occurred during practice in the new gymnasium on January 18 of that year. It was a day when architectural standards were much less stringent than those of the present day. There was a pipe presumably used for carrying water that protruded above the floor on the eastern out of bounds area of the new gymnasium. At a practice that day Howie Crittenden while running after a ball "kicked" the pipe with his big toe. Because of the injury Crittenden missed the road trip to Eastern Kentucky and Morehead and at least one more game.

The proud Thoroughbreds ended their season by breaking even in the OVC and avenging an earlier loss to powerful Oklahoma City

Crittenden continued his torrid scoring pace and the Cuba junior averaged 21 points a game for the year. He was joined at guard by Dick Kinder with a 15 point average. Big Jim Gainey provided strength at center with a 10.7 average, with Mikez at forward averaging 9.0 a game. Fran Watrous at 7.5 and John Powless at 5.8 rounded out the major scorers for the year. All six of them were expected to return for the 55-56 season.

1955-56 • 15-10

Murray opened the 1955-56 season with six returning lettermen that included Crittenden, Mikez, Powless, Darnell, Watrous, and Kinder. Pre season polls all but ignored Murray, but as polls often do, they were wrong. Playing six road games before Christmas that included New Mexico A&M, Texas Western, Middle Tennessee and Louisville, Murray State posted a 5-3 record that included winning a holiday tournament hosted by West Texas State.

After the Texas trip the Racers returned home to play in the hotly contested Kentucky Invitational Tournament to be held in the armory in Louisville. The teams playing included Louisville, Arizona State, Bowling Green of Ohio, Ohio University, Morehead, Eastern Kentucky and Murray. Their first opponent in the tournament was unbeaten Morehead who boasted the top offensive team in the nation.

The speedy Racers exceeded the 100-point mark for the third straight game to upend Morehead in an exciting record breaking performance 106-97. The game set tournament records for the most points scored by a team with Murray's 106 and most points scored by two teams. Western, Louisville and Eastern survived their first round game and the excitement heightened for the Murray faithful.

With only four minutes to go Murray led Eastern 92-72 and would have reached the century mark for the fourth straight game had not Alexander removed the starters. Center Quitman Sullins was given much credit for crashing the boards for 12 rebounds and was followed closely by 6-4 forward Tom Darnall with 10. Crittenden was fantastic connecting on 16 of 17 free throws, and scoring a game high 30 points. Dick Kinder chipped in 19 points in a great effort for the Racers.

The stage was set for the game with Western who had upended Louisville then led by the fabulous 6-8 in Charlie Tyra and Wickliffe star Phil Rollins who scored 37 points. Those two splendid athletes had led Louisville to a #8 national ranking when the tournament began.

The Armory in Louisville was filled to capacity and Murray fans filled the hotels and excitedly enjoyed the food at the Blue Boar Cafeteria as they cheered their Racers on. Murray jumped to an early lead over the Toppers and at halftime led by 17. But the Toppers came roaring back in the second half cutting the lead to seven with 10:40 remaining. The game went down to the wire but when the final buzzer sounded in the Louisville Invitational Tournament in 1955 the winner was Murray 74-69 over Western.

The *Sun Democrat* sportswriter described the scene. "When the final horn sounded, Murray fans rushed to the floor and with the aid of other Racers hoisted Crittenden and Kinder to their shoulders and carried them to the bench."

"I believe that's the greatest Murray team I've ever seen," said Ted Hornback, Western's respected assistant coach after the championship game. "We'll be glad to get rid of Crittenden and Kinder. You can expect 35 to 40 points out of them every game. Those kids will beat you."

In the Shield of that year there is a large photo of Governor A.B. Happy Chandler who later was Commissioner of Baseball presenting the championship trophy to coach Rex Alexander.

The Racers returned home to a heroic welcome as hundreds of Murray fans met the team at Eggner's Ferry bridge and led a parade to the campus. News reports stated that earlier in the day the team had lunch in Bowling Green and circled the campus there proclaiming their victory over the Toppers.

Paducah Sun Sportswriter Bill Carter in his column described the gentlemanly Alexander commending him for not running the score up against Eastern in the tournament. He described Alexander's coaching job as amazing. He noted that midway in the Western game with big Jim Gainey gone from the lineup Alexander adopted a high-low post placing Sullins at the head of the circle and a forward on the base line. "The Racers began to click immediately," opined Carter.

The excitement of this tournament win filled Murray State followers with pride and on the heels of the tournament the team returned to Racer Arena to play the University of Arizona and soundly defeated them 93-73. They then lost to Western on the road by 11 and returned home to beat Middle by 22. Morehead avenged the earlier loss to the Racers in the tournament by handing Murray a rare home court loss 75-73 on Feb. 4th. Murray then beat Eastern and a good Siena team but lost to nationally ranked Memphis State at Memphis.

After winning three straight games the team faced a formidable schedule for the remainder of the year. The schedule included both Memphis State and Louisville who was the ranked 5th in the nation. They lost to Memphis State by 6 points 100-94 and to Louisville by 13.

This was a season filled with great OVC teams and a daunting schedule, Alexander's team ended the year with a respectable 15-10 mark.

The story of the year was the career performance and records set by Howie Crittenden of Cuba. In the Memphis State game he scored 37 points giving him a career total of over 2,000 and establishing a new Kentucky collegiate mark.

Sports Editor Bill Carter of the *Paducah Sun Democrat* described Crittenden's inimitable play in a February 14th editorial.

"Yet, to me, scoring has always been incidental for Howie. I've been watching him play for six years. But I went to see his passing, dribbling, defense, and clutch play. He can pick up 20 points accidentally, without making an effort to score. But I've never seen him matched as a playmaker.... Howie will gain nationwide recognition over his scoring record. But, around here, we know this talented youngster, the best college player in the state of Kentucky today, is a playmaker first, a scorer second."

1956-57 • 11-13

The post Crittenden era began with five returning lettermen and two transfers. Tall Quitman Sullins returned and the Darnall brothers from Hornbeak, Tennessee showed great promise. Also returning were Gerald Tabor, Sherill Marginet, John Powless and Fran Watrous. Wingo High School Stars Frank Waggoner and Ken Wray along with Dale Alexander from Murray High joined these talented players. Gene Landolt, who ended up in Murray after playing in the North-South game with Garrett Beshear joined Alexander as assistant coaches.

The team began the year by winning four of five and losing only to Georgia Tech by three on the road. Then they went to Hardin-Simmons, New Mexico A&M and Arizona and lost all three games though each game was close until the end.

Pete Waldrop remembers the game against West Texas and a traumatic event that occurred in Racer Arena. Forward John Powless was driving in for a shot and the West Texas player undercut him. He crashed to the floor and a hush came over the crowd. Waldrop recalls, "Dr. C.C. Lowry was the team physician and he rushed on the floor and professionally and carefully held Powless head until the ambulance with its attendants and their stretcher could arrive. It was later discovered that his neck was broken and he of course was out for the year.

Powless, from Flora, Illinois made quite a mark for himself as a tennis player at Murray by never losing a match in three years of varsity competition and went to the semifinals of the NCAA tournament. Powless became a coach and served as head coach at the University of Wisconsin for eight years.

The Thoroughbreds, as the *Shield* still insisted on calling them, then won at Ky. Wesleyan and took on Southeastern Conference powerhouse Mississippi State in Hattiesburg. The *Shield* reported on the game, "The contest was tied eighteen times with neither team getting much of a lead before the final three minutes when the Breds pulled away on foul shots. All five of the Murray starters scored in the double figures. Final score Murray 91, Mississippi State 80."

The Thoroughbreds played competitive basketball that year in a very strong Ohio Valley Conference. Western Kentucky was nationally ranked and in competition for the conference crown. They beat Murray twice. Murray swept the series with Middle Tennessee and Eastern Kentucky but lost both games to Western and Morehead who fought it out for the conference crown.

The team finished slightly below the 500 mark at 11-13. They were led in scoring by Quitman "Skeeter" Sullins who averaged 16.6 points a game. Terry Darnell, a tall and talented guard chipped in 12.7 a game and was followed closely by Gerald Tabor with 12.3 and Sherrill Marginet with 11.5.

1957-58 • 8-16

Quitman Sullins and Terry Darnall led the way for the Thoroughbreds this year playing a strong road schedule and a talented OVC card.

After winning at Kentucky Wesleyan they lost both to Florida State and Alabama on the road. The remainder of the pre-Christmas schedule included Fresno State and William and Mary in the Evansville Holiday Invitational Tournament.

Terry Darnall recalls the Kentucky Wesleyan game because of his guarding a legendary Kentucky high school player King Kelly Coleman, "He was one heck of a ball player. He scored 30 on me that night but I was able to score 29. He didn't defend me as closely as I did him but he was very strong and would hold you a lot."

The New Year began with Murray's signature victory of the year. Louisville came to Murray on New Year's Day of 1958. Racer Arena was filled with proud fans celebrating the holidays with their families. The Breds did not disappoint them sending the talented Louisvillians home with a 75-51 licking.

The team continued its win streak by defeating Western in a barn burner as Quitman Sullins tipped in two points as the horn sounded to give the Racers a 57-55 victory.

Murray State lost to Mississippi State twice that year and also lost twice to Memphis State.

Even in a losing season there are bright spots. The bright spot in 1958 came in the next to last game. OVC foe Marshall had an excellent team that led the nation both in scoring and in free throw percentage. Terry Darnell hit a shot just before the halftime buzzer and the Racers went on to thrill the fans by winning a high scoring affair 98-92. Darnall recalls the game well, "We loved to run with the ball and that night we simply outran them. To score that many points with no three point shot was really something."

6 foot 9 inch Skeeter Sullins finished the year with a 12.7 average followed closely by Guard Terry Darnall with 12.3, Tabor with 10.0, Wingo star Ken Wray with 8.3 and Sherrill Marginet at 5.5. Gene Herndon from nearby Almo contributed 5.1 points a game.

The Racers ended the year with an 8-16 record but in points per game they trailed their opponents by only four – 69.9 to 65.9.

1958-59 • 10-15

The 1958-59 season began with a new coach. Dr. Ralph Woods and Athletic Director Roy Stewart hired Milwaukee native Cal Luther. Luther was a smart and charismatic man who would serve as Murray State's head coach for 16 years, becoming a legend in the process. He was in his early thirties when he came to Murray after coaching at DePauw (Indiana) for four years.

Rex Alexander remained at Murray coaching the freshman team, the Tennis Team and teaching physical education.

Luther's first team was led by Terry Darnall, Ken Wray and Dale Alexander, all veterans from the previous year's squad. Joining them was the tall and talented Chicago native Ken Peterson. The Racers dressed only 11 men and played a very strong non-conference schedule.

Luther won his first two games, beating Texas Wesleyan 70-56 and New Mexico A&M 66-51. The team lost at Ole Miss by six but returned to beat Ole Miss at Racer Arena by a one sided score of 80-60. Murray native Dale Alexander led the scoring with 25 points. The Oxford quintet had been repaid.

In the fourth game of the season the Racers carried nationally ranked Mississippi State to the wire before losing by one. Peterson held All-American center Bailey Howell who was then averaging 30 points a game to 18. Dale Alexander, Peterson, and Terry Darnall led the scoring with 14, 13 and 12 point performances.

Eastern Kentucky was very strong that year and beat the Racers twice. Murray also lost twice to Western but split with a good Morehead Club. The Racers signature victory that year was a 96-71 drubbing of Florida State in Murray on February 9. A poor record on the road led to a 10-15 finish.

The team was led by senior guard Terry Darnall who finshed the year with a 14.1 scoring average and 191 rebounds. Darnall hit 76% of his free throws. Dale Alexander averaged 11.9 a game, Mike O'Riordan 10 and big Ken Peterson chipped in 9.6 a game and pulled in 230 rebounds. Ken Wray finished his Murray career by averaging 4.9 points a game and savvy South Marshall star guard Harold Wilkins showed promise by averaging 9.6 for the Racers.

Terry Darnall was an All-OVC selection for the second straight year. Everybody likes to score, but I tried to be a team player," he said. "Basketball is a team game."

WHERE DID WE GET THE NAME "RACERS"?

Rainey T. Wells first gave the athletic teams the nickname of Thoroughbreds in June of 1928, according to Dr. Carr's history of the early days of the university. In a day when Man O' War was a household word and the horse remained a nostalgic symbol it was a perfect nickname. But times change, and fans response also change. Athletic team followers remaining in sync with their teams constantly throw out variations of the original nickname as they excitedly describe the team they cherish. They do the same for the players. The wordsmiths of the day consisting primarily of reporters and broadcasters quickly adopt the nicknames they hear and perhaps originate their own.

Murray State was no different. Reading accounts of Racer teams in newspapers, yearbooks, media guides, and listening to "old timers" remember, one finds a constant search for nicknames.

The variations of the nickname Thoroughbreds came early as local sportswriters seeking to humanize the horse nickname referred to the basketball team as the "Men O' War." That name didn't seem to stick, and a rather common nickname began to emerge both in the sports pages and in the yearbooks – it was "The Racehorses." After a few years that name was shortened simply to "Hosses." During Harlan Hodges coaching tenure when his teams began fast breaking the nickname "Hodges Hosses" was commonly used. Some creative writers seized on the Race Horses theme and began writing about the "Ramblin' Racehorses."

Also in the 30's some erudite sportswriters utilizing the English idiom for nobility or more probably referring to the bloodlines of a thoroughbred nicknamed the team the "Bluebloods."

As late as the early fifties some used the well-known term "Big Blue" as a nickname, and it was not unusual to see the term "Big Blue Netters" when describing the basketball team.

It becomes obvious to anyone writing about the team that the nickname "Thoroughbreds" is simply too long. It takes forever to type it, and even longer to make sure the spelling is correct. Surely many thought that in the day of airplanes and automobiles it was no longer a "horse and buggy" world.

Some tried to satisfy the spelling and the length problem by simply calling the team the "breds." That word had little meaning really, but it served as a reminder of the original name and many continued its use.

Then the word that has stuck for over 58 years evolved. In a day when Murray State basketball was creating great excitement on the national stage by traveling to New York, Connecticut, Louisiana and Texas to play, Murray publicity director Erl Sensing always creative mind began diligently seeking a new name to describe this team. This was a fast-breaking team that often scored in the eighties and nineties and name Thoroughbreds simply didn't seem to fit. Besides it was simply too long.

A basketball program requires the support of many and particularly those who are in charge of publicity. In 1947 season there appeared on the Murray scene a tireless and creative publicity director for the athletic department. His name was Erl Sensing and he was destined to make quite a mark before he left in 1954. He was central in establishing the famous North-South classic at Murray and those who knew him said, "He wrote more copy than any two newspapermen in the state."

Sources close to Coach Harlan Hodges gave Sensing the credit for originating the nickname "Racers." His label took root, and in the January 28, 1952 edition of the sports page of the *Paducah Sun Democrat Edd* Kellow writing in a column he labeled "Timeout" publicly proclaimed the Murray team as the "Racers." The team after a couple of bad games was experiencing resurgence and he described it this way. **"The Racers had to win to gain back their self-respect as well as confidence."**

By the time the yearbook was published late in the school year of 1952 the editor of the Shield first used the nickname "Racers" when describing the basketball team. Interestingly in that year book the editor was all over the map and in 4 short paragraphs he used the nicknames, Racers, Breds, Hosses, Big Blue Netters, Race Horses and Blue Bloods. But it was the Racer nickname that stuck, and quickly all teams, except the baseball team, began to use it in their literature, and the sportswriters and broadcasters followed suit.

HARLAN HODGES

from Nancy Hodges Darnell's recollections of her father

The man who would establish Murray State Racer basketball as a program to be reckoned with on the national stage very nearly launched his coaching career on the gridiron instead of the hardwood.

The mere fact that Harlan Crews Hodges was in consideration for a head coaching job as a football and basketball coach at the same time is a testament to his talent as a leader of collegiate athletes. A graduate of Southern Illinois University, with a master's degree from the University of Michigan at Ann Arbor, he further proved his commitment to student athletes in his post-coaching career by dedicating himself to the field of education full-time.

Despite his relatively slight build (He was listed as 5'9", 150 pounds as a high school senior.) and later success in the realm of basketball, Hodges made his first mark in the athletic world as a football player. He was selected by Spalding as an Illinois All-State high school honorable mention right tackle in 1920, earning him scholarship opportunities. His collegiate football career featured a brief stint as SIU's backup quarterback.

Ironically, Hodges was never listed on a basketball roster anywhere, so his immense success in his first head coaching job must have come as something of a surprise. In 12 years at the helm of the West Frankfort High School Redbirds in West Frankfort, Illinois, he racked up a 72 percent winning percentage. Hodges would lead the team to three regional tournament titles and two sectional titles. The Redbirds also made it to the state tournament four times during Hodges' tenure. It was after spending one year as the head basketball and track coach at the Missouri School of Mines that he returned to SIU as an assistant basketball and football coach.

Harlan Hodges

Along the way, he soaked up knowledge from every hoops mentor he could find, including Henry Iba, Adolph Rupp, Ray Meyer, Ed Hickey, and Clair Bee. He studied Ward "Piggy" Lambert's book, "Practical Basketball," which outlined the Purdue coach's fondness for the fast break offense and the methods of UCLA legend John Wooden. The now out-of-print book apparently contained quite a bit of useful information, as copies of it were going for $140 at one time on Amazon.com.

Hodges would also draw on experiences from those outside of the basketball world in his quest to not just be a good coach but also an exceptional leader of men. Two of his early examples were Dr. Melvin Deweese, a nationally recognized Memphis ophthalmologist whose early research writings are still available online, and Dean Akridge, a Fredonia, Kentucky, resident who used leading by example to expand his father's retail business.

Hodges was keen on developing his coaching skills over any type of athletic reliance, as he wrote at one point, "Some great athletes are poor coaches. I think this is true in all events. They spend too much time in doing, not coaching."

Despite his burgeoning basketball knowledge, Hodges still found himself firmly entrenched enough in the world of SIU football that the university was prepared to offer him the heading coaching reins of its program. He was attracting interest from college basketball programs as well, leading to a telephone call from Ed Kellow, then-sports editor for the *Paducah Sun-Democrat*, prior to the beginning of the 1948 season broaching the subject of him taking the men's head coaching job at Murray State.

Hodges detailed in his personal notes that Kellow directed him to contact MSU Athletic Director Roy Stewart. Kellow would also state that Hodges had the support of "Mr. Paxton," alluding to *Paducah Sun-Democrat* owners the Paxton family (the Paxton family still owns the *Paducah Sun* today). Hodges, who was in his mid-40s at the time, would recall his initial interview at MSU in the following passage:

> *"This was on Thursday. I called soon, and he asked me to come that day. I said it will be late, as I had football practice that afternoon. The rain came about the time I left Carbondale, and it rained all the way to Murray. As I drove up to the Administration Hall, the (acting) president and committee were coming out."*

Among those present at the meeting were Stewart, Marvin O. Wrather, Dean William G. Nash, Preston Ordway, and Carlisle Cutchin. The meeting began after 10 p.m., and after an hour or so of laying out the university's offer, Wrather asked Hodges if he had any particular demands. After Hodges listed his preferences, Stewart took him to see the Carr Health Building, where the then-Thoroughbreds were playing their basketball games. Wrather rejoined Hodges and Stewart following the brief tour and initiated the following converstation:

> **Wrather:** *"Mr. Hodges, if we give you a three-year contract and you sign it, and you go back to SIU and they give you $1,200 more to stay, would you break it?"*
> **Hodges:** *"If I sign it, I'll be here."*

Hodges would note later on that had he not signed a contract with MSU that night, he "would have been a football coach forever." While he anticipated his decision would be supported by his wife, Helen, her response upon hearing the news of his new basketball coaching career was less than enthusiastic.

"When I got home the next day," Hodges wrote, "I told my wife, Helen, what I had done. She asked, 'Why?', and began to cry. I said, 'Helen, I have always wanted to have my coaching tested, learn if I can compete with the best, and this conference is a very good test.'" Helen evidently got over her husband's decision, as the two remained married until Harlan passed away just four days prior to what would have been their 64th wedding anniversary.

As the life of a men's college basketball coach in 1948 was not quite what it is today, Hodges had some duties stipulated in his contract beyond the hardwood. He was required to teach 18 semester hours at the university, help coach the ends on the football team, and help out as a football trainer as needed. He also acted as a scout for the MSU football program, sometimes logging as many as 20 scouting hours in a single weekend.

Toiling away in the less than ideal confines of the Carr Health Building (he would describe the facility as "a good P.E. building, but a very poor gymnasium."), Hodges gradually built the MSU program up over the course of his first three seasons as head coach. The crowning achievement of those first three seasons occurred February 24, 1951, when MSU clinched the Ohio Valley Conference Tournament championship playing at the Armory in Louisville. To win the championship, the Thoroughbreds had to beat Western and Eastern Kentucky universities on the same day.

Hodges and his players were given a hero's welcome when they returned home from Louisville. *Paducah Sun-Democrat* writer Dix Winston would describe the scene on February 25, 1951, with the following words:

"Students, alumni, rabid fans and any other natives who never heard of Coach Harlan Hodges and the Murray State Thoroughbreds started gathering on the west fill of Eggner's Ferry Bridge after the noon hour and waited faithfully until 5 p.m. A little brass band struck up several times during the wait..."

Before the day was over, Hodges had been presented a key to the city of Murray, wrapped in blue and gold, by Judge Hall Hood.

MSU had not joined the NCAA at this time, though, so their only hope of an extended post-season run rested with a potential National Invitational Tournament (NIT) birth. Despite the school's Top 20 ranking that year, they were passed over and forced to watch lower-ranked teams such as Lawrence Tech, LaSalle, and St. Bonaventure move on. Outrage over the snub was so high the Kentucky General Assembly even registered its disapproval, noting that the Thoroughbreds had won both the regular season championship and conference tournament.

Before he was finished at MSU, Hodges led the team to five Top 20 finishes in the AP poll, peaking with back-to-back rankings at number 16. As great a coach as Hodges was, however, he could not have achieved his high level of success without the play of legendary athletes such as Bennie Purcell, Garrett Beshear, and Howie Crittenden.

Crittenden, who would become an All-American while playing at MSU, was one of several players Hodges recruited from the "North-South Cage Classic." Hodges came up with the idea for the tournament, which featured high school talent, as a way to draw more national publicity to MSU's program. Future stars such as Tom Gola, Bob Pettit, Gerald Stockton, Max Hooper, and Gayle Rose would all participate in the tournament at one time or another.

Hodges' remarkable success as a high school coach led to West Frankfort constructing a new gymnasium, but he had already left the school before its completion. Ironically, he would do the same thing at MSU, as the university had begun construction of a new gym in 1954 – the year Hodges left Murray State to become the new head coach of the University of Idaho Vandals men's basketball team in Moscow, Idaho.

Crittenden would later write, "When Coach Hodges announced he was leaving Murray State, I was devastated. I truly loved playing for him. During the two years I played for Coach Hodges, I was never upset with anything that he said or how he treated me. He was a first-class gentleman, and he was like a father figure to me."

Unfortunately, Hodges never matched his level of success at MSU while he was at Idaho. After piling up 106 wins versus just 66 losses as the Thoroughbreds/Racers head coach, he compiled a 52-77 record for the Vandals. None of his University of Idaho teams ever made a tournament appearance, and he resigned as head coach there on April 30, 1959.

Hodges' legacy would not be limited to the basketball court, however. After leaving the University of Idaho, he became the superintendent of the Anna-Jonesboro Community High School in Ana, Illinois, a position he would hold for five years. He returned to MSU in 1964 as a teacher in the education department, a position he held until his retirement in 1973.

Although he may have finished his time at MSU off the court, Hodges is widely regarded as the coach who put Racer basketball on the map, drawing national attention not only to the school's basketball program but also showcasing it as a place students could receive a quality education at a lower cost. He was perhaps best described in three simple words by Don Stephenson, a retired school administrator and member of the 1951 OVC championship team: "A fine gentleman."

BENNIE PURCELL

by Will Aubrey

Bennie Purcell is fond of saying that he's been on scholarship all his life. If that's so, there can be no question that he's earned it. Few people anywhere have accomplished half as much in their lives as the affable Purcell. And no star in the Racer constellation has ever burned brighter.

An All-Ohio Valley Conference basketball player as a junior at Murray State, Purcell surpassed that by being named an All-American as a senior. He was a member of MSU's first OVC championship team in 1951. And in 1952, the Racers, under his leadership, finished second at the prestigious NAIB tournament where he was named the most valuable player.

Skipper Patrick, a writer for the Associated Press, wrote that Purcell was "the greatest basketball player ever to play in an NAIB basketball tournament, bar none."

Following his senior year he toured with the College All-Americans who played a series of games against the famed Harlem Globetrotters. Drafted by the NBA's Baltimore Bullets, he was the last player cut and turned down an opportunity to play in the Eastern League for a spot on the Washington Generals, a team that toured with the Globetrotters.

Following his career with the Generals he coached high school basketball for a number of years before returning to Murray State as an assistant to Cal Luther. And finally, despite never having played tennis as a youth, he topped it all off by leading the Murray State tennis team to 10 OVC titles, being named coach of the year eight times.

Bennie Purcell

Along the way he has been inducted into five different Hall of Fames including the NAIA Hall of Fame, the Murray State Hall of Fame, the Kentucky Tennis Hall of Fame, and the Intercollegiate Tennis Hall of Fame.

Purcell grew up in Mount Vernon, Illinois during the depression years of the 1930's and the war years of the 1940's. Like many Illinois towns of the era Mount Vernon was a little wild, with gambling houses and all manner of other vices.

"Mount Vernon was wide open at that time.," Purcell recalled. "There were hookers and everything else. Then Adlai Stevenson became governor of Illinois and cleaned it all up."

Still, Purcell was focused on athletics and quickly became an avid baseball fan.

"Mount Vernon is as close to St. Louis as Murray is to Paducah." he said. "So we went to St. Louis a lot and I saw lots of baseball games. I saw the World Series, the Cardinals and Browns in 1944. I saw six games of that World Series."

"I saw my first major league baseball game in 1937 and Dizzy Dean was pitching against Carl Hubbell."

And when he wasn't at the ballpark he was listening to the games on the radio.

"We were both Cardinals and Cubs fans because we could get both games on the radio," he noted. "And I listened to both of them. A lot of the time we'd have two radios and try to listen to the Cardinals and the Cubs because they both played in the afternoon. There weren't any night games back then."

But as much as he enjoyed watching baseball, when it came time to play he preferred a game still in it's infancy – basketball.

"I started playing basketball in third grade and was channeled right on in," he recalled. "Mount Vernon had won the state in Illinois four times so it was one of those deals where you were channeled into basketball as soon as it looked like you were an athlete. It was the main thing. You practiced three nights a week if you wanted to play.

"The gym that we had in grade school was terrible but it was open all the time. You could go up there any time you wanted to. You could go in there and turn the lights on. It was nothing probably but a fire trap but that's where I learned to basketball. I was always one of the better players because I was quick. That was what gave me an edge."

Despite his obvious talent and the success he would enjoy later on, Purcell's first experience with high school basketball was humbling.

"I was on the freshman team and our freshman coach was the assistant football coach and he was meaner than a snake," Purcell recalled. "I put the ball on the floor and started to shoot and a guy blocked it. Well, the coach took me out of the game and cursing the whole time he said, 'I've been warned against you and heard you weren't worth anything. I know it now. Get yourself down to the end of the bench.' And that was my introduction to high school basketball."

Fortunately Purcell didn't let that discourage him and as he honed his game over the next three years he had the staunch support of his parents, Floyd and Audrey Purcell.

"Mount Vernon won the state tournament back when my dad and mom were in high school," he noted. "So they were interested in basketball from then on. Neither of them were athletes but they were interested in athletics and were very supportive."

During Purcell's youth the game of basketball was in a state of flux as it evolved from the staid, low scoring game invented by James Naismith to the thrilling, high scoring sport that would capture the hearts and minds of millions of Americans.

"There wasn't anybody teaching the jump shot back then," Purcell said. "When I first started high school we were taught to shoot a one handed push shot. My high school coach's brother was a coach up at Northern Illinois. And between my junior and senior year of high school he called my coach and said, 'There's a guy up here, a junior high coach, teaching people to shoot the damnedest shot I've ever seen. They jump off the ground and shoot this crazy looking shot but it goes in.'

"So my coach went up there and watched this guy in the summer and saw how he was teaching it and came back and started teaching us to shoot a jump shot. So I didn't have a jump shot till then. And I shot it just a little bit my senior year. I still had that push shot. The year I laid out all I did was shoot jump shots. And that's when my game went to another level and it was because I had a jump shot. There just wasn't anybody shooting jump shots."

"After I left, Mount Vernon won the state tournament two years in a row – undefeated – with these kids he taught to shoot jump shots that were freshmen when I was a senior."

During Purcell's junior and senior years Mount Vernon was the top ranked team in the state yet lost in the sectionals both years. But his athletic exploits weren't limited to basketball, though they would have been if it had been up to him.

"Our coach coached football, track and basketball so I had to play football and had to run track," Purcell said. "But that was just because you had to be out there."

It was during high school that Purcell got his first exposure to Murray State basketball.

"Our coach brought us down and we saw Murray State play DePaul down in Paducah," he said. "And our folks took us to see Illinois play a couple of times and SIU but we weren't big SIU fans. We were probably more St. Louis U. fans.

"The difference growing up in Illinois... Everybody here is a Kentucky fan. That wasn't done in southern Illinois. We weren't automatically Illinois fans. And of course we were close to St. Louis and listened to their games on the radio all the time so were more St. Louis U. fans than Illinois or SIU."

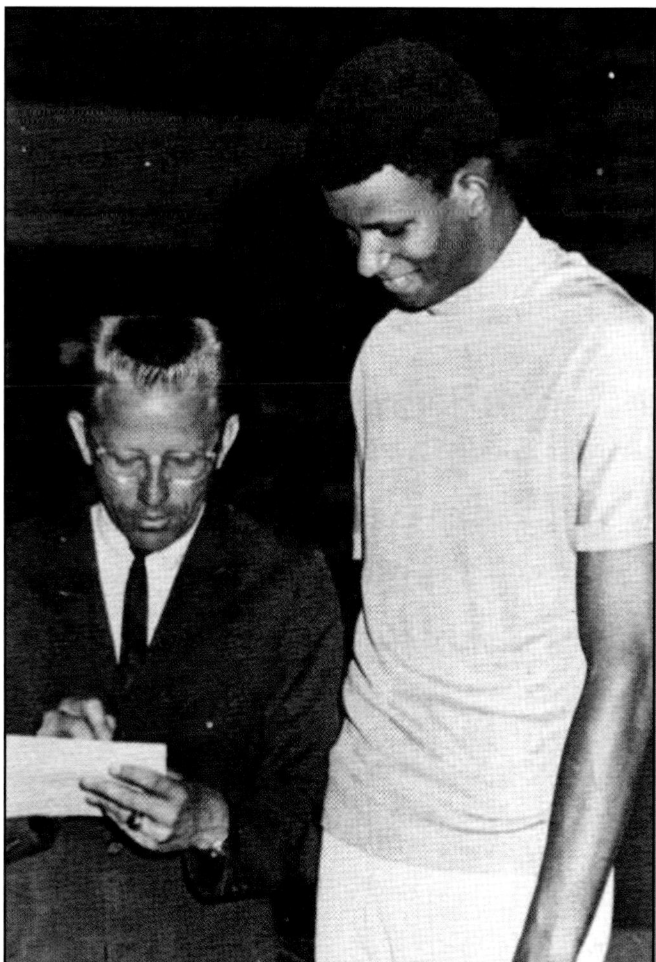

Coach Purcell and prize recruit Will Luter, a 7-0 center.

But, for the most part, what he knew of those teams was what he heard on the radio or read in the newspaper as there was no television in those days. As a result, Purcell says he didn't really have anyone to pattern his game after.

"There wasn't any television so what you heard or read was all you knew," he said. "That made it hard to pattern your game after anybody. Later on when I saw T.V. I learned to put the ball behind my back and make behind the back passes because I saw other guys do it.

"Seeing so many other players on television gives today's players a tremendous advantage. It makes an unbelievable difference. I never saw a guy throw a behind the back pass when I was growing up or dribble behind their back. So I didn't practice doing those things."

Following his senior year at Mount Vernon Purcell decided to play college ball at Bradley University in Peoria, Ill. Today, Bradley is on the periphery of the college basketball world, a middling program in the no-name Missouri Valley Conference. But it wasn't always that way.

In the late 1940's and early '50's the Braves were among the nation's elite as they were the country's top ranked team on five different occasions and finished as the national runnerup in the NIT, NCAA and National Campus Tournament.

So when Purcell went to Bradley he figured to make a splash on a national scale. Fortunately for Murray State it didn't quite work out that way.

"When I got up there, inside the first three days, I turned my ankle playing basketball so bad that I couldn't walk," he said. "So I decided not to stay."

He came home and set out a year. But he continued working on his game.

"I played about 140 games of basketball the year I sat out," he said. "I played in every independent league around. I've been on scholarship all my life.

"That year that I sat out all I did was go down to the gym in the mornings about 9:30 or 10:00 and shoot baskets till noon. Then I'd go eat and come back and shoot more in the afternoon and then I'd go play at night."

At the end of that year, Harlan Hodges got the head coaching job at Murray State. At one time he had been an assistant coach at West Frankfort High School so he knew about Purcell and asked him to come to MSU.

"When I came down here to Murray there were 100 guys trying out for 15 scholarships," Purcell recalled.

But he got one of those scholarships and went on to start over half of the games as a freshman. As a sophomore, he was a fixture in the starting lineup for a team that finished 18-13 and recorded victories over powerhouses Seton Hall and Brooklyn College as well as Memphis State.

There were no NCAA restrictions on practice time in those days and the Racers hit the hardwood twice each day, practicing in the mornings and afternoons. That along with a surprise revelation at the end of the year helped Purcell take his game to an entirely new level.

"I didn't wear glasses until the end of my sophomore year at Murray State," he recalled. "I didn't know my eyes were that bad. We had some eye exams and they said, 'Boy your eyes are bad.'

"And so I put those glasses on and that's when I really became good because I hadn't been able to see and didn't know it. Back then they didn't give you eye exams at school. I never had an eye exam in grade school or high school the whole time. It was like a new world when I put those glasses on."

In those days Murray State played it's games in the North Gym at the Carr Health Building and it was almost impossible to get a ticket because every game was a sellout. Oddly enough, on one occasion Purcell had trouble getting in himself.

"As a student you couldn't get in unless you had your I.D," he said. "Well one time I'd lost my billfold. And Preston Ordway was the business manager and he wouldn't let me in. I told him my billfold had been stolen and he said, 'That's tough you'll have to pay to get in.'

"And I told him there was no way I was going to pay to get into the game to play. Hodges had to come out and pay a dollar to get me in."

The next year (1950-51) saw the Racers win their first OVC regular season and tournament titles after being ranked 10th in nation in the Associated Press preseason poll.

Despite winning the regular season title the MSU was seeded second in the OVC tournament because seedings were based on overall records not conference records. And bookmakers made the Racers the fourth choice in the field.

Western Kentucky won a coin flip which allowed them to choose whether they wanted to be in Evansville's bracket or Murray's. The Hilltoppers chose Murray's half and WKU assistant coach Ted Hornback was ecstatic.

"What luck," he said. "Boy! Boy! I think we have a better chance of getting to the finals now. I think our personnel is better suited to beat Murray than Evansville."

He would live to regret those words as the Racers beat both Western and Eastern on the final day of the tournament to secure the title. When the team returned to Murray they found 2,000 fans waiting for them at the Eggner's Ferry Bridge over the Tennessee River. It was like a county fair.

But as successful as that season was, Purcell and his MSU teammates would have an encore the next season as they came within one game of winning a national championship.

In the late 40's and early 50's there were three major postseason college tournaments – the NIT, the NCAA and the NAIB. In 1948 the champions of those tournaments played a round robin tournament to determine which team would represent the United States at the Olympics.

Following their OVC championship in 1951, Murray State was invited to the NAIB tournament but, expecting an NIT invitation, they declined. That was understandable because the NIT was the most prestigious tournament in the land.

Unfortunately Western got an NIT bid and the Racers were left sitting at home. In 1952 MSU would not repeat it's mistake.

"We thought the '52 team was going to be the best we'd ever had," Purcell said. "Gene Garrett, Garrett Beshear and myself were All-OVC as juniors and we were all back. We won 11 straight games and then Gene Garrett got drafted in the army.

"The guy that took his place was Bobby Clark. He played two games and then they drafted him. So we lost a starter and our number one reserve."

During that 11 game winning streak Murray State celebrated road wins over Houston, Texas and Baylor. Following the loss of Garrett they would lose four straight games but closed with a rush, winning seven of their final 11 regular season games heading into the OVC tournament in Louisville where they lost to Western Kentucky in the final, 47-45.

Presented with an NAIB bid, the Racers quickly accepted. They ran off four straight victories before losing to Southwest Missouri in the national final in Kansas City, Mo. And they might have won a national title but Purcell, the team's leading scorer, injured his wrist in the second game. Then the team's second leading scorer, Garrett Beshear, got word that his father had died.

Both Purcell and Beshear played in all the games, but they can't have been at 100 percent. Still, MSU fans got to welcome home the national runner-ups.

"When we came back from Kansas City a big bunch of people met us and we had a ceremony at Lovett Auditorium honoring us," Purcell said. "And that's when they retired my number because I was the most valuable player in that tournament."

It was the first time Murray State had ever retired anyone's number.

1952 College All-Americans. Back row: Coach Ray Meyer, DePaul University; Carl McNulty, Purdue University; Rod Fletcher, University of Illinois; Bob Zawoulak, St. Johns University; Bill Mikvy, Temple University; and Coach Claire Bee, Long Island University. Center row: Leroy Leslie, Notre Dame University; Lee Terrell, North Carolina State; and Nick Kladus, Loyola University. Front row: Jim Ivenson, Kansas State University; Bennie Purcell, Murray State College; and Sam Miranda, Indiana University.

Garrett Beshear

by Sid Easley

Garrett Beshear was indeed a legend in his own time and had the age to prove it. He was 27-years-old when he entered college at Murray State as a freshman in the fall of 1949. Sports writers during his playing days wrote volumes about his age. Some who paid little attention to the facts would give his age as 35 or even higher.

Beshear was born at a "wide place in the road" in Hopkins County, Kentucky by the name of Ilsley. He had been an outstanding basketball player in high school for the Nortonville Badgers. One of the "old timer" basketball fans in the area named "Poss Rogers" recalled one of Beshear's memorable high school games: "We were playing Kuttawa and the great Joe Fulks. It was Beshear against Fulks, and Garrett outscored him and out rebounded him too. He was among the greatest players I've ever seen and I've seen all of them around here."

Beshear reached 19 shortly after he graduated from High School in 1941. War was raging in Europe and most then knew it would only be a matter of time before boys at home would ony be called to defend their country. It happened, and Beshear entered the Army and served for 4½ years. Western had recruited him out of high school, but when he returned from the Army he chose not to go to college for a time and worked at home. His father was a revenue agent in the days when there were moonshine stills all around west Kentucky. He knew Garrett's basketball ability and felt he was wasting it by not playing, but most of all he knew there was no substitute in the post war world for a college education.

Garrett Beshear

Finally in the summer of 1949 Garrett made the decision to enroll at MSU. As a veteran he could use the GI Bill and also thought he could convince those in charge that he should receive a basketball scholarship. His first cousin was Rex Alexander. Rex had graduated in the spring of 1949 and would later become Murray's assistant and head coach. Alexander was two years younger than Beshear. Doris Alexander, wife of Rex, recalled, "Rex worked hard to get Garrett to come to Murray."

Getting Beshear here was one thing, but impressing Coach Hodges, who had a keen eye for talent, was another. Here was a rugged and slightly stooped 27-year-old married guy with a child who had spent 4½ years in the Army and hadn't played organized basketball since high school, almost 10 years before. And it didn't help that his recommendations were coming from cousins rather than other coaches who had seen him play. Hodges was skeptical.

Erl Sensing, the college's publicist at the time, remembered that Beshear "came to Murray without a scholarship." Though Beshear was a humble fellow, he did not lack confidence in his ability to play basketball. Bennie Purcell was a sophomore Beshear's freshman year and remembers Beshear coming to practice for the first time and a conversation he had with Coach Hodges. The two were discussing Garrett's going out for the team and at some point in the discussion Garrett became exasperated and said to the coach, "I can make it because I'm better than anything you have out there."

By early December in his freshman year Hodges realized he had a gem, and offered him a scholarship. At the close of Beshear's playing career Hodges showered him with glowing compliments and in a *Paducah Sun Democrat* article Hodges proudly said, "he had an extraordinary will to excel."

From the minute he arrived on campus at the ripe old age of 27 he became something of a celebrity simply because of his age. But age soon was forgotten as this 6 foot 4 sneaky fast, and somewhat unorthodox, inside player began to make his mark in Murray State basketball annals. The statistics of the four years when viewed in their entirety reveal an astonishing fact. Murray lost only six home games during the four-year career of Garrett Beshear. "No man is an island," and certainly having Bennie Purcell in his front court for three years and Howie Crittenden for one helped make him the legend he became, but nevertheless he left holding the Murray scoring record with a total of 1716 points in his career.

During his career he hit 40 percent of his shots and made 619 field goals. In 1952-53 he set a record for points scored in a single season with 643. Today he remains in 9th place in career scoring in the Racer record books. For his sustained excellence he was the first Racer and first conference player to have been named to the All-OVC team for three years, and today is one of only nine to have been so honored.

Two Racer greats who played with him and joined him in Murray's Hall of Fame recalled their friendship and respect for Beshear.

Purcell roomed with him on the road, played with him for three years, and knew him as well as anyone. He gave him this compliment. "I played with four All-American centers including Bill Spivey from Kentucky, and Clyde Lovellette from Kansas. A good center must be capable of putting himself into a position to receive the ball, and Garrett was absolutely the best of them all to be able to get in position to get the ball."

Howie Crittenden, who was a freshman when Beshear was a senior, agreed. "He had big hands and could catch the ball in almost any situation. I threw it to him behind my back, between my legs, and over my shoulders, and some way he would always come up with it. The same was true on the fast break. He was uncanny in his ability to catch a ball that was thrown him from behind and over his shoulder on the break. He would just come up with it."

Everyone who ever played with Beshear mentions his ability to fake. All said it was comical to watch those guarding him jumping all over the place when he started his fake moves.

Purcell noted his ability to make the outlet pass. "The fast break is totally dependent on that rebound and quick outlet pass. Beshear was a master at it – just so quick."

Dean Akridge played with Beshear during Beshear's senior year. "He was always a presence – always after you. He was a smart player and knew how to pace himself so he wouldn't wear out. But he always wanted the ball, and you knew you had better get him the ball if you wanted to get some playing time. He and Coach Hodges were very close – almost a father-son relationship."

Sensing wrote some inimitable prose in attempting to portray the real Beshear to *Courier Journal* reporter Tommy Fitzgerald on February 27, 1951.

"I don't know how to describe Garrett Beshear to you, but have you ever noticed his eyes in the heat of a basketball game. There is a sort of glassiness to them as if he's entranced, completely carried away with what he's doing. Kind of like the eyes of a prophet if you know what I mean. Fanatical zeal, I guess is what you'd call it. Maybe you mean an uncontrollable lust to kill we heard that some soldiers have in combat. In boxing and sports in general we call it the killer instinct."

Purcell may well have summed up Beshear as a basketball player better than any. When you play with a fellow you get to know him, and Bennie had some of the most thoughtful reflections on Beshear.

"He had the confidence that he could score on anybody who played against him, and when you played with him you had that same confidence in him. His age and experience coupled with natural athletic ability undoubtedly bred that self-confidence."

Marvin N. Gay Jr., who wrote for the *Louisville Times,* said of Beshear the week before he last appeared in the OVC Tournament in Louisville: "Fabulous, almost unbelievable Garrett (Daddy) Beshear comes into town this week for his lone appearance of the basketball campaign and when he departs the Ohio Valley Conference Tournament likely will have a standard that will hold up for years, possibly forever."

Beshear ended his playing days in the spring of 1953, receiving the degree his father wanted him to get, and immediately was hired as the coach of Hazel High School in Calloway County. "He won the District tournament the first year there," remembers Murray raconteur Pete Waldrop.

In 1954 the basketball coaching position at Murray Training School opened, and Beshear opted to return to work at Murray State as the coach of its laboratory school. He held that job for 14 years. When a new gymnasium was built for the Training School the Murray State Regents named it after him. The new Gymnasium, which would later become the home of the National Scouting Museum, was named "Garrett Beshear Gymnasium."

Local fans and Murray State faculty and staff never forgot the great Beshear as a player and a coach, and retained their affection for him. Dr. James Frank recalled a treasured story about Beshear's relationship with Dr. Ralph Woods the President of the College.

"Garrett loved to fish and would often be up at daylight to get in a few hours on the lake before school opened. Dr. Wood's was a workaholic and his wife Elizabeth was always alert to the times when he needed to 'take off.' Dr. Woods would never listen to her, but she knew that he would do anything for Garrett, and that a fishing trip with him was the best medicine he could take. One spring day she called Garrett and told him that Dr. Woods needed to take a few hours off, and asked him to call Dr. Woods for a fishing trip. Garrett assured her he would, and called Dr. Woods. It went this way. 'Dr Woods this is Garrett Beshear. Do you think you could take off a couple of hours this afternoon to go fishing?' Dr. Woods in his inimitable deep professional voice quickly responded. 'Well Garrett, I guess if you can get off, I can too.'" Dr. Woods would relax, and the two fishing buddies would treasure their day together.

Beshear's father passed away unexpectedly at the age of 49 while Garrett and the Thoroughbreds were preparing to play in the finals of the NAIB tournament in Kansas City. It was Garrett's junior year. Purcell recalls that the loss of Garrett's father at that time cast a damper on the entire team, but Beshear played, and played well, as always.

Often we cannot escape our family health history, and sadly on July 24, 1968, at the young age of 46 years, Garrett Beshear too died of a heart attack. He was suddenly struck while in East Lansing, Michigan at a Driver's Education seminar representing the University School. His obituary revealed that he was born May 19, 1922. He was survived by his wife Lucy, his mother Ethel, and sons Gary and William Keeney.

All those who had known him mourned his loss and paused to reflect on the skilled basketball player and the wonderful gentleman who made a lasting contribution to Murray State Basketball

Sensing searched for the real Garrett Beshear. "The finest thing that can be said about Beshear, though, is not a log recitation of his records and his basketball skill. Rather, it is his splendid sportsmanship. In him no opponent has ever met anything except a top-notch basketballer giving his all to win – under the rules of the game."

Hodges showed his profound respect and affection for his player when he wrote. "As his coach, it was my privilege to see his qualities in daily operation. No imminent opponent, however formidable, could daunt that courageous athlete. Repeatedly, he would say, 'Don't worry coach, we'll take this one. I know it.'"

At Beshear's death much was written about him by those who loved and respected him.

"Garrett was one of those fellows who had a friendly hello, was quiet, unassuming, efficient, and modest.' *Editorial, Murray Ledger and Times*

Vernon Shown, beloved Murray State staff member and University School Principal said this about him: "There was absolutely no pretense about him. He didn't have the ability to 'put on.' He never tried to be anyone but Garrett Beshear. He had regard for all – from the janitor and the campus worker to the president of the college."

Bill Powell, respected columnist for the *Paducah Sun Democrat,* eulogized him in his column.

"...he was a competitor in everything he did. As much as he loved to win – even if it simply were out-fishing a friend – he was a good loser. I have never known anyone with a greater sense of fair play that Garrett Beshear. He didn't replay ball games and try to justify whatever turned against him and his team; he merely looked ahead with iron determination to winning the next time.

But, in a way, Beshear had a contradictory personality. He was humble and a well-balanced athlete and sportsman. But he didn't hesitate, in his days of stardom, to say how good he thought he was."

Purcell recalled that Dayton had a big time team and came to Murray with every intention of earning an easy victory. But Murray won, and Beshear, who was almost 31 at the time, scored 40 points.

On the way out of town the Dayton team stopped to eat, and someone asked how the game came out.

"We got beat, and a hump-backed old man scored 40 points on us," a Dayton player said sardonically.

Howie Crittenden

by Sid Easley

On December 11, 1955 Howie Crittenden scorched the nets with 41 points to tie a Murray State scoring record. It was the first game in Murray's new arena. Thirty-eight hundred proud and excited fans saw Crittenden tie Bennie Purcell's single game scoring record. Crittenden's points and brilliant floor game led Murray to a 104-84 victory over OVC foe Middle Tennessee.

This game was simply another record setting event in the storied basketball career of Howie Crittenden from the crossroads village of Pilot Oak and Cuba High School in Graves County, Kentucky.

"There wasn't anything else to do in Pilot Oak in my time but play basketball," Crittenden said. "I played on an outside goal near the grocery store every chance I got. Soon I was playing with a group of boys that included my friend Charles 'Doodles' Floyd. I was a skinny and short little kid, even shorter than my twin sister, and didn't begin growing until about the 8th grade. I think you probably inherit competitiveness, but a good work ethic is indispensable. When I began receiving a little recognition for my basketball ability I just never quit working at it.

"I had a wonderful high school coach, Jack Story, who was ahead of his time. He was smart, and he knew the fundamentals of the game. He always admired my peripheral vision and he taught me to look one way and pass the other, to never look at the ball when I dribbled, and to dribble and pass with either hand. I was at my best with the ball in the middle of a fast break. I could see the entire floor and could hit the open man with a sharp pass from behind my back with either my right or left hand. They didn't keep assists in those days, but I sure had a lot of them. I scored a lot, but my floor game was my strength.

"In high school I would dribble the ball down the Pilot Oak road for two miles or more on a pitch dark night. There was no traffic in those days, and if you do that enough you learn where that ball is going to be when it bounces back to you. Coach Story told us to pick up rocks as we walked down the gravel road and throw them behind our back at fence posts on either side of the road without looking at the posts."

One gets an idea of Crittenden's basketball philosophy in his reply to the question of what makes a good coach. "Above all a coach must know the fundamentals of basketball, and know how to teach them. And a good coach must know how to teach defense," he said. "You gain respect for a coach because of his knowledge of the game, and for his ability to help you become a better player.

Howie Crittenden

"There are many intangibles, but always a coach should treat you like he would want to be treated. You expect a coach to correct you, and to discipline you, but screaming at you or doing other crazy things has no place in the game and is counterproductive."

Crittenden paused in the conversation and remembered one crucial thing he learned from Story that he never forgot. "It was the best basketball advice I ever received," he said. "We were in the 8th grade and sitting outside listening to Coach Story talk about basketball. He turned to me and said, 'Howard, see that big tree over there. Run as fast as you can run and touch it, and run back to where you started.' So I took off running as fast as I could, there and back. Then Coach Story looked at me and said, 'now pick up that basketball and dribble it to that tree and back, just as fast as you ran – back and forth.' I tried it, but with the ball I went a lot slower. He then said to us all, 'if you want to be a great basketball player you have to learn to *move as fast with the ball, as you do without the ball.*' I remember that advice to this day. I followed it myself, taught it to the kids I coached, and I share it with every kid I talk to about basketball."

Crittenden's "Hoosier-like" high school team had won the Kentucky State Tournament in his senior year. He was considered the number one high school player in Kentucky in 1952, and after the North-South All-Star game in Murray, he was named a high school All-American.

With those credentials, he was avidly recruited by numerous colleges. Adolph Rupp came to see him play, visited him at school in Cuba and offered him a scholarship to Kentucky. Western Kentucky's Ed Diddle came to Crittenden's house more than once and, "my parent's loved Coach Diddle. He was down home just like us." Memphis State wanted Crittenden as well as South Carolina. Peck Hickman from Louisville promised him a starting position and numerous benefits.

So why did you come to Murray he was asked, "Well, Kentucky was going to be on probation the following year, and that was a problem for me, but frankly I wasn't that excited about playing for Rupp. I didn't want to go to Memphis, but Western was another matter, and it was all because of Coach Diddle who was just a great fellow.

"Then one day I was in school at Cuba, and the Principal came to class and got me. He said the Graves County School Superintendent 'Baby' Deweese and my father were in the office and wanted to talk with me. I was scared to death, not knowing why my father was there or what was wrong. 'Baby' spoke up and said, 'Howie come on and go with us over to Murray. They want to talk with you about playing basketball over there.' I was barely 19 at the time and wasn't about to question the superintendent.

"We drove to Murray and went into the boardroom of the local bank where about eight or nine businessmen with suits were sitting around the room. The president of the bank then took over.

"It was 1952, the Korean War was winding down, and we were living on a little 30-acre farm in Graves County. We were poor, and Daddy didn't have a job. He was crippled from a bout with polio when he was four. The president of the bank sat by my father in that room, and the first thing he said was, 'We want you to come to Murray and play basketball. Your daddy needs a job and I believe we can find him one with the highway department. He will have a job as long as you play here.'

Howie Crittenden fakes a shot during the Murray-Western game.

about my grades there either. 'You sure won't flunk at Western,' he said to me."

Crittenden's career at Murray was an extension of his storied high school career. He started the first game he ever played at Murray and played that year with the great Garrett Beshear. "He was just a great player," Howie said. "He was fast, had a quick first step, and was always alert in catching my passes. He was over 10 years older than I, and was like a coach on the floor."

"I shall never forget the night we played at Wichita State my freshman year. I had one of those nights where the ball always goes in for you. I even hit a desperation shot from near Wichita's free throw line to end the half, and had 25 points going into the dressing room. When we came out for the second half I was feeling good.

"I was speechless. Then he started talking about spending money and the list went on. I regained my senses and there sat my father. There was no way I was going to turn down a job for my father. I then sort of mumbled about not having clothes to wear like the other kids. The president of the bank responded quickly. 'So and so sitting right over there owns a clothing store right here on the square, and he will fix you up.' With that I was headed for Murray, and my daddy had a job. I had only seen Murray play one time while I was in high school.

"Recruiting was different in that time, and Murray folks were not content to be second. One coach handed me a blank sheet of paper and told me to write down whatever I wanted to come play for him. The Memphis coach offered to move our whole family to Memphis. Diddle assured me that 'everything I needed at Western would be provided,' and that I wouldn't have to worry

"We were warming up before the half started and Beshear looked over at me, and in a fatherly voice said, 'freshman – come here.' I thought he was going to tell me to keep it up. But he said, 'Throw that damn ball into me, I'll be hot this half.' I did what he said," Crittenden laughed.

Crittenden was named to the All-OVC team his sophomore and junior years, and undoubtedly would have been his senior year but for some strange reason the OVC did not name an all-conference team in 1956. He was Honorable mention All-America his junior and senior years.

Crittenden was a prolific scorer, piling up points with a barrage of consistency – freshman 14.4 avg., sophomore 21.0 avg., junior 21.3 avg. and senior 21.2. Perhaps his greatest single achievement occurred when he held the record for the most points scored by any Kentucky college player in a four-year career. He held the Murray 4-year scoring record for 33 years. When his career at Murray ended he had played in 104 games and scored 2,019 points. The record was finally broken by Jeff Martin in 1989. When looking at this point total one must be cognizant of the fact that there was no bonus free throw in that time and the three-point shot was unheard of. Crittenden retains the Murray four-year scoring record for players playing all their games before the three-point shot was allowed.

Howie Crittenden hangs in the air.

Though he was a record setting scorer, knowledgeable fans view Crittenden's strength as his ball handling and playmaking ability. This fact becomes apparent when you look at the school records that he holds to this day. His 222 free throws made in 1953-54, and 214 made in 1954-55 at a time when there was no bonus awarded remain the best in Murray history. He made 19 free throws in each of the games against Morehead, Eastern Kentucky and Western Kentucky in 1954-55. Shooting that many free throws (a record setting 731 in his career) is a tribute to the unmatched playmaking and ball handling ability of Crittenden.

After his last game as a college player, the sports editor for the *Paducah Sun* summed up his ability with these words. "Yet, to me, scoring has always been incidental for Howie. I've been watching him play for six years. But I went to see his passing, dribbling, defense, and clutch play. He can pick up 20 points accidentally, without making an effort to score. But I've never seen him matched as a playmaker…."

"I always worked hard," Crittenden remembered. "I lived in Murray during the summer and worked for college maintenance in digging trenches, foundations and ditches. Robert Glenn Jeffery from Murray worked with me. The coach would give me a key to the gym and every day during the summer for two hours I was in the Carr Health building by myself in 95 degree heat shooting, dribbling and practicing. I had done the same thing in high school, so college was no different. I always wanted to get better."

As his college career came to a close the pros came calling. "I wanted to play for the St. Louis Hawks," he said. "Pettit and Hagan were there and I thought there would be a guard slot open for me.

"But the New York Knicks drafted me first. They had a poor team, and I didn't want to go to New York anyway. Pro basketball in those days paid almost nothing. I needed the money, and a career after basketball was what was most important to me. I knew what it meant to be poor, and this was no time to take risks."

"At that time there was a National Industrial

Howie Crittenden making a layup against Kentucky Wesleyan.

League where large corporations such as Caterpillar, Phillips 66, and Goodyear had teams. It was a forerunner of the ABA. You worked for the company, played basketball, and retained your amateur status. It paid well for the time. "I played for the Peoria Caterpillars for three years, and the league finally folded."

Crittenden was on the All-Star team all three years and was named to the AAU All-American Team each year. Crittenden is most proud of being selected to be a member of the first USA Team to go to Russia in 1958, "It was during the Cold War, and Russia was considered our enemy. We toured in Russia for a month, and played the Russian all-stars. We never lost a game."

When asked about the great players he played against in his career, he quickly named Jerry West and Oscar Robertson. "They were great players. I felt comfortable guarding West, but if you backed off him at all he could fill it up. He was just an incredible shot.

"Charlie Tyra and Phil Rollins from Louisville were outstanding players, and so were Dan Swartz from Morehead and Jack Adams from Eastern. There were many other great players.

"In those days Murray played a very difficult schedule. We had moved from NAIA to Division I and were required to play a certain number of Division I teams. That meant we played outstanding teams on the road, mostly, but we played some good teams in Murray, too."

As is so often the case in life, success breeds success. Crittenden's achievements on the basketball floor carried over into his professional life. He was an academically gifted student taking Advanced ROTC and carrying a double major. He served as basketball coach at Metropolis High School in Illinois and later at Calloway County High. His coaching career was interrupted for a year when his Army Reserve unit was called up and 1st Lt. Crittenden spent one year in Fort Chaffee, Arkansas. He also was named assistant coach at the University of Missouri under Bob Vanatta. But "Boots Jeffrey, Superintendent at Calloway called me and insisted I return and take the principal's job in 1966," Crittenden remembered.

He remained as principal at Calloway County for eight years. In 1974 he was named principal of Kentucky's largest high school, Henderson County, and served in that capacity for 21 years. For his many accomplishments he was named Kentucky Principal of the Year in 1989-90 and was elected President of the Kentucky Principal's Association in 1990.

TERRY DARNALL

by Sid Easley

Terry Darnall was recruited by Kentucky, Tennessee, Memphis and Murray. "It was a no brainer for me,' remembered Darnall. "I liked Murray from the beginning. My brother played here."

Darnall grew up in Hornbeak, Tennessee, located a few miles south of Union City. "My mother was an all-state basketball player in Tennessee. We lived next door to the local gymnasium and I was in there all the time."

Darnall earned all-state honors as a junior and senior. His high school team had a combined record of 75-3 during those years.

"Harlan Hodges recruited me and then he left. I played three years under Rex Alexander and one year under Cal Luther," recalled Darnall.

Darnall is exceedingly modest. He downplays his career, but those who saw him play tell a very different story. Bennie Purcell said, "Terry was one heckuva player."

Luther said of him, "He was one of the best all-around athletes I ever coached. He had it all – coordination, toughness, strength and competitiveness. He was a natural, and how I wish I could have had him longer."

At 6-3, Darnall was a tall guard for his day. He had a great jump shot and as a rugged west Tennessee farm boy he never let anyone run over him. One of Murray State's legendary stories involves Darnall.

"We were playing Memphis State," Darnall said. "Bob Vanatta was their coach. They had a very good player named Bob Swander, but he seemed to enjoy elbowing anybody who came close to him, and for the most part he got by with it. We were playing in Murray and he began to sneakily put his shoulder and elbow to me every time we came close to one another. He did it twice to me that night.

"I had enough of it, and I told him, 'You do that again and I'm gonna take care of you.' We lined up for an out of bounds play and sure enough here he came with a big elbow right in my stomach. 'I cold-cocked him.' They threw me out of the game, but he was out for the season. Memphis wouldn't play Murray for several years after that. But we had the film to show what really went on. We played at Memphis later in the year and the crowd there was after me. They threw stuff on the floor and harassed me the whole game."

Terry Darnall

Darnall had a great career at Murray. He was twice all OVC and led the team in scoring his senior year.

After college Darnall became quite a tennis player and won the senior circuit state doubles title in Tennessee more than once. He became a successful business man in Jackson, Tennessee where he still lives. His love for Murray State basketball has never waned, and on many game nights he is seen standing in the corner of the CFSB Center with his great friend, Bennie Purcell.

THE 1960S

by Jimmy Wilder

1959-60 • 12-11

The players who were difference-makers for the 1959-60 Racers hardly resembled the cast that took the court the season before, Cal Luther's first as Murray State's coach. And as Murray's 12-11 record indicates, the new faces had a positive impact on the direction the program was headed.

Even though leading scorers Terry Darnell and Dale Alexander were gone from the 10-15 team of the year before, Luther wasn't fretting when practice began for the '59-60 season.

In Jarrell Graham (DePauw), Ron Greene (Bradley) and Larry Bale (Campbellsville), Luther had three transfers who he felt would challenge returning starters Mike O'Riordan, Ken Peterson and Harold Wilkins for meaningful playing time. And in Gene Herndon, he had a junior redshirt who might give the Racers an upgrade in the paint.

The 6-5 Herndon averaged 5.1 points and 5.6 rebounds a game in '57-58 and was expected to be a starter in '58-59, but he sat out after being injured in the preseason. He recovered from his foot problem to start every game in '59-60, leading Murray in scoring (15.4 ppg) and rebounding (11.6 rpg) and joining O'Riordan and Graham on the All-OVC team. O'Riordan was Murray's second leading scorer (13.4 ppg) and rebounder (11.1 rpg).

Graham (12.4 ppg) and Greene (10.8 ppg) were also double figure scorers. Bale (9.3 ppg) and Wilkins (6.3 ppg) shared the fifth starting spot.

Luther changed his offensive philosophy, opting to go long stretches with three guards and two forwards on the court together. Peterson, the tallest player in the OVC at 6-11½ and a natural center, saw his scoring and rebounding averages drop from 9.7 and a team high 9.2 in '58-59 to 2.1 and 3.8.

Choosing athleticism over size posed match-up challenges for the Racers against Louisville, Miami (Fla.), Western Kentucky, Eastern Kentucky and Tennessee Tech.

Coach Peck Hickman's Louisville's Cardinals, a NCAA Final Four participant in 1959, had a strong inside presence in 6-11 Fred Sawyer and 6-7 Bud Olsen and beat the Racers twice, 78-72 at Louisville and 74-67 at Murray. Olsen scored six straight points to give the Cards a 67-60 advantage with 1:53 remaining in their win at Louisville. At Murray, Sawyer had 27 rebounds, a plethora of blocked shots and 16 points as Louisville rebuffed a comeback by the Racers, who pressed most of the second half, cutting a 50-35 deficit to four points before the Cards expanded their lead to 62-50 with 5:15 remaining.

Coach Bruce Hale's Miami Hurricanes handed the Racers a 92-80 loss in Miami on their way to a 23-win season and a NCAA Tournament game against Western Kentucky. The Hurricanes trailed Murray 74-68 before going on a 24-2 run in the final seven minutes. Forward Ron Godfrey was the catalyst for Miami's win, scoring 32 points and hitting 12 of 12 free throws. In the NCAA tourney, Western beat Miami 107-84, lost to eventual champion Ohio State and beat Ohio 97-87 in the Mideast Regional consolation game.

With records of 10-2 and 9-3, Western Kentucky and Eastern Kentucky were the OVC's top two teams in '59-60, splitting their games against the Racers. Murray beat the Toppers 87-62 and beat the Colonels 73-54 in the Racer Arena.They also split their games against Tennessee Tech, winning 73-67 in Murray in their Feb. 27 season finale.

O'Riordan's 26 points keyed the Racers' win in January against Western, which had a starting front line of 6-8 Harry Todd, 6-6 Charles Osborne and 6-4 Al Ellison. Greene (18 points) and Graham (14 points) also helped take down the Toppers, and Joe Wilmore, another guard, came off the bench to score 12 points.

Graham (20 points), Herndon (17 points) and Greene (15 points) led the Racers in scoring in their Feb. 14 win against Eastern, which came into the game leading the league with an 8-1 record. It was an especially sweet outcome for the Racers because the Colonels had beaten them 84-69 at Richmond.

Four nights before Murray played Western at Bowling Green on Feb. 20, Luther was in Diddle Arena for a Western-Eastern game, scouting the Toppers.

Play ended 13:28 into the contest, when EKU coach Paul McBrayer took his team to the locker room and never returned, following a hard foul by his 6-7 center Ralph Richardson on WKU guard Bobby Rascoe and an ensuing fracas, after which Richardson told McBrayer that WKU coach Ed Diddle, had put his hands on him.

McBrayer's response to the incident resulted in the game being recorded as a forfeit, producing the impetus for the Toppers to win all four of their upcoming OVC games and their eighth league title, all with Diddle as their coach.

Western's first win after the Eastern game came against Murray, 65-56, with the Toppers overcoming a Racer 12 point first half lead.

Wins against Western, Eastern and Tech represented the Racers' most noteworthy of the season, but the most crowd-pleasing came on Feb. 1 when they beat East Tennessee State 113-68 at Murray, setting a new school single-game scoring record. O'Riodan (20 points), Herndon (19 points) and Greene (18 points) led Murray's offensive charge against East Tennessee, and John West, a 6-5 reserve forward, added 12 points.

The Racers' most grating loss came on the road in their next game, when Morehead beat them in overtime, 96-87.

Murray State didn't get its Feb. 16 home rematch against the Morehead because snow and ice made for hazardous driving conditions, preventing the Eagles from making the trip to Murray. Impassable roads also resulted in the cancellation of a Tech game at Morehead. Thus, the Eagles played only 10 league games (they won three), Murray and Tech played 11 and the other OVC teams played their full compliment of 12 games.

In what must be described as an unusual re-scheduling arrangement, Murray would play Morehead three times in the 1960-61 season, weather-permitting. Tech and Morehead would also have an identical scheduling arrangement in '60-61.

1960-61 • 13-10

A 13-10 record and fourth place finish in the Ohio Valley Conference were not quite what Cal Luther anticipated coming into the 1960-61 Murray State season.

Not with the Racers tying Tennessee Tech for third place in the OVC standings and returning nine lettermen (eight of them seniors) and all five starters from the 12-11 team of '59-60.

Not with league coaches voting Murray State the third best team in the OVC in their preseason poll, behind Western Kentucky and Eastern Kentucky and comfortably ahead of (in order) Morehead State, Tennessee Tech, Middle Tennessee State and East Tennessee State.

Not with their schedule calling for the Racers to play 13 games at home, two against Morehead, a 5-14 team in '59-60 whose best player, guard Herbie Triplett, had graduated.

Not even with Murray going on the road to face St. Bonaventure, Memphis and Mississippi State, who were projected to be among the elite teams in America.

What Luther didn't have in '60-61 was an answer for how to win the close ones, or how to win away from home. When the Racers needed defensive stops, they often couldn't keep their opponents from scoring.

At season's end, the Racers had lost six games by a total of 15 points (four in the OVC), won just two of 10 road games and been torched for 90 or more points five times. Western, Eastern, Morehead and East Tennessee guard Tom Chilton, the nation's second leading scorer, were the league's headline makers, leaving Luther to ponder what might have been.

The following is not a misprint. Morehead won 19 games (nine in the OVC, one in the NCAA Tournament) and played its last five games in Freedom Hall, site of the 1961 NCAA Tournament Mideast Regional.

There's a two-part explanation for the Eagles playing five consecutive games in Freedom Hall:

First, Morehead, Western and Eastern tied for first in the OVC round-robin title chase, setting up a playoff in Freedom Hall to determine the conference representative in the NCAA tourney. Coach Bobby Laughlin's Eagles earned that right, beating EKU 55-54 on March 6 and following-up with an 80-72 overtime win against WKU on March 8.

Second, in In the NCAA tourney, Morehead added to the lore of its Cinderella season by beating Xavier 71-66 in Freedom Hall. Kentucky then eased past the Eagles 71-64 in a second round game and Louisville routed them in the regional consolation game, 83-61. That win allowed the hometown Cardinals to forget for a few moments their 56-55 loss two nights earlier against unbeaten and No. 1 ranked Ohio State, the 1961 tourney runner-up.

Perhaps the win against Morehead also offered some measure of satisfaction for Cardinal fans who were still steaming from Louisville's in-season losses to Eastern Kentucky (80-74 at Richmond on Feb. 8) and Western Kentucky (96-80 in Freedom Hall on March 1).

Murray's OVC résumé for '60-61 shows a 7-5 record that breaks down this way: the Racers lost both of their games against Eastern (75-73 at Murray on Jan. 9 and 110-77 at Richmond on Feb. 11), swept their two games against Middle and East Tennessee and split their two games against Morehead, Western and Tech.

Actually, Murray beat Morehead twice, 85-80 in overtime in Racer Arena on Feb. 3 when Jarrell Graham scored a career high 32 points, and 95-78 on Feb. 4. However, only the first win counted in the conference standings.

In a "must win" game for both teams on Feb. 13, the Eagles beat Murray 91-88 at Morehead, handing the Racers their fourth league loss and for practical purposes eliminating them from OVC title consideration.

The sting of that setback didn't last long as the Racers defeated Western 95-87 on Feb. 18 before an estimated 7,000 spectators in 5,500-seat Racer Arena and then earned a season split with Arkansas State, winning 73-59 at Murray on Feb. 22. Graham (28 points), Gene Herndon (22 points) and Larry Bale (21 points) powered the Racers past Western, which four weeks earlier had beaten Murray 79-77 when Bob Jackson made two free throws on the Toppers' last possession. Herndon's 18 points set the scoring pace against A-State, followed by Graham's 16 and Mike O'Riordan's 15.

Murray's season ended Feb. 25 against Tech with Herndon scoring 29 points in a 92-89 road loss.

Herndon (14.8 ppg) and Bale (12.0 ppg) were the Racers' No. 1 and 3 scorers, but their offensive numbers only partly explain why they earned All-OVC honors. Herndon was a beast on the boards at times, averaging a team-best 14.3 rebounds a game, getting 20 or more on three occasions and grabbing 27 in a 70-59 home win against Stetson, which beat the Racers 80-67 the year before. Effusive praise came Bale's way for his defensive effort against East Tennessee's Chilton, who scored "only" 18 points in Murray's 83-63 road win on Jan. 30. Chilton led the nation in scoring coming into the game and for the season averaged 32.1 points a game, trailing only Frank Burgess (32.4 ppg) of Gonzaga in the national stats.

The NCAA's No. 3 scorer in '60-61 was All-America forward Tom Stith of St. Bonaventure, which embarrassed the Racers in their second game of the season, 92-39 at Buffalo, N.Y. The Bonnies ranked third in the final Associated Press poll, won two games in the NCAA Tournament and ended the season with a 24-4 record.

How good was Memphis, which beat Murray 70-60? Coach Bob Vanatta's Tigers, like St. Bonaventure a NCAA Independent, won 20 of 22 games in the regular season and participated in the National Invitation Tournament, where they were beaten 81-69 by Holy Cross, the tourney's third place finisher.

And what about Mississippi State, which beat the Racers 94-81? Coach Babe McCarthy's Bulldogs won the Southeastern Conference championship, but sat out the NCAA Tournament for the second time in three years because the state legislature banned all Mississippi intercollegiate teams from playing against African-Americans.

1961-62 • 13-12

At first glance, a 13-12 overall record and a fifth-place finish in the OVC (5-7) would seem to be a mediocre season. But given the Racers' inexperience, including the loss of every letterman but one from the previous years' team, there was room for optimism by the end of the year, as well as some highlights to savor. Ron Greene, who averaged 8.8 points per game in 1961-62, shouldered the responsibility of leadership, being the lone letterman to return. But a group of sophomores led by Jim Jennings helped the Racers make respectable showings against high-powered teams like Memphis State and Mississippi State, and even enabled them to upset a strong Eastern Kentucky team in Richmond. Jennings, a 6-6 center from Dayton, Ohio, hit a last second jumper from the top of the key to beat Eastern 82-80 and end the Colonels' home winning streak at 38 games. Jennings led the team with a 20.5 per game scoring average and led the conference with a rebounding average of 17.1 per game. Joining Jennings' class were guards Al Varnas and Scott Schlosser, who would become regular contributors for the remainder of their careers at Murray State.

The Racers won five of their first seven games, all of them at home, all non-conference foes. They beat Mississippi Southern, San Fernando, Arkansas State, Northwestern Louisiana, and Jacksonville, losing to Miami and Mississippi State. There was some consolation in losing at home by only 69-57 to the Bulldogs, who would be ranked as high as fifth in the nation that year. Team captain Greene (who would coach Mississippi State in the 1970s) led the team with 19 points. The Racers traveled south to participate in the Gulf South Classic tournament in Shreveport. They beat Louisiana Tech 69-61, and lost to Centenary 81-69 and to Memphis State 79-67. The bright spot: Jennings scored 79 points in three games and set a Racer record by grabbing 31 rebounds against Louisiana Tech. Not surprisingly, he made the all-tournament team.

After beating Middle Tennessee and losing to Tennessee Tech, the Racers pulled the upset of the season, defeating Eastern Kentucky 82-80 in Richmond. Jennings led the Racers with 25 points. Unable to build on this success, they lost to Western Kentucky, Morehead, and East Tennessee. Greene scored 29 in the loss to the Buccaneers. After beating Regis 71-69, they lost to Memphis State for the second time that year and entered conference play again. Once again, Jennings hit a jump shot in the final seconds, this time to beat Middle Tennessee 69-68 in Murfreesboro. They swept Eastern for the season with a win in Murray 75-66, Jennings leading the way with 21 points. The Racers were victims of high-scoring opponents in their next two losses, first to Morehead 74-66, then to eventual OVC champion Western 96-77 at Bowling Green. Morehead's Granville (Granny) Williams scored 34, while Western's Bobby Rascoe dropped in 38 against the Racers. The Racers traveled to Jonesboro and beat Arkansas State 80-74 on the strength of four Ron Greene free throws in the last 26 seconds. Back in Murray for their final game of the season, the Racers lost in overtime to Tennessee Tech 68-66. Coach Ed Diddle's Western Kentucky Hilltoppers, who went 11-1 in OVC play, defeated Detroit 90-81 in the NCAA Tournament, and then lost to Ohio State in the regional semifinals 93-73.

1962-63 • 13-9

Since he began coaching the Racers in 1958, Cal Luther's teams gradually improved during the 1960s. The 1962-63 season continued that trend, as the Racers' overall record of 13-9 was the best in eight years. Much of the credit for that record goes to Luther, of course, but also to returning players Jim Jennings, Al Varnas and Scott Schlosser, now juniors, as well as newcomers John Namciu and Gene Pendleton. On the negative side, the Racers of 1962-63 did not live up to their pre-season status as the favorites to win the OVC. Part of the reason for their disappointing 6-6 record in the OVC (tied for fourth) was an untimely ankle injury to star center Jim Jennings, which occurred just before the first conference game with Middle Tennessee, keeping him out of action until the Western Kentucky game at Bowling Green, when the Racers were 1-2 in conference play. As he did the previous year as a sophomore, Jennings came through in the clutch in that game, hitting a last second shot to beat the Hilltoppers 73-70.

To start the season, the Racers beat the first four teams they faced, New Mexico A & M (90-55), McKendree College (79-46), and Arkansas State (94-76). Oglethorpe College gave the fast breaking Racers some trouble with their slowdown tactics, but the Racers prevailed 50-45. After losing to Bradley in Peoria 79-78, the Racers polished off their pre-OVC schedule by defeating Emporia State 67-44 and San Francisco College 83-63. Missing the injured Jennings, the Racers began conference play by losing at Middle Tennessee 86-82 and at home to Tennessee Tech 78-67 before beating Eastern Kentucky 89-78 in Murray. Guard Al Varnas had 28 points and 16 rebounds in the win, and sophomore Gene Pendleton added 19 points. Next came the last-second win over the Hilltoppers, marking Jennings' return to the lineup, then losses at East Tennessee 72-70 and to Morehead 90-73 at home. Jennings had 22 points and 24 rebounds as the Racers avenged their earlier loss to East Tennessee by beating the Buccaneers 79-58 in Murray. Varnas had 20 points in the win. The Racers hosted Memphis State and almost pulled off an upset, losing 60-58 on a last-second shot by Hunter

Beckman. Arkansas State beat the Racers in Jonesborough 75-62, avenging the early season blowout in Murray. As if fired up by the embarrassing loss, the Racers crushed Middle Tennessee 109-73 in Murray. Jennings had 28 points and 24 rebounds, while Varnas had 15, Namciu and Schlosser 13 each and reserve Butch Hill 12, typifying the balanced offensive attack the Racers had all season. Murray State got its fourth victory in a row over Eastern Kentucky with a 91-88 win at Richmond. Traveling down to Morehead, the Racers weren't as fortunate, losing 90-86 to the Golden Eagles. Beating Western 87-74 in front of a near-capacity crowd at Racer Arena gave Murray State a sweep of the Hilltoppers that year. Western's Bobby Jackson was ejected from the game for slugging Jennings, but the punch seemed to have little effect on the Racer center as he scored 19 points and pulled down 17 rebounds. Varnas and John Namciu had 21 points apiece. The Racers beat Tennessee-Chattanooga in Murray 79-60, using reserve players extensively. They lost the last game of the season 84-61 to Tennessee Tech in Cookeville. This was a must-win for Tech as they ended up in a tie with Morehead for the OVC crown, each team with identical 8-4 conference records. Tennessee Tech won the playoff game and went to the NCAA tournament, losing big to Loyola of Chicago in the first round.

1963-64 • 16-9

- *OVC Regular Season Champion*
- *OVC Tournament Champion*

The 1963-64 season was a breakthrough year for many reasons. Most importantly, Stewart Johnson, who had played on the freshman team the year before, became the first African-American to play varsity basketball at Murray State, as well as the first black college player in the OVC and one of the first in the southeast. The efforts of Coach Luther and the administration deserve much credit for integrating the basketball team and setting an early example for other programs in the South. In addition, Johnson's courage in pioneering such social progress stands out as one of the highlights of this season. There were other accomplishments as well: OVC Coach of the Year for Luther and Player of the Year for senior Jim Jennings. The Racers won the OVC for the first time in 13 years and advanced to the NCAA Tournament. Johnson and Jennings made the All-OVC team. The Racers recorded their fifth win in a row against arch-rival Western Kentucky. Murray State Hall of Famer Bennie Purcell, a star on the 1951 OVC championship team (the last time the Racers won the conference) came on board as an assistant coach.

The Racers began the season with comfortable wins over McKendree College (83-68) and Oglethorpe (83-57). Known for their fast-break offense, the Racers also showcased a stingy defense, leading Oglethorpe by a score of 32-6 at one point. Jim Jennings' 28 points wasn't enough against Bradley, and the Racers lost 85-78 to a Braves team that was ranked in the top-10 in the nation at the beginning of the year. The Racers followed up the loss with three high-scoring lopsided wins in a row against non-conference foes Arkansas State (93-63), Tennessee-Chattanooga (109-88), and Central Missouri (111-60). The non-conference schedule got tougher after that, and the Racers dropped three in a row. First, they lost at home 79-74 to a West Texas team that outrebounded them. They lost 86-71 at Dayton and to Loyola of the South in New Orleans 105-88.

OVC conference play and a return to Racer Arena may have helped Murray get the hot hand against Middle Tennessee, shooting 53 percent in a 98-68 win. Jennings had 19, Gene Pendleton 17. Jennings' 31 points wasn't enough to overcome Tennessee Tech, who beat the Racers 70-67 in Cookeville. Going for their fifth victory in a row over Eastern Kentucky, the Racers went into a stall with a two-point lead late in the game but lost 67-63. Returning to Murray, the Racers beat Western Kentucky 86-77 and then lost at home to East Tennessee 62-61 in double overtime. Comfortable wins over Austin Peay in Clarksville (98-82) and against Morehead in Murray (102-89) kept MSU in the race. Like the previous year, the Racers lost to Arkansas State in Jonesborough after beating them in Murray earlier in the season. This time the Red Wolves defeated the Racers 85-74. Murray bounced back from this loss. After beating Middle Tennessee 86-79 and sweeping Eastern Kentucky with a 93-87 victory, the Racers took over first place in the OVC. Al Varnas hit a free throw with 11 seconds left and the Racers completed a sweep of the Austin Peay Governors with a 69-68 victory in Murray. In beating Western Kentucky for the fifth straight time, the Racers' Scott Schlosser held Hilltopper star Darel Carrier to just one field goal, and Murray State won 85-77. Then the Racers beat East Tennessee (96-76) and returned home to clinch the OVC title with an 88-82 win over Tennessee Tech. Gene Pendleton had 36 points as the Racers closed out the regular season with a road win over Morehead 89-84. In the NCAA Tournament, Murray, a 30-point underdog, jumped to a 13-point lead against defending national champion Loyola of Chicago, but then missed 10 shots in a row and eventually lost 101-91. Although the Racers scored more points than Ramblers in field goals, they scored 12 less points from the free throw line, making the difference in the game. Jennings led the team with 24, while Varnas had 21, Johnson 18 and Pendleton 15.

1964-65 • 19-7

Though they didn't make the NCAA Tournament as they did the previous year, the Racers continued to improve as a program with the best overall record since 1943. Their 19-7 record unfortunately included five OVC losses, good for a third place finish in the conference. Other highlights included an OVC Christmas Tournament win and a victory over powerhouse Texas Western in the Sun Devil Classic tournament in Tempe, Arizona. Stu Johnson and John Namciu were named All-OVC, each of them averaging 20 points per game for the season, Johnson with 367 rebounds. Johnson's average of 14.1 rebounds per game was second in the conference. Though not named All-OVC, sophomore Herb McPherson averaged 18.6 points per game. Not much was expected of a team that lost three key players to graduation: Jim Jennings, Al Varnas and defensive standout Scott Schlosser. But they started strong and overachieved with a 12-0 home record, despite having their troubles on the road.

The Racers opened the season defeating Arkansas State 73-71. On the road against Canisius, they came from ten points down to defeat the Golden Griffins 92-81. They lost to Bradley in Peoria 76-74 and then came home to beat Oglethorpe (74-66) and New Mexico State (72-69). Then they traveled to Tempe for the Sun Devil Classic where they beat Don Haskin's Texas Western team in the first round 65-58. The following year, this same team would win the NCAA Championship with a defeat of #1 ranked Kentucky. Though the Racers lost in the championship game 107-96 to Arizona State, Stu Johnson was named tournament MVP. The Racers swept through the OVC Christmas Tournament in Louisville by beating pre-season OVC favorite Morehead 89-82, Tennessee Tech 79-75, and Western Kentucky 77-68. In the first official conference game of the season, Western got a rematch in Bowling Green and prevailed in overtime 71-70. The Racers dropped two more conference games, both on the road, to East Tennessee 69-68 and to Tennessee Tech 93-91. Then they went on a six-game winning streak against Eastern Kentucky (86-84), Austin Peay (97-75), Centenary (93-76), Middle Tennessee (90-76), Tennessee Tech (92-79) and East Tennessee (85-71). When they went on the road and lost to Eastern Kentucky and Morehead, they were officially out of contention for the OVC title. But that didn't stop them from winning their last five games. They beat Austin Peay 96-89 in Clarksville and won the last four in Racer Arena against Loyola of New Orleans (83-73), Middle Tennessee on Herb McPherson's last second jump shot (91-89), NIT-bound Western Kentucky (103-91), and Morehead (84-75).

John Namciu ended his career at Murray State with 1,003 points making him a member of the elite 1,000 point club.

1965-66 • 13-12

Though the 1965-66 team was somewhat inexperienced, it finished third in the OVC and marked the beginning of exciting college careers for explosive guard Don Duncan and dominating center Dick Cunningham. Two notable highlights in an otherwise average year, record-wise, were Herb McPherson's record breaking 44-point game against Middle Tennessee, and a defeat of Austin Peay, in which the Racers hit 24 of 24 free throws, an OVC record. Knowing what we know now about Cunningham's future at Murray State, as well as McPherson's, it seems odd that a team with such rebounding strength (Cunningham and Johnson) and scoring punch would end up with a mediocre overall record of 14-12. But Cunningham was as yet unproven, and Johnson, who had been brilliant his sophomore and junior years, had an off year, hitting only 36 percent from the field and averaging 13.8 points per game. McPherson averaged 21.2 points per game and was the lone Racer picked to the All-OVC team. Transfer Don Duncan, who fearlessly drove to the basket, created and made what seemed impossible shots, was the surprise of the season, the second leading scorer on the team with a 15.7 points per game average. Another newcomer, Milt Pitts, rounded out the balanced scoring attack with 13.8 per game. It was in rebounding that the Racers excelled, led by big men Cunningham and Johnson. The Racers outrebounded their opponents 1308 to 1132. Cunningham, who averaged 11.2 points per game, led the team with 390 rebounds (15.8 per game), and Johnson had 270.

The Racers began their season by beating up on non-conference foes Parsons College (101-88) and Hardin-Simmons (92-18). Canisius avenged last year's loss to the Racers with an 87-81 victory at Buffalo, and the Racers came back home, only to be upset by Abilene Christian 82-78. They rebounded with lopsided wins against San Fernando State (110-79) and East Carolina (104-84). The Racers then traveled to Peoria to play Bradley, a team they had lost to for three years in a row. Make it four: Bradley won 78-64. At the OVC Tournament in Louisville, the Racers beat Middle Tennessee 86-65 and then lost to Eastern Kentucky 79-73 in the second round. Murray started out its OVC schedule by beating Middle Tennessee again, this time in Murfreesboro 89-73. After building a 21-point lead against East Tennessee, the Racers lost 74-72 at home, a devastating loss. But they bounced back on the road to defeat Morehead 86-79 and Eastern Kentucky 79-78 to avenge the earlier loss to the Colonels. In a break from conference play, the Racers defeated the Mexican Olympic team 83-58, but lost to Arkansas State 63-61 in Jonesboro. Showing their resilience once again, the Racers went down to Clarksville and beat Austin Peay 108-77, hitting the record-setting 24 of 24 free throws. Don Duncan scored 30 points. Western Kentucky came into Racer Arena and took a 41-point lead before the Racers made it respectable with a 101-84 loss. This was a Western team that went 14-0 in the OVC and advanced one round in the NCAA Tournament. After losing to Western, Murray traveled to Dayton and lost 99-86. Returning to Murray against Middle Tennessee, Herb McPherson got the hot hand and scored 44 points in a 107-81 game. Coach Luther took him out of the game with five minutes left when he had 37, and assistant coach Purcell, who held the Racer scoring record with 41, asked Luther to put McPherson back in so he could break the record. He was 17 of 26 from the field and hit 10 of his 11 free throws. Murray lost to Tennessee Tech (83-76) and East Tennessee (104-94) on the road, and returned to Murray to beat Eastern Kentucky 100-91. After losing at home to Morehead 83-94, the Racers gave the Western Kentucky Hilltoppers a good game but lost 71-59. They ended the year with a win over Austin Peay (80-73), which put them into a tie for third place in the OVC.

While Johnson had a bit of an off year, his accomplishments as a basketball player at Murray State were historic. In addition to breaking the color barrier with class and dignity, Johnson scored 1275 career points, putting him 23rd on the all-time list. His is ranked fourth in career rebounding. He went on to star for many years in the American Basketball Association, breaking a single-game scoring record with 62 points.

1966-67 • 14-9

Though Stu Johnson and Milt Pitts would not return for this season, the Racers were loaded with talent and experience. Long-range sharpshooter Herb McPherson was back for his senior year, as were starters Don Duncan and Dick Cunningham. Talented newcomers included Bill Chumbler, a transfer from Mississippi State who attended Lowes High School in nearby Graves County, and 6-4 forward Rick Haverstock.

Cunningham led the nation in rebounding, and McPherson, who averaged 21.8 points per game, was tenth in the nation in free throw percentage. The team's 89.1 per game scoring average made it the highest powered offense in Racer history. This team also set the Racer record for rebounding average per game: 53.9.

In spite of all these superlatives, the Racers finished 14-9 overall and 8-6 in the OVC, good enough for second place. Part of the reason the Racers didn't do better was a formidable non-conference schedule and an unusually strong OVC, dominated by Western Kentucky.

Some brilliant spots in a solid season: Murray dealt mighty Western its only OVC loss in the final game of the season, and Cunningham and McPherson made All-OVC. Western only lost two games all year and was ranked as high as third in the nation.

The Racers set a single-game scoring record in a 121-65 win over Georgia Southern to start the season.

McPherson led the team with 30 points. In Buffalo, Canisius' Andy Anderson scored 41 as his team defeated Murray 78-69. Back in Racer Arena, Murray beat Southwestern at Memphis 99-60, with McPherson scoring 20 points, Cunningham 15. McPherson had 25 and Bill Chumbler 18 in a 101-85 loss to Bradley in Peoria.

At home, the Racers won three non-conference games in a row, downing Louisiana College 105-83, Oglethorpe 90-75 and Emporia State 99-91. After being down by 17 points, the Racers came back but lost to Western 94-83 in the first round of the OVC Christmas Tournament. The Racers came home and beat up on MacMurray 100-79, and Dick Cunningham set a school record for rebounds with 36, breaking Jim Jennings' record of 31.

Conference play began with a 105-93 loss at Morehead. Don Duncan led the Racers with 30 points, and McPherson had 28. Murray beat Eastern Kentucky 86-76 behind a balanced scoring attack: Chumbler 20, Haverstock 17, Cunningham 18, Duncan 13 and McPherson 14. Cunningham's 20 rebounds helped Murray get past Tennessee Tech 72-70, but East Tennessee came to Murray and beat the Racers 86-79.

After blowing a 27-point lead in the second half, the Racers prevailed over Middle Tennessee in overtime 96-93. Chumbler had 30 in the road win. Two OVC wins in a row against Austin Peay (92-91) and Middle Tennessee (91-75) put the Racers at 5-2 in the conference, still in the race.

Austin Peay beat the Racers 117-94 in Clarksville by shooting 56 percent from the field. In Bowling Green, Clem Haskins' 33 points led Western over Murray in overtime 88-79. A reserve on Eastern Kentucky's team hit a free throw with no time remaining, giving the Colonels a 71-70 win over Murray in Racer Arena.

Dick Cunningham had 25 points and 31 rebounds, the best game of his career to that point, as Murray avenged an earlier loss to Morehead with a 99-89 win. McPherson had 26 points. In Johnson City, McPherson's 21 and Chumbler's 19 led the Racers to a double overtime win over East Tennessee 88-86.

A 89-86 loss to Tennessee Tech in Cookeville set the stage for the final game of the season against the Hilltoppers in Murray. In front of a crowd of 7,500, the Racers handed Western their second loss of the season and their first conference defeat 75-69. In his last game as a Racer, McPherson led the team with 24 points, and Cunningham pulled down 23 rebounds and scored 14. Don Duncan, in his final act as a Racer, also scored 14. Western, who played without an

1966-67. Front row: Head Coach Cal Luther, Billy Chumbler, Tom Moran, Ron Romani, Keith Lambert, Don Duncan, Assistant Coach Bennie Purcell. Second row: Manager Ronnie Dickerson, Rick Haverstock, Gary Quint, Gary Wilson, Rick Miller, Herb McPherson, unknown manager. Back row: Manager Walter Moore, Craig Roeder, Dick Cunningham, Jim Stocks.

injured Clem Haskins in the loss to Murray, would go on to lose to Dayton in overtime in the first round of the NCAA Tournament.

1967-68 • 16-8

• OVC Regular Season Co-Champion

Starters Dick Cunningham and Bill Chumbler returned to lead the Racers to a record of 16-8 and a first place tie for the OVC crown. Eventual MSU hall of famer Claude Virden joined the Racers as a sophomore after a year at Paducah Junior College and led the team in scoring with a 17.9 average. He would make an immediate impact and help begin a run of winning basketball that took the program to a new level. Guard Don Funneman would earn a starting position, contributing his hustling and intense defense to the Racers. Chumbler and Cunningham would average 15.5 points per game, and Cunningham continued his dominance of the boards, pulling down 479 for the year. This season, however, was the year of a near-miss, like a shot rimming out of the basket.

To open the season, the Racers traveled to Nashville for the OVC Holiday Tournament. They beat Austin Peay 77-68 and Western 83-75 before losing in the finals to Tennessee Tech 67-60. They beat Louisiana College and Howard Payne at home before traveling to Buffalo for always-tough Canisius. The Racers lost 71-68, and came close in Peoria after that, losing to the Bradley Braves 83-78. Chumbler had 20.

Next came a string of six straight wins, first over non-conference foes Culver Stockton (98-74) and Butler (in Indianapolis, 86-74), and then over Middle Tennessee (77-74), Morehead (83-67) and Eastern Kentucky (71-67). To make it six, the Racers traveled to Cookeville and beat Tennessee Tech 92-91. Riding that streak, the Racers cruised into Johnson City to face East Tennessee and star Harley "Skeeter" Swift, who would win OVC Player of the Year in 1968. The Bucaneers beat Murray in this, their first clash of the year, by a score of 91-82. Murray then beat Austin Peay 91-82 in Clarksville, and then Middle Tennessee 91-72 in Murfreesboro.

They beat Austin Peay for the third time that year, this time in Racer Arena by a score of 85-70. After losing at Western 79-78, the Racers traveled to Richmond and defeated Eastern Kentucky 68-66. They lost to Morehead 101-80 and returned home for another showdown with East Tennessee. The Racers won this one 105-72, in front of an overflow crowd of 7,000 at Racer Arena. Virden had 22, Chumbler 19, and Tom Moran 18. The Racers used a pressing defense led by Don Funneman, who had to leave the game after a hard intentional foul. Little did the Racers know that they were not finished facing the Bucs.

The Racers beat Tennessee Tech in Murray 81-67, Virden leading the way with 23, Cunningham had 18, and Chumbler 15. This win would set up what could have clinched the OVC in a showdown with Western in Murray. But the Racers lost 86-83, forcing them into a tie with East Tennessee for the OVC title. This was the final home game for Dick Cunningham and Billy Chumbler, who scored 21 points each. Virden led the scoring with 22. In the playoff game at neutral Richmond to decide who would get the NCAA bid, the Racers lost to East Tennessee 79-75. The Bucs went on to upset second-ranked Florida State 79-69 in the NCAA Tournament before losing in the next round to Ohio State.

Dick Cunningham ended his career at Murray State and went on to a successful NBA career, including a championship with the Milwaukee Bucks. He holds the OVC record for career rebounding at 18.2 per game, as well as the OVC record for rebounding average in a single season (21.8 in 1967 when he led the nation in rebounding). He is 19th on the MSU scoring list with 981 points. The Racers would also miss the competitive spirit and the long-range shooting of Bill Chumbler, who would graduate and go on to a highly successful career as a high school coach.

1968-69 • 22-6

• OVC Regular Season Co-Champion

In many ways the 1968-69 season was the culmination of the recruiting, mentoring and strategy of coaches Luther, Purcell, and Alexander in the 1960s. The Racers, picked to finish sixth in the OVC, won the title in a playoff with Morehead, Luther was named coach of the year, Claude Virden OVC Player of the Year. The overall record of 22-6 was the best in 26 years.

They were undefeated at home, 15-0, and 11-3 in the OVC. Virden and transfer Hector Blondet were

After tying Morehead for the 1969 Ohio Valley Converence Championship, the Racers beat the Eagles 94-76 in a playoff game at Bowling Green to determine the league's representative to the NCAA Tournament (upper left). However, they lost 82-62 to Marquette in the first round of the NCAA at Carbondale, Ill. (next three pictures).

All-OVC. Aside from Blondet, newcomers Jimmy Young, Ron Johnson, and Frank Streety cracked the starting lineup and made major contributions. Young averaged 11.2 points per game, Johnson 10.5, and Streety 6.6.

The Racers beat some teams they hadn't beaten in a while, in particular Canisius and Bradley. They did something they failed to do the year before: win a playoff game for the OVC title. This time they did it in convincing fashion, downing Morehead 94-76 in Bowling Green.

The Racers won their first six games over Texas-Arlington (91-83), Trinity (89-76), San Fernando State (96-67), Carson-Newman (76-61) and Bradley (66-63), all at home, and then traveled to Buffalo to beat Canisius 76-67.

Playing the University of Kansas for the first time, the Racers lost 72-59 in Lawrence. Before beginning OVC play, they beat Georgia Southern and Abilene Christian before losing to Hardin-Simmons in Abilene. Their first conference game did not bode well for the Racers, as they lost on the road 111-78 to Morehead. Little did they know, at this point, that they would have two more meetings with the Eagles.

1969 NCAA Tournament Murray-Marquette game.

Murray followed up that loss with a streak of seven wins in a row, two against non-conference foes Pan-American and Louisiana College and the rest against OVC rivals Eastern Kentucky, Tennessee Tech, East Tennessee, Middle Tennessee and Austin Peay. Western Kentucky put a stop to the winning streak with an 84-82 win in Bowling Green. The Racers won five more conference games in a row, including 91-89 home win over Morehead, before losing to East Tennessee 87-81 in Johnson City.

That made the next game against Western a must-win to stay in the conference race. The Racers delivered with an 89-79 win in Murray. They won the playoff against Morehead and advanced to post-season play for the first time since 1964. Unfortunately they would be playing without captain Don Funneman, who dislocated his shoulder against Morehead. In the NCAA Tournament, the Racers lost 82-62 to a Marquette team that went on to beat Kentucky in the next round. Virden scored 17, Blondet 15 in the loss. Murray would return all five starters the following year, losing seniors Jim Stocks and Ron Romani.

JIM JENNINGS

by Sid Easley

Seldom, if ever, has the Ohio Valley Conference sported a Player of The Year who was offered a recording contract with Universal Records in Nashville during his playing days. It happened to Jim Jennings, a 6 ft., 7 in. record setting left handed center, who played at Murray State for three seasons from 1961 through 1964.

"Jerry Crutchfield, a graduate of Murray, was in the recording business in Nashville and invited me down to try out after seeing me perform with a band on campus. We played for fraternity and sorority parties, and several events in the area," recalled Jennings. "I sang and played several instruments including the guitar and keyboard. We were from a musical family, and I made a career of music playing at major resorts, night clubs, and hotels, mostly in Florida, for almost 40 years.

"In fact they offered me a recording contract in Nashville, but in those days you had to do your own advertising so they told me I would have to quit Murray State and go on the road to sell my records.

"I wasn't going to do that," said Jennings. "I loved college life and I loved Murray – still do," he said. "Murray was just a very special place and everyone there treated me like a king. Dr. Woods, the president, was a good friend. I loved Coach Luther, Rex Alexander, Bennie Purcell, Professor Jim Frank, and so many more.

"I was All-City First Team in Dayton, and had several college offers, including Stanford. But Louisville dazzled me by inviting me to the 1960 NCAA Final Four in Freedom Hall. They even gave me a Les Paul Guitar. I signed with them, and led their freshman team in scoring and rebounding.

"But I was unhappy in Louisville. It was a commuter school, and lacked the campus life I had expected of a college. The dorms at Murray, the Hut, and the caring atmosphere of students, faculty, and townspeople made my time at Murray unforgettable.

"Coach Hickman accused Murray of recruiting me. That wasn't true. One night in my freshman season at Louisville I had a great night and scored 33 points. I walked off the floor and there stood Lubie Veal, a staunch Murray fan. He said, 'We thought we were going to be able to recruit you out of high school to play at Murray State.' I said, 'Tell Coach Luther I'm transferring out of Louisville, and I'll play basketball at Murray State if they'll give me a scholarship.' My high school coach had been good friends with Luther.

"Before long I was driving to Murray to go to school.

"I have never been sorry. We had some wonderful players, and some great teams – especially my senior year," recalled Jennings.

"Luther installed a 3 out and 2 under offense that enabled us to have 3 or more options every time we got the ball. My senior year we averaged 85 points a game, were OVC

Jim Jennings

Champions, and went to the NCAA tournament in Evanston, Illinois. Loyola of Chicago had some outstanding teams in those years and they were our first round opponent.

"We played a great game against Loyola, and had a good chance to beat them. At one time early in the game we led them 24-8," he recalled. "Michigan was ranked #1 that year, and had Cazzie Russell. Had we beaten Loyola we would have played Michigan, and as I recall they only beat Loyola by four in the next game. We got better as the season progressed. Stu Johnson and I played inside, and John Namciu, Gene Pendleton, Al Varnas and Scott Schlosser were outside. Namciu had played in Canton, Ohio, and we discovered after I got to Murray that we had played against each other in high school. He was a great player and was injured late in the year, and that hurt us in the tournament.

"The Western games were always so very competitive. I recall playing in the Red Barn my junior year, in the last game played in that place. Boy, it was tough to win there. We were tied with a very short time left in the game.

"A Western player was headed to their goal wide open and it looked like there was no stopping him. John Namciu was trailing the guy, and fearlessly dived head first and slapped the ball forward right into the hands of one of our players. We broke back down the floor and the ball came to me. I leaned in and then back, and made a fall away jumper. I was fouled, and I can still see those Western players with their seats right beneath our basket yelling and waiving their towels trying to distract me from hitting that free throw. But I hit it, and we won the last game ever played in Western's house.

"But basketball is a team game. I got the glory by making the basket and the free throw, but Namicu won the game by giving up his body and making that headlong dive for the ball."

Jennings choked up as he described a memorable event in his playing days, "My mother was my greatest fan. Whenever she could get our games on the radio she was listening and praying. One night we played Eastern and I hit the winning shot. Mother was listening on the radio and I told Coach Luther that Mother was praying for us tonight.

"The year we won the conference championship my mother and stepfather drove the 400 miles from Dayton to Murray to see me play. Sadly, Mother was terminally ill with cancer, but she was determined to come see me play for the championship.

"To win the championship we had to beat Tennessee Tech. Mother was in the stands, and I had an incredible game. The fans swarmed onto the floor after the win, and in celebration put me on their shoulders. I looked up in the stands, and saw my mother crying. I ran up in the stands where mother was standing and put my arms around her. She looked up at me and said, 'Jimmy this is the happiest day of my life.' She died later that year at the young age of 45."

She was right to be proud of him. He led the team both in scoring and rebounding all three of his years at Murray State. He was a three-time all OVC First Team pick and was named Conference Player of the Year in 1964. Bradley University, who had top ten teams in those years, named him to the first five of their all-opponent team. He averaged 19.3 points a game for

his three-year career finishing at 18th on the all-time scoring list with 1,370 points. He would move up on the list to 8th if you excluded the "three point shot players," and like all of them he said wistfully, "sure wish we had the three point shot in those days."

At Murray the 6-7 lefty pulled down 1,147 rebounds – an average of 16.2 rebounds a game, tying him for third place in MSU history. "I seemed to have an innate sense of where the ball would come down on a rebound, and made a lot of points on offensive put backs," he remembered. He recalled the memorable voice of the Racers, Chuck Shuffett saying to him as he concluded his career at Murray, "Jim, you were a great scorer while you were here, but I believe you will be remembered most for your rebounding."

Jennings fondly recalled the coaching he received at Murray. His free throw percentage increased each year – from 59% to 61% and finally to 76% his senior year. When asked how he improved so much his senior year, he gave all the credit to Coach Luther. "I was shooting the ball with one hand which was a fad in those days. Luther suggested that I might improve if I would guide the ball with the other hand. I practiced that all summer. It paid off my senior year."

Jennings remembered Cal Luther as an exceptional coach. "I played at Louisville under good coaches, so I had a comparison.

"Coach Luther prepared us so very well for a game. He was smart, and he was thorough. He gave us confidence. The one thing I remember about Cal was his ability to alter his strategy during a game. We always had a thorough game plan, but Cal had this amazing ability to adjust to whatever the other team threw at you."

Like all great Murray players, Jennings agreed that there was no substitute for hours, days, and years of practice. "I loved the game, and I never tired of playing. I remember in my junior high years playing basketball in a local gym in Dayton from 8 in the morning until 8 or 9 every night."

STEWART JOHNSON

by Kim Trevathan

Athletes demonstrate courage in different ways: playing with an injury, taking the shot when the game is on the line, subduing inner demons to make crucial free throws in front of a hostile crowd. Stewart Johnson was a masterful basketball player whose courage transcended these on-court situations. As the first African-American varsity player at Murray State (1963-66) and practically in the entire southeastern United States, Johnson demonstrated nerve, talent, dignity, and forbearance in a tumultuous time that tested the fortitude of the best people and brought out the worst among those who were ignorant and fearful of change.

A 6-8 forward from Clairton, Pa., Johnson was the best shooting big man ever to play at Murray State, according to Bennie Purcell, who noted that many of Johnson's shots came from the 25-30 foot range. Playing in the era before the three-pointer, Johnson ranks 22nd on the all-time MSU scoring list, and fourth in career rebounding. He played for the duration of the American Basketball Association's existence – nine years – and broke an ABA record by scoring 62 points in a game against the Miami Floridians.

Though Johnson made history when he came to Murray State as a freshman in the fall of 1962, it was Coach Cal Luther who prepared the way for that breakthrough. In the spring of 1960, after his second season with the Racers, Luther met with Athletic Director Roy Stewart to discuss the possibility of recruiting African-American players. At that time there were no black basketball scholarship players at any of the Ohio Valley Conference schools and none in the Southeastern Conference or the Atlantic Coast Conference.

Stewart, President Ralph Woods, and Dean Marvin Wrather met several times to discuss Luther's proposal and agreed that, in Luther's words, "despite the current racial problems in the South this was a positive action whose time was overdue in the Ohio Valley Conference and other conferences in the area." With the Board of Regents' approval, Luther was given the green light, this in a year when four black students at North Carolina Agricultural and Technical College staged a sit-in at a segregated Woolworth's and triggered nonviolent protests against segregation across the South.

As Luther phrased it, the leaders of Murray State "demonstrated great foresight, courage, and understanding in reaching their decision."

Stewart Johnson

Johnson was not, in actuality, the first black basketball player at Murray State. A year before he arrived, Tom Officer, from Washington, Mo., played on the Racers' freshman team. Although Officer "toughed out" his freshman year, according to Luther, and excelled both on the court and academically, the on-campus racial tension and the harassment he faced took a toll on him. In the fall of 1962, after Johnson had arrived and befriended Officer, racial tension on campus and nationwide escalated as James Meredith became the first black student to enroll at the University of Mississippi, and President John F. Kennedy had to send 5,000 federal troops to quell the riots that ensued. An ugly incident occurred at Murray State that showed the negative forces that Luther and his players were up against. From a high-rise dorm room window, hung an effigy of Tom Officer, his name clearly printed on the black jersey, for all the students to see on their way to class.

Officer's parents, learning of the incident, came to Murray State that very day, packed his belongings, and took him back to Missouri. Johnson, understandably, was seriously considering an exit himself. Luther acted quickly. He called Johnson's father, a police officer who, as Luther put it, was "a very intelligent, strong individual who had dealt with racial discrimination personally and professionally all his life." Luther had previously talked at length with Johnson's father about the challenges his son would face in the South as a pioneer of racial equality and anti-discrimination.

After the effigy incident, Johnson's parents visited Murray State, met with President Woods and Athletic Director Stewart, as well as some of their son's professors. Luther assured Johnson's parents, once again, that he would do everything in his power to make their son's experience at MSU a positive one. With his parents' support, Johnson decided to stay. Luther remembers what Johnson's father said that day: "I know that you and the college officials are sincere in your interest in keeping Stewart safe here and helping him get a good education. My son is no quitter; he was raised different than that. His mother and I know it's not going to be easy, but it's something that has to be done and we'll all benefit from it. I'm leaving him in your hands."

Luther said that the elder Johnson emphasized to his son that what he was doing was good for the community, good for basketball, and good for humanity.

It wasn't all easy from there, but at least Johnson had resolved to stick it out, and Luther was ready to help him in any way he could, in spite of being harassed himself and having to change his phone number. Murray, Luther noted, was segregated at the time. Blacks and whites did not dine out together; if you were black, you sat in the balcony at the theater. The freshman game at Tennessee Tech had to be canceled because there was no place that the team could stay, with Johnson along.

Luther said people would routinely shout insults at Johnson from the stands during games. The young player, who married during his time at Murray State, would come back from away games to see racial slurs and threats on his apartment in married student housing. Luther said Johnson "demonstrated courage on a daily basis," learning how to shut out the abuse and not even acknowledge its existence.

As a freshman, he averaged 22.8 points per game on a team that went 8-5.

The 1963-64 Racer Program, published at the beginning of the season, was clairvoyant in its prediction about Johnson's role on the team: "Thoroughbred fans are counting on this sophomore giant [Johnson] to give this year's Varsity squad the added height and scoring punch they will need to be a conference contender."

Not only were they a contender, they won the conference with an 11-3 record, and for the first time in Racer history advanced to the NCAA Tournament, where they lost a hard-fought contest, 101-91, to defending champion Loyola of Chicago. Johnson was second in scoring on that team, with at 16.4 points per game.

Jim Jennings, the team's leading scorer that year, said he "thought the world of Stew Johnson." Jennings remembers him as an unselfish player who "moved well for a big guy and had a great touch on his jump shot." He said that Johnson did a remarkable job contributing the way he did as a sophomore, having to learn a new offense and adjust to stiffer competition.

Jennings remembers an incident which demonstrated Johnson's ability to use humor during times of crisis. Flying on a small Beechcraft from a game in New Orleans, the team had a scare when one of the plane's engines began emitting smoke and eventually stopped functioning. The pilot informed Coach Luther and the team that they would have to make an emergency landing in Greenwood, Miss.

"Greenwood, Mississippi?" said Johnson, incredulous. "Just leave me up here."

Jennings said they all got a big laugh from that comment.

Johnson showed up to play his junior year 20 pounds heavier, and the program that year notes that he would be the lone "big man" on the 1964-65 squad, after the graduation of Jennings.

That year he increased his scoring to 20 points per game (tied with John Namciu for the team lead) and also led the team in rebounds with 367. He was selected all-OVC, as he was for his sophomore year.

Early that year, the Racers beat Texas Western in the Sun Devil Classic at Arizona State. The following year, with virtually the same team, Texas Western would beat the University of Kentucky for the national championship, a historic win because the Miners were the first team with an all-black starting lineup to play in the NCAA Tournament.

"Without question he was one of the best long range shooters to play in the ABA."
– Gene Rhodes, former Kentucky Colonels Coach

"I had 16 assists one night, they were all to Stew. He scored 62 points against the Floridians. He could really shoot it from anywhere."
– Skeeter Swift, former All OVC player at ETSU and teammate of Stew's on Pittsburgh Condor ABA Team.

In the Sun Devil Classic, Johnson scored 34 in the loss to Arizona State in the finals and won the Most Valuable Player award in the tournament. The team flew to Louisville directly after that and won the OVC Holiday Tournament, beating Western Kentucky in the final 77-68. The Racers finished 19-7, third in the OVC with a 9-5 record.

Johnson tailed off a bit his senior year, but averaged a respectable 13.8 points per game, as well as pulling down 270 rebounds on a team that tied for third place in the OVC.

Although he was drafted in the third round by the New York Knicks, Johnson opted to sign with the Kentucky Colonels of the American Basketball Association. This was the league with the red, white, and blue basketball, the wide-open offenses, and the three-point shot, which the NBA did not adopt until 1979. It was a league well-suited to Johnson's talent as a long-range shooting big man.

Johnson played nine seasons in the ABA, averaging 16.3 points per game, an all-star in 1973, 1974, and 1975. He used his long-range shooting talents to their best advantage in what was then known as the outlaw league, even though it featured some of the game's best players in Julius Erving, Rick Barry, Connie Hawkins, and George Gervin.

Gene Rhodes, former coach of the Kentucky Colonels said of Johnson, "Without question he was one of the best long-range shooters to play in the ABA."

Johnson didn't remain with the Colonels for long. He was traded to the New Jersey Americans after that first year, and ended up playing for 12 different teams (seven franchises) during his ABA career: Kentucky, the New Jersey Nets, the Houston Mavericks, the Pittsburgh Pipers, the Pittsburgh Condors, the Carolina Cougars, the San Diego Conquistadors, the Memphis Sounds, the Baltimore Claws, the San Diego Sails, and the San Antonio Spurs.

He had his best years with San Diego, averaging 22.1 points per game in 1972-73 and 20.1 the next season. When he scored 62 points against the Floridians, he beat Denver Rocket Spencer Haywood's record of 59. In that game, Johnson hit 25 of 44 from the field, but only hit one three-pointer. He hit 11 straight free throws at one point. "We tried four or five guys on him," said Coach Bob Bass of the Floridians. "He just couldn't be stopped." Bass's words take on some irony, considering that the night before, against the Virginia Squires, Johnson's scoring total was a mere three points.

Johnson's one-game scoring record was short-lived, as Zelmo Beaty scored 63 in a game that same season. Johnson ranks ninth on the all-time ABA scoring list with 10,538 points.

After the ABA folded in 1976, Johnson took his talents to Europe, where he played for teams in France and Iceland. He was a player-coach for an Icelandic team.

Known as "Big Stew" to his teammates, Johnson left a legacy of class, dignity and courage, an example of leadership that went far beyond his stature. Jim Jennings remembers a team portrait in which the big men, including him, Johnson, and Stan Walker, sat in the front row. Johnson, a bit taller than Jennings and Walker, sat between them, and Jennings said he looked over at Walker, whose face was completely visible above Johnson's head. "He was all legs," said Jennings.

Jennings noted that at times, Johnson had his doubts about staying at Murray State because he was one of the few blacks enrolled at the college. Shooting around in the gym, Jennings, a senior, had a "heart to heart talk" with the sophomore. "I told him we all loved him and that we had a great team," said Jennings. Transferring to another school, he told Johnson, there would be no guarantees.

"None of us would really know what it was like to be a black person in that environment," said Luther. "I admired his mental strength and the way he handled situations."

Luther also emphasized the strength of Johnson's family. "He was brought up to do things right," Luther said. "He had a great set of parents, with a good solid Christian background."

Johnson was inducted into the Murray State Athletics Hall of Fame in 1979.

HERB McPHERSON

by Kim Trevathan

Growing up in Gas City, Indiana, Herb McPherson could not remember many days from the fifth grade on when he didn't shoot a basketball. If it snowed, he shoveled to clear the court. As a student at Mississinewa High School, he would arrive at 6:00 in the morning, and the custodian would have to let him in so that he could shoot free throws and jumpers in the empty gym.

"It paid off when I got to college," said McPherson.

McPherson was probably the best long range shooter ever at Murray State, according to former assistant coach Bennie Purcell, who should know since McPherson broke the single-game scoring record that he and Howie Crittenden had held at 41 points. McPherson shattered the record with a 44-point performance against Middle Tennessee in 1966, his junior year.

If Purcell hadn't been sitting on the bench that night, aware that his record was under siege, McPherson might not have broken it.

"Cal [Luther] took him out with about five minutes left in the game, and he had 37 points. I told him to put him back in so he could break the record."

McPherson said that he wasn't aware how close he was to the record until Purcell informed him of it. "That put a little extra pressure on me," he said.

He ripped a 20-footer to break the record, and the crowd in Racer Arena roared, knowing that history had been made.

Purcell handed him the game ball afterwards and said, "Records are made to be broken, and I wanted you to break it."

Herb McPherson

To say McPherson was hot that night would be an understatement. He hit 17 of 26 from the field and ten free throws as the Racers trounced the Blue Raiders 107-81.

McPherson was a prolific scorer all three of his years on the Racer varsity. During his sophomore year, on a team that finished 19-7 and featured All-OVC players Stew Johnson and John Namciu, he averaged 18.6 points per game and 10.4 rebounds. He got better each year. His junior year, he averaged 21.2 per game, and during his senior, part of a high-powered offense that averaged over 89 points per game, McPherson averaged 21.8. He was All-OVC his junior and senior years.

Luther's preference for a run-and-gun offense was one of the reasons that McPherson chose Murray State when schools such as Purdue, Tennessee, South Carolina, Georgia Tech, and Ball State were recruiting him.

"I knew if I went to Murray State, he'd let me shoot it, and that's what I liked," said McPherson.

Luther was more than a coach to McPherson. "He helped me as a person. He had a big impact on my life."

As Luther tells it, McPherson almost left Murray State because he missed his high school sweetheart, Lauraine. She was still a senior in high school when McPherson was a freshman at Murray State, and according to Luther, the young man could not concentrate on his studies or on basketball. McPherson left a note with his roommate saying he was going to drop out of school and move back to Gas City.

Luther arranged a meeting with McPherson, Lauraine, and

both sets of parents, who wanted their children to remain in school. He flew up there in a private plane to meet with them all. A deal was made. Lauraine would finish high school, Herb would stay at Murray State, and at the end of the school year, if the young couple still felt the same way about each other, the parents agreed to give them permission to marry. They married that summer, and both graduated from Murray State with teaching certificates. Of the trip that had Luther negotiating as a sort of pre-marriage counselor, he said, "It was a trip I'll never forget. I'm happy to report that as of this interview, they have been married 47 years."

McPherson noted that he wasn't the only married player on the Racers his sophomore year; seven other teammates were married.

In a career full of highlights, McPherson remembers one win more than any other. During his sophomore year, the Racers played in the Sun Devil Classic at Arizona State and beat Texas Western the first game of the tournament. This was the Texas Western team, coached by Don Haskins, that went on to beat number one ranked Kentucky for the national championship the following year, 1966, a historic moment in college sports since Texas Western started five black players for the first time in NCAA tournament history.

McPherson, who noted that Murray State had integrated its team, felt it was not only a great win over a great team, but that it was a historic time in college basketball, and it was great for him to be a part of it.

Stewart Johnson, the first black varsity player in the OVC, was on that team, and he was McPherson's roommate on road trips. "We were great friends," said McPherson. "He had a great personality and was very intelligent. My wife had just about a perfect 4.0 grade point average, and when Stew took classes with her, he matched her A's."

McPherson's other memorable highlight was his last game as a Racer. He scored 24 points against a Western Kentucky team that came into Racer Arena ranked third in the nation and undefeated in the OVC at 13-0. "I think that was probably the highest ranked team that Murray State has ever beaten," he said.

McPherson was drafted by San Diego in the NBA and also had a chance to play in Europe, but he elected to enter the teaching profession. He and his wife

taught at the high school they graduated from for many years. The McPhersons' daughter, Stephanie Lockwood, is now the principal of that institution, Mississinewa High School.

Inducted into the Murray State Hall of Fame in 1989, McPherson ranks 12th overall in career scoring, though he's the number one scorer among players who were limited to three years of varsity competition. His 44-point performance against Middle Tennessee is still a record among players competing before the adoption of the three-pointer.

"I have a special place in my heart for Murray State," said McPherson. "Murray was a great place for a young, married couple to live."

DICK CUNNINGHAM

by Kim Trevathan

Lurch. The Jolly Green Giant. Herman Munster. A house running down the court. These were just a few of the nicknames for Dick Cunningham, the Racers' all-time leading rebounder, who led the nation in that category in 1967 and still holds the OVC career record for rebounds per game at 21.8. He also holds the OVC record for career rebounding average at 18.2.

Cunningham broke Jim Jennings' MSU record for rebounds in a single game with 31, and snatched 36 rebounds against MacMurray, more than any other player in the nation pulled down in a game during the 1966-67 season.

Twice All-OVC, Cunningham was selected as the MVP in the 1967 OVC Tournament.

At 6-10, 245 pounds, Lurch (The nickname comes from a character in the TV series *The Addams Family.*) could have played on any college team in the country, yet he chose Murray State. Cal Luther, who recruited him, had established a connection with prospects from basketball-rich Stark County, Ohio, near Canton, and that gave him an advantage when it came to recruiting Cunningham.

In 1967-68, his senior year, Cunningham, Claude Virden, and Billy Chumbler led the Racers to a tie for the OVC Championship. They lost 79-75 in a playoff game to East Tennessee State, who went on the win a round in the NCAA Tournament against Florida State.

Though known for his size and his rebounding, teammates and coaches remembered Cunningham's strength as phenomenal.

"He didn't know his own strength," said Rick Haverstock, an MSU teammate who played against Cunningham in high school. Haverstock said that he and Cunningham were on their way to practice one day and came upon the threshold to the weight room, where serious lifters and football players were working out.

Dick entered and walked up to a squatter stand with a weight so heavy that the bar was bowed. He bent his 6-10 frame underneath the bar, "did several squats without much effort, put the bar back on the rack, and walked out without a word," said Haverstock. The football players and serious lifters stared at him without comment, their mouths open in amazement.

Haverstock's job was to guard the opposing team's center while Cunningham concentrated on rebounding and triggering the fast break style that Luther loved. "Dick would have people hanging off him," said Haverstock. "He had the biggest hands of anyone I've ever met."

Luther noted that Cunningham also had great "natural jumping ability."

Cunningham's size, strength and rebounding ability attracted offers from both the NBA and the ABA. In 1968, he was the second round pick of the Phoenix Suns and was also drafted in the second round by the ABA's New York Nets.

Traded by the Suns to the Milwaukee Bucks, he played in the NBA for seven seasons, six of them as backup for the Bucks' Kareem Abdul Jabbar, known then as Lew Alcindor. Cunningham was a member of the 1971 Milwaukee team that won the championship against the Baltimore Bullets, sweeping them 4-0. Jabbar said that practicing against a player of Cunningham's size, talent, and strength helped him make the transition from college to the NBA.

Cunningham was more than a rebounding machine though.

Luther recalls that Cunningham's wingspan, big hands, and touch made him a great tipper. "He could tip the ball from one side of the basket to the other and score," said Luther. Herb McPherson, a teammate of Cunningham's and also an MSU Hall of Famer, said that Cunningham had a great jump hook and a good turnaround jump shot.

Cunningham averaged 15.5 points per game his senior year, when the Racers tied with ETSU for the OVC title. During his junior year, Cunningham averaged 15 points per game and seemed to thrive on the pressure of playing conference opponents. He had 25

points and 31 rebounds in a win over Morehead his junior year, as well as 23-rebound performance in a win against eventual OVC Champion WKU, then ranked third in the nation.

With 981 points, Cunningham ranks 19th on the Racers' all-time scoring list. In his sophomore year, he led the Racers in field goal percentage at .512.

McPherson also praised Cunningham's ability to pass the ball. "When he got double-teamed," said McPherson, "Dick could kick it outside to the shooter. He could throw a bullet outlet pass, as if throwing a baseball."

Many teammates noted the legendary Cunningham screen, not only as beneficiaries of it, but also as victims in practice. Jimmy Young, a freshman when Cunningham was a senior, called the picks "devastating." Young said, "Sometimes he'd stand over you and laugh as you lay on the floor."

Denny Potts, a teammate who had played football in high school, said that running into a Cunningham screen was "like hitting a goal post," though for the big man, said Potts, the impact was probably like a mosquito glancing off him.

Though fierce and competitive on the court, Cunningham was known for being a laid-back jokester and a great friend off the court. Assistant coach Bennie Purcell said that he "had a great personality," and that he "drew people to him."

Haverstock remembered Cunningham's "Herman Munster laugh. Everything was funny to him." Haverstock and others recalled that Cunningham's vehicle of choice was a Volkswagen Beetle. Seeing a giant in such a tiny car made for a humorous sight around campus, in keeping with Cunningham's joking demeanor.

Potts, who at 5-6, was introduced at the games next to Cunningham, said he "thought the world of him." During a time when dunks were illegal in college basketball, Potts and Cunningham did a stunt that entertained the crowd during warmups, Potts catapulting off Cunningham's back for slam dunks.

Ron Romani, a 6-9 teammate, remembers the time that Cunningham playfully grabbed him around the neck, lifted him off the ground and bounced him off his hip as they walked to the cafeteria for Thanksgiving dinner.

Despite his reputation as an easygoing jokester,

difficult to antagonize, Cunningham could be intimidating. Luther recalls an away game against a strong Dayton team that had a seven-footer named Henry Finkel. Don Duncan, "a tough little guy," said Luther, was driving to the basket when Finkel hit him in the air. As Duncan lay on the floor, dazed, Finkel stood over him and taunted him, said Luther. Duncan regained his senses and stood up, ready to fight, and that's when Cunningham stepped in, with his chest stuck out, and said, "Why don't you pick on somebody your own size?" The seven-footer turned and walked away.

Haverstock said the only time he remembered Dick losing his temper during a game was against Canisius in Buffalo, New York, a contest in which the officiating seemed particularly slanted to the home team's advantage. As he and Cunningham were walking off the court after a timeout, Haverstock said, a Canisius player walked up and elbowed Cunningham in the chest "for no reason."

"We looked at each other and he tore after the guy," said Haverstock. "There was a lot of pushing and shoving at their bench and they almost caused a riot." Things calmed down and they were able to finish the game, but Dick caught grief from his mother, who had traveled from Ohio to watch the game and disapproved of his behavior.

Haverstock noted an incident in practice in which Cunningham reacted with some irritation to an elbow thrown by teammate Rick Miller. "He grabbed Rick, who was 6-5, 185 pounds, by both biceps, raised him up to eye level, and said, 'Don't ever do that again.' Then he put him down and walked away."

Almost as legendary as his ability was Cunningham's appetite. Luther recalls the Murray tradition of a welcome back party for students on the court square. There was free food and drink there, and a couple of guys challenged the Jolly Green Giant to an eating contest. "They didn't last long," said Luther. He said Cunningham ate twenty-something hamburgers and he could not remember how many milkshakes he consumed.

After taking Cunningham and the team to Sue and Charlie's, a restaurant known for its all-you-can eat catfish entrée, Luther remembers the rest of the team having to wait, while the cooks fried batch after batch of catfish that Cunningham continued to devour, playing pinball in breaks between orders. The owner requested that Luther let him know ahead of time if he was bringing the team, so he could have more fish ready.

Potts, who grew up in Philadelphia watching the 76ers, said that Cunningham was not quite as tall as Wilt Chamberlain but "thicker." He said you rarely saw guys that size who were so athletic. In particular, he remembers an exploit that he witnessed during a physical education class that he and Cunningham were taking. One of the activities required students to play soccer. Potts said that Cunningham kicked the ball off the ground "90 yards in the air." Potts said that the NFL was interested in Lurch because of his size and agility and the fact that few teams had players of that height and strength.

Purcell remembered taking the team water-skiing on Kentucky Lake. "Dick got up and was doing pretty well, but he broke the rope, he was so strong," said Purcell.

Having had one of the most successful NBA careers of any player in Racer history, eight years in the league, Cunningham retired after a serious ankle injury and coached at Canton Catholic High School for a few years. He was inducted in the Murray State Hall of Fame in 1986.

CLAUDE VIRDEN

by Kim Trevathan

Sometimes an athlete is so gifted, so natural, that his performance looks effortless, as if he's on a higher level than other players, who seem to huff and puff and strain next to him. Claude Virden, a 6-6 forward who played for the Racers from 1968-71, was one of those athletes. Teammate Jimmy Young, a Racer Hall of Famer himself, said Virden was "smooth as silk." Coach Cal Luther said it looked like Virden "was gliding," like the ball "flowed out of his hand."

That's what it looked like to others. To Virden, basketball was about challenges and working hard. "Nothing was easy for me," he said. "If I had a weakness, I'd go out and work on it." Watching Virden play at Murray State, you'd think he was the model of consistency. But this was a guy never satisfied, always looking to improve. "When I had a bad game, I wasn't pleased with myself," he said. "Sometimes, even when I had a good game, I wasn't pleased."

Virden grew up in Akron, Ohio and transferred to Murray State after a year at Paducah Junior College, where he averaged 21 points a game. On a Racer team with stars such as Dick Cunningham, Bill Chumbler, and Tom Moran, Virden still made an immediate impact, leading a balanced offensive attack with 17.8 points per game. He also led the team in free-throw shooting (85.5 percent) and field goal percentage (47.5).

Virden, who according to Luther, "had a picture-book jump shot," kept scoring with consistency the next two years, ending his career at Murray State with a 21-point-per game career average, good for fifth in the all-time Racer rankings. He was OVC Player of the Year in 1968-69 and made All-OVC twice.

Claude Virden

In the 1968-69 season, he averaged 23.5 points per game and shot over 50 percent from the field. He led the team in rebounding and had the highest free-throw percentage (81.7). Virden said it was "one of those magical years that you try to take advantage of. We won a lot of close games and everybody clicked together."

In particular, Virden remembers beating Morehead State twice that year after losing the first game to them 111-78. The Racers beat them in Murray by two and clobbered them 94-76 in Bowling Green in a playoff game for the OVC title. That Murray State team, which also featured MSU Hall of Famers Jimmy Young and Hector Blondet, lost to Marquette in the first round of the NCAA Tournament, playing without senior guard and defensive force Don Funneman.

Young, as a sophomore, remembers Virden's encouragement of underclassmen. "He told us, 'When you're open, shoot it.'" Young, along with others, emphasized that though Virden was a pure shooter, he had an all-around game. "He played awesome defense," Young said.

Teammate Jim Stocks , who played one-on-one against Virden as they both grew up in Akron, said that Virden had "a quick first step" that made it easy for him to drive around people.

Assistant coach Bennie Purcell called Virden an "uncanny rebounder," who not only had a quick jump but seemed to be able to position himself perfectly for rebounds. Luther remembered Virden's ability to rebound his own misses and put them in.

Virden was also a defensive standout. Purcell said that Virden was usually assigned to guard the best forward on the other team,

and Luther said "he had that great agility to cover the sideline and trap the middle man" when the Racers employed a full court press.

Purcell said that because of his varied talents, Virden was "the greatest forward to ever play at Murray State."

In Virden's senior year, he led the Racers' high-powered offense with a 20.4 points per game average on a team that finished 17-9 overall and second in the OVC. Luther said that Virden got better each year he played at Murray State, finishing with a very strong senior year. Virden himself noted the importance of conditioning and discipline that Luther ingrained in his players.

Growing up in Akron, Virden was fortunate enough to be mentored by NBA-great Gus Johnson who was a few years ahead of him at Central High School. Johnson, an NBA Hall of Famer for the Washington Bullets and other teams, was a 6-6 forward like Virden would be. He used to take the younger player to the park to play in pickup games. These weren't just ordinary pickup games, said Virden. There were crowds watching. Johnson, said Virden, would always play against him, never on the same team. "He was like a giant to me," said Virden of the experience of playing against Johnson.

These high-level pickup games during his younger years started a pattern that Virden recognized as important in the development of his game. "Playing against good competition makes you stronger and more confident," he said. Growing up, he always tried to play against the older guys, recognizing that this would improve his game.

Stocks remembered that college teams, including the Racers, weren't all that interested in Virden his senior year of high school, when he was slowed by a sprained ankle. "They were more interested in this 6-8 guy," said Stocks, "but I helped persuade them that Virden was a great player. He was flat-out gifted."

Luther, who had already recruited extensively in Ohio, getting stars such as Dick Cunningham, Stocks, and Rick Haverstock, said he didn't get to see Virden play in a high school game, but watching him on film was enough to get his attention. "I was always looking for shooters," said Luther, and this guy could shoot.

Virden said that visiting Murray State won him over. "It was a beautiful campus," he said, "and people were great to me, very friendly." Stocks was a sort of big brother to Virden, helping him adjust to the move from Akron, an urban environment, to small-town Murray.

Not only were they among the first African-Americans at Murray State, Stocks noted, but they were moving from a place where there was a lot of entertainment to a place "with nothing much to do." On breaks, he and Virden would ride in the same car for the 13-hour drive to Akron. For a while, Stocks drove the whole way, until he convinced Virden to get his driver's license so he could help out. "We helped each other through that whole time, and supported each other after Martin Luther King was assassinated," he said, noting that Coach Luther gave them time off to attend a memorial.

Luther himself was an important person to Virden beyond his role as a basketball coach. Virden said the coach was "an amazing guy, like a parent to us. He and the other coaches cared about us and kept us out of trouble. I decided to come to Murray State because of Coach Luther."

Virden also remembers that Murray State's facilities were much nicer than the places they visited in the OVC, "Murray State was first-class compared to other teams' facilities."

Luther remembers Virden as a "terrific kid, well-mannered and well-liked by teammates. He was a quiet guy, not vocal, but he expressed himself on the basketball court. Claude is high on my list as a player and a person. I've always had a soft spot in my heart for Claude."

After graduation, Virden was drafted into the army and served a year and a half, mostly in Virginia, though he also traveled to Greece, Germany, and Syria, where he played on a military team that won a championship. Though he was able to play basketball in the army, Virden said that once he started playing professionally, he was behind in his conditioning. Though drafted by the Seattle Supersonics, Virden signed with the Kentucky Colonels from the ABA.

A starter for the Colonels in 1972-73, Virden averaged almost 10 points a game on a team that made it to the league championship. A knee injury curtailed Virden's season and eventually ended his professional career.

"Being hurt like I was, I couldn't play like I wanted to, so I called it a career," he said.

Virden, who now lives in Akron, played competitive basketball into his mid-forties. Now 65, he still stays in shape by working out at the gym. He was excited to watch the 2012 Racers in a rematch with Marquette, hoping that they would avenge the 1969 loss that his team suffered in the tournament. As we know, it was not to be.

Virden was inducted into the Murray State Athletic Hall of Fame in 2002. He finished with 1,490 career points, 13th on the MSU all-time scoring list. His 778 career rebounds puts him at 10th all-time at MSU. During his three years, the Racers won two conference titles and placed second the other year. Overall, the team was 65-23.

Aside from his work ethic as a player, his talent, and the support he got from teammates and coaches, Virden noted one other quality that helped him excel as a player: "I love the game of basketball," he said. "You've got to love the game."

Billy Chumbler

by Kim Trevathan

Fiery, talented player, Hall of Fame coach and influential mentor, Billy Chumbler has reached many lives through the game of basketball. A guard for the Racers from 1967-69, Chumbler was known for his outside shot, his hustle, and his intense desire to win. That desire to compete and the ability to hit the outside shot have not diminished over time. Chumbler, who retired from full-time coaching in 2005, won a silver medal for three-point shooting in the 2012 Senior Games at the Villages in Florida, an event which draws 80,000 participants from all over the country. He hit about fifty percent of his shots and had to chase down his own rebounds.

Chumbler was one of the most recruited high school players in the country when he graduated from Lowes, in Graves County, Kentucky in 1963. The all-time leading scorer at Lowes with 2080 points, he got 36 scholarship offers and was heavily recruited by Adolph Rupp at the University of Kentucky. Watching him score 42 and 38 points as a junior in two games at the Louisville Invitational Tournament, UK's assistant coach told Chumbler's father, the principal at Lowes, that he would sign him right away if he could.

First team all-state in his junior and senior years, Chumbler chose Mississippi State because he wanted to play in the SEC, and he wanted to play right away, something he feared wouldn't happen if he went to UK. He led the Bulldogs' freshman team in scoring (21 ppg), and in his sophomore year, he led the varsity in scoring at 14 points a game. Then fate intervened. Chumbler fell in love with a young woman who was attending Murray State and moved to Murray to marry her and to play for the Racers.

Billy Chumbler

One big difference he noted right away. "Everybody was into basketball," he said, a contrast to Mississippi State, where football was all anyone seemed to care about. Chumbler also noted that the OVC was a stronger basketball conference than the SEC.

"The OVC was loaded with talent," he said, noting that good African-American players were admitted into the conference at a time when the SEC was still segregated.

Chumbler stayed busy that summer. He took chemistry and physics and played in highly competitive summer basketball games with coaches Cal Luther and Bennie Purcell, as well as Hall of Famer Howard Crittenden, former player and future coach Ron Greene, and Adrian "Odie" Smith, from Farmington, who played for the Cincinnati Royals. "I got a lot better playing in those games," he said.

Luther, who had followed Chumbler during his high school years, knew from an earlier summer basketball camp that he was a competitive young man. He said that Chumbler's team got to the finals of the camp tournament, but Chumbler, who had had some run-ins with a certain official, refused to play in the finals with that official calling the game.

"That's the way he approached the game," said Luther. "All out on everything."

In Chumbler's junior year, playing alongside MSU Hall of Famers Herb McPherson and Dick Cunningham, he averaged 16.2 points per game on a team that beat Western in the final game of the season and finished second in the OVC. This was a team that set the school record for scoring, averaging nearly 90 points per game.

McPherson said that Chumbler was "a great competitor, a great shooter, who had a great love for basketball and always gave 100 percent, even in practice. He helped us win a lot of basketball games."

One game in particular illustrated Chumbler's performance in the clutch. Against a strong Middle Tennessee team at Murfreesboro, the Racers had an 18-point lead at the half. "Coach Luther told us that they would come back," Chumbler remembered, "and we all said 'yeah, yeah.'" Luther was right. The Blue Raiders came back and took a two-point lead. With five seconds left, Chumbler was fouled while shooting. He hit the first free throw, no problem. Then he happened to glance beneath the goal, where Middle's bench was.

One of the Blue Raiders stood up and grabbed his throat as Chumbler waited for the ball to shoot his second free throw. "You're going to choke, Chumbler!" he called out. All this did was make Chumbler bear down more, as he made the shot and sent the game into overtime.

In overtime, he hit two free throws to ice the game that Murray won 96-93. He hit all 12 of his free throws in that game and scored 30 points.

Luther said, "He's a guy that always wanted to take the shot late in the game."

Chumbler was captain of the team his senior year, leading the 1967-68 squad to a tie for the conference championship. They lost to East Tennessee in a playoff game for the NCAA bid. On a team that included MSU Hall of Famers Claude Virden and Dick Cunningham, Chumbler averaged 15.5 points per game, second to Virden.

Purcell says Chumbler was "one of the better guards we've had here." As a long-range shooter, Purcell put him in the same class as his teammate, Herb McPherson, and Jimmy Young, who was a freshman during Chumbler's senior year.

Both Luther and Purcell noted that Chumbler was not one to back down from confrontations. "He'd fight you in a second if you wanted one," said Purcell.

Luther said that Chumbler's aggressive style of play sometimes "aggravated" opponents, "If he got fouled hard, he would get up and square off with people."

Chumbler graduated from Murray State with a double major in psychology and physical education, and then got his master's degree from MSU in School Administration.

After he left Murray, Chumbler embarked upon a remarkable coaching career that touched the lives of many players, fans, and entire communities.

Inducted into the Illinois Coaches Hall of Fame in 1993, Chumbler has a record of 780-288 as a high school coach. Bob Swisher, longtime Paducah sports journalist, said this about Chumbler's coaching style: "He could be fiery, demanding, and even mad. He was Mr. 'You do it my way.' And they did; they did it his way 780 times."

Chumbler coached at Century High School in Illinois, Cairo High School, Paducah Tilghman, and Trigg County.

Now he divides his time between a home on Lake Barkley and a home in Florida, where he lends his expertise to the elite Monteverde Academy, as a volunteer assistant. He fishes competitively and recently placed second in a Bassin' USA tournament held at Lake Barkley.

HECTOR BLONDET

by Kim Trevathan

With a chance to beat Murray State and his best free throw shooter at the line, Eastern Kentucky's coach waved his players away from their places along the lane. Racer forward Hector Blondet crept up behind the free throw shooter, rubbed his shortly cropped head, and said, "Don't be nervous, it's just you and me here."

Apparently, Blondet's comic strategy worked, and Eastern's best free throw shooter missed. Coach Cal Luther, who related this story, said soon after Blondet's head rubbing, they put in a rule that prohibited opposing players from touching a free throw shooter.

Blondet played for the Racers' from 1968-71 when they had a combined record of 58-20. He averaged 14.6 points per game, second to Claude Virden, on the 1968-69 team that won the OVC and went to the NCAA Tournament.

Luther designed his 1-3-1 offense with Blondet in the middle to take advantage of his ball handling abilities. "He could fake so well that teams couldn't defend against him," said Luther. "He was the best I've ever had at finding the open man."

Blondet, a six-foot-five-inch forward who could drive to the basket and score, was known best for his ball handling and his ability to ignite the crowd. "He was the kind of player who had the ability to turn a game around," said assistant coach Bennie Purcell.

Blondet averaged 16 points per game his junior year and 14.5 his senior year.

Luther said that Blondet personified the sports cliché of a great ball handler having eyes in the back of his head. He could execute the no-look pass as well as the behind-the-back pass. Blondet was "a very clever player," according to Luther, and he did not put any restrictions on him.

Jimmy Young, Blondet's roommate, said that he had "all kinds of moves to the goal," in addition to being a great passer. Blondet used to tell Young, "Get open, man, and I'll get you the ball. I know you can shoot it."

In addition to being a talented player, Blondet was an entertainer. "He played to the fans," said Purcell, and you never knew what he would do. "He might throw a behind the back pass from one free throw line to the other."

Once Blondet, while waiting for the other team to come out of the huddle, sat down on the front row with him and ate a couple of handfuls of popcorn with the fans. He was still chewing when play resumed.

Hector Blondet

Young describes Blondet as "a cat," who once snuck out of the dorm after curfew, leaving pillows under the covers in an attempt to fool Coach Luther.

"He was a free spirit," said Luther, "and a couple of times I had to discipline him. But he was such a good kid, you couldn't be upset with him. He was loved by his teammates as well as the fans."

One Courier Journal writer called him the "Happy Warrior."

Racer fan and Murray native Gary Moore remembers that the name "Hector Blondet" seemed an uncanny fit for the man: "He was fun, different, and cool" like his name. Moore remembers seeing Blondet off the court wearing an "all-weather coat," in contrast to the letter jackets that most players wore. It gave Blondet a "cosmopolitan look," said Moore, who remembers thinking, "So that's what guys in New York wear."

Blondet was All-City at Boy's High in Brooklyn, the same school that Kareem Abdul Jabbar, Connie Hawkins and other great players had attended. Recruited by Purcell, he played a year at Paducah Junior College before transferring to Murray State.

Drafted by the NBA's Portland Trailblazers and the ABA's Virginia Squires, Blondet went on to star for the "Cardenales de Rio Piedras" and the "Capitanes de Arecibo" teams in the National Basketball League in Puerto Rico.

Known as "El Mago" or the Magician, Blondet played in two Olympics for the Puerto Rican national team: in Munich in 1972, where he averaged 16 points per game; and in Montreal in 1976. In 1971 he starred on the Puerto Rican national team that won a silver medal in the Pan Am Games. Blondet played professional basketball in Puerto Rico until he retired in 1984.

Luther said he was "very proud" of Blondet for representing his country in two Olympics. "El Mago" died of an apparent heart attack in 2006 at the age of 59.

THE 1970S

by Will Aubrey

1969-70 • 17-9

Murray State entered the 1970's having won back-to-back conference championships in 1968 and 1969. Fans expected that success to continue as the new decade began. After all, the Racers had five starters back including OVC Player of the Year Claude Virden.

Head coach Cal Luther's only concern seemed to be front court depth.

"We should be deep enough at guard," he said before the season started. "But let us lose a couple of front court men on fouls and we're in trouble."

An 83-51 victory over Tennessee Wesleyan in the opener at Racer Arena seemed to signal that another championship was in the offing. Hector Blondet and Claude Virden led MSU with 21 and 19 points respectively while Ron Johnson scored 10 points and grabbed 16 rebounds.

After beating California-Riverside 87-76 in their next game the Racers headed out on their first road trip of the year, losing at Canisius 84-75 and beating Seton Hall 90-81.

They were 3-1 when they opened OVC play at Racer Arena against Austin Peay on December 11.

Murray State came into the game having won 10 in a row against Peay in Murray. But an overflow crowd of 7,200 saw the Govs take a 16-15 lead in the early going. The lead ballooned to six at 21-15 after a technical foul was called on Luther. But the Racers reeled off 14 straight points to take a 29-21 advantage.

MSU led 68-57 with 4:08 left to play when a brawl broke out at midcourt. Blondet was ejected for Murray as was Peay's Terry Young. Four free throws by MSU's Jimmy Young and three by the Govs' Howard Wright left the Racers with a 72-60 advantage. Four minutes later they were celebrating an 85-72 victory.

Young led the Racers with 21 points while Virden had 17. Johnson had 15 points and 11 rebounds and the 6-4 Blondet had 11 points and an incredible 16 rebounds.

Murray State headed to Bradley following an 83-69 victory over Abilene Christian. In those days Bradley was a top notch program. They had won 60 games in a row at home against non-conference opponents and they had no doubt that the Racers would be their 61st victim.

For a while it looked like they were right. Bradley led at halftime 35-29. But Murray State's toughness made the difference in the second half as they limited the Braves to just six rebounds and rolled to a 72-60 upset victory.

Virden led the Racers with 25 points and 18 rebounds while Johnson had eight points and 10 rebounds.

"The big difference was the boards," Bradley's head coach Joe Stowell said. "Murray was just better organized. And that's a credit to Cal."

Murray State returned home for a 112-71 victory over William Penn. But they closed out the first semester with a 72-69 loss at Butler.

OVC play began in earnest when Morehead State came to town on January 3. The game was nip and tuck throughout the first half. And it was still in doubt with 8:01 left and the Racers on top 61-59. But MSU went to a 1-3-1 zone trap and that keyed an 8-1 run that put the game away.

"We could have gone to the trap earlier but we didn't want them to have time to adjust," Luther said. "They finally got some layups off it late but it didn't matter then."

Blondet led the way with 27 points as the Racers won 79-72. Ten games into the season Murray State was 8-2 overall and 2-0 in the OVC.

Three straight wins followed in quick succession as the Racers beat Eastern Kentucky and Parsons College at home before upending Tennessee Tech on the road, 87-78.

The winning streak ended with a 75-71 loss at East Tennessee State. That was followed by losses at Kansas and Western Kentucky. The loss to WKU left the

Racers 4-2 in the OVC, two games behind league leading Western.

Murray State got back on track with lopsided victories over Louisiana College and Austin Peay. With Tennessee Tech up next the Racers needed a victory to hang on to second place. And that's exactly what they got as they beat the Golden Eagles in Racer Arena 76-70.

Virden had 24 points and 14 rebounds while Johnson had 13 points and 14 rebounds.

The Racers beat Middle Tennessee next to keep their title hopes alive, but then proceeded to lose four of their next six games. One of those losses was a 79-78 defeat at Eastern Kentucky in which the clock mysteriously went from 10 seconds left to play to no time left in a single tick. Luther fumed but Eastern's players left the floor. The OVC commissioner, Art Guepe, ruled that Eastern was the winner and the teams did not have to finish the game.

They finished the OVC season with a disheartening 77-75 loss at home to Western. The defeat snapped a 28 game home court winning streak.

The Hilltoppers were led by 7-footer Jim McDaniels who scored 23 points and grabbed 12 rebounds.

MSU closed out the season with a 98-96 loss at Loyola (La.). Virden, who averaged 20.4 points and 11.5 rebounds, was a first team All-OVC selection and won the conference's Player of the Year award.

1970-71 • 19-5

As the 1970-71 season got underway head coach Cal Luther wasn't sure what to expect. He had five of his top seven scorers back – Jimmy Young, Hector Blondet, Ron Johnson, Bill Mancini, and Ron Williams. And he had Les Taylor who had been widely regarded as the top freshman in the OVC the year before.

But Claude Virden, one of the best to ever wear a Racer uniform, had been lost to graduation. There was no one taller than 6-7 on the roster. And the varsity had struggled to beat the freshman team in an exhibition, 87-81.

"Our freshmen are good, but not that good," Luther said with concern. "The varsity was outrebounded badly and I'm petrified by the thought that this is a sign of things to come.

"We couldn't win a title, not the way we've been playing like Ned and the First Reader. My choice to challenge Western is Eastern Kentucky. If we're going to win it will be because we're going to force the other team into errors.

The rest of the coaches in the OVC weren't buying Luther's lack of optimism though.

"He's most dangerous when he has a young, rebuilt team which he can spring on the conference," Middle Tennessee's Jimmy Earle noted.

And Western's head coach Johnny Oldham said of Luther, "He's the man we have to watch. I can't think of a coach I respect more. Matter of fact he's one of the few coaches I know who changes offenses every year."

The Racers dispatched MacMurray 101-50 in their home opener. But they had to rally to prevail against the University of California at Davis 68-61 in the second game of the season.

Murray State hit just 10-of-31 shots in the first half against UC-Davis and trailed 30-23 at halftime. But the Racers bounced back in the second half as they hit 58.3 percent of their shots and took the lead for good with 13:52 to play.

Despite Luther's concern about rebounding, MSU won the battle of the boards 41-37 as Johnson grabbed 10 rebounds himself. Taylor led the team with 20 points while Young had 17.

MSU ran its record to 4-0 with victories over two more "small college" opponents as they edged Howard Payne 83-81 and crushed Illinois College 113-60.

When questioned about the schedule Luther explained, "Let's face it, Murray has been tough as hell for the past 10 years and I'm not able to get name schools in here because the chances are excellent that we'd kick their butts.

"In 10 years I've been able to get Bradley to come to Murray twice. Last year we almost beat Kansas at Lawrence and you can bet that they're not going to come to Murray to play."

Through four games Taylor was averaging 16.7 points and 10.5 rebounds. Not bad for a 6-3 sophomore who was seeing his first action with the varsity.

"We're asking a tremendous amount of him on both ends of the floor," Luther said. "For instance, he's the point man on our pressing defense which means that he has to scramble all over the floor. At the same time he is our leading rebounder and leading scorer."

The Racers suffered their first loss in a 97-63 blowout at 10th ranked Villanova. But they bounced back by beating Federal City and Baldwin Wallace before opening the conference season at Eastern Kentucky on January 2.

MSU led Eastern 79-70 with 11 seconds left when Luther asked the head official if he and the players on the bench could leave. The official answered, "Just make sure you have a substitute available in case somebody gets hurt." So Luther literally cleared the bench with 11 ticks left on the clock.

When asked about the incident he explained, "I'll tell you when I decided to do it. Last year when the commissioner ruled we didn't get another chance."

The Racers won 81-74 as five players reached double figures. Blondet and Young led the way with 19 points each.

With four wins in their next five games the Racers were 12-2 and 3-1 in the OVC when fifth ranked Western Kentucky came to town on January 23. The Hilltoppers were also 12-2 overall but they were a step ahead of MSU in the conference as they sported a perfect 4-0 record in OVC play. Western had an 18-game OVC winning streak.

The game had been sold out for months.

"I've often wondered what an enterprising person could steal during a Murray game," Luther mused. "The whole city police force will be at tonight's game, along with about half of the state police. I'm aware of this because about half of them have hit me up for tickets. I oblige where I can because it never hurts to be friends with the law."

The arena was packed two hours before the game started.

"I was just a kid but I was at that game," long time MSU radio announcer Neal Bradley said. "People were sitting on the steps between the aisles and they were standing 15 deep around the top of the arena. It was an absolute zoo."

While Western was warming up fans caught basketballs that strayed into their midst and gleefully tossed them around the arena.

The game was nip and tuck from the outset and Western led 41-37 at halftime. Early in the second half Taylor posted himself up against the Hilltoppers' 7-foot All-American Jim McDaniels. He whirled and muscled the ball through the hoop, striking McDaniels in the face with his elbow. The Western star retreated to the dressing room but was soon back on the floor.

With the game winding down Western took a 71-70 lead on a jump shot by Jim Rose. The Racers stormed back down the floor and with 17 seconds left Williams launched a long jump shot that fell inches short of the rim. Fortunately Taylor was there to grab the rebound and stick it in the basket.

McDaniels had a chance to tie the game but his hurried 15-footer with about 10 seconds to play caromed hard off the glass and into the hands of a Murray player. Williams was fouled with seven seconds left and missed the front end of a 1-and-1. Taylor grabbed the rebound and was fouled. He hit the front end of a 1-and-1 and missed the second shot. But the Racers grabbed the rebound and ran out the clock.

At the beginning of the year Luther had worried about his team's ability to rebound the ball. But it was proving to be a strength, not a weakness.

Murray State cracked the Associated Press Top-20 at #19 after the win over Western.

Up next was Austin Peay. And in those days that generally meant an easy victory. Peay had only beaten Murray State once since joining the OVC in 1962. And the Govs were coming off of a 35 point loss to Western Kentucky.

But Young, who was from Clarksville, said there was no way the Racers would take them lightly.

"We've won the big ones, and we've worked too hard to blow it all now," he declared. "Every game we play from here on is a big one, and I'm sure we'll be ready for Austin Peay.

"Shoot. I'd just die if we went over there and lost to them. We haven't been beaten by Austin Peay since I've been playing at Murray and I sure don't want to start losing to them now."

Murray State rolled to a 90-76 victory over the Govs behind 26 points from Taylor and 20 from Blondet as Peay double-teamed Young wherever he went and held him to just two points.

"Jimmy only got three shots," Luther said. "He decoyed to one side and we passed the ball to the other. They cared more about stopping him than they did about beating Murray State."

A week later MSU beat Peay again 81-58, this time in Racer Arena. And they followed that with an 89-78 victory at Morehead. With two minutes left in the first half the Racers led the Eagles 48-24 and they were never seriously threatened. Taylor and Young led all scorers with 26 points each. With that victory Murray State moved up to #17 in the AP Top-20.

Unfortunately, the season was about to take an unexpected turn, in more ways than one. The Racers' nine game winning streak ended with back-to-back losses to Eastern Kentucky and East Tennessee State. They dropped out of the Top-20. Blondet injured his groin muscle and Taylor turned his ankle.

So when MSU met Western Kentucky in Bowling Green with the title on the line on February 27, the Racers weren't at their best.

"Earlier in the week I thought Hec would be the one who wouldn't be able to go," Luther said the day before the game. "But Les' ankle injury has failed to respond as well as we had hoped while Hec's pulled muscle has loosened up considerably.

"We must, of course, choke off the big guy. McDaniels is a tremendous talent, the best ever in our league as far as I'm concerned. And he poses a terrific problem for our defense. Our only hope is to limit his number of opportunities."

The Western star wasn't buying what Luther was selling though.

"That man is a fine coach," he said. "And he always has his team ready to play."

A record crowd of 14,277 filled Diddle Arena as Western upended Murray State, 73-59. The Racers trailed by 15 at halftime and by 22 midway through the second half. Taylor and Blondet came off the bench to lead MSU with 18 and 14 points respectively.

The Racers bounced back by beating Middle Tennessee in the season finale, 92-69. Young wound up leading the team in scoring at 16.1 points per game. Taylor was second at 15.8 and was named to the all-conference team.

1971-72 • 15-11

With just three lettermen back and only nine players on the team head coach Cal Luther knew the 1971-72 season might be trying at times. But there was also reason for optimism.

Les Taylor was back for his junior year after averaging 15.4 points as a sophomore along with Bill Mancini (8.5 ppg) and Ron Williams (8.4 ppg). And sophomore Marcelous Starks had averaged 19.6 points and 20.6 rebounds for the freshman team the year before.

Still, no one could blame Luther for being concerned about the team's lack of depth.

"With only nine players on the squad and only three of them experienced we'll be in real trouble if we lose a man on fouls," he cautioned.

The Racers opened the season at home with a 79-66 victory over Arkansas Tech as Taylor scored 40 points and grabbed 13 rebounds. Williams had 14 points while Starks scored 10 points and grabbed 10 rebounds.

They dropped an 81-80 decision to Cheyney State in the second game of the season before bouncing back to beat Illinois State and Western Carolina.

Next up was a trip to Peoria, Ill. to face the Bradley Braves. After having lost the first seven times they played Bradley, the Racers came into this game having beaten them three times in a row.

At halftime Murray led by 13 but the Braves switched to a zone defense at the beginning of the second half and went on a 17-5 run. It was nip and tuck the rest of the way and with five seconds left the Racers trailed 74-73 when Taylor hit a six foot jump shot to win the game 75-74.

Williams led MSU with 22 points, Taylor had 14 and Starks again registered a double-double with 10 points and 10 rebounds.

The Racers beat Oral Roberts 94-87 before heading to Evansville for the Purple Aces' holiday tournament. They beat Pacific in the first round before losing to Evansville in the championship game.

They were back home on January 8 for a 72-55 victory over Louisiana College. Unfortunately, Taylor broke his hand in that game and press reports indicated that he would be out for at least five weeks.

"It's a tremendous blow," Luther said. "Not only is he #1 in scoring, he's also the best defensive man, a strong rebounder, and our team leader."

With Taylor out the Racers lost three of their next five games. At the time of his injury he was the leading scorer in the OVC and eighth in the nation. He returned after just three weeks but was obviously limited as he scored just eight points in a 73-64 victory at Middle Tennessee.

Murray State was clearly a different team without Taylor at full strength as they lost five of their next nine games. When the Racers played host to Middle Tennessee in the penultimate game of the season they were fighting just to reach .500 in OVC play. They came away with a 52-46 victory as Taylor scored 20 points and Starks netted 17.

But they lost the final game of the season, dropping a 70-68 decision at Austin Peay to finish 6-8 in OVC games. Taylor was a first team all-conference selection and was named OVC Player of the Year.

1972-73 • 17-8

The NCAA implemented two significant changes in the rules for the 1972-73 season. They eliminated free throws on the first six fouls of each half unless a player was fouled in the act of shooting. On the seventh foul teams were awarded one free throw and if they made it they were awarded a bonus attempt. This resulted in 15-20 fewer free throw attempts per game.

"I like it," MSU head coach Cal Luther said. "The most boring thing about the game is to watch some guy shooting free throws."

They also allowed freshmen to play for the first time since World War II.

With three of their top five scorers back, including OVC Player of the Year Les Taylor, the Racers expected to return to the top tier of the Ohio Valley Conference. And a 99-79 victory over Samford in the home opener affirmed those expectations.

Luther started Taylor, normally a forward, at guard against the Bulldogs and he responded with 13 first half points as MSU used a pressing man-to-man defense to roar to a 56-38 halftime lead. Taylor wound up with 21 points while Marcelous Starks scored 17 points and grabbed 11 rebounds. Mike Coleman had 15 points and 11 rebounds.

After an 86-57 victory over Tennessee Wesleyan and an 83-71 win over Missouri Southern, the Racers were receiving votes in the Associated Press Top-20 poll as they headed to Lawrence, Kansas to play the Jayhawks.

With 8:57 left Kansas led 57-39 but Murray State went on a 24-10 run to make it 67-63 with 45 seconds to play. The Jayhawks executed down the stretch though as they pulled out a 69-63 victory. Taylor led the Racers with 15 points. Coleman had 14, and Starks had 10.

After dropping a 79-78 decision at #14 Oral Roberts, MSU won three of its next four games, beating Jackson State, Fairfield, and William Jewell and losing to Canisius.

Murray State was 6-3 but the fans were unhappy with the schedule. And they made enough of a fuss about it that Luther addressed their concerns in an interview published in the *Ledger and Times*.

"I think our schedule compares with anybody's, he said. "For instance, Minnesota plays the same Corpus Christi team we beat last year by 33 points. They play the University of Wisconsin Milwaukee Branch and the University of California Irvine Branch.

Missouri, one of the top teams in the country, plays Louisiana Tech and South Alabama. Memphis State plays such teams as West Missouri, South Florida, and Florida Tech."

MSU was still receiving votes in the AP poll as it headed to Richmond for its OVC opener against Eastern Kentucky. But neither team was at full strength. Luther was unsure of Coleman's status after he sprained his ankle against William Jewell. And EKU had five players sick with the flu, three of them starters.

Coleman wound up playing and he scored 14 points in the 75-70 Racer victory. But Eastern's best player, Charlie Mitchell, was unable to play. Taylor led the way for MSU with 22 points.

"We didn't play well enough defensively to put it away in the first half," Luther said. "We certainly shot well enough. But our defense and our floor mistakes kept us from getting a really big lead."

The Racers dropped an 82-75 decision at Morehead but bounced back with victories at home over East Tennessee and Tennessee Tech. With Western Kentucky coming to town on January 27 Murray State was 9-4 overall and 3-1 in the OVC.

The Hilltoppers were deliberate early on and led 14-10 with 11:56 to go in the first half. But the Racers scored 24 unanswered points and the rout was on. Taylor scored 30 points on just 16 shots as MSU rolled to a 99-80 victory.

MSU won seven of its next nine games and was a game back of league leading Austin Peay when it traveled to Bowling Green for a rematch with Western on February 26. With Peay losing to Middle Tennessee earlier that day a win would have put the Racers in a tie for first place.

And with six minutes to play Murray State led 60-53. But the Hilltoppers rallied for a 67-66 victory.

There was still reason for optimism though. All the Racers had to do to grab a share of the title was beat Austin Peay in Murray in the final game of the season. They had won 20 straight games at home and 15 in row against Peay at Racer Arena.

An overflow crowd started lining up more than two hours before game time to watch MSU try to beat the Govs and their marvelous freshman, Fly Williams. Williams was the fifth leading scorer in the nation at 29.4 ppg.

But it was the Govs' senior Eddie Childress who stole the show as he hit 11-of-14 shots and scored 25 points to lead Peay to a 75-73 victory.

Taylor was named OVC Player of the Year for the second consecutive season as he and Coleman were both named to the all-conference team.

1973-74 • 12-13

For the first time in four years the Racers began a new season without Les Taylor. But head coach Cal Luther did have six of his top seven scorers back. Still, Murray State was no match for Kansas as they opened on the road with a 103-71 loss to the Jayhawks. Jesse Williams led the Racers with 19 points while Mike Coleman had 14 and Marcelous Starks had 10.

They bounced back with an 82-78 victory over Howard Payne two nights later at Racer Arena. MSU never trailed but the game was close throughout as the hometown fans got their first look at 6-6 freshman guard Grover Woolard.

Woolard showed some razzle-dazzle in the first half, dribbling behind his back and firing a one-handed pass to Starks for a layup. By halftime the Racers had a 46-39 lead but they saw that margin cut to a single point in the second half. Fortunately they had an answer every time the visitors made a run and came away with the four point victory.

Coleman led all scorers with 27 points to go with his 11 rebounds; Williams had 16 points; Starks had 15 points and an amazing 19 rebounds; and Henry Kinsey came off the bench to score 12 points.

After running their record to 3-1 with victories over Arkansas College and Louisiana College the Racers lost four of their next seven games, including their OVC opener against Eastern Kentucky.

It looked like they were going to lose a second straight home game as they trailed Morehead 53-36 with 16:37 left to play. But a 23-4 run put the Racers on top 59-57 as Coleman took charge on his way to a game high 34 points before fouling out with eight minutes to play.

"When he fouled out one of the kids on the bench said to me, 'Well, we can still do it,'" Luther noted after the game. "I said to him, 'Hell, what do you mean? We are going to do it!"

With just 11 seconds left Morehead led 72-71 when the Eagles' Arch Johnson stepped to the line for the one-and-one. He missed, the Racers got the ball to Starks in transition. He made a layup and hit a free throw to seal the 74-72 victory.

Victories at East Tennessee and Tennessee Tech gave MSU a three game winning streak. But just when it looked like the Racers were hitting their stride, it suddenly seemed like they couldn't get a break as they lost six straight games by a total of 32 points.

A 79-75 loss at Western Kentucky was followed by a 74-71 loss to Middle Tennessee at Racer Arena. Another home loss to McNeese State was followed by losses at Austin Peay, Morehead, and Eastern Kentucky.

Murray State was 9-11 overall and 3-6 in the OVC when Tennessee Tech came to Murray on February 16. Tech held a one point lead at halftime but the Racers seized the lead at the beginning of the second half and held on for a 78-75 victory. Coleman led the charge with 20 points while Woolard pitched in with 19 and Starks had 14.

A victory over East Tennessee in the next game was followed by losses at Middle Tennessee and at home against Western Kentucky.

The Racers closed out the season at home against Austin Peay with the Govs needing a victory to clinch the conference championship. Peay had the OVC's leading scorer, Fly Williams who was averaging 27.6 points. But Murray's Coleman was second at 24.6.

Peay was heavily favored but MSU stunned the visitors, winning 74-71 behind 24 points from Jesse Williams. Starks had 16 points and 10 rebounds while Coleman went for 12 and 10.

Following the season Coleman was tabbed as a first team All-OVC selection.

1974-75 • 10-15

Cal Luther had served as both athletic director and basketball coach since 1970 and following the 1973-74 season he was told by university president Constantine Curris to choose between the two positions. He opted for the administrative job and Curris selected his top assistant, Fred Overton to replace him.

With only two of the team's top six players back from the previous season it looked like a rebuilding year. But there was no evidence of that in the early going.

The Racers opened the season on the road with an 86-76 victory at Baylor.

"We didn't seem at all tense," Overton noted. "The thing that really impressed me was that they tried everything to stop us but they couldn't. They ran a press, they played man-to-man, and they played zone but they couldn't stop us."

Junior forward Jesse Williams led the way for Murray State with 26 points and 11 rebounds. Senior guard Henry Kinsey had 18 points, Zach Blasingame had 14, and Grover Woolard had 12.

"We've all known Kinsey has been great," Overton said. "He was one of the best high school guards to ever come out of the East. He did a really great job directing traffic for us. Give him a couple of more games like this and he is going to be hard to contain."

MSU ran its record to 2-0 with a 79-69 win at Texas.

"The big thing was the team effort," Overton said. "Everyone on the floor gave something extra and that's all a coach could possibly ask for. A lot of times you don't see it in practice. But you can never tell what a group of kids will do when they get on a floor and get as emotionally involved as we did."

The Racers won despite getting just two points from Kinsey. Blasingame led the way with 20 points and 14 rebounds. Larry Moffet had 19 points and 13 rebounds. Williams had 19 points and Woolard had 15.

Four more wins followed against lower division teams before losses at Memphis and at home to Samford left MSU with a 6-2 record. A win against Mississippi College pushed them to 7-2 heading into their OVC opener at Morehead. But they would make the Death Valley trip at less than full strength. Blasingame, who was averaging 14.1 points a game, was out with a sprained knee.

As it happened there was little need to worry. Kinsey came off the bench at Morehead to spark the Racers to a 93-88 victory. He scored 24 points and grabbed seven rebounds. Throw in some fancy dribbling and length of the court passes from Kinsey and Woolard and the Eagles' crowd was stunned.

"I just couldn't believe that was Murray," one Morehead fan told the Ledger and Times. "I thought they were supposed to be down this year. They looked to me like they will easily be the best team in the conference this year. I've never seen a team operate like they did in the second half. They were almost perfect."

Jeff Hughes also tallied 24 points for the Racers while Williams had 22 and Woolard had 13.

Spirits were running high when MSU took the floor at Eastern Kentucky two nights later. But the Colonels dealt them a 104-95 defeat.

Despite getting Blasingame back for their next outing the Racers went into a tailspin. Losses to Tennessee Tech and East Tennessee State left them 1-3 in the OVC and there was enough unrest among the fans that Ledger and Times sports editor Mike Brandon felt the need to write a column in support of Overton.

"About half a dozen people last night at the Calloway County game asked me what's wrong with the Racers... Let's be completely honest about it. Baylor and Texas, where the Racers opened this season with a pair of 10 point wins, have big names, yes. But not for basketball. They would do well to win three or four games in the Ohio Valley Conference. Both teams were big and rather slow. And, Murray, having a great deal more speed, was able to use that to their advantage.

"So now we're off to a 1-3 conference start and we've lost two straight at home and everyone's talking about how they aren't going to come and watch the team anymore... So there's nothing wrong with Murray this year. Instead, take a positive look and try to understand what's right with the OVC.

"Freddie Overton has promised to build quite a basketball program here. And he will do it. You say how? By recruiting some of the best, and I mean best, players in the country."

Losses to Indiana State and Middle Tennessee followed Brandon's column. And Kinsey quit the team along with backup guard Donnie Woods.

The losing streak continued as Murray State dropped games at Western Kentucky and Austin Peay and then lost at home to Oral Roberts.

Victories over Eastern Kentucky and Morehead stopped the bleeding but they were followed by five straight losses at the end of the season.

"A lot of games could have gone our way with a little more strength," Overton said after losing to Austin Peay in the final game of the season. "We got in a lot of deep holes we couldn't get out of because of periods when we did not play with a great deal of excitement. We never quit but one of the greatest motivating things, depth, was gone."

Williams was named to the OVC's all-conference team at the end of the year.

1975-76 • 9-17

There was every reason to be optimistic about Overton's second season. He had his top three scorers back – Jesse Williams (20.8 ppg), Grover Woolard (16.6 ppg), and Zach Blasingame (15.3 ppg). Jeff Hughes (6.2 ppg), the top scorer off the bench, was also back.

But it was apparent from the outset that something was missing.

The Racers opened on the road at Kansas and they were never in the game as they dropped a 72-56 decision.

"We got down real quick and tried to catch up in a hurry," Overton said. "And as a result we took some bad shots and shot ourselves right out of the game. Instead of executing our offense, we just threw it up there. Once we learn the lesson and it sticks with us we'll be a fine club."

Williams led the way for MSU with 18 points while Woolard had 14 and Blasingame had 10.

Murray State bounced back for a 75-60 victory over Fort Lewis in their home opener only to be savaged in the local paper.

"When the guy sits on the edge of the bed and rubs his eyes and talks about not being able to sleep because he has a bad case of insomnia, he need not go out and spend his money on Sominex," Ledger and Times sports editor Mike Brandon wrote. "We've got something better right here in Murray. They're called the Murray State Racers.

"They worked wonders Monday night in the Sports Arena as they put 4,000 fans to sleep while beating some team called Fort Lewis College 75-60. There were a few exciting moments, once a cheerleader slipped on some ice and fell."

Blasingame led the Racers with 17 points while Williams had 14.

"Offensively, we never seemed to get our second wind," Overton said. "We just couldn't get people to get the ball down the floor. We like to try and fast break but somewhere down the line we seemed to have lost it. If we can keep playing good defense and get the fast break going the way we can then we should be a pretty good club."

MSU ran its record to 2-1 with a victory over Tennessee Wesleyan but then they lost five in a row. That streak came to an end with an 82-78 victory over New Orleans. But that was followed by a 74-70 loss to Austin Peay in the OVC opener.

Heading into their January 17 home game against Eastern Kentucky the Racers were 3-7 overall and 0-1 in the OVC. But Williams had one of the best games in MSU history as he scored 38 points to lead them to an 87-85 victory. Williams made 16-of-23 shots from the field and 6-of-8 free throws.

"He's just unbelievable," Overton said. "He is a bona fide pro prospect. He has so much talent at the offensive end. Sure we were going to him. We have been for four years.

"He's a winner. He has never played second fiddle even when we were losing. His unwavering faith is fantastic. He was telling me at Kansas we'd be all right when conference play started. We're in the running now."

Unfortunately they weren't in the running for long as they lost three of their next five games. Among those defeats was a crushing 92-68 loss at Western Kentucky.

As they prepared to play Middle Tennessee on February 2 the Racers had won just seven games all year. And they were 2-4 in conference play.

They did manage to right the ship against MTSU as they rolled to a 71-60 victory in front of 2,500 fans at Racer Arena. Williams led all scorers with 22 points. Blasingame had 12 as did Victor Jordan.

Five straight losses followed that victory. MSU then managed to beat Tennessee Tech and East Tennessee State but they closed out the regular season with a loss at Middle. And they bowed out in the first round of the OVC tournament with an 82-71 loss at Austin Peay.

Williams earned his second consecutive berth on the OVC's all-conference team.

1976-77 • 17-10

With a roster that was almost entirely new it was hard to know what to expect from the Racers in Fred Overton's third season as head coach. The only familiar faces were Grover Woolard and Zach Blasingame. And things looked bleak early on.

Murray State opened the season in the University of New Orleans Tip Off Tournament and they were blown out by the Privateers in the opening game, 105-76. A second round 83-82 victory over Northeast Louisiana evened their record at 1-1 and they were competitive in an 81-66 loss at Kansas in their next game. Blasingame saw limited action in all three games.

Finally, in the home opener against Butler, the Racers seemed to hit their stride in the second half of an 85-70 victory. After trailing 36-32 at intermission they dominated the second half.

"We moved the ball and looked for each other instead of playing 1-on-1 like we usually do," Woolard explained. "We ran our plays and played together. And we played a lot more aggressive on defense."

"Harmony is what it was," Blasingame agreed. "We were looking for the open man and going to him."

Junior college transfer Mike Muff led all scorers with 32 points while Blasingame and Woolard each had 17. Donnell Wilson came off the bench to grab 12 rebounds.

"That's the best ball game Zach has had at home," Overton said. "The big thing about Zach is his attitude. He was a starter for two years and he didn't get to play much on our road trip. Zach knew he could play if he got the opportunity. The way things turned out tonight, he got the opportunity and made the most of it. There's a great lesson in that."

Five straight victories against lower division teams boosted the Racers to 7-2 overall as they headed to Nevada to play in the Las Vegas Classic. They dropped the opener to UNLV 104-77 but bounced back to beat Bradley 83-80 in the consolation game.

Muff led the way in MSU's victory over the Braves as he scored 26 points and grabbed 12 rebounds. Jimmy Warren had 16 points, Danny Jarrett had 15 points and 12 rebounds and Blasingame had 10 and 7.

Following a 15 day layoff the Racers hit the road as they made the Death Valley trip to Morehead and Eastern Kentucky. After losing to Morehead 79-71 they eked out a controversial 71-70 victory at EKU.

With MSU leading 71-70 Eastern's Tyrone Jones hit a jumper as the buzzer sounded but the officials ruled that it came after time had expired. Warren led the Racers with 19 points, Muff had 17, Wilson had 10 points and 11 rebounds, and John Randall had 10 points.

After beating Tennessee Tech 73-65 and East Tennessee State 80-62 the Racers were 11-4 overall and 3-1 in OVC play.

But it looked as though their winning streak would end against first place Middle Tennessee. With 36 seconds left they trailed 70-64 but a furious rally carried them to a 71-70 victory. Randall scored five of MSU's seven points down the stretch including the game winner, a tip-in with six seconds left.

"This was one of those unbelievable games that you only read about," Overton said. I've experienced it vicariously that way. But when you actually go through it, seeing it happen to a bunch of kids who have worked so hard. Well it's something you hope for all your life as a coach."

Muff scored 23 points to lead the Racers.

MSU followed that improbable victory with one that seemed even more unlikely, an 89-87 double-overtime win in Bowling Green over Western Kentucky. It was their first win in Diddle Arena since 1964.

With12 seconds left in regulation the Hilltoppers led 65-61 when a jump ball was called at Murray's end. So MSU's 6-8 John Randall and Western's 6-0 Steve Ashby got set to jump it up at Murray's free throw line.

But before referee Ralph Stout tossed the ball up, Randall whispered something to him. Stout stepped back in disbelief and said, "What?"

"I asked the official if I could tip it in the basket," Randall explained. "He said it was all right so I tried my luck. I tried it once in junior college and hit the rim."

Randall's tip hit the rim, hit the backboard, hit the rim again and rolled in. Then, in the next seven seconds, the Racers committed a foul, watched Western miss two free throws, hit two free throws of their own, stole the ball, and hit two more free throws to take a 67-65 lead with five seconds left. Unfortunately Ashby threw a length of the court pass to Aaron Bryant who scored at the buzzer to send the game into overtime.

With 10 seconds left in the first overtime Western's Tom Shinn went to the line with the Hilltoppers' leading 77-75. Shinn missed both free throws and MSU's 5-9 freshman guard Lenny Barber came out of nowhere to get the rebound. Barber got the ball down the floor quickly and hit a 20-footer to force a second overtime.

With 12 seconds left in the second overtime the score was tied, 87-87. MSU got the ball to Warren who hit a 15 footer from the left corner to seal the victory.

"He spent an hour after practice working on that shot yesterday because he had been missing it," Overton said.

"I shot 100 of them after practice because I had a bad game Saturday," Warren agreed. "It seemed like it helped. I had to take that shot and I felt like I was going to make it."

Overton praised his team's resiliency, "Many times tonight it was awfully hard to look up there at the clock and think we had a chance to win. But these kids just will not be beat. When it comes time to do it they do whatever it takes."

The Racers won four of their next six games and still had a shot at the conference title when Western came to town on February 19. Fans expected another miraculous finish as MSU nearly erased a nine point deficit in the final four minutes.

Randall stepped to the free throw line for a bonus opportunity with two seconds left and MSU down by a single point. But his attempt rolled off the rim giving the Hilltoppers an 82-81 victory.

"I thought Freddie had pulled another miracle out of the hat," Western's head coach Jim Richards said. "He did it at our place last time and he's been doing it all over the league."

"I guess everyone in the stands thought we would win," Overton agreed. "I have to admit I never thought we'd lose it. I hate to lose it. I never like to lose anything to Western."

That loss seemed to take something out of Overton's team though as they proceeded to lose their next three games as well.

Mike Muff and Grover Woolard both received All-OVC honors.

1977-78 • 8-17

With three of their top six scorers back the Racers were expected to build on the previous season's second place finish in the OVC and challenge for the championship. But a season opening 78-74 victory over Arkansas-Pine Bluff caused alarm bells to ring.

6-7 center Mike Muff led the Racers with 19 points and nine rebounds while Donnell Wilson had 18 points and 10 rebounds. But OVC title contenders are not supposed to struggle with lower division opponents.

A 75-72 victory over Bethel did little to ease the fans' concern and that win was followed by losses at Samford, Kansas, and Indiana.

The Racers returned home to play Mississippi College on December 12. It was supposed to be an easy victory. It turned out to be an embarrassing defeat as MSU was beaten 70-62.

The Racer Arena crowd booed loudly when head coach Fred Overton called time out late in the game with Murray State trailing by 14.

Mississippi College head coach Doug Hines cautioned people not to read too much into the victory, "I know the calibre of basketball in the Ohio Valley Conference. Our basketball is not that calibre... We don't have a great team. We just have a good team."

Muff led the Racers with 30 points and nine rebounds while Warren had 10 points.

"I don't know what to say," Overton remarked. "It was just unbelievable. It sure wasn't very enjoyable. I thought we got a good effort but somewhere along the way we just missed 'em."

Following the loss to Mississippi College, Overton suspended forward John Randall along with guards Robert "Bobo" Jackson and Lenny Barber for "disciplinary reasons." The Racers responded by thrashing Georgia College 82-62.

"It's a lot of fun to coach and win," Overton said. "The three guys who were suspended... They're my people. And I'm responsible and concerned for them. They'll have to adjust to my philosophy in order to return."

Muff scored 28 points to lead MSU in the victory.

"I let the kids take themselves out during the game," Overton said. "The kids all pull for one another. When a guy comes out he puts himself back in when he's ready. I learned this from Dean Smith. But you have to have the people to do it and we did tonight."

The fun didn't last. MSU lost its next game at home to Livingston, their second loss at home to a lower division team. They followed that by losing three of their next four, including their first two OVC games against East Tennessee State and Tennessee Tech.

Heading into their January 14 home game against Morehead the Racers were 4-8 overall and 0-2 in OVC play. Morehead was also struggling at 3-7 and 0-2. But they had one of the top scorers in the country in Herbie Stamper (24.6 ppg).

At halftime it looked like Stamper might get 40 as he hit 10-of-14 shots and scored 22 points in the first half. But the Racers held the vaunted outside shooter to three points on 1-of-9 shooting in the second half en route to a 69-60 victory. How did they do it? By playing zone.

"The thing that amazes me is that Stamper won't shoot against a zone," Overton explained. "He ought to fill it up against a zone but he won't shoot. So the only way to play Morehead is a zone."

Muff led the Racers with 25 points while Warren had 13 and Wilson had 10.

Unfortunately Murray State was unable to build on that victory. They dropped their next five games, and among those defeats was another loss at home to a team from a lower division.

This prompted Overton to announce that he would resign after the season was over because he had failed to achieve the "winning success" he had hoped for.

"I still believe, and so does this team, that we can win every game left on our schedule," he declared. "We are playing very good basketball at the present. This team has worked hard, they play together, and they are strongly committed to winning. Hopefully everyone will stay behind them the rest of the way.

"We have the greatest fans in the world. My only regret is that we did not win more games so that they could really have shown their true Murray State spirit."

Two more losses followed Overton's resignation. The Racers then rallied to win three of their final five games.

Muff was named to the OVC's all-conference team at the end of the season.

1978-79 • 4-22

Ron Greene was chosen to take over the program following Fred Overton's resignation. Greene had played for the Racers in the early 60's. He had just been named Southeastern Conference Coach of the Year after leading Mississippi State to a runnerup finish in his first year there and turned down a substantial pay raise to take the job at Murray State.

"Murray State has always meant a lot to me," he told the Murray State News. "I owe any success I've had to MSU and hope to repay the university for what it has given me.

"Financial reasons are not always the most important reasons anyway. There is no place like home and Mississippi State was just not home."

Greene was taking over a team that was coming off the worst season in school history. He knew that he faced a monumental task and he knew it couldn't be done overnight. So he set out to rebuild the roster from the bottom up.

Fans grew restless as the season started with six straight losses. The streak ended with a 75-65 victory over Tennessee-Martin at Racer Arena.

"It wasn't the NCAA but it sure felt like it," Greene said. "We were still tight though. We would miss a wide open layup and they would come down and get a 40-footer and that would keep the pressure on."

Allen Mann led the Racers with 19 points, Roy Taylor had 16, and John Randall had 12.

Murray State ran its record to 2-6 with a 67-59 victory over Campbell College.

"We're gaining experience with each game and I hope we really get together as a team by January," Greene said. "We're gaining confidence and we're playing smarter but we've still got a long way to go. Compared to a V-8 automobile, I'd say we were hitting on five cylinders."

Randall and Taylor led the way with 14 points each. Keith Oglesby had 13.

Unfortunately the Racers were unable to derive any momentum from the victories over UTM and Campbell. They closed out the month of December with four straight losses and then they dropped their first four games of the new year.

There were roster issues as well. Taylor (13.8 ppg) was declared academically ineligible for the second semester. Mann and Bobo Jackson were dropped from the team for "continuous training violations." David Lowry was suspended for one game because of a training violation.

With Western Kentucky coming to town on January 20 the Racers were 3-15 overall and 0-2 in OVC play. The Hilltoppers were 8-5 overall and 1-1 in conference play and everyone expected them to hand MSU another loss. But everyone was wrong.

Murray State set a school record as they hit 27 of 39 shots from the field for 69.2 percent. And they upended their arch rival 67-65.

"This game doesn't necessarily mean the start of something good," Greene noted. "It was just a typical Murray-Western game like when I played in college."

Kenny Hammonds led MSU with 17 points while Tom Adams had 11.

Greene's caution in appraising the significance of the win over Western was prescient as the Racers lost their next eight games.

MSU was 3-21 when it headed to Bowling Green on February 19 for a rematch with Western. While the Racers had been losing eight games in a row the Hilltoppers had won 8-of-10 games. And although Randall had been reinstated Oglesby was limited by a back injury.

Despite all that Murray State pulled off another upset as it beat Western in Diddle Arena 66-64, sweeping the Hilltoppers for the first time since the 1963-64 season. To make the victory even sweeter for Racer fans it knocked Western out of the chase for the OVC crown.

"I've felt like this was coming all year," Greene said. "We've been close so many times and still lost that I didn't think we had this one won until I heard the buzzer."

Randall led MSU with 24 points while Hammonds had 17, and Mann had 15.

The Racers closed out the season with a loss at Austin Peay but Randall and Hammonds were both named to the all-conference team.

JIMMY YOUNG

by Kim Trevathan

The Racers trailed nationally ranked Oral Roberts University by one, with only seconds left in the game. Guard Jimmy Young sidled up to forward Hector Blondet, who was inbounding the ball and said, "If I'm open, man, get it to me. I'll make it."

Blondet obliged and Young ripped the long-range game winner from the dead corner.

"I was never afraid to take that shot," Young said. "You've got to be willing to be the goat in order to be the hero."

A two-time All-OVC selection, Young played at Murray State from 1967-1971, on teams with superstars such as Claude Virden, Les Taylor, Ron Johnson, and Blondet. The highlight of his Racer career came in his sophomore year when Murray State beat Morehead 94-76 in a one game-playoff to win a bid to the NCAA tournament. It was a "team effort," he said, particularly satisfying because Morehead had beaten the Racers twice already that season.

"Hard-nosed" is how Coach Cal Luther and his assistant Bennie Purcell describe Young. "He hustled in practice just like he did in a game," said Purcell.

Young said "hard-nosed" to him meant he "couldn't stand to get beat."

The Racer teams that Young starred on rarely lost. Aside from the 1968-69 team that went to the NCAA tournament, the Racers went 17-9 Young's junior year and 19-5 his senior year, when the Racers finished second in the OVC behind Western, who made it to the final four that year. Young led that team with a 17.8 points per game average.

He had incredible range according to Purcell. Long time Racer fan and Racer Insider publisher Lindy Suiter put it this way, "I haven't seen many college players shoot the deep ball as well as Isaiah Canaan. But Jimmy was right there with him. You couldn't leave him open even if he was 25 feet from the basket because he could shoot it from anywhere. There's no telling how many points he would have scored if they'd had the three-point shot back then."

Jimmy Young

Luther added that Young was "very strong in his upper body" and was one of the "best clutch shooters" during the 16 years he coached at Murray State. "Young had great mental toughness," said Luther, "was" a great free-throw shooter and "tough and aggressive" on defense.

He was often double-teamed and you didn't want to foul him. He holds the school record for single-season free throw percentage, shooting 89.6 percent in 1969-70.

Young, who says he can still shoot, said a 30-footer was just as easy as an 18-footer for him.

Scoring 1,128 points during his career as a Racer, Young's total would have been much higher had the three-point shot been used during his playing time. "He would have averaged 30-35 points a game," said Purcell.

Young, recruited by Purcell, did average 35 points as a senior at Montgomery County High School near Clarksville, Tenn. His father, James G. Young, coached him in high school, a fact that opposing teams used to try to get under his skin at away games, when they unfurled banners calling him "Daddy's Baby."

Basketball was a sport for which Young showed talent early on, playing on the eighth grade team when he was in the fourth grade. He was pretty good at baseball as well and turned down an offer to sign with the Pittsburgh Pirates organization out of high school.

Heavily recruited by teams such as Western Kentucky, Alabama, Auburn, and Mississippi State, Young chose Murray State because it was close to home and because, he said, "Murray seemed more interested than any other team."

He said playing at MSU was "four of the best years of my life, an awesome experience. That was a special crowd in Racer Arena that backed us like crazy."

After college, Young said he got better as a player. He played basketball in independent leagues with former Austin Peay and Vanderbilt players until he was 31, teaching physical education in elementary and middle schools. After graduating, he thought the Indiana Pacers were going to draft him, but he said it didn't work out.

"I know I could have played in the pros," he said, noting that his strong wrists and quick release would have made him a valuable outside shooter in the pro game, with the three-pointer.

Like his father before him, Young now coaches the Montgomery County High School basketball team, where he has racked up over 450 wins. He said coaches Luther and Purcell were big influences on him, that he "respected them so much" and through their examples realized he wanted to coach and teach P.E.

Luther calls Young "a coach's dream…one of the finest basketball players who ever played here."

"Tell coach Luther and Bennie I made 52 three-pointers in a row today," Young said during a 2011 interview. "I've been blessed with good health, I try to walk six miles a day and I still have a good jump shot."

Les Taylor

by Will Aubrey

In the late 1960's college basketball was still something of a curiosity. Very few games were shown on television and there was virtually no network coverage. The NCAA tournament wasn't televised nationally until 1969. And the first national regular season telecasts didn't occur until 1974.

There was no three-point line, no shot clock, most state schools in the south wouldn't sign black players, and dunking was against the rules.

There weren't any recruiting services either. Of course, college coaches still knew who the best high players were. And when Les Taylor graduated from Carbondale High School in 1969 he had offers from more than 150 different schools. He was the starting center for a team that reached the final eight of the Illinois state tournament.

Murray State had an edge though.

"I had coached high school basketball in Mount Vernon, Ill.," former MSU assistant coach Bennie Purcell noted. "Les played for a guy that I had coached. So that gave me an advantage.

"We were lucky to get him. Everybody was after him. He was all-state in Illinois. But he didn't take the ACT until the summer after his senior year and a lot of schools had used all their scholarships by then."

In those days the Courier Journal provided extensive coverage of the state's regional universities. And Taylor explained his choice to the C-J's Paul Borden, "I didn't want to stay at home so I didn't go to Southern Illinois. But at the same time I didn't want to go too far from home, so Murray, which is about 130 miles from Carbondale was a perfect compromise."

Les Taylor

Taylor only played for three years because freshmen weren't eligible in his day. But he is still 15th on Murray State's career scoring list with 1,477 points after averaging 15.8 as a sophomore, 25.6 as a junior, and 22.4 as a senior. He was a three-time All-Ohio Valley Conference selection and was named OVC Player of the Year as a junior and senior.

Taylor was an unusual player, though. At 6-3 ½ you would expect him to play guard or maybe small forward. But he played power forward.

"I think he's the best power forward we ever had," Purcell said. "He was strong. He scored or was fouled almost every time he got the ball because he was so strong. And he really didn't take a lot of shots. He was a great rebounder too."

Taylor averaged 8.9 rebounds as a sophomore, 8.3 as a junior, and 6.0 as a senior.

As a sophomore Taylor went up against Western Kentucky's 7-0 All-American Jim McDaniels. Early in the second half, with the Racers trailing, he posted up against McDaniels. He whirled and muscled the ball through the hoop, striking McDaniels in the face with his elbow.

It sent a message to the Western star that Taylor would not be denied. And he had two huge offensive rebounds late in the game that helped propel MSU to a 73-71 victory.

As a junior he scored 40 points and grabbed 13 rebounds against Arkansas Tech. He was eighth in nation in scoring until he broke his hand. Initial reports indicated that he would be out for five weeks but in a testament to his toughness he only missed five games.

Taylor insisted that he hurt

his hand when he jammed his knuckle against a basketball. But there were those who said that basketball looked a lot like an opposing player's skull.

When Taylor was a senior, head coach Cal Luther started him at guard in the home opener against Samford. He responded by scoring 13 points in the first half.

A few weeks later he scored 30 points in a 99-80 rout of Western Kentucky.

Taylor's father died when he was two years old and his mother worked hard to support the family.

"My mother had a lot of jobs to support us," he told Borden when he was a senior at Murray State. "And she was sick most of the time. She's diabetic. When I was in high school she was taking insulin pills. Then when I graduated she was up to taking shots. Now she's taking two shots a day."

He didn't even try out for his high school team as a sophomore because he didn't think he would get a fair shake from the coach. And college was the furthest thing from his mind.

"I really didn't think about going to college until the second half of my senior year in high school," Taylor continued. "My guidance counselor told me I had a good chance at a scholarship and that I should work to get my grades up.

"I never thought of college before because my first goal was to get out of high school. I just took these things step by step."

Racer fans are glad one of those steps brought him to Murray State because he remains one of the best to ever wear the Blue and Gold.

Marcelous Starks

by Kim Trevathan

Most people probably don't know that one of the more successful professional players to come out of Murray State was none other than Marcelous Starks. That's because his prime years were spent in Europe, playing for teams in France, Italy, and Spain.

Starks played for Murray State from 1970-74, with stars such as Les Taylor and Jimmy Young. He starred on Coach Kayo Willis' undefeated freshman team in 1970-71, alongside Murray State Athletic Hall of Famer Steve Barrett, a guard who excelled on the hardwood as well as the baseball diamond.

When the 6-8 Starks arrived at Murray State from Chicago, Willis told him, "Listen, you're going to be my star player." Les Taylor (1970-73), an MSU Hall of Famer who was from Carbondale, helped convince Starks to come to Murray at a time when he was considering USC and Detroit. Taylor said, ""Come down here and you play with me, we'll have a real good team."

Starks said it was an adjustment moving from Chicago to Murray, which he said, was "country." He told of a time when he was riding in the car with Les Taylor on Highway 641 South near the Tennessee border, where Calloway Countians would drive to buy beer. "Les slowed down to like ten miles per hour as we started to cross these railroad tracks," said Marcelous. "He told me to buckle my seat belt. I didn't know what was going on." A state trooper pulled over Taylor and Starks soon afterward, and after determining that they hadn't been drinking, let them go.

Marcelous Starks

"After my freshman year, I got used to Murray," Starks said.

After playing on the undefeated team his freshman year, Starks was told by Coach Willis, "You're on your way." He stepped into his role as a starter on the varsity and led the team in rebounding while scoring 14.3 points per game.

When Starks was a junior Mike Coleman joined the team and contributed 17.4 points per game. On a Racer squad that finished 17-8 and tied for second in the OVC standings, Starks pumped in 15.8 points per game and shot 61 percent from the field. Coach Cal Luther said Starks' touch was so soft that the ball was like a marshmallow when it left his hands and bounced around on the rim before going in, more often than not.

Starks was joined that year by fellow Chicagoan and future Murray State Hall of Famer, Jessie Williams, a pure shooting forward that Starks persuaded to come to Murray.

He remembers beating a much bigger Western Kentucky team 99-80 in Murray, a feat that made him realize what a great coach Cal Luther was. He said Luther worked them hard on defense, and as a result they could often beat much bigger teams.

"He was the best defensive coach in the OVC," said Starks. "Defense won us a lot of games. When

you're small you've got to play defense to win the game."

During his senior year, after Taylor's graduation, Starks led the team in rebounding with 319, his 13.8 points per game was second on the team behind Mike Coleman.

The turning point in Starks' career came in the Tennessee-Kentucky All-Star Game in 1974. At 6-8, he was the biggest player on the Kentucky team, coached by Denny Crum, and the Tennessee team had a much bigger lineup that featured some players who were going to be first-round draft picks in the NBA.

Crum told him, "I'm putting all my money on you. You're playing the whole game and we're going to run them to death." Starks said that's what the Kentucky team did, ran them out of gym. He had 22 points, 17 rebounds and won MVP of the game, important for him because he got the attention of several pro scouts in attendance.

He got a tryout with the Chicago Bulls but didn't make the team. He played in the Eastern League, where a Frenchman saw him play and asked, "Do you want to play in the French Riviera?" Starks signed with Antibes and was the best player on the team, averaging 25 points per game and 17 rebounds. His second year he got even better, averaging 27 points and 18 rebounds, earning him another look by the Bulls.

Once again, it came right down to the end, but Starks, faced with playing in the Eastern League again, signed a three-year contract with an Italian team. He played on teams in Barcelona, Bologna, and Naples, winning championships with the Spanish and Bolognese teams. Playing in Europe, he won six MVP awards, three in Italy, one in France, and two in Spain, as well as many rebounding awards.

Starks ended his 14-year professional career in 1990. He now works as a scout out of Italy, the Dominican Republic, and Brazil. He has placed about 20 American players in Europe, Asia, and South America.

CAL LUTHER

by Jimmy Wilder

Cal Luther's hiring in 1958 as Murray State head coach led to a renaissance in Racer basketball that produced more than wins, Ohio Valley Conference championships and two NCAA Tournament appearances. His fiery demeanor and up-tempo, ball pressure style of play were fan friendly, making tickets to games in 5,500-seat Racer Arena a coveted possession.

And at Luther's behest, president Dr. Ralph Woods and the Murray State Board of Regents gave their approval in 1961 for him to recruit African American players. It was a decision that forever changed the landscape of the OVC and positioned Murray State to become a presence on the national stage.

"When I came to Murray I was too young to know how hard it would be to get the program going again," said Luther, who replaced Rex Alexander at the age of 29. "But I wanted to be a Division 1 head coach and Murray had a lot of appeal to me."

"I worked my butt off to build a championship program," he said. "I had some good times and some tough times, particularly in my early years. The fans were great, and I was blessed to be able to coach some really good players. I have wonderful memories and friendships from my days at Murray State."

What follows is a capsule look at Luther's 16 years as Murray's head coach.

- His 241-154 record represents the second most wins in school history, surpassed only by the 267-100 mark compiled by Carlisle Cutchin, the school's first coach.
- His teams were 173-38 in Racer Arena, where they had a 27-game winning streak, beginning Nov. 30, 1968 against Texas-Arlington (91-83) and ending Feb. 28, 1970 against Western Kentucky (77-75). Western's victory completed a perfect 14-0 OVC title run for the Hilltoppers, while Murray State finished 9-5 in the league and in second place.
- Luther had fourteen consecutive winning seasons and his teams won four OVC championships.
- In 1964 and 1969, Luther's Racers earned automatic invites to what was then a 25-team NCAA Tournament.
- He was selected OVC Coach of the Year in '64 and '69, making him the league's first two-time recipient.
- Luther's 13-10 squad of '60-61 was 2-0 against OVC champion Morehead State, which beat Xavier 71-66 in the NCAA Tournament and lost to Kentucky, 71-64.
- His 1961-62 team defeated Eastern Kentucky, 82-80 in Richmond on forward Jim Jennings' jumper just ahead of the buzzer, ending the Colonels' 38-game home court win streak.
- His 16-9 Racers of '63-64 claimed the Ohio Valley Conference title and earned Murray's first ever appearance in the NCAA tourney. But he was hung in effigy on campus in January of '64 after the Racers lost at home to East Tennessee State, 62-61 in two overtimes, dropping their league mark to 2-3 and their overall record to 7-7. Luther's team then won its last nine OVC games to finish two games ahead of league runner-up Eastern Kentucky in the standings (one of Murray's wins

Cal Luther

was against East Tennessee State, 96-76, on Feb. 24).

In the NCAA Tournament, defending champion Loyola of Chicago came from 13 points down to beat the Racers, 101-91, at Evanston, Ill. Loyola lost its next game, 84-80 to Michigan, which placed third in the tournament by beating Kansas State, 90-80, in the consolation game.

- In December of 1964, Murray won the OVC preseason tournament in Louisville, but in January lost consecutive road games against Western Kentucky (71-70), East Tennessee State (69-68) and Tennessee Tech (93-91). The Racers recovered from those setbacks to post six straight victories and finish 19-7 overall. They placed third in the conference behind Eastern Kentucky and Western.
- Murray and East Tennessee State shared the OVC championship in '68, but the Buccaneers represented the conference in the NCAA Tournament, thanks to a 79-75 playoff win over the Racers. East Tennessee beat Florida State 79-69 in the NCAA tourney and lost 79-72 to Ohio State, a Final Four participant.
- Luther's 22-6 team of '68-69 was undefeated at home (15-0), shared the OVC championship with Morehead State, and qualified for the NCAA Tournament by beating Morehead in a playoff, 94-76. In the NCAA tourney, Marquette beat Murray 82-62 at Carbondale, Ill. Marquette then defeated Kentucky, 81-74, and lost 75-73 to Purdue, which advanced to the national title game before losing to undefeated UCLA, 92-72.
- Beginning in the 1968-69 season and continuing through '70-71, Murray State won four straight games against Bradley, a perennial Missouri Valley Conference power. The first win came in Racer Arena and the other three came on the Braves' home court, two in the 1970-71 season. Following those losses, Bradley's athletic director declined Luther's request to extend the series.
- The 1970-71 Racers won 19 of 24 games and were ranked in the Associated Press poll for four consecutive weeks, twice getting as high as No. 17. Following a 73-71 home win over No. 7 Western Kentucky, Murray State first cracked the AP Top-20 at #19 on Jan. 23, and with a 17-2 record on Feb. 17, the Racers made their way to #17.

Murray State then encountered a late-season swoon, losing three of its last five games and relinquishing first place in the OVC to Western Kentucky, which placed third in the 1971 NCAA Tournament.

Soon after his second losing season (12-13 in 1973-74) and a fifth place league finish, Luther was told by president Dr. Constantine Curris to choose between being Murray's head coach or its athletic director. He opted for the administrative position, and Curris tapped Fred Overton, Luther's top assistant, to replace him on the bench.

"The AD duties had expanded," Luther said, "and I thought Fred would do a nice job as Murray's head coach. But things didn't work out real good for either of us."

Following a third losing season in four with Overton as coach, Curris replaced him in 1978 with Ron Greene of Mississippi State, the Southeastern Conference coach-of-the-year. Curris also changed athletic directors in '78, moving Murray State baseball coach Johnny Reagan into the position.

Luther, who had served eight years as AD, taught one more year in Murray's physical education department before first becoming the athletic director and then the men's basketball coach at Longwood (Va.) College, whose athletics program was transitioning from NCAA Division III to NCAA Division II.

Luther was born in Valdosta, Ga., grew up in Milwaukee, Wis., and graduated from Bay View High School in 1946 as a three-sport letterman (football, basketball and track). Drafted into the U.S. military, he served 20 months in the 82nd Airborne, volunteered for the paratroopers, and was assigned to Fort Benning, Ga., where he trained and started on the base's national service championship basketball team.

After his discharge from the Army, he enrolled at Valparaiso College, played basketball, got married just before his senior year and earned his degree in 1951. He then accepted a graduate assistantship at the University of Illinois, aspiring to be a coach and teacher.

"A couple of my high school coaches were very positive influences in my life," he said. "I thought maybe I could be like them and help young people."

Good fortune awaited Luther upon his arrival at Illinois. "The freshman basketball coach quit for a head coaching position at a Chicago high school and they were short a person," he said. "I was able to get affiliated with the program as coach of the freshman team."

No pay was involved, but at the end of the year athletic director Doug Mills called him into his office and gave him an envelope. There was a $500 check in it. "Mr. Mills said I'd done a good job and the basketball staff wanted to show its appreciation," Luther said.

The monetary reward was much needed by the Luthers, who were barely getting by financially, residing in an attic apartment. Also forthcoming was an offer from head coach Harry Combes, whose Illini had won two straight Big Ten championships, for Luther to be a "full time" assistant. He proved an effective recruiter, and when the head coaching position at DePauw College in Greencastle, Ind., came open in 1954, he applied.

"I knew I was a long shot candidate and had to figure out a way to get an interview," Luther said. "I called DePauw's athletic director and told him I was coming to Indianapolis to speak at an alumni meeting. I asked if I could stop by for an interview. He said I could. I spent my last dime for a new suit. The interview went good, and some members of the board were called to come meet me. The AD said I was their man."

DePauw was a private school, offering no athletic scholarships and competing in the NCAA Division II Indiana Collegiate Conference (other members were Ball State, Butler, Evansville, Indiana State, St. Joseph's and Valparaiso). Luther coached the Tigers for four years, compiling records of 8-11-1, 13-8, 12-9 and 12-12.

The Tigers won the conference championship in 1957, participating in the first NCAA College Division postseason tournament and losing 77-62 to eventual runner-up Kentucky Wesleyan. Luther was recognized as the conference Coach-of-the-Year.

"I'm proud of what we accomplished at DePauw," Luther said. "There were two Naismith Hall of Fame coaches in the league (Tony Hinkle of Butler and Arad McCutcheon of Evansville), and the league, overall, was very competitive."

How did DePauw's home game against Wabash in Luther's inaugural season end in a 67-67 tie? Actually it didn't.

According to the scorebook signed by the officials, DePauw beat Wabash, 67-66. But the Wabash coach complained at the half and after the game that his team hadn't been credited with a made free throw. "He said we cheated them," Luther said. "My manager told me he thought Wabash had made another free throw in the first half. The next day my boss called to see if Wabash would agree to a five minute overtime when we played them at their place, but the coach said 'no.' Under the circumstances, I didn't want us to count the game as a win, so we listed it as a tie."

And how did Luther wind up at Murray State in the summer of 1958?

"During the '57-58 season, (Murray State athletic director) Roy Stewart started looking for a new coach," Luther said. "Coach Stewart, Dr. Ralph Woods (Murray president) and M.O. Wrather (Dr. Woods' special assistant) drove to Evansville to see us play Evansville. We were ahead at halftime and they headed back to Murray. We lost the game, but I guess they liked what they saw."

Once the season ended, Stewart and Woods had Luther come to Murray for an official interview. "Dr. Woods was ready to hire me when I got there," Luther said. "There was no negotiation of a contract. I was going to get paid $4,500. My wife and our kids could live in Swan dorm and I would watch over the athletes, most of whom were football players."

Luther learned early on that the Racers' overall talent level didn't match up to what most of their league rivals had. He made recruiting a priority, going after the best players in west Kentucky, and then widening the net to include high school players from nearby states as well as transfers from two- and four-year institutions.

He scheduled aggressively and for his first season lined up two games against Mississippi and Mississippi State and single games against Florida State and New Mexico State. It was not a year to highlight on a resume, as a 10-15 record and a last place finish in the OVC would indicate. But Murray almost pulled off one of the nation's most noteworthy upsets, losing at home in December to eventual SEC champion Mississippi State, 63-62.

Despite facing Baylor, Louisville, Memphis State and Miami (Fla.), things picked up the next season, record-wise, when Gene Herndon of Almo, Ky., joined transfers Larry Bale (Campbellsville), Jarrell Graham (DePauw) and Ron Greene (Bradley) as new faces in the starting lineup. The Racers were 12-11 overall and 7-4 in the league, tied with Tennessee Tech for third place.

Racer basketball began to sizzle soon after Luther was allowed to recruit African-Americans. His first signee, Tom Officer, a combo guard/forward from Washington, Mo., near St. Louis, excelled on Murray's freshman team in '61-62. However, Officer never suited up for the varsity, withdrawing from school early in the fall semester of 1962 because of some racial issues that had occurred on campus.

Luther brought in another black player in the fall of '62, Stewart Johnson, a coveted 6-9 forward from Clairton, Pa. Johnson, who was to be Officer's roommate, led Murray's freshman squad in scoring and established himself as one of the OVC's top performers as a three-year starter for the Racers.

By Johnson's senior year, there were two more African-Americans on the Racer varsity squad, Don Duncan, from Centralia, Ill., Junior College, and Milt Pitts, from Xavier. However, the new source of talent prompted some schools from the South to refrain from scheduling Murray State. Securing lodging for his Racers and finding places to eat team meals were also a challenge.

Besides being given the OK to recruit African-Americans, Luther said another key component to his

Murray State success was the approval by Stewart for him to secure additional funding for recruiting. He sold ads for game programs twice brought the Harlem Globetrotters to Murray for games against the Washington Generals.

One year Luther arranged for the St. Louis Hawks and Cincinnati Royals to play an NBA exhibition game in Racer Arena, and an overflow crowd attended, resulting in a $9,000 windfall for Racer basketball.

Luther's only full-time assistant in his first five years at Murray State was Alexander, who had been Murray's head coach for four years. In 1963, money was budgeted for Luther to hire a hand-picked assistant, and former Racer All-American Bennie Purcell of Mt. Vernon, Ill., was his choice.

"Bennie was coaching high school basketball in Illinois and coming to our games when he could," Luther said. "We had become friends, and I wanted him on my staff. He was an excellent judge of talent. He was passionate about Murray State. We worked well together, because we had respect for each other."

Purcell assisted Luther through the 1969-70 season, after which he took over the head coaching duties of Murray State's men's tennis program. Luther then hired Overton, a Hopkinsville, Ky., native who was an assistant at Pepperdine College and a former player and coach at Austin Peay, an OVC nemesis of the Racers.

Just how did recruiting, the lifeblood of college basketball, evolve for Luther at Murray?

"We needed to recruit players we could win with," he said, "and my thought process was to get them wherever we could. I mailed letters to high school coaches all over Kentucky and the states I was targeting, asking them to list by specific categories the top prospects they knew.

"I only got a seven or eight percent return on my first-year mailings, but I hit on a gimmick that got the return up to around 68 percent after that. The dad of a former player of mine at DePauw was a big shot in advertising in New York, and he told me, 'Free is the magic word. You've got to give the coaches something free.'

"I started promising them a monograph about various aspects of basketball if they'd complete and mail back the recruiting questionnaire I had sent them. That's how I got the names of Jim Jennings, Stewart Johnson, John Namciu, Herb McPherson, Dick Cunningham, Claude Virden, and many of our other top players."

And what did the coaches get? They received written insights from Luther on such topics as how to break the press or how to play a match-up zone.

Luther said former *Paducah Sun-Democrat* sports editor Ed Kellow, who was coaching high school basketball in Chicago, Ill., helped get Chicago-area kids interested in Murray State.

Center Ken Peterson and forwards Mike O'Riordan and Frank Smikoski were already enrolled at MSU when Luther came on board. Guard Al Varnas of Chicago made his Racer debut in 1961 and was a double figure scorer in each of his three varsity seasons, earning All-OVC honors in '62-63.

For most of Luther's tenure, the NCAA did not wield the compliance power it now has, and recruiting rules were somewhat lax and hard to enforce. There was no national signing day or national letter of intent – only conference letters of intent. Players were sometimes still being pursued after they had attended their first college classes. Such was the case with Johnson, who was still being pursued by two colleges soon after he had enrolled at Murray State.

Luther perfected a jazzed-up halftime routine in which recruits were escorted to the Racer Arena court and introduced by the public address announcer, who extolled their feats. Luther also utilized other means to add to the Racer stable.

In 1965, a year after enticing Leonard Poole, an electrifying point guard from Hardinsburg, Ky., to enroll at Murray State, Luther went all out to get Butch Beard, a high school teammate of Poole's. He showcased Beard by holding a "Butch Beard Day" in downtown Murray and staged a parade for him from downtown to campus when he came for his recruiting visit.

Luther thought Beard was a lock for the Racers, but he wound up attending the University of Louisville, where he became an All-American and an eventual NBA first-round draft pick.

The summer of '65 had tragic results for Poole, who drowned in late July while trying to save a younger brother who was swimming in the Rough River Reservoir near Hardinsburg. His brother made it to shore safely.

Poole and Cunningham, a center from Canton, Ohio, were the stars of Murray's 1964-65 freshman team that won 12 of 15 games, with the 5-10 Poole being the leading scorer and the 6-10 Cunningham, an eventual pro, setting the pace in rebounding. "Leonard was a special kid who would have been a terrific college player," said Luther, who spoke at Poole's funeral. "He had great quickness and ball handling skills. He could dunk and could really shoot."

A life-changing experience for Luther came in 1971 after he was announced as the University of Minnesota head coach at a Saturday press conference in Minneapolis and then called Murray State president Dr. Harry Sparks the next day asking if could return to Murray as coach of the Racers.

According to Luther, Dr. Sparks said, "Sure, get back down here." And he did. "But things were never the same after that," Luther said. "My whole life turned upside down. I still haven't gotten over the disappointment of the Minnesota experience.

"I thought Minnesota was going to be a dream job. But it didn't take long to find out that coaching there was not the right environment for me."

Luther's pursuit of the Minnesota coaching vacancy came after Murray's 19-5 season of 1970-71. The hiring process was unconventional and the eventual outcome was surreal.

Though no contract was signed prior to the press conference announcing his hiring, Luther said he had agreed to a salary of $20,000, which would make him the second highest paid coach in the Big Ten conference, behind Ohio State's Fred Taylor.

In the late 1960s, Minnesota struggled to produce a consistent winner in basketball, and in 1971 first-year coach George Hanson got the ax after his 11-13 Gophers placed fifth in the Big Ten. Luther, Dick Harter of Penn and Bill Musselman of NCAA Division II Ashland (Ohio) College, emerged as the leading candidates to succeed him. They were brought to Minneapolis under assumed names and stayed at a hotel near the airport, where they would be interviewed by a committee.

"The interviews began at 7 a.m. on a Wednesday morning and each lasted an hour. Harter went first and Musselman went second," Luther said, "All three of us waited around the hotel after our interviews, and later that day they offered me the job. I was ecstatic."

Luther said Harter was furious when he got the news and reportedly responded with unflattering comments. Musselman tempered his remarks and once Luther came back to Murray, he was named Minnesota's coach.

While in Minneapolis, Luther was instructed to remain in the airport hotel until the day of the press conference. By Thursday, he began to get bad vibes about what he might be undertaking. He was told he must keep a particular assistant coach from Hanson's staff, and he learned the Minnesota athletic director was about to be fired.

"I was able to speak with the other full-time assistant coach and a trainer for basketball," he said. "I wasn't comfortable with some things I heard.

'I knew I must get out of the hotel, and on Friday an assistant athletic director took me to the school. I saw where the black players were being housed and it was awful."

The deal-breaker came Sunday at a brunch attended by a recruit from a Texas junior college and a prominent booster. "I could never make eye contact with the kid," Luther said. "The booster told me he would help get me money to use for any needs of the players."

Upon hearing that, Luther excused himself from the table they were sitting at, saying he had a headache and needed to take something for it. "I left the room for a few minutes, found a pay phone and made a call to Dr. Sparks," he said.

The eight years Luther served as Murray State athletic director after Stewart's retirement in 1970 proved helpful in his return to college athletics at Longwood, once an all-girls school, in 1979. But the coaching itch never left him and in 1981 he became the Lancers' men's coach, a position he held for nine years.

Luther resigned at Longwood in April of 1990 and headed to Egypt to coach the Egyptian National Team in the FIBA World Championship. But he returned to the United States in August because of a family health issue.

In December, University of Tennessee-Martin athletic director Don McLeary had to replace coach Tom Hancock, and contacted Luther to gauge his interest. Luther's wife endorsed the idea of him coaching once again, and seven games into the 1990-91 season, he was introduced as Martin's interim coach.

McLeary removed the interim title in April of '91, and Luther coached at Martin for eight full seasons, before "retiring" in 1999. The retirement was short lived as he acquiesced to a request from Bethel (Tenn.) College president that he be the school's coach for the 1999-2000 season.

While at Longwood, Luther compiled a 136-105 record. He was the Mason-Dixon Conference and Kodak Division II South District coach-of-the-year in 1988. The Flames won 19 games that season and were league co-champions. He had one 20 win season (20-7 in 1988-89) and a two-time All American in forward Jerome Kersey, who finished second to Michael Jordan in the 1987 NBA slam dunk contest and averaged 19.2 points per game for the Portland Trail Blazers in the 1987-88 season.

Wins were not the norm for Luther at UT Martin or Bethel, where he had records of 72-163 and 6-27. Still there were some of significance, and his time at both schools did nothing to tarnish his resume.

Luther managed only one victory against Murray State, 74-73, on Feb. 6, 1999 at Martin. It was a memorable victory, coming in the last game he coached against Murray State. His final game at Bethel, a 78-74 victory against Indiana Southeast in the Kentucky Intercollegiate Athletic Conference Division II Tournament, was career win number 500. For anyone counting, that win gave Luther a 500-489-1 career record. It should be mentioned that he is a member of the Ohio Valley Conference and Murray State Hall of Fame.

Luther and his wife have resided in Martin since August of 2006, and he remains connected to UT Martin basketball, joining Chris Brinkley on the radio broadcasts of Skyhawk men's and women's games when Tom Britt is not available to do the color. Each October he spends several days in Santa Barbara, Calif., helping coach John Moore of Westmont College install his team's offense in preseason workouts. And each year he attends at least one Murray State Racer home game.

"I think he'd still be coaching if someone would offer him a job," says Purcell, not entirely in jest.

JESSE WILLIAMS

by Kim Trevathan

Jesse Williams, from Chicago, was the epitome of class on the court and off. Twice all-OVC (74-75, 75-76) Williams, a 6-7 forward, had the purest jump shot that Coach Fred Overton had ever seen. "Jesse was in his own zone when he played," said Overton. "He was a competitor and he loved to score."

And score he did. In his junior year, Williams averaged 20.8 points per game, and he improved to 21.1 his senior year. He is eleventh on the all-time Racer scoring list. Overton said he would have averaged 30 points per game if he'd played during the three-pointer era.

Williams was recruited by Overton, who saw him playing in a Christmas tournament in Chicago. He played at Hales Franciscan School in the tough Chicago Catholic League, averaging 28 points a game his senior year. He made all-city, all-state, and prep all-American. At the Christmas tournament Overton forged a relationship with the budding star, and after he visited Murray State and met head coach Cal Luther, he signed on, choosing the Racers over, among others, Louisville, who "really made a run at him," said Overton, at a time when the Cardinals were highly ranked.

Williams was a natural shooter with a "perfect" shot, said Overton. "He had good rotation, a good arc, and he squared up nicely to shoot the ball."

Luther, who coached Williams his freshman and sophomore years, said he "developed and matured" as a player while at Murray State. He learned how to handle pressure defenses and improved as a ball handler, said Luther. "He became a great perimeter shooter who could handle the ball great."

Jesse Williams

Mel Purcell, son of Coach Bennie Purcell, recalls that Williams used to run down the court with his thumbs up after making a shot.

As a freshman Williams started most of the year and averaged 7.2 points per game. The team went 17-8 and tied for second in the OVC, and Williams was honored as Freshman of the Year in the conference. Gaining 18 pounds in the off season, he improved to 10.7 points per game his sophomore year, before breaking out as the star of the team during his junior and senior years.

He took on a leadership role his junior year after the loss of four starters: Marcelous Starks, Steve Barrett, Mike Coleman, and Darnell Adell. The Racers also had a new head coach that year in Fred Overton, who took the helm as Luther concentrated on his duties as athletic director. Though the Racers had a down year, Williams responded to the leadership challenge, ending the year third in the OVC in scoring, and among the leaders in field goal percentage (55.8%), rebounding, and free throw shooting.

He had his best year as a senior after "working like a Trojan to improve his game over the summer," according to Overton.

Williams is remembered as much for his character as for his talents as a player. Teammate Marcelous Starks, also from Chicago, helped talk Williams into coming to Murray State. He remembers Williams as a "great guy."

Luther recalls his "studious personality," that he was very analytical and well-spoken. "I really thought a lot of Jesse," said Luther. "He was a really good kid who had his feet on the ground. He wanted to be able to do something for himself when he got through with basketball."

Overton said that before each game, Williams would read from the New Testament. "He was a fine kid, a really fine kid," said Overton. "He would come by the office and we'd talk. He was everything we wanted and we were fortunate to get him."

After graduating from Murray State with a degree in business, Williams got a seat on the Chicago Board of Trade.

THE 1980S

by Will Aubrey

1979-1980 • 23-8

• OVC Regular Season Champion

After suffering through a dispiriting 4-22 campaign in his first season as head coach of the Racers, Ron Greene knew better days lay ahead. He had lain the groundwork for success and he was confident Murray State was ready to contend for an OVC championship.

"When you measure the strengths of this team you have to start with our quickness," he said before the season began. "We may lack impressive overall size. But I think it's more important to see how big we play than to measure how big we are."

The Racers returned just two of their top five scorers from the previous year, all-conference forward Kenney Hammonds and center Allen Mann. But Greene brought in a talented group of recruits who were expected to make an immediate impact.

Gary Hooker transferred in from Mississippi State where he was one of the Bulldogs' top-15 all-time leading scorers. Hooker had been selected in the 1979 NBA draft.

Freshmen Lamont Sleets and Glen Green were also expected to play immediately. Sleets averaged 32 points and 11 rebounds as a high school senior at Eminence High School and Green averaged a double-double as a high school senior. Green was also the leading scorer for the winning team in the Kentucky high school all-star game.

The home opener against Roosevelt College produced an easy 106-74 victory. Hooker led the way with 31 points and 18 rebounds.

But Greene knew tougher games lay ahead. And he was right, as Pan American beat the Racers 67-65 in the opening game of the McDonald's Classic in Wichita, Kan. With less than 20 seconds left the game was tied and Murray State was in the four-to-score when Pan American's Billy Bailey stole the ball and went the length of the floor for a layup to win the game.

Hooker led the way again with 25 points and 14 rebounds while Sleets and junior college transfer Jerry Smith each had 14 points.

The Racers were much sharper in the consolation game as they crushed San Francisco State 74-43. Hammonds, who had struggled through the first two games, poured in 14 points and grabbed 11 rebounds.

"Basically, we're pretty pleased," Greene said. "It was good to come back after a heartbreaking loss the night before. Our players came on strong and did a nice job.

"It's good to see Kenney Hammonds bounce back to his old form. The thing that pleased me most was his 11 rebounds."

Murray State was 2-1 as they returned home to play Arkansas State. ASU had already beaten Auburn and they had lost a nail-biter at Memphis State.

"They'll be the best team we've played to date," Greene warned.

But they were no match for the Racers as MSU rolled to an easy 68-46 victory.

Victories over Georgia Southern and Towson State at Racer Arena pushed Murray State's record to 5-1. But two heartbreaking losses followed – a 72-71 defeat at Memphis State and a 65-63 loss at Texas.

After splitting games with Missouri-St. Louis and Akron, the Racers were 6-4 heading into OVC play.

Before opening conference play at Tennessee Tech Greene declared, "It starts for real Monday. Tech is playing well right now and playing with a lot of emotion."

But Murray State eked out a 72-71 victory before returning home to play Morehead.

"In the second half against Tech we played pretty good team basketball," Greene said. "We were glad to get that one."

Next up was a home date with the high scoring Eagles. Morehead was coming off a 99-84 victory over Xavier. They were led by 6-6 forward Greg Coldiron. Coldiron scored 18 points against Xavier and was hitting a ridiculous 83.3 percent of his shots from the field.

"They gave a brilliant display of shooting against Xavier. They ran them back to Cincinnati," Greene cautioned fans before the game. "It's important for us to play good defense against their shooting."

Heading into the game, three Racers were battling injuries. Green was hampered by a hip pointer, reserve center Michael Bates had a twisted knee, and backup guard Walt Davis had a sprained ankle.

It was, nonetheless, a lopsided affair as Murray State cruised 85-67, giving Greene his 200th career victory. The second half was signature Ron Greene basketball as MSU employed the four-to-score for the full 20 minutes with the spread attack producing 10 layups off backdoor cuts.

"We executed it about as well as we could have," Greene noted. "We played well and held our poise."

Hooker led the way with 28 points and 17 rebounds. But after the game it was learned that he had a partially detached retina due to a blow he had taken to the eye.

The Racers kept rolling anyway with victories over Eastern Kentucky and Samford. They lost Hammonds to a stress fracture in his foot following the EKU game which would cause him to miss the rest of the season. But they were unbeaten in conference play when they headed to Bowling Green on January 17 to play Western Kentucky. The Hilltoppers were also unbeaten and tied with MSU for the conference lead.

Unfortunately, Hooker was still unavailable and Greene announced his intent to start Davis in Hooker's place.

"Hopefully someone will step up," he said before the game. "Not too many teams around the country have Hookers. It's time to start talking All-American. We're obviously not going to slip up on Western but I think we'll be ready."

He was wrong. The Hilltoppers rolled to a lopsided 68-48 victory to take sole possession of first place.

But the Racers bounced back by winning at Middle Tennessee 68-62, again without Hooker. Four players scored in double figures and Mann just missed a double-double with 10 points and nine rebounds.

"The guys did a great job," Greene said after the game. "They really hustled. It was like the Spartans holding off the Carthaginians. It was about as pleasing a win as we've had."

Hooker was back for the next game, as MSU made the trip to Clarksville to face Austin Peay.

The All-American candidate was clearly rusty though as he scored just six points. And things looked bleak late in the first half with the Govs in front 32-23. But the Racers cut the lead to four by intermission. And they owned the second half as they posted a convincing 62-51 victory.

Hooker bounced back in the next game though as he poured in 20 points and grabbed 10 rebounds in a 75-68 victory at Georgia Southern.

Akron was up next. The Zips had beaten Murray three weeks earlier and the Racers had payback on their minds as they crushed the visitors 100-74, stealing the ball 15 times in the process.

"We just felt like we owed them something," Sleets said. "We were sluggish in the first game. Tonight we played hard and ran them into the ground. We overplayed them on defense. We were trying to mess with their heads."

Sleets led the way with 26 points, Mann had 17

1979-80 men't basketball team.

points and 11 rebounds and the Racers set a team record with 33 assists.

Murray State was riding high with four straight wins and they would win four more to run the streak to eight before playing Western at Racer Arena on February 16. MSU came into the game with a 9-1 mark in conference play while Western was 8-2. With just one game left, a win by the Racers would have clinched the title.

The game was played before an overflow crowd despite the fact that it was televised live on WPSD-TV out of Paducah.

1980 NIT

It looked like Murray State had it won but they missed 4-of-8 free throws down the stretch including their final two as the Hilltoppers won again 56-55.

"You have to shoot the one plus ones down the line," Greene said. "We've been in pressure situations and made them. Hopefully next time we will."

The Racers beat New Orleans and Peay to close out the regular season, sharing the conference championship with Western. Then they edged Morehead 77-74 in the first round of the OVC tournament to advance to the final for a rematch with the Hilltoppers in Diddle Arena.

Unfortunately, Western won again, 54-51, as Sleets hit just 5-of-17 shots.

"I'm not sure the crowd affected either team," Greene said. "But it sure was a factor. We played as well as we could in the first half. When we got bumped around it was hard for us. We just did not execute well in the second half."

Hooker was named OVC Player of the Year just ahead of Sleets who was second in the voting. Hooker, Sleets, and Green received all-conference honors.

The Racers were invited to play in the NIT where they would face Jacksonville in the first round.

"It is a great reward for our players to have an opportunity in postseason play," Greene said. "We are very appreciative the NIT committee recognized us as a quality team. We are also happy to be going to Florida."

And he made sure his players had fun on the trip, allowing time for them to enjoy the ocean and the beach. But if the trip was something of a joy ride, the game was more like a visit to the dentist's office.

Both teams were very patient on offense in the first half as each hit just seven shots. And the Racers trailed 19-16 at the break. But they bounced back in the second half as they outrebounded the Dolphins 21-8.

MSU took its first lead at 40-39 with 4:38 left in the game. The margin reached seven points at 46-39 but Jacksonville rallied and the Racers hit five free throws down the stretch to seal the 53-49 victory. Green had 15 points and eight rebounds while Hooker and Smith had 11 and 10 points respectively.

"They tried to sag in the middle and give up the outside shot," Smith noted. "Glen penetrated their defense though."

Murray State stunned Alabama in the second round 70-62. And this was a Crimson Tide team that had beaten Kentucky by 14 points earlier in the year.

"I just told our guys to go out and play like it was shirts and skins and forget it was Alabama," Greene said.

The game could be used as a teaching aid for coaches as Greene was masterful in the way he modulated the tempo, pressing at times and using the four-to-score at other times.

"We wanted to press them occasionally to get the rhythm," he explained. "But I felt it would be difficult to run up and down and exchange shots with them."

Sleets led the way with 25 points while Hooker hit all nine of his shots from the field and scored 21 points.

"We felt all we had to do was play a good game and remember the fundamentals," Sleets said. "The four-corner helped a lot. It took the crowd out of the game and we were able to execute it. We don't have anybody to fear."

Hooker echoed that sentiment, saying, "A basketball player is a basketball player."

MSU moved on to play Illinois for a trip to New York and a spot in the semifinals. They came up just a little short, losing 65-63, but they earned some respect in the process.

"They're as good as any team in the Big Ten," Illinois center Derek Holcomb said.

And Greene was proud of his team's effort.

"I was very pleased and proud of the way we hung in there," he noted after the game. "If Illinois had come to Murray we might have had some fun. We'll be back."

Hooker finished the season as the fifth leading rebounder in the nation at 12.3 per game.

1980-1981 • 17-10

With Gary Hooker and Allen Mann gone, some people expected the Racers to take a step backward. But head coach Ron Greene wasn't one of those people.

"Everything that helped us win last year should be in abundance again this year," he said before the season began. "We have some fine new players and they should help us in our rebounding and our team quickness, an aspect of the game we stress."

Foremost among the newcomers were Tony Slaughter and Brian Stewart. Four starters from the previous year were back – Lamont Sleets, Glen Green, Kenney Hammonds, and Jerry Smith. Of course, Sleets and Green were only sophomores and Hammonds was coming off of a significant injury. So despite the experience on hand the Racers were still a young team.

And that was evident in a season opening 59-41 loss at Indiana. But the young MSU squad bounced back nicely with an 82-69 home opening win over Quincy. Hammonds hit 10-of-12 shots as he scored 24 points and grabbed 10 rebounds. Green had 18 points and 14 rebounds.

Still, Greene was less than pleased.

"Either we have an awful lot of work to have a sound defense or they can shoot the ball pretty well," he said after the game. "We must improve our man-to-man defense. We need to take a good look and see where our breakdowns are. There isn't much time to work on our weaknesses."

The rest of the pre-conference campaign was an up and down affair. MSU beat Wisconsin-Parkside and Northeast Louisiana before losing three straight to Arkansas State, Gonzaga, and Maine.

A 69-60 victory over Southeastern Louisiana at Racer Arena snapped the losing streak. But that was followed by a loss at Towson State.

The hot and cold pattern continued as OVC play began with a win over Morehead and a loss to Eastern Kentucky.

With Western Kentucky coming to town Murray State was just 5-6 overall and 1-1 in the OVC. The Hilltoppers were 8-4 and 2-0 with wins over St. Louis and Evansville.

WKU's head coach Clem Haskins made it clear that he feared the Racers' quickness.

"If we get off to a good start we are going to slow it up and spread it out," he said. "I know they are ready to go after us and I know we cannot run with Murray State."

As it happened, neither team seemed interested in running up and down the floor. Both played tight zone defenses that slowed the game down but Murray led 22-19 at the half.

The second half saw MSU push the lead out to seven points at 40-33 but Western fought their way back and tied the game at 55-all to force overtime.

With the game tied 57-57 and just six seconds left in overtime Western's Mike Reese missed a 20-footer. Murray State's Brian Stewart grabbed the rebound and threw the ball to Sleets as he darted into the backcourt. Reese fouled Sleets to prevent an easy basket with one second left.

Western called two timeouts to try to ice the sophomore. But Sleets calmly made both free throws to seal the 59-57 victory.

Green and Sleets each had 14 points while Hammonds had 12.

"Coach Greene wanted me to have the ball toward the end," Sleets said. "I have the experience but there was a lot of pressure on me."

The Racers kept rolling with a 74-70 victory over Middle Tennessee and a thrilling 70-69 overtime win against Austin Peay.

The game against the Govs was close throughout but Peay led 54-48 when Sleets hit an underhanded shot from beyond the baseline while being knocked out of bounds.

Peay still led 62-60 with one second left. Murray called timeout and Green asked coach Greene if they could run a play that he and Hammonds had been practicing.

Green stood near midcourt and threw an alley-oop as Hammonds cut to the basket, grabbed the ball in mid-air and stuffed it to tie the game and send it into overtime.

"Our first option was to look for Kenney on the alley-oop," Green said. "He goes up about as high as I have seen anyone. I have thrown him a couple before and he always puts it through."

"Coach Greene knows we practice it a lot," Hammonds said. "So he said to go for it."

The Racers were still down by one late in the overtime period. But Stewart hit an 18 footer to win it as the clock ran out.

"Lamont just told me to take charge," Stewart said. "I just felt it was what I had to do."

The winning streak reached four games with a victory over Tennessee Tech. Then the Racers lost to Akron before winning their next five games.

That streak ended with back-to-back losses to Middle Tennessee and Western Kentucky. But MSU closed out the regular season by beating Austin Peay and Akron and then they beat Middle in the OVC tournament to set up a rematch with Western in the final.

The Racers came up just a little short, losing 71-67. But the story of the game was the officiating.

Fans always complain about officials and so do coaches. You can generally take that with a grain of salt. But when a sportswriter goes so far as to write a special column about the officials, that's worth noting.

The Ledger and Times' David Hibbets had this to say about the officiating in the OVC final, "In a game in which so much rested on every call it was the whistle that resulted in two technicals on Greene and a totally erroneous charging call on forward Tony Slaughter as WKU center Craig McCormick was coming over his back while both were going up in the air.

"Supposedly Slaughter was guilty of bumping back into McCormick when the WKU center did not even have position.

"The officiating crew at the OVC championship game became so glaring that Austin Peay assistant coach Walter Ayers began complaining directly to the trio from his seat at the press table.

"Now it is not normally considered to be a proper or fair policy to place the blame on the officials for a loss, especially in so critical a game. But Saturday night's fiasco resembled a steal."

Stewart was named to the all-freshman team while Sleets and Hammonds were all-conference selections.

1981-1982 • 20-8

• OVC Regular Season Champion

In his second and third years at Murray State head coach Ron Greene had led the Racers to their most successful back-to-back seasons in nearly a decade. And with eight players back everyone expected the 1981-82 season to be more of the same.

Six of the returning players – Lamont Sleets, Glen Green, Brian Stewart, Kenney Hammonds, Walter Davis, and Tony Slaughter – had starting experience. Transfers Ricky Hood and Mike McDuffen were starters prior to enrolling at MSU.

"We're very enthusiastic about our chances for a strong showing," head coach Ron Greene said before the season. "I'm hopeful we can improve on the 17 wins we had last year. We have the depth and experience a team needs for success. We look stronger on paper."

In fact, Murray State appeared to loaded, on paper. On the court, they looked overconfident and disinterested in their home opener as they edged Missouri-Kansas City 66-61.

"Our quick-shooting was off, we had poor defense at times, and they played their own game and controlled the ball," Greene said. "The important thing though was that we found a way to win. I'm glad this one is over. I'd like to forget it as soon as possible."

The Racers looked better in an 84-67 victory over West Virginia Tech. But they dropped a 71-65 decision at Southern Illinois. And more importantly, they lost Sleets to a broken ankle.

Things got worse with a 50-48 home loss to Arkansas College in the next game as MSU missed the front end of seven 1-and-1 opportunities.

"When you play and people foul you, you have to make them pay the price for fouling," Greene said.

The media was less than kind.

The Ledger and Times' Jim Rector noted, "(Greene) denied the team was falling apart due to the lack of Sleets in the lineup and he said the Racers weren't looking ahead to Notre Dame."

Hammonds grumbled, "He is giving everybody a shot. I'm not sure why the vets don't start out on top. I'm going to stay on top of things, that's for sure. And I try not to be a bad example, even when I'm sitting on the bench."

Murray State was 2-2 having just lost to an NAIA school, its best player had a broken ankle, players were grumbling about playing time, and a trip to South Bend to play the powerful Fighting Irish was up next. To say things looked bleak would be an understatement.

And then, suddenly, things changed.

Greene arranged for MSU's offensive end to be in front of the Racers' bench in the second half against Notre Dame. Never mind that this meant the Notre Dame student section was behind the basket they were shooting at. And the same players who couldn't make free throws against Arkansas College were rock solid at the line as Murray State upset the Irish 56-54.

"We talked about it before the game," Greene said. "I elected to have the team in front of me where I could talk to them."

Green led the way for MSU with 15 points.

Victories over conference foes Akron and Youngstown State followed in quick succession before the Racers hit the road again to face Bradley. They came away with a 58-56 victory as Davis hit two free throws with 23 seconds left to win the game.

"It was a great win for us," Greene said. "It's hard to compare it with Notre Dame though. Name-wise, nationally, the win over Notre Dame was more impressive. But talent-wise Bradley was superior."

The winning streak reached six games with victories over Ferris State and Eastern Illinois. But the Racers were crushed 77-58 at Evansville and 71-54 at Western Kentucky.

In the loss to the Hilltoppers, MSU hit just 25 percent of its shots in the first half and the usually dependable Green went 2-for-12 from the field. After the game Greene promised the Racers would bounce back.

And that's exactly what they did, drubbing Austin Peay 70-49 the next time out.

Hammonds had only started four games all year and had seen his playing time dwindle as the season progressed. But he was back in the lineup against Peay and he responded with 17 points as the crowd roared in appreciation every time he left the floor.

"Everything happens for those who wait," Hammonds said when asked about his playing time. "I had to wait as a freshman and now I've had to wait as a senior. I love the people here. They've been so good to me."

Hood and Green each had 13 points and Hood led all rebounders with eight.

Racers over Notre Dame, 1981.

And suddenly the Racers were rolling again as they won five straight heading into a rematch with Western.

"I'm proud of the way our guys rose to the occasion," Greene said. "They're certainly playing crowd pleasing basketball, and, I might add, coach pleasing."

Even though Western had won handily in Bowling Green the Hilltoppers' head coach, Clem Haskins, said he expected a close game.

"Murray has an excellent, well drilled team," he noted.

"We caught them just right when they were here. I'm sure they'll be out to even the score with us."

Early on, it looked like Haskins had overestimated the Racers as Western led by 11 points twice in the first seven minutes. They still led by eight at halftime. But Murray State refused to give up.

"There was no way they were going to beat us at home," Hammonds said. "That's like letting a stranger come into your house and beat you up. You're not about to let that happen. That's why I kept telling 'Ice' (Glen Green) to keep his head up. It's not over till the last shot."

In this case, Hammonds was right. His tip-in with 46 seconds left gave the Racers their first lead. And with two seconds left Hood hit two free throws to put it away.

"That's how we spell relief – 63-60," Davis said.

The victory gave MSU sole possession of first place in the OVC. But they won just three of their next five games. Especially troubling was a 70-53 blowout loss at home to Middle Tennessee as the Racers shot just 27.6 percent in the second half.

"They outplayed us in every way," Greene said. "We ran into a veteran ball club with a few seniors who decided they didn't want to hang it up yet."

MTSU's Jerry Beck tormented the Racers with 20 points and 11 rebounds.

Murray State bounced back again by beating Tennessee Tech 60-58 in their final home game to give Greene his 250th victory and clinch a spot in the conference tournament. Green missed a 10-footer with nine seconds left but grabbed the rebound and put it in for the winning basket. The junior led all scorers with 20 points. Hammonds had 16 and Hood had 10 points to go with his 10 rebounds.

After the game Greene complained that Hood wasn't taking enough shots.

"I had to holler at Hood tonight to shoot more," he said. "My coaches were always hollering at me not to shoot. Whenever I came in range I let loose.

"The way we've been playing lately I was just tickled to death to get out of here with a victory. That secures one of our goals for the season, reaching the OVC tournament."

The Racers won their final two regular season games on the road to clinch a share of the conference championship.

Murray State ran into Middle Tennessee again in the OVC tournament and the Racers again struggled to find the basket. They made just 26 percent of their shots in the first half and trailed by as many as 13 points. In the second half they shot just 36.7 percent from the field while Middle hit 70.6 percent of their shots. But somehow the Racers fought their way back into it only to lose 56-54 in overtime.

Beck, who was named OVC Player of the Year, again led Middle with 19 points. Hood and Green both had 16 for MSU and were both named to the all-conference team.

"I felt good when we went into overtime," Greene said. "But they found a way to win and we didn't."

The Racers went on to play Nevada-Las Vegas in the NIT, losing 87-61.

1982-1983 • 21-8

• *OVC Regular Season Champion*

With 20 victories in two of the last three seasons and two conference championships head coach Ron Greene had established Murray State as one of the top programs in the OVC. And with five of their top six scorers back for the 82-83 season everyone expected the Racers to win the title again.

So no one expected Murray State have any difficulty with West Virginia Tech in their home opener. Then again, expectations are like rocks in your path, waiting to trip you up.

The Racers certainly tripped over West Virginia Tech as they hit just 1-of-12 three point attempts in losing to the Golden Bears, 84-75. Ricky Hood led MSU with 20 points as he hit 10-of-13 shots but it wasn't enough.

"Tonight's loss was a very, very bitter pill to swallow. I think our guys read too many press clippings and they're not able to handle it," Greene said after the game. "I thought we should be a better team than what we showed tonight because of our experience. But we're a finesse team. We're not going to blow people away."

Greene's players must have taken that as a challenge because two nights later they blew away Bradley, the defending Missouri Valley Conference and NIT champion, 90-67.

The Braves came into the game with two guards, Willie Scott and Barney Mines, who had combined for

1982-83 Racers

45 points in their 90-82 victory over Loyola (Chicago). Greene frustrated them by switching between a 1-3-1 and 2-3 zone, limiting them to a combined 14 points.

"I think that's the first game I ever coached that my team didn't play man-to-man a minute," he said after the game. "But playing zone helped us on the boards and it took away their penetration."

Glen Green led the Racers with 31 points and a career high 14 rebounds. Hood and Lamont Sleets each had 19 points.

Murray State won its next three games, the first two blowouts over Southern Illinois and McNeese State, before heading to Eastern Kentucky to open conference play.

It was Green's birthday and he celebrated by scoring 27 points to lead MSU to an 86-63 win over the Colonels. Sleets and Hood had 21 and 15 respectively.

"We just wanted to come up here and make a good showing," he noted. "To come up here to Death Valley and win both games would show that we are the elite of the conference."

And that's exactly what the Racers did as they completed the Death Valley sweep with a 96-89 victory over Morehead.

Next came a trip to Birmingham, Ala. for the UAB Classic. The opening game against Fordham was no contest as MSU rolled to a 93-63 victory. Brian Stewart hit 9-of-12 shots and along with Sleets scored 19 points to lead the way.

Hood, who had 13 points and five rebounds, was disappointed in his performance and blamed it on an off night. Hood grew up in Montgomery, Ala. and had been recruited by UAB so he was anxious to play the Blazers in the championship game.

"I'm looking forward to a better game against UAB," he declared. "I wanted to play UAB because it will be in front of a lot of my hometown friends and relatives. When I go home I'd like to be able to brag a little bit about beating them. We all want to win this tournament and we think we can play with anybody."

Hood proved as much the next evening as he scored 29 points, many of which came on thunderous dunks, to lead the Racers to an 81-75 victory. Green had 23 points and was named MVP of the tournament. Hood, Green, and Sleets all made the all-tournament team.

"I think the real Racers stood up tonight," Greene said amid cheers from his players. "And stood over the rim a few times too."

Murray State proceeded to run its conference record to 4-0 by beating Youngstown State 92-83 and Akron 90-79 despite losing Vada Martin who was sidelined due to academic problems. Martin, a starter at forward, had averaged 6.9 points and 4.6 rebounds.

Sammy Curran took Martin's spot in the lineup and scored 11 points against Akron.

"I think I'm just as good as Vada," he said after beating the Zips. "I feel confident we can do it without him."

Hood led the Racers with 25 points while Sleets

had 23 and Green had 20. A hush fell over the sellout crowd in the second half when Sleets hit the floor hard and limped off the court. But it proved to be a minor ankle injury.

Akron's best player was Joe Jakubick, a lanky, awkward looking guard with an uncanny knack for getting his own shot. He spread his legs like a cheerleader on his jump shot and held the ball over his left shoulder. Two of his 33 points against the Racers came on a 360-degree jumper in the lane.

"He's the best we've played against," Curran said. "That 360 of his came off the blind side. I've never seen anything like it."

"He's wild," Hood agreed. "I've never seen anybody play like that. He's just a good player. I don't care how awkward he looks."

Victories over Eastern Illinois, Tennessee Tech, SIU-Edwardsville, and Middle Tennessee pushed the winning streak to 14 games before MSU dropped a 75-65 decision at Southeastern Louisiana.

They got back on track with an 81-77 victory over Austin Peay that left them 15-2 overall and 7-0 in the OVC. The Govs led by as much as 12 points as they hit 10-of-21 three-point attempts. But the Racers rallied and took the lead for good with 1:45 to play.

"I told these guys to do things the easy way and not try to do things so flashy," Greene said. "I'm the one who's paid to think. I'd rather they didn't think too much. Basketball is a game of habit. We were very fortunate to get out of here with a win. But good teams do that."

Green led MSU with 26 points while Stewart had 17 and Sleets had 13.

Following the victory over Peay the Racers headed to Youngstown State where they came away with a 79-74 victory. But they weren't as lucky at Akron as Jakubick scored 47 points in leading the Zips to an 84-76 victory.

"That's what happens when you're on top," Greene said. "Everybody plays better to knock you off. Jakubick's an All-American. We didn't have anybody to stop him. And we tried everybody – the popcorn vendor, the guys selling Pepsi in the stands, and anybody else we could have gotten."

Green led Murray State with 25 points while Sleets had 19.

The loss sent the Racers into a bit of a tailspin as they dropped three of their next six games. But they closed out the regular season by beating Eastern Kentucky and Morehead to clinch the conference title outright. That also gave MSU two consecutive 20-win seasons for the first time in 30 years.

"Now we're the OVC champions," Greene said. "No matter what happens next weekend in the OVC tournament that can never be taken away from us."

Murray State was clearly the class of the league and with MSU hosting the OVC tournament at Racer Arena fans had visions of the NCAA tournament dancing in their heads.

MSU was slated to play Akron in the semifinal round and although the Zips had beaten the Racers earlier in the season they had lost seven of their last eight games. Murray State was expected to win easily.

And for a while it looked like they would do just that. With 10 minutes to play they led by nine points. With six minutes left they led by seven. But Akron never gave up. With 1:35 left they took a 57-56 lead and when the final horn sounded the Zips were on top, 65-61.

"You can't put in enough time and effort just to see it all go down in one game," Greene said disconsolately. "One game... It just doesn't seem right. We knew it would be tough but we thought somehow... But it wasn't to be."

Asked about the NIT Greene said, "That's a tough question to answer right now. We'd be honored to play in it. But right now I'm kind of angry deep down inside. You've really got to want something real bad (an NCAA bid). It's hard to give it up for something else."

Sleets hit just 2-of-15 shots. Green led the Racers with 19 points while Hood had 18.

Jakubick paced Akron with 22.

Green shared the OVC Player of the Year award with Jakubick and was named to the all-conference team along with Sleets and Hood.

MSU did go on to play in the NIT, losing at home to Wake Forest 87-80.

1983-84 • 15-13

Before Ron Greene took over as head coach of the Racers, Murray State had won four OVC championships. Then Greene won three in his first five years.

But with all-conference players Glen Green and Ricky Hood lost to graduation he knew that winning a fourth crown was going to be difficult.

"Glen and Ricky meant a great deal to our team last year and we're going to be hard pressed to replace them," he said before the season. "They were not only extremely talented, but they gave us that valuable experience every team must have to win consistently."

Of course the cupboard wasn't completely bare.

Lamont Sleets, an all-conference player himself, returned at one of the guard spots after averaging 16.9 points as a junior. Sleets was already fourth on Murray State's career scoring list. Brian Stewart, a three year starter at point guard, was also back after averaging 8.1 points the previous year.

Vada Martin was back at one of the forward spots after averaging 6.9 points as a sophomore. And 6-11 Mike Lahm, a transfer from Loyola Marymount, was expected to make an immediate impact at center.

"There's no question we will have talent on our team but a great deal of it is unproven talent," Greene cautioned. "That will be particularly true along the front line. I feel good about this team though. And if our players perform on the court like they look on paper we will have a chance to contend for the conference title again."

Of course no one expected Sleets to battle injuries all year long. The senior guard started the season on the bench with a pulled hamstring. But Murray State won its first two games anyway, beating Missouri-Kansas City 80-49 and Tennessee State 65-58 in overtime.

TSU tried to slow the Racers down and led 23-19 after the first half of play. But Greene went to a full court press in the second half and with five minutes left to play MSU led 46-40. The lead reached seven at 55-48 before the Tigers rallied to force overtime with the score tied 58-58. MSU completely dominated the extra period, outscoring the visitors 7-0.

"I tried to tell our players that Tennessee State was a good ballclub," Greene said. "They are well coached, disciplined, and physical. Right now, though, our players are listening but not hearing and looking but not seeing."

Craig Talley led the Racers with 24 points while Sleets' replacement, Willie Holland, had 17.

Sleets was back for the next game but MSU proceeded to lose three in a row on the road.

Next up was a date with Metro Conference opponent Southern Mississippi at Racer Arena. MSU led by as many as 12 points but in the end it all came down to the last shot. With Murray State trailing 63-62 and 11 seconds left to play Sleets took it the length of the floor, bobbing and weaving through defenders. With four seconds left he launched a 10-footer that circled the rim before dropping through.

"Did everybody know that tricky play," Greene quipped after the game. "I was never so glad to see that thing trickle in there. I had a sinking feeling there with 11 seconds to go."

Sleets scored 28 points while Stewart had 11.

The Racers reeled off four more victories, three against NAIA schools, to push their record to 6-2.

But they stumbled in their OVC opener at Akron, losing 89-77. Senior Joe Jakubick led the way for Akron with 35 points.

"Jakubick is just amazing," Greene noted after the game. "Time and time again he gets the job done."

MSU lost despite shooting 55 percent from the field and having five players reach double figures. Martin led the Racers with 27 points.

"We played well enough to win," Greene said. "It was the kind of game where with a few calls going our way we could have won it."

But the loss sent the Racers into a tailspin as they dropped four of their next six games. Heading into a February 3 game with Austin Peay at Racer Arena they were 8-7 overall and 2-4 in conference play.

The game against Peay was part of the OVC's late night television package which showcased the conference on regional television at 10:30 on Friday evenings. It was Murray State's fifth appearance on Friday Night Live and they ran their record in those games to a perfect 5-0 by beating the Govs in overtime, 90-85.

Talley and Lahm came up big for the Racers as Talley scored 25 points while Lahm had 17 points and 10 rebounds.

Murray State went 5-4 the rest of the way despite losing Sleets for five games due to back problems. But they were thumped by Morehead, 80-64, in the first round of the OVC tournament. Sleets and Talley were named to the OVC's all-conference team.

1984-1985 • 19-9

Some things just can't be explained. The 1984-85 Racers came into the season with high expectations, rolled to an 18-3 record and were on the verge of cracking the Top-20. Then they collapsed, losing six of their last seven games.

At the beginning of the season head coach Ron Greene was optimistic even though Murray State was coming off of a 15-13 season the year before.

"We have experience inside and we've recruited taller, stronger players overall which ought to make us a better rebounding team and more effective defensively," he noted. "I also believe our perimeter shooting is going to improve considerably but we did lose two veteran guards, Lamont Sleets and Brian Stewart, who will be tough to replace."

The front line of Vada Martin, Craig Talley and Mike Lahm returned intact and JUCO transfers Chuck Glass, Zedric Macklin, and Owen Bronston figured to make an immediate impact at guard. Bronston had been an honorable mention junior college All-American.

Still, there was concern when MSU lost its exhibition opener to Marathon Oil, 81-70. But those fears were allayed somewhat when the Racers beat West Virginia Tech 78-62 to start the regular season. Macklin led the way with 17 points while Martin and Glass each had 15. Bronston came off the bench to score 12.

Following that victory the Ledger and Times quoted one fan as saying, "Maybe there's hope after all."

Greene was more effusive, "Tonight we showed sparks of good signs for the season ahead."

After an inexplicable loss to Lincoln Memorial in their next game the Racers bounced back with a 58-50 victory over Evansville. With 11:53 left to play MSU had a 45-44 advantage. But Glass and Martin were both in foul trouble so Greene went to the four-to-score.

At one point the Racers held the ball for seven minutes without taking a shot as the Aces chased them around the court in a game of keep-away.

Macklin again led the way with 14 points while Lahm had 12 and Talley had 10. Bronston failed to score and MSU got just eight points from its bench. As the season wore on this would be a recurring theme as the starters scored 85 percent of the Racers' points. If Bronston didn't score they didn't usually get much from their bench.

Still, the wins began to pile up. Five straight victories followed the win over Evansville. By January 9 Murray State was 10-2 and ranked 35th in the nation by USA Today's Jeff Sagarin, one spot ahead of Kentucky.

And they looked the part as they opened OVC play with an 86-69 thrashing of Austin Peay. The Racers shot 72.5 percent from the field and 90.5 percent in the second half.

"Only 90.5 percent," Greene asked rhetorically after the game. "Well I always strive for perfection and it looks like I didn't get it again."

Macklin had a game high 22 points while Talley, Martin, and Bronston each had 16.

By early February the Racers were 18-3 overall and 8-1 in OVC play. Their only loss in conference play had come at Eastern Kentucky when they were assessed two technical fouls for having players listed with incorrect numbers in the scorebook. The resulting free throws provided EKU with their margin of victory.

And then the wheels fell off.

It started with a 53-51 double-overtime loss at Tennessee Tech. At the time it didn't seem like such a big deal.

"I thought we had a good effort overall and I thought we were in pretty good shape to win it," Greene said. "But we turned the ball over at critical times. I'm proud of the effort. Like I told them, this can either be a stumbling block or a stepping stone. This isn't the end of the world."

But four more losses followed the defeat at Tech. The final loss in that string of defeats came at Racer Arena as MSU was beaten 76-70 by Eastern Kentucky. And the Colonels again benefited from two technical fouls lodged against the Racers for having incorrect numbers in the scorebook.

Murray State closed out the regular season with a 76-58 victory over Morehead and wound up fourth in the conference. But they lost their opening game in the OVC tournament at Middle Tennessee, 63-60. Martin and Talley were both all-conference selections.

1985-86 • 17-12

At the end of the 1985-86 season head coach Ron Greene left Murray State to take over the program at

Indiana State. He was replaced by his assistant Steve Newton.

"We want to maintain the excellence that has been established here in the last seven years," Newton said before his inaugural season. "In order to take our program to another plateau in Division I we must recruit and retain Division I student athletes who have the ability and potential to pursue these goals."

And what was Newton's ultimate objective?

"Our long range goal is to finish at the top of the OVC, secure an NCAA bid, and advance further than any team in MSU history," he declared.

Those were lofty goals for a program that hadn't even been to the NCAA tournament since 1969. And Newton knew it would take time to achieve them.

He had five returning players and two starters back as he embarked on his first season as a head coach. But he also had 10 newcomers. So it wasn't surprising that the Racers were picked sixth in the OVC's preseason poll of coaches and sports information directors.

Still, the season started with a bang as MSU crushed William Penn, an NAIA school, in the opener 78-53. The Statesmen made it close for a half as Murray State led 32-26 at the break. But Newton shifted to a full court press in the second half and the Racers went on a 24-4 run to put the game away.

Chuck Glass led MSU with 18 points and nine rebounds while junior college transfer Glenn Sanders ran the point and scored 16 points with five assists and five turnovers.

"I was very pleased with our team's businesslike attitude," Newton said after notching his first victory. "They had good quickness but we had about an eight minute stretch there after halftime when our pressure got to them and our defense created some situations for us."

He also made it clear that he hadn't settled on a starting lineup – "I imagine we'll be the type of ballclub this year that whoever is delivering, whoever is doing the best job is going to be out there on a given night. That kind of competition will be healthy for this team throughout the year."

Newton's expectation proved to be on the mark as 10 different players would find themselves in the starting lineup over the course of the season. And just three would average more than 6.4 points.

Though they struggled at times, the Racers ran their record to 3-0 with victories over Indiana-Purdue Fort Wayne and Wisconsin-Stevens Point. A loss to Utah State in the opening round of the Illini Classic dropped them to 3-1. But they bounced back with a 63-61 victory over Eastern Kentucky in the consolation game.

The Colonels led by 17 with 8:04 left to play but Murray State went on a 24-5 run the rest of the way. Glass hit a jump shot with 50 seconds left to give MSU the lead. And a late free throw closed out the scoring.

Glass led the Racers with 23 points while Zedric Macklin had 14.

Over the next seven games Murray State won big at Evansville and notched victories at home against Bowling Green, Southern Illinois, and Kentucky State. But there were also blowout losses at Alabama, Memphis State, and New Orleans.

That stretch was followed by three straight losses at Western Kentucky, Middle Tennessee, and Tennessee Tech leaving MSU 8-7 overall and 0-2 in conference play.

So when Youngstown State came to town on January 18 the Racers were in a must-win situation. But they rose to the occasion with an 82-74 victory as Macklin scored 29 points. Freshman Jeff Martin had 18.

"Zedric asserted himself and I think he finally decided his concentration wasn't going to be bothered," Newton said. "He isn't a real physical player, but I think he decided he was going to take charge out there and not worry about being bumped around and take the ball to the basket the way he is capable of doing."

Five more victories followed in quick succession. But the Racers stumbled down the stretch, losing four of their last six regular season games. They beat Austin Peay in the first round of the OVC tournament but then lost in the second round to Middle Tennessee, 85-81.

Glass had the best year of his career as he averaged 18.2 points and 6.8 rebounds and was an All-OVC selection. Martin and fellow freshman Don Mann averaged 11.7 and 6.4 points respectively. Both were named to the OVC's all-freshman team.

1986-87 • 13-15

Steve Newton's second team was even younger and more inexperienced than his first. He had just seven lettermen back, all with just a single year of experience. Add to that two Division I transfers, Craig Eversoll (Virginia Tech) and Wayne Tiller (Tennessee) along with a couple of junior college transfers, two redshirt freshmen, and two true freshmen and it's easy to see why they were called the Kiddie Korps.

But Newton made it clear that he was laying the foundation for success down the road.

"This is by design," he said. "We'll field a young team this season. But we're looking to evolve toward balance and consistency in our personnel and our program.

"Last season we needed to implement our system. Now we need to build on the positives of last season."

The Racers looked impressive in their opener against William Penn as they cruised to a 79-50 victory. Jeff Martin led the way with 24 points and eight rebounds.

Still, Newton was less than pleased.

"Our schedule is going to get much tougher," he said. "We're going to have to execute better than we did tonight to be competitive against some of the teams we will be playing."

They did play better in beating Belmont 94-92 the very next night. Don Mann led the attack with 21 points while Martin had 16, Eversoll had 15, and Doug Gold had 12.

The Rebels came into the contest having already played nine games. With nine seconds left they trailed by a single point and they had the ball. But a steal by Gold sealed the victory for MSU.

Belmont's head coach, Rick Byrd, was very complimentary in his post game remarks – "I really enjoy playing here. Coach Newton is a first class coach and the people here treat me really well. Murray State is a first class organization."

After a 2-0 start the Racers lost four straight. Two of those defeats came by a single point against Southern California and Mercer.

So when they headed to Lafayette, La. for the Bayou Classic in mid December it was difficult to be optimistic. But they beat Tennessee-Chattanooga 76-67 in the first round. And they topped host Southwestern Louisiana 81-70 to win the championship.

Mann had 30 points in the win over the Ragin' Cajuns while Martin had 27 and Tiller had 13.

"We set the tempo early and kept the crowd out of the game," Mann said. "I thought we played pretty well."

Mann was honored as the most valuable player in the tournament and Martin joined him on the all-tournament team.

Following a 78-74 loss at Minnesota the Racers reeled off three straight victories beating Kentucky State, Evansville, and IUPUI. They were 7-5 heading into their OVC opener against conference favorite Middle Tennessee at Racer Arena.

Middle was 9-2 and they played like it as they beat MSU 64-57. Martin lead the Racers with 21 points while Mann had 19.

"We knew we had to play a half court game," Newton said. "I can't fault our effort. We just ran into too many guns and we couldn't handle their beef inside. They just wore us down."

The Racers won three of their next five games. They were 10-8 overall and 3-3 in conference play as they headed to Clarksville to play Austin Peay at the end of January.

They came away with a 61-59 victory as Mann hit two free throws after the final buzzer. Mann had hit a three-pointer with 36 seconds left to tie the game at 59. Martin led all scorers with 22 points.

"We wanted to get the ball in Don's hands," Newton said. "He's awful tough in the clutch. He wants the ball when the game is on the line."

Unfortunately the season went south after that as MSU lost six straight games. Wins over Youngstown State and Austin Peay closed out the regular season. But an 89-75 loss to Eastern Kentucky in the first round of the OVC tournament brought it all to an end.

Martin and Mann were both named to the all-conference team as they averaged 21.2 and 15.5 points respectively.

1987-88 • 23-9

• *OVC Regular Season Champion*
• *OVC Tournament Champion*

After two straight lackluster campaigns the Racers were picked fifth in the OVC at the beginning of the season. But head coach Steve Newton was undaunted. He was convinced they were deeper and more experienced than they had been the previous two years and expected to contend for a championship.

Then before the season began starting point guard Don Mann was suspended following an incident in one of the dorms. Linzie Foster and Lorenzo Doyle were also suspended and both had been expected to compete for a spot in the starting lineup.

Mann and Foster would rejoin the team at the end of the first semester but their absence was felt early on.

Despite all that MSU was impressive in winning their home opener against William Penn, 97-49. Jeff Martin led all scorers with 21 points while centers Carl Sias and Robert McClatchey combined for 18 points and 15 rebounds.

"I think we took a big step forward in maturing," Newton said. "I'd have to say that it offered us what we wanted to see and we had the opportunity to get up and down the floor in transition, probably more than we will later on. The ability to play a lot of people and look at different combinations was good for us."

But if anyone thought Mann wouldn't be missed they were disabused of that notion in the very next game, a 77-70 loss to Southern Illinois. Martin scored 34 points. It wasn't enough though as just one other Racer reached double figures and MSU made just 4-of-15 three-pointers.

Newton said the team was relying too much on Martin in Mann's absence – "They're looking to him and he's being asked to carry a big, big load both offensively and defensively."

The Racers won just two of their next five games before heading to Lafayette, La. for the Bayou Classic. But spirits were high as Mann was ready to make his return.

With the Mann hitting five three-pointers and scoring 19 points MSU crushed Eastern Washington in the first round 84-57.

"His impact is dramatic," Newton said. "Don gives us impetus and energy at point guard. We were able to get the ball into the paint from the perimeter which is something we haven't been able to do in previous games this season."

Martin was even more impressive as he hit 13-of-15 shots and scored 31 points.

Foster also returned from suspension and came off the bench to score six points and grab eight rebounds.

The Racers fell behind early in the championship game against Southwestern Louisiana as they struggled with the Ragin' Cajuns pressure defense. They were down by 14 at the half, 43-29.

A furious second half comeback trimmed the lead to a single point at 55-54. But the Racers couldn't get over the hump, dropping a 64-62 decision despite 23 points from Martin and 16 from Sias.

Murray State split its next four games as they beat Bethel and Tennessee State and lost to Memphis State and Western Kentucky. They took Memphis to overtime before losing 76-70.

Years later Martin recalled, "We lost that game but it showed us we could play with anyone."

Finally, the Racers were ready to roll as they started a five game winning streak by whipping Eastern Kentucky 95-84 at Racer Arena. Martin poured in 36 points, Mann had 26, and Foster had 10.

"Jeff's great," Mann said after the game. "He's just unstoppable. Down the stretch he just took over."

The streak ended with a 74-71 loss to Austin Peay. Mann scored 31 points while dishing out seven assists and Martin had 23 points. But it just wasn't enough.

With 30 seconds left Murray State trailed 69-68 following a layup by Martin and Newton called timeout. There was just one problem. The Racers were out of timeouts so they were charged with a technical foul.

"I wasn't aware we were out of timeouts," Newton said after the game. "I should have been, but I wasn't."

The loss left Murray State and Austin Peay tied for the top spot in the conference at 6-1. But they wouldn't have to wait long for the tie to be broken as they played again in Clarksville two nights later.

This time the Racers came out on top as they rolled to a 42-27 halftime lead en route to an 83-70 victory. Martin led the way with 29 points while Mann had 23. Foster came off the bench to score 11 points and grab 11 rebounds.

"It feels good to come down here and win," Foster said. "This shows we're for real. This was just one game though. We have six more to go and we have to win them all."

Following a 78-70 win over Tennessee State in Nashville and a 71-64 victory over Youngstown State in Murray, the Racers headed to Death Valley with an 8-1 record in OVC play.

Morehead State pushed them to the limit before falling 77-75 as Sias had his best game of the year. The senior poured in 18 points and grabbed 10 rebounds.

The Eagles' Tony Curry hit a layup to tie the game at 75 with eight seconds left and Newton promptly called timeout.

"I told Don to penetrate as far as he could and then look for Jeff or the shot," he told reporters after the game. "Jeff was due to hit one but I also told Carl to be available since he had the hot hand."

Mann took it to the basket and drew a foul. Then he hit two free throws with three seconds left to give MSU the victory. Mann led all scorers with 21 points while Martin struggled as he made just 7-of-18 shots and scored just 14 points.

"When Jeff doesn't get his 30 we struggle," Newton said. "We were fortunate that Carl was able to pick up the slack for us."

Next up was Eastern Kentucky and the Colonels were riding a 17 game home court winning streak. Martin was back in form as he scored 32 points but the Racers trailed by as many as 16. And with 5:30 left to play they were still down by 14, 72-58.

A 15-4 run trimmed the lead to three at 76-73. EKU's Jeff McGill hit two free throws to make it 78-73. But Mann and Martin both hit jumpers to cut the lead to a single point. And then Martin made two free throws with 10 seconds left to give MSU a 79-78 victory.

"I'm very proud of our comeback," Newton said. "We displayed the poise and patience of a championship ballclub."

1987-88 men's basketball team. Front row: George Kimbrough, Terence Brooks, Jeff Robbins, Scott Ricks, Paul King, Greg McQueary, Lorenzo Doyle. Second row: Athletic Assistant Greg Whobrey, Dion Elliot, A.J. Mensey, Assistant Coach Charles Cunningham, Head Coach Steve Newton, Assoc. Coach Mark Bernsen, Don Mann, Donald Overstreet, Trainer Paul Newman. Third row: Student Assistant Coach John Wyatt, Robert McClatchey, Linzie Foster, Doug Gold, Carl Sias, Chris Ogden, Jeff Martin, Athletic Assistant Rick Metcalf.

Murray State reeled off three more victories as they closed out the regular season with wins over Tennessee Tech, Middle Tennessee, and Western Illinois.

The Racers were 13-1 in conference play and 19-8 overall heading into the OVC tournament. They had won eight games in a row and 13 of their last 14.

They were on a roll and it showed as they crushed Eastern Kentucky in the semifinals at Racer Arena 76-60. Martin led the way with 32 points, Sias had 19, and Mann had 15. They held EKU to 33 percent shooting from the field.

"We challenged our team with our defensive effort," Newton said. "We felt like it was going to be a key, especially to handle their transition game and keep them out of their fast break attack."

The final was a rematch between the Racers and the Govs. The two had split during the regular season. Everyone expected a war and that's exactly what they got.

It wasn't pretty though as Martin made just 6-of-18 shots and Mann was 2-of-16. At halftime Austin Peay held a tenuous 37-35 advantage but the Racers went on a 20-6 run at the beginning of the second half to take a 55-43 lead. Then Peay scored 12 of the next 14 points to get within two at 57-55.

It was nip and tuck the rest of the way. With two seconds left and MSU leading 72-70 Peay's Vincent Brooks launched a three-pointer that rimmed out. Sias got the rebound for the Racers. He was fouled immediately and hit 1-of-2 free throws to seal the victory.

Sias had missed a free throw earlier in the year against Western Kentucky that would have sent the game into overtime. But he said he didn't think about that when he went to the line.

"Honestly, all that was going through my mind was that I was going to make it for my mother," he said. "I dedicated this game to her."

MSU vs North Carolina State, NCAA.

MSU vs. Kansas, NCAA.

Martin led all scorers with 22 points while Mann and Chris Ogden each had 10. The Racers were headed to the Big Dance for the first time since 1969, or to put it another way, for the first time in the modern era.

Their reward was a first round game in Lincoln, Neb. against perennial power North Carolina State and their legendary coach, Jim Valvano.

Cheryl Whittaker was Newton's secretary at the time.

"We had to drive to St. Louis in a snowstorm to catch a plane to Nebraska," she recalled. "And we had to stay in a dormitory at the University of Nebraska. All the other teams were set up in hotels so that tells you what they thought about Murray State."

It seemed as though no one gave the Racers a chance. And with the Wolfpack leading 32-24 late in the first half things looked somewhat bleak. But back to back three-pointers by Mann and Paul King cut the lead to two and by halftime the Racers held a 41-36 advantage.

They built the lead to nine in the second half and held on. With seven seconds left King hit the front end of a 1-and-1 to put MSU up 78-75. But he missed the second shot and N. C. State got the ball to sharpshooter Vinnie Del Negro for one final three-pointer.

"When I missed the second one I didn't even follow it for a rebound," King said. "I found Del Negro and tried to get on him. I figured he'd be the one to take the shot."

Del Negro pushed it up the sideline but King kept him from getting a good look at the basket and his final shot rimmed out.

Martin led all scorers with 23 points while Mann had 16 and Ogden had 12.

"It's a dream come true for this ballclub," Newton said. "These guys just never believed the doomsayers.

Martin and Don Mann getting the net after winning the 1988 OVC Tournament.

Don Mann hoisted the 1988 OVC Tournament trophy for his teammates moments after the Racers won their first trip to the NCAA tournament in 21 years.

1987-88 award winners

Linzie Foster, who got the nod at center despite being undersized at 6-6, scored 12 points and grabbed eight rebounds.

"Every day I go hard in practice," Foster said. "I want to give 110 percent. I try to leave everything I have out on the court."

Martin led MSU with 21 points while Mann had 12.

After running their record to 2-0 with a 96-83 victory at Lamar the Racers headed to Bowling Green for a first round game in the Western Kentucky Invitational against Missouri Valley power Tulsa.

Martin completely dominated the game against the Golden Hurricane. Midway through the first half the score was Murray State 25, Jeff Martin 15, and Tulsa 14. Martin finished with 34 points as the Racers won 86-63.

"Obviously we were able to get some pretty good shots at the hoop from Martin," head coach Steve Newton said. "And he rose to the occasion and put the ball in the hoop for us."

Unfortunately, Newton's charges lost to Western Kentucky in the final. Then, after getting blown out at Louisville, they won just four of their next seven games. A 3-0 start had devolved into a 7-5 mark as the Racers headed to Clarksville for their OVC opener against Austin Peay.

Martin scored 28 points to become MSU's all time leading scorer but Mann struggled, making just 3-of-14 shots, and the Racers lost, 84-75.

"One game doesn't make a season," Newton said. "They're the team to beat just like last year. But you have to play them one at a time."

Next came an 80-78 overtime victory against Lamar at Racer Arena. Lamar's center Adrian Caldwell had his way inside as he scored 20 points and grabbed 10 rebounds.

But Martin offset that with a game high 37 points.

We told them to go out and play some shirts and skins and they did. I couldn't be prouder of their effort."

Murray State dropped a 61-58 decision to eventual national champion Kansas in the second round.

Martin set a school record for most points in a single season. He was named OVC Athlete of the Year and Player of the Year. Mann joined him on the all-conference team and Newton was named OVC Coach of the Year.

1988-89 • 19-11

• *OVC Regular Season Champion*

Following MSU's stirring upset of North Carolina State the previous year expectations were sky high. After all, Jeff Martin and Don Mann were back for their senior year along with two other starters, junior Chris Ogden and sophomore Paul King.

The only starter missing from the team that beat N.C. State was center Carl Sias and no one believed his 8.7 points and 5.7 rebounds would be hard to replace.

After a 68-49 victory over visiting Oakland City in the opener it appeared the common wisdom might be correct.

Mann scored 11 points and dished out 13 assists, and King had 12 points.

With 5:32 left the visitors led 62-54 but the Racers went on an 11-3 run to tie it at 65. Lamar didn't buckle though and it took a three-pointer from King with three seconds left to send the game into overtime.

"There were some big offensive plays in the game but we made several big plays on defense as well," Newton said. "Even when we got down we made the big plays and that's what it takes."

The Death Valley trip was up next and the Racers' defense was stifling in a 79-66 win at Morehead. The Eagles made just two of their first 20 shots and at halftime were shooting just 19.6 percent from the field.

"We needed a win badly," Newton said. "Our guys said before the game, 'It's Racer Time!' That's more like the Racer team I know."

Martin led all scorers with 25 points and moved into third place on the OVC's career scoring list.

Murray State was even more dominant in a 63-40 win at Eastern Kentucky as the Colonels shot just 31.2 percent from the field.

"It was good to see an outstanding defensive effort in both halves," Newton said. "We put together our best 40 minutes of the year on the defensive end."

It was the first time MSU had ever swept Morehead and Eastern on the road in consecutive seasons.

Wins over Tennessee Tech, Tennessee State, and Middle Tennessee ran the Racers' winning streak to six games leaving them 13-6 overall and 5-1 in the OVC. Up next was a rematch with Austin Peay.

With Western Kentucky leaving the OVC in the early 80's the Govs had become Murray State's principal rival and the Racers were eager to avenge the loss they had suffered in Clarksville.

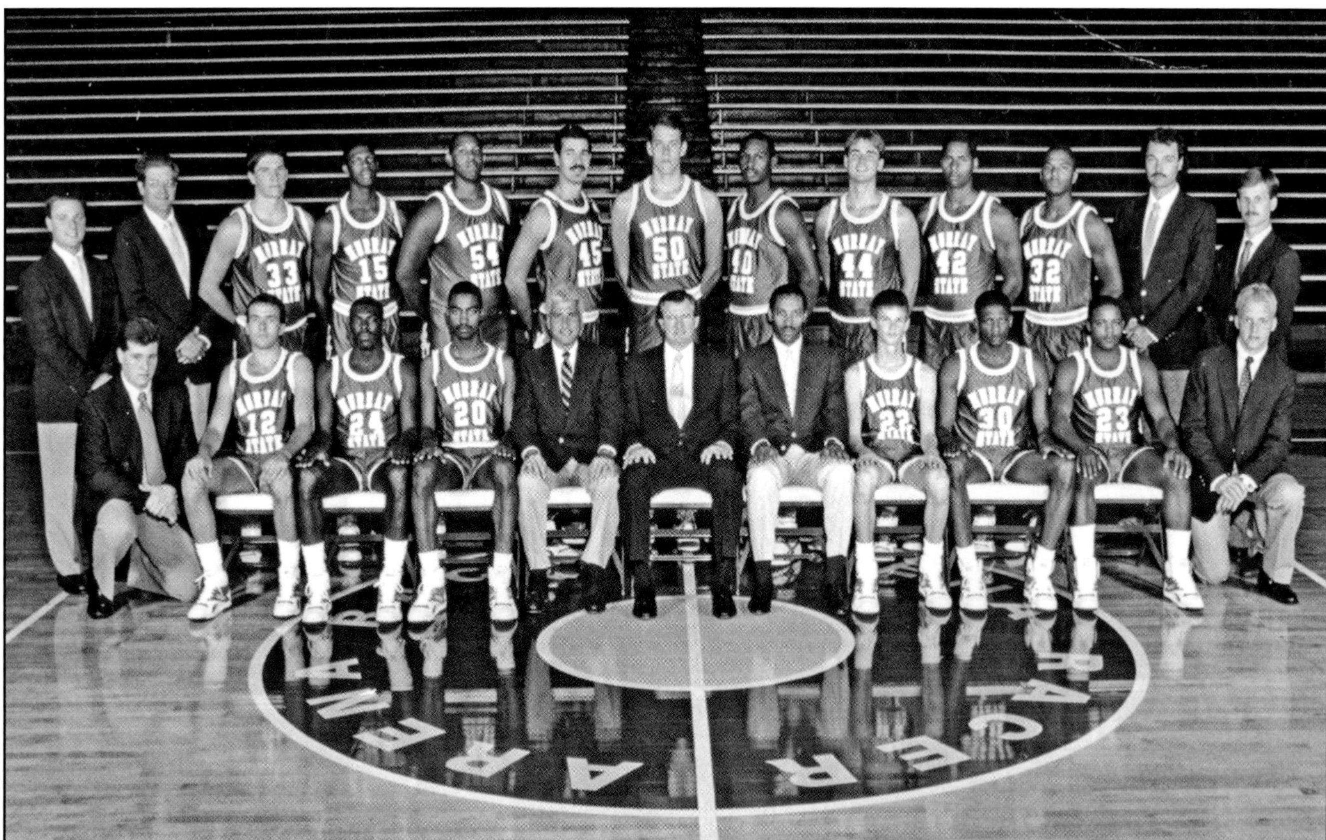

1988-89 men's basketball team. Front row: Manager Brad Pritchett, Jeff Robbins, Terence Brooks, Michael Gray, Associate Head Coach Mark Bernsen, Head Coach Steve Newton, Assistant Coach James Holland, Mitch Cothran, Paul King, Don Mann, Manager Lance Akridge. Back row: Volunteer Assistant Coach John Lykins, Part-time Assistant Coach John Wyatt, Mike Land, Jeff Martin, Popeye Jones, Ismael Rosario, Steve Wendt, Chris Ogden, Doug Gold, Linzie Foster, Donald Overstreet, Graduate Assistant Coach Rich Metcalf, Trainer Paul Newman.

MSU led most of the way but Peay mounted one comeback after another. It took 25 points from Martin and six free throws by Mann in the final 33 seconds to secure the 72-64 victory. Mann wound up with 13 points and six assists.

"I love playing against Peay," he said after the game. "But everyone tries to hype the game up more than it is. This game we got into our offense a lot better. We just had to get the ball where it needed to go."

That usually meant getting the ball to Martin which Mann said was becoming more difficult.

"As we play more and people scout us more, they all start doing a better job of trying to stop Jeff," he noted. "They put more pressure on me so I won't see him when he pops open."

Nonetheless, Newton had high praise for his leading scorer.

"Jeff just did a super job," Newton said. "He carried a lot of luggage out there tonight. He's having to work awful hard to get his hands on the basketball and then to get a clear shot the last couple of games."

Unfortunately the Racers lost three of their next five games. They were 16-9 overall and 8-2 in the OVC, tied with Middle Tennessee for first place, when Eastern Kentucky came to town on February 25.

Martin poured in a career high 38 points and Mann added 23 as Murray State scored 61 first half points en route to a 97-66 victory.

"It could have been this way all year," Martin said. "We just had a couple of games where the shots didn't fall like that."

The Racers seemed to be hitting their stride as the season wound down.

"We have worked real hard to orchestrate our season so we would be peaking at the right time," Newton said. "We feel like we're where we want to be."

Lopsided victories over Morehead and Tennessee State followed so the Racers headed to Nashville to play Austin Peay in the first round of the OVC tournament having won five of their last six games.

All year long MSU had shot the ball well and outrebounded their opponents. But against the Govs they struggled to find the basket as they shot just 37.7 percent from the field. And they were dominated on the boards as Peay outrebounded them 49-36.

Martin scored 16 points but made just 6-of-15 shots while Mann had 13 points but hit just 2-of-11 shots. Without Ogden's 15 points on 7-of-11 shooting it wouldn't have even been a game.

As it was, the Racers trailed most of the way. They were down 69-62 with 57 seconds left. A three-pointer by Mann that would have cut the lead to four was off target. A deuce by King made it 69-64 with 40 seconds left but it was too little, too late as Peay came away with a 72-64 victory.

"We're proud of what this team has achieved," Newton said. "I'm just disappointed we didn't play one of our better games in the tournament. I feel so bad to have played so many fine basketball games during the season and to have it end like this. It just wasn't meant to be."

MSU accepted an invitation to the NIT but lost its first round game at Penn State, 89-73. Martin and Mann were both named to the all-conference team and Martin was once again honored as OVC Athlete of the Year and OVC Player of the Year.

GARY HOOKER

by Kevin Stewart

Gary Hooker played just one season at Murray State, but his impact was tremendous.

The Racers went from 4-22 the year before Hooker to 23-8 in 1979-80 to establish the greatest turnaround in college basketball history.

But Hooker's connection to Racer basketball goes back much further than that one season – back to his days as a skinny high school kid hanging around Harlem. Hooker had talent, and that was his ticket out of the neighborhood and into college.

When Steve Newton convinced the youngster that Mississippi State was the right destination for that ticket, the bond to Murray State was set. Newton was Ron Greene's assistant coach in Starkville, Miss., and witnessed the 6-foot-5 forward evolve into a solid player in one of the country's top leagues, the Southeastern Conference.

Hooker started some games as a freshman and became a full-time starter as a sophomore. When Greene was named head coach of the Bulldogs for Hooker's junior year, 1977-78, Hooker expected his playing time and production would, naturally, increase.

Greene has always been into the psychology of coaching and the handling and progression of players. Develop trust between player and coach and leadership will emerge from the player. As part of that process, Greene felt Hooker needed a place on the bench instead of starter's status as the Bulldogs and their new coach grappled early that season. Hooker played plenty, and contributed plenty – in fact he averaged 14.3 points a game over his three-year stay in Starkville – but he just didn't start a lot of games under Greene.

Gary Hooker

In an article in the Paducah (Ky.) *Sun* newspaper, Greene recalled, "He didn't like it. He didn't like it at all. No player does. But he didn't pout. He tried to win his position back, which is what a great player will do."

Slowly trust formed from Greene's tough-love approach. "I respected (Greene) because he treated me as an individual," Hooker said in the article.

The bond Greene sought grew. And so when Greene after one season left to take Murray State's job, Hooker felt he had to follow. Newton was also headed to Murray to be Greene's assistant, and Hooker had grown close to both coaches.

"(Greene) has been like a father to me," Hooker told *Sun* writer Barry Forbis. "He tells me not what to do, but how to go about it.

"He's been very good to me. He's more than just a coach. Any kind of problem I got I can go to him. This Christmas, I didn't have any funds to get home, and he said, 'Do you want to go?' He said, 'I'll loan you the money to get home if you'll pay me back when you get back.' So he put me on the bus, and I went back home to see my family...

"Coach Newton went up into the ghetto and got me. He said I've got the ability and they could teach me how to use it. He could talk to my father, and that's something most people can't do. He told him I probably wouldn't be home for four years, but they'd take care of me."

And after sitting out a year following the transfer, Hooker was ready to take care of the Racer's opponents for Greene and Newton.

Teaming with freshman phenoms Lamont Sleets and Glen Green and aided by returning starter Kenney Hammonds off that four-win squad, Hooker and

the Racers surprised most and amazed many. The 23 wins was the fourth most in school history, dating back to the '25-26 season.

The Ohio Valley Conference was a playground of sorts for the Racers. They whipped every league opponent twice except for Western Kentucky, and finished tied with the Hilltoppers atop the OVC with a gaudy 13-1 record. In the loss at Western Kentucky, Hooker didn't play due to an eye injury suffered two games before the big meeting. And Hammonds also missed the game and the rest of the season after suffering a stress fracture in his foot.

Hooker gave the Racers scoring (18.6 points) and a defensive presence. And boy, could he rebound. His 12.3 average was fifth-best in the country.

"Gary Hooker was the best rebounder, pound-for-pound, that I every coached," Greene said. "Gary could do something that very few players could match. When the ball went up, players could jump with Gary, get just as high as he did. But when they needed to keep on jumping, keep on rebounding, on that same play, they couldn't keep up with him. He was still way up there on his third, fourth jump, rebounding the ball, tipping the ball, shooting it. No one could keep up with him in that regard."

Glen Green

by Kim Trevathan

Murray State basketball certainly needed a shot of something when Glen Green first stepped foot on campus in the fall of 1979.

"Glen Green was as smooth as Southern Comfort," recalled coach Ron Greene, alluding to a liqueur quite popular at the time.

Southern Comfort, it seems, wasn't meant to be guzzled from the bottle or swallowed bottoms-up style from a shot glass, but instead sipped like fine wine, to be enjoyed and appreciated. Greene saw the comparisons, "Glen was refined, a smooth player, a fine player from the start, but he also got better with age."

Indeed. A starter as a freshman, the 6-foot-5 guard and sometimes swingman out of Henderson County (Ky.) High School closed out his Racer career in 1982-83 as the Ohio Valley Conference Player of the Year. Considered one of Murray's greatest all-around players, Green averaged 20.1 points, shot 81 percent from the free-throw line, 50 percent from the 3-point line, handed out over 100 assists and produced a combined 65 steals and blocks as a senior.

The glory days of the early 1970s were filled with stars like two-time OVC Player of the Year Les Taylor and the talented Mike Coleman. And winning seasons were the standard in the 1960s under Cal Luther. Murray State did not have a losing season in the decade. That trend continued into the early '70s.

Glen Green

But in the six year's prior to Greene's arrival, Murray State suffered five losing seasons. Greene got a whiff of the losing problem right away. In his first year the Racers won only four of 26 games.

So Greene and assistant coaches Steve Newton and Mike Dill tackled the recruiting wars with vigor, and signed Green along with Eminence (Ky.) High School star Lamont Sleets. With Mississippi State transfer Ricky Hood, a 6-6 junior jumping-jack, now eligible, Greene had the talent to stage a reversal of fortune.

Few, however, imagined that the group would go 23-8 in '79-80, establishing the greatest won-loss turnaround in college basketball history.

And Green was a key ingredient. Freshman jitters weren't allowed. He averaged nearly 10 points a game and was second in assists and third in rebounds. He averaged 10.2 points as a sophomore and 14.9 as a junior.

Versatility was Green's forte, even though he played mostly inside in high school.

"Glen turned out to be quite a perimeter player," Greene said. "He could play a swingman spot, or he could go to the point. He could play the one (point guard), two (swing or shooting guard) and the three (small forward) and be successful for us at each spot. That made him such a valuable player."

Green was certainly valuable as Murray State made a postseason run in March of 1980. A loss to host Western Kentucky in the OVC Tournament finals pushed the Racers into the National Invitational Tournament. There, they took on the big boys and beat them. The Racers won at Jacksonville, 53-49, and at Alabama, 70-62, before bowing to host Illinois by two, 65-63.

Against Jacksonville, Green scored four points as part of a Racer rally that helped cement the victory. Green sank two free throws with 4:39 left that gave Murray State its first lead, 40-39, then added a key layup later. Green led his team with 15 points and also pulled down eight rebounds.

As a junior, he blocked a last-second shot to preserve a signature victory at Notre Dame, which had blossomed into one of the country's top programs in the 1970s. That victory was the first of six straight early in the year and part of a run of 15 wins in 17 games that fueled a 20-8 record and another trip to the NIT. The Racers also played in the NIT in Green's senior season.

"The players called Glen 'Ice' because with him, you never knew if we were up 10 or down 10, or if the score was tied, he was smooth and cool at the same time," Greene remembered. "He was the glue-ish type player that every coach looks for. It's difficult to find a player who can do all the kinds of things well that Glen Green did well."

LAMONT SLEETS

by Kim Trevathan

Full throttle. That's how assistant coach Mike Dill described LaMont Sleets' style of play. To accomplish what the 5-10 guard did at Murray State from 1979-1984 (he redshirted one year due to an injury), Sleets had to go all-out, full throttle from start to finish.

He's one of only two MSU players to make All-OVC in each of his four years as a Racer. (Isaac Spencer is the other one.) At the end of his college career, Sleets was second in career steals (191), first in career assists (459), and second in career scoring (1902). He averaged 17.1 points per game, with a personal single-season high of 18.3 points per game his senior year. Known for his long-range jumpers, Sleets' scoring total would have been much higher had he played with the three-pointer in effect all four years of his career.

Dill remembers one particular talent that set Sleets apart, "Lamont was very fast and could run down the court at full speed, stop on a dime, and get great elevation on a jump shot. That's a very hard thing to do."

Sleets said this was a skill that he practiced a lot because he knew that playing a big man's game, he needed an edge to get his jumper off.

The other thing that Dill remembers most about LaMont Sleets was his desire. "He loved the game of basketball, and gave you 100 percent effort all the time," Dill said. "He wanted to prove he could play at the Division I level."

Play he did, with a quiet intensity that inspired his teammates and his coaches. Coach Ron Greene said Sleets was a "quiet unassuming guy, who led by example. He let his actions do the talking."

Lamont Sleets

Sleets' actions were instrumental in the success of the teams he led. He played on three OVC championship teams and three National Invitational Tournament teams, including the 1980 quarterfinalist team.

His freshman year, said Sleets, was the "most memorable." He'd "never won anything in high school," and that 1979-80 team won the OVC and beat Jacksonville and the University of Alabama in the NIT before losing by two to Illinois. "It was all new to me," said Sleets, "being that successful. I played with great guys. Everybody got along and we all worked together for a common goal."

Former Alabama Coach C.M. Newton said Sleets was one of the best guards he saw all year after Sleets scored 25 points in the win over the Crimson Tide.

Sleets followed that up with a strong sophomore year (1980-81) in which he led the team in scoring at 16.7 points per game and was selected as the most valuable performer in the OVC tournament, scoring 48 points over two games.

Sleets said he started playing basketball at an early age in the streets of tiny Eminence, Kentucky. His heroes were Dave Bing, who played for the Detroit Pistons, and Julius Erving. "I watched the ABA a lot," he said.

Although he played a lot of basketball, Sleets' first love was football. He was going to start at quarterback heading into his freshman year of high school, but some problems with his knees kept him out of sports entirely that year. He actually played in the band his freshman year, but once he was healthy, he got more interested in basketball than football. Enter Sleets' desire.

"Everybody said I was too small," he said, "and that's what motivated me to play basketball."

Motivation led him to stardom at Eminence, where he scored 1,944 points in his three-year career, including averaging 32 points a game his senior year.

Sleets had gotten the attention of some big schools, including Michigan. Greene, who noted that Sleets was "a very coachable young man," saw his potential as a shooting guard, even though he was playing forward in high school.

It didn't hurt either that his parents and grandparents liked both Greene and Dill. He enjoyed his visit to Murray State and appreciated the personal interest they took in him. Although Louisville showed some interest, Denny Crum's preference at the time was for big guards.

What Louisville missed out on, Murray State profited from. Sleets became a star almost immediately, the second leading scorer behind Gary Hooker on the team that advanced to the NIT quarterfinals.

Even though he was small, Sleets could elevate. Greene said he was one of the better dunkers on the team. With a muscular build and a fearless demeanor, Sleets was "not afraid of physical contact and would go to the basket hard," said Dill.

Sleets said that Greene advised him to grow his hair out to look taller. "Every inch counts in basketball," he told Sleets.

In his junior year (1982-83), after sitting out all but three games in 1981-82 because of a foot injury, Sleets teamed up with 6-6 point guard Glen Green to win an OVC regular season title and make an appearance in the NIT, where they lost to Wake Forest 87-80. Green's nickname was "ice," and opponents would fear an ice and sleet storm when they took the court against the Racers.

Before his senior year, Coach Greene called Sleets "the best guard under six-feet in the nation."

Sleets responded with his strongest year, averaging a team-leading 18.3 points per game. Though he had some people calling him about opportunities in professional basketball, Sleets' had developed some serious back problems that made him decide to call it a career.

"I catch hell sometimes for not doing it," he said. "But I enjoyed playing and I decided I'd had a good run."

Dill said that in addition to being "about as good a guard as you could have at that level," Sleets was "a pleasure to be around, an outstanding person. He was a team player and he expected everyone else to give 100 percent."

If you search Sleets' name on the Internet, you may find a story which claims that he invented the high-five. Sleets always maintained that the story wasn't true and the writers who originally concocted the story later admitted it was all a hoax.

Sleets now lives in Eminence with his wife and kids. He moved back, he said, "to take care of my parents, since they took care of me growing up."

Sleets was inducted into the Murray State Athletic Hall of Fame in 1994. Dill, who introduced Sleets at the Hall of Fame Banquet, called him a "great representative and ambassador of Murray State."

RON GREENE

by Will Aubrey

Over the years, Murray State has lost a number of coaches to higher profile programs. Steve Newton left for South Carolina; Mark Gottfried went to Alabama; and Mick Cronin moved his clipboard to Cincinnati.

That's life at the mid-major level. Fans have come to expect it.

But against all odds, defying all reason, there was one occasion when the door swung the other way.

In 1978, Ron Greene guided Mississippi State to a second-place finish in the Southeastern Conference and was named the SEC Coach of the Year.

That same year, Fred Overton guided the Racers to a dismal 8-17 record. There was talk of dropping to Division II.

Instead, in a move that shocked the college basketball world, Murray State convinced Greene to leave one of the most powerful conferences in the nation for an Ohio Valley Conference school that had suffered four losing seasons in five years.

If you wrote a film script like that, it would be derided as hopelessly unrealistic. But loyalty can be a powerful thing.

Greene grew up in Terre Haute, Ind., where basketball inspired fervor that was almost religious in it's intensity.

"It was an amazing era," he recalled. "Television wasn't as prevalent then, so we played ball whenever we could. We'd meet on Saturday mornings at 10 a.m. and play three-on-three. If you got beat, you might not get back on the court for an hour, so you played like the devil. At 10 o'clock that night, we were still playing."

Ron Green

At Gerstmeyer High School, Greene played for one of the best teams in the history of the state. He and five of his teammates earned Division I scholarships to places such as Kentucky, Indiana, Kansas, and Bradley.

In 1956 and 1957 they made it to the state finals – only to lose to Crispus Attucks and the legendary Oscar Robertson.

"We had a very balanced team," Greene recalled. "The top six players averaged between 10 and 15 or 16 points. I was somewhere there in the middle. A lot of people thought we were one of the best offensive teams to ever play in the state of Indiana."

A lot of people also thought Greene was an exceptional player. When the Silver Anniversary Indiana All-State team was announced in 1957, Greene was one of those honored.

After high school, he enrolled at nearby Bradley. One of the top teams in the nation at the time, the Braves had just won the NIT championship, which in those days was considered just as prestigious as the NCAA title.

Greene was only there for a single semester, though.

"I got sick and didn't really recover very well from it, so I came back home," he recalled. "That's when Cal Luther had just taken the job at Murray State. He had coached at DePauw University in Greencastle, Indiana, so he knew about me and I ended up coming down here along with a high school teammate of mine, Bill Newton.

"He had a green and yellow Buick, and Bill and I slept in the back seat all the way down here. We didn't think we were ever going to get here because it's a

long way. He told us he watched us in high school, but he didn't think he could recruit us to DePauw. But since Bill left Kansas and I left Bradley, he wanted us to come to Murray State. We both said yes. I stayed, but Bill left after one semester, I think."

It would turn out to be a fortuitous decision for both Greene and MSU.

"I played for one of the winningest high school basketball coaches in Indiana history, Howard Sharpe," Greene declared. "Any success I have had can be attributed to playing for him and Cal Luther.

"Coach Luther was one of the best teachers the game has ever known. There are bigger names, but no one was a better teacher than Cal Luther."

The teams Greene played on at MSU were always competitive but never posted gaudy records. They did have their moments though.

"When I was a senior, we went to Eastern Kentucky and they had won 40 in a row at home," he recalled. "We had some young guys on the team. I was a senior and the captain, and I just didn't tell them we weren't supposed to win. They didn't know any better and I didn't tell them. We broke Eastern's 40-game home winning streak."

By that time, Greene had already decided he wanted to be a coach.

When he was a junior, while sitting in an adolescent psychology class, it hit him that he hadn't really grown up.

"That was the year I kind of discovered myself," he recalled. "Before you can help anyone else, you have to understand and know yourself. That happened to me in adolescent psychology class.

"My degree from Murray State prepared me for coaching as well as anything could have. I majored in physical education and I minored in business administration and psychology. That gave me a background in business and human behavior, as well as basketball."

Following graduation, Greene stayed at Murray State and earned a masters degree, as well as an ROTC commission in the Army. He also helped coach the Racers' freshman team.

When he had completed his tour of duty, he got a call from Luther.

"Coach Luther said that he had a friend at Loyola University in New Orleans who was looking for an assistant coach. He asked if I'd be interested, and I said yes," Greene recalled. "It didn't pay very much, but I wanted to be a college coach."

"So I went down there and I got hired. That year, we played Texas Western in El Paso and it didn't seem like we got the ball across half-court the whole game. I turned to the head coach and said, 'I don't think I can help you here. I think I need to get some of those guys on their team to come and play for our team.'"

Texas Western won the NCAA championship that year, defeating Kentucky in the title game.

"That first year, we were warming up and getting ready to play Michigan State," Greene said. "I was talking to the head coach, Bill Gardner, and Father Smith, the school president.

"When we left, Father Smith shook my hand and said, 'Coach, it was nice to meet you. I hope you don't beat us too badly.' He didn't know who I was. So, I said, 'Father, I hope I don't beat you too."

A year later, Greene became the head coach despite being just 28 years old and Loyola enjoyed it's first winning season in six years.

"In my second year we had a little difficulty with some of the players," he recalled. "They got intoxicated in the school cafeteria and turned their trays over. So I fired them all. We were 11-1 at the time with wins over Michigan State and LSU. But we finished 12-10.

"We didn't do very well after I fired our top four players. But I thought that was what we needed to do. and I figured the Jesuits would too. They weren't very happy about it though."

After another year at Loyola, Greene moved across town to the University of New Orleans which was just starting it's athletic program. But he wasn't just the basketball coach; he was the athletic director, too."

In his first year at UNO, the Privateers finished 18-5. The next year, he guided them to a 23-1 record and a No. 1 ranking in the Associated Press Division II poll.

While at New Orleans, Greene took the Privateers to Division I and was essentially the founder of the Sun Belt Conference.

"I sat down with a pen and paper and looked at urban universities that were not playing football – good places, great cities like New Orleans," he said. "I came up with UNC-Charlotte, South Alabama, Jacksonville, South Florida, and Georgia State. And they joined us in forming the Sun Belt."

From there, he would go to Mississippi State, where his team would battle Kentucky (a team that went on to win the NCAA championship) to the wire on national television.

"They rarely took more than one team from each conference then," Greene said. "But we were good enough to win the national championship that year, too."

Then it was time to come home.

"Marshall Gordon, the vice president for university relations at Murray State, asked me if there were any coaches I could recommend for them," Greene said. "I gave him a couple of names, and he said he didn't expect I'd be interested in discussing the job.

"Well, I said since it was my alma mater I'd be willing to listen. But I was really just being courteous. So we got together and he asked me what it would take for me to come to Murray State, and I outlined about 15 or 20 things. At breakfast the next morning, he said it was done and asked me to come and take a look."

Greene did just that. After meeting everyone and touring the campus, his mind was made up. He was going to say no. But before he could, Gordon asked him to sleep on it first.

Around 3:30 or 4 in the morning, Greene changed his mind.

"My alma mater needed me and I answered the call," he said. "It probably hadn't happened before or since, a coach leaving an SEC school for an OVC school.

"I took my son, David, to visit the campus at Mississippi State, and he said he couldn't understand why I left. I asked him if he thought I had rocks in my head, and he told me he thought they were boulders."

While at Murray State, Greene took a program on the brink of collapse – a program with three OVC titles in its history – and led it to three conference championships in six years.

It didn't come easy, though. The Racers were a dismal 4-22 his first year. At Christmas time of that year, The Murray State News ran a story headlined "The Hanging of Greene."

"We completely turned the roster upside down," he recalled. "But we beat Western twice that year. Our second year, we went 23-8. That was the biggest turnaround in the history of the NCAA at the time."

Of course, no coach can be successful without great players. And Greene excelled at finding them, sometimes by spotting greatness in players others didn't want.

Lamont Sleets and Glen Green are prime examples of his recruiting acumen.

"A lot of people looked at Sleets and said, 'He's not a very good point guard because he doesn't handle the ball very well,'" Greene recalled. "But he played forward for Eminence High School. He was a 5-9 forward, but he was the best dunker I ever had. He could jump up and do a 180 and jam it.

"He was like Calvin Murphy. He could take one step beyond the circle at mid-court and jump up and bomb it. He was physical, too – a strong kid and a very good player. Glen Green was 6-7 and thin. Ole Miss said he was too skinny and wouldn't be able to handle the beating in the SEC. Fine. We put Sleets at two-guard and Glen at the point. That gave us a 6-7 point guard and a 5-9 two-guard. It's all about putting the right people in the right places."

Sleets was a four time All-OVC selection and is the sixth-leading scorer in MSU history. Green was a two-time All-OVC selection and is the 10th-leading scorer in school history.

But the most impressive player Greene brought to Murray State may have been Gary Hooker.

"Hooker was 6-4, but he could jump three times by the time the other guy went up once," Greene said. "He was Freshman of the Year in the SEC at Mississippi State.

"When Jim Hatfield replaced me at Mississippi State, he called me and said, 'I understand Hooker may be a problem.' I said that he wasn't for me. But he said he didn't want him so I said, 'Send him to me.'"

In his one year with the Racers, Hooker averaged 18.6 points and 12.3 rebounds while shooting 55 percent from the field.

But Greene's impact wasn't limited to the basketball court. He had the basketball offices moved to Stewart Stadium, where they remained until the new practice facility was built in 2012. When he took the job at MSU, the four basketball coaches were using the nurse's quarters in the Carr Health building as an office.

He also had the floor at Racer Arena replaced with a Tartan surface because the old floor had buckled as a result of a leak in the roof. In addition, he improved housing for the players, getting them 7-foot beds so their legs didn't hang off the end.

The bottom line is, Greene didn't set out to build a team. He wanted to build a program. That's why his assistant, Steve Newton, won four OVC titles after he left.

Ron Greene laid the cornerstone for whatever success the Racers enjoy today. And along the way, he entertained the fans and always maintained a sense of humor.

"One technical I got, the referee was coming by and he stopped in front of me. So, I took my glasses off and put them on him," Greene said. "He didn't think that was very funny."

Of course, one can't talk about Greene's legacy without mentioning "The Play."

"The best play I've ever been associated with as a coach – we were playing Austin Peay at Racer Arena, there was one second on the clock and we were down two," he recalled. "We took it out in front of Austin Peay's bench.

"We put Sleets under the basket and ran him right at the ball. Two people followed him up the lane. Kenny Hammonds was at the hash mark across from where we in-bounded the ball. As Sleets came out, he ran toward the basket and Glen Green alley-ooped it to him. Hammonds caught it with one hand and dunked it.

"Fans were getting in their cars and listening to the radio, and they turned around and started coming back in. We won in overtime."

One of Greene's few disappointments in his years at the helm of the Racers was not reaching the NCAA Tournament.

In his second season, Murray State shared the conference title with Western Kentucky and lost in a playoff. In his fourth and sixth seasons, the Racers lost the OVC Tournament final to Middle Tennessee and Akron, respectively.

Greene's signature victory came on December 7, 1981 as his Racers beat Notre Dame in South Bend, Ind. 56-54. The Fighting Irish were coached by one of the top names in the game at the time, Digger Phelps. They were a perennial top-25 program. And they had John Paxson who would later win an NBA title as a starter for the Chicago Bulls.

"We chartered a plane and stayed in a classy hotel in the Chicago area," Greene noted. "Our boosters were able to go out on the football field and see the 'Golden Dome.' So it was a neat trip. And to cap it off with a victory was huge. I still have a plaque on the wall of my office with the score on it.

"After the game Digger wrote me a nice note and congratulated me on how well our team played. Of course they didn't play us again."

His signature play was the Four-to-Score. The Racers would spread the floor and whip the ball around the perimeter. If the other team came out to apply pressure they would use backdoor cuts to get wide-open layups. Opponents had to choose between letting the Racers run out the clock and giving up easy baskets.

At first the fans didn't like it. But they came around. By the end of Greene's second season everyone would stand and sing "Amen" when the Racers spread it out.

If he had gotten his way they'd have been singing that song in a new arena though.

"I learned a lesson about politics," he observed. "I wasn't very political. But when I was considering coming to coach at Murray State, Gov. Julian Carroll called me to try to get me to come.

"I told him if I came he'd have to build us a new place to play. He promised that he would. My mistake was that I forgot to ask him when. Twenty-some years later, it finally happened."

That, along with concern about his aging parents, led him to leave Murray and return to Terre Haute to coach Indiana State in 1985.

"I wanted to be with my parents as they were getting older," he said. "They passed away four years later.

"But the job at Indiana State provided a challenge without an opportunity. The only time they had really won there was when they had Larry Bird.

"Looking back, I wish I had stayed at Murray State, and I think my parents did, too. They didn't really want me to come. They knew the situation at Indiana State better than I did, and they knew I was happy here. They probably would have been happier if I could have just brought them down here more often. It ended my college career. On the other hand, I did see my mom and dad every day."

In retrospect, Greene says he should have relied more heavily on Luther.

"It's important to have mentors, and I wish I had done a better job of staying in touch with Cal Luther," he said. "Bob Knight never made a move without consulting Fred Taylor. The North Carolina group never makes a move without consulting Dean Smith.

"Indiana State only had 10 winning seasons in 40 years. I just thought since I had done it before I could do it again. I went to Bob Knight and asked him if he could help me get back in coaching, and he cussed me out a little bit and told me I should have called him before I took the Indiana State job, not after."

Following his stint with the Sycamores, Greene coached the Nashville Stars in a 6-foot-5 and under professional league. But the league folded and he returned to Murray to became the head basketball coach at Calloway County High School.

The Lakers had never had any success on the hardwood. But, true to form, Greene turned the program around. After his first year, Calloway had a winning season every year until he retired in 2001. In 2008 Greene became the head coach at Murray High School. He coached the Tigers for three years before retiring again in 2011.

He remains a fixture in the community, attending games at the CFSB Center and cheering on his alma mater.

JEFF MARTIN

by Will Aubrey

If you asked 10 fans to name the best player in Murray State history you might get half a dozen different names. And it's really an impossible question to answer. But Jeff Martin would have to be in the conversation.

Martin is the all-time leading scorer in the history of college basketball in the state of Kentucky. He won the Ohio Valley Conference Player of the Year award twice and was named OVC Male Athlete of the Year twice. He is one of 11 players in MSU history to earn all-conference honors in three consecutive seasons.

He holds six school records – most points in a single season, most points in a career, most field goals in a single season, most field goals in a career, highest 3-point field goal percentage in a single season, and highest 3-point field goal percentage in a career. He is among the top-10 in five other categories. And it's worth noting that he is third in career blocked shots.

Martin wasn't just a scorer either. He was one of the best all-around players to ever wear a Racer uniform. And yet, it was almost an accident that he wound up at Murray State.

"Shortly after I was hired I got a call from one of our fans in Paducah," former MSU head coach Steve Newton recalled. "He had overheard a conversation about a player who was visiting Paducah Community College. We did some research and found out that it was Jeff Martin from Cross County High School in Cherry Valley, Ark.

"I sent Mike Dill, one of my assistants to take a look at him and he found Jeff shooting in the gym in his street clothes. Well, Mike called and said, 'He's hit 10 shots in a row. Do you think we ought to recruit him?' And I said absolutely, let's bring him in for a visit."

Jeff Martin

Cherry Valley was so small it made Murray look like a sprawling metropolis by comparison.

"It was a town of about 500 people," Martin recalled. "Everyone knew everyone else. The kids I played with when I was little are the same kids I played ball with in junior high school and high school.

"I started playing organized ball in the fifth or sixth grade. I played football, basketball, and baseball. I played everything. I liked football better than basketball. We played a lot of football when I was growing up. We played basketball too but we played more football than anything else.

"I grew up in a competitive atmosphere. My sister Diane was all-state in basketball. To this day I still haven't beaten her. My brother Wayne was all-state in football and basketball and he went on to play at Arkansas and in the NFL for the New Orleans Saints. We always took sports seriously."

Martin starred in both football and basketball at Cross County, playing alongside his brother.

"From my sophomore through my senior year we went 35-2 in football," he said. "My sophomore year we went undefeated in the regular season and lost in the playoffs. My junior year we went undefeated in the regular season and lost in the semifinals. My senior year we went 14-0 and won the state championship. I played receiver and free safety.

"My junior year we played Harding Academy in the playoffs. We were 12-0. But they beat us by one point. I've never seen such disappointment. Our players, fans and coaches were all crushed. I saw my brother break down and he was a tough guy. We played that same team the next year in the playoffs and we beat them."

As a senior, Martin earned all-district honors and was named to the all-state playoff team. In four playoff games he intercepted five passes.

He also excelled on the hardwood as he strove to emulate one of the game's all-time greats.

"I really admired Kareem Abdul Jabbar," he recalled. "I liked him because he was so consistent. He scored in double figures in almost every game. And I always wanted to be consistent.

"In basketball we were just so-so my sophomore year. But we were good my junior and senior year. When I was a junior my brother was a senior. He averaged 20 points and I averaged 18. We both made all-conference, all-region, and all-state. He was a great athlete.

"We got beat in the regional by a team that... Well everyone gets bad calls now and then but we had some tough calls go against us. I won't say that they cheated but they pretty much did. They were an all-white school and we were mixed."

Martin averaged 32 points, 16 rebounds, and five blocked shots as a senior, while shooting 58 percent from the field and 80 percent from the free throw line. But until coach Dill made his way to Cherry Valley it looked like he might not even play Division I basketball.

"Arkansas State had offered me a partial scholarship," he recalled. "And I had some offers from Central Arkansas and some other NAIA schools. Murray State was the only Division I school that offered me a full scholarship.

"I was from a small town and I was a 6-5, 175 pound center. No one knew whether I could shoot or play on the wing. They just saw a skinny kid who could score around the basket."

When he got to Murray, Martin quickly discovered that college basketball was going to be more demanding than he had expected.

"I remember my first day on campus, we played a pickup game that night," he recalled. "There was this guy, Owen Bronston. He had played my position the year before. And he was shooting it from deep right in my face and yelling, 'Christmas!'

"He was really good. I remember going back to my room and thinking I really had to get with it. I was also a little ticked off because I'd never had anyone talk trash to me before. And I think that drove me more than anything.

"I wasn't one of the highly recruited guys. We had some highly recruited players from Ohio and St. Louis. So I didn't know what to expect. But after playing against those guys in practice I wasn't surprised that I got to start as a freshman."

That first year (1985-86) Martin averaged 11.7 points while shooting 47.2 percent from the field. By midseason the Racers were starting two freshmen, Martin and Don Mann. It was an up and down year as they finished 17-12 overall and 8-6 in OVC play. But they were a perfect 14-0 at home.

"My freshman year I won the team's Defensive Player of the Year award," Martin recalled. "I guarded the other team's best player. If I scored, I scored. If I didn't, I didn't."

The next season saw Martin develop into one of the best players in the league as he averaged 21.2 points while shooting 52.3 percent from the field and 40.5 percent (15-for-37) from 3-point range in the first year after the adoption of the new rule.

"I didn't think anything about it," he admitted. "I didn't make a conscious effort to shoot the 3 until I was a senior. When I came off of a pick wherever I caught it, that was where I shot it from. I had more 3-point plays than I did 3-pointers. In one game against Morehead I had six 3-point plays."

Unfortunately, Murray State stumbled to a 13-15 record, 6-8 in OVC play and just 8-5 at home.

"We had some good players," Martin declared. "Sometimes we played well and sometimes we didn't. There were a lot of good teams in the league then. Going 17-12 and 13-15 was difficult because we had all won a lot of games in high school."

The 1987-88 season looked like a repeat of the previous two years as the Racers won just six of their first 13 games. But once conference play began they got on a roll, winning 16 out of 17 games at one point. And Martin was better than ever, averaging 26 points while shooting 55.8 percent from the field and 35.4 percent from behind the arc.

"The turning point in that season was the game at Memphis State," Martin said. "We lost in overtime. But after that we knew that we could play with anybody. We got into conference play and some of those teams had beaten us with joy the year before. Somebody acting up like that always irked me.

"We only lost one conference game that year and that was to Austin Peay at Racer Arena. I remember Lake Kelly (Austin Peay's head coach) running his mouth after the game and telling people Murray State wasn't as good as everyone thought. That was on a Saturday and we played them again on Monday at their place. I didn't talk to anyone the rest of that weekend. I was mad. All I wanted to do was play them again and beat them. And that's what we did."

"I remember that game," Newton said. "We were down 10 points and I called time out and was talking about bracing up defensively and shutting them down. And Jeff said, 'We're okay. Just get me the ball five times and we'll be tied.' So, that's what we did. We wound up beating them 83-70."

Murray State rolled into the NCAA tournament on a 10 game winning streak. Their reward was a first round game against highly regarded North Carolina State, a game the Racers would win 78-75.

"To me it was just another game," Martin said. "We knew we were playing a good team. But we had played against good teams. After we won we had another game so we couldn't really enjoy it until we got back home. The gym was packed when we got back. We knew then that we had done something special.

"After the season I got a chance to go to the Olympic tryouts in Colorado Springs. John Thompson was the coach. That was an experience I won't forget. David Robinson was there. Alonzo Mourning was there, all those big name players. I saw that I could play with those guys and that gave me confidence. That's what got me started thinking about the NBA. Before that it never even crossed my mind."

Much was expected of Martin and the Racers the next year and they did well. He averaged 25.7 points and set the single season school record for 3-point field goal percentage as he hit 65-of-131 attempts for 49.6 percent. The team finished 19-11 overall and tied for the conference championship with a 12-2 record in OVC play. But they lost to Peay in the conference tournament and failed to make it back to the NCAA.

Looking back, Martin treasures his memories of the fans and the unique atmosphere in Racer Arena.

"It was a special place," he recalled. "You could literally feel people against the back of your legs when you took the ball out. Some of my best memories are from the games we played against Austin Peay there. We had fans, they had fans, and that place was rockin'."

Martin's legacy is inextricably connected with that of teammate Don Mann as they both held down spots in the starting lineup from 1986-1989.

"Don and I were suitemates the whole four years I was there," he noted. "We were close on the court and off the court. We never had any special signals though. I never had to point at the rim and he never had to give me a nod. He would just throw it up and he knew I was going to get it. I can't remember a time when he threw a bad pass."

Newton says Martin was so good they had special practice rules for him.

"We gave him a red shirt that he wore during practices," Newton said. "We wouldn't allow anyone to draw a charge on him and we wouldn't allow him to take a charge. We told our other players if Jeff got a breakaway not to try to block his shot or draw a charge because we were afraid he'd get injured.

"He was a great shooter, perhaps the best in the history of Murray State. He had great range but he also had strong post-up moves. He drew a lot of double teams and box-and-one defenses. But they never slowed him down."

Following his career at Murray State, Martin was taken early in the second round of the 1989 NBA draft by the Los Angeles Clippers. In two years with the Clippers he averaged 6.7 points and 2.0 rebounds per game.

Martin continued his career in Europe where he played through the 2000-2001 season. During that time he had brief stints in the CBA and IBL. Through it all, Murray State was never far from his thoughts.

"I bought a house in Murray in 1991 and I kept it for 15 years," he said. "I'd come back in the summer time and play pickup games. In 2001 I went back to school and got my masters in occupational safety at Murray State.

"My jersey was retired my second year in the NBA. I didn't actually find out about it until after the fact.

'Then in 2004 I was inducted into the Hall of Fame. It took a while and I was kind of like, 'Hey, what took so long?' But it meant a lot to me because of all the great players who've played at Murray State. I try to make it back whenever I can and I follow the Racers as best I can."

DON MANN

by Kevin Stewart

Nobody at Murray State ever sent regional rival Memphis State a thank-you note in the spring of 1985, but someone should have.

Thanks to some very bad decisions by Memphis State, some very good things happened to Murray State.

At Dyersburg High School about halfway between Murray and Memphis, Don Mann was a smallish (5-9) but talented point guard who made all-state in 3A, Tennessee's largest school classification. Mann wowed enough folks his senior year of 1984-85 to woo Memphis State into offering a full athletic scholarship.

But NCAA investigators had their eyes on Tigers' coach Dana Kirk and the offer to Mann turned to mush – in the end the captain of a sinking ship offered only half a scholarship. Kirk went to prison and Memphis State was stripped of its NCAA Tournament appearances from 1982 through 1986.

Having told college recruiters throughout the year that he was a Memphis man, Mann now had few options. The army might be the place to go, he thought – he needed the money. Then Murray State coaches witnessed Mann's magic at a postseason all-star game in Nashville, and Racer head man Steve Newton became convinced Memphis State's loss was Murray State's gain.

Newton was right in a big way. Mann finished a brilliant career in 1989 as Murray State's all-time assist leader (531), a member of the 1,000-point club and arguably the player who powered Murray's greatest team ever.

Along with all-time MSU scoring leader and classmate Jeff Martin, Mann and the Racers captured Murray State's first NCAA Tournament victory with an upset by a #14 seed of #3 seed North Carolina State in 1988 during Mann's junior year. Mann then cemented his place in school history when the Racers lost by a whisker, 61-58, to eventual national champs Kansas which featured the famous Larry Brown as coach and college Player of the Year Danny Manning.

"Some of the locals around Dyersburg were rooting for me to go to Memphis State, but when the full scholarship turned into a half scholarship, I didn't know what I was going to do," Mann recalled fondly. "I didn't have much time to make a decision. So I visited Murray and I loved it.

"It wasn't too small and wasn't too big – kind of what I wanted anyway – but big enough to get some national exposure as a ballplayer."

And for the next four years Mann exposed the country to play that brought him national praise as one of the country's top little men. Mann says ESPN's Dick Vitale either coined or greatly helped promote the moniker "M&M Boys," which other media quickly adopted.

Martin was a 6-6 swing forward who became an excellent 3-point shooter. He had an uncanny knack of scoring inside and his mid-range jumper was deadly. When Newton signed the pair to scholarships in the spring of 1985, Murray State's future was set. Swinging around picks by big men like Carl Sias and Chris Ogden, or running the court like a rabbit, Martin was always a target for Mann's pin-point passes.

"We got along right off the bat," Mann remembered. "We were suitemates (roommates) for all four years. But even in the beginning, when we'd be playing pickup games and pick sides, we always made sure we were on the same team. Some nights just me and him would go shoot baskets and do that until our arms got sore."

As a freshman, Mann started half the games and was named to the Ohio Valley Conference All-Freshmen squad. Mann was second-team All-OVC as a sophomore and a first-teamer as a junior and senior.

The Dyersburg Dynamo made up for a lack of height with other qualities. He was a man in motion, a jitterbug on the court with a body that defied speed – 175 pounds with square shoulders and a barrell-bodied midsection.

A sense of timing and speed motored drives to the hoop, or to open spots on the floor where a vertical jump pushing 40 inches made the lefty's shot-put jumper a thing of beauty. He took charges with the best. He played defense with a sense of urgency.

There were other attributes also at work, intangibles according to Newton, an assistant coach to Ron Greene before taking the reins for the Racers for Mann's freshman season.

"Some colleges, some of the high-majors, might have thought Don was too small to play, but what they didn't realize is that he has a huge heart and he made up for lack of size by playing a lot bigger than he was," Newton revealed.

Mann was always competitive.

"I would describe myself as tenacious and very competitive, and very much a team player," he said. "I would always put the team in front of myself. I would rather pass than shoot, but I had the ability to shoot the ball well.

"We just had a great group of guys at Murray when I was there. Jeff was a prolific scorer and we had a group of guys who were just as close off the court as we were on the court."

The Racers won 17 games during Mann's freshman season. With heavy senior losses the Racers struggled in 13-15 in Mann's sophomore year when Martin led everyone in scoring and Mann was second, a trend that repeated itself the next two seasons.

But it was during that sophomore year ('86-87) that Mann developed a penchant for producing in key situations. At conference rival Austin Peay on New Year's Eve 1986, Mann grabbed the ball with the game tied, drove the court and was fouled with no time showing. He calmly sank both shots for a 61-59 victory.

Then on Feb. 27 in Murray State's final regular-season game, also against Austin Peay, but this time at Racer Arena, Mann banked in a long 3-pointer as time expired for a 69-68 win.

And over his junior and senior seasons, Mann repeatedly took charge at critical points in big games.

"Don just loved to have the ball in stress situations," Newton figured. "He loved being in charge of the basketball game when the game was on the line.

"There was no one better than Don. He knew who the shooters were and he knew how to get the ball to them. He was a very intelligent point guard with a great assists-to-turnovers ratio and he was very dependable."

A 78 percent free-throw shooter as a junior and a 77 percent shooter as a senior, Mann averaged 15.8

points in '87-88 and then 13.4 as a senior when Martin was one of the country's leading scorers at 25.7 points.

As a junior, Mann's two key foul shots helped the Racers to the upset of North Carolina State, 78-75. By most accounts, Mann controlled the game's tempo. His two free throws with 19 seconds gave the Racers a 77-73 edge.

"I absolutely wanted the ball," Mann said of his playing days. "I think it was confidence, my upbringing, just who I am, even now. I'm not afraid to make a mistake and I take full ownership of it.

"I had two kids early in my life but rather than run away from that like some of my friends did, I stuck in there with my girlfriend who ended up being my wife, and I helped her raise our kids."

Against Kansas following the upset of the Wolfpack, Mann put up a mid-range jumper with just seconds remaining. The shot rolled off the rim. A new high point in Murray State basketball wasn't in the cards.

"I got a call from Larry Brown later," Newton recalled. "He wanted to know how we felt at Murray State having the second best team in the nation. Brown reminded me that we played his team closer than any other team did on their way to winning the national championship."

As seniors, Mann and Martin couldn't quite capture the magic of their junior seasons, but still won 19 games and tied for the OVC regular-season championship. Austin Peay upset the Racers in the OVC Tournament and Murray State ended the season with a first-round loss at Alabama in the National Invitational Tournament.

Mann got a measure of revenge scoring 29 points when Memphis State played in Racer Arena his senior season, a game the Tigers won, 73-62.

As of 2011, Mann was a supervisor for a steel company in Decatur, Ala., but he recalls the NCAA Tournament runs and his days as a Racer as if they were yesterday.

"We had a great bunch of guys that really wanted to win," he said. "I was always comfortable and confident in my ability to handle the ball no matter who we were playing or what the score was.

"We never panicked if we got behind. We would listen to our coaches, and we were disciplined enough to set up the right play if the fastbreak wasn't there.

"I was just glad that fate led me to Murray State. I wouldn't trade it for the world."

THE 1990S

by Will Aubrey

1989-90 • 21-9

• *OVC Regular Season Champion*
• *OVC Tournament Champion*

After four years of relying on Jeff Martin and Don Mann head coach Steve Newton knew he would have to find a new formula for success. With only two returning starters, Chris Ogden and Paul King, and seven new faces on the roster the question was clear. Were the Racers rebuilding or reloading?

Newton sounded a note of caution at the beginning of the season, "We're in a rebuilding cycle," he said plainly. "It will be difficult replacing four seniors and 56 points a game.

"I believe we have good chemistry and balance though. We have three seniors who have experienced success in the Ohio Valley Conference, and we have the ingredients of a very competitive team in a well balanced league."

Over the years Murray State had generally opened the season with a home game against someone like Oakland City or William Penn. Most Division I schools do that. But the 1989-90 season began on the road with a game against arch rival Western Kentucky at Diddle Arena.

The Hilltoppers hadn't lost a home opener since 1978 when #1 Duke beat them at Diddle. So what chance did the Racers stand with a group of kids who were just getting to know each other? As it turned out, a very good chance.

They led by 17 points with 10:47 to play. But Western used a full court zone-press to spark a furious rally and with 31 seconds left the score was tied at 64. Then with three seconds left to play junior college transfer Greg Coble stepped up to the foul line and sank two free throws to give Murray State a 66-64 victory.

"I guess I thrive under pressure," Coble explained. "We shoot them every day in practice and I guess the practice paid off."

Coble's clutch play would become a recurring theme.

Ronald "Popeye" Jones led the Racers with 19 points and 13 rebounds. Ogden also had a double-double with 14 points and 11 rebounds, while King added 13 points. Ogden and King played every minute of the game.

"That was basketball 101," Newton said. "That was a group of guys who just wouldn't get beat. They did what they had to do to win. You have to give Western credit. They could have given up and folded, but they kept fighting back."

"I had a little headache before the game. Now I have a migraine. Poise and patience are things that come with experience. I thought Chris and Paul did a good job of calming us down."

Unfortunately the Racers followed that victory with losses at St. Louis and Eastern Illinois. Murray State was 1-2 and in need of a victory when unbeaten Southern Illinois came to town on December 9.

The Racers led by 12 midway through the second half but SIU chipped away and tied the game on a 35-footer by Rick Shipley as the horn sounded at the end of regulation. Shipley crashed into Jones after the shot but no foul was called.

With 48 seconds left in the first overtime period the Salukis led 91-87 but Ogden scored on a putback and then Coble hit two free throws to send the game into a second overtime.

With 1:41 left in the second overtime SIU's Kelvan Lawrence scored to draw the Salukis withing a single point. Then as Ogden inbounded the ball Shipley stole it and laid it in. However, the basket was nullified when Shipley was tagged with a technical foul for slapping the ball while it was still out of bounds. SIU's head coach Rich Herrin was called for a technical foul for protesting the call and thrown out of the game when he bumped an official.

Murray State shot four free throws, making two to go up by three points. Then Shipley hit a three-pointer to send the game into a third overtime, with the scored tied, 100-100.

SIU outscored the Racers 14-8 in the final overtime for the 114-108 victory.

Even so, Newton declared, "We've never been prouder of our guys in defeat. The Racers took a number of major steps tonight."

Freshman point guard Frank Allen had been struggling to find the basket in the first three games but he exploded for 35 points against SIU, hitting 10 of 19 shots from the floor and 13-of-14 free throws.

Two more losses followed as MSU dropped a 71-69 decision to Georgia Southern before getting blown out at Evansville, 93-69. The losing streak came to an end with a 71-68 victory over Southern California College.

"It wasn't pretty but it was in the right column, especially for a basketball team that has gone through what this team has," Newton said.

King led the way with 17 points. Ogden had 16, Allen had 15, and Jones had 10 points to go with his 11 rebounds.

Murray State won five of its next six games to carry a 7-6 record into its OVC opener against Morehead at Racer Arena. The victories came against a collection of lightly regarded opponents but those games gave the Racers an opportunity to gain some confidence and eliminate the youthful mistakes they had made earlier in the season.

With his team on a roll, Newton sounded an optimistic note, "We do expect to be the best. We're starting the defense of our title, and it is up to someone else to dethrone us.

"This team is going to have to play like veterans. We are going to have to overachieve. We've played like veterans here lately and we are very proud of that."

Jones dominated the game against Morehead, scoring 24 points and grabbing 17 rebounds as Murray State rolled to a 79-55 victory.

"We just hope it's the sign of bigger and better things for Ronald," Newton said. "He did a nice job of posting up tonight, and he'll hunt you up from down there and kick the ball back out."

Jones, who had shed an enormous amount of weight during the offseason, delighted the crowd with the first dunk of his career.

"I could do it last year but I didn't get the chance," he said. "We're just getting it together as a team. I've got to thank the guys for looking me up inside."

Ogden had 15 points, Coble had 12, and King had 10.

The Racers were on a roll and what had seemed like a rebuilding year was beginning to look entirely different. For the first time, Newton seemed optimistic when asked whether Murray State could win another OVC crown.

"It's a definite possibility," he said. "It's up for grabs and we feel we're going to be a factor in the race."

The Racers ran off five more victories to push the winning streak to nine. They made it 10 with a 66-58 win over Austin Peay at Racer Arena on February 3 and when the teams met two days later the Govs were determined to get revenge.

But it looked like Murray State had the game well in hand with a 12 point lead at halftime. A frenzied rally by Austin Peay got the Govs back in the game though. And they held a late lead at 53-52 before a 6-2 run by MSU gave the Racers a 58-55 victory.

"We kind of got caught up in the game and they did a nice job of picking the pace up," Coble said. "We finally got our minds back in the game and slowed it down and got the ball inside."

Ogden had 15 points to lead the Racers while Jones had 14 points and King had 12.

The Racers extended their winning streak to 12 games with a thrilling 90-89 overtime victory over Tennessee State. Coupled with an Arkansas loss to Baylor it gave Murray State the longest winning streak in the nation.

It was anything but easy though.

TSU led by 17 points in the first half before the Racers stormed back. Then Murray State frittered away a seven point lead in the second half as poor free throw shooting and turnovers down the stretch allowed TSU to send the game into overtime. The Racers rolled to an 88-82 lead in the extra period and then held on for the victory.

"The thing I was most proud of was the way we battled back tonight," Newton said. "When you're out on top everyone is coming at you and I think, after the first half, our guys realized that. I'm proud of the way we worked in the trenches for this victory.

"We've got to do a better job of taking care of the ball in pressure situations though. That's something we're going to have to work on because championship teams have to take care of the ball."

Victories over Georgia Southern and Tennessee Tech pushed the winning streak to 14 games. But the Racers stumbled down the stretch as they lost two of their last three regular season games.

With the OVC tournament at Racer Arena everyone assumed MSU have an easy time of it. It didn't turn out that way though.

With 4:50 left in the first half of the semifinal game against Austin Peay the Racers found themselves trailing 38-22. It looked like all the hard work they had done during the regular season might be for naught.

But they chipped away and cut the lead to 11 at the half. Then they forced Peay into turnovers on four of their first five possessions of the second half. And with 15 seconds left Murray State led 68-61. Then Nate Jones and Tommy Brown hit three-pointers for Peay to cut the lead to a single point.

With the Govs out of timeouts King just held the ball after the second three-pointer and let time expire. The game clock shut off before showing that time had run out but after an official timeout and a huddle at the scorers' table the game was called.

"It was another day at the office," Newton joked. "That was one of our better comebacks since I've been here."

Jones scored 24 points and grabbed 15 rebounds to lead Murray State. Allen and Ogden each had 12 points while the little used Ismael Rosario came off the bench to score 10 points.

The Racers moved on to play Eastern Kentucky and their Mongoose offense in the finals. The Colonels stationed three players out near mid-court, with their center in the middle and their best ballhandlers on either side. Then they put their quickest player and best corner shooter near the baseline.

They would hold the ball out near mid-court and run the shot clock down to 10 or 15 seconds before attacking. The last thing you wanted was to let them get a lead. But that's exactly what Murray State did.

With 4:43 to play the Racers trailed by eight points, 51-43. But MSU rallied and trailed by just three with under two minutes to play. A three-pointer by King tied it at 57-all and then the Racers held EKU scoreless the rest of the way to secure the 64-57 victory.

Murray State's reward was a 16 seed in the NCAA tournament and a game against fourth ranked Michigan State in nearby Knoxville, Tenn. No one gave the Racers a chance. Steve Newton was referred to as "Frank" Newton and one reporter asked what the "Murray" in Murray State meant.

"The great thing about this team and this season is that we were in a rebuilding year and weren't supposed to be here," Newton said. "This reminds me a little of 87-88 when we advanced out in Lincoln. We're used to the underdog tole and it doesn't affect us in a negative way."

Jones put on a show for the ages as MSU took the Spartans to overtime before falling, 75-71. The sophomore center scored 37 points, hitting three shots from beyond the arc in the process. He also pulled down 11 rebounds.

With 16 seconds left in regulation and Murray trailing 65-62 Newton called timeout to set up a play for Allen. The freshman point guard couldn't get free though and Coble wound up with the ball 25 feet from the basket.

He had made just 27 percent of his three-point shots during the regular season. But he didn't hesitate. He let it fly and it ripped through the net to send the game into overtime.

No one should have been surprised. He told everyone that he thrived under pressure at the beginning of the season. Unfortunately the Racers ran out of gas in the overtime period.

Jones and Ogden were first team all-conference selections while King was named to the second team. Jones was named Player of the Year and Newton was tabbed as Coach of the Year.

1990-91 • 24-9

- *OVC Regular Season Champion*
- *OVC Tournament Champion*

As the Racers began their quest for a fourth consecutive conference championship inexperience was once again a concern. But despite having six new players on the roster head coach Steve Newton was optimistic.

"I think we have a good blend again," he said. "I think the newcomers will compliment the veterans we have. I'm hopeful that we have enhanced our depth. That's one area we concentrated on."

Of course MSU did return three starters as well as sixth man Greg Coble from the previous year. Player of the Year Ronald "Popeye" Jones was back as were guards Frank Allen and Paul King.

And the Racers had the look of a seasoned team as they rolled through the Puerto Rico Classic to open the season. An 81-68 victory over Bucknell in the first round gave Murray State it's 1,000 victory. They reached that mark faster than any school in history, making it in their 65th year of competition.

"To reach this milestone is a tribute to our staff and numerous staffs before us, and to our players and the hundreds before them," Newton said. "I think that it shows what kind of program we have at Murray State. The timing of history worked out where it didn't happen at home. But we're just happy to make history."

Jones led the Racers with 32 points as MSU bounced back from an early 10 point deficit to secure the victory.

"Coach told us no matter what our reputation was, or what we did last year, we had to earn everything this year," Jones said. "We realized that we had to start earning this year in the second half."

After beating Old Dominion in the second round Murray State squeaked past Nebraska 81-79 in the championship game. Jones scored 22 points and was named tournament MVP. It was his fourth consecutive such award. Allen had 21 points.

"We felt going in that we had to take away their transition game and on each offensive possession, play the clock and make them work on defense," Newton said. "We kept them off the offensive boards and kept them from running, so they didn't get as many shots as they did in their first two games. Our guys did a great job."

MSU returned home for an easy 78-61 victory over Georgia Southern before hosting Western Kentucky on December 1. The winless Hilltoppers gave the Racers fits before falling, 97-91.

"It was everything we had warned our guys it would be," Newton said. "It was really the worst case scenario that you could lay out... We hadn't felt defeat and they hadn't won a game. In fact, they had been embarrassed. I knew exactly what we were going to be faced with."

Murray State probably would have tasted defeat for the first time if Allen hadn't exploded for a career high 38 points.

"I really think if I were facing Frank, I'd really try to stay on him and not gamble much," Newton said. "He can obviously burn you."

Jones had 22 points and 12 rebounds while King chipped in with 12 points.

Unfortunately, the Racers dropped two of their next three games, losing at Memphis State and at Arkansas State. So they were 6-2 when they made the short trip to Carbondale to play Southern Illinois.

Midway through the second half MSU trailed 62-54 as Allen struggled to find the basket. The sophomore made just 5-of-21 shots but he came up big when it mattered most. With just 28 seconds left he hit a three-pointer that put the Racers on top to stay as they eked out an 83-77 victory.

"I thought I was going to have a big night," Allen admitted. "But I kept missing everything. I missed my last six in the first half. I missed about six more in a row in the second half. But coach called the play for me down the stretch, and I knew that last one was going in the moment it left my hands. It had to go in. I couldn't keep missing."

While Allen struggled Jones and Coble kept MSU close. Jones had 26 points and 20 rebounds while Coble hit 10-of-15 shots on his way to 25 points and 10 rebounds.

The win broke a four game losing streak against the Salukis.

At 7-2 the Racers seemed to be on the right track. And back to back lopsided wins over Prairie View A & M and U. S. International pushed their record to 9-2. But they proceeded to lose three of their next four games. Particularly galling was an 88-70 loss at home to Division II North Alabama.

When Austin Peay came to town for the OVC opener on January 5, Murray State was 10-5 and coming off of back to back losses. But the Racers managed to eke out a 71-66 victory despite committing 29 turnovers.

Sixth man John Jackson led the way with 19 points. Coble had 18 points, Allen had 11 and Jones had 10 points and 17 rebounds.

With 10 seconds left MSU held a 69-66 lead and Allen was at the line for a one-and-one. He missed the first shot but Peay's players didn't react. So he grabbed his own rebound was fouled again and made two free throws to seal the victory.

"I knew it was a one-and-one," Allen said. "I guess they thought it was a two shot foul. I was shocked that I missed it and shocked that none of them moved."

The Racers won four of their next six games and were coming off of an 80-55 rout of Morehead when they rolled into Richmond to play Eastern Kentucky on January 28.

With six minutes left the Colonels held a 19 point lead but MSU mounted a furious rally only to fall short in the final moments. The 87-82 defeat dropped the Racers to 4-2 in conference play, a game back of EKU and Tennessee Tech.

"It was a tough day at the office," Newton said with a sigh. "We ran into another highly motivated basketball team to say the least."

"We were fired up and Murray's got to expect that," the Colonels' head coach Mike Pollio said. "You don't win three championships and come in and slip past people. We were in the mood to do business. We knew we had to win. The pressure was on us."

Allen led MSU with 19 points. Jones had 12 points and 13 rebounds but made just 4-of-15 shots from the field.

With Jones hobbled by a sore hamstring and a sprained ankle things looked bleak for the Racers as they headed to Austin Peay. He played anyway but was forced out of the game when he reinjured the ankle in the second half. After watching his teammates fall behind 54-53 with 9:28 left, Jones had the trainer retape his ankle and he went back in the game.

The Govs fouled him four times in 30 seconds putting Murray State in the bonus and he hit four free throws to key a 12-7 run that put the Racers back in control. The big man's 24 points and 15 rebounds led the Racers to a 79-71 victory. Coble had 18 points and Jackson had 15.

"I played with Chris Ogden for two years," Jones said. "I knew what he was going to do and he knew what I was going to do. It's getting that way with Tree (Jackson). I know when he's going to shoot and when he's going to pass and he knows the same about me."

MSU clinched the conference crown with a 65-64 victory at Tennessee State on February 18. Jones hit a free throw with two seconds left to put the Racers up by one and then TSU's Leo Parker missed a three-pointer at the buzzer.

Popeye Jones, 1990

"I'm glad our guys found a way to win," Newton said. "Championship teams have traditionally won the close ones, and credit our senior leadership for pulling us through this one."

Jones had 22 points and 21 rebounds while seniors Coble, Jackson, and King had 18, 11, and 10 points respectively. It was the fifth game of the season in which Jones had at least 20 rebounds.

The Racers closed out the regular season with a 91-86 victory over Middle Tennessee and then crushed Morehead 89-61 in the OVC tournament to advance to the final where they once again faced Middle.

Both teams were on a roll. Murray State had won eight in a row and 10 of its last 11 games. Middle had won 10 of its last 12. The Racers had swept the regular season series though, winning by four points on the road and by five at home.

The game itself was something of an anticlimax as the Murray State rolled to a 79-67 victory and earned a berth in the NCAA tournament.

"Last year I was excited," Coble said after the game. "I'm not as excited this year. I guess it's routine."

Jones scored 21 points, pulled down 18 rebounds, and was named tournament MVP for the second straight year.

"Murray played an outstanding basketball game," MTSU head coach Bruce Stewart said. "They got all the contested rebounds and all the loose balls because of their physical, aggressive style of play. Popeye Jones is just a fantastic basketball player. He and the rest of the Murray team just physically whipped us."

The Racers were headed to the NCAA tournament for the third time in four years and one of the host cities was just a few hours away.

"I really want to go to Louisville," Jones said. "I want to be somewhere close for our fans because they've been great to us."

Unfortunately, Jones didn't get his wish. Murray State was seeded 13th and sent to Atlanta to face fourth seed Alabama.

Despite being the underdog Newton was confident his players wouldn't be intimidated.

"We're going to play a good old fashioned Kentucky shirts-and-skins game," he declared. "Kentucky has a great tradition of basketball. Basketball is a way of life and everyone splits it up in shirts and skins on the playgrounds and school yards. We're not looking at their reputation. We're going to toss it up in a shirts and skins game."

But MSU couldn't find the basket in the first half as the Tide rolled to a 23 point advantage. Jones hit just 5-of-16 shots as he was double-and-triple-teamed all night. The Racers did mount a late rally, scoring the final 10 points of the game to make the final score a respectable, 89-79.

Jones led the nation in rebounding and was once again named OVC Player of the Year. Coble joined him as a first team all-conference selection while King and Allen were named to the second team.

1991-92 • 17-3

- *OVC Regular Season Champion*
- *OVC Tournament Champion*

In July of 1991 the Racers' head coach Steve Newton resigned to take over the program at South Carolina. Athletic director Mike Strickland and university president Ronald Kurth moved quickly to replace him and less than a month later Arkansas assistant coach Scott Edgar was announced as the 10th head coach in the history of the program.

"It's quite obvious that it's a great moment of joy, elation, accomplishment," Edgar said. "Murray State has always been known as an outstanding basketball program. Today I assume full responsibility and will begin to accomplish my mission and my goal, which is to not only maintain, but create a newer and higher level of excellence in the basketball program."

Edgar also promised to implement Arkansas' "40 Minutes of Hell" style of play – "I would like to play fast, aggressive, entertaining basketball, and run and press."

The Racers were seeking an unprecedented fifth consecutive OVC championship and it didn't matter to the fans that they would do so with a new coach and eight new players. Another banner was expected.

Edgar did have six players back from the previous year, including two-time OVC Player of the Year Ronald "Popeye" Jones and second team all-conference point guard Frank Allen. Although Allen was ineligible for the first semester because of academic difficulties.

"Popeye can have another All-American year," Edgar said. "I'll find out a lot more about him as the year goes on but he's one of the best rebounders I've ever seen.

"The thing Frank gives us is experience. He's played in 60 games and that makes a big difference."

MSU opened the season with a 102-66 victory over Illinois Tech at Racer Arena. But the Ledger and Times' David Ramey called it the most disappointing 36 point victory in the history of basketball.

"I think it's obvious that it wasn't the prettiest game and we didn't play up to our full potential," Edgar said. "But I would rather play short of our full potential and win than play to our full potential and lose."

Jones led the Racers with 15 points and 18 rebounds. Maurice Cannon also had 15 points and five other players reached double figures.

The victory over Illinois Tech was followed by losses at Southern Illinois and Memphis State. Then the Racers traveled to DeLand, Fla. to play in the Hatter Classic hosted by Stetson where they dropped a one point decision to Monmouth in the opening round. They finally snapped the losing streak by drubbing North Carolina – Asheville 105-81 in the consolation game.

Murray State was 2-3 when they hosted Middle Tennessee in the OVC opener on December 14. Middle had been picked as the co-favorite to win the league along with Eastern Kentucky. And for a while it looked like the Racers would have their hands full.

At halftime MSU held a tenuous 37-33 advantage. And Middle led 42-39 early in the second half. Then the Racers scored the next 26 points en route to a convincing 98-74 victory.

"All we did was extend the defense," Edgar said. "We ran a man-to-man full court and we didn't look to trap as much. We wanted to go toe-to-toe with them and make them earn every inch of the floor."

Jones led the way with 20 points and 20 rebounds. Darren Hill and Cedric Gumm each had 16 points as five players reached double figures. Allen came off the bench to score six points in his first action of the season.

"Frank is used to playing point guard the last two years," Edgar said. "And a few times he set up at the point. I told him that Cedric was doing a good job so go play two-guard."

But instead of triggering a resurgence the victory of Middle Tennessee was followed by six straight losses. Murray State was a disappointing 3-8 when it headed to Clarksville for their second OVC game of the season.

"It's a big ball game," Edgar said. "Our goal is to win another OVC title, and to do that we have to win at least half of our road games. I'm expecting a war against Austin Peay."

It was every bit the battle that Edgar expected. Peay led 39-38 at halftime and they still led by one with seven seconds left when Cannon rebounded a missed Austin Peay free throw. He raced down the floor, taking the ball all the way to the basket where he crashed into the Govs' Rick Yudt after releasing what would have been the game-winning shot.

If the official had called a blocking foul on Yudt then Cannon would have gone to the line with a chance to win the game. But he called Cannon for charging instead giving Peay the 86-85 victory.

"I didn't think it was good call," Cannon said. "I saw a clear lane to the basket but I saw the guy coming. I came to a stop and he went under me."

"I've got to be careful of what I say but I didn't think it was a charge," Edgar agreed. "My kids did everything they had to do to win."

Allen led the Racers with 25 points. Jones had 20 points and grabbed 15 rebounds. Cannon and Gumm had 15 and 14 points respectively.

The string of losses ended two days later with an 86-76 victory over Southeast Missouri at Racer Arena.

"I feel as good after this win as any game I've ever won as a player or a coach," Edgar said. "That includes the win that sent us to the Final Four at Arkansas. I didn't tell the kids before the game, because I didn't want to put too much pressure on them, but we needed this win bad."

For a while it looked like they weren't going to get it as SEMO held a 68-57 lead midway through the second half. But a 10-1 run by the Racers got them back in the game and then they outscored the visitors 19-7 the rest of the way.

Jones led the way with 23 points and 10 rebounds. Cannon had 20 points and Allen had 17.

MSU split its next four games, losing at home to Virginia Commonwealth before sweeping a road trip to Tennessee Tech and Tennessee State and then dropping a home game to Eastern Kentucky.

When Morehead came to town on January 27 the Racers were 6-11 overall and 4-2 in the OVC. The Eagles were struggling too at 8-9. and they were coming off of three consecutive losses. But they had the the nation's leading scorer, Brett Roberts (28.1 ppg).

Murray State rolled to a 49-37 halftime lead and then pushed the margin to 21 in the second half. Morehead mounted a late rally to get within seven with a minute to play but the Racers held on for an 87-83 victory.

Roberts led all scorers with 39 points. Allen led Murray with 22 while Jones had 15 points and 10 rebounds.

"Popeye Jones was definitely the difference in the ball game," Morehead's head coach Dick Fick said. "He's so effective on the boards and shoots the ball so quickly it's hard to defend him. And Frankie Allen really set a good tempo there in the second half for them and took the ball to us."

Victories over Middle Tennessee and Eastern Illinois pushed the winning streak to three games. Then the Racers headed to Morehead for a rematch with the Eagles.

Murray State led 45-37 at halftime but Morehead rallied and with 2:19 to play held a four point lead of their own. Allen hit a three-pointer with a minute left that gave the Racers an 80-79 lead but a free throw by Morehead's Doug Bentz sent the game into overtime.

With seven seconds left in the extra period Allen hit two free throws to give Murray the 93-91 victory. In the first 35 minutes of the game he scored just nine points. But in the final 10 minutes he scored 15.

"I just wanted it, I really did," he said. "I missed some easy shots in the first half, but you just have to keep putting it up there. Right now I'm very happy with the way we're playing I have a lot of confidence in my teammates. I know somebody's going to make a key pass or grab a key rebound."

Morehead's Roberts led all scorers with 35 points Jones led the Racers with 30 points and 15 rebounds. He also had a team high five assists.

Back-to-back wins over Eastern Kentucky and Tennessee State pushed MSU's winning streak to six games. And when Tennessee Tech came to town on February 17 the Racers were in position to clinch a share of the OVC title with a victory.

Allen scorched the nets so his teammates could cut them down. The junior scored a career high 39 points as he hit 14-of-21 shots from the field and 8-of-10 free throws. But it almost wasn't enough as MSU eked out a 103-99 victory in overtime.

The junior was more concerned with his defensive play though, "I struggled a little bit tonight," he said, laughing when he realized how silly it sounded. "I didn't play too much defense and that bothers me."

"When I came here I really wanted to win the OVC in my first year," Edgar said. "Right now I'm proud to be a part of the great Murray State basketball tradition."

Jones had 24 points and 14 rebounds against Tech and after the Racers won two of their last three regular season games to win the title outright many expected him to be named OVC Player of the Year for the third time in a row.

That didn't happen though. Despite being named Athlete of the Year he lost the Player of the Year award to Morehead's Brett Roberts. Allen was the only other Racer named to the all-conference team.

Jones and his teammates took out their frustration on Morehead when the teams met in the OVC tournament in Lexington as Murray crushed Roberts and the Eagles 109-77. Jones scored 17 points and grabbed 14 rebounds in just 19 minutes of action. Allen had 22 points and Cannon scored 25 points in less than 24 minutes.

Roberts made just 3-of-14 shots as he was held to a season low 10 points.

The OVC final was a bit of an anticlimax as MSU rolled past Eastern Kentucky 81-60. Their reward was a date with Edgar's former employer, third seeded Arkansas in the NCAA tournament.

"Guys get your running shoes ready because they will run," Edgar told a large crowd of players and fans when the pairing was announced. " Fans get ready to holler because the Hog fans will be hollerin'. I'd like to beat them at both.

"They won't have any trouble getting up for us. Any team with Popeye Jones won't be taken lightly."

The game was nip and tuck through the first 32 minutes as Arkansas clung to a tenuous 61-59 lead with eight minutes left. But they outscored the Racers 19-10 down the stretch to claim an 80-69 victory.

Allen scored 25 points to lead the Racers while Jones had 17 points and 15 rebounds.

"He's the toughest big man I've had to defend," Arkansas' Oliver Miller said of Jones. "He'd take the ball up with two hands and I'd try to block it and he'd shoot with one hand. It really ticked me off. He's got great skills and he's a great competitor."

1992-93 • 18-12

Three-time first team all-conference player Ronald "Popeye" Jones was gone. But head coach Scott Edgar did have three returning starters to rely on as he headed into his second season – Frank Allen (17.6 ppg), Maurice Cannon (13.4 ppg), and Cedric Gumm (9.5 ppg).

The schedule was brutal though, as MSU was slated to open at Indiana in the Preseason-NIT in addition to playing at Evansville and Mississippi and hosting Texas at Racer Arena.

"My main concern is to prepare my team for the OVC and get us into the NCAA tournament," Edgar explained. "One way I can do this is by challenging my players with a competitive schedule outside the league. We know we have our work cut out for us this year, but it's always going to be that way."

The Racers dropped their November 18 opener to Indiana 103-80 but Edgar was undaunted.

"The thing I know now is that with practice we're going to have a very good basketball team," he declared. "We'll be prepared in March to play teams the caliber of Indiana. The biggest thing we need right now is practice. We play again December 1 and I know we'll be a much better team."

Allen led the way against the Hoosiers with 19 points. Cannon had 11 as did freshman Marcus Brown.

As it happened, Edgar wasn't happy with his team's play in their next game as they struggled to beat Campbellsville, an NAIA school, 103-90. And that win was followed by losses to Rice and Boise State.

But the Racers showed signs of finding themselves in an 87-78 overtime win at Evansville on December 19. Edgar had been telling anyone who would listen that his team was improving in practice, they just hadn't shown it in a game yet.

Allen hit 5-of-6 three-point attempts and led MSU with 36 points. Gumm had 19 while Cannon and Brown each had 13.

"I think I needed to pick it up this game," Allen explained. "It's up to the seniors to step up and lead the team. We've been playing pretty good, but not as good as we're capable."

Two losses followed the victory over the Aces as the Racers lost at Virginia Commonwealth 83-77 and then got blown out at St. Louis 94-58. A 68-64 win at Florida International got them back on track and then they exploded in a 124-71 victory over Pikeville at Racer Arena.

"Everybody needs games like this," Edgar said. "It's hard to gain confidence when you're splitting and fighting for your life on the road.

6-11 junior Antione Teague blocked nine shots to break the school record.

"The fact that the tallest guy they had was 6-5 had something to do with it," he explained humbly.

"If he's active he can block a lot of shots against anybody in the country," Edgar declared. "He may have goal-tended a few, but at least he was going for the ball."

Jerry Wilson led the way for MSU with 21 points. Allen had 18, Brown had 17, and Teague had 12, as did Lawrence Bussell.

A 75-65 triumph at Mississippi pushed the winning streak to three games. The Racers led 16-6 midway through the first half and closed the game with a 13-2 run to seal the victory.

Allen's 22 points led all scorers. Gumm hit 6-of-9 shots from the field and 8-of-8 free throws for 20 points.

Murray State was dead even at 5-5 when they made the trip to Clarksville for the OVC opener against Austin Peay on January 9. Allen struggled, making just 10-of-29 shots. But he hit two three pointers in overtime to give the Racers an 82-76 victory.

"I know I'm going to make something big happen down the line," he said. "I know I'm not going to hit every shot. But sooner or later I'm going to make a big one. I've got a lot of confidence in myself. That's what I thrive on."

Allen led all scorers with 26 points. Cannon had 16 and Wilson had 10.

"It's tough to win over here," Edgar said. "We didn't play great but the kids did some great things and we found a way to win."

The Racers won four of their next six games and they were 5-1 in conference play when Tennessee Tech came to town on January 30. Tech's center John Best, the leading scorer in the OVC, hit a 12-footer to send the game into overtime but Allen hit two three-pointers in the extra period as MSU edged the visitors 117-112.

"We're going to have trouble matching up with people who have good inside scoring," Edgar noted. "Our interior game is improving but the strength of our team is on the perimeter."

Allen hit just 8-of-25 shots but scored 29 points to lead the Racers. Gumm had 23, Antwan Hoard had 18, Cannon had 16, and Brown had 10.

"Some people stepped up for us," Allen said. "Everybody's picking their spots right now with their play, but we're not playing great as a team."

Victories over Middle Tennessee and Southeast Missouri pushed the winning streak to five games. It reached six with a 100-74 win at Tennessee-Martin.

From the outset members of UTM's various fraternities did their best to rattle Edgar, shouting things like... "You're a Rick Pitino wannabe!" and "You're not from Arkansas! You're wearing shoes!"

Edgar got the last laugh though. The Racers crushed the home team and late in the game the PA guy announced that Arkansas had beaten Pitino's second ranked Wildcats.

"I got two wins tonight fellas," he said after the game. "I got one here and one in Arkansas."

Gumm led six Racers in double figures with 16 points. Allen continued to struggle from the field as he hit just 4-of-17 shots but scored 10 points.

Unfortunately, MSU lost it's next two games at Eastern Kentucky and Morehead. An 88-69 victory over Austin Peay at Racer Arena kept its title hopes alive. But Tennessee State put an end to that with an 82-75 win in Murray that clinched the crown. Carlos Rogers, who would go on to play in the NBA, led the Tigers with 20 points and 14 rebounds.

"I think the thing that impresses me the most is that they won a championship on a team's home floor, which has dominated the league for so long," Edgar said. "They were awfully good tonight."

The Racers split their final two regular season games, winning at Tennessee Tech and losing at Middle Tennessee. Then victories over Peay and Eastern Kentucky in the OVC tournament put them in the final against TSU.

They couldn't get past the Tigers though as Carlos Rogers scored 16 points and grabbed 11 rebounds to lead the Tigers to victory.

"All in all they were the best team in the OVC this year," Edgar said. "Night in and night out, they proved it throughout the year and they proved it up here."

Allen received recognition as a second team all-conference selection while Hoard was named to the All-Newcomer team.

1993-94 • 23-6

• OVC Regular Season Champion

Hopes ran high at the beginning of Scott Edgar's third season as head coach of the Racers. MSU was talented, deep, and experienced.

""I'm very excited to get this season underway," Edgar said. "This is the first year since I came to Murray State that I have more returnees than newcomers.

"I feel like we have a good collection of athletes and a certain amount of depth. I think all of our returning players had some bright moments last year and most of those came toward the end of the season."

The Racers returned four of their top six scorers from the year before – Cedric Gumm, Antwan Hoard, Marcus Brown, and Jerry Wilson. But they were no match for second ranked Arkansas in the opener. The Razorbacks rolled to an easy 93-67 victory in the first game at 20,000 seat Bud Walton Arena.

"Early in the game I thought Scotty's kids were in awe of the arena," Arkansas' head coach Nolan Richardson said. "Our team was fired up and played great defense for the first seven minutes. That was the telling point of the game."

Brown led MSU with 13 points despite hitting just 1-of-10 shots from the field.

"The team has a lot of work to do but as head coach I have a lot more work to do," Edgar said. "I thought our team was going to come out ready, but from the tipoff we had to play catchup. We came out and made a lot of mistakes like stepping out of bounds and falling down."

The Racers bounced back with an easy 89-71 victory over Campbellsville in their next game. It was a coming out party of sorts for freshman Vincent Rainey who hit 4-of-7 shots and scored nine points. Rainey had been considered one of the top high school players in Memphis and chose Murray State over Maryland and Missouri.

"My confidence hasn't been up," he said. "I know my playing time is based on what I do. Coach Edgar showed confidence in me by playing me and I wanted to show my appreciation. I think I've been trying too hard but tonight I let it come to me."

Brown led the team in scoring for the second consecutive game with 14 points. Gumm had 12 and Hoard had 11.

"This was a chance to develop the whole team," Edgar said. "This team is only going to be as good as its bench."

A victory over Florida International and a three point loss at St. Louis left the Racers 2-2 when Mississippi came to town on December 22. Everyone expected the 5-1 Rebels to provide a stern test for Murray State but it didn't turn out that way as the Racers ran them off the floor. It was 58-33 at the half and MSU coasted to an easy 87-68 victory.

"Against a good team like Mississippi we can't play any better than we did in the first half," Edgar said. "I know the ball bounced our way, but we were getting after them defensively, hitting the threes, and getting on the boards."

It was an emotional game because little used reserve Anthrius Carter made an appearance after being stabbed in the chest just a few days earlier. Carter was introduced as an honorary starter.

"I wouldn't say it made us play any better, but it was great to see him here and not in the hospital," Brown noted. "Last week was so emotional. We have to thank the fans for caring and showing their support of Anthrius."

Brown led the MSU with 26 points while Gumm had 20 and Hoard had 18.

The Racers won three of their next four games with the only loss coming to Toledo in the championship game of the Toledo Invitational. With a 6-3 record they hit the road to begin OVC play at Morehead.

Over 50 fans followed the team in sub-freezing temperatures to the mountains of eastern Kentucky. The Racers were anything but cold themselves though as they rolled to a 36 point halftime lead en route to a 116-91 victory.

"It was just one of those things," Edgar said. "You hope to have a couple of these at home, but you never dream of having one on the road. We couldn't have done any better."

The game marked the debut of Alabama transfer Marcus Jones who came off the bench to score 15 points. William Moore had 21 points, Gumm had 15, and Lawrence Bussell had 12.

Three straight victories followed as MSU won at Eastern Kentucky and then beat Middle Tennessee and Tennessee Tech at home. So the Racers were 10-3 when Memphis State came to Murray on January 19.

Brown had a game for the ages as the 6-3 guard scored 29 points, grabbed nine rebounds, had six assists and four steals. He hit 9-of-12 shots from the field, 3-of-4 from long range, and 8-of-9 from the foul line.

"He was the best player on the floor tonight," Edgar said. "I've been pretty lucky at Tulsa and Arkansas to be around some pretty darn good players but I don't know any sophomore who does what he does. He practices hard every day and he's a warrior on the floor."

Brown had been the best player on the floor most nights as Murray State was winning nine of their last 10 games.

"I've been feeling it for the last two months to be honest," he said. "My shot has come on. It's just confidence. I didn't think they had anybody that could check me tonight."

Gumm had 16 points and Jones had 11.

Wins over Tennessee-Martin and Tennessee State pushed the Racers' record to 13-3 but they came crashing back to earth with an 83-81 loss at Austin Peay.

"I've been down here three times," Edgar said. "It's always close at the half then they widen the gap to 10 in the second half and we fight back late. Any time Murray State and Austin Peay get together it's like a title game."

Jones led MSU with 29 points but he missed a 14-footer as time expired that would have sent the game into overtime.

Brown was in foul trouble the entire game and fouled out after playing just nine minutes.

"That was the disappointing thing," Edgar said. "You take any team in the country and their best player only plays nine minutes, it's going to hurt."

Bussell had 15 points and Gumm had 10.

Four straight wins followed the loss at Peay as MSU pushed its record to 17-4 overall and 10-1 in conference play, 1 ½ games ahead of the second place Govs who were 7-2. But three straight wins at home by an average of five points caused Edgar to use the word slump.

If that's what it was, a road game at Middle Tennessee proved to be just what the hoops doctor ordered as the Racers crushed MTSU 116-86.

"We haven't been finishing games like we should have," Hoard noted. "We want to play the whole 40 minutes and put a whippin' on people."

Jones led all scorers with 21 points while Brown had 16, Gumm had 15, and Rainey and Moore each had 11.

A win at Tennessee Tech pushed the winning streak to six games. But it looked like it would end at Southeast Missouri. With 4:31 to play the Racers trailed by 18 points. But a furious comeback got them to within a single point with two seconds left and Jones at the free throw line. He calmly sank both shots to give MSU a 96-95 victory that clinched the regular season OVC championship.

"To tell you the truth I've thought about that situation many times," Jones said. "When I stepped up to the line I told Marcus Brown, 'It's money. Put it in the bank.'"

Jones led all scorers with 34 points. Brown had 16 and Moore had 10.

"If you never give up," Edgar said. "Miracles can happen."

The Racers won their final two regular season games and beat Morehead soundly in the OVC tournament semifinals. But they came up short in the final against Tennessee State as the Tigers prevailed, 73-72.

With 21 seconds left Murray State held a one point lead but TSU had the ball. The Racers were in a full court press but Tennessee State's Carlos Rogers was left wide open under the basket behind the defense. Rico Beasley threw him the ball and he dunked it to win the game.

"We were in a 1-2-1-1 and we didn't rotate," Edgar said. "Obviously there was a breakdown. The ball was going to get in Rogers' hands somehow whether we were in man or zone. Credit the guy who found him."

Rogers led all scorers with 39 points. Jones had 20, Brown had 19, and Wilson had 11 for MSU.

The Racers closed the season with a 66-58 loss to Bradley in the first round of the NIT.

Brown was a first team all-conference selection., Gumm was named to the second team and Jones was named to the All-Newcomer team.

1994-95 • 21-9

- *OVC Regular Season Champion*
- *OVC Tournament Champion*

As head coach Scott Edgar prepared for the season he knew it wouldn't be easy to win another conference crown. Six of the top eight scorers from the previous year had been lost to graduation.

"We'll be doing a lot of experimenting with combinations early," he said. "But hopefully by January we'll be able to compete once again for the OVC title."

He did have a first team all-conference player back in Marcus Brown. And although Brown was the lone returning starter, William Moore and Vincent Rainey had made major contributions off the bench the previous year. So the cupboard wasn't entirely bare.

The season got off to a rollicking start with a 138-88 victory over Campbellsville at Racer Arena.

Oddly enough, Brown didn't reach double figures as he finished the game with just nine points. Rainey hit 9-of-11 shots and led the way with 24 points. Moore had 17 as did junior college transfer Larry Johnson.

Walk-on Jarrod Martin thrilled the crowd with nine points. The 5-8 guard missed a dunk in the waning moments though.

"I just didn't have the legs tonight," he said. "On a good day I can usually dunk with two hands."

The 138 points set a new school record as did the 81 points MSU scored in the second half.

"This is just one game and it's not against a Division I opponent," Edgar said. "But I think this team could be really special."

With so much youth Edgar still expected that there would be a few hiccups and it didn't take long for them to show up as the Racers lost three of their next five games. They were 3-3 after dropping a 53-48 decision to Youngstown State in the first round of the US Air Classic in Dayton, Ohio.

They got back on the right track with a 116-97 victory over Prairie View A & M in the consolation game. MSU roared to a 64-46 halftime lead and coasted home from there. Moore led five Racers in double figures with 24 points. Brown had 18 and Rainey had 16.

Back home, they kept things rolling with a 105-63 victory over Pikeville. The final score was deceptive though. Pikeville actually led late in the first half and trailed by just seven at the break. That's when Rainey took over, scoring 22 of his game high 26 points in the second half.

"At halftime I was a little upset with myself," he admitted. "I remembered how we've lost a few games lately that we shouldn't have. That reminded me how much I hate to lose and that I would do anything tonight to win."

Brown had 20 points and 6-6 Mississippi State transfer Greg Anderson had 15.

"I never thought winning was in doubt," Edgar said. "Our depth, speed, and pressure traps were all factors in the game. The same shots were there for Pikeville in the second half that were there in the first, but fatigue started to set in for them. When they started missing that meant fast breaks for us."

Two more wins followed as Murray State beat Milligan College 102-82 before beating Alcorn State on their home court 111-100.

OVC play began at home with a 70-66 victory over Morehead.

The Eagles were coached by Dick Fick, as colorful a coach as the OVC has ever seen. Fick was theatrical, rotund, and loud. He would grab his tie and feign hanging himself and he once collapsed in a mock faint after what he thought was a particularly bad call. For a time, ESPN gave out a weekly Dick Fick award to the college coach who showed the most emotion during a game.

"I call him the Fat Man and we're good friends," Edgar said of Fick after the game. "And I've been saying all along that the Fat Man is laying low up in the woods waiting for everybody.

"You have to give them all the credit in the world. With one break or one shot they come in here and win."

Brown and Anderson led the Racers with 20 and 15 points respectively. Anderson had the biggest basket of the evening as he hit a three-pointer with 45 seconds left to put the Racers up by four.

MSU won three of its next five games. So when Austin Peay came to town on January 28 the Racers were 11-5 overall and 4-2 in OVC play. Peay was struggling at 5-10 and 2-3 in conference play but they had one of the top players in the OVC in Bubba Wells.

With 2:21 to play the Govs looked like certain winners as they held a 73-60 advantage. But Murray State mounted a furious rally as the Racers repeatedly took the ball to the basket, drew a foul, and scored with clock stopped. During that final stretch they made 10 free throws without a miss.

But with seven seconds left they were still behind 79-78, inbounding the ball at Peay's end of the floor. Brown raced all the way down court and launched a 14-footer that clanged off the rim. Fortunately, Anderson was there to tip it in as time expired.

"That's the biggest play I've ever had," he said after the game. "I'd pay a million dollars to have that same feeling again. That was my only rebound all day wasn't it?"

Though some of the crowd of 5,303 left with two minutes to play many were on their feet or on the court celebrating at the end.

"For all the fans that left the game early, they have to have more faith," Anderson said. "It's not over until there are triple zeroes on the clock."

Brown led the Racers with 28 points while Rainey and Anderson each had 17.

"This was a must game," Edgar said. "We've already lost two games on the road and we have a monster in here on Monday night."

That monster was Tennessee State, the league leader at 7-1. By beating the Tigers MSU would have a share of first place. But they came up short, dropping a 72-65 decision. An 82-79 victory over Southeast Missouri followed the loss to TSU. But losses at Eastern Kentucky and Morehead put the Racers' title hopes on life support.

When the team got back home, Edgar let them see what sunrise in Murray looked like by practicing at 6 am.

And the Racers got back on track with a 114-90 victory over Tennessee Tech. Moore hit 6-of-9 three-pointers and led the way with 30 points while Rainey had 26 and Brown had 21.

"We've been playing not to lose and playing scared," Moore said. "Tonight we got the monkey off our back."

Edgar said that he had decided after getting swept on the Death Valley trip that he would change the offense and try to create chaos with more pressing and trapping.

"The easiest thing to do is play someone who is predictable," he said. "I had been running only two plays, plays for Brown and Rainey. I think we only ran those a few times today. I've been too concerned with other teams and not us. I've been watching too much tape and reading too many scouting reports."

Four more wins followed as the Racers got hot while Tennessee State was faltering. And after a 107-75 victory over Tennessee-Martin in the regular season finale Murray State found itself sharing the title with the Tigers despite losing to them twice during the regular season.

MSU's lone senior, William Moore, led the onslaught against Martin with 18 points.

"This is what I was looking for," he said. "I didn't think we could finish first after we lost to Tennessee State for the second time. I thought it was over."

"I'm happy for all the kids but most of all Will," Edgar said. "When the season started we dedicated it to Will."

TSU continued its slide. While Murray was beating the Skyhawks the Tigers were getting blown out at home by Jackson State. And they wilted in the OVC tournament too as they lost to Austin Peay in the semfinals.

The Racers beat Peay for the third time, 92-84 in the championship game.

"I give a lot of credit to coach Edgar for turning us around and getting us up at six in the morning," Moore said. "That was the turning point right there, because ever since then we haven't lost a game."

"He tried to stop the six o'clock practices, but everybody said keep it going," junior Fred Walker said.

Brown led the way in the title game with 28 points. Rainey had 17 and Anderson had 11.

"I have the easy part," Brown said with a grin. "I just shoot the basketball. My teammates find me and set screens for me. Will does a great job running the team and Vincent really stepped up his offense this year."

The Racers were headed to the NCAA tournament for the first time since 1992.

Marcus Brown, 1995 NCAA.

"I'm happy for everyone who follows Murray State basketball but I'm happiest of all for William Moore because this was his last chance," Edgar said. "Next to that, I'm happy for the young men who put forth all the work and put up with me all year."

Brown was named OVC Player of the Year and Rainey was a second team all-conference selection.

MSU's reward was a first round game against second seeded North Carolina.

"The bottom line is if you want to be the best you have to beat the best," Edgar said. "We're not only playing one of the top teams, we're playing one of the top programs in the country."

Carolina had two players in the running for the national Player of the Year award, 6-5 forward Jerry Stackhouse and 6-10 center Rasheed Wallace. But Wallace sprained an ankle in the ACC final and it was unclear how much he would play.

As it turned out the big guy played just 16 minutes and Murray State led by as many as six points in the first half. The Racers still led 42-41 at halftime but the Tar Heels took control in the second half and won by 10, 80-70.

Wallace's 7-2 backup Serge Zwikker scored 22 points while Stackhouse had 25. Brown led the Racers with 26. Rainey had 21, and Moore had 14.

"I remember in the first half North Carolina's Dante Calabria was on Rainey," MSU radio announcer Neal Bradley said. "As he ran by the press table I heard him call out to a teammate, 'You've got to help me. I can't guard that guy!'"

1995-96 • 19-10

• OVC Regular Season Champion

Scott Edgar left Murray State to take the head coaching job at Duquesne in early April of 1995. Press reports indicated that the Dukes offered $40,000 more than he was making at MSU.

"I knew that when we hired Scott four years ago that this day would come," athletic director Mike Strickland said. "He did a marvelous job for us, and elevated our program to another level. When you're successful like Scott is you're going to have opportunities to move up."

A university search committee narrowed the list of candidates to replace Edgar down to five finalists, Murray State assistant coach Kenny Roth, Arkansas assistant Mike Anderson, UCLA assistant Mark Gottfried, Florida assistant Robert McCullum, and Vanderbilt assistant Buzz Peterson.

The administration moved quickly and Gottfried was announced as the Racers' new head coach.

"This is my first head coaching job and I'm flattered and thankful that you believe in me," Gottfried said. "Every year you look at the standings in other conferences and you try to figure out which of those jobs might be yours someday. I've always looked at Murray State as one I've wanted. I enjoy being in the hunt for a championship. Murray has been good for a long time and I have no intention of letting that slip."

Gottfried's uncle, Mike Gottfried, had been head football coach at MSU in the late 70's and early 80's.

The team Gottfried inherited appeared to be loaded with it's top two scorers (Marcus Brown and Vincent Rainey) back from the year before and seven seniors. He was, nonetheless, cautious when discussing the outlook for his first season.

"People can't forget, although we have a veteran basketball team, it is a transition year," he noted. "With a new coach and a new system, things are going to be different this year. The players are excited, as am I, but I've got to be realistic and have some patience. It's going to take some time for us to get to know each other."

Even so, the Racers got off to a fast start with a 108-62 victory in their home opener over Berry College. Senior point guard Kenneth Taylor led the way with 18 points as he hit 7-of-9 shots from the field and 3-of-4 three-point attempts. Greg Anderson had 19 points, Rainey had 18 and Brown had 11.

"We definitely need Kenneth to be a good team," Gottfried said. "His role will change from game to game, but he shot it well tonight. I'm really happy for him. I understand that we were playing a team that was over-matched but I like the way we played."

Unfortunately, it was discovered after the game that Taylor had injured his right leg. He was diagnosed with a stress fracture. He wound up playing in just 14 games and only got two other starts.

The Racers kept winning anyway as they beat Western Michigan and Drexel before dropping an 88-76 decision at Purdue. Back in the friendly confines of Racer Arena they beat visiting Arkansas State 94-82. The Indians were coached by Dickey Nutt, brother of Houston Nutt who at the time was head football coach at Murray State.

Brown led all scorers with 27 points. Anderson had 23 and Rainey had 18. Anderson also had nine rebounds.

"Marcus Brown and Vincent Rainey are two of the best guards we've seen so far," the ASU head coach said. "They may be the best two we'll see all year long."

MSU split its next four games, losing to Western Michigan and Louisville and beating Washington (Mo.) and Ashland. OVC play was scheduled to begin on Saturday, January 6 with the Racers at Tennessee State. But weather intervened.

Despite a winter storm Murray State arrived in Nashville at noon on the day of the game and held its shoot-around at the Gentry Center. Then when the team got back to their hotel at 3:15 pm Gottfried received a call telling him the game had postponed.

"I was told that it was icy outside the gym and on the hill leading up to the Gentry Center," Gottfried said. "But we drove right up to the front door and so did some of our fans."

He also pointed out that games were played at Vanderbilt and Middle Tennessee that night and insisted that the game be rescheduled for Sunday or Tuesday.

TSU head coach Frankie Allen wanted the game rescheduled for late February.

OVC officials told Gottfried to go to Cookeville on Sunday for a game against Tennessee Tech the next day.

Gottfried was not pleased, "The question I raised was: 'If you think I can drive to Cookeville, certainly we can drive to TSU's arena.'"

So Murray State wound up playing Tech on Monday and TSU on Tuesday. Following a 64-63 defeat at Tech Gottfried was unhappy with the officiating.

"At the end of the game we had two possessions and Marcus has the ability to get to the foul line," he explained. "We ran two plays for him and they bump and ride him and he doesn't get to the line.

"We've got 16 conference games and this is just one. We'll have to steal one along the road. We've just got to get mentally prepared to go play at Tennessee State."

Brown led the Racers with 20 points. Anderson had 11 and freshman Darren Dawson had 10.

MSU bounced back with a 71-67 victory at TSU the next night to even their conference record at 1-1.

Back home, the Racers beat Eastern Kentucky and Morehead before going down to Martin and whipping UTM 80-68. After a six point loss at St. Louis ended the winning streak they headed to Clarksville for a date with Austin Peay.

The matchup featured two of the highest scoring guards in the country, MSU's Brown and Peay's Bubba Wells. Gottfried put senior Fred Walker on Wells and he shadowed the Govs' star wherever he went, holding him without a field goal in the first half.

Wells did bounce back with 17 points in the second half but it wasn't enough as MSU prevailed, 71-64.

Brown led the Racers with 30 points while Rainey had 18. In addition to hounding Wells wherever he went, Walker grabbed 20 rebounds.

"I didn't pay any attention to all the hype before the game," Brown said. "I just wanted to get a win. And Bubba Wells knows who Fred Walker is now. Vincent and I had our shots going and Fred rebounded like a wild man."

Two nights later the Racers eked out a road victory at Middle Tennessee, 73-72. MSU led by four points in the final seconds but a meaningless three-pointer at the buzzer cut the lead to one.

After shaking hands with MTSU head coach David Farrar, Gottfried let out a scream, "Let's go home baby!" Then he went over to where the MSU fans were seated to lead the cheers.

Rainey led the way with 32 points while Brown had 20.

The Racers proceeded to beat Southeast Missouri at Racer Arena and they had a chance to put a

1995-96 men's basketball team.

stranglehold on the OVC title with a victory over TSU. But the Tigers did something no one else had done all year. They beat the Racers on their home court, 78-72.

So when Murray State hit the road to Morehead on the Death Valley swing they didn't have any breathing room. As it turned out, they didn't need any as they beat the Eagles soundly, 81-66.

Rainey led the way with 24 points. Brown had 22 and Anderson had 11. Taylor played for the first time in two months and hit his only shot to finish the game with three points.

"I'm so glad to have him back," Brown said. "I missed my guy, parenthesis, exclamation point."

The Racers won four of their next five games to clinch the conference championship. But the regular season finale against Austin Peay was a shocker. The Govs crushed Murray at Racer Arena, 80-65. And Rainey went down with a bad ankle sprain.

"We're a much easier team to guard when either Marcus or Vincent isn't in the game," Gottfried said. It doesn't take a genius to figure that out."

Brown led MSU with 28 points while Wells, at the time the nation's leading scorer, led the Govs with 26.

After beating Tech 85-71 in the semifinals of the OVC tournament MSU found itself facing Peay again with an NCAA tournament berth on the line. And with a second left it looked like the game was headed for overtime with the score tied, 68-68.

Peay's Reggie Crenshaw had just rebounded a missed shot by Brown and was cradling the ball, waiting for overtime. Then with 0.7 seconds left Rainey reached in and was called for a foul. Crenshaw hit two free throws, Peay had a 70-68 victory and a trip to the Big Dance.

"This is hard to swallow emotionally," Gottfried said. "To get the rug pulled out from under you like that is hard to swallow."

It should be noted that Brown played the game with a bruised foot that was black and blue. He was shadow of his usual self and scored just 11 points. Rainey was just a week removed from a serious ankle sprain but he led the Racers with 23 points despite missing two minutes of the second half after being knocked to the floor.

"Vincent Rainey was magnificent," Gottfried said. "He got knocked out cold and came back in the game."

Murray State dropped its final game of the season, an 89-85 loss at Missouri in the NIT.

Brown and Rainey were both first team all-conference selections. And Brown was named Player of the Year for the second year in a row.

1996-97 • 20-10

• OVC Regular Season Champion

• OVC Tournament Champion

On paper it looked like Murray State might struggle in Mark Gottfried's second season as head coach. After all, the Racers would be without four players who started the year before, including two-time OVC Player of the Year Marcus Brown.

But they looked like a juggernaut in a season opening 84-45 thrashing of Belmont. Vincent Rainey, a senior, led the way with 22 points. Junior college transfer De'Teri Mayes had 18. And sophomore Darren Dawson came off the bench to score 12 points as he hit 4-of-5 three-point attempts.

"We played pretty well in some areas," Gottfried said. "Overall we're happy with it. It was a difficult game to play because they take so much time off the clock."

Rainey was cautiously optimistic, "The biggest thing for this team is time. We have tremendous heart and a never-say-die attitude. Our only questions are rebounding and depth."

An 85-75 victory over IUPUI ran MSU's record to 2-0 and hopes were high as the Racers headed to Murfreesboro to play Middle Tennessee State.

Unfortunately, the two questions Rainey had about the Racers came into glaring focus. MTSU outrebounded them and Murray's lack of depth was apparent as all but three of their points came from four players. The result was a humbling 85-72 defeat.

"I still think we're going to be a good team," Gottfried said. "Middle Tennessee was underestimated by all of us. They've beaten Providence and played Alabama to the wire."

"We've only played Division II schools and they've played six games already against teams like Providence, Alabama, and New Orleans," Rainey agreed.

Mayes led the Racers with 28 points and Rainey had 18. Aaron Page scored just three points and was 0-for-10 from the field.

A couple of 20+ point victories over Alcorn State and Campbellsville at Racer Arena ran MSU's record to 4-1 with a three game road swing against Arkansas State, St. Louis and Auburn up next.

With 23 seconds left against ASU Mayes hit a three-pointer from the corner to give Murray State a 69-68 lead. Instead of calling timeout the Indians' head coach Dickey Nutt let his team try to score before MSU could get its defense set and it paid off.

Forward Mark Kiehne missed a jump shot from the baseline but Jabari Myles came down the middle of the lane and got the tip-in. Mayes missed a last second three-pointer that would have won the game for Murray State.

"I thought we did just about every thing we needed to do to win the game," Gottfried said. "We just came up 3.8 seconds short."

Mayes led the way for the Racers with 22 points. Rainey had just nine points and Gottfried said his team "was its own worst enemy" because it didn't get the ball to Rainey enough.

Losses at St. Louis and Auburn followed in quick succession. But another victory over Alcorn State, this time on the road, snapped the losing streak.

Chad Townsend, 1997

And MSU evened it's record in OVC play at 1-1 with an 80-68 victory at Tennessee-Martin on January 6. With 500 Racer fans in attendance it almost felt like a home game.

"I think our guys, mentally, were ready to get into our league," Gottfried said. "Every team in America zeroes in on the league this time of year."

Junior point guard Chad Townsend echoed that sentiment, "It's conference play. It's time to get down."

Rainey led the way with 28 points while Mayes had 21.

"The biggest thing is I just want to get back to Racer Arena," Rainey said. "We haven't had a home game in a month. And we know that even though we don't get good crowds in the preseason it will be packed for Austin Peay."

Unfortunately the Racers still had one road game before hosting Peay, at Eastern Illinois. And they lost 76-64. So when Peay came town on January 11 they were just 6-5 overall and 1-2 in OVC play. After starting the season 2-8 the Govs came into the game having won four in a row and they were 3-1 in conference play.

Murray was still smarting from a loss to Peay in the championship game of the conference tournament the year before. But this game was more than a showdown between two arch rivals. It was also a showdown between the league's two best players, Rainey and Peay's Bubba Wells.

This time Rainey and the Racers came out on top. Rainey outscored Wells 33-32 and grabbed 12 rebounds as MSU won 85-78.

"He's going to rise up," Gottfried said of Rainey. "He's the definition of competitive greatness. He's a great competitor who loves the battle."

Freshman Michael Turner was the first of three Racers to get a crack at defending Wells. Rainey and

Mayes took their turns on him later in the game. Gottfried said he wanted to front Wells with the 6-7 Turner and it was a challenge the freshman relished.

"It was a big assignment," he admitted. "He had 35 and 39 in his last two games. So I said if he got 34 or below today I would have done something."

MSU beat Tennessee State 87-75 two days later before hitting the road again to face Eastern Kentucky and Morehead.

With 6:40 to play the hapless Colonels led by 14 points, 56-42, and it looked like a major upset was in the offing. But with 13.7 seconds left the Racers were within a single point at 59-58. Gottfried called timeout and set up a play for Rainey.

The senior got the ball off of an in-bounds pass at the top of the key.

"I tried to go to the hole as soon as I got the ball," he said. "The guy who was on me was a good defender. But when I hesitated he relaxed and I went by him."

Rainey took it all the way to the rim and laid it in to give the Racers a 60-59 victory.

"He's going to get the last shot for us most of the time," Gottfried said. "He's our only senior and if we go down I want him taking the last shot."

The three game winning streak came to an end at Morehead as Murray dropped an 86-78 decision.

Southeast Missouri, Eastern Illinois, and Tennessee Tech were tied atop the OVC at 5-2. Murray State and Austin Peay were tied for fourth at 4-3. But the Racers' next four games were all at home and two of those games were against conference co-leaders SEMO and Tech.

First up was SEMO. And with 16.5 seconds left the score was tied 75-75. Gottfried called timeout to set up a play against the Indians man-to-man defense. But SEMO switched to a zone so when Townsend took the in-bounds pass Gottfried called out for him to just take his man.

Townsend started to the right of the lane, beat his defender to the left and lofted a shot just inside the free throw line. It rolled in and the crowd went wild.

"Chad kind of improvised," Gottfried said. "But I wanted him to put it on the floor. He'd been having a great game."

1996-97 men's basketball team.

The Racers won despite being outrebounded by five as SEMO's 6-10 Bud Eley grabbed 20 boards to go with his 34 points.

Rainey led Murray State with 25 points. Mayes had 19 and Townsend had 16.

MSU went on to beat Middle Tennessee State, Tennessee Tech, and Tennessee-Martin at home to take sole possession of first place in the conference. Next they beat SEMO on the road to run their record to 14-6 overall and 9-3 in the OVC.

And then, suddenly, everything changed. The Racers were blown out at Tennessee State, losing 84-68. Then they lost by 12 at Austin Peay. Finally, they lost 89-62 at Tennessee Tech after leading by four at halftime. They had played four games in seven days and lost the final three.

"I'm embarrassed," Gottfried said. "I'm embarrassed for the team and the program. We have a team that plays hard. And we did that for the first 20 minutes, but not the last 20 minutes. We collapsed in every phase of the game in the last 20 minutes – offensively, defensively, and at the free throw line. I don't have an answer. I don't know why."

"I talked to coach Gottfried about that losing streak after the season was over," Murray State's radio announcer Neal Bradley said. "He told me then that he thought the team was just mentally and physically exhausted."

At 14-9 overall and 9-6 in conference play it looked like the Racers were dead in the water.

And then, suddenly, everything changed again. Back at Racer Arena MSU cruised past Morehead 82-65 despite being outrebounded as Mayes led five players in double figures with 25 points.

"Today we played good, not great but good," Gottfried said. "No other conference in America makes you play four games in seven days in four different cities and then come home and play three games in five days. That's a lot of games for a team without much depth."

Despite the difficult schedule the Racers won their next three games to finish the regular season on a four game winning streak and tie Peay for conference championship.

Their reward was a date with Middle Tennessee in the semifinals of the OVC tournament. The teams had split during the regular season with Middle winning in Murfreesboro by 13 and MSU winning in Murray by six. So everyone expected a close game.

Everyone was wrong. The Racers held MTSU scoreless for the first 10 minutes en route to a 74-48 victory.

"Tonight our defense was good but I think Middle Tennessee had one of those nights where there's a lid on the rim and it's not going to go in," Gottfried said. "It's a nightmare for a coach when you have one of those nights."

Townsend led MSU with 22 points. Mayes had 21 and Rainey had 10.

Arch rival Austin Peay awaited Murray in the final. And once again the Racers would have to try to find a way to contain Bubba Wells.

Gottfried admitted that he'd spent a lot of time thinking about Wells, "One night I rolled over in bed to give my wife a kiss and I said Bubba."

All that thought did little good as Wells scorched the nets, scoring 38 points in the final. But despite that and despite having both Rainey and Mayes foul out, the Racers prevailed, winning 88-85 in overtime.

With 12 seconds left in regulation Murray State trailed 69-66. But Gottfried called timeout and designed a play for Mayes to get the ball at the top of the key. The 6-3 junior caught the ball cleanly and drilled a turnaround jump shot from 20 feet to send the game into overtime.

With a minute left in overtime the score was tied at 79. But both Mayes and Rainey were already on the bench with five fouls.

"I definitely felt like the game was on my shoulders," Townsend said. And he held the team together down the stretch.

Aaron Page tipped in a miss by Townsend with 36 seconds left. Then he hit two free throws to put MSU up 83-79. Layups by Dawson and Townsend made it 87-83. Then after a basket by Wells, Dawson hit a free throw to give the Racers an 88-85 advantage.

After a final, desperate fling by Wells missed the mark Murray's players ran onto the court in jubilation, piling on top of Townsend. Gottfried was in the middle of it all, shirt untucked, hair mussed, and tears in his eyes.

"Our guys just kept making the plays that had to be made," Gottfried said. "I'm very thankful for that.

A year ago I had to fight back tears but it was because I was on the other side."

Townsend was named tournament MVP and Mayes was Newcomer of the Year. Rainey and Mayes were first team all-conference selections and Townsend was named to the second team.

The Racers were given a 15 seed in the NCAA tournament and matched up against 8th ranked Duke. And they gave the heavily favored Blue Devils fits before succumbing 71-68.

At halftime the game was tied 35-35. But Duke went on a 16-4 run to seize control in the second half as Jeff Capel scored 18 of his game high 25 points.

Murray State rallied gamely though and Rainey launched an 80 foot desperation shot at the buzzer that would have sent the game into overtime. But it bounced off the rim.

"We were one athletic defender away," Gottfried said. "We were going to have a tough matchup and we knew it was going to be Capel, Trajan Langdon, or Ricky Price. And tonight it was Capel.

"That was a fear of mine going into the game. I was hoping they wouldn't expose our weakness but ultimately they did."

1997-98 • 29-4

- *OVC Regular Season Champion*
- *OVC Tournament Champion*

Having won nine of the last 10 OVC titles it was no surprise that the Racers were picked to win the league again despite losing all-everything Vincent Rainey to graduation. With preseason Player of the Year De' Teri Mayes and last season's OVC tournament MVP Chad Townsend along with talented newcomers Isaac Spencer, Rod Murray, and Duane Virgil Murray State appeared to be loaded.

"Offensively, we're right where we want to be," Gottfried said. "I like our unselfishness. We've got guys who could average more points, but they're more interested in winning. Our goal is to be the best defensive team in the country."

The Racers faced a stiff challenge right out of the gate. Instead of opening the season at home against a Division II team as they had usually done in the past, they opened on the road against Atlantic-10 power Dayton. At halftime Townsend and Mayes were a combined 1-for-11 from the field but surprisingly the score was tied 29-29. In the second half they hit 10-of-19 shots and MSU eked out a 76-69 victory.

"We have the luxury of senior guards and you can bet your bottom dollar that makes a difference," Gottfried said. "De' Teri is an excellent shooter and when it's not going in the hole you have to keep letting him go and hope that he makes some."

Mayes finished with a game-high 23 points.

"Coach Gottfried will never tell me to quit shooting," he said. "The guys kept encouraging me. I was rushing it a little bit and I was anxious early on. I was getting frustrated with myself. But it's hard to turn down a shot. I forced some tonight but I knew it would eventually come."

Back at home the Racers beat Belmont 79-59 and then proceeded to win the first and only Racer Thanksgiving Classic by beating Western Illinois and Idaho State.

Next up was the OVC opener against Eastern Kentucky. The Colonels came in with an 0-3 record, having lost to Berea, Florida International, and Miami (Fla.). So everyone expected Murray State to have an easy time of it.

Defying expectations, Eastern led throughout most of the first half and despite giving up the lead hung tough in the second half. With 1:54 to play the Racers held a tenuous 57-54 advantage. But they outscored EKU 7-4 down the stretch to secure a 64-57 victory.

"Eastern Kentucky did a heck of a job against us," Gottfried said. "They prepared well for us. That just shows you how good our league is. They were picked ninth in our conference but they won't finish ninth."

Mayes led the way for Murray State with 22 points.

"This was a great win in conference play," he noted. "No team is going to come in here and let us embarrass them."

As it happened, Mayes was wrong. In their very next game the Racers ran Morehead out of the gym in a 91-69 victory.

Murray State ran its record to 9-0 with victories over Morehead, Washington (Mo.), Campbellsville, and Western Kentucky. And when the Racers played Michigan in the first round of the Puerto Rico Holiday Classic they were playing for a spot in the top-25.

1997-98 men's basketball team.

The Wolverines were too big though and they used their size to great advantage as they cruised to an easy 76-53 victory. Michigan's starting front line outscored Murray State's 41-2 and out-rebounded them 30-16.

But MSU had an easier time with 12th ranked Arkansas in the second round, beating the Razorbacks 94-83 behind 42 points from Mayes.

"They just beat us," Arkansas' legendary coach Nolan Richardson said. "They've got a nice ball club. They're aggressive, rangy, and quick. Mayes is better than anybody we've got."

The senior guard had 10 rebounds to go with the 21 points he scored in each half.

"He'd be pushing for some All-America teams if our league had a higher profile," Gottfried said.

The Racers closed out their trip to Puerto Rico with an 84-76 overtime victory over Iowa State. With 20 seconds left in regulation Murray State trailed 71-66 but two three- pointers by Townsend and Mayes sandwiched around an Iowa State free throw sent the game into an extra period. The Racers then outscored Iowa State 12-4 and moved to 11-1 on the season.

"I'm so excited for our program and our players," Gottfried said. "This was one of the most unbelievable games I've ever been involved with. I hope this will give our program a real shot in the arm and give our players confidence."

Mayes led MSU with 27 points and Townsend chipped in with 16.

"We're never going to give up," Townsend declared. "We'll keep fighting until the end. It's up to De'Teri and me to make shots like we did at the end of regulation and we came through."

Back on the mainland the Racers again found themselves working overtime. But the outcome wasn't pleasant as they lost at Middle Tennessee 76-71 despite a phenomenal game by Spencer who had 22 points and 17 rebounds.

"This is hard to swallow," he said. "Last year (sitting out under proposition 48) we never went to the road games, and we didn't know coming in what kind of atmosphere to expect. It's hard to win on the road in the conference. We'll just have to find a way."

And that's exactly what the Racers did as they crushed Tennessee Tech in Cookeville two nights later 95-72.

"We played defense the way we have to play it where we're down, our shoes are squeaking and we're talking to each other," Gottfried said. "We got away from that a little bit the last game and we need to play good defense to win. I thought it was really good tonight."

Mayes led the way with 19 points while Spencer had 16 and Virgil had 14.

Four more wins followed as Murray State beat Indiana-Southeast, Tennessee-Martin, Eastern Kentucky, and Eastern Illinois. So the Racers were on a roll when Southeast Missouri came to town on January 17 and it showed as they ran the visitors out of Racer Arena 101-66.

It was a night when everything went right.

Spencer had slipped on a patch of ice the night before and twisted his knee. There was some question whether he would even play but he had one of his best games of the year as he exploded for 24 points and 11 rebounds.

Aaron Page caught a pass that spun him completely around but he calmly set his feet and drilled a three-pointer. He hit all four of his three-point attempts.

Virgil and Marvin Gay who had combined to shoot 52 percent from the free throw line all year were a perfect 6-for-6 from the stripe.

And newcomer Aubrey Reese, who was averaging just 2.9 points hit 5-of-6 shots and scored 13 against SEMO.

"We came out fired up today," Spencer said after the game. "My knee hurts a little bit now, but it didn't when the emotion was pumping. I thought it would slow me down but it didn't."

"Everything was right today; everybody was involved," Mayes said. "Coach (Tevester) Anderson (Gottfried's top assistant) stressed to us about having the killer instinct to see if we could put a team away when we have a lead on them, and we did today."

Back on the road again, the Racers lost at Austin Peay 80-72 falling to 7-2 in conference play, one game behind league leader Middle Tennessee.

"You've got to give them all the credit," Gottfried said. "They came out here to play and they played a great basketball game. They did everything they needed to do to win. It was probably the best game they've played all year."

Townsend led the Racers with 20 points while Mayes had 17. James Stewart paced the Govs with 25 points as he went 3-for-4 from three-point range. The loss left MSU a game behind Middle Tennessee in the conference standings.

Murray State got back on track two nights later with a 96-84 victory over Tennessee State.

When Middle Tennessee came to town on January 29 the Racers were tied with Eastern Illinois for second, one game behind the Blue Raiders. After Murray escaped with a 78-75 victory over Middle all three were tied for first at 9-2 in conference play.

"We really needed this one. We didn't want to go two games behind them," Mayes said after scoring a game high 30 points. "That's a great team, a big time team. You've got to

1998 OVC Tournament

tip your hat to them because it's easy to come in here and get intimidated by our crowd, but they didn't."

The overflow crowd of 6,011 fans wasn't able to breathe a sigh of relief until a last second three-point attempt by Middle's Freddie Martinez went awry.

"I was thinking, 'Here we go again,'" Gottfried said. "They don't go away. They've got guys who can shoot. But I thought we defended the last shot very well."

After beating Tennessee Tech and Morehead the Racers took sole possession of first place with a 94-66 victory over Tennessee-Martin. It was a five point game early in the second half but a 33-9 run by MSU put it away.

Mayes led all scorers with 37 points and Page had 14.

"I felt good coming in and the other guys did a good job of getting me the ball," Mayes said. "The other guys did all the work by penetrating and dishing. All I did was catch and shoot. I've got to thank my teammates for this."

Mayes hit 14-of-21 shots and 6-of-11 three-pointers.

"De'Teri was unbelievable," Gottfried said. "He was out of this world. Obviously, that was the difference in the game. And when Aaron comes in and hits a couple his confidence level rises. I'm excited about how we're playing right now. "

Murray State closed out the regular season with four more victories to win the OVC crown. Then they beat Tennessee Tech in the first round of the conference tournament to set up a third meeting with Austin Peay.

The two teams had split a pair of close games during the regular season. But this time the Racers crushed the Govs 81-56 as Mayes scored 25 points and Spencer tallied 17 while making all seven of his shots from the floor. Townsend finished with 17 points.

Then they ran past Tennessee State 92-69 in the championship game to secure a spot in the NCAA tournament. Spencer led the way with 20 points and Townsend had 19. Virgil went 7-for-7 from the field and scored 15 points.

Townsend was named tournament MVP. Mayes and Townsend were both first team all-conference selections. Spencer was named to the second team.

Duane Virgil

Both Spencer and Murray were named to the All-Newcomer team. And Gottfried was named Coach of the Year.

"Our guys don't feel like they're through," Gottfried said. "We're looking forward to being in the greatest show on earth. Our guys see a bigger picture than just participating in the NCAA tournament. We want to move through it.

Murray State was ranked 25th in the final Associated Press poll of the season and was given an #8 seed in the NCAA tournament. Unfortunately they lost to #9 Rhode Island in the first round 97-74.

1998-99 • 27-65

- *OVC Regular Season Champion*
- *OVC Tournament Champion*

A little more than a week after Murray State was eliminated from the 1998 NCAA tournament head coach Mark Gottfried left to take the head coaching job at the University of Alabama. It took just two days to find his replacement as MSU selected Gottfried's top assistant, Tevester Anderson, to be the 12th head coach in the history of the program.

Anderson was introduced in a press conference held in the brand new Regional Special Events Center, the first event to take place in the facility.

"I'm so thankful and happy this day has arrived," he said. "I've been around a long time and I've helped a lot of programs. But now this program is in my hands. My goal is to take this program to another level. We not only want to get to the NCAA tournament; we will win and move through it. I assure you of that."

With Isaac Spencer, Rod Murray, and Duane Virgil back Anderson was confident his front line could match up with anybody.

"I really like what we have up front," he said. "They were good last year and they've gotten bigger, stronger, quicker, and more experienced. I'm very excited about Isaac Spencer. He had a very good sophomore year and by the end of the season he may have been our best player."

The backcourt was another matter entirely. When Chad Townsend and De'Teri Mayes graduated the previous spring the Racers lost one of the best guard tandems in school history. Anderson knew he would have to rely on Aubrey Reese and Marlon Towns.

Reese had played sparingly as a sophomore, averaging just 4.6 points. He did shoot well from the floor, 48.9 percent overall and 37.5 percent from three-point range. And he had proven himself to be a solid ball handler.

Towns had played his freshman season at Arkansas and like Reese he had seen limited action. He was a highly regarded high school player though, having been chosen as the top player in the state of Tennessee when he was a senior and one of the top 30 players in the nation. He came to Murray State from Northern Oklahoma College where he averaged 18 points and 15 rebounds and was tabbed by CNN/SI as one the top mid-major newcomers in the nation.

In the opener against Southern Illinois Reese and Towns struggled. Reese scored nine points but was 2-for-7 from the field and 5-for-10 from the foul line. And Towns scored just one point as he missed all seven of his shots from the floor and made just 1-of-3 free throws.

Spencer led the Racers with 16 points. Virgil had 15 and Murray had 11.

1998-99 men's basketball team.

With just under five minutes to play SIU led 62-57 and Towns was out of the game, having been taken off the floor on a stretcher after a blow to the head. But Murray State scored the final eight points of the game to win it 65-63.

"It was certainly not beautiful but a win's a win," Anderson said. "Getting the win was the most important thing. That was our goal."

It was clear though, that Reese and Towns would have to play better for the Racers to reach their ultimate goal, an OVC championship.

After a victory at Belmont MSU crushed Arkansas-Little Rock 91-66 in the first round of the Sooner Classic as Towns hit 5-of-10 three-point attempts and Reese dished out 10 assists while committing just two turnovers.

But the Racers' guard play was shaky again in a 68-64 victory over Oklahoma in the championship game as their starting backcourt committed 11 turnovers and hit just 6-of-20 shots. Fortunately, they made up for that by outrebounding the Sooners 46-23.

"I'm very happy. I'm just overjoyed," Anderson said. "I thought if we could control the boards we'd beat this team. Our goals were to outrebound them and outrun them. We could have gone ahead early but some unforced turnovers cost us."

Spencer grabbed 14 rebounds, scored 13 points, and was named tournament MVP.

"We were so confident," he said. "We knew we could beat this team and we did. Our defense really helped us tonight. Coach Anderson did a good job of setting up defenses to keep them off balance."

Conference play got under way with a trip to Death Valley to play Morehead and Eastern Kentucky on December 3. And the Racers' guards signaled that they were coming of age with a scintillating performance in a 90-59 victory over the Eagles.

Reese hit 8-of-14 shots and 3-of-6 three-pointers as he scored 19 points. And Towns hit 3-of-4 three pointers and 6-of-7 free throws for 17 points. Murray and Spencer also had big games as they scored 16 and 15 points respectively.

Three more wins pushed the Racers' record to 8-0. And at 2-6 Western Kentucky didn't seem to be much of a threat when they came to town on December 19. Oh, Anderson cautioned that anything can happen in a rivalry game. But his fears proved to be unfounded as Murray State rolled to a 69-57 victory.

Murray and Spencer led the way with 17 points each.

"I knew I played well against them last year," Murray said. "And I wanted to do the same this year. We all know about the rivalry. But Isaac and I were able to give the team a lift tonight."

After dropping two-out-of-three games in the Rainbow Classic in Honolulu the Racers returned home and returned to OVC play against Tennessee Tech. Murray led five players in double figures with 14 points as MSU rolled to a 75-53 victory.

"It was a game that I had some concerns about," Anderson said. "We challenged our guys to suck it up and give a good effort. And they rose to the challenge."

The win over Tech started a four game home stand for MSU which Anderson said would be crucial if the Racers wanted to win another OVC championship.

"I feel like we need to win all four of these games," he said. "We need to come in here and take care of business. You don't need any slip-ups at home in this conference."

Anderson got just what he wanted as Murray State beat Middle Tennessee, Tennessee-Martin, and Morehead to run its record to 14-2 and 6-0 in conference play. Southeast Missouri was also unbeaten in the OVC so when the two teams met in Cape Girardeau on January 14 sole possession of first place was on the line.

With five seconds left Murray State trailed 70-69. Having to inbound the ball under SEMO's basket, Anderson put the game in the hands of his point guard, Reese. The junior quickly made his way downcourt and hit an off balance jumper in the lane with one-tenth of a second left to give MSU a 71-70 victory.

"Coach Anderson just told me to make something happen," Reese said. "I saw a double-team coming so I just leaned in and I was lucky that it went. I tried to put it at the rim and I was hoping I would get fouled. That was the biggest shot I've ever made in my life."

Spencer led all scorers with 22 points. Towns had 15; Reese had 13; and Virgil had 12.

"It shows the kind of character Aubrey has to take adversity and deal with it like that," Anderson said. "I told him to go coast-to-coast with it and the fact that he did it shows he has the heart of a champion."

The Racers then beat Eastern Illinois on the road 86-73 and returned home to beat Tennessee State 81-71. They ran their record to 18-2 before a record crowd of 8,352 at the RSEC by drubbing Austin Peay 89-58. Spencer led six players in double figures with 16 points and 10 rebounds.

Three more wins pushed Murray State's winning streak to 11 games and its record to 21-2. But the streak ended on February 6 at Tennessee-Martin.

UTM's head coach Cal Luther had announced his retirement earlier in the season. Luther had coached the Racers in the 60's and 70's. And Martin played an inspired game in beating MSU 74-73.

That loss was followed by a 62-51 defeat at St. Louis. So the Racers returned home to play SEMO, having lost two in a row. MSU led the OVC at 13-1 while the Indians were second at 12-2. But Anderson downplayed the importance of the game.

"It won't decide anything," he said. "If we win we will be two ahead and if they win we will be tied. It will only put the winner in a better position.

"I think the past two games are pretty much behind us. We're healthy and we've got more energy so I think we'll be okay."

SEMO led 26-17 in the early going but Murray State ratcheted up the defensive pressure and the Indians were helpless. At halftime the Racers trailed 28-26. At the beginning of the second half they went to a full court press and that keyed a 13-0 run that essentially put the game away as MSU won it 62-52.

The Indians only made five shots from the floor in the second half.

"We would like to have pressed earlier," Anderson said. "But to do that you have to score and we couldn't score much in the first half. We always talk about coming out and playing well the first five minutes of the second half, and we turned the game around at that point tonight."

Reese led all scorers with 16 points.

The Racers closed out the regular season by beating Eastern Illinois at home and Tennessee State on the road before dropping their final game at Austin Peay.

Wins over Tennessee Tech and Morehead in the OVC tournament set up a third game against Southeast Missouri in the final.

And just like the first time the two teams met SEMO led by one, 61-60 with just over five seconds to play. In a scene right out of the movie Hoosiers, Anderson initially called a play for someone other than Reese who had beaten the Indians on a last second shot a month earlier.

"We were considering a different play because the first time against SEMO we had Aubrey drive the floor," Anderson explained. "But he said, 'Coach, I'll get it for you.' So we gave him the ball again. When you want a big play Aubrey is the man to get it for you."

Reese streaked down the floor and lofted an off-balance runner over SEMO's 6-10 center Bud Eley as time expired. And he hit it again, giving MSU a 62-61 victory.

Radio announcer Neal Bradley's call was played repeatedly on ESPN, "Reese will bring it up the floor. Two seconds, one second... Shot at the buzzer by Reese... It's good! It's good! He did it again! He did it again! He did it again! Reese does it again! Reese hits it at the buzzer! Reese hits it at the buzzer! And the Racers are going dancing for the third time in a row!"

"I was thinking shot all the way," Reese said. "I didn't have a lot of time to think about what I was going to do. I didn't worry about who was on me. I was just thinking about making the shot."

Reese and Virgil led MSU with 16 points apiece. Spencer had 15 points and 14 rebounds.

Spencer and Reese were named first team All-OVC and Murray was a second team honoree. Anderson shared the Coach of the Year award with SEMO's Gary Garner.

The Racers went on to play Ohio State in the NCAA tournament, dropping a 72-58 decision.

LAST GAME IN RACER ARENA

by Steve Parker

Record books will show that Murray State hosted Tennessee State on Saturday, Feb. 21, 1998 in an Ohio Valley Conference men's basketball regular-season game. What records won't show is what the game actually meant to the glorious history of Racer basketball, because the thousands of Racer fans who flocked to the MSU campus on that uncharacteristically warm February day weren't there to just watch a basketball game. They were there to witness the end of an era.

When a dear friend or colleague retires or moves on to another station in life, it's only fitting to throw a going-away party. And that's exactly what Racer fans were doing on that historic Saturday afternoon – saying farewell to long-time family member who wasn't exactly moving on, but rather being replaced. Predictably, a sellout crowd of 6,154 Racer fans turned out to witness the final regular season game in venerable and tradition-rich Racer Arena.

It was described by the *Murray Ledger & Times* as a "festival-type atmosphere." Free posters to mark the occasion were given away to fans, and a trumpeter stood at midcourt to capture the spirit of Racer Arena so that it could be let out the next season when the Racers opened up the brand new 8,600-seat Regional Special Events Center on the other side of campus. But, as is customary with Racer basketball, the highlight of the day for many fans was the return of numerous greats from the past who traveled back to Murray to help mark the event.

In addition to local luminaries such as Bennie Purcell and Howie Crittenden, some not so often seen stars of the past returned, as well. Most notably,

Popeye Jones was fortunate enough to find a break in his NBA schedule to return to a Racer basketball game for the first time since his rock star-like career ended in 1992.

All former players gathered on the floor at halftime for a ceremony marking the history of Racer Arena. Among those in attendance were Paul King and Sheila Smith, both of whom had their numbers retired.

As for the game itself, it provided plenty of suspense if not the typical excellence that was the hallmark of the 1997-98 Racers.

One of MSU's most dominant teams ever, Mark Gottfried's '97-98 Racers rolled through league play and had wrapped up the regular season OVC title before the Feb. 21 game against Tennessee State, which was good because the Racers were seemingly distracted by the atmosphere. Murray State suffered one of its worst shooting performances of the season, hitting just 32 percent. But with stars such as De'Teri Mayes and Isaac Spencer, the Racers hung on for an 81-76 victory. Mayes, who would be named OVC Player of the Year the following week, poured in 27 points while Spencer chipped in with 22. The victory moved MSU's record to 26-3 and the Racers finished OVC play with a 16-2 mark.

Consequently, Murray State hosted Tennessee Tech on Tuesday, Feb. 24 in the first round of the OVC Tournament, which would be the true final game in Racer Arena and the answer to a trivia question years down the road. In the "actual" finale, the Racers had little trouble with the Golden Eagles, posting an 84-63 win.

FIRST GAME AT THE CFSB CENTER

by Justin McGill

Since 1998, Murray State University's most recent arena has played host to a wide variety of events. The Regional Special Events Center, renamed the CFSB Center after a $3.3 million donation from the bank in 2010, has been the site of everything from the Barnum & Bailey Circus to concerts by the likes of Tim McGraw, large youth religious gatherings (like Youthfest '98, the first event ever held in RSEC) to boat shows.

In the end, however, it all comes back to the Racers.

Former Racer head coach Ron Greene said a facility to replace Racer Arena was first promised in 1978. Ground was finally broken for the project in January 1994.

Pre-season exhibition games were played in the arena, but the first official contest took place on Nov. 14, 1998, when the Murray State hosted Southern Illinois. MSU led by as many as 17 points in the first half but fell behind the Salukis in the second half, trailing 62-56 with less that five minutes to play.

The intensity of the crowd had subsided during the SIU run, but that all changed when Racer guard Marlon Towns went to the floor after taking an elbow to the head from an opposing player. That situation presented the Racer faithful with their first big challenge – could they impact a game the way they historically did in Racer Arena?

The answer was an emphatic "Yes!"

Fueled by the crowd, the Racers scored the final nine points of the contest and won 65-62, led by Isaac Spencer's 16 points.

The announced crowd of 7,633 stands today is still one of the largest crowds for a Racer basketball game in the history of the arena, although it was bested by

two OVC wins later that same season – January 23, 1999 against Austin Peay (8,352) and February 11, 1999 against Southeast Missouri State (8,602).

Aside from the game itself, the evening was special for several other reasons. Restless Heart singer Larry Stewart sang the national anthem. The mini-blimp made its first appearance.

And, the trumpeter who captured the "spirit of Racer Arena" during the final season of play there released the spirit with a blast of his trumpet prior to the game.

Many times since then, that spirit has revealed itself, wreaking havoc on opponents and guiding the Racers to victory.

In 43 seasons at Racer Arena, the Racers held a record of 457-126, a mark capped by an 81-76 win over Tennessee State in front of an announced crowd of 6,154 in the regular-season finale and an 84-63 win over Tennessee Tech in the first round of the OVC Tournament.

In 13 seasons at the CFSB Center, the Racers are 151-30 with only one season in which MSU won less than 10 games at home.

The name may have changed, but that's all. In the end, the Racers are tough to beat at home.

Nov. 14, 1998 was a big day for Racer athletics as the football team hosted Tennessee State in a contest to determine that season's Ohio Valley Conference champion. The game took place at Roy Stewart Stadium, adjacent to the brand-new RSEC. The football Racers lost a 46-44 barn-burner on a Tiger touchdown with 1:32 left in the fourth quarter.

STEVE NEWTON

by Steve Parker

Just like the previous 86 games as the school's basketball coach, he looked and carried himself like a Baptist minister. He covered the approximately 30 feet of hardwood with the usual composure. As he approached his more famous and more accomplished counterpart, his left hand held the familiar rolled-up game program while the right hand was free of any objects. It and he, were ready for the big moment.

It only lasted a matter of seconds, and it didn't seal a major financial deal or guarantee, but don't tell Steve Newton that it was just a post-game formality.

"It was the best handshake I think I've ever had," Newton said of his post-game exchange with the losing coach – North Carolina State's Jim Valvano.

It was likely Newton's greatest moment as a head coach. The handshake came after his Racers, an unknown long shot from an anonymous school in western Kentucky, upset one of the elite programs of college basketball. Playing in the NCAA Tournament for the first time since 1969, the Racers stunned N.C. State 78-75 in a first-round game in Lincoln, Neb.

Steve Newton illustration.

In the previous 61 seasons of basketball Murray State had its share of successful teams and iconic players, but this was different. This was on a national stage. This was in the era of ESPN. And, though it was hardly the mega event that it would later become, this was the Big Dance.

Under an assortment of head coaches, the Racers would become regular guest stars in CBS' college basketball series from the late 1980s to the present day. On a seemingly regular basis, Murray State delivered an occasional eye-opening individual performance, an entertaining story line and even tantalized college basketball with a couple of near upsets. Without question, Murray State has a place in March Madness, and it can all be traced back to Steve Newton.

When Newton was hired to replace Ron Greene as Murray State's ninth basketball coach in 1985, he had a clear vision of where he wanted to take the Racer program. Cal Luther made the Racers matter again in the Ohio Valley Conference during his 16-year tenure, and Greene added vision and a memorable NIT run to the program's history. But there was still the missing piece to a strong tradition of winning basketball.

"We wanted to go to the NCAA

Tournament and we wanted to advance," explained Newton, who was familiar with the Racers' history after serving for seven seasons as an assistant coach on Greene's staff. "We set up a war room where we had on the wall what it would take for us to get there."

Newton's entire coaching career had been spent as an assistant coach up until he met with then-MSU president Dr. Kala Stroup for lunch at the Dakota Feed and Grain restaurant in 1985. From that lunch meeting came Newton's chance to lead his own program. And, as was his custom, he was prepared for it.

Spend any time around Newton and his attention to detail and meticulous planning is apparent. His plan for the Racers' ascent into the upper reaches of college basketball was just one in the long line of Newton plans. One of the earliest plans was how to make basketball a career once his playing days were done.

That Newton chose basketball as his vocation should not come as a surprise. A native of Terre Haute, Ind., Newton grew up in the epicenter of high school basketball. If kids from Texas make football a way of life, kids raised in Indiana are drawn to the roundball as players and, later, coaches.

"I made a decision early in life that I wanted to coach," Newton said. "My goal was to make $10,000."

Newton stayed in Terre Haute to play college basketball for Indiana State University and Duane Clee. He was a standout for ISU from 1961-63 and in 1984 earned a spot on the school's Silver Anniversary Team. He's prone to tell people that his No. 33 was retired by his alma mater, and will leave it to the listener to figure out that Indiana State legend Larry Bird sported No. 33 when he was leading the Sycamores to a historic Final Four run in 1979.

After coaching high school basketball following graduation, Newton fulfilled his dream of coaching college basketball when a hometown connection paid dividends.

Newton played prep basketball at Terre Haute's Gerstmeyer Technical High School, a powerhouse in the Indiana high school ranks. It also happened to be the alma mater of the second-year head coach at Division II Louisiana State-New Orleans, Ron Greene. Though Greene was ahead of Newton at Gerstmeyer, each played for the highly respected Howard Sharpe, once the winningest coach in Indiana high school basketball.

"I stayed in touch with Ron by sending him articles from our high school while he was at Loyola," Newton recalled. "I tried to keep him up to date on players in our area and the Midwest."

While in New Orleans, Newton was part of a coaching staff that saw the school advance to four NCAA Division II Tournaments, and "cut his teeth" recruiting and scouting. He also met his future wife, Kathleen Meyn.

After the successful run at New Orleans, Newton moved on to Mississippi State in 1978 to work for head coach Kermit Davis, Sr. Moving to Starkville gave Newton his first glimpse into major-college basketball, and it also introduced him to a future long-time colleague in Mike Dill. Newton and Dill would work together under Davis, Sr., for one season until a familiar face would become their new boss. In 1977-78, Greene was lured away from New Orleans and named the new Mississippi State head coach. Greene, Newton and Dill would work together for one season (actually eight months) in Starkville before Greene would pack up and bolt the SEC for the OVC.

Murray State may have had emotional pull for Greene, who was a former player at MSU, but Newton and Dill had no connections to the small-conference school. "Rebuilding was the key word. The program was at a low ebb," Newton said of the situation in Murray. "I was told, 'Steve, hit the road and get us some players.'"

In the seven seasons Newton served as Greene's top assistant, the Racers not only returned to the upper echelon of the OVC, they laid the infrastructure that would serve Newton well in his next position at MSU.

After reviving Racer basketball over seven seasons, including a magical NIT run in 1980, Greene packed up and headed home to Terre Haute to coach Indiana State.

As for Newton, he felt it was now or never if he was ever going to be a college head coach. "I had 16 years preparation to be a head coach and I was coming to a point in my career where I needed to be a head coach," said Newton, who had been an associate head coach under Greene. "To be honest, I had decided that if it wasn't to be then I needed to prepare myself for another career."

At that fateful lunch with Stroup, Newton laid his cards on the table, as well as his plans for the program. Stroup heard enough and ended her search at what is known in Murray as "Five Points."

"It was a great lunch," beamed Newton.

With the tradition of the program, as well as recent success in the NIT under Greene, Newton felt Murray State was on the cusp of achieving what many in Murray hungered for: an NCAA Tournament berth. "It was all about winning the conference and the OVC Tournament championship," said Newton. We put a laser on that. Everything we did was geared to that."

However, all the plans and goals couldn't overcome the facts before Newton's first season in 1985: the roster lost a lot of talent the year before and the Racers were a middle-of-the-pack team at best. Murray State posted a 17-12 record in 1985-86 and '86-'87 was even worse. At 13-15, it was the last losing record a Murray State team would post, as of this writing.

"It was rebuilding time for sure," said Newton, who had long-time friend and colleague Mike Dill as his associate head coach during those early years. "We spent those two years with a broad recruiting brush and a plan to find the right players."

That broad brush swept across Cherry Valley, Ark., and Dyersburg, Tenn. to collect all-time MSU greats Jeff Martin and Don Mann, respectively.

"They were our cornerstones, no question about it," Newton explained of the duo that would become known as the M&M Boys. "You had to have the great point guard and a scorer, someone who could create his own shot, especially in crucial situations. The M&M Boys were legendary and I was blessed to be able to coach them. I knew we weren't far away when we got them."

Martin and Mann played key roles during those first two losing seasons, and Newton and his staff were putting the pieces around the two juniors that would pay dividends in 1987-88. From Webster Groves High School in St. Louis, Newton found power forward Chris Ogden and defensive stopper Paul King. Spotting a hole at the center position, Newton drove over to Fort Campbell to lure 6-foot-8 Carl Sias out of the military and into the center position.

In '87-'88, Murray State wrapped up its non-conference schedule with a 5-6 record and seemed to have little momentum going into OVC play, where they were tabbed for a fifth-place finish in the pre-season prognostications. But the Racers won five-straight OVC games to set up a showdown with pre-season favorite Austin Peay. Racer Arena was rocking on that Saturday, but Lake Kelly's talented Governor team was not impressed and won 74-71. In a quirk in scheduling, the Racers had to travel to Clarksville on Monday to face the Governors for a second time in three days. With an OVC title perhaps hanging on that game, the Racers responded by posting an 83-70 victory.

"It showed the character of our guys and they made up their minds that they weren't going to lose back-to-back," Newton said.

Murray State would roll through the rest of conference play with a 13-1 record and wrap up the school's first title since 1983. Entering the OVC Tournament as the No. 1 seed, Newton was confident his team would be focused and the Racer Nation would be ready. As the top seed, the Racers would serve as hosts for the semifinals and championship game of the OVC Tournament.

"I think (Racer Arena) was as much of a home-court advantage as you could find, so it was huge," said Newton, whose team fashioned a 10-3 record that season in the 5,500-seat facility. "Our fans are second to none. I think eventually this led to the tournament being moved to Nashville because the league began to feel like we had too much of an advantage."

Newton's Racers hosted the OVC's postseason tournament three times in his six seasons, each time claiming the championship. But there was nothing like the first. Eastern Kentucky was dispatched 76-60 in the semifinals, setting up the rubber game against rival Austin Peay. Murray State chiseled out a 3-point lead in the final seconds and when the Governors' desperation '3' missed the mark, pandemonium ensued. For the first time since 1969 the Racers were going to the NCAA Tournament.

"We reached the opportunity to play in the Big Dance," Newton said of his initial thoughts after the 73-70 win over the Govs. "It was a great achievement, but as a coach you begin to worry about seeding and where will we play, who will we have to compete against."

Despite the lack of a pairings party and accompanying CBS cameras or autograph sessions that are common at the school today, the Racers learned they would be a No. 14 seed playing No. 3 North Carolina State in Lincoln, Neb. Murray State now knew where they were going, and even if the fans didn't know how to handle the pre-Big Dance hoopla, the head coach knew his team would be fine.

"We were not the least bit leery of our ability to compete. We played a good schedule and had some good wins," the coach recalled. "More importantly, our players knew how to win and expected to win."

Facing a major program with a superstar head coach just five years removed from famously upsetting the University of Houston for the 1983 national championship, the Racers faced their stiffest test of the season. And site officials must have expected Murray State to last only one game in Lincoln, as well, since the Racers were assigned to stay in a campus dormitory while the other "high profile" teams slept in nice hotel beds.

As for the plan going into the game? Newton broke the game down into its simplest terms.

"How are we going to approach it? If we played this team out on an outdoor court, just played shirts and skins, how would we do?" Newton asked the team. "Oh, coach, if we played shirts and skins we would win. So we started talking about shirts and skins. And they picked up on it and they really believed they could win the game.

"Let's not talk about just getting there, let's advance. Let's be Cinderella."

Still, the plan had to be executed by the players and as they did all year, Newton's team responded. Getting 23 points from Jeff Martin and 16 from Don Mann, the Racers pulled off a 78-75 upset. "I think it worked in our favor that North Carolina State didn't give us the respect that maybe they should have," the coach stated. "I think we caught them at the right time."

Murray State ran out of time in its second-round game two days later, falling 61-58 to Danny Manning and the Kansas Jayhawks. There was no trip to the Sweet 16, but the Racers gave coach Larry Brown's Jayhawks their toughest game on the way to a national championship.

That summer, Brown made sure Newton knew how difficult KU's game with the Racers really was. According to Newton, Brown asked, "'Steve how did you feel about finishing second in the nation? I asked him what he meant and he said, 'Well, you played us closer than anyone else. You were our toughest game.' That's quite a compliment."

Newton and his team returned to a heroes' welcome replete with handshakes, congratulatory notes, and a new normal. More than one Racer fan mentioned to Newton that the team should make it to the Sweet 16 the following year, and while expectations were bordering on unreachable, Newton said he cherished coaching at a school with high expectations. "I came home one night after we got back (from the NCAA Tournament)," explained Newton with a smile, "and told my family that we've created a monster."

The following season (1988-89) saw a freshman "big" man from Dresden, Tenn., join Martin, Mann, King and Ogden on the roster. But the addition of

Popeye Jones couldn't keep the Racers from being upset in the semifinals of the OVC Tournament after winning its second-straight regular-season title. Instead of a NCAA Sweet 16 berth, the Racers settled for the NIT. But that was just a small detour for Newton and his program.

Popeye Jones' brilliance helped ease the loss of Martin and Mann, and in 1989-90 and 1990-91, the Racers won 21 and 24 games respectively. They collected two more OVC titles and two more trips to the NCAA Tournament. In the 1990 Big Dance against No. 1 seed Michigan State, Jones introduced himself to the nation by scoring 37 points in a thrilling 75-71 overtime loss. It's still the only time a No. 16 seed has taken a No. 1 to overtime.

The Racers had high hopes of advancing in the 1991 NCAA Tournament in Atlanta, Ga., when they drew a No. 14 seed. However, they also drew an Alabama team which featured three future NBA players, including Robert Horry and Latrell Sprewell, and fell 89-79.

That night in Atlanta was Newton's last as the Racers' coach, as the lure of the SEC was too great and he accepted the head coaching position at South Carolina. "I had always dreamed of getting to the Final Four. The opportunity to get there (from the SEC) was too great to pass up," said Newton.

It was difficult leaving the school which gave him his first head coaching job, but he was coming off of an incredible four-year run that will be difficult for future Racer coaches to match. In that span the Racers won four OVC titles, had four OVC Players of the Year (Martin and Jones) and four OVC Athletes of the Year (Martin and Jones.) "Those four years, we had four championships and we left the fifth one in tact for Popeye's senior year."

In his six seasons as the Racers head coach, Newton had an overall record of 116-65 (64 percent), and became only the second coach in OVC history to lead his team to four consecutive league titles. He was named OVC Coach of the Year twice (1988, 1990) and recruited and coached 15 All-OVC selections in addition to four OVC Player of the Year selections. He was inducted into the OVC Hall of Fame in 2006 and the MSU Hall of Fame in 2010.

His accomplishments are lengthy and his legacy will last a lifetime. Someone may come along and match his coaching accomplishments, but Steve Newton will always be the coach that created the "monster" that was – and still is – Murray State basketball.

Greg Coble, Steve Newton and Popeye Jones.

Paul King

by Kevin Stewart

Paul King saw the signs of it very early on during his basketball career at Murray State.

He realized it even more as he grew into an unfamiliar role – during those first practices, during those first games, during those first conversations with coach Steve Newton.

Finally, when he understood for sure that he was indeed Newton's starting two-guard, the entire concept seemed all at once blatantly written in stone: King was going to have to sacrifice, be the unsung leader, play the best defense, lead instead of be led.

Newton needed the kid from the Webster Groves community in west St. Louis to create a foundation for his program that would last four years. King didn't disappoint his new coach.

King's jersey hangs in the rafters of Murray State's Regional Special Events Center in part because he embraced a role that helped him become the first Racer to play on four straight Ohio Valley Conference championship teams from 1988 to 1991.

Winning regular-season crowns is usually a good sign of things soon to come, and so it was. With King at starting guard for four years, the Racers won three OVC Tournaments and played in one National Invitational Tournament and three NCAA Tournaments.

"Paul King did exactly what we asked of him his entire career," Newton said. "We had shooters. What we needed was a big guard who could give us stability, leadership and play strong defense. Paul did that and more. He really developed into an all-around great player and he has four championships to prove it."

Paul King

That wasn't exactly King's plan coming out of St. Louis, where the 6-foot-4 guard was the Metro area's Mr. Basketball. He was used to hanging 20-plus points on opponents. In fact, it wasn't his plan at all to come to Murray State. He only did so because a former high school teammate, Chris Ogden, was playing in Murray. Ogden told King he might as well come visit. Murray State would pay for the official recruiting visit, he'd get free grub and the pair could hang.

Big East Conference teams, especially Georgetown, had expressed interest, but when assistant coach Mark Bernstein turned on the charm and King found he liked the visit much more than expected, his future was set.

"I kind of gave up going (to the East Coast). I didn't want to go to a Missouri school, but I wanted to be close enough to drive home," King recalled. "And I felt I had a chance to play right away as a freshman at Murray."

What King didn't know was that his life as a high-scoring guard was at an end. The Racers were expecting plenty of firepower with the return of standout juniors Don Mann and Jeff Martin, and they got it. Mann averaged nearly 18 points a game and Martin was one of the country's leading scorers at 26 points per game.

"I started to realize that I was going to have to sacrifice a lot of what I was used to," King said. "I was used to winning and playing. I started all four years of high school and we probably lost no more than 10 games. But I was also used to shooting the ball when I wanted to.

"I adjusted that year and I kept on adapting into my sophomore season. I had to change from getting a large volume of shots to playing a certain role, and I think that role was important to the success of those teams at Murray."

Newton called upon King to perform some of the most difficult, unheralded tasks. He wanted King to be a rebounding guard, a defensive specialist, a passer before a shooter. But when situations arose dictating that King must shoot, Newton expected him to do so with decisiveness and accuracy.

"Paul became an excellent 3-point shooter and he was always an offensive threat," Newton said. "But he did so many other things for us that he was always invaluable."

King's team-first sacrifices continued into his junior and senior seasons.

Again there were players whose specialties were scoring. Popeye Jones, a year younger than King, came on as a crowd favorite at Racer Arena and developed into a scoring and rebounding machine. Frank Allen, two years King's junior, was a shooting guard with great range. And Greg Coble came in from the junior college ranks to add scoring punch to the backcourt.

Off the court, the tranquility of small-town America worked well for the big-city kid.

"I really remember the fairness I was given as a freshman and the opportunity I had to play. And that bled over to off the court. Some of the boosters treated me like a son," said King, who returned to his hometown of Webster Groves and started his own insurance and investments agency. "Everything was in place for me to get an education and maximize my basketball career.

"I really didn't know until I came in as a freshman that the county was dry, so that was probably good for someone who might be tempted by the extra-curricular activities. So I think all that helped me to stay focused. I thought it was a great environment for a kid fresh out of his parents' house on his own for the first time."

King quickly experienced the thrill of big-time college basketball. The Racers went from OVC regular-season and tournament champions in March of 1988 to the NCAA Tournament fish bowl, upsetting North Carolina State before falling to eventual national champions Kansas by three points.

The Racers settled for the NIT the following year as King gained a growing reputation as one of the best defensive players in Murray State history. In the 1980s and into the 1990s, nearly every college team worth its salt tried to sign a big guard, a player in the 6-4 to 6-7 range who could take advantage of smaller guards by posting up inside or shooting over them. And so college teams then also had to develop defenses against

those oversized guards. If teams were lucky, they would find a player like King, who could handle both big and small guards.

With long arms, fast feet, a deceivingly powerful build and a great mind for defense, King evolved into a defensive stopper. He was human Velcro.

"I just always felt like I needed to contribute on both ends of the floor," he said. "I took the attitude that if I scored on you then turned around and let you score on me, nothing was gained.

"I had a secret. I had a style where I always let the offensive player commit to his move, then I'd cut him off. Then I learned his tendencies, his style, and I knew what to do to stop him. I had to anticipate. I'd take their best moves away from them. "I took pride in my defense. I didn't want anybody scoring on me."

As a junior, King took part in one of Murray State's greatest postseason games – a three-point overtime loss to top-seeded Michigan State in the NCAA Tournament. No 16 seed had ever come that close to beating a top seed.

During King's senior season in 1990-91, the Racers won 11 of their last 12 games before entering the NCAA Tournament. Ironically, in his final game, King's offense kept the Racers close in an 89-79 loss to Alabama. He scored a game-high 25 points on 6 of 13 shooting and 10 of 12 free throws.

"I almost didn't play that game because my grandmother (Beatrice King) had just passed away," King recalled. "But I decided to play and I kind of reverted to my high school days. I dedicated the game to my grandmother, then went out and scored 25. That was a good way to end my days at Murray State."

Popeye Jones

by Will Aubrey

Few players have excited the imagination of Racer fans the way Ronald "Popeye" Jones did in the early 1990's.

A three-time All-OVC selection, Jones earned Player of the Year honors in 1991 and '92. He was also named Athlete of the Year in '91 and '92, meaning that out of all the thousands of athletes in all the sports that the OVC sponsors he was deemed to be the very best.

He is Murray State's all-time leading rebounder, is fourth on the career scoring list, and was named MSU's Player of the Century in a January, 2000 Racer Insider poll.

Not bad for a kid from Dresden, Tenn. who only had two scholarship offers coming out of high school.

"There wasn't much to do in Dresden except play ball," he recalled. "I started out playing baseball but it wasn't long before I began playing football and basketball too. Our school was so small everybody played all three sports.

"So, I never had the opportunity to concentrate on one sport and work on getting better. When it was baseball season I played baseball. When it was football season I played football. And when it was basketball season I played basketball."

Popeye Jones

Despite growing up 45 minutes from Racer Arena, the youngster never made it to a Murray State game. He was a Pacer fan, a UT-Martin Pacer fan.

"I grew up eight miles from the University of Tennessee at Martin and I went to a lot of their games," he recalled. "But they didn't offer me a scholarship. I was 6-8, weighed 320 pounds, and the coach there didn't think I could play. Austin Peay didn't recruit me either. Their head coach Lake Kelly said he'd retire if a team I played for ever beat him in a college game."

Despite being named Tennessee's Class A Mr. Basketball, the only D-I schools to offer Jones a scholarship were Murray State and Lamar.

"I felt Murray was a perfect fit for me," he recalled. "They had a lot of tradition. I remember watching the Ron Greene Show on Sunday nights when I was growing up and after that the Steve Newton Show. I watched them beat North Carolina State on TV and then one of the assistant coaches called me after the game. That really meant a lot to me. I had never dreamed that I would play basketball on TV.

"When I came to Murray for my recruiting visit I met Jeff Martin and Don Mann and they asked me if I was a football player or a basketball player. After I signed I didn't touch a basketball all summer. I played baseball. I was a pitcher and a shortstop. Even as a kid I played shortstop. I think it helped me develop my hands. I didn't move very well but I was always positioned well. We won a state championship my junior year.

"Even though it was only 45 minutes away when I left to go to Murray when as a freshman I felt like I was going far away to go to school. And then when I got there and went for my physical I was too heavy for the scale. I had to go get weighed where the football linemen got weighed, over in the mail room."

By the team the season started Jones was down to 285. He wanted to redshirt but head coach Steve Newton knew he needed Jones on the floor even

though his lack of conditioning limited his playing time.

"He was a signature signing for us," former Racer head coach Steve Newton declared. "He had a major impact on basketball at Murray State University. He took us to another level. And he's a legendary figure in Murray."

Jones played in all 30 games, averaging 5.8 points and 4.6 rebounds as the Racers finished 19-11.

"At the end of the season coach Newton told me he was bringing in some players who were pretty good," Jones recalled. "He told me if wanted to play as a sophomore I needed to go to summer school and work out and get myself in shape. When I left his office I thought that if Murray State was going to give me a scholarship I owed it to them to become the best basketball player I could be.

"During that offseason I really dedicated myself to getting in shape. I was on the track every morning before class. I was in the gym in the afternoons after class. I ran pass patterns for Michael Proctor who played quarterback on the football team. I did whatever I could to get in shape."

Newton still marvels at how hard Jones worked that summer: "He wore number 54 and I told him that was how many pounds he would have to lose if he wanted to play as a sophomore. And he lost the weight. That's really an amazing feat in itself if you think about it."

His transformation certainly shocked his teammates.

"When the other guys got back on campus that fall they could see that I was a different player," Jones said. "They were like 'Holy crap! What did you do? Where did all the weight go?' And as the season unfolded they put a lot on my shoulders to carry the team."

The 1989-90 season started with a thrilling 66-64 victory at Western Kentucky. But that was followed by five straight losses.

"We had lost Jeff Martin and Don Mann from the previous year's team and it took us a while to adjust," Jones explained. "We had a freshman point guard in Frank Allen and I was just a sophomore. So it took us a while to get it together.

"But we got really close as a team. We had each others' back. We enjoyed playing together and we played unselfishly. We played defense and we had a little swagger about us. We felt like we could beat anybody."

It showed, as they won 17 of their next 18 games. Jones averaged 19.5 points and 11.2 rebounds and a 64-57 victory over Eastern Kentucky in the OVC tournament final sent the Racers to the Big Dance. Unfortunately, they were seeded 16th which meant they had to play fourth ranked Michigan State.

"We felt that we were much better than a 16 seed," Jones said. "We thought we could beat anyone in America. We got off to a slow start at the beginning of the season but we felt like we should have had a higher seed because of the run that we had made down the stretch.

"Paul King and Chris Ogden were the only guys we had who had played in the NCAA tournament before and they were our leaders. They told us not to be scared, that we were as good as anybody. And we believed it."

They played like it too as they took the heavily favored Spartans to overtime before dropping a 75-71 decision. Jones was unstoppable as he scored 37 points and grabbed 11 rebounds. He took seven three-pointers and hit three of them. That seemed to take Michigan State by surprise despite the fact that he had hit

44 percent of his shots from behind the arc during the regular season.

"At first they tried to guard me with their center and he gave me the outside shot," Jones recalled. "Then they tried putting a smaller guy on me so I posted him up and started shooting my jump hook.

"I never worked on my outside shooting much but in high school I always took that shot from the top of the key. There was no way I was going to take that shot as a mere freshman though. But my sophomore year I started taking it in practice and that gave coach Newton the confidence to let me take it in a game. He never questioned me taking that shot. But I didn't want to abuse it either because we had guys who were better three-point shooters than I was."

Greg Coble hit a three-pointer just before the buzzer to send the game into overtime. But the Racers had nothing left for the extra period.

"We just got tired," Jones said. "I know I did. That was the first time all year that I basically played the whole game. My calves started to cramp in the overtime and during timeouts the trainer would rub my calves and give me Gatorade. But coach Newton didn't feel like he could take me out."

Jones was even better as a junior. He averaged 20.2 points and 14.2 rebounds while leading the Racers to a 24-9 record and a second consecutive trip to the NCAA tournament where they dropped an 89-79 decision to an Alabama team that was better than anyone at the time imagined.

"We kind of expected to go back," Jones recalled. "But we didn't know what we were going up against in Alabama. They were the most athletic team we had ever faced. It was a track meet and they ran by us and jumped over us.

"They had Latrell Sprewell, Robert Horry, and James 'Hollywood' Robinson, all future NBA players. And they had other great athletes too. They were by far the most talented team I played against while I was in college."

After the season Newton left to take the head coaching job at South Carolina and Scott Edgar was hired to replace him. The two men couldn't have been more different.

Newton believed in fundamentally sound, half-court basketball. Edgar believed in a frenetic, full court

style of play. Newton was laid back and calm on the bench while Edgar was, well, fiery would be a bit of an understatement.

"It was really hard for me when coach Newton left," Jones said. "I was really close to him and I knew his system. But I understood. He got the opportunity to coach in the SEC. You can't really turn that down.

"What upset me was that there were some rumors that I was going to declare for the NBA draft. There was no way. I didn't think I was good enough and I didn't want to leave college. I loved the college life and hanging out with my friends. There was another rumor that I was going to transfer. But I didn't want to do that either. Murray was like my second home. I still have great friends there."

It took the players a while to adjust to the new style of play as MSU lost nine of their first 12 games.

"It was totally different for us all," Jones recalled. "We had to learn to trust coach Edgar. He came in with that Arkansas, '40 Minutes of Hell,' style of play. And the practices were brutal. They weren't long but they were brutal. They were the hardest practices I was ever part of, even harder than the NBA.

"When everyone went home for the holidays and we stayed there and practiced... Boy, boy, boy... Those were the toughest practices you could imagine. It paid off though. Every drill was all-out, full court. We didn't do much half court stuff.

"But we adjusted and so did coach Edgar. He had come from Arkansas where the guards pushed the pace and the big guys rebounded and blocked shots. But he started encouraging our guards to get the ball inside more and that slowed the game down a little."

The adjustments paid dividends as the Racers won 11 of their last 12 games and made it back to the Big Dance where their reward was a game against Edgar's former employer, the Arkansas Razorbacks. MSU lost 80-69 but Jones scored 17 points and grabbed 15 rebounds.

He wound up averaging 21.1 points and led the country in rebounding at 14.4 per game. The NCAA record book lists him 10th in career rebounds in the modern era (post 1973).

Asked to reflect on what it was like to play basketball at MSU, Jones' thoughts quickly turned to Racer Arena.

"It was just a joy to play there," he said. "Opposing teams didn't like it though. When I was in Boston I used to joke with coach (Rick) Pitino about him not wanting to play us when he was at Kentucky. And he said, 'No, I didn't want to play you guys. And I definitely didn't want to play you in Racer Arena!'

Following his senior year, Jones was drafted in the second round by the Houston Rockets.

"I didn't get a guaranteed contract," he said. "So I played my first year in Italy. The Dallas Mavericks had a scout over there who saw me play and they traded for my rights and brought me to Dallas the next year.

"Dallas had won 11 games the year before I got there. So we were building something. I enjoyed playing with guys like Jason Kidd, Jim Jackson, and Jamal Mashburn. From there I went to Toronto.

"Then I hurt my ACL in 1997 and that really set me back. I played another seven years but I was never the same. I had numerous 20 rebound games though. It was great getting to play with and against guys like Michael Jordan and Charles Barkley."

Jones played 12 years in the NBA for six different teams. He twice averaged a double-double for the Dallas Mavericks. And he once grabbed 28 rebounds in a single game. After his playing career ended he worked as an assistant coach, first with the Mavericks and more recently with the New Jersey Nets.

But he's never forgotten the time he spent at MSU.

"I'm proud to say that I'm a Racer. I wanted to get my degree and I wanted it to be from Murray State," he said. "So after I retired from the NBA I told my wife it was the perfect time. The independent studies program was great for me and the people who worked with me were terrific. When that degree came in the mail right around Christmas time in 2005 I told my wife that I didn't need a Christmas present because I had just received it.

"As a former MSU athlete, becoming an alumnus of the school meant a lot to me. Murray State took a chance on a 300-pound small-town boy that many universities thought couldn't be successful in basketball. I'll always be grateful for the opportunity they gave me."

SCOTT EDGAR

by Steve Parker

It was a late night at the end of July 1991, which meant Scott Edgar was in the car en route to another recruiting stop. But instead of going from Union City, Tenn., straight to Louisville, Ky., he decided to detour to a small west Kentucky town which served as the home of Murray State University.

At the time, Edgar was the top assistant coach at the University of Arkansas, but he was being mentioned as a candidate for the vacated Murray State coaching job. So, his spur-of-the-moment drive to find Murray wasn't for entertainment, it was a reconnaissance mission.

"I thought I could find it but I didn't," said Edgar, recalling the late-night run to Calloway County. "I think I ended up in Martin (Tenn.). It was around midnight so I just forgot about it and headed to Louisville."

One month later, Edgar arrived in Murray as its newest head basketball coach, but after a rocky start in his first season, many Racer fans were hoping the rookie head coach would once more forget about it and head on down the road.

"We went 30 days without a win," recalled Edgar, adding he was aware of the rumblings around town.

It wasn't just the losing. The young coach was introducing the "40 Minutes of Hell" style he coached at Arkansas to an audience used to half-court defense and work-to-get-the-best-shot offense. Furthermore, Racer fans accustomed to the calm, cool demeanor of Edgar's predecessor, Steve Newton, were a little leery of the fiery, expressive Edgar.

"It was a different style on the court and different style on the sidelines," admitted Edgar. "I was more high strung then. It was A-to-Z different from what they were used to."

With the help of senior Popeye Jones, the Racers hit their stride once conference play started in January and eventually wrapped up the program's fifth Ohio Valley Conference championship in a row. Most importantly, Edgar silenced any doubters by guiding the Racers to their third-straight trip to the NCAA Tournament.

"That was big because you feel apart of it now. You're the coach, but you have to earn the right to be there," Edgar said of advancing to the Big Dance. "The measuring stick at Murray State is the NCAA Tournament."

Scott Edgar had finally arrived in Murray, Ky.

Growing up and attending college in Pittsburgh, Pa., Edgar never considered coaching as a career. In fact, "he fell into it," by accident. A basketball and baseball player at the University of Pittsburgh-Johnstown, Edgar wrapped up his playing career in 1978. One of his former mentors was the basketball coach at New Mexico Military Institute, and offered Edgar the opportunity to join his staff.

"Like everyone else, I wanted to have a longer playing career," said Edgar, who went to New Mexico to help his former coach. "It was never my design to get into coaching. Basically, I needed three credits and I could get them in New Mexico."

During his three-year stint at New Mexico Military, Edgar came across a man who would not only elevate his interest in coaching, but also give him a career. In the late 1970s and early 80s, Nolan Richardson was the head coach at Western Texas Junior College where he was highly successful. Edgar got to know Richardson over the years and when Richardson landed the head job at the University of Tulsa in 1980, Edgar was one of his first hires.

After five successful seasons at Tulsa, which included an NIT championship, Richardson left for the University of Arkansas in 1985 and took Edgar with him. It didn't take long for Richardson to work his magic with the Razorbacks. It took three seasons to reach the NCAA Tournament, and the Hogs got all the way to the Final Four in 1990 and the Elite 8 in 1991. During those last two seasons, as the Razorbacks were becoming one of the elite programs in the country, Edgar started to consider moving from assistant to head coach.

While Richardson was working his magic in Fayetteville, Steve Newton was doing the same thing in Murray. In August 1991, Newton was lured from Murray State to South Carolina, and a national search was on for his replacement.

"I didn't really know a whole lot about (the MSU program)," said Edgar. "Remember, this was in the early 1990s before the internet and a lot of other things. The only way you knew about the OVC was if you stayed up late on Saturday night for the OVC's Pajama Party on ESPN at midnight."

Then-Racer athletic director Michael Strickland couldn't resist the young assistant from Arkansas who would bring exciting, up-tempo basketball to Murray. And, Edgar couldn't pass up the chance to take over a program on the rise.

"They (Racers) were coming off four OVC championships and they had Popeye Jones coming back," said Edgar. "That would get anyone's attention.

"Ironically, I was passed on by Morehead and Austin Peay," Edgar said of previous job interviews. "As it turned out the Lord delivered me to the cream of the crop in that conference."

From the first day on the job, Edgar set out to implement his 40-minute, full-court pressing style. Only problem was, he inherited a half-court roster. Gone from the previous season was Paul King, Greg Coble and John Jackson. One starter who was returning, however, was one of the best players in MSU and OVC history: Popeye Jones.

"You can't describe how huge it was to have him," Edgar said of the two-time OVC Player of the Year. "It's a blessing to coach somebody that good in your entire career, but we're talking about a coach in his first year."

Even with the future NBA player leading the way, Edgar couldn't negotiate the first portion of his inaugural season, despite notching his first career win over Illinois Tech. Heading into mid-December at 3-3, the Racers would drop six in a row to fall to 3-9. Steve Newton's last two teams at MSU lost nine games all season.

"I should have fired the guy who made the schedule," noted a laughing Edgar, rattling off the likes of Western Kentucky, Evansville, Missouri and Texas as opponents during the losing streak. But Edgar sensed his team was getting better as 1991 was coming to an end. Plus, junior guard Frank Allen, suspended for the first semester, was coming into form. "People in town kept coming up to me and saying, 'Coach, you'll be fine when the OVC starts.'"

A win at Southeast Missouri on Jan. 13 snapped the losing skid and woke up the Racers. Winning seven games in a row at one point, Murray State rolled to the regular-season title.

At the OVC Tournament in Lexington, the Racers came in as the team to beat, but also had a score to settle. The night before the tournament started, Morehead State's Brett Roberts edged

Popeye Jones for OVC Player of the Year. In a semifinal matchup against Roberts' Eagles, the Racers got on the board first with Jones drilling a 3-pointer from the top of the key. Game over. Racers 109, Morehead 77. In the championship game, MSU dispatched EKU 81-60 to earn the school's third-straight trip to the NCAA Tournament.

"Of all the teams I had, that team breezed through the OVC Tournament," Edgar recalled fondly.

Eleven days later, the Racers were matched up against a familiar foe – at least to Edgar. As the No. 15 seed in the Midwest, MSU drew No. 2 seed Arkansas.

"No game that first weekend had the atmosphere of that game," Edgar said of the matchup against his former boss (Richardson) and players that he helped recruit. "During the pregame, several of the Arkansas players went up into the stands to hug my wife (Elaine)."

Edgar's Racers made a late run, but couldn't overcome the talent and depth of the Razorbacks, falling 80-69. MSU managed only a 17-13 record in Edgar's first season, but a regular-season OVC title and a berth in the NCAA Tournament proved he was more than capable of guiding the Racers.

Year two of Edgar's tenure would begin with a nearly brand new roster, but no Popeye Jones. Edgar signed "maybe 10 guys that year," he said, noting there was no limit to how many players a coach could sign in those days. Along with senior Frank Allen, the Racers featured returning letterwinners Cedric Gumm, Scott Sivills, Bo Walden and Jerry Wilson, and junior college transfers Antoine Teague, Antwan Hoard, Lawrence Bussell and Tony Bailey.

One player, a freshman no less, stood out to Edgar even as early as preseason conditioning. "Early on (Marcus) Brown was leading every sprint in the fall," Edgar said of the 6-foot-3 forward. "I kept telling the rest of the guys, 'That boy is going to take someone's spot.'"

He did. When MSU opened the 1992-93 season at Indiana, Brown was in the starting lineup against Bobby Knight's Hoosiers. Though Brown impressed in his first season, the Racers finished 18-12 and couldn't overcome a surprising Tennessee State squad in the regular season or the OVC championship game.

Most of the team returned the following year, plus Edgar added freshman Vincent Rainey. With Brown emerging as a star, the Racers bolted out of the gate with a 13-3 start to the season. Included in the victories were wins over Ole Miss and Memphis, both at home. Edgar, who recruited the city of Memphis heavily, called the win over the Tigers "a highlight" of his career.

A two-point loss at Austin Peay was the only stumble in OVC play as the Racers' rolled to a 15-1 record and the conference title. MSU wasn't just winning games, they were mauling their league brethren. Running players in and out, Edgar's Racers didn't wear teams down, they drove them into submission on most nights.

Heading into the OVC Tournament with 25, 26, 29 and 32 point wins against league foes, it seemed as if all the Racers had to do was make sure the team bus didn't break down on the way to Nashville.

A 104-86 win over Morehead in the semifinals pitted Murray State against Tennessee State in a rematch of the previous year's title game. Led by 6-11 center Carlos Rogers, the Tigers were the defending league champs, but were swept by the Racers in the regular season by 11 and 16 points in two meetings. A

Harlan Hodges, Jim Frank, Scott Edgar

tighter-than-expected game went into the final seconds before Rogers got loose for a wide-open layup to send TSU to its second-straight NCAA Tournament.

As for Murray State, it ranks as one of the most crushing losses in recent history.

"It's one of those games I will never go back and watch on tape," Edgar said of the 73-72 defeat. "The worst thing was that TSU was staying in our hotel and I had to listen to that fight song all night."

Despite being the league's best team by a wide margin, the Racers had to settle for an NIT bid. Though they played valiantly, the still hurting Racers fell 66-58 at Bradley.

The following season, 1994-95, the Racers lost much of their depth, but still had two of the best players in the league in Brown and Rainey. With that duo leading the way, MSU had a nice season going until the team was swept on the Death Valley swing to drop to 5-5 in the league.

"I knew I had a good team. All I had to do was call plays for Marcus and Vince," said Edgar. "When we lost at Morehead and went to 5-5 in the league, I told the team, 'Look, I brought you guys here to play and all I'm doing is calling plays.'"

So, instead of calling plays, Edgar got his team up for 5 a.m. practices. He threw the playbook away, stopped watching film and led the Racers on an eight-game winning streak that would be good enough to win the coach's third OVC title in four seasons.

The Racers drew North Carolina in the first round of the NCAA Tournament in Tallahassee, Fla. MSU led Hall of Fame coach Dean Smith's Tar Heels at halftime, but eventually fell to Jerry Stackhouse and Rasheed Wallace, 80-79, in a closer-than-the-score indicated contest.

What came next for Edgar was what he calls one of the "poorest decisions of my life."

Having won three OVC titles and earned two NCAA Tournament berths in four years, Edgar was on the list of up-and-comers in the coaching ranks, so when Duquesne came calling, it was difficult to turn down a school based in his hometown of Pittsburgh.

But the up-tempo, pressing style didn't work at Duquesne, and after three seasons Edgar was let go. He would go on to serve as an assistant at TCU, UAB and Tennessee before landing the head coaching job at Southeast Missouri. During his two seasons SEMO, Edgar had the Redhawks on the rise until the NCAA placed the men's basketball program on probation. Through all of that, leaving Murray State ranks as one of his biggest regrets.

"Other than the people I chose to be on my staff at SEMO, the worst professional decision I made was leaving Murray State and going to Duquesne," said Edgar, now the head coach at Eastern Oklahoma State College.

Of all the coaches who have come and gone at Murray State, none have more fondness for Murray State than Edgar. He stays in touch with many of his former players and keeps tabs on the Racers.

When he brought his Southeast Missouri team into Murray in 2006, Edgar didn't play up his return. Instead, he told them the truth about the Racers: "This is the best team in the league and the measuring stick in the OVC."

Scott Edgar would know about the Racers' proud tradition. He was one of its architects.

FRANK ALLEN

by Eddie Sheridan

Former Murray State basketball standout Frank Allen once said he considered "college the best four years of my life." One look at a list of Allen's accomplishments at MSU will show why he made those four years pretty special for Racer fans as well.

Allen, a 6-foot 3-inch guard from Memphis, burst onto the MSU and Ohio Valley Conference basketball scene as a freshman in 1989. He immediately snagged the Racer's starting point guard role, which was no small accomplishment considering that year's team also featured all-time MSU greats Popeye Jones, Paul King and Greg Coble.

Allen struggled to find his shot over the course of the Racers' first three games that season, but then exploded against Southern Illinois for 35 points, making 10 of 19 shots from the floor and 13 of 14 from the free-throw line. There would be more performances like that for Allen, and it validated coach Steve Newton's decision to insert the freshman into the starting lineup.

Newton would coach Allen during his freshman and sophomore years at Murray State, and the former Racer head coach grew to appreciate his point guard's fearless style of play.

"Frank Allen was a somewhat unconventional player," Newton said. "He played instinctive basketball, and he had great, deep range when shooting. He could shoot from anywhere."

Allen's range was on full display during his career at MSU, as he led the team in three-pointers made during each of his four seasons, the only Racer to ever accomplish that feat. His 251 career threes are second only to Isaiah Canaan.

"I always had good range," Allen said. "Since high school, I could pretty much cross halfcourt and just let it go. That's something I was blessed with."

Frank Allen

His shooting prowess and cool on-court demeanor were also present at the free-throw line, as he is eighth on MSU's career list of free-throws made with 428 and sixth in career free-throw percentage at 82.9 percent.

While Jones may have been the Racers' most recognizable face during the 1989-90 season, Allen played no small part in turning what was supposed to be a rebuilding year into a surprising success story. The team would go on to win the OVC Tournament, setting up a first-round NCAA Tournament matchup with top-seeded Michigan State.

As much as the odds were stacked against MSU emerging as the OVC's NCAA Tournament representative that year, the likelihood of them achieving a victory over the Spartans was nearly impossible. A 16 seed has never beaten a top seed in the NCAA Tournament, and Michigan State was the fourth-ranked team in the country at that time. Still, the Racers nearly did the impossible, led by a monstrous performance from Jones and a piece of clutch shooting from Allen.

While Jones' explosive 37-point, 11-rebound performance is what most Racer fans remember from the game, it was a three-pointer from Allen with 1:07 left in overtime that knotted the score at 71. In the end, though, the Spartans would score the game's final four points and claim a 75-71 victory.

This would be the first of three trips to the NCAA tournament for Allen. Along the way, he would compile a list of impressive regular-season accolades. He was named to the OVC's All-Freshman team for 1989-90, the All-OVC second team for the 1990-91 and

1992-1993 seasons, and was a first-team All-OVC selection in 1991-92. He was also named to the OVC's All-Tournament team in 1990 and 1992, showing his talent as a post-season performer as well.

Allen's next shot at the NCAA tournament would come in 1991 against the Alabama Crimson Tide. Unfortunately, this tournament appearance would prove to be a sour one for the sophomore guard, as he hit only 2-of-14 shots from the floor and saw the Racers fall to the Latrell Sprewell and Robert Horry-led team by a score of 89-79.

He would redeem himself the following year, though, in a first-round matchup against Nolan Richardson's Arkansas Razorbacks. This particular tournament pairing garnered national media attention, as new Racer coach Scott Edgar had served as an assistant under Richardson for 11 years before taking the MSU job. Allen would score a game-high 25 points, but the Racers still lost to the Razorbacks 80-69.

This would prove to be Allen's last appearance in the NCAA tournament, as the Racers were defeated 82-68 in the OVC Tournament finals his senior year by Tennessee State.

Over the course of four seasons, Allen averaged 14.6, 14.1, 17.6 and 16.7 points per contest. He joined Jones and Scott Sivills as the only Racers to play in three consecutive NCAA Tournaments. While he may have experienced some ups and downs toward the latter part of his MSU career, there is no denying Frank Allen remains one of the Racers' all-time greats.

MARCUS BROWN

by Steve Parker

Talk to him long enough and it will become apparent that Marcus Brown has the confidence required of someone who has accomplished so much in his life. But also present during the conversation will be hints that the former Murray State Racer was – and is – never satisfied.

For instance, bring up the 1995 game at the University of Louisville in which Brown was simply the best player on the Freedom Hall floor. He scored 35 points, dished out seven assists and pulled down eight rebounds. Said Brown: "I probably should have had 48 but I missed a lot of easy shots."

One of the greatest single-game performances in MSU history and he sees the warts and not the beauty.

"My mom always gets on me. She says, 'Give yourself some credit once in a while. You did great,'" explained Brown. "But I always felt I could do a little better."

That attitude led to a basketball metamorphosis that has rarely been seen at Murray State. Playing his freshman year as an athletic but undersized post player who didn't seem to have backcourt skills, Brown arrived for his sophomore season poised to be in the starting backcourt.

"He told me after his freshman season that he was going to go home and work on his game, and come back next year and take somebody's spot," remembered his coach for the first three seasons at MSU, Scott Edgar. "And, man did he do that."

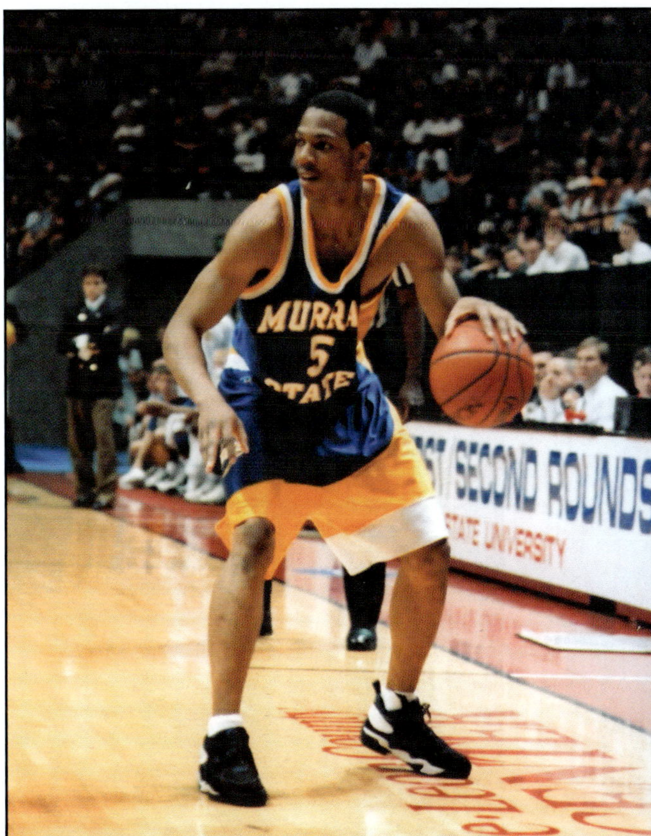

Marcus Brown

Major growth would continue throughout his career until Marcus Brown was one of the top guards in all of college basketball.

Growing up in West Memphis, Ark., Brown established himself as one of the top athletes in the state of Arkansas, particularly when it came to track and field as he was an accomplished high jumper. In fact, Brown had scholarship offers from such big-time programs as UCLA and Arkansas. But his heart was with basketball, despite the fact that the profile of the schools interested didn't equal that of his track suitors. Not surprisingly, Brown had his eye on Nolan Richardson and the Arkansas Razorbacks. Deep NCAA Tournament runs and national exposure made Arkansas one of the big boys of college basketball. But other than a few cursory phone calls and letters from Razorback assistant coach Scott Edgar, Brown wasn't a high priority for the Hogs. But then in the spring of 1991, the dynamics changed.

Brown said he knew of Murray State from its NCAA Tournament appearances on television and the notoriety of Popeye Jones, but it was his relationship with Edgar that tilted the outcome in the Racers' favor.

"Scott got the (MSU) job before my senior year, so I went from seeing him in Arkansas gear to Murray State gear," Brown explained of his days with his AAU team, the Arkansas Wings. "Then, my first game my senior year in high school, (MSU assistant)

Kenny Roth showed up and I stunk up the gym. But they stayed with me."

Edgar and Roth were in hot pursuit of Brown, and despite heavy interest from Arkansas State and Jackson State, as well as his track offers, Brown chose to attend MSU. "I was just led to Murray State to be honest," explained Brown. "I woke up one morning and told my mom that I was going to Murray State before I even visited the campus."

Brown arrived at MSU in 1992 as part of Scott Edgar's first recruiting class and his early work as a freshman paid off as the 6-foot-3, 160-pound Brown made an impression with his tremendous hustle, maturity and athletic ability. He was so impressive, in fact, that in the 1992-93 season opener at Indiana, Brown was the starting small forward guarding the Hoosiers' Calbert Chaney.

"We go to Indiana and Scott says, 'I'm putting you on Chaney,'" Brown remembered. "I said, Okay, let's go. I'm just going to play basketball, and try to stop this guy the best way I know how. I was just going to rebound and defend. As long as the team won I didn't care."

MSU lost to the Hoosiers that night, but Brown showed the tenacity that would take him to great heights later on in his career. That freshman season, he played in every game of the Racers' 18-12 campaign. He averaged a respectable 8.9 points per game, nearly all of those points coming around the rim as the freshman forward was just a minor threat from outside. Like all great players are prone to do, Brown would learn from his first season of college basketball.

As he left for the summer in 1993, he had "enough banging with the big guys," especially at just 6-foot-3, 160 pounds. "I was realistic. If I wanted to make it to the next level or even be a decent Division I player, I had to make a move," he said.

"Project Perimeter" started in the summer for Brown, who lifted weights and ran miles upon miles to build strength in his legs. But his primary emphasis was on shooting jumpers to hone his form and expand his range.

"I lived in the gym that summer," said Brown. "West Memphis (High School) had small rims and I shot the ball all the time, working on my range...By the time I landed back in Murray in 1993 there was hell to pay."

Right out of the gate, in preseason pickup games, Brown proved to his teammates and coaches that he was a guard. Actually, he was THE guard. And, "Hell to Pay" may have been the unofficial theme of the 1993-94 season. Going 10-deep and pressing the entire 40 minutes, the Racers rolled through the OVC with a 15-1 league record. MSU won

10-straight games to close out the regular season, but to move on to the NCAA Tournament, they would have to win the OVC Tournament. An OVC Tournament championship seemed like the closest thing to a sure thing as possible, and after dispatching Morehead State 104-86 in the semifinals, the Racers moved on to Saturday night to face defending conference champ Tennessee State. Despite the fact that Brown sprained his foot in the Morehead game and TSU boasted 6-11 center Carlos Rogers, few thought the championship game would be anything other than a formality, especially since the Racers beat TSU twice in the regular season by 11 and 16 points respectively.

In a game that was tight from the beginning, the Racers saw Rogers convert a layup in the final seconds to pull a 73-72 upset.

"It's still hard to swallow, not because we lost to TSU, but because of all the work we put into it and how we bonded as a team," explained Brown, who was named first-team All-OVC as a sophomore. "We got a lot out of that season, but not the ultimate prize."

Brown started every game his sophomore year, and proving that his goal of becoming a Division I guard was an unquestionable success, he hiked his scoring averaged up from 8.9 ppg as a freshman to a remarkable 18.7 ppg as a soph.

With the individual transformation complete, Brown set his sites on team success heading into his junior year. "I was fed up after losing it the year before. I said, 'I'm sorry. We're winning it this year.'"

But before he took to the court, Brown detoured into an old neighborhood – track and field. According to Brown, MSU track coach Wayne Pate asked Racer assistant Kenny Roth if Brown was interested in high jumping in the OVC Championships being hosted by MSU in April. Though he only got to practice for two days, Brown amazingly jumped a meet best 6-10 to win an OVC title. "That was fun. I never thought I'd win an OVC title in track."

As for basketball the next season, 1994-95 started well, but the team hit a slump midway through the OVC portion of the schedule. With all the depth and size gone from the year before, Scott Edgar was leaning on Brown, point guard William Moore and sophomore swing man Vincent Rainey in a more half-court approach. A two-loss trip to Death Valley brought the Racers back to the pack in the league race, and sent Edgar back to the basics, including practices at 5 a.m.

In the midst of Edgar's boot camp, the Racers started clicking on all cylinders, rolling to both the regular-season and tournament titles. Cutting down the nets in Nashville following the OVC Tournament championship game victory over Austin Peay was emotional for Brown. "Getting over the hump and bringing back a banner to put up in Racer Arena put a smile on my face," noted Brown, the tourney MVP. "That's what you come to Murray State to do."

In the first-round NCAA Tournament game against North Carolina, Brown introduced himself to the nation by scoring 26 points in an 80-70 loss. "We were playing North Carolina on a neutral floor and we let them off the hook," said Brown. "I still have nightmares about that one."

For the season, Brown averaged 22.4 ppg and was named OVC Player of the Year, the first such Racer to win the honor since Popeye Jones in 1991. And, Brown also earned OVC Male Athlete of the Year. But, as is customary at Murray State, its head coach was being courted by bigger schools and Edgar couldn't resist the pull of going to his hometown to coach Duquesne University in Pittsburgh, Pa.

Murray State named UCLA assistant coach Mark Gottfried as Edgar's replacement. Said Brown: "Mark didn't try to change a lot of things, which was good. But he really emphasized me and Vincent."

Gottfried moved Brown to the point guard slot and the move proved valuable to both player and team. Playing a full 40 minutes in 11 games his senior season, Brown averaged 26.4 points per game to rank among the nation's leaders. He said that the game "came easy to him" his senior season, which was apparent in two outings in particular. In addition to his 35-point game at Freedom Hall, Brown set the school's single-game scoring record with 45 points against Washington on Dec. 16, 1995.

MSU won its third-straight OVC title and took aim at the OVC Tournament and back-to-back trips to the NCAA Tournament. After dispatching Tennessee Tech in the semifinals, the Racers met old rival Austin Peay in the championship game. Like two seasons prior in the agonizing loss to Tennessee State, Brown entered the 1996 OVC Tournament championship game with a sprained foot. This time, a phantom foul call on Rainey put Austin Peay at the free throw line to win the game in the final seconds. Agony once again hit Brown and his teammates in Nashville.

"Another crappy ending," was how Brown described the team's fate in 1996. But Brown said he wasn't destroyed after the shocking ending. "It helped me learn some things. When you win a lot like we do at Murray, you get spoiled, so I think that loss helped me as a player and a person later one. It shaped my character."

Brown was again named OVC Player of the Year, becoming the fourth Racer in history to earn back-to-back honors. He finished his career with 2,236 points, which ranked second all-time in school history at the time, and his 26.4 ppg scoring average in 1995-96 is still a school record.

But unlike previous seasons, there was no more next year to look forward to after the team finished up with an NIT loss at Missouri. At least there was no *college basketball* season to get ready for.

After his breakout junior year, followed by a scintillating senior year, Brown was drawing attention from NBA scouts. He had realized professional basketball could be part of his future midway through his sophomore year, "Once I got going the game was coming easier for me. I would watch TV and see guys doing things that I could do, so I thought, 'Man, I could make some money with this.'"

The Portland Trail Blazers thought Brown was good enough, too, selecting him with the 17th pick of the 2nd round in the 1996 NBA Draft. He played the 1996–1997 NBA season with the Trail Blazers, averaging 4.0 points, while shooting 41 percent from 3 point range in his rookie season. He then signed with the Vancouver Grizzlies for the 1997–1998 season, but a torn ACL kept him from appearing in any games. A brief stint with Detroit in 1999 was his last in the NBA, as Brown, ever practical, made a wise business decision. Instead of chasing an NBA dream, which would mean bouncing from team to team, Brown chose to head overseas where more lucrative contracts and stability awaited.

From 1999 to 2011, Brown played in the Euroleague, making stops in France, Italy, Turkey, Russia, Spain and Lithuania. Retiring prior to the 2011-2012 season, Brown is widely regarded as the most successful American player ever to play overseas. It wasn't the NBA, but he made a living – a great living – playing the game he loves.

One of Brown's first trips back to Murray since his college career came in February 2009 when he was being inducted in the MSU Athletic Hall of Fame. Also on that night, Brown had his No. 5 retired, truly cementing his place among MSU's all-time greats.

"There was nothing little about it," recalled Brown of the occasion. "It really was special. No matter what I do, my kids will always see my number hanging in the rafters. I was so emotional because I was sharing the moment with my family and my extended family – my Murray State family."

Yet, even on such a momentous occasion, Marcus Brown couldn't let go of the drive and the habit of never being satisfied.

"When I was out on the floor for the ceremony, I looked up in the rafters and saw all those NCAA Tournament banners," he recalled, "and it still pisses me off to the highest degree that I only did it once."

VINCENT RAINEY

by Kevin Stewart

Vincent Rainey was 6-foot-3, maybe 6-4, and a very successful forward at the Division I level.

Believe it or not!

As a mid-major, it has always been Murray State's lot to turn the undersized into supersized, the meek into monsters, the somewhat-stars into superstars.

But the final X-factor apparently lies inside each player – the measure of heart and soul, the level of guts and determination.

Rainey had plenty of all. He came to Murray State as one of the top five high school players in the state of Tennessee. And, he chose the Racers over the likes of Missouri and Maryland.

"Vincent's great attribute was his competitive nature. He loved to play the game and he played it with a great passion," said Mark Gottfried, who coached Rainey during his junior (1995-96) and senior seasons ('96-97) after Scott Edgar left Murray State to coach at Duquense.

"Vincent was always in the gym, always sweating, always working. He just had a passion, a drive, a desire to be as good as he could be. And I don't say that lightly. He really was that kind of a person and a player.

"He was an emotional guy. He had a tough home life coming out of Memphis, had a close relative in prison and no dad, so I think his passion became basketball. He lived and breathed it."

Murray State won 83 games during Rainey's time, averaging nearly 21 wins a season, and the Racers played in two NCAA Tournaments and two National Invitational Tournaments. They were Ohio Valley Conference champions or co-champions each year.

"Vincent wanted to win and he knew how to win," said Chad Townsend, the team's point guard during Rainey's senior season.

Rainey turned his lack of height into an advantage.

"For a power forward to have to guard him was a hard matchup because he was so quick and so crafty around the rim," Gottfried said. "And he was just stronger and, many times, faster than the smaller forwards."

Rainey's drives from the wings to the hoop were legendary. He was a blur, lightning in sneakers. He'd push the ball ahead as if playing with a horizontal yo-yo, looking like an NFL receiver stretching the ball forward toward the goal line. First defenders usually fell by the wayside. If some giant of a defender remained, Rainey would stop, coil his knot-muscled legs, and power through or up-and-over the defense.

The meek to monster transformation took place quickly, soon after his freshman season. Rainey scored five points as a freshman, then really blossomed in the 1994-95 season. His average soared to 18.8 while playing a pretty good Robin to Murray State's Batman, junior Marcus Brown, who averaged 22.4 points while earning his first OVC Player of the Year award.

After the basketball banquet following his

As a senior, Rainey averaged 21.9 points, 8.2 rebounds and shot 77.4 percent from the line.

During that senior season, with Brown gone but high-scoring shooting guard D.T. Mayes moving in from the junior college ranks, the Racers beat Austin Peay 88-85 in overtime in the OVC Tournament championship, and then nearly knocked off second-seeded Duke in the NCAA Tournament. Rainey scored 23 points and grabbed 10 rebounds, both team highs, as the No. 15 seed Racers fell short, 71-68.

Rainey had his share of monster games. In December of his senior season at home against Alcorn State, he poured in a career-high 43 points while hitting 15 of 22 field goals and 12 of 15 free throws. He scored 33 and ripped off 12 rebounds that year in a win against arch-rival Austin Peay. And in the regular-season finale, Rainey hung 32 points on Tennessee State. He also had 13 boards and made 12 of 13 free throws in that game.

Rainey's legacy includes hitting a late 3-pointer against Duke that helped pull the Racers within upset range, and a last-second heave from 75 feet that hit the backboard, a shot that had it fell would have forced overtime.

Following the game, Rainey asked Duke coach Mike Krzyzewski for his autograph.

Believe it or not!

freshman year, Edgar and his wife came across Rainey dribbling his way to the Carr Health Building for a late night shoot around.

"I remember Coach saying 'Me and (Marcus) Brown promise you a championship next year,'" Rainey told *Ledger and Times* sportswriter Steve Parker in 1995. "When I came here I was thinking… Murray State, I could go in with my potential and get by.

"The biggest thing tht made me come back was my mom. She raised me by herself and she taught me to never quit, no matter what. I wanted out of here last year but she knew that I wouldn't be giving myself a chance."

Brown took the honor for a second time as a senior by sporting a 26.4 scoring average while Rainey poured in 19.4 points.

Rainey finished his career with 1,888 points, good for sixth at the time on Murray State's all-time scoring.

MARK GOTTFRIED

by Steve Parker

Anyone who followed Murray State basketball from 1995-1998, would agree that that three-year period was about as good for the Racers as any other period in school history – Ohio Valley Conference titles, NCAA Tournament appearances, wins over big-time opponents. But forget about the numbers. Murray State basketball was cool in the waning years of the 1990s.

And, why wouldn't it be? Its coach was cool. Mark Gottfried dressed cool, acted cool on the sidelines, and his teams played cool. He was a resident of Los Angeles for eight years while an assistant coach at UCLA, so he understood cool.

But on the morning he was to be introduced as Murray State's 11th head coach, Mark Gottfried was cold. As in cold feet.

Mark and his wife, Elizabeth, flew into Murray and were housed at the Curris Center, MSU's student union building which has residential suites for the University's guests. When he woke up just hours before accepting the new job and introducing himself to hundreds of Racer fans and media, he had something to tell Elizabeth.

"I told her, 'I'm not taking it. Let's go back to L.A.,'" Gottfried remembers telling his wife. "We discussed it for a while and finally I said, 'No, let's do it.'"

Boy, did he do it. An OVC title all three years he was the Racer coach, two trips to the NCAA Tournament and big-time wins with some of the program's best players of all time. He was one of the biggest hires in MSU history, regardless of the sport, but it wasn't easy luring him from California.

Mark Gottfried

In eight seasons at UCLA, Gottfried worked under head coach Jim Harrick to build the Bruins' program back to national prominence. That effort peaked in 1995 when UCLA once again ascended to the top of the college basketball world by winning its 11th national championship.

While UCLA was making its run to the NCAA title, 1,885 miles away in Murray, Ky., a coaching search was underway because Scott Edgar chose to leave Murray State for Duquesne.

Opting to continue a trend started with Edgar, MSU athletic director Mike Strickland targeted young, up-and-coming assistant coaches from prominent major-college programs. At that moment, there was no more prominent program than UCLA and the Bruins had a young, up-and-coming coach. And, Gottfried was on Strickland's list.

But Murray State was not on Gottfried's radar, who was busy celebrating the Bruins' national championship.

Following the title game on Monday, the team appeared on The David Letterman Show on Tuesday, were VIPs at Disneyland on Wednesday and threw out the first pitch at the Los Angeles Dodgers' game on Thursday.

"There was so much happening with our team," Gottfried recalled. "I was so caught up in the euphoria of everything that was going on that I really couldn't think about anything else."

As the celebration died down a week later, Gottfried

agreed to meet with Strickland and the search committee, but he was still not interested in leaving Los Angeles. He even told Elizabeth, that he was just going for the interview and had no intention of taking the job.

Still, he joined a finalist pool of young assistants which included MSU assistant Kenny Roth, Vanderbilt's Buzz Peterson and Arkansas' Mike Anderson.

Gottfried was the final candidate to visit and he changed his attitude from not being interested in the job to going all out for it, for someone else.

"On the way to Murray, I had a layover in the airport in St. Louis and I called Buzz Peterson who had just interviewed," said Gottfried, who knew Peterson from the recruiting trail. "I asked him, 'Do you want the job?' He said yes, so I told him, 'I'll help you get the job. I'm going to spend the whole interview talking you up.'"

Gottfried's "Vote For Buzz" campaign took a turn when he arrived in Murray. "I went in for the interview and I liked it. I met with Mike Strickland and the search committee and was thinking, 'Gosh, this is a great place.'"

So, after trying to sabotage his own candidacy, and almost backing out hours before the announcement, Gottfried was introduced as MSU's 11th head coach in April of 1995.

As for Buzz Peterson? "Whenever I run into Buzz out on the road, he always thanks me for getting him the Murray job," a laughing Gottfried explained.

Peterson may have had a better shot at becoming Murray State's coach if not for Racer football.

From 1978-1980, Racer football was under the direction of Mike Gottfried, who happened to have a brother, Joe, coaching basketball at Southern Illinois University-Carbondale. Joe had a son, Mark, who as a youngster spent many days in Murray and on the MSU campus visiting his uncle, Mike. "I remember Ron Greene, and Lamont Sleets, and Racer Arena. I was very familiar with that era."

Furthermore, Mark's sister, Christy (Logan), is a graduate of Murray State and once worked in the MSU football office. Mark says his familiarity with Murray State during the 1980s forced him to at least agree to an interview in 1995.

"If I had not been familiar with Murray, I might not have interviewed," he explained. "I knew how the fans felt about basketball and I loved Racer Arena."

It would have benefited Ron Greene had Mark Gottfried decided to attend MSU out of high school, but Mark chose Oral Roberts after a standout out prep career in Carbondale, Ill., and Mobile, Ala. He was named to the Freshman All-American Team in his first season at ORU, but transferred to the University of Alabama where he started 98 consecutive games. Alabama advanced to the NCAA Tournament's Sweet Sixteen in all three seasons he played. He holds the school records for most 3-point shots made in a single game with eight in a 1987 game against Vanderbilt, and for career 3-point field goal percentage (.485, 81–167). He was selected by the Detroit Pistons in the seventh round of the 1987 NBA Draft, though he never played professionally. Instead, he spent three years touring with Athletes in Action, then attended graduate school at UCLA for two years.

He joined Harrick's staff in 1987 where he began a coaching journey that would lead him to his first head coaching job. However, despite inheriting a team which reached the NCAA Tournament the year before, Gottfried had his work cut out for him. He may have been a great hire for MSU fans, but his new team didn't want anything to do with him.

"At our first team meeting, three players showed up," recalled Gottfried, noting only Marcus Brown, Vincent Rainey and Kenneth Taylor bothered to come meet their new coach.

Gottfried eventually lured the remaining cast of characters to a team meeting – he threatened to pull their scholarships if they didn't show up – but he had a battle on his hands to win the hearts and minds of his players.

"The first few weeks were a disaster," he explained. "We had seven seniors and they had such loyalty to Scott, which was understandable. They didn't want a coaching change. They had been to the NCAA Tournament the year before (vs. North Carolina), their coach leaves, and now they have a new guy.

"It was not like they had won 10 games the year before and were dying for a change."

Despite resistance, the 1996 Racers gradually came around. Led by Brown, who was moved from shooting guard to combo guard to get the ball into his hands as much as possible, the Racers won 19 games to capture the program's third OVC regular season title in a row.

"You learn at UCLA that the season begins in March, the other games are all exhibitions," noted Gottfried. "Murray State is the same way. You could go 25-2 and win the OVC regular-season championship, but if you lose in the OVC Tournament the fans are not satisfied."

In the '96 OVC championship game in Nashville, the Racers lost to Austin Peay when the Governors converted two free throws with two seconds remaining in a tie game to win 70-68. It would have been bad enough just to lose the championship game and be denied a trip to the Big Dance, but the '96 Racers had their hearts ripped from their chests. Austin Peay's last-second free throws were set up by a disputed foul call on Rainey that remains one of the most controversial moments in Racer history. Immediately after the foul was called, ESPN cameras cut to Gottfried who promptly fell to the Municipal Auditorium floor with an "I-can't-believe-that-just-happened" expression on his face.

"That (loss) never leaves me," Gottfried said, disappointment still apparent in his voice 15 years after the infamous night. "I felt so bad for our seniors. From that first team meeting where three guys showed up to

winning the regular season championship and then to have it end when an official makes a horrible call. I still remember going into the locker room and thinking, what do I say to these guys? They just got screwed out of the NCAA Tournament."

More disappointment followed 11 days later when the Racers narrowly missed upsetting Missouri in the first round of the National Invitation Tournament in Columbia, Mo. Gottfried was slapped with a rare technical foul in the final moments and Mizzou survived 89-85.

On the long bus ride home to Murray, Gottfried turned his sights to 1996-97. He was losing Brown and six other seniors, so he planned to "change the program from the inside out."

What resulted would cause Gottried to proclaim, "I am probably more proud of that team than any of the teams I coached at Murray." But not because all of his changes were effective. On the contrary, very few of Gottfried's plans worked as designed.

In addition to Rainey, now one of the top players in the OVC, the Racers were going to add nine new players that would greatly enhance the roster's talent level. Gottfried was counting on one player who sat out the prior season (Chad Townsned), and seven new recruits. But not just any recruits, however, perhaps the best recruiting class in program history. Unfortunately, only shooting guard De'Teri Mayes, slender post player Arnell Hamilton, both junior college transfers, and freshmen Mike Turner and Aaron Page were eligible for the '96-'97 season.

With an undersized lineup that revolved around Rainey (6-4), Townsend (6-1) and Mayes (6-2), the Racers slowly developed into an OVC contender. But they needed Dick Fick's Morehead State team to knock off league-leading Austin Peay on the season's final night to give the Racers a tie atop the OVC heading into the tournament.

Playing for the first time in the brand new Nashville Arena, the Racers ripped Middle Tennessee 74-48 in the semifinals to set up a championship rematch with Austin Peay. In a see-saw battle, Mayes drained a clutch 3-pointer at the top of the key as time expired to force overtime. In the extra period, Rainey and Townsend fouled out, leaving the Racers to battle APSU's Bubba Wells with Mayes, Hamilton, Page, Matt

Harris, and Darren Dawson. Harris came up with a key steal and dunk in OT while Hamilton blocked a shot in the final seconds to secure a trip to the NCAA Tournament for the Racers.

MSU headed to Charlotte, N.C., two weeks later for a date with mighty Duke in the first round of the tournament. Normally, that matchup would mean trouble for the Racers, but Mike Krzyzewski's No. 2-seed Blue Devils resembled Gottfried's 15th-seeded Racers – guard oriented.

In a late-night battle of two scrappy teams, the Racers stayed even with the Blue Devils throughout the game, but were down three in the final seconds. Rainey's desperation full-court heave bounced off the glass, sending Murray State home with a 71-68 defeat.

"We were up at the half, but at the 14-minute mark, Trajan Langdon hit a couple of threes to put them up four or six points," Gottfried recalled. "But they never could pull away. Outside of that stretch, we played them even."

Finishing 20-10 with an OVC co-championship and tournament championship was an incredible accomplishment for Gottfried's second team, but the final seconds had barely ticked off the clock in the Duke game when the thoughts of all Racer fans and coaches turned toward 1997-98.

Though Rainey would be moving on, Gottfried would bring back Mayes and Townsend to form the best backcourt in the OVC. As for the rest of the roster? Help was definitely on the way.

Assistant coach Tevester Anderson lured the duo of Duane Virgil and Marvin Gay from Trinidad by way of West Palm Beach (Fla.) Community College and Division I transfer Michael Floyd was a key veteran. Most anticipated of all, four players who were on campus but sat out the '97 season as Proposition 48 casualties, were finally eligible. MSU intramural basketball's loss was Gottfried's gain.

Isaac Spencer, Rod Murray, Ray Cunningham and Aubrey Reese were all expected to play major roles in their first seasons of eligibility, and the anticipation of seeing the foursome only added to the high expectations heading into the season. Anticipation of Gottfried's '97-'98 team was so great, the team was brought onto the Stewart Stadium field and introduced during a Racer football game.

Right out of the gate, Racer fans' high expectations were met when Murray State opened the season against a very good Dayton team. Veteran guards Mayes and Townsend were joined in the starting lineup that night and every night to follow by newcomers Spencer, Murray and Virgil. They rolled into Dayton and came away with an eye-opening 76-69 victory.

"Getting on the bus to come home that night, I remember thinking, this team has a chance to be good," Gottfried recalled. "I wanted us to be a Top 20 team, and I thought we had a chance to get there."

MSU had little trouble through the early portion of their schedule and when they left E.A. Diddle Arena with a decisive 86-75 win over rival Western Kentucky, the Racers were 9-0. Up next, a trip to San Juan, Puerto Rico for the Puerto Rico Holiday Classic.

Facing Michigan in the first round, the Racers were tasked with stopping massive Wolverine center Robert "Tractor" Traylor. A win by MSU would not only set the Racers on the path to a spot in the Top 25, but would also signify one of the greatest victories in school history. But for the first time that season, the Racers displayed uncertainty and were pushed around by the Big Ten foe, losing 76-53.

"Michigan just manhandled us," explained Gottfried. "The guys were so down. We had a come-to-Jesus meeting in my hotel room that night. We had to get their spirits up and convince them that we were still a good team."

A day later, the Racers responded by beating Nolan Richardson's Arkansas team 94-83 in a game that is noteworthy for Mayes' game-high 42 points and the fact the Racers beat the Razorbacks much worse than the 11-point margin might suggest. The Puerto Rico tournament ended with Murray State beating an up-and-coming Iowa State team, coached by Tim Floyd, 84-76.

"We came back from Puerto Rico 11-1 and we were probably going to be ranked. Then we lost at Middle Tennessee the next game out," Gottfried recalled of the Racers' lethargic effort in a 76-71 OT loss to the Blue Raiders to open January.

Losing at Middle may have been disturbing for Gottfried and the Racers, but it was not the last speed bump in January. The Racers didn't go into a tailspin on the floor – they actually reeled off six straight wins following the loss at MTSU – but events in Alabama would serve as a pothole on seemingly smooth road to the OVC title. In mid-January, the University of Alabama announced that head basketball coach David Hobbs would not return the following season. Racer fans were well aware that Alabama was not only a high-profile job, it was also their coach's alma mater. Plus, six of Gottfried's players were from Alabama, so they were in-tune with what was going on back home.

Of course, the media "rolled into Murray," according to Gottfried, with a writer from Montgomery coming to Murray to do a feature on hometown heroes Spencer and Murray – and broaching the "Alabama situation" with Gottfried. It came to a head in Clarksville, Tenn., when a reporter from the *Birmingham News* showed up to talk to Gottfried at the Racers' shootaround just hours before MSU was to take on Austin Peay. Later that night, the Racers lost 80-72, but it would be the team's last loss until March.

With Mayes earning OVC Player of the Year, the Racers finished league play with a 16-2 mark and a three-game margin. In the OVC Tournament, they dispatched Tennessee Tech (84-63) and Austin Peay (81-56) in the first two rounds, setting up a championship matchup against Tennessee State.

"Going into the championship game we were 28-3 and I remember thinking: we cannot lose this game," Gottfried said. It wasn't an arrogant thought. It was a demand. I did not want to sit there on (NCAA Tournament) Selection Sunday worrying if we were going to get in."

Gottfried had little to worry about, as the Racers took control early and cruised to the finish line with a 92-69 championship victory. There would be no weighing the chances of an at-large bid on Selection Sunday, but the CBS-televised tournament draw was still painful for Gottfried. Desipite getting a No. 9 seed, which at the time was the highest in school history, the Racers would play Rhode Island of the Atlantic 10. The Rams just happened to be coached by none other than former UCLA coach Jim Harrick. Gottfried voiced his displeasure over the draw, but it wasn't only because the NCAA – in Gottfried's mind – put together an emotional matchup between teacher and pupil.

"I spoke with Jim probably thirty times that year, so we knew each other's teams," recalled Gottfried, still carrying a grudge against the tournament committee's pairing. "It was frustrating because we had a chance to make some noise and not only did we draw one of the hottest teams, (Harrick) knew what to take away from us offensively."

Squaring off in Oklahoma City, Okla., the Racers jumped out to a quick 10-point lead before the first TV timeout. After that, it was all Rhode Island as the Rams took control and rode home with a 97-74 first-round win.

In the interview room following the game, Gottfried discussed the loss. In the hallway leading from the interview room back to the Racer dressing room, the questions pertained to the coach's future: "Was this your last game at Murray State?" "Are you going to Alabama?"

It was believed by most observers, including anyone associated with the Racers, that Gottfried was going to be coaching the Crimson Tide come next basketball season. Gottfried insists that he never discussed the job with anyone from Alabama during the season, saying he "was the flavor of the month," because of the team's success that year. He was not only on Alabama's short list either, as Arizona State also met with the him to discuss their job opening, according to Gottfried.

"Believe it or not, it got tricky (with Alabama)," Gottfried said after it was determined he was a candidate at Alabama. "The (Alabama) athletic director did not offer much money. It was not a done deal right off the bat, especially with Arizona State involved. It took a couple of weeks."

All speculation was put to bed on March 25, 1998, when Gottfried was named the next Crimson Tide head coach. "It was not as easy as people think to take that job," he noted. He had a tremendous team coming back the following season had he stayed. And, he had developed an attachment to the school and program that he tried – twice – to pass on.

"I have a great appreciation for those three years, they were some of the most fun I've had in coaching. I couldn't have asked for a better place to coach for a first job," said Gottfried who coached the Crimson Tide for 11 seasons before resigning in 2009, "I hope I was good for Murray because Murray was good to me."

Gottfried accepted the head coaching job at North Carolina State in April of 2011. In two seasons with the Wolfpack he is 48-24, having reached the Sweet Sixteen of the NCAA Tournament in his first season.

CHAD TOWNSEND

by Kevin Stewart

When Murray State coach Mark Gottfried needed someone to go to war on the basketball court, Chad Townsend knew exactly what he wanted.

In the early 1990s, Townsend was in the army overseas as part of the restoration and follow-up to the actions of the Desert Storm war.

In 1997-98, the 6-foot-1 guard from Kerrville, Texas was out in front of Gottfried's Racers carrying the banner for MSU's young troops, leading the way to a 29-4 record and a Top 25 ranking, only the second season in school history to finish nationally ranked in the prestigious Associated Press poll. Murray State took the final spot at No. 25 in the March 10th voting by the nation's top sportswriters and television and radio media. In 1951, the Racers finished 17th in the poll and in 2012 they finished 12th.

Townsend only played two years, but he was the leader of the '96-97 squad, which won 20 games and nearly upset Duke University in the NCAA Tournament, and the team the following year that made its mark on the Top 25.

Townsend led the Racers in assists and steals in both seasons while averaging 13.2 points.

The warrior in Townsend certainly came out in the postseason. He was the most valuable player in both the 1997 and 1998 Ohio Valley Conference Tournaments, both won by the Racers.

The fierceness and fighting spirit Townsend displayed on the court surfaces just as visibly when he talks about that 71-68 loss to Duke, a first-round game of the Southeast Regional in hostile territory at Charlotte, N.C. Duke was a No. 2 seed and ranked 10th in the country. Murray State was a 15 seed.

The mighty Blue Devils tied the Racers at 35 at halftime. And despite a 16-4 Duke run early in the second half, the Racers hung close, pulling within 70-68 in the closing seconds on 3-pointers from Townsend and Vincent Rainey.

Steve Wojciechowski made a free throw with 2.3 seconds left, and Rainey's 75-footer bounced off the backboard.

"Um, yeah, we had an opportunity to win," Townsend recalled, his voice stalling a bit. "If I hesitate here, it's because we could have and should have won that game. That's the one that got away.

"I look at that game and I don't see it as that we were lucky to hang around. I see it as Duke was lucky to come out with the win."

Chad Townsend

Townsend's emotions are understandable. The Racers were on a roll with six straight wins, including an 88-85 overtime triumph over Austin Peay and OVC Player of the Year Bubba Wells in the OVC Tournament championship. Townsend scorched the Governors for 28 points.

"One of the biggest hangups I have about the OVC is that we have to play our tournament so much earlier than all the bigger conferences, and we have so long to wait before that first NCAA Tournament game," Townsend said.

The Racers played eight games in 17 days ending in the OVC finals. But they had to wait 13 days before facing Duke. The layoffs are largely created by television network contracts.

"We were really rolling after the Austin Peay game and then we had the long layoff," Townsend said. "Myself, D.T. (Mayes) and Vincent (Rainey) had bad shooting nights against Duke. If just one of us had shot better, we would have beat them."

Townsend's recruitment to Murray State was anything but typical. He went to an NAIA college to play baseball, then walked-on to the basketball team. He later joined the army and honed his skills playing on camp teams.

Friends and commanders in the military encouraged him to continue his education, and to do so through basketball. So soon upon leaving the service after three years, Townsend took a stab in the dark that paid off.

"He actually paid a $400 entry fee to go to a junior college exposure camp," Gottfried recalled. "I was out recruiting and got home on July 30th (of 1995). The last day of the recruiting period was July 31st, and (assistant coach) Tevester Anderson called me that night and said, 'I found us a point guard.' I hadn't even seen Chad play."

Townsend sat out a year as a transfer, but that time practicing with the team and the experiences of a worldly 25-year-old proved invaluable when he was called to lead much younger players.

"He really learned our system in that year, really learned how to become a point guard," Gottfried said. "Just as important, he was an older, more mature guy who had been half-way around the world with Desert Storm, so nothing was going to rattle that guy."

In '96-97, Townsend focused on getting the ball to the senior Rainey and the junior Mayes, the fabulous one-two, jump-shooting punch that averaged 21.9 points and 21.2 points, respectively, as Townsend racked up a Racer-record 212 assists.

In '97-98, Mayes was back, but youngsters filled much of the roster. First-year players Isaac Spencer and Rod Murray exploded onto the scene. Spencer led the team in rebounding and was second in scoring and Murray was second in rebounding and had the fourth-best scoring average.

With Townsend running the show, commanding the troops, the Racers won 18 of their last 19 games

before the NCAA tournament, where they lost to Rhode Island, 97-74.

"In 1997, with Vincent and D.T., we weren't that athletic but we had a team that could really shoot the ball," Townsend said. "The next year was a different dynamic. We had young guys who could run the floor and were athletic. We got better and better. My job was to keep us focused, keep the younger guys on track.

"Coach Gottfried really pushed me to lead that team, to be his eyes out there. We really fed off each other.

"With age comes experience. I'd been in the army and I'd been through a lot of life by the time I got to Murray. I think that maturity and that experience made a big difference in the player I became."

De'Teri Mayes

by Steve Parker

As Murray State has risen to become one of the winningest college basketball programs in the country, a logical question is "how?" Coaches, fan support, financial commitment, facilities and coaches have all played a part. But the primary contributor to the Racers' winning ways is players. More often than not, MSU has fielded the most talented teams in the Ohio Valley Conference, in addition to having the league's top player. Many times that leading player came out of nowhere, arriving with little fanfare, but emerging as a superstar. Steve Newton called those players "diamonds in the rough." The former Racer coach found two in Jeff Martin and Popeye Jones, and Scott Edgar found Marcus Brown.

But perhaps no player came from as far in the rough as De'Teri Mayes. In fact, one could argue that De'Teri Mayes never even got to the rough.

Thumbing through the MSU basketball record book, it doesn't take long to determine that Mayes was a big-time performer for the Racers. The 1997-98 OVC Player of the Year, Mayes' career scoring average of 21.26 points per game is the best all-time at MSU and his 103 made 3-pointers during the '97-'98 is the most ever by a Racer player in one season. He only played two seasons for Murray State, but that's two more than he played in high school.

Because De'Teri Mayes, the Racers' 19th all-time leading scorer, did not play high school basketball.

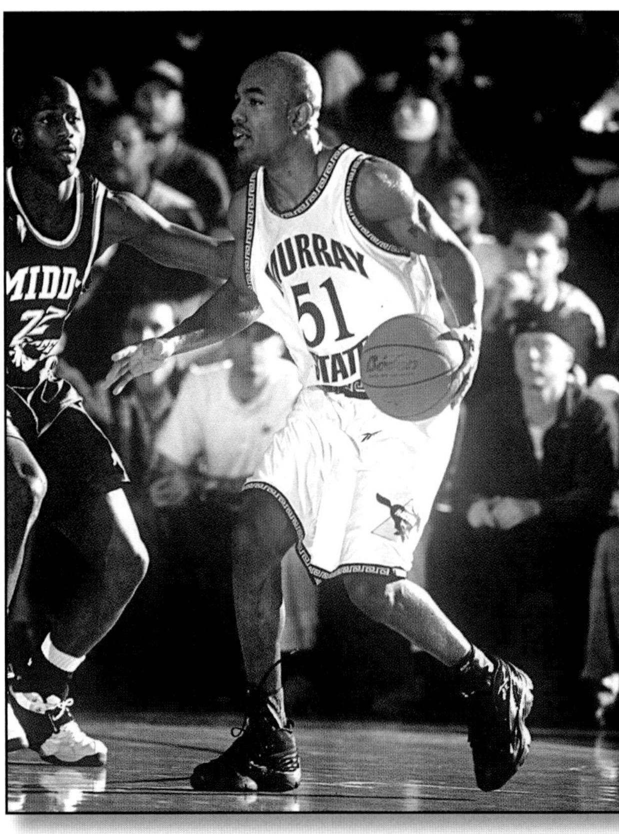

De'Teri Mayes

Growing up in Montgomery, Ala., Mayes had a deep love for the game of basketball, but he had to play his basketball on neighborhood courts. Bad study habits led to poor grades, which made him ineligible to compete for Carver High School. Finally, as a senior Mayes became academically eligible but the coach said he was too far behind the rest of the team to be able to join. Crushed, Mayes transferred to nearby Robert E. Lee to pursue his diploma, but not basketball.

After high school, Mayes continued to work on his game with his cousin, Greg Harris, who believed Mayes could play in junior college if he found the right situation. So, the two scheduled tryouts with several Alabama junior college coaches and Mayes made up his mind that he would attend the first school to offer him a spot on its roster. That school was Wallace State Community College in Hanceville, Ala. Shortly after he signed to play at Wallace, the previous coach left and Paul Brown took over.

Mayes enjoyed a solid freshman season at Wallace, but Brown told him after that first season that if he wanted to play at the Division I level he had to do more than drive to the basket. Working that offseason on his shooting, Mayes came back as a much-improved sophomore. After shooting 29 percent as a freshman, Mayes boosted his 3-point percentage up to 42 percent as a sophomore, averaged 24.0 ppg and became Wallace's all-time leading scorer.

Suddenly, a Division I career looked possible and, thanks to his coach's previous relationship with Murray State assistant coach Tom Kelsey, Mayes came to the attention of the Racers. When then-head coach Mark Gottfried got involved, he had one question for coach Brown. "I asked him, 'If De'Teri Mayes gets 15 points a game, would you be surprised?'" recalled Gottfried. "He said, 'yes,' and I asked him if it was because that was too many, and he said it was because it was too few."

So Mayes signed with Murray State, completing his goal of one day playing basketball at the highest level.

"I always said one day I was going to play college basketball," Mayes told the *Racer Insider* in a 1997 interview. "To sign at a Division I school after not playing high school, it's something to look back on and be proud of. I'm proud that I didn't quit because I didn't play high school ball. Don't get me wrong, I wanted to play high school basketball bad, but back then I wasn't focused. You only get so many chances and I realized I got another chance in junior college and I wasn't going to blow it."

He didn't blow his chance at Murray State, either.

With senior Vincent Rainey leading the way for the 1996-97 season, Mayes teamed with point guard Chad Townsend to lead the Racers in Mark Gottfried's second season. In his seventh college basketball game, he scored 20 points in a loss to Auburn in Birmingham, Ala. Later, in his first OVC game against Middle Tennessee, he went off for 28.

Mayes' impact on the program was immediate and his impression on Murray State's coaches and fans was positive. Said Gottfried, "He really has fun playing and he's exciting to be around. He very rarely has a bad day, and I think he probably appreciates the opportunity to play as much as anybody because he had to wait a little bit longer to play."

Perhaps the most memorable shot of his first season came in the OVC championship game against Austin Peay when his 3-pointer from the top of the key forced overtime. The Racers would defeat the Governors in OT and advance to play Duke in the first round of the NCAA Tournament. Despite Mayes' 17 points, the Racers fell 71-68. For the season, Mayes scored at a 21.0 ppg clip and earned a spot on the All-OVC team.

Heading into his senior season, excitement swirled around the team with the anticipation of Isaac Spencer, Rod Murray, Auburey Reese, Duane Virgil and Marvin Gay joining Mayes and Townsend on a loaded roster. Showing the talent and depth that was expected of that team, the Racers got off to a 9-0 start before heading to the Puerto Rico Holiday Classic. In the first round game against Michigan, the Racers were physically overmatched for the first time all season and lost 76-53 to the Wolverines.

A day later, the Racers would get back on track in a major way by knocking off coach Nolan Richardson's Arkansas Razorbacks, thanks mainly to a performance by Mayes that will go down as one of the top games ever by a Racer. Mayes scored 21 points and pulled down five rebounds... in each half.

Powered by 5 of 7 shooting from 3-point range, Mayes finished with a career-high 42 points and called it the best game he ever played. It left an impression on Nolan Richardson, who said, "Mayes is better than anybody we've got."

Mayes and the Racers steamrolled through the rest of the season, winning the OVC in a walk and rolling through the OVC Tournament to earn the program's second straight NCAA Tournament appearance. In its first-round game against Rhode Island, the No. 9-seeded Racers never found their footing and lost 97-74 to the Rams for a disappointing end to one of the best seasons in Racer history.

Mayes' improbable collegiate career came to a sad conclusion, but his efforts didn't go unnoticed. His 21.5 ppg average earned him OVC Player of the Year honors, and later he would be named the OVC Male Athlete of the Year, a rarity for Racer basketball players.

His immense talent and unbridled enthusiasm for the game made the always smiling Mayes a favorite among Racer fans, whose only regret was that they only got to enjoy the De'Teri Mayes Experience for two glorious seasons.

AUBREY REESE

by Steve Parker

In the long and storied history of Murray State basketball there have been great players and great moments. Rarely, though, have the two crossed paths. That is until Aubrey Reese let go of a one-handed floater that instantly became part of Racer lore.

Reese's "Great Moment in Racer History" came in the biggest moment this side of the NCAA Tournament: the Ohio Valley Conference Tournament championship game. His floating one-hander at the buzzer gave Murray State a one-point victory over Southeast Missouri to give the Racers the 1999 tournament title. A nation-wide audience watching on ESPN saw the Racers punch their ticket to the NCAA Tournament, and also became aware of the name Aubrey Reese.

He may have cemented his place in Racer history with the floating miracle, but his Racer career was much more than one game-winning shot. His numbers and awards leave no doubt as to how important Aubrey Reese was to Racer basketball. And, as his heroics in 1999 proved, Reese was a strong-willed leader who didn't shy away from the biggest moments.

He arrived in Murray from Auburn, Ala. The athletic point guard, who was also a highly recruited football player, was signed by then head coach Mark Gottfried who constantly raved about the 6-footer's toughness and "moxie." Reese sat out his freshman season under Proposition 48 guidelines along with Isaac Spencer, Rod Murray and Ray Cunningham. As a sophomore in 1997-98, Reese was a backup to senior point guard Chad Townsend. He averaged only 4.6 points per game, but he showed glimpses of what could be expected in the years ahead. In a blowout loss to Michigan during the Puerto Rico Holiday Classic in which the Racers looked overwhelmed by the bigger, more physical Wolverines, Reese continually drove the ball right at them and finished with a better-than-it-looked 10 points. All season Reese was more than capable backup to Townsend as the team won the OVC title and earned a No. 9 seed in the NCAA Tournament.

Aubrey Reese

As the 1998-99 season dawned, the Racers were loaded in the frontcourt with all three starters returning, but first-year head coach Tevester Anderson had to replace his backcourt. Newcomer Marlon Towns, a one-time Arkansas signee, was expected to replace De'Teri Mayes, but many questioned Reese's ability to handle the starting point guard duties.

Right out of the gate, Reese proved more than capable of leading the team, especially when the Racers got off to a 9-0 start which included a 68-64 win over Oklahoma in the Sooners' own Thanksgiving tournament. If he was solid in the first nine games, he became a star at the University of Hawaii's Rainbow Classic. Facing a solid Florida State team in the third and final game of the tournament, Reese took over in the second half to force the game into overtime. Though the Racers lost 80-76, Reese finished with 29 points and it was apparent that another Racer great was born.

Reese and the Racers rolled to the 1999 OVC regular-season championship, but to snare the coveted berth in the NCAA Tournament, the Racers would have to win the OVC Tournament. True to form, the two best teams – Murray State and Southeast Missouri – met in the championship game with everything on the line.

The game, played in Nashville Arena, was a seesaw affair that was as intense as expected. Reese, a junior point guard, hit a short jumper to give the Racers a 60-58 lead with 11 seconds remaining. Following a timeout, fans, coaches, players and a national television audience watching on ESPN expected SEMO to pound the ball inside to 6-foot-11 big man Bud Eley for a potential game-tying two-point basket. Instead, Indian point guard Kahn Cotton, being guarded by Reese, pulled up from way beyond the 3-point line and drained what most thought was the game-winner with five seconds left on the clock.

In the ensuing timeout, first-year Racer head coach Tevester Anderson didn't waste time drawing up an elaborate final play. He wanted the ball in Reese's hands. Said Anderson: "Aubrey's done it three or four times throughout the year. He has no conscience."

Reese took the inbounds pass from center Duane Virgil and raced the length of the court, floating a soft one-hander over Eley's outstretched hand. Reese's 16-footer splashed through the net as the buzzer sounded, giving the Racers a 62-61 victory.

Earlier that season, Reese hit a similar shot at the buzzer to beat SEMO 71-70 in Cape Girardeau, Mo. "I'm sick of him," Southeast Missouri coach Gary Garner said after the OVC Tournament loss.

Reese, who earned a reputation as a fierce competitor during his three-year career, was not going to have his junior season end with an opponent sticking the game winning shot in his face. "Instead of being the goat, I had to switch right back and be the hero," said Reese, the tournament MVP. "[Cotton] made a good shot and I knew I had to come down and make an even better shot."

Proving that he had put the heroics behind him, Reese came back to score 26 points in the Racers first-round NCAA Tournament game loss to Ohio State. His 26-point effort was second-most all-time among MSU players in the NCAA Tournament, trailing only Popeye Jones' 37 against Michigan State in 1990.

As a senior in 1999-2000, Reese proved that the breakout season the year before was no fluke. Whether

it was winning a one-on-one duel with dynamic Detroit point guard Rashad Phillips, or scoring 32 points in a win over Rutgers of the Big East, Reese proved to be one of the top players in the OVC but one of the best point guards in the nation.

His efforts were rewarded when he was named OVC Player of the Year after averaging 20.4 points per game and leading the Racers to a 23-9 record and another OVC title. Unfortunately, Southeast Missouri was able exact some revenge in the tournament championship game with a 67-56 victory.

Reese wrapped up his Racer career with a 13.7 ppg average in 98 games and his name is prominent throughout the record book. Though he attained 1,000-point club status at Murray State before turning in a long professional career overseas, numbers alone don't do Aubrey Reese justice. Prolific players of the past may have had more skill and natural basketball ability than he did, but over his three-year career he displayed as much toughness and determination as any player to ever wear an MSU uniform.

ISAAC SPENCER

by Kim Trevathan

As the Racers' second all-time leading scorer, known for his fierce finishing moves to the basket, Isaac Spencer is pretty modest about his talents. When asked how he shot 63 percent his freshman year (fourth in the nation, third-best ever for a Racer) Spencer said it was because he was playing on a great team, surrounded by good players like De'Teri Mayes, Chad Townsend, and Rod Murray, a team that went 29-4 overall, 16-2 in the OVC, losing to Rhode Island in the 1998 NCAA Tournament.

Spencer's entire career at Murray State was characterized not only by individual accomplishments but also excellent teams. In his four years as a Racer (1997-2001) Spencer led Murray State to two NCAA appearances and three OVC titles. The Racers' record during Spencer's four years: 109-39. Spencer and LaMont Sleets are the only two Racers to be awarded All-OVC honors all four years.

At 6-6 he wasn't big for a power forward, yet he is ranked fifth on the Racers' career rebounding list, with 976, right behind MSU legends Popeye Jones, Dick Cunningham, Jim Jennings, and Stew Johnson. He's fourth for most career blocks, with 127, and he has the record for most points scored in the CSFB Center - 42 against Tennessee State, his last game as a Racer in 2001.

From Montgomery, Alabama, Spencer's dream was to play at the University of Alabama. Not basketball, but football. Growing up, he said he never watched a lot of basketball on TV; it was football that ignited his passion as a spectator. But with a mother who coached AAU basketball, Spencer said he basically grew up in the gym, and by the time he began to attend Jefferson Davis High School, the premier athletic school in Montgomery, it was clear that as an athlete, he would find his destiny on the hard court, not the gridiron.

With Rod Murray as his high school teammate, Spencer's team had a record of 83-13 his last three years there. They won a state title their junior year and always played in front of packed gyms, often with college recruiters in attendance. Though Murray's talent was more celebrated in high school, Spencer won Alabama's Mr Basketball, averaging 22.5 points and 10 rebounds per game his senior year. He was considered the most highly touted prospect to ever come to Murray State.

Spencer was recruited by bigger schools than Murray, and he almost went to Clemson, but academic problems kept him from going there. Recruited by Coach Mark Gottfried and Assistant Coach Tevester Anderson, who would become the head coach Spencer's sophomore year, he decided to go to Murray State because he knew it was a "strong basketball school," and he would get a chance to play right away, as soon as he was eligible.

Isaac Spencer

instead of the coveted 13. "I've never taken tails again after losing that toss," he said.

Spencer wasted no time making an impact once he became eligible. His freshman year he averaged 13.8 points per game, tied for second on the strong 1997-98 team, and had the incredible field goal percentage of .633. He shot 100 percent from the field in four games. It should not come as a surprise that he was named OVC Newcomer of the year.

Typical of Spencer's team-oriented philosophy, he said that the greatest highlight of his Racer career came at the end of that season, when MSU beat Tennessee State in the last game at Racer Arena. Spencer hit the game-winning shot and remembers the magically charged atmosphere at that game, full of ceremony and a frenzied crowd. Popeye Jones was there. Think of the pressure that the possibility of losing that game brought on and you understand the glory and significance of Spencer's making that shot. That Racer team lost to Rhode Island in the NCAA Tournament and ended the season ranked 25th by the Associated Press.

While Spencer had to sit out a year to get his grades up, he did more than just hit the books. He hit the weight room and added 20 pounds of muscle. Not only that, he became a presence on campus. According to the Racer Insider, "Not long on the MSU campus, Ike knew everyone and everyone knew Ike. That's not just students, either. Spencer knows the janitors in most buildings and his teachers all know the ever-smiling face of Isaac Spencer." (from "Ike and Rod," Feb. 5 1998).

He was roommates with his old high school teammate, Rod Murray. Surveying their dorm room, one got the sense of the differences in their personalities, Murray's side was neat as a Marine barracks, Spencer's section looking like a tornado had hit it. Spencer said he lost a coin toss with Murray about who would get the number 13, which Spencer had in high school. Murray won the toss and Spencer said his friend still reminds him about having to take 31 as his number

His sophomore year, Spencer was joined by MSU great Aubrey Reese, and the Racers went 27-6, including a conference record of 16-2. For Spencer it was a year of adversity, a season of playing in pain with a back injury, which he aggravated in the NCAA Tournament loss to Ohio State. Demonstrating his toughness and desire, Spencer led the team in scoring (16 points per game) at a sizzling field goal percentage of .527. After the season, he had surgery for a herniated disc.

In Spencer's junior year he averaged 19.9 points per game and led the team in rebounds, adding some variety to his game after the back injury, developing close and medium range shots to go with his relentless inside game. That team had big wins over Big East power Rutgers, a highly regarded Valparaiso team, and avenged the loss to Rhode Island in the 1998 NCAA tournament with an 80-74 win in the Sun Classic.

His junior year also marked one of Spencer's

biggest disappointments, the end of the Racers' 47-game home winning streak against Southeast Missouri State. At the time, he said, Murray State was tied with Duke for the longest home winning streak. It was Spencer's first home loss since middle school.

For the 2000-2001 season, Spencer was the lone senior, the undisputed leader of the team. Coach Tevester Anderson, at the beginning of the season, emphasized Spencer's leadership role and his suitability for it. "He wants to win more than anything, and it rubs off on his teammates," said Anderson.

Though the team didn't make it to the NCAA tournament, Spencer went out in style. In his final home game he had the record-setting night, scoring 42 points. How did he do it? "I had to shoot a lot," said Spencer, laughing. He said that they'd just come off a terrible loss to Tennessee Tech, in which he felt he didn't play well, and before the Tennessee State game, he just "felt good coming into the gym and knew it was going to be a special game." He said he used to circle the Tennessee State games on the calendar because he always did so well against them.

Spencer is remembered as much for his personality as for his performance on the court. Coach Anderson called him his "best goodwill ambassador." He remembered going with Spencer to different high schools, where he spoke to kids from the heart with no notes. "He's the best I've seen at that," said Anderson. "Charles Barkley would probably be second." Anderson called Spencer "our best recruiter."

Anderson also remembered Spencer's fondness for Krystal burgers, a craving that tantalized him in Krystal-less Murray. On trips home to Montgomery, Spencer said, he used to always stop at the Clarksville exit to get his Krystal fix.

Anderson called Spencer a "coach's player. He would do whatever you asked him to, off and on the court."

The Racer Insider's Lindy Suiter remembered how hard Spencer played, that he was a crowd favorite, "fiery, who played with a smile on his face."

"For his size," said Suiter, "he was one of the best rebounders ever at Murray State. He was very explosive off the floor, a real power player."

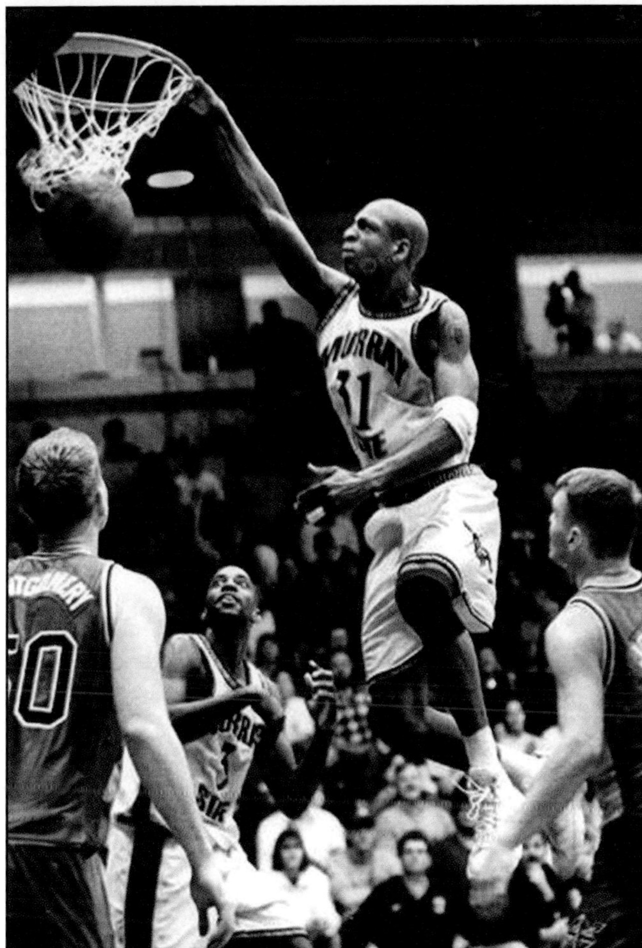

After his remarkable career at Murray State, Spencer went on to play for nine years in Europe for teams in France, Spain, Holland, the Philippines, Korea, and Finland. He said he had to adjust to the European game, which was different from the fast break, dunking American style. It was difficult at first, he said, but he got better and better. He enjoyed playing in Europe against former teammates such as Ray Cunningham, who played for a Finnish team, and Aubrey Reese, who played in Germany.

Spencer said he stays in touch with teammates such as Cunningham, Reese, Murray, and Mayes. Part of what keeps them together is coming to terms with the tragic death of teammate Kijana Howard, who had a heart attack and died on the court at the school that he transferred to from Murray State. Spencer said that the teammates call each other every year on the day that Howard died.

At the time of this writing Spencer lives in Salt Lake City, working in the oil fields near Vernal, Utah. He said the hours are a little crazy, but he doesn't mind the work. He dominates the 35-and-over league. "Nobody can guard me," he said.

Hardly anybody could stop Isaac Spencer when he set his sights on the basket. One of the truly greats at MSU, he was a great finisher, a "hard knocker," said Coach Anderson, who "had the will to succeed on the offensive end."

2000-2013

by Will Aubrey

1999-2000 • 23-9

• *OVC Regular Season Champion*

With six straight conference titles the Racers were the dominant program in the Ohio Valley Conference in the late 90's. And with four starters back for the 1999-2000 season they were expected to hang another banner. But head coach Tevester Anderson was enigmatic when asked about the team's prospects.

"We'll be a much different team than we were last year, but with four starters back our experience should give us a chance to be successful," he said. "How successful that will be, I don't know."

Isaac Spencer and Rod Murray were back to man the forward spots. Both had earned all-conference honors the previous year as Spencer averaged 16.0 points and 7.1 rebounds while Murray averaged 12.3 points and 5.0 rebounds.

Another all-conference player returned at point guard as Aubrey Reese was back after averaging 14.7 points the year before. And his running mate, Marlon Towns, was also back.

The only question mark was at center where Mike Turner would be called on to replace the graduated Duane Virgil. Turner and Virgil were as different as ice and fire. Virgil was a 6-9, back to the basket, post player. Turner was three inches shorter, was far more comfortable facing the basket, and more likely to shoot a three-pointer than dunk the ball.

He just didn't have the size to defend the post the way Virgil had. And Anderson acknowledged as much.

"With our lack of size we won't be as good defensively as we were last year," he admitted. "We'll have to press more and look to trap to take advantage of our quickness. But I do think we'll be better offensively because we'll be able to push the ball up the floor."

As the season got underway Towns found himself on the bench. He was suspended for the first four games due to a violation of team rules. And Rod Murray was out with an ankle injury.

Nonetheless, the Racers got off to a fast start as they beat Colorado-Colorado Springs 90-63 in their home opener. Aaron Page started in place of the defensive specialist, Towns. He had a steal and a blocked shot to go with six points. Ray Cunningham started in place of the high flying Murray and scored 20 points on 9-of-14 shooting.

Next up was a trip to St. Charles, Mo. for the Hoop and Quill Classic and a first round game against Rutgers from the Big East Conference. Page and Cunningham started again as the Racers prevailed 87-83 behind 32 points from Reese who hit 12-of-14 free throws, many of which came late and helped seal the victory.

Mike Turner

"Free throw shooting is important," Reese said after the game. "The ball is going to be in my hands late in the game and I have to make free throws."

"It's really important to get wins against teams from big conferences," Anderson said. "We came out and showed we could compete with anybody in the country. Too much is made of our opponents and people don't give us enough credit for our heart and effort. We just find a way to win."

Following a 78-58 pasting of Valparaiso in the second round the Racers advanced to play Southern Mississippi in the final. The Golden Eagles had humiliated Nebraska in the first round 75-48 before edging Evansville in the semifinals.

The game was close throughout as Southern Miss held Reese in check, limiting him to six points and 2-for-14 shooting from the field. But Spencer had a huge game as he hit 12-of-19 shots and scored 30 points.

Just before the final horn Reese launched a shot from midcourt that rimmed out as the Racers lost 65-62.

After the game Anderson said, "That's the kind of shot Aubrey usually makes."

Of course no one "usually" makes half court shots but everyone had come to expect late game heroics from the senior guard.

Murray State made the trek to Clarksville next to face arch-rival Austin Peay. It had been four years since they had last beaten the Govs at the Dunn Center so no one expected it to be easy.

Midway through the second half the Racers trailed 51-48 when Anderson switched defenses from man-to-man to zone. The result was a 13-3 run that put the game away.

"I thought when we changed defenses it turned the whole game around," Anderson said. "We went to our 1-3-1 zone and they really had problems with it."

Four MSU players scored in double figures as Reese led the way with 19 points.

The Racers returned home to beat Detroit Mercy 77-68 on ESPN before taking their 5-1 record to Bowling Green to face Western Kentucky. The Hilltoppers were 0-5 and decided underdogs despite playing at home. MSU's Isaac Spencer was wary nonetheless.

"Western Kentucky knows that the best time to catch us is coming off an emotional win," he said. "But we're excited about this game and we're going to be ready for them."

There was little evidence of that excitement or readiness during the game though, as Western crushed Murray State 92-70 behind 32 points from Lee Lampley.

"What can I say?" Anderson asked rhetorically after the game. "We just got an old fashioned butt whipping tonight. Going into the game I knew they weren't an 0-5 team.

"You can talk till you're blue in the face, but how can you convince a bunch 18-to-20 year old kids that an 0-5 team could give them some problems. I can't see one positive thing coming from this game."

The Racers bounced back to beat Alabama State and South Alabama before losing to Kent State in the first round of the Sun Classic in El Paso, Tx.

But they followed that loss with an 80-74 victory over Rhode Island in the consolation game as Spencer scored 21 points and grabbed 11 rebounds.

"Any time you defeat a team like that you have to feel good about it," Anderson said. "We didn't keep our composure against Kent State but we were able

1999-2000 men's basketball team.

to do that tonight. We sucked it up and played hard down the stretch."

Murray State laid an egg in their next game, a 95-67 blowout loss at Purdue. But they bounced back nicely with wins over Tennessee-Martin and Eastern Illinois. That set up a battle for first place in the Ohio Valley Conference when Southeast Missouri came to town on January 15.

The Racers had beaten SEMO in the OVC tournament final on a last second shot by Reese the previous year. The Indians were eager to exact some measure of revenge. And that's exactly what they did as they handed MSU an 84-78 defeat.

Murray State trailed 35-33 at halftime. But when the second half started they quickly built a 43-38 advantage and SEMO's head coach Gary Garner was tagged with a technical foul. When the lead reached 10 points at 53-43 Garner picked up his second technical and was ejected.

"That's one of the oldest ploys in the game," Anderson said. "If your team isn't playing well and the game is slipping away you get yourself thrown out of the game. The referees fell for it and we weren't able to get a call the rest of the game."

Garner's ejection seemed to energize the Indians as they went on a 20-4 run to take control. With 51 seconds left the Racers trailed 77-74. Then, when Towns went to inbound the ball he was assessed a technical foul for taunting and SEMO sealed the victory by hitting 7-of-10 free throws down the stretch.

"When I picked up the ball I said, 'it's our ball,' and threw it back to the referee," Towns explained. "And he called a technical foul."

Reese scored 29 points in the loss which ended Murray State's 47 game homecourt winning streak, the longest in the nation at the time.

Now in second place in the OVC the Racers knew they had to bounce back strongly against Austin Peay. So Anderson shortened his bench, choosing to go with his best, most experienced players. And it paid off as Murray State eked out a 77-75 victory in overtime.

Reese had 27 points and Spencer had 23 as both played all 45 minutes. Only seven players saw action for the Racers and the seventh man played just six minutes.

"This was an important win for us," Anderson noted. "We were still hurting from the loss to Southeast Missouri. I thought it was a real test of character."

With the Death Valley trip to Eastern Kentucky and Morehead up next the Racers were 11-5 overall and 4-1 in OVC play.

"The Death Valley swing is tough," Anderson said before making the trip. "We've always done well out there but it does concern me because we're not playing as well as we can right now. Eastern Kentucky and Morehead both have good teams. It's going to be a challenge for us."

And he was right. Murray State won an 82-77 squeaker at Eastern Kentucky as all five starters scored in double figures.

The game at Morehead was even closer as the Racers eked out an 87-86 victory in overtime. MSU won despite an off night from Spencer who hit just 2-of-11 shots as Reese scored 21 points.

"We don't like games to be this close," Reese said. "But you have to give them a lot of credit. They played really well. No game is an easy win for us anymore. We know that no matter who we play we have to play 40 minutes every time out."

Reese's comments proved to be prophetic as the next three games were decided by a total of five points – an 81-79 loss at home to Middle Tennessee, a 75-74 victory over Tennessee Tech, and a 77-75 loss at Tennessee State.

But the Racers returned home and got back on track with lopsided victories over Tennessee-Martin and TSU. Then a win at Eastern Illinois left them 17-7 overall and 10-3 in conference play as they headed to Cape Girardeau for a rematch with league leading Southeast Missouri.

Murray State won handily, 77-60, and reclaimed first place in the conference behind 24 points from Reese and 22 from Spencer.

The Racers' pushed their winning streak to six games with victories over Eastern Kentucky and Morehead State. A loss at Middle Tennessee in the penultimate game of the regular season cost them sole possession of first place. But they clinched a tie for the title by beating Tennessee Tech in Cookeville in the final game.

After crushing Tennessee State and Eastern Illinois in the first two rounds of the OVC tournament, MSU appeared to be on a roll. Fans expected the final against SEMO to be a repeat of the rout in Cape.

And it started out that way as Murray State led 21-9 in the early going. But when it was over the Indians were on top 67-56.

Reese's final game as a Racer was the worst game of his career. He hit just one shot in 18 attempts.

When asked what went wrong after the game he replied, "I don't know. It was just one of those nights."

Actually, the entire team had one of those nights as the rest of the Racers hit just 18 of 53 shots or 33.9 percent from the field.

"We got off to a very fine start," Anderson said. "But sometimes when you do that you find out that it's fools' gold. Once we got ahead by 10-12 points we got out of our offense and started taking quick shots."

Reese and Spencer both earned all-conference honors and Reese was named OVC Player of the Year.

2000-01 • 17-12

Murray State rolled into the 2000-01 season having won seven consecutive conference championships. And most Racer fans expected that to continue. But everything has to come to an end and MSU's string of championships was no exception.

The Racers began the year minus three players who started the previous year – Aubrey Reese, Mike Turner, and Rod Murray. And they were also without key reserves Aaron Page and Marlon Towns. In retrospect it's amazing that they were picked to finish second in the OVC, behind Austin Peay, despite having lost five of their top seven players.

Head coach Tevester Anderson sounded a note of warning at the beginning of the season, "This must be some kind of joke because we have way too many new players and this league's too talented. I believe we have a chance to be that good by the end of the season, but we're not that good right now.

"We're very young and we'll be weak fundamentally early on. We have nine players who have no Division I experience at all."

Anderson also warned that the league was very much improved.

"The talent is far superior to what it was when I came into the OVC," he said. "Some of the teams that we won the league with a few years ago wouldn't win it now."

Those words would seem prophetic by the end of the season as the OVC was ranked 16th in the nation by the Sagarin Ratings, an all-time high.

The Racers lost another starter, Ray Cunningham, following the second game of the season. Cunningham was suspended after he ran afoul of the law.

Justin Burdine started the year at point guard but was displaced by Kevin Paschel and eventually moved to shooting guard. Isaac Spencer had spent his entire career at power forward but, in an attempt to prepare him for a pro career, Anderson moved him to small forward. That experiment failed and by the end of the season Spencer was back at his natural position.

Despite their youth the Racers got off to a great start, winning four of their first five games. They beat Western Kentucky 83-81 and they beat UAB 84-72 in overtime.

Murray State found themselves trailing at UAB by 16 points with 11 minutes left. At that point Anderson switched from man-to-man to a matchup zone he called the 3-D. The Blazers never solved it and MSU outscored them 18-6 in the extra period to win going away.

Spencer led the way with 20 points while sophomore Chris Shumate had 19.

Unfortunately that victory was followed by five losses in the next six games. During that stretch the Racers were pounded by Southern Illinois 94-79 and Colorado 98-71. They did give Louisville fits before falling 89-86 and they won at Nebraska, 79-71.

MSU entered OVC play with a 5-6 record but they won five of their first six conference games and with a four game road trip looming it appeared they had righted the ship. Unfortunately they lost three of those four, the last an 84-79 overtime defeat at Austin Peay.

With their backs against the wall the Racers rallied, winning six of their final eight games. Spencer was incredible, scoring 29 against Eastern Illinois, 27 against Morehead, 20 against Eastern Kentucky, 26 against Tennessee State, and 42 against Tennessee Tech.

The season ended with a 97-71 blowout loss to Eastern Illinois in the semifinals of the OVC tournament. The Racers just couldn't find a way to stop Kyle Hill (28 points) and Henry Domercant (27 points).

Spencer was a first team All-OVC selection and Burdine was a third team selection.

2001-02 • 19-13

• *OVC Tournament Champion*

The Racers began the post-Isaac Spencer era with cautious optimism. They were again picked to finish second, behind Tennessee Tech, in the OVC but head coach Tevester Anderson wasn't so sure that was warranted.

"I don't like our team very much right now," he said at the time. "We have kids who have a lot of talent, but it's going to take some time in putting that talent together. We're just not at that level right now."

Most thought he was sandbagging, including Tennessee Tech head coach Jeff Lebo, "There's no doubt about that. He's been around long enough to know how the deal works. Everybody knows the road to a championship still goes through Murray."

The Racers did return two regular starters in Chris Shumate and Andi Hornig along with four part-time starters – Justin Burdine, Antione Whelchel, Cuthbert Victor, and Kevin Paschel. So the cupboard wasn't entirely bare.

And the season began with lopsided victories over Division II opponents West Florida and Colorado-Colorado Springs. So spirits were high when Murray State rolled into Bowling Green to play the Hilltoppers on November 24. Western had already beaten Kentucky by 12 and was ranked 25th in the nation.

For a while it looked like the Racers would have an easy time with their arch rival as a capacity crowd of 8,117 saw them roar to an 18-9 advantage. But their shots stopped falling and Western rallied. By halftime the Hilltoppers were up 48-35 and they won going away, 101-77.

"We really didn't play the kind of ball I thought we could for 40 minutes," Anderson said after the game. "We did for the first 8-10 minutes, but we got winded and we didn't execute when we started subbing.

"Western is a very good and experienced team, but we should've played much better. We missed a lot of putbacks in the first half, we weren't cohesive and our offense wasn't very efficient because we went one-on-one a lot."

MSU followed that loss with wins over Chattanooga and UAB at the RSEC.

For the second straight year they found themselves in a deep hole against UAB as the Blazers had a 19 point lead (55-36) with 11½ minutes to play.

Then Anderson went to his bench and shifted to the matchup zone he had employed successfully against UAB the year before.

Reserves Antonio Henderson, Rashard Harris, James Singleton, and Cuthbert Victor along with starting point guard Kevin Paschel held the Blazers to just three field goals the rest of the way as they pulled out a stirring 74-69 victory.

"We've been in a situation like this before and we've come back to get it done," Paschel told reporters after the game. "The biggest thing we had to do was play real good defense. The coaches keep telling us that if we play well defensively, then our offense will come around. And it did."

The Racers were 4-1 but an alarming trend started to take shape with a loss at Indiana State. They just weren't consistent. And with a trip to Louisville for the Billy Minardi Classic on the horizon that was more than a little troubling.

Anderson was definitely concerned so he altered his starting lineup for the game against Virginia Tech in the opening round of the BMC. Burdine and Shumate were benched in favor of Victor and Singleton.

The Racers responded with a 66-63 victory over the Hokies. Following the game a reporter from the Courier Journal asked Anderson how it felt to get a victory over a team from the Big East. He replied, "I'm undefeated against the Big East."

But the lineup change did not alter the see-saw pattern of the season as the Racers lost to host Louisville 84-69 in the final. They followed that with a 69-65 victory at DePaul and a 103-72 victory over Tennessee State.

After the victory over the Blue Demons Anderson noted, "I'm real proud of this basketball team. I think they showed a lot of resiliency in bouncing back from the loss to Louisville. This was a big win for our program.

"Our bench came in and really played well," Anderson noted. "Guys like Rod Thomas, who hasn't played in a while, came in and gave us some big minutes when our starters had to be out. And Justin Burdine did another great job for us."

Burdine came off the bench to score 25 points and it looked as though the Racers were on a roll. Unfortunately the wheels were about to fall off.

Murray State lost eight of its next 10 games. They lost at Chattanooga 71-58. Gardner Webb embarrassed them at the RSEC, 80-66. Tennessee Tech routed them in Cookeville, 78-59. And they gave up 92 points to both Eastern Kentucky and Morehead in back-to-back to losses.

With a 3-5 record in conference play and the team in a tailspin, failing to qualify for the OVC tournament was a distinct possibility.

Injuries were partly to blame for the slide. Shumate had contracted a mysterious illness and didn't play after the Indiana State game. Harris and Hornig suffered knee injuries in mid-January. And Singleton was hampered by an ankle injury.

All of these complications hindered the Racers. But, Shumate's illness may have hurt the most.

"When he became ill I felt like it wasn't going to hurt us very badly," Anderson said in late January. "But, it hurt us worse than I thought. We miss his shooting quite a bit. And, when he's on the floor he makes other players better because he draws defenders and he can execute the offense. Defensively, Whelchel and Victor fill the small forward role very well. But the small forward needs to be a scorer and they haven't shot the ball consistently well."

He seemed at a loss when asked how the Racers could get back on track though.

"I've talked to other coaches that have been here," he noted. "I asked Scotty Edgar what he did when he was down and he said he just worked his tail off. When your back's against the wall that's when you have to work the hardest. And that's what we're trying to do."

The fans and the media were up in arms as some questioned whether the team cared and others called for Anderson to be fired.

"I took it hard because Coach T recruited me and most of the other players," Victor said at the time. "So, we had a team meeting and we decided that he was not going to lose his job because of us."

"It was really hard for us when we went into that little slump," Whelchel said. "But, we pulled together. We didn't let it get us down. When everybody counted us out, when everybody said our season was over, when it was rumored that Coach T was through, that motivated us instead of getting us down. And, then we started taking better shots and playing as a team. When we started doing that we became very successful."

As the first week of February began Anderson drew a metaphorical line in the sand. It was time for the losses to stop. He met with each player individually and scheduled practices at 6 a.m.

"I didn't spend too much time thinking about the adversity," he said. "I felt like we had the talent to win and I believed I had our players ready to win."

Not many Racer fans shared that belief, but those who did made the short drive to Martin, Tenn. on February 2 and they witnessed the rebirth of the team and earned Anderson's heartfelt appreciation.

"I'll never forget the fans that went with us to Martin because they're the core fans," he said in a voice strained with emotion.

The importance of that game at Martin cannot be overstated. It was the first of four games in seven days, a stretch that would determine whether the Racers would become road kill or contenders. And, it came after a week of soul searching and two-a-day practices with the first practice each day coming before sunrise. A loss after so much introspection and hard work might have finished the team while a victory would validate their efforts.

They took the floor with the cheers of their diehard fans ringing in their ears and they blew the Skyhawks away, 92-74.

"We were playing extra hard for Coach T," Paschel said. "He showed us the way with those practices at six in the morning. And that showed during the Tennessee-Martin game. We really played hard and we played as a team. It was really, really important that we won at UT-Martin. It showed that if we played hard and shared the ball we could win."

Murray State wound up sweeping the week to push their record to 13-11 overall and 7-5 in the OVC. Among those four wins was a 19 point drubbing of league leader Tennessee Tech, a team that had routed them a month earlier.

Some players would have been intimidated, facing the Golden Eagles after being so thoroughly dominated by them in Cookeville. But, the Racers knew no fear.

Antione Welchel

"We weren't worried," Victor said. "We knew we could beat any team in the OVC. We just played badly at Tennessee Tech. But, beating them proved to us that we were the best team in the conference."

The winning streak reached seven games before MSU lost to Morehead at the RSEC in the final game of the regular season. But, that turned out to be a blessing in disguise.

"When we lost to Morehead it woke us up and showed us that we could be beaten," Paschel said. "We had won seven in a row. And that eighth game told us that if we don't come out and play really hard we can be beat. It showed that night because we didn't really get on track until the end of the game. I think it made us play even harder when we got to Louisville."

Actually, it made them play even harder in the OVC tournament opener against Eastern Illinois at the RSEC as they put on a show Racer fans may never forget, suffocating the Panthers with incredible defensive intensity as they challenged not just every shot, but every dribble. And, that game marked the emergence of Whelchel as the team's defensive stopper.

"It's flattering to have a coach tell you he wants you to guard the other team's best player," Whelchel said. "That's what coach asked me to do right before the Eastern Illinois game when we beat them by a hundred. And, I kind of accepted the challenge and I think I proved myself. I did a good job on Henry Domercant and then I did a good job on Ricky Minard when we played Morehead."

Whelchel exaggerates when he says the Racers beat EIU by a hundred. The actual margin was 47. But, after having lost to the Panthers by two earlier in the year at home and beating them by one at their place the blowout was completely unexpected. Indeed, most fans were worried about the game. Fortunately, the team wasn't.

"We just wanted to show everybody that we were for real and that the seven game winning streak wasn't just luck," Paschel said. "We were determined to come out, share the ball and play as a team. And, we knew we would beat them. We didn't know by how much but we knew we would beat them."

At the OVC tournament in Louisville's Kentucky International Convention Center the Racers easily dispatched a Morehead squad that had swept them during the regular season as Whelchel shackled Minard before facing conference champion Tennessee Tech.

"I enjoyed the court and how the seating was and our fans were incredible," Paschel said. "They never sat down. They always cheered for us. When the games got close they still cheered. It was a great atmosphere. But, we didn't gawk at our surroundings. We were really focused. No one was going over here or over there to look around. Everybody was in their rooms waiting on the games. That's all we talked about was game issues and what we do when we get there."

That business like focus caught the attention of Tech coach Jeff Lebo who said you could tell the difference between his team and the Racers in the way they walked through the hotel. He complained that the Golden Eagles were hanging over the railings and goofing around while MSU was focused and composed, as though they had been through it before – which of course they had. But, credit for that focus goes to the coach.

"When Coach T takes us on the road he always tells us it's a business trip," Paschel said. "It's never for enjoyment. You can have fun after you win the game."

Sometimes, OVC teams get a reputation for playing finesse basketball because they aren't as big as some of the teams from the power conferences. But, the game between Tech and Murray State was a physical battle that was won in the trenches. And that's what the Racers expected going in.

"We knew it was going to be a battle," Paschel said. "Some of the players on our team had read newspapers where Coach Lebo said it was going to be a football game. So we knew it was going to be a defensive battle and we just wanted to win it on the defensive end."

Winning such a battle requires an iron will and an enormous amount of energy. MSU's iron will was forged during their losing streak earlier in the season and they got an extra dose of energy as soon as they ran out onto the floor.

"Murray State has always had good fans," Whelchel said. "But instead of being two hours away in Nashville it was an extra couple of hours in Louisville. And, to see that many people there just made us want to play that much harder. When we came out and saw our side double Tennessee Tech's side that just made us want to win it even more."

The Racers led for most of the game. But Tech took a 69-68 lead with just over a minute to play. Burdine hit a runner in the lane with 9.1 seconds left to make it 70-69. Then with about two seconds left the Golden Eagles' Cameron Crisp scooted around a screen only to find MSU's defensive stopper, Whelchel, all over him. All he could do was throw it at the basket.

"I was hoping it wouldn't go in," Whelchel said. "When Beasley took out JB I went out to pick Crisp up and made him take a bad shot. And I was like 'Don't go in, don't go in, don't go in!' And, from the time he missed it until we started celebrating I can't remember anything. I can't remember the follow shot. I can't remember anything."

Whelchel's plea was answered as both Crisp's heave and Damien Kinloch's follow shot clanged harmlessly off the rim. And then, it was time to celebrate.

"It felt really great because we had so much adversity throughout the season," Paschel said. "We were in seventh place at the end of January and then to jump up to third and win the tournament was just a great

2002-03 men's basketball team.

feeling. I think we really deserved the title because of the way we fought back and played as a team."

Burdine was a first team all-conference selection and Singleton was named to the second team.

After their 70-69 victory over Tech the Racers went on to play Georgia in the NCAA tournament. MSU got off to a great start and led 25-11 before Georgia took control. The Bulldogs pulled away in the second half and cruised to an 85-68 victory.

2002-03 • 17-12

The 2002-03 season began with great optimism. For the first time in a couple of years the Racers were picked to win the Ohio Valley Conference.

James Singleton was a first team preseason all-conference selection and Cuthbert Victor was a second team selection.

The roster was stacked as Murray State returned four starters and eight of their top nine players. They also welcomed back Chris Shumate who sat out much of the previous season with an illness. And they added Rick Jones to the roster, a guard who had previously played for two years at Vanderbilt.

The Racers opened the season with lopsided victories over Division II opponents SIU-Edwardsville and West Florida. Next up was Southern Illinois.

The Salukis had beaten Texas Tech and Georgia in the NCAA tournament the year before. And while MSU was beating up on D-II opponents SIU was beating Colorado State and George Mason. So everyone expected a tough, hard-fought game.

Everyone was wrong.

Murray State got off to a good start and led 11-10 five minutes into the game. SIU went on a run and led 23-18 with 9:04 left in the first half. And then the nightmare began.

Over the next eight minutes the Salukis outscored the Racers 26-0. It was over by halftime. MSU didn't get closer than 24 in the second half and wound up losing 85-56.

"That's never happened to me in my career," Tevester Anderson said when reporters asked about the scoring drought. "If anyone would have told me that this team I have this year, with the guards that can shoot the ball pretty decently, I never would have thought this could happen."

The Racers bounced back with an 83-72 victory over Western Kentucky. Next came a blowout loss at Auburn but they won 4-of-6 after that.

One of those four victories was an astonishing 85-39 demolition of Indiana State.

The Racers blocked the first three shots the Sycamores took and held them to 23 percent shooting from the field as they played suffocating defense.

Five MSU players scored in double figures as Rick Jones led the way with 18 points and five three-pointers. James Singleton had 11 points, 14 rebounds and five blocked shots.

The Racers were 7-4 heading into conference play.

Their first conference game was against the team picked second in the league, Tennessee Tech. Tech was without starters Leigh Gayden, who was out with an injury, and Jason Harrell who had been kicked off the team. But Anderson was still concerned.

"They're missing some guys, but they're still a dangerous team," he said before the game. "A lot of these guys have been on two OVC championship teams so they know how to win."

Six minutes into the game Anderson was disgusted with the play of his starters so he put them all on the bench.

"Yeah, he sent a message to us," forward Antione Whelchel said. "If we don't produce, he's yanking us out of the game. And the five guys that came in played better than we did."

When they got a chance to atone for their poor play in the second half the starters did just that as they held Tech without a field goal for 7½ minutes and won going away 64-52.

Unfortunately the Racers were never able to build any momentum. The victory over Tech was followed by three losses in four games. Then a three game winning streak was followed by two losses. Every upswing was followed by a reversal.

The fans were up in arms and Anderson was asked to step down before the season ended. But he and his players never quit.

They finished the regular season in fourth place and advanced to the semifinals of the OVC tournament where they lost in overtime to Austin Peay, 59-56.

2003-04 • 28-6

• *OVC Tournament Champion*

After Tevester Anderson was encouraged to retire following the 2002-03 season Murray State moved quickly to hire his replacement using the script that had worked so well for them in the past. Go after the hottest young assistant coach you can find.

This time they turned to Louisville assistant Mick Cronin.

Cronin had spent two years with Rick Pitino at Louisville and before that he worked under Bob Huggins at Cincinnati for six years.

He promised a return to the kind of fast paced basketball Racer fans had seen a decade earlier from Scott Edgar's teams.

When he was introduced to the fans he said, "We're going to play a full-court, pressing style of basketball that should be very exciting. We expect to average 75 shots a game."

The athletic department quickly fashioned a media campaign built around what Cronin promised. The slogan "Catch Us if You Can" could be seen all over town.

The rest of the Ohio Valley Conference was unimpressed as the Racers were picked third on Media Day. And Cuthbert Victor was MSU's only preseason all-conference selection.

The favorites were Austin Peay and Morehead.

Murray State started the season with lopsided victories over Wagner, West Florida, and SIU Edwardsville. It was expected that their first real test would come against Southern Mississippi at the RSEC on November 29.

The Golden Eagles played in Conference USA with heavyweights like Louisville, Cincinnati, Memphis, and Marquette. And they had won their first two games.

The outcome stunned everyone: Murray State 94 – Southern Mississippi 54. Rick Jones and Antione Whelchel each scored 16 to lead the six Racers who reached double figures.

After leading 36-23 at the break, MSU completely dominated the second half, outscoring the Golden Eagles 58-31 over the final 20 minutes, including 31-8 over the final 7:38.

"If they play like that, they'll win a lot of games in a lot of places," Southern Miss head coach James Green said. "We've taken a few hits over the years, but I don't remember anything like giving up 58 points in a half. Then again, I try to forget about games like this one."

A 73-67 road win over Texas Christian, another member of Conference USA, pushed MSU's record to a gaudy 5-0. Up next was archrival Western Kentucky.

The Hilltoppers were 0-4 and they were coming off of a 30 point loss to Louisville. But Cronin didn't expect to have an easy time of it.

"It'll be a tough challenge because anytime you're trying to beat somebody whose back is against the wall, you know you're definitely going to get their best shot, which is okay," he said. "It'll just make us better. So, hopefully, it'll be a war and we'll come out of there with a win."

Sometimes you should be careful what you wish for. Western Kentucky gave the Racers fits in the first half and led 40-35 at intermission. The second half was a seesaw affair but Western had a chance to win the game on a halfcourt shot by Jamal Brown at the buzzer. Fortunately Brown's fling rimmed out.

MSU scored first in the first overtime and built a five point lead. But a three pointer by Mike Wells with six seconds left sent the game into a second overtime with the scored tied 89-89.

The Racers outscored WKU in the second overtime 11-6 to secure the victory, 100-95, as Cuthbert Victor scored 26 points and pulled down 20 rebounds.

Following a 100-80 victory over Chicago State, MSU played host to another regional rival, Southern Illinois. The Salukis were 6-0.

They had embarrassed the Racers the year before and it looked like they might do it again as they held a 44-29 advantage with 16 minutes left to play. With 12:15 left they still trailed by 12. And then Murray State unleashed a 16-2 run over the next four minutes.

SIU responded with a 6-0 run to take a 58-54 lead with 6:25 to play. But the Racers countered with a decisive 11-0 run over the next five minutes.

JUCO transfer Kelvin Brown led MSU with 20 points while Victor scored 19 points and grabbed 15 rebounds.

"I couldn't be happier with the win," Cronin said. "I do wish it had been a little easier, but that just wasn't going to happen against a team like SIU. Our crowd

2003-04 men's basketball team.

was definitely a factor down the stretch. They really got involved during our run in the second half and our guys fed off of that. Our crowd was tremendous and I can't thank them enough for their help tonight.

"You're never out of a game when you play the way that we play. Our kids know it and believe in it. Our full-court press was the difference in the game tonight. We forced some turnovers that led to some easy baskets and I knew that we were going to have to do that to have a chance at winning."

The Racers were 8-0. They weren't averaging 75 shots a game because nobody does. But they were averaging 87.8 points on 62 shots per game and they were listed 18th in the nation by one of the computer rankings.

A 70-49 loss at 18th ranked Pittsburgh brought them back to earth. And then a loss at 11th ranked Louisville followed victories over Georgetown College and Delaware State.

Conference play got underway with a trip to Death Valley which the Racers swept, beating Morehead 97-75 and Eastern Kentucky 82-71.

MSU had run and gunned their way to a 12-2 record heading into a home game against Samford. The Bulldogs were just 6-7 but they were the polar opposite of the Racers.

They averaged just 47 shots per game as they walked the ball down the court, spread the floor, used backdoor cuts to get layups, and pick-and-pop plays to get open looks from the perimeter.

Before the game Cronin expressed his concern over the contrast in styles. "It's like going to the dentist preparing for Samford," he said. "It's been a rough week. Samford definitely has me scared to death."

He was right to be scared as the Bulldogs used an 18-0 run in the first half to grab a lead they would never relinquish. After trailing 23-6 in the early going MSU made a couple of runs but could never get over the hump as they dropped a 61-58 decision despite 17 points from Brown.

"We were held accountable tonight for our lack of defense, our lack of rebounding and our lack of effort in practice," Cronin told reporters after the game. "We ran into a team that was very disciplined and knew exactly how to attack us. We were overconfident, and we forgot what had gotten us to 12-2. Samford did a great job of passing and shooting, and they beat us.

"We can't handle success, and I'm just trying to figure out why our guys think they're so good right now. This team hasn't had success yet. Success is hanging from the rafters of our building with those OVC championship banners. Those teams won conference titles and they had success. That's how you judge success around here."

The Racers won eight of their next nine games and they were 10-1 in OVC play heading into a February 14 game at league leader Austin Peay. The Govs had played a brutal non-conference schedule, winning just three of their first 10 games against the likes of Louisville, Kentucky, and Memphis. But they were a gaudy 12-0 in conference play.

Once again MSU would be facing a team that preferred to walk the ball up the floor and take time off the clock as they ran their offense.

"We have to establish our tempo and our style of play," Cronin said before the game. "We're not going to win a game in the 50s with them. They're a devastating team defensively, and they know how to win. I don't think their talent gets enough credit because of their style of play.

"Unlike us, they're not scoring in the 90's a lot, so their kids don't average the numbers that are as impressive to a lot fans and people around the league. But if you want to go player-for-player, they've got great players."

The game was doubly important because it was the only time the two teams would play during the regular season. It was billed as the game of the year in the OVC and it definitely lived up to that billing.

Peay came out and physically challenged the Racers at the outset, turning the game into something that resembled a wrestling match more than anything else. And despite losing starting guard Adam Chiles in the first half when he dislocated his shoulder, Murray State didn't back down.

Senior Kevin Paschel came off the bench to fill in for Chiles and the Racers led at halftime 33-31. With 6:50 left it was tied at 43-all. But the Govs went on a 9-2 run that put the game away.

Whelchel led the Racers with 17 points while Victor had 13 points and eight rebounds. But it wasn't enough as Peay prevailed 63-56.

"We battled all night long through a lot of tough situations," Cronin said after the game. "We really wanted to continue to play our style of basketball after the injury to Adam, but we had to be careful so Kevin wouldn't fall out from exhaustion. We played hard, but we just didn't execute as well as we could have, and we didn't hit the open shots when we got them."

MSU proceeded to win their last five regular season games, finishing 14-2 in conference play, two games behind Peay and their perfect 16-0 mark. With Chiles out Paschel took over as the starting point guard and Jones backed him up. Paschel averaged just 5.4 points and three assists during that stretch. But, with the exception of the game against Texas A & M Corpus Christi in which he committed eight turnovers, he was a solid floor general.

No one would have ever thought of Jones as a point guard. But he averaged 11 points and twice had four assists while Chiles was out.

Chiles was back for the OVC tournament although

Chris Shumate

he was clearly not 100 percent. And the Racers rolled into the final against Peay having crushed Tennessee Tech 92-75 and Morehead 94-72.

"This is probably the way it should be," Cronin told reporters before the game. "It's a shame, because I think we're both (NCAA) tournament teams, but the reality of the situation is that only one of us will be able to go."

The game was close throughout. Cronin made a subtle change in his offense as he put the ball in the hands of point guards Paschel and Chiles and set ball screens for them so that they could break down the defense.

Paschel capitalized by creating scoring opportunities for his teammates as he dished out five assists while Chiles scored 12 points as he hit 5-of-11 shots from the field.

"They were able to really get down into our defense and it caused a lot of problems," Austin Peay coach Dave Loos said. "Having two guards like that is a real advantage for them."

With 1:19 left Brown was called for a technical foul for arguing with an official and Maurice Hamptom came off the bench to hit two free throws for Peay to cut the Racers' lead to 58-55. But the Govs got no closer as MSU prevailed 66-60 behind 13 points and nine rebounds from Cuthbert Victor.

Victor was named OVC Player of the Year and the Most Valuable Player of the OVC tournament. Shumate was a second team all-OVC selection.

Following the OVC tournament Brown and Chiles were arrested and charged with possession of marijuana among other things. Brown was suspended but Chiles was allowed to remain on the team and play in the NCAA tournament against Illinois.

Losing Brown was a serious blow. Although he had lost his spot in the starting lineup in early February because of an earlier violation of team rules, he was clearly one of the best players on the team. He had averaged 12.7 points and 4.1 rebounds while shooting 51.2 percent from the field. He was an offensive threat in the low post and made it difficult for opponents to double team Victor.

And with Illinois starting two players over 6-10 Brown's size and his ability to score in the post were sorely missed. Victor had 15 points and Shumate scored 13 but the outcome was never really in doubt as the Illini rolled to a 72-53 victory.

2004-05 • 17-11

The Racers went into the 2004-05 season without 10 players who had been on the team the previous year as they were hit hard by graduation. But they were still picked to win the Ohio Valley Conference.

"My biggest worry about this team is that they will think they're going to win just because last year's team won," head coach Mick Cronin told reporters on Media Day. "That won't win us any games. No one we play will care about that. I'm wiping last year out completely."

The team figured to revolve around point guard Adam Chiles who was back for his senior year and was a first team preseason all-conference selection. But Chiles was dismissed from the team before the first game after being arrested for driving under the influence and possession of marijuana.

So the backcourt was manned by two transfers, Keith Jenifer and Trey Pearson. Jenifer had been a starter as a freshman at Virginia and Pearson had started as a freshman at Mississippi.

Sophomore Shawn Witherspoon stepped into a starting role at one of the forward spots. But the rest of the lineup was unsettled and as the season progressed took on the appearance of a game of musical chairs.

It was obvious from the very beginning that making it back to the NCAA tournament was not going to be an easy task. The Racers opened the season at the RSEC against SIU-Edwardsville, a Division II team they had beaten by 25 points the year before.

This time the game was close throughout and the visitors had a potential game-tying three-pointer rim out with 1:19 left. Murray State prevailed in the end as Pearson scored 28 points and Jenifer pitched in with 12. Small forward Issian Redding, a JUCO transfer, scored 14 points in his debut.

"They were the kind of team that could exploit our inexperience," Cronin said after the game. "They're physical, set really strong screens, and they're a veteran team that executes offensively and has the experience of having played together for a while."

The Racers played better in routing Arkansas Tech

81-50 in their next game. They pushed Missouri to the limit before losing to the Tigers in Columbia 59-55. And then they returned home to beat Texas-San Antonio 69-58.

But they were beaten soundly at home by Western Kentucky next and then they dropped an 80-71 decision at Southern Illinois to fall to 3-3. Those losses were followed by wins over Delaware State and UC-Davis. But MSU finished pre-conference play with a 5-5 record after losses to St. Mary's and UAB.

They started OVC play with home games against Morehead and Eastern Kentucky in early January.

"We're slowly getting guys into what we want them to do and still learning what they can do," Cronin said before playing Morehead. "Ten games isn't much time to grow up, but we've got to go now.

"Our guys have a target on their backs because of last year's success and the pre-season poll. My concern going into the league is that our opponents are thinking we're the team to beat. For us to win this league, we have to get great play from Trey Pearson, Keith Jenifer, Darnell Hopkins and Shawn Witherspoon. They have to be solid for us to have a chance in the OVC."

Witherspoon exploded for 33 points against Morehead and Pearson chipped in with 12 as Murray State crushed the visitors 83-61. They both played well against Eastern Kentucky too with Pearson scoring 24 points and Witherspoon 16 in the 80-78 overtime victory.

Hopkins and Jenifer didn't score much in either game but Jenifer hit two free throws with 0.3 seconds left to beat EKU.

"I can't say enough about Keith," Cronin said after the game. "I was real happy with the way he stepped up late. He had 13 deflections, three steals, and nine assists in 43 minutes. His outstanding defense was real big for us."

The Racers followed that victory with a 55-47 loss at Samford. Five wins in their next six games put them at the top of the OVC with a 7-2 record. But back-to-back losses to Southeast Missouri and Tennessee Tech dampened their title hopes.

And then the pattern repeated itself as MSU won five of their final six regular season games only to lose at home in the first round of the OVC tournament to Southeast Missouri.

Pearson received first team all-OVC honors after averaging 14.5 points and finishing in the top five in the league in points per game, field-goal percentage, assists, steals, three-point percentage, and three-pointers made.

2005-06 • 24-7

- *OVC Regular Season Champion*
- *OVC Tournament Champion*

Not surprisingly the Racers were once again picked to win the OVC at the beginning of the 2005-06 season and Trey Pearson was named preseason Player of the Year. Head coach Mick Cronin acknowledged that they should be the favorite.

"Being picked first this year seems more legitimate than last year," he said on Media Day. "It's more assuring knowing what your strengths and weaknesses are. Last year, we were trying to figure out what those were. This time around, we've got a lot better feel for what we have."

"I think the tough thing last year was that we were picked to win the league because of Adam Chiles. He was probably the best guard in the Ohio Valley Conference. We would not have been picked to win the conference without him. So when I had to dismiss him from the team we had a bunch of young guys saddled with unrealistic expectations."

A fall trip to Canada for a series of exhibition games gave Murray State a head start on the season. But they won just two of their first four regular season games with the losses coming at Cincinnati and to Tennessee at the Gaylord Entertainment Center in Nashville.

Pearson got off to a good start with 18 points against the Bearcats and 21 against Campbellsville. But he struggled badly against Texas-San Antonio and Tennessee as he made just 5-of-21 shots and 1-of-13 three-pointers.

So Cronin benched him for the OVC opener at home against Eastern Kentucky, choosing to start Issian Redding in his place. Redding responded with a career high 21 points to go with four rebounds as MSU won easily, 80-51.

"Coach was jumping down our throats earlier in the week for turning the ball over in practice, not taking our time," Redding said after the game. "We came back and just slowed it down and started executing."

"You're not always going to get an open shot after

two or three passes," Cronin explained. "I'm real proud of Issian. He has worked extremely hard in the summer and early fall, and everything is beginning to work out for him."

Few people noticed it at the time but this signaled a shift in style of play that would become obvious as the season wore on. In their first four games the Racers had taken an average of 67 shots per game. The rest of the year they averaged fewer than 57 shots.

Two days later Morehead State came to town and got the same treatment accorded EKU as MSU crushed the visitors 92-40. Six games into the season the Racers were 4-2 overall and 2-0 in conference play with a trip to Jacksonville State and Samford on the horizon.

"Jacksonville State is formidable because they're experienced," Cronin said. "They return their top six or seven players. They only have one new guy starting. And they're scoring a lot of points.

"Samford is Samford. They do what they do. The biggest challenge for us involves our center, Pearson Griffith, because his man is a three-point shooter when you play Samford. And that's tough on him. If we can continue to defend the 3 the way we have our odds go up because that's what they do, spread you out and shoot the 3."

Cronin also said that he planned to keep Redding in the starting lineup and bring Pearson off the bench. It didn't work out that way though.

Pearson was back in the starting lineup at Jacksonville State and he responded by making 4-of-6 shots and scoring 13 points as the Racers rolled to a 91-72 victory.

In Cronin's first two seasons Murray State was 0-2 against Samford so there wasn't any reason to take the Bulldogs lightly. And yet it appeared that was exactly what happened as MSU lost 61-50.

"We were going down no matter who we were playing," Cronin said. "Samford played hard and I give them all the credit, but we were overconfident. We missed numerous offensive and defensive assignments."

A 57-53 loss to Southern Illinois at the RSEC dropped the Racers to 5-4 overall. Over the last three games starting point guard, Keith Jenifer, had made just 3-of-14 shots. He had also committed 11 turnovers while dishing out just five assists.

So Cronin benched him. He moved Pearson to the point and started Darnell Hopkins at shooting guard.

The move paid immediate dividends as Hopkins reached double figures in four consecutive games, all Racer victories. Against Eastern Illinois he scored 23 points while making all eight of his shots, seven of which were three-pointers. Over the same stretch Pearson had 19 assists and just four turnovers.

Murray State was 6-1 in conference play and in first place when 4-2 Austin Peay came to town on January 12. The game was close early but the Racers used

2005-06 men's basketball team.

a 14-8 run at the beginning of the second half to take control. Freshman Tyler Holloway came off the bench to hit four three-pointers and score 16 points in the 67-56 victory.

"We know he can shoot the ball," Cronin said of Holloway. "But the tough part sometimes is getting him open. He was able to get free because the guys guarding him were going under our screens, and our guys recognized it and got him the ball."

The winning streak had reached five games. Unfortunately it would end there as MSU dropped it's next outing, a 59-54 defeat at Eastern Illinois.

"On the way home after that game there were a couple of players laughing in the back of the bus," Racer play-by-play man Neal Bradley said. "Cronin was livid. He asked how they could be laughing after they just lost to the worst team in the country."

The defeat dropped MSU into a tie for second place in the conference with Samford at 8-2, half a game behind 9-2 Tennessee Tech. A 79-73 win over Tennessee-Martin set up a battle for a share of first place as the Racers hosted Tech on January 26.

It was an ugly game with both teams playing suffocating defense. But Murray State came out on top, 55-51.

"When you have two athletic teams with that much talent, it's hard to find baskets out there," Cronin noted after the game. "I thought it would come down to turnovers and easy baskets. Fortunately we won the game with our defense and making enough free throws at the end. I'm proud of our guys, this was a big win."

The victory left the Racers tied for first place with Samford at 9-2. They were still tied for first when Samford paid a visit to the RSEC on January 30. And having lost three straight to the Bulldogs, Cronin embraced the role of underdog.

"We have to go into this game with the underdog mentality," he said. "We need to go in like we're 10 points down at the start and not supposed to win.

"From a motivational standpoint, I'm not going to have to do much. Our guys obviously understand the situation and everyone is going to be talking about the game in the next couple of days."

Samford's style of play made them difficult to deal with. They spread the floor on offense and if you crowded them they used backdoor cuts to get uncontested layups. If you didn't crowd them they shot three-pointers. Forward J. Robert Merritt was third in the nation in three-point field goal percentage at 47.6 and center Travis Peterson wasn't far behind him at 40.9.

The Bulldogs' offense took the strengths of a man-to-man defense and turned them into weaknesses. So Cronin junked the man-to-man he generally employed. He used a variety of zone defenses instead. And it worked better than even he could have imagined as the Murray State crushed Samford 59-38.

"I knew I wanted to play zone against them," Cronin said after the game. "It goes against conventional wisdom because they shoot the 3 so well. But it allowed us to defend the perimeter without giving them layups."

Griffith and Shawn Witherspoon both had double-doubles for the Racers. Witherspoon had 15 points and 11 rebounds while Griffith had 11 points and 10 rebounds.

The Racers kept rolling with a 69-68 overtime victory at Austin Peay. Witherspoon missed a 19-foot jump shot with six seconds left but Pearson grabbed

Pearson Griffith

the rebound and while still in the air nailed a five-footer for the win.

"Coach just told everybody to crash the boards when the shot went up," Pearson said. "The ball just came my way. I didn't really know how much time I had, so I just put it on the glass. I knew that if I missed, we would have a big guy there to get the rebound."

The winning streak reached six games with a 78-72 victory over Jacksonville State. And then the season took an odd twist. Pearson missed a team workout and disappeared for a couple of days. As a result he was suspended for two games.

The Racers didn't miss a beat though as they recorded lopsided victories at Eastern Kentucky (62-45) and Morehead (71-56) with Keith Jenifer starting at the point. Jenifer had 15 points at Eastern Kentucky and forward Justin Orr had 15 points and 10 rebounds at Morehead.

When Pearson returned for the February 16 game at Tennessee State he was Jenifer's backup. That would be his role for the rest of the season and he flourished in it. At the time of his suspension he was averaging 9.7 points and shooting 40.2 percent from the field. After his return he averaged 12.6 points and shot 54.4 percent from the field.

The Racers ended the regular season by winning 11 of their last 12 games. Then victories over Tennessee-Martin (65-52) and Jacksonville State (69-64) in the OVC Tournament set up a rematch with Samford in the final.

MSU spanked Samford again 74-57 to secure a spot in the NCAA tournament. Cronin was named OVC Coach of the Year and Witherspoon was a first team all-conference selection.

Griffith was named MVP of the OVC Tournament after averaging 9.3 points, six rebounds, and 3.7 blocked shots over three games.

"I could only bench press 95 pounds when I came here, but now I can bench 260 or 265," the 6-10 senior noted. "I got tired of everybody making fun of me. Coach Cronin just told me to get in the weight room and get stronger, and I've become a better player because of it."

"He's the reason we feel confident that we can make some noise in the tournament," Cronin declared. "He's a great equalizer against bigger teams."

The Racers played defending national champion North Carolina in the NCAA tournament. Eight minutes into the game Witherspoon broke his foot. But Redding filled in admirably as he scored five straight points and Murray State led at halftime 31-30.

With 1:03 left the game was tied 65-65. But Carolina's Tyler Hansbrough hit a layup with 46 seconds left and then with 17 seconds left Marcus Ginyard hit two free throws to seal the 69-65 victory for the Tar Heels. Pearson missed a three-pointer and a jumper, and Hopkins missed a layup in the final minute for the Racers.

2006-07 • 16-14

Mick Cronin left Murray State at the end of the 2005-06 season to take the head coaching job at Cincinnati. Billy Kennedy, an assistant at Miami (Fla.) was hired to take his place and Racer basketball entered a new era.

Unfortunately, Kennedy inherited a depleted roster. Keith Jenifer, Darnell Hopkins, Issian Redding, Pearson Griffith, and Charles Johnson had all exited via graduation. Justin Orr, Marqis Wright, and Mike McCoy all decided to transfer. And Kennedy had to suspend Trey Pearson before the fall semester began.

Only four players returned from the previous year – Shawn Witherspoon, Tyler Holloway, Rob Kennedy, and Tony Easley. Witherspoon was still recovering from a broken foot, Holloway and Kennedy had seen limited action as freshmen, and Easley had redshirted.

"I didn't know what I was walking into," Kennedy admitted. "I didn't know I was going to have to build a team from scratch. But I think God was protecting me from seeing that because if I had known everything I wouldn't have taken the job."

Kennedy brought in 10 players, five junior college transfers, three freshmen, and two Division I transfers. The D-I transfers, Ed Horton and Dwayne Paul, came from Birmingham Southern and were key additions. They were able to play immediately because Birmingham Southern had decided to drop to Division-III in basketball.

Despite all that the Racers were picked fourth in the OVC on Media Day and received three first place votes while Witherspoon was named preseason Player of the Year.

"Shawn is in his fifth year and his third head coach," Kennedy said. "He's won championships and has toughness and character. To have him lead is a great blessing. We're going to lean on him more than he's ever been leaned on in the past. We do hope that he'll score more than he has in the past."

Witherspoon had averaged a career high 10.6 points as a junior. But his foot never healed properly and he would have problems with it all season. As a result he saw his average fall to 10.3 points as a senior.

Murray State started the season with three losses in the Shamrock Invitational hosted by St. Mary's. They even lost to a Division-II team, Seattle-Pacific. Never mind that the Falcons were one of the best D-II teams in the country. Racer fans were in a panic. A 73-72 victory over NAIA's Belhaven only served to heighten their concern. The Racers trailed by 11 points in the first half. But JUCO transfer Bruce Carter scored 20 points and dished out five assists to lead them to victory.

Following a 62-46 defeat at Southern Illinois MSU was 1-4 but they bounced back with a 53-50 victory over Eastern Illinois at the RSEC in their OVC opener. No one reached double figures but Witherspoon scored seven points and pulled down nine rebounds.

"In the first half I thought we played defense the way I want to play for about 17 minutes," Kennedy said. "We held them to 10 points in the first 17 minutes. It's hard to get much better than that. Unfortunately, we let up the last three minutes of the first half and the first five minutes of the second half."

The Racers lost three of their next five games though. Heading into a December 19 home game against Jacksonville State they were 4-7 overall and 2-1 in OVC play. JUCO transfers Kevin Thomas and Ray George joined the team for the game against JSU.

Thomas had injured his knee during preseason workouts but he played brilliantly, scoring 12 points and hitting 3-of-five three-point attempts. George, who had been forced to wait until the end of the first semester before he was eligible to play, saw limited action.

Murray State won two of their next three games but it was obvious that Thomas' knee was not fully healed. Following an 86-83 victory at Tennessee State a decision was made redshirt him.

George scored 12 points and dished out five assists at TSU, signaling that he could be a major contributor. But the Racers lost three of their next four games.

George had moved into the starting lineup and MSU won their next four, beating Southeast Missouri, Samford, Austin Peay and Jacksonville State. With six games left they were 12-11 overall and 10-5 in the OVC.

Then the Racers proceeded to lose two of their next three games and George was back on the bench. Horton had taken over at point guard and he led the team to three straight wins to close out the regular season.

But the season ended with a 70-60 home loss to Samford in the first round of the OVC tournament. Still, the Racers finished in a tie for second in the conference and Carter was a second team all-league selection. Not bad for a major rebuilding year.

2007-08 • 18-13

Murray State was again picked fourth in Billy Kennedy's second season and senior Bruce Carter was a preseason all-conference selection. The Racers also returned six other players who had started at one time or another the previous year.

The roster appeared to be loaded. But Kennedy sounded a note of caution.

"The problem is that we're still building a program." he noted. "We have one guy who has played on a championship team – Tyler Holloway. And he was a backup. The other Murray State teams that won championships had guys who had already experienced that.

"We're still trying to build a championship culture. Playing hard every day, playing without excuses... We're not at that level right now. I'm hoping by the end of the year we will be."

The Racers edged Rider 66-65 at the RSEC in their first game of the season. The game was tied with 3.5 seconds left but MSU had the ball. Kevin Thomas took the inbounds pass at midcourt and took it to the basket. He was fouled with .2 seconds left and hit 1-of-2 free throws to seal the victory. Kevin Thomas had 13 points and three steals while Danero Thomas had 15 points and five rebounds.

Up next was a trip to Bowling Green to face longtime rival Western Kentucky.

"They're forcing teams to turn the ball over and they score off their defense," Kennedy said of the

Hilltoppers. They have the ability to score in a hurry. They're very athletic, talented, and experienced."

They were also too much for the Racers as MSU committed 27 turnovers en route to an 87-63 loss. The lone bright spot was the play of Holloway. The junior hit all five shots he took, including three three-pointers and did not commit a single turnover.

The loss to Western was followed by wins over Avila and Arkansas State and a loss at Mississippi State.

The Racers opened conference play at home by losing a 59-58 squeaker to Eastern Kentucky and crushing Morehead 63-44. Carter scored 13 points and Holloway had 11 as MSU held Morehead to 26.1 percent shooting.

A victory at Jacksonville State gave the Racers a 5-3 record, 2-1 in conference play. But Samford was up next and the Bulldogs always seemed to give Murray State fits.

This meeting would be no different. But Carter hit two free throws with 2.7 seconds left to give MSU a 64-62 lead. Then he intercepted Samford's inbounds pass and thinking the game was over tossed the ball toward a referee.

But the ball went out of bounds and the officials gave Samford the ball with 0.4 seconds left. The Bulldogs' Josh Bedwell threw a pass to Travis Peterson who hit a three from the right wing for an apparent victory. There was just one problem. The clock never started.

After the officials huddled at the scorers' table Samford was declared the winner. There was no replay monitor but the controversy caused the OVC to require replay monitors for all future conference games.

"OVC games are too competitive, and we have too much invested to not utilize every means available to ensure our officials have every tool necessary," Ohio Valley Commissioner Jon A. Steinbrecher explained. "We owe this to our student-athletes, coaches, and fans."

Unfortunately the loss to Samford started a four game losing streak for Murray State as they suffered blowout losses Chattanooga and Belmont before dropping an 83-80 decision at Eastern Illinois.

They then proceeded to win eight games in a row, the last being a 62-34 demolition of Samford. The game was over at halftime with the Racers holding a 45-20 lead as Carter led the way with 19 points and 11 rebounds.

Everything seemed to going MSU's way as they headed to Clarksville to play Austin Peay with first place on the line. But the Govs sent them home with a 92-87 defeat. And that was just first of five losses the Racers would suffer in their final nine regular season games.

They did beat Tennessee Tech in the first round of the OVC tournament but lost to Tennessee State in the semifinals. Carter was a first team all-conference selection after averaging 14.5 points and 5.6 rebounds.

2008-09 • 19-12

The 2008-09 season was supposed to be the year Racer basketball returned to its accustomed place atop the OVC. Murray State was picked first in the annual preseason poll of coaches and sports information directors and MSU's Danero Thomas received preseason all-conference honors. Thomas, a junior, had had averaged 12.3 points while starting all but one game the year before.

It was the first time in three years that the Racers had been picked to win the OVC. But when head coach Billy Kennedy was asked what it felt like to have a bullseye on his back, he laughed.

"I've had a bullseye on me ever since I stepped up to the podium and took the job as the Murray State basketball coach," he declared. "If you come to Murray State to play basketball you come to win and you come to win championships. So I'm not losing any more sleep this year than I did the first week of practice when I got here two years ago."

The Racers started the season with a victory over Lyon College and followed that by winning at Arkansas State. Then they crushed Western Kentucky at the RSEC 89-61.

Freshman Ivan Aska scored 20 points and Isacc Miles, a transfer from Creighton, had 15. Murray State led 44-23 at halftime and they were never threatened as they shot 56.4 percent from the field. The Racers held WKU to 39.6 percent and outrebounded them 39-27.

"Our guards got Ivan the ball in great spots and he finished," Kennedy said. "He finished with his left hand. He finished with his right hand. He dunked, he drove the ball, and then he made a 15-footer. He's not shy about shooting the ball."

Three more victories followed as MSU beat Indiana State, St. Catharine, and Eastern Kentucky. But they lost a close one at Morehead (79-74) and to make matters worse they also lost sophomore Jewuan Long to a knee injury. Although Long had averaged just 4.3 points he was one of the team's best defensive players.

The Racers lost three of their next four games and then junior center Tony Easley injured his ankle in a loss to Niagara. At the time of his injury Easley was averaging 6.4 points and 5.5 rebounds and was coming off of one of the best games of his career.

He played just four minutes at Tennessee-Martin as MSU lost 75-71 and just three minutes in a 75-71 victory over Tennessee State. He didn't play at all in the next game, a 58-57 loss to Austin Peay.

"Losing Jewuan hurt us badly, especially in the Morehead game," Kennedy said. "Not having him down the stretch could well have cost us that game. And then it hurt us big during that stretch of road games that followed.

"And then not having Tony Easley for a while made it harder for us to score in transition because he runs the floor well and he can finish."

With Easley back, the Racers won 11 of their final 14 regular season games. And they beat Tennessee State in the first round of the OVC tournament.

But in the semifinal against Austin Peay they had one of those nights where they just couldn't throw it in the ocean. They shot 32.8 percent from the field and they were 0-of-15 from three-point range.

"In games like this, you have to make shots," Kennedy said. "We had opportunities in the first half to catch up, but they played like a veteran, seasoned, tough-minded team. Defensively, they were very good."

Thomas was a second team all-conference selection. Miles and Aska were named to the all-newcomer team. And Aska was named Freshman of the Year.

2009-10 • 31-5

- *OVC Regular Season Champion*
- *OVC Tournament Champion*
- *NCAA Tournament victory over Vanderbilt*

They say that history is what happens when you aren't paying attention. Certainly no one expected the 2009-10 season to be historic.

Oh, everyone expected the Racers to be good. Murray State was tabbed as co-favorites with Morehead by OVC coaches and sports information directors. And three MSU players were named to the OVC's preseason all-conference team: Ivan Aska, Isacc Miles, and Danero Thomas.

Expectations were high, and head coach Billy Kennedy embraced those expectations.

"This is our best chance to win it since I've been here," he said before the season began. "There is always pressure here in Murray. You can't go anywhere in Murray without people expecting great things, and that's just a way of life around here."

But no one expected history to be made.

And although Murray State played well in the season opener at California, they came up short 75-70.

Then they won four straight games heading into the OVC opener at the RSEC against Eastern Kentucky.

The Colonels led almost every step of the way. They led by three at halftime and led by nine with 6:06 to play. It looked like the Racers were done. But they rallied and with 11 seconds left the game was tied, 60-60.

It was the kind of game they had lost so many times over the previous three years. But this time there was a difference. This time they had a transfer shooting guard named B.J. Jenkins who asked for the ball. He asked for the ball despite the fact that before the final shot he was just 2-of-8 from the field.

"I wanted the ball," Jenkins said, "because I felt like I owed my team because I was playing so horribly. I felt like I had to make a shot to make up for what I was doing earlier."

He got the ball on the left wing with 2.6 seconds left and drilled a jump shot for the 62-60 victory.

The Racers completely humiliated co-favorite Morehead in the next game, crushing the Eagles 86-56. Danero Thomas led the way with 18 points becoming the 35th member of MSU's 1,000-point club.

"Defensively we came out with a good effort and we had a good night shooting the ball," Kennedy said. "We've got a chance to be a good team when we use our depth like we did tonight."

"I'm proud of Danero. He's been through the tough times with us when we were first starting here. I'm glad to see him reach that milestone."

The Racers split their next four games, beating East

Tony Easley

Tennessee State and Chattanooga and losing to Louisiana Tech and Western Kentucky.

With SIU-Edwardsville up next MSU was 9-3 overall and 2-0 in the OVC.

They proceeded to win their next 17 games, breaking a school record in the process.

In 10 of the previous 12 years MSU had lost at Austin Peay. This group of Racers flushed the Peay in Clarksville 69-53 behind 14 points from Jenkins, 12 from Miles, and 10 from freshman Isaiah Canaan.

"It's a good win, but we have more work to do," Jenkins said. "We're right back at it. So, we can't enjoy it too much. It does feel good for guys like Danero, Tony, and coach Kennedy who have never won here before."

The streak also included a 92-68 thrashing of Jacksonville State at the RSEC. Jenkins led the way with 19 points and four other players reached double figures as Miles had 16, Aska and Canaan each had 11, and Easley had 10.

And then there was the 77-45 road win at Tennessee-Martin, a game the Racers dominated from the outset. They led 46-23 at halftime and were able to substitute freely in the second half. They shot 56.6 percent from the field and held Martin to 24.6 percent. They hit 8-of-18 three-pointers while Martin hit just 1-of-11.

Canaan and Aska led the scoring with 13 each. But Easley was also a major factor as he scored eight points, grabbed seven rebounds and blocked seven shots. It was one of nine games during the season in which Easley blocked at least four shots as he wound up setting the single season record with 95. He bettered the previous record by 16.

Following the win over the Skyhawks, Kennedy expressed concern that it was all coming too easily.

"What I'm concerned with is getting a false sense of success," he said. "Sometimes you pick up bad habits by beating teams like that. It's important we get back to doing things the right way. I didn't get a good evaluation in watching the Martin game as far as what we want to be and the teams we have to face coming up."

The Racers kept rolling though as they crushed Tennessee State 76-54. Heading into the rematch with Austin Peay at the RSEC they were 21-3 overall and 12-0 in OVC play.

But the 14-10 Govs played like they expected to win. They led at halftime and led throughout most of the second half.

With four seconds left Peay's John Fraley made two free throws to tie the game at 63. Then, instead of calling a time out, MSU inbounded the ball to Miles who raced down the floor and hit a jump shot as time expired to win the game. He was just 2-of-8 from the field before hitting the game-winner.

"I was counting down in my head really," Miles said. "We did it in practice a couple times, me and B.J. We always work on the 5, 4, 3, 2, 1, and it came down to that situation."

Thomas played one of the best games of his career as he scored 23 points, made 4-of-6 three-pointers and grabbed 11 rebounds.

The Racers clinched the regular season OVC championship on February 16 against Southeast Missouri as they cruised to an 80-68 victory. But that was almost overshadowed by a midcourt shot Canaan hit from his knees.

"I'm just thankful," Kennedy said. "We got a good group of guys. We have good support here at Murray State. It's just been a quick four years.

"When I first got the job here, really, the first day I was wondering why because it was a tough situation. But it's just a tribute that God is faithful and he got us through it and I'm very thankful for it."

Canaan's shot was ESPN's Play of the Day and the YouTube video got over two million views.

The Racers closed out the regular season by winning two of their final three games with the loss coming at Morehead. Then they rolled through the OVC tournament, beating Morehead in the final 62-51.

Canaan led the way against the Eagles as he scored 16 points, hitting 3-of-5 three-pointers in the process.

"I just came into the game and tried to get into the flow of it and not force anything," he said. "The guards on our team are like the engine for a car. We try to get the other guys going and tonight it worked."

"It is very humbling to be the head coach at Murray State University and represent a great community and basketball tradition," Kennedy said. "We stepped up tonight when things weren't going well for us. We have a bunch of MVP's on this team and it was a big night for all of us."

Canaan was named MVP of the OVC Tournament and Freshman of the Year. Miles and Jenkins were first team all-conference selections while Easley and Thomas were named to the second team. And Kennedy was named Coach of the Year.

Murray State drew Vanderbilt in the first round of the NCAA tournament and although Vandy was favored the Racers were undaunted.

"I think we have a team that can win in the NCAA tournament," Kennedy said. "My goal when I came here was to build a team that could go into the tournament and have a chance to win. We're going in there to win."

"I think it's the perfect matchup for us," Easley said. "We've come into this whole season where we feel like we're pretty good, and nobody's really recognized us, and I think it's one of those games we can really show off to the world that we're a big-time team and we're worthy of this."

And that's exactly what they did.

The game was a see-saw affair as the lead changed hands eight times. With four seconds left Murray State had the ball with Vandy leading 65-64.

Isaac Miles, Murray vs Vanderbilt, NCAA.

B.J. Jenkins, Murray vs Vanderbilt, NCAA.

Murray's victory over Vanderbilt.

It almost didn't matter that the Racers lost to Butler 54-52 in the second round. Of course the Bulldogs made it all the way to the final game where they lost a squeaker to Duke.

The 2009-10 Racers won more games than any other team in school history, set a single season record for assists, set a single season record for blocked shots, won 17 games in a row to set a new school record, and won a game in the NCAA tournament for the first time in 22 years.

The Racers' opponents shot just 38.7 percent from the field. That was the best defensive field goal percentage of any MSU team since the 1957-58 season.

National champion Kentucky only hit 37.4 percent of their shots in 1957-58. It was a different game back then. The Racers' defense was so stifling it was as though they sent their opponents back in time 50 years.

After a timeout the Racers' Jeff McClain inbounded the ball to Miles who was immediately double-teamed so he quickly passed it to Thomas. Thomas put down one dribble to free himself then rose up and nailed a jumper from the right wing to win the game 66-65. And then pandemonium ensued as Thomas was mobbed by his teammates.

"I was trying to find a hole so I could breathe," he said with a laugh. "Everybody was just piling up on me, but I didn't really care, we were celebrating."

"It was a miracle play," Kennedy said. "It was something I drew up at the end of the game, something we've never done before."

It was the Racers' first win in the NCAA tournament since 1988. Lindy Suiter, a longtime fan and publisher of the Racer Insider attended both games.

"Of course the win over North Carolina State was special because it was the first one," he recalled. "But this one ranks right up there, it's right up there with it. It's special for my dad, too because he was the one who started me out as a Racer fan."

Murray State student Lyndsey Magness told the Paducah Sun, "I'm pretty excited. I can't hardly think straight. I'm so excited. After it happened I was shaking and almost fell over the seat in front of me. But it made it worth the trip definitely. I think it kind of makes it worth the tuition, too."

2010-11 • 23-9

• *OVC Regular Season Champion*

Following their victory over Vanderbilt the Racers became media darlings. ESPN's Andy Katz posed the question – "With all but two of its top-10 scorers returning, why can't Murray State win just one more game and be a Sweet 16 team in 2011?"

The Sporting News had Murray State ranked 35th in the nation. The Racers were ranked ahead of West Virginia, Dayton, Marquette, UCLA, and Clemson.

CollegeHoopsnet.com listed them 41st and CollegeInisder.com picked them 47th. One preseason mid-major poll had them 10th, ahead of teams like Dayton and Xavier. Every preseason publication picked the Racers to win the OVC and tabbed at least two of their players as first team All-OVC selections.

Even better, Lindy's College Basketball Preview ranked the Racers 31st in the nation and gave them a page all their own. The other 10 teams in the OVC were limited to a paragraph each.

Lindy's ranked Murray State higher than Louisville, UCLA, Wisconsin, Memphis, Notre Dame, and Maryland.

OVC coaches and sports information directors concurred as the Racers were once again picked to win the league. And four MSU players were preseason all-conference selections: Ivan Aska, Isacc Miles, B.J. Jenkins, and Isaiah Canaan.

The season started with a 50-39 victory over East Tennessee State. The play was uninspiring as the Racers were outrebounded by nine and hit just 37.8 percent of their shots.

But it was a victory and they played well defensively as they held the Bucs to 33.3 percent from the field and forced 25 turnovers. ETSU's 6-8 power forward Isaiah Brown had scored 25 points at Kentucky but MSU held him to just seven points.

"No one got frustrated and I thought that was a key in us winning the game," head coach Billy Kennedy noted. "I think that helped us because I thought they got frustrated at times and I liked our composure tonight."

Spirits were high as the Racers headed to Ole Miss but the Rebels were not accommodating. They led by 11 at halftime and pushed the lead to 23 in the second half. A late rally by MSU made the final score 77-61.

The Racers returned home for an 84-70 victory over Rheinhardt before heading to Los Angeles to play Stanford in the 76 Classic. Stanford was young but they had signed the 16th ranked recruiting class in the country the previous year. Jenkins scored 15 points and the Racers won 55-52 after leading by 11 at the half.

"I liked the way our seniors stepped up," Kennedy said. "I thought they had good poise and composure and that's what we were missing some days in practice and in our last game."

Losses to UNLV and Oklahoma State followed. It was a tired, jetlagged team that headed to Eastern Kentucky for their OVC opener and it showed. The Colonels led 25-12 with 3:20 left in the first half.

The Racers rallied to cut the lead to three at halftime and they pulled out a 74-72 victory as Canaan scored 17 points and Aska chipped in with 16 points and eight rebounds.

"I thought we would win the whole time," Kennedy declared. "I like our team. I like our guys. We've

2010-11 men's basketball team.

been on the road a bunch and I was really proud of our composure. Our guys didn't get rattled."

MSU wasn't as lucky at Morehead as they dropped a 75-65 decision to the Eagles. Morehead's big man, Kenneth Faried was the consensus favorite for Player of the Year and he played like it as he scored 21 points and grabbed 10 rebounds.

"We can play so much better," Kennedy said. "My mistake has been assuming that the defensive intensity we had last year and the defensive commitment and valuing the ball offensively would carry over. It hasn't. We've seen that in practice and it comes out against good teams."

The Racers regrouped and won six in a row. Traditional rival Western Kentucky was one of their victims. The Hilltoppers head coach Ken McDonald had made it clear that he would prefer not to play MSU in the future and the Racers took exception to the slight, dealing the visitors a 69-60 defeat.

Canaan came off the bench after starting the first 10 games of the season. But he led the way for Murray State with 19 points as he hit 5-of-8 three-pointers. When he hit one he would turn and nod at the fans.

"I was feeding off the crowd," he said. "Every time it was going up, they were saying it was going in, so I just smiled at them and thanked them for guiding it in for me."

Jenkins had nine points and 10 assists.

"I just wanted to come in and create for other people," he noted. "My shot hasn't been falling lately, so I figured I would try and do something else to help the team win. My teammates made me look good."

The winning streak ended in controversial fashion with a 66-64 loss at home to Austin Peay.

With 1:49 left in the game Miles had the ball on the left wing when the whistle blew. The official immediately indicated that the whistle was inadvertent and time was out on the floor.

During the timeout, an ESPNU announcer beckoned the official over to the press table. After he conferred with the announcer all three referees went to the replay monitor. About 10 minutes later they announced that a technical foul had been called against Miles, ostensibly because his elbow made contact with an Austin Peay defender.

Neither the officials or the ESPN announcers were available for comment after the game. But it was clear what had happened. An ESPN announcer called one of the officials over and alerted him to the fact that Miles might have accidentally struck the defender with his elbow.

The OVC acknowledged after the game that there had been no contact and said the officials erred in the way they handled the situation. But the damage was done. MSU was 10-5 overall and 3-2 in conference play.

The Racers won 10 of their next 12 games but the losses were inexplicable as they were beaten by two of the weakest teams in the league: Eastern Illinois and Southeast Missouri.

They went into the final weekend of the regular season needing to beat both Morehead and Eastern Kentucky to clinch the regular season championship and they did just that as they beat Morehead 70-62 and EKU 66-56.

Seniors Miles, Jenkins and Jeff McClain led the way against Eastern Kentucky. Miles and Jenkins had 23 and 18 points respectively. And McClain had nine points and eight rebounds.

"Maturity and toughness," Kennedy said. "Our seniors knew what was on the line. They wanted to win a conference championship. They demonstrated that and produced. The guys who really wanted to do it as a team, the truth came out and you saw those guys."

MSU came up short in the OVC tournament as they lost to Tennessee Tech 64-59. And then they lost a first round NIT game at Missouri State 89-76. Canaan received first team All-OVC honors. Jenkins and Miles were named to the second team. And Kennedy was tabbed as Coach of the Year for the second year in a row.

2011-12 • 31-2

- *OVC Regular Season Champion*
- *OVC Tournament Champion*

Billy Kennedy accepted the head coaching job at Texas A & M in May of 2011 and assistant coach Steve Prohm was announced as his replacement on May 23. Kennedy left Murray with a career record of 107-53, back to back regular season Ohio Valley Conference championships and a win over Vanderbilt in the 2010 NCAA tournament.

"When I first took the job at Murray State the

program was in such difficult shape," he recalled. "I wasn't prepared for that when I got the job. But I was patient, I had great help, and we stayed the course. I think we turned the corner in my third year. Then we had that special run the next year. We were very fortunate that everything fell into place because that doesn't happen very often in college athletics.

"But I wouldn't have been successful without Steve Prohm, not only at Murray State but throughout 12 of my 13 years as a head coach, I will definitely miss him. He's prepared to be a head coach, he loves Murray and believes in it, and I'm sure he'll do a great a job. And none of it would have been possible without an athletic director like Allen Ward. Allen allowed me to do my job in a way that made it possible to win big. I'm very thankful that he was there during my five years in Murray."

There were rumors that Kennedy's replacement would be some high profile assistant from one of the "big schools." But in addition to Kennedy, Prohm had the players on his side. And that always carries a lot of weight.

"It didn't take long to realize that Steve Prohm was the right man to lead this program and build upon the success we have enjoyed the past few years," Ward said when Prohm's hiring was announced. "He's a bright, up-and-coming young coach with impeccable character and is fully prepared for this opportunity.

"Steve's passion for Murray State and Racer Basketball is contagious. That's one reason he received such overwhelming support from the community and from both current and former players. No one will work harder to make sure Murray State builds upon its winning tradition."

For Prohm it was a little surreal. But at the time he had no idea just how surreal it would get before his first season was in the books.

"It's a dream come true," he said. "I worked toward this since I was a freshman in college. You work every day and... I knew about Murray State. Coach (Mark) Gottfried actually came to Alabama when I was leaving. But I had known about Murray forever. This is a special place to me. When you're in a community that truly embraces the basketball program, truly embraces the coaches and the players, and you know how much it means to them... The only thing I think about every day is that I can't let those people down."

Although Prohm had been at MSU for five years, his assistants were all new and he had five new players coming in. He figured it would take time to get everyone on the same page. So he scheduled an August trip to Canada to help the players and coaches get to know each other.

"It was really beneficial," he said. "The basketball part of it was good but the social part of it was great. We got to know the players better, they got to know us better, and they got to know each other better. When they walked in for our first meeting of the fall semester it was like they had been together for a year already."

At the beginning of the season the Racers were a bit of a Rorschach test for fans. What you thought of them said more about you than it did about them.

Some people looked at the roster and said they had lost three starters from the year before – Jeff McClain, B. J. Jenkins, and Isacc Miles. Others pointed out that they had four players back who had been starters in the past – Isaiah Canaan, Ivan Aska, Jewuan Long, and Ed Daniel.

Coaches and sports information directors around the OVC adopted the former view, picking the Racers third in their preseason poll.

And the opener against Harris Stowe at the CFSB Center provided ammunition for both points of view. Murray State led the lightly regarded NAIA squad by just seven points at halftime before rolling to a 76-49 victory.

"These games are tough," Prohm said. "Everybody thinks because you're playing an NAIA, Division II team or whatever, that you're just going to come in and be up 20 or 30 points. It doesn't work that way. Harris-Stowe is very well coached team. They spread the floor and gave us problems. I was worried and concerned. We prepared the same way we do for any team."

Donte Poole led four players in double figures with 18 points.

An 80-69 victory at Morgan State and an 83-41 romp over Tennessee Temple back in Murray pushed the Racers' record to 3-0. But the first real test was up next, a trip to Birmingham, Ala. to play defending Conference USA champion UAB.

The Blazers led 31-28 at halftime and with 10:20 to go they led 49-37.

"I called timeout and I told them they could either get beat by 20 or they could make it a game," Prohm

2011-12 men's basketball team.

recalled. "Then we started to play defense, started to make some shots, and before you knew it, we were back in the game."

MSU closed with a 25-6 run to win it 62-55. Poole scored all 11 of his points during that run. Canaan led all scorers with 19. Aska had 18 points and seven rebounds.

With a 5-0 record the Racers headed north to play in the Great Alaska Shootout where they faced host Alaska-Anchorage in the first round. The Seawolves were a Division-II team but Prohm knew better than to take them for granted.

And at halftime it was obvious his concern was warranted as Murray State trailed 24-23. The Racers bounced back in the second half though and led 62-51 before settling for a 64-62 victory.

San Francisco was up next and the Dons boasted a couple of imposing post players in 6-9 Perris Blackwell and 6-8 Angelo Caloiaro. They were San Francisco's top two scorers and rebounders. But Murray State's Aska and Daniel shut them down, holding them to a combined 12 points and four boards.

The Racers led 30-19 at halftime and held on for a 70-67 victory as Poole and Canaan led the way with 22 and 21 points respectively while combining to hit 8-of-13 three-pointers.

"I'm very proud of our kids," Prohm said. "They continue to compete and play hard. If you do that and play with character and toughness you can do very good things. We were very good defensively in the first half and that gave us a good chance to win."

Southern Mississippi awaited MSU in the final. The Golden Eagles were 4-1 with victories over highly regarded Colorado State and New Mexico State.

For a long time it looked like the game would be a rout. The Racers bolted to a 17-8 lead with 12:42 to play in the first half. They led by 12 at halftime and by 14 early in the second half.

But Southern Miss rallied and sent the game into overtime tied 69-69. Then they took a three point lead in OT. After leading the whole game MSU had its back against the wall. The Racers were behind and their shots had stopped falling. A lot of teams would have folded.

Not the Racers. They bore down on defense and held the Golden Eagles scoreless for the rest of the overtime and with 53 seconds left Canaan hit a three-pointer to send the game into double-overtime.

Poole was on the bench with five fouls so Prohm called on Stacy Wilson who came in and scored eight points in the second overtime as Murray State rolled to a 90-81 victory. Canaan led all scorers with 36 points as he hit 6-of-11 three-pointers and grabbed eight rebounds.

By winning the championship the Racers put Murray State's name alongside that of the 33 other teams that have won the Great Alaska Shootout. Teams like North Carolina (1980, 1985, 1997), Louisville (1982), Kentucky (1979, 1996), Duke (1995), and North Carolina State (1978, 1983).

"When you get up there and walk into the arena you see banners from all the elite college basketball programs," head coach Steve Prohm noted. "That was a great motivation for our kids to be able to hang a Murray State banner up there."

Canaan was named Most Valuable Player and Poole joined him on the all-tournament team.

After dispatching Western Kentucky 70-59 in Bowling Green the Racers returned to the CFSB Center to play Dayton on December 4. Before the season began Prohm expressed his hope that the game would be a sellout. But the crowd fell far short of his expectations as only 3,857 showed up.

The Flyers were 5-2 with victories over Wake Forest and Minnesota but Murray State ran them off the floor. The 75-58 victory pushed the Racers' record to 9-0.

Canaan led all scorers with 21 points. Latreze Mushatt came off the bench to score 14 points as he hit 6-of-8 shots from the field.

"I think we were really locked in defensively," Prohm said. "We held them to 23 points in the first half. Any time you can hold a team like that to 58 points you've put yourself in a good position to win."

Memphis was up next. The Tigers were 5-2, ranked 20th in the nation, and they had just beaten OVC favorite Austin Peay by 31 points. They had one of the best guards in the country in 6-6 Will Barton. Barton was coming off a game at Miami (Fla.) in which he scored 27 points and grabbed 14 rebounds.

Add over 17,000 hostile fans to all that and it appeared the deck was stacked against Murray State. There were omens to the contrary though.

Memphis had just hired a new football coach. Their choice? Former Murray State quarterback Justin Fuente.

And when the PA announcer introduced the Tigers' starting lineup and head coach he suffered a monumental brain cramp. With Josh Pastner's visage on the huge video screen above midcourt the announcer introduced him as John Calipari, the Tigers' former head coach.

The Racers rolled to an early 11-2 lead. They led by five at the half and with 1:58 to play they led by 11, 71-60. Memphis went to a full court press late in the game and Murray State had to withstand a furious rally to prevail, 76-72.

Donte Poole led the Racers with 20 points as he hit 6-of-8 three-pointers. Ed Daniel had 13 points, nine rebounds and four blocked shots. Isaiah Canaan had 15 points and Ivan Aska had 12.

Asked whether Murray State should be ranked in the top-25 Daniel said, "I think we should but it really doesn't matter. We're just going to come out every day and work as hard as we can.

"We've had some very good wins," head coach Steve Prohm said. "We beat Memphis. We beat Dayton and they have a very good program. We beat Southern Miss and I think they've only lost one other game. They beat New Mexico State twice and they are very good. And we won in tough environments at Western Kentucky and UAB."

Dick Vitale was convinced, as he tweeted that he was putting Murray State in his top-25.

"We knew we could beat this team," Jewuan Long said. "We don't even really see it as an upset. When I met with Coach Prohm before the season began I told him there wasn't anyone on our schedule that we couldn't beat."

The Racers were 10-0 and playing loose. And according to Poole, Prohm deserved all the credit for that.

"He's just a real good guy," Poole said. "And he trusts us to run the game sometimes. If we see something the defense is doing he lets us call something. He just gives us a little bit more freedom and we kind of feel more comfortable with it."

When the Associated Press Top-25 was released the next day Murray State was 24th. It was the first time since 1998 that the Racers had been ranked.

After lopsided victories over Lipscomb and Arkansas State the Racers were 12-0 heading into their first

OVC game of the season against Tennessee-Martin. The Skyhawks were just 3-10 and there was some concern MSU might overlook them.

"I talked to our team about that," Prohm said. "Last year Central Florida started the season 13-0 but they struggled in conference play. We have to raise our level another notch. Martin will come in here excited to play. We've gotten a lot of notoriety so I expect them to play extremely hard and give us their best shot."

The students were away on Christmas break but 6,000 fans showed up anyway and they were treated to a show as the Racers demolished Martin. They led 16-5 in the early going and with 11:11 left in the second half it was 64-29. The Skyhawks closed the gap against MSU's bench players down the stretch but the final score of 78-54 was still convincing.

"I'm excited to get the first OVC win," Prohm said. "This was a tough game because it's the first conference game. And then it's a Christmas game. These guys have a foot out the door but we really had to get them focused and locked in. I thought our energy was great."

Poole led the Racers with 15 points. Aska had 12 and Canaan had 10.

Aska broke his hand in a 73-40 romp at Eastern Illinois. The Racers were 14-0 and ranked 19th in the AP Poll. But they had to prepare to face Eastern Kentucky without their starting center.

"The funny thing about it, I was playing in the game when it broke but I still had my left hand so I kept playing," Aska noted. "I could feel the pain but I didn't know it was broken."

Mushatt started in Aska's place and although he scored just two points he grabbed 10 rebounds. Even so, the Racers were outrebounded by nine and faced some tense moments before gutting out a 76-67 victory.

"We missed Ivan in terms of just having a veteran presence on the floor," Prohm said. "But we will have a few days to work on getting the rotation right without him. Getting out-rebounded like that really concerns me though."

Poole scored 22 points to lead MSU. Daniel and Canaan each had 16. And Wilson had 13.

A trip to Clarksville to play arch-rival Austin Peay looked dicey without Aska. The Govs had struggled since losing burley 6-8 center John Fraley to an injury early in the season. But he was back and without Aska it was hard to see how the Racers could match up inside.

Of course when you scorch the nets from the perimeter inside play is less important. And that's exactly what Canaan did for Murray State. He scored 22 points in the first 10 minutes and finished with 37 as he hit 7-of-8 three-point attempts in leading the Racers to an 87-75 victory.

And it was Daniel's turn to take up the slack Aska's absence created as he scored 19 points and grabbed 11 rebounds.

Murray State was 16-0 and ranked 15th in the nation.

A crowd of 5,839 turned out to see the Racers cruise past Jacksonville State for their 17th victory. And then a sellout crowd of 8,691 saw them edge Tennessee Tech 82-74.

The win over Jax State set a new school record for consecutive victories to start a season. And the victory over Tech broke the record for the longest winning streak at any point during a season.

Attendance had been growing all season. In November crowds at the CFSB Center averaged less than 2,500. By the end of December they were pushing 6,000. But no one had expected a sellout.

Poole led the Racers with 28 points and eight rebounds. Canaan had 24 points and Long had 11.

"It was a great environment," Prohm said. "I'm really proud of the fans that came out. We set an attendance record. We're having to figure things out on the fly and make adjustments with Ivan out. But I couldn't be prouder of our guys."

Two days later the Racers cracked the top-10 in the USA Today/ESPN Coaches poll at #10.

Attention from the national media reached a fever pitch. ESPN did a 30 minute mini-documentary on Racer basketball. Wherever you turned your TV or radio dial you found people talking about Murray State.

MSU fans began following the team on road trips in large numbers and opposing fans showed up in droves to see the Racers. Over 6 ,000 turned out to watch Murray State win 66-60 at Morehead. And a capacity crowd in excess of 4,000 saw them crush SIU Edwardsville at the Vadalabene Center.

The victory over Edwardsville pushed MSU to 20-0. When Syracuse lost their first game of the season that same night they announced it on the intercom at

USA Today Coaches Poll			
RK	TEAM	RECORD	PTS
1	Kentucky (31)	23-1	775
2	Syracuse	23-1	740
3	Ohio State	20-3	715
4	Missouri	21-2	673
5	North Carolina	20-3	639
6	Baylor	21-2	635
7	Florida	19-4	536
7	Murray State	23-0	536
9	Duke	19-4	525
10	Kansas	18-5	480

USA Today Coaches Poll

Kroger. Murray State was the last unbeaten team in the nation. The Racers would finish the season with six consecutive sellouts at the CFSB Center.

MSU returned home to host Eastern Illinois on January 28, and Aska returned to action. The senior came off the bench to a standing ovation with 14 minutes left in the first half and hit a layup less than a minute later. He wound up scoring eight points and grabbing three rebounds in 21 minutes of action.

"I thought he played well," Prohm said. "But I think the best moment was the fans showing him their appreciation. For them to stand up and give him a standing ovation was just awesome."

Poole and Canaan scored 18 points apiece as Murray State cruised to a 73-58 victory.

With the Racers undefeated and ranked in the top-10 ESPN gave them a TV game and matched them against St. Mary's in the Bracketbuster. Fans started making music videos about the Racers and students began a campaign to bring Dick Vitale to Murray.

The hysteria surrounding the program was at an all-time high.

MSU led the OVC at 9-0 and Southeast Missouri was second at 7-2. So a lot was on the line when the two teams met at in Murray on February 2. The game was a sellout and so many media outlets requested credentials for the game that additional press seating was added on the second level of the arena.

The Racers handled the pressure well as they rolled to an 81-73 victory. Canaan scored 32 points, 24 of which came in the second half, as he hit several deep three-pointers.

"I thought I did a pretty good job on him in the first half," the Redhawks' Corey Wilford said. "Then he started pulling from halfcourt in the second half. There wasn't anything I could do about that."

Prohm was just happy the Racers won to push their record to 22-0 overall and 10-0 in OVC play.

"We were very fortunate to get out of here with a win," he said. "This was a huge game in the conference race. The undefeated record is special but we're seeking a conference championship first. SEMO was really ready to play."

A victory at Tennessee-Martin left 7th ranked MSU undefeated at 23-0. But the streak ended with a 72-68 home loss to Tennessee State. Before another sellout crowd.

The Racers led 48-35 with 14:45 left to play but a 21-7 run by TSU put the visitors up 56-55 with 7:17 left. It was nip and tuck the rest of the way but the Tigers made more plays down the stretch when the game was on the line.

"They did some things that we haven't really seen," Long said. "They switched on ball screens and we didn't execute the way we're supposed to. Defensively, we let them drive the ball and get open shots."

Murray State got the ball with a chance to tie or take the lead three times in the final 10 seconds but each possession ended in a turnover. With 3.5 seconds left a length of the court in-bounds pass from Ed Daniel sailed out of bounds, effectively sealing the Racers' fate.

"He was supposed to throw it right to the free throw line to Ivan," MSU head coach Steve Prohm said. "It's basically the Homer Drew play with Donte and Isaiah running and Ivan's got either one of them. We work on it during every shoot-around and Ed makes great passes but it was just off the mark tonight."

Of course that single play didn't determine the outcome of the game.

"They got eight offensive rebounds in the second half and that was one key," Prohm said. "And then I have to do a better job in some areas to make sure we do a better job of executing. But I'm extremely proud of our guys. It was an amazing run.

"I love every one of those guys. Isaiah was the last one out of the locker room and he said, 'We're alright coach.' The impact those 14 guys have had on this town... I've never seen anything like it. They've impacted this community in so many more ways than people even know. Just because we lost tonight shouldn't end all that. But now we have to be totally locked in on trying to win a conference championship."

Canaan led the way for Murray State with 31 points but Donte Poole was the only other player to reach double figures as he finished with 10. Canaan scored 18 of MSU's 28 second half points.

Robert Covington led four TSU players in double figures with 17 points. Kenny Moore had 16; Patrick Miller had 12; and Jordan Cyphers had 10.

Following a bounce-back 82-63 victory over Austin Peay it was announced that Vitale would come be in Murray for the game against St. Mary's. A 75-66 win at Southeast Missouri ran MSU's record to 25-1 overall and 13-1 in the OVC, clinching the regular season title. It also set the stage for the most hyped home game in the history of Racer basketball.

Donte Poole

Murray State was ranked 14th in the coaches poll while the Gaels were 23-4 and ranked 16th. Students camped out the night before the game to make sure they could get a good seat and ran into the arena as soon as the doors were opened. Fans made signs and dressed up in all sorts of wild costumes.

It was a zoo. But there was also a basketball game to be played.

"We have to defend and get back on defense," Prohm said. "We need to make St. Mary's play in the halfcourt, and not give them anything easy. We have to make sure we rotate defensively, keep the ball out of the paint, and contest three-pointers. If we share the basketball, don't turn it over and make sure we get to the free-throw line, we will be alright."

In other words, all they had to do was what they had done all year. And that's exactly what they did as they rolled to a 65-51 victory behind 23 points from Canaan who hit 5-of-8 three-pointers.

"It's amazing what God can do," head coach Steve Prohm said. "We talked a lot this season about staying on our wall and I've had so many people emailing us that they were praying for our team and we really appreciate that. We've talked about how phase one of our wall has been built. That was our regular season conference championship. Phase two of our wall was built today, being undefeated in non-conference play. Phase three of our wall will be completed down in Nashville and phase four – the NCAA Tournament."

Murray State closed out the regular season with road victories at Tennessee State and Tennessee Tech. Then they routed Tech 78-58 in the semifinals of the OVC tournament. Awaiting them in the final was TSU, the only team that had beaten them all year.

With 5:31 left it looked like their wall might not be completed as Racers trailed 50-43. But Poole came to the rescue, hitting a three-pointer and a shot from the elbow to cut the lead to two.

A layup by Aska and two free throws by Daniel tied the score, 52-52. As the clock wound down

Canaan tried to penetrate and when he was cut off. Fortunately, he found Long who hit a floater to give the Racers a 54-52 victory.

"That final play definitely wasn't drawn up for me," Long said laughing. "Isaiah drove in and my man helped on him," Long said. "When he passed off to me, my man closed out too strong and I was able to get around him and get off the floater."

Before the game winner, Long had made just 1-of-6 shots from the floor.

"Jewuan's made big shots for us all season long," Prohm said. "He's a fifth-year senior, and I've got a lot of confidence in him. He hadn't made a lot of shots all night, but that's his shot. What we really wanted to do was screen a screener into a ball screen for Isaiah, but they jumped out on him. Jewuan got it, drove it and made a terrific play."

Murray State was rewarded with a #6 seed in the NCAA tournament at the Yum Center in Louisville where they would play #11 Colorado State. And despite not shooting the ball well, they crushed the Rams 58-41.

The Racers forced CSU into 14 second half turnovers on their 35 possessions and held them to 28 percent shooting.

"Murray State's team defense in the second half was tremendous," Colorado State head coach Tim Miles said. "With their physicality they got us off the attack. We turned the ball over and we shot poorly because of Murray's intensity."

The Racers had trailed 24-23 at halftime.

"It wasn't a pretty game in the first half," Prohm said. "We talked to the team about it at halftime. We had one steal and only had nine deflections. That wasn't our style of basketball. I thought our toughness level in the second half was tremendous. To hold them to 17 points... I loved our toughness and energy."

Canaan led the Racers with 15 points. Poole had 13 including the team's first eight. Poole suffered a broken nose in the second half but was able to return to the game.

After MSU's previous NCAA victories over North Carolina State in 1988 and over Vanderbilt in 2010 there was wild jubilation. This time there was joy but it wasn't unbridled and it was mixed with relief.

That relief turned to tears after a 62-53 loss to Marquette in the second round.

With 7:36 to play the Racers had led 46-41. But a 13-2 run by the Warriors turned the tables and Murray was never able to get closer than four points the rest of the way.

Canaan and Poole were both named to the OVC's first team all-conference squad. Poole was named MVP of the OVC tournament. And Canaan was a first team All-American selection.

Aska earned second team all-conference honors. Prohm was named OVC Coach of the Year and Basketball Times National Coach of the Year.

The season ended in tears, the way it does for every team except the national champion. But the story of this season wasn't the way it ended. It was the way the glorious way it played out, all season long.

2012-13 • 21-10

• OVC West Division Champion

The media attention surrounding the Racers after their magical run to the top-10 in 2012 continued all summer. Isaiah Canaan and Ed Daniel drew rave reviews at the NBA Skills camps they attended. Dick Vitale said Canaan was one of the top three players in the country. And several pundits had Murray State in their preseason top-25.

So, expectations were through the roof. But those expectations may have been unreasonable.

After all, the Racers lost three starters to graduation. Latreze Mushatt, a part time starter the year before, tore his Achilles tendon in the summer. And Zay Jackson, who had been expected to start in the backcourt, was suspended before the season even began. Brandon Garrett and Dexter Fields would start in place of Mushatt and Jackson. But that meant that every one of the subs would be a freshman.

Nonetheless, a preseason poll of Ohio Valley Conference coaches and sports information directors tabbed Murray State as the team to beat. And early on it looked like all the hype might have been justified.

The Racers opened at home against Brescia and rolled to an 88-43 victory as Stacy Wilson scored 21 points. Freshman Jeffery Moss demonstrated that he could provide some scoring punch off the bench as scored 11 points.

Murray State followed that victory by crushing Auburn 79-59 in the opening round of the Charleston

Classic as Canaan hit 9-of-12 shots and scored 26 points. Moss had eight points off the bench.

"It was all business in the locker room, because we expected to win," Canaan said. "We prepare hard and prepare to beat bigger teams, and that's what we were able to do tonight. There wasn't any reason to celebrate tonight, we won a game, and now we have to go out again tomorrow night and win another game."

And that's exactly what they did, as they erased a 14 point deficit to beat St. John's 72-67. Stacy Wilson led the way with 23 points and Ed Daniel notched a double-double with 15 points and 11 rebounds.

"We work hard and we feel like we can beat anyone in America," Daniel said. "If you ask us, we think we can play with anyone, and that's what happened tonight."

After three games the Racers had already beaten a team from the SEC and one from the Big East. It seemed like another magical season was underway. There was reason for concern though. Moss injured his knee against the Red Storm and was unavailable for the title game against Colorado, a game the Racers lost 81-74. Although he returned to action in the next game, a 79-72 victory over Old Dominion at the CFSB Center, he wasn't the same player and wouldn't score more than three points over the next eight games.

Even so, the Racers won six in a row before dropping back-to-back decisions at Dayton and at home to Valparaiso. They were 9-3 when they headed to Tennessee-Martin to open conference play on January 3.

They beat the Skyhawks 73-62 as Canaan scored 18 points; Wilson had 16 and Moss returned to form with 14. The game also marked the return of Mushatt who logged an uneventful seven minutes.

Murray State won six of its next eight games to set up a clash with league leader Belmont at the CFSB Center on February 7. The Racers were 16-5 overall and 7-2 in the OVC, leading the West division. Belmont was 19-4 overall and 10-0 in conference play, leading the East Division.

With 35 seconds left the game was tied 74-74. Canaan hit a three-pointer to give the Racers the lead and they went on to win it 79-74. He scored a game high 26 points out-dueling Belmont's Ian Clark who had 22 points.

"I always believe that the next shot I take is going to go in," Canaan said. "I took what the defense gave me. Ed (Daniel) set a great screen; the defender backed off of me and I took it. I've made those throughout my career, and I believed it was going to go in."

The victory pulled MSU within one game of Belmont in the loss column. The Racers kept rolling with a 69-48 victory over Tennessee State at the CFSB Center. But back to back losses at SIU-Edwardsville and Eastern Illinois eliminated any chance they had at securing the top seed in the OVC tournament.

They seemed to right the ship with victories over Morehead and South Dakota State. But then they closed out the regular season with a 69-68 loss at home to UT-Martin and an 84-68 blowout defeat on senior night against Southeast Missouri.

Despite the late season swoon the Racers won the West Division of the OVC and went into the tournament as the #2 seed. They advanced to the final against Belmont by beating Eastern Kentucky 81-73. And with 47 seconds left in regulation they looked like they were headed back to the NCAA tournament as they led the Bruins 62-58.

But Ed Daniel missed two late free throws and Belmont scored twice to send the game into overtime. With 25 seconds left in the extra period the Racers had the ball and intended to hold it for the last shot. But Canaan dribbled it off of his foot at mid-court and lost it out of bounds. With one second to play Belmont's Kerron Johnson hit a 12 footer over Ed Daniel to give the Bruins a 70-68 victory.

"I just dribbled it and it was a mistake on my part, I was dribbling like regular, but I guess my foot was in the way. I just dribbled it off my foot," Canaan said. "It's tough. We hate losing as a team, and just losing a championship game is real tough."

But Prohm wouldn't let his star take the blame.

"This one is hard to stomach, because we should have closed the game," he said. "I take the blame, but we should have been able to close that game. That's the bottom line."

Canaan finished the year averaging 21.8 points. Wilson checked in at 13.5 and Daniel became one of only a few players in school history to average a double-double, 13.2 points and 10.0 rebounds.

Canaan shared the OVC Most Valuable Player award with Belmont's Clark. And Daniel joined him as a first team all-conference selection.

TEVESTER ANDERSON

by Will Aubrey

From the very beginning, basketball was an important part of Tevester Anderson's life. From hot summer days in Canton, Miss. when, as a child, he tossed a rubber ball about the size of a softball at a backyard goal, to his days at Auburn coaching players like Charles Barkley, to his tenure as head coach at Murray State and later at Jackson State, his life followed the rhythms of the game.

Canton was, and still is, a small town about 15 miles from Jackson, a poor rural section of Mississippi. And, when Anderson was a boy it was deeply segregated.

"My mother and father were poor and we worked very hard," he said. "I've cut pulp wood. I've chopped cotton. I've plowed cotton. I've done all of those things. My grandfather owned a farm and my mother and father were sharecroppers for my grandfather."

In those days, blacks in Mississippi lived in a world apart. They went to separate schools; they couldn't eat in restaurants with whites; they couldn't even drink at the same water fountains as whites. Some even lost their lives to racial violence.

But, Anderson never dwelt on these things. In fact, he always refused to even discuss them.

"I never wanted people to feel sorry for me or see me as a pioneer," he said. "I never watch movies about segregation and I don't think about those things. Some blacks are upset at what happened in the past and hate white folk. But, I'm not like that. I wouldn't have been able to achieve what I have if wasn't for white people like Joe Iupe."

Iupe gave Anderson a job at a men's store in Canton when he was a teenager.

"Joe was a white guy, but he was like a father to me," Anderson explained. "He took special care of me and paid me decent wages. He said I was the most thorough person he had ever seen.

"He was a big Mississippi State fan. And, when Mississippi State played Ole Miss, or LSU, or Georgia he'd bite his fingernails until his fingers were bleeding."

Iupe was one of Mississippi State's biggest boosters and when Anderson was coaching at Auburn he took him around the campus and introduced him to everyone, showing them what a success his "son" was.

Anderson played basketball at Madison Training School and later at Rogers High School under the tutelage of James Jones Jr.

"He learned basketball from books," Anderson said of Jones. "I think he was a genius. We won because he was very detailed. He couldn't teach you how to shoot or some other things, but he paid great attention to detail.

"I cared as much about him as I did my Daddy. He was just like my Daddy. A lot of my values come from him – caring about others and respecting all people, having manners, and taking care of your players."

Those who have heard Anderson speak won't be surprised to learn that in

Tevester Anderson

addition to his athletic exploits he won the Future Farmers of America state public speaking contest while in high school.

Following his years at Rogers he was awarded a basketball scholarship to Campbell Junior College. After two years there he played a single season at Philander Smith, a traditionally black school with an outstanding academic reputation. Then he transferred to Arkansas – Pine Bluff where he earned his degree.

"I was always the guy who guarded the other team's best player," Anderson recalled. "I always guarded guys who were 6-4 or 6-5 and wouldn't let them get the ball. I was considered an outstanding defender."

Following his graduation from UAPB Anderson planned to go to medical school. But, those plans were put on hold, as it turned out permanently, when he got a call from his former high school coach.

"I was asked to come and coach one year at Rogers High School by my former coach," he said. "I couldn't say no. And, I've been coaching ever since."

As it turned out, he spent nine years at Rogers. During his tenure there he won two state championships and developed a reputation as a tough minded disciplinarian. In 1971 he moved to Atlanta where he became the coach at West Fulton High School, winning state titles in 1975 and '76.

But, despite this success his coaching career nearly came to an end in 1980.

"I was considering getting out of coaching because of the financial deal," Anderson said. "I was going to go to work for New York Life Insurance Company. I took the test and they told me I made the highest score anybody had ever made on their test. But, I was offered the head coaching job at DeKalb County. I was going to have an integrated team. And, I wanted to see if could take some guys from the suburbs and win the way I did with inner city kids.

"They hadn't had a winning season in four or five years. My first year there we went 20-5 and won the regional championship. The next year I left and went to Auburn University."

At Auburn, Anderson worked as an assistant under Sonny Smith, helping recruit players like Chuck Person, Chris Morris, and Charles Barkley.

"Charles was a very energetic guy, very athletic and smart," Anderson recalled. "He was very funny. If I'd kept notes of all the things he said I could probably write a book myself."

In his first SEC game Barkley scored 27 points and pulled down 18 rebounds against Kentucky at Rupp Arena. But, it's another game against the Wildcats that sticks out in Anderson's mind, or perhaps sticks in his craw.

"We had beaten Kentucky by 18 points at Rupp Arena," he said. "They had Charles Hurt and Melvin Turpin – those guys. And Joe Hall, the Kentucky coach was getting a lot of heat. Well, they came to play us at Auburn and to this day I believe they made a deal with the officials.

"Their strategy was to get Barkley out of the game. First play down the floor Hurt gave Charles a forearm and knocked him down, no call. Next time down the floor he knocked him almost into the stands – no call. Then the next time he knocked him into the sidelines again. But, as Charles came back on the floor he kind of brushed by Hurt and the officials threw him out of the game. And, Kentucky wound up beating us in overtime."

After five years at Auburn (1981-1986) Anderson joined Hugh Durham's staff at Georgia and he was there until Durham was fired in 1995. Not long thereafter he got a call from Mark Gottfried who had just gotten the head coaching job at Murray State.

"I was going to go with Oliver Purnell up at Dayton," Anderson said. "And, I was sitting at home one afternoon when Mark called. He told me that he had gotten the job at Murray State. I knew that, but I wasn't going to call him for a job. I didn't call anybody for a job. He asked me to come and work with him. So, I came to take a look at the place and he had his uncle Mike with him. It was a big sell.

"Mike told me what a great place it was and I liked it so I took the job. And, Mark told me wherever he went he'd take me with him and I'd have a job. So naturally my goal was to come to Murray and win and then go somewhere else."

Anderson and Gottfried bonded quickly and they set their sights high.

"Mark was a special guy to work for," Anderson said. "He treated me like I was somebody special and I worked hard to make the program the best it could be.

"We never talked about being mid-level Division I. We always talked about being upper level Division I. If you talked to us about someone who would be a great OVC player we didn't want to hear that. We wanted guys who could be great SEC players. We didn't always get those guys but we got our share."

After three years as Gottfried's assistant Anderson became the Racers' head coach when Gottfried moved on to Alabama.

"When Mark left it was a very tough decision not to go with him," Anderson admitted. "But I enjoyed Murray so much and had made such great friends in the community I just had to stay. When they offered me the position as head coach it was like a dream come true."

In five years he compiled a record of 103-52, winning two Ohio Valley Conference regular season championships and two OVC tournament championships. He reached 100 wins faster than any coach in MSU history and took the Racers to the NCAA tournament in 1999 and 2002.

During his tenure Murray State had at least two players earn All-OVC honors each year. And in 2000 Aubrey Reese was named the OVC Player of the Year.

Anderson was an innovator too. He appointed offensive and defensive coordinators, something few basketball coaches have attempted. And his team occasionally employed a unique match-up zone called the 3-D.

The 3-D sparked many a come back but Anderson always refused to answer any questions about it. He treated it like a state secret, shrouded in mystery.

His teams beat more highly regarded opponents on a regular basis. Oklahoma, Rutgers, Rhode Island, UAB (twice), Nebraska, Virginia Tech, and DePaul all tasted defeat at the hands of the Racers.

Following MSU's victory over Virginia Tech in 2002 a reporter asked Anderson how it felt to beat a team from the Big East.

"I'm undefeated against the Big East," was his quick reply.

Anderson feared no one and neither did his players.

But despite his success he was heavily criticized in some quarters when Racers lost eight of 10 games during the 2001-02 season.

"That hurt," he admitted. "But, I didn't have time to think about it. All I thought about was playing. I thought I had our guys ready to play. I couldn't wait till the games started.

"I never complained. I never said one thing about my job. Not one time. Because I didn't want our players to ever think it was about me. I wanted them to think it was about them having success together. Not saving anybody's job. I knew that if they played together as a team they would be successful."

And that's exactly what happened. The Racers won 10 of 11 games down the stretch and won the OVC tournament as they beat Tennessee Tech 70-69 when

Justin Burdine hit a runner in the lane with just a few seconds remaining.

"It was the best feeling of my life when we won the OVC tournament," Anderson said. "It was kind of like when I confessed Christ. I had prayed to God and he came to rescue me. But, you pray to God to lead you and guide you. Not to help you win, but to crown your head with wisdom and knowledge and the ability to lead. That's what you pray for. And, I felt like that he heard my prayer and came to the rescue."

Murray State went on to play Georgia on the first round of the NCAA tournament. And they raced to a 25-11 lead early in the game.

"I thought we were playing as well as anyone around going into that game," Anderson said. "But when we got that big lead our guys thought it was going to be easy. I tried to get them to settle down and be a little more deliberate but the only one that did that was Cuthbert Victor. Then Jarvis Hayes got it going and it slipped away from us in the second half."

The Racers finished 17-12 the next year and lost in the semifinals of the OVC tournament. At the end of the season Anderson was encouraged to retire.

"I was very surprised," he recalled. "I think that decision had been made before the season ever started though. They came to me before the season was over and said that even if I won the championship they wanted me to step down."

Anderson certainly had the respect of his peers.

"Tevester was always very professional and he beat me more than I beat him," former Southeast Missouri head coach Gary Garner said. "His players always played hard. No team ran the floor better than Murray State. He was always very pleasant and was one of those guys you always enjoyed talking to. I liked everything about Tevester except losing to him."

Austin Peay's Dave Loos echoed those sentiments.

"I thought he always represented himself and Murray State very well," Loos said. "He was a gentleman and a good coach. His teams always played hard and I think that's a credit to him and the way he ran the program."

As for Anderson himself, he'll always be a Racer.

"I have fond memories of Murray State," he said. "It was a great place to coach and a great community. I still have good friends there and in the end I believe everything happens for a reason. And hey – Go Racers."

After retiring from Murray State, Anderson took the head coaching job at Jackson State and coached there until 2013 when he finally retired for good. He took Jackson State to the NCAA tournament in 2007 and in 2010 he took them to the NIT.

JUSTIN BURDINE

by Will Aubrey

They say it's not how big you are that matters, it's how big you play. And, although Justin Burdine was small by college basketball standards at just over six feet tall, he played big, very big.

He holds the school record for three-pointers in a game with nine. He's second in three-pointers made in a single season with 99 and is fifth in career three-pointers with 198.

As a junior he was a third team All-OVC selection and a first team selection as a senior. He'd remind you that he also won three Fan Jam slam-dunk contests.

Few players in Murray State history have had the ability to dominate a game the way Burdine could. As a senior he scored at least 20 points 19 times. He scored 25 or more eight times. And he scored 33 or more three times. He hit at least four three point shots in 10 different games.

"When he got on a roll he could shoot from anywhere," former MSU head coach Tevester Anderson said. "He was just unreal when he got in a zone."

But Burdine played big at the other end too, delivering spectacular blocks and a bevy of steals that he turned into dunks. He could pick off a pass and go end to end for a jam in less time than it took for the announcer to call his name.

"In those days digital cameras had a two second delay," Racer Insider photographer Marilyn Aubrey said. "Justin was so fast I could never get his picture unless he was at the free throw line."

When he was a junior Murray State beat Eastern Illinois at the RSEC 92-77 behind 27 points from Burdine. EIU's coach Rick Samuels was asked how the Panthers could lose so decisively to a team they had beaten soundly in Charleston a month earlier.

Justin Burdine

"Justin Burdine," he said, slowly and emphatically. "Justin Burdine changes the game."

Burdine grew up in Savannah, Tenn., a small town south of Jackson, about two hours south of Murray.

"Savannah and Murray are very similar," he said. "That was one of the big reasons for me coming to Murray. Savannah is exactly like Murray except for the university. The people are the same. We've got the same stores, the same restaurants. We've got Pickwick Lake right down the road. It's just the same."

Although basketball takes a back seat to football in the Volunteer State, Burdine always preferred the round ball to the oblong one.

"I played basketball as far as back as I can remember," he said. "There's a picture of me with a chicken bone in one hand and a basketball in the other one."

Still, basketball was just a diversion for him when he was young. His passion was baseball and that's what he poured his heart into.

"Basketball was fun, but it was just something to do," Burdine noted. "I was more serious about baseball. I loved baseball back then.

"Then I started watching basketball. And I just kept playing. People told me I was getting better and I started growing a little bit. I started to focus more on basketball. I just got to playing it so much that I got to love it more than baseball. And I quit baseball in eighth grade."

Burdine credits his middle school coach for developing his where-did-he-go end to end speed.

"My middle school coach had a drill," he said. "He'd bounce the ball at the other free throw line and you had to grab the ball and get to other end and score in less than three seconds. We practiced that every day. I kept working on that in high school and it paid off."

At Hardin County High School Burdine averaged 21 points as a junior and 23 as a senior, earning all-district, all-region and all-state honors. As a senior he was a first team all-state selection. His coach at HHS was the colorful but demanding Anthony Gilchrist.

"He was an excellent coach," Burdine said. "He'd get after you though. He'd get out there and cuss you out, kick you out of practice – he'd do all those things.

"One time during practice somebody threw the ball away and he turned around and threw his paper up against the wall and broke his ankle. One game he was hollering and screaming at the refs, he was jumping up and down and turned around and hit the bleacher with his hand and he broke his hand. And then he jumped up one time and busted the seam in his pants. So he was a colorful coach. But he was a great coach."

It's said that you can tell just as much about someone from how they handle failure as how they handle success. And, despite the success he enjoyed at Hardin County, Burdine experienced failure too.

"We played a double overtime game against Bolliver one year," he recalled. "They were undefeated in the conference and they came to our gym. After the first overtime I got fouled with one second on the clock and missed both free throws.

"We won anyway, but I was ready to hang it up after that game. I ended up fouling out in the middle of the second overtime. I was crying after the game and I didn't go to school the next day. It just hurt me because I felt like I let the school down."

As heralded as he was coming out of high school Burdine had plenty of options when the time came to select a college. And, for a while, it looked like he might go to Tennessee. But his father, Prentis Burdine, talked him out of it.

"I considered Tennessee, Arkansas – Little Rock, and Arkansas State as well as Murray," Burdine recalled. "My girlfriend was going to Tennessee so when I told my Dad I was going to Tennessee he thought I was chasing the girl.

"We had rounds about that. He said, 'You're going up there chasing that girl. You're not going up there to get an education, you're not going to play ball. You're going to be with her all the time.'"

Mark Gottfried was the head coach at MSU and his assistant Tom Kelsey led the Racers' effort to recruit Burdine. But Anderson, then an assistant on Gottfried's staff, was involved too.

"I saw Justin play in Florida in the national AAUs and really liked the way he stroked the ball," Anderson recalled. "I thought he played aggressively, but I didn't know how aggressively. So, I came back and told Mark I thought we needed to take a look at him.

"When I went to see him in practice I asked him how good a shooter he was. He said he was pretty good and stood behind the out of bounds line on the baseline and began knocking them down with ease, one after another – rip, rip, rip. He could dunk the ball and was very athletic too."

It may have taken a couple of looks to convince the Racers' staff to offer Burdine a scholarship. But he was sold on Murray after one look.

"When we came up here and visited Murray I just fell in love with Coach Gottfried, Coach T, Coach Kelsey and all those guys," he said. "They took me around town and it seemed like home. They told me I was going to get to play and things like that. So, that's why I decided to come to Murray."

The playing time didn't come right away, though. In fact, Burdine played so little as a freshman that in retrospect it might have been a good idea to redshirt him. He didn't see much more action as a sophomore and it really wore on him.

"My freshman and sophomore years I was frustrated because I wasn't getting to play," he recalled. "We were winning games and making it to the tournament. But I worked hard in the preseason and worked hard in practice. I just felt like I needed to play just a little bit. Just a little bit would've been fine with me."

Frustrated with not getting to play, Burdine turned to the party scene.

"I wasn't having fun playing basketball so I tried to make up for that in my social life – going to parties and all that," he said. "But it was different when I was a junior and senior. I concentrated on basketball. I wasn't really a party person anyway."

He didn't spend all his time going to parties, though. He made regular trips to the Carr Health Building's North Gym with Aubrey Reese where the senior passed on his savvy and schooled the youngster in the finer points of the game.

Burdine began his junior year as the starter at point guard. That wasn't to last long, though. After 12 games he lost his spot in the lineup to Kevin Paschel. But, that may have been a blessing in disguise because he got to play more shooting guard, which was his natural position.

As a starter, Burdine averaged an unspectacular 11.6 points. He averaged an incredible 17.9 coming off the bench. Perhaps that's why he was able to accept the change in roles with such equanimity.

"Coach T and I sat down and talked about it," he said. "And, I just wanted to do what was best for the team. And that's what I was doing by playing point guard in the beginning. I didn't really handle the ball well enough to play the point but Kevin wasn't ready yet so I didn't have much choice. I was never the type of person to sit around and complain about not getting to play or not getting to start."

Burdine began his senior season as the starter at shooting guard and averaged about 20 points as the Racers got off to a 4-2 start. And then, almost inexplicably, he found himself coming off the bench again.

"That bothered me a little more because I didn't really understand it," he admitted. "Coach T was like, 'We don't have any scorers coming off the bench.' But, we had Antonio (Henderson) and Rashard (Harris). They were coming off the bench when I started and doing a great job. So, I didn't understand it. But, I said, 'Okay coach. For the team, I'm going to do it.'"

Burdine's friends and family found it difficult to accept too. All the while he was trying to be a team player, he had people telling him that he was the best player on the team and deserved to be starting. That wore on him as did the mental and physical demands his new role entailed.

"When I got in the game everyone else was already warmed up and going full speed," he noted. "It took me two or three minutes to catch up to the game. And, it took a toll on me physically. I'd come in after the first media time out and play all the way through the half. I really didn't get a break until halftime."

But, unlike the previous year, neither Burdine nor the Racers thrived with him coming off the bench. His average dropped two points per game and the Racers went 4-7. So, Anderson put him back in the starting lineup for a home game against Eastern Illinois in mid-January.

He responded with 21 points and he averaged 22.1 points down the stretch. The Racers won 11 of their final 16 games and at one point they won seven in a row.

Anderson credits Burdine for the turnaround.

"Justin gave us great senior leadership," he said. "When he was in the game you knew we had a great chance to score some points. But, he also rebounded and played better defense. And he became a better ballplayer because of it. He was also more disciplined after he got his starting job back."

Murray State went into the OVC tournament as the third seed but they were the hottest team in the league, having won seven of their final eight regular season games.

In the first round they played an Eastern Illinois team that had already beaten them twice. No problem. The Racers rolled to a 103-56 victory behind 21 points from Burdine.

In the semifinals they played Morehead, another team that had beaten them twice. Once again, no problem, as they cruised to an 89-75 victory with Burdine's 26 points leading the way.

In the final they played top seeded Tennessee Tech. The first time the two teams had met Tech won by 19. The second time MSU won by 19. But the championship game was a nip and tuck affair that came down to the final minute of play with Murray State up by a single point.

"That was the worst and best time of my life in two possessions," Burdine recalled. "On our next to last possession one of the players for Tennessee Tech stole the ball from me at midcourt and went down and scored. That goes back to my lack of ball handling skills. I was crushed. I felt like I had let the team down.

"When we got the ball back I was determined to score. I didn't want to get called for charging so I pulled up for a little floater in the lane and it went in. They got the ball one last time but we stopped them.

"I ran over and jumped on the press table after the game. We were all hollering and screaming, even Coach T. It was a great feeling."

After their 70-69 victory over Tech the Racers went on to play Georgia in the NCAA tournament. MSU got off to a great start and led 25-11 before Georgia took control. The Bulldogs pulled away in the second half and cruised to an 85-68 victory.

"We were confident going into that game," Burdine recalled. "And we shot the ball well in the early going. But their size and strength took a toll on us in the second half."

Following his career at Murray State, Burdine played briefly in the Continental Basketball Association. After his stint in the CBA he finished his degree and purchased a sporting goods store in Jackson, Tenn. Through it all, he has remained a Racer fan.

"I come to five or six games a year," he said. "And when they played Vandy in the NCAA tournament in 2010 my whole family was gathered around the TV. We went crazy when Danero Thomas hit the jump shot at the end to win the game."

JAMES SINGLETON

by Will Aubrey

Tevester Anderson wasn't exactly impressed the first time he saw James Singleton.

"I was just playing around the first time he came to look at me," Singleton recalled. "I didn't even know who he was. And, then told me I was lazy, would have to redshirt and put some weight on my bones before I could play for him. I couldn't believe he was recruiting me and saying things like that. Then he saw me in a game and he said, 'Wow!'

"Coach T was the first head coach to recruit me. It's okay to have assistant coaches come to see you. But if the head coach comes, you know they're really interested."

Before enrolling at Pearl River Junior College, Singleton played at Hirsch High School in Chicago, Ill.

"It's a small school, not a big time basketball school," he noted. "And, I didn't play basketball until my sophomore year. I ran track, played football, volleyball, baseball, and was on the wrestling team. Playing volleyball helped me learn how to block shots. It helped me learn where the ball was going to be.

"I learned how to play basketball in Florida. I had gone down there in the spring of my sophomore year. I couldn't do anything. I couldn't jump or anything."

Singleton had gone to Jacksonville, Fla. to stay with his sister and just happened to hook up with a former college player who lived across the street.

"The guy's name was Art Davis," he recalled. "He saw me at the playground and told me that if I wanted to learn how to play he'd teach me. He was a former college basketball player and he could really jump. I met with him at 6:30 every morning for four months and he taught me the game."

Davis worked extensively with Singleton on all aspects of the game – shooting, jumping, passing, and dribbling – because at the time the youngster was unskilled and in the middle of a growth spurt which threw his timing off.

"Before working with Art I had no left hand," he said. "Heck, I had no right hand. He took my shoestring and tied my right hand behind my back to make me use my left hand. And, he gave a tennis ball to squeeze to build my strength. I'd squeeze it until it busted and then he'd give me another one."

James Singleton

When he left Chicago for Jacksonville, Singleton was six feet tall. When he came back in the fall of his junior year he was 6-6. His friends were stunned and so was Hirsch High School's basketball coach Lavelle Abrams.

"When I first dunked on somebody in practice they had never seen me do that before," he said. "Everybody was shocked. They couldn't believe I dunked it. Coach called off the rest of practice. He was shocked too."

"He was almost like Bobby Knight. He always wanted the best out of you. He never let you quit or give up."

Growing up in Chicago, Singleton was, of course, a huge Bulls' fan.

"I loved the Bulls," he

said. "I loved Michael Jordan, Scottie Pippen, and (Dennis) Rodman. I wore Rodman's number one year in high school. I was a DePaul fan too. But, Pat Kennedy (the DePaul head coach) told me I wasn't good enough to play for him."

Singleton first attracted the attention of college scouts as a senior at Hirsch when he registered a triple-double against Bowen High School. A scout saw the game and told Abrams he was interested in the 6-6 leaper. After that, Singleton worked even harder because he saw an opportunity to get a college education.

Perry Clark, the head coach at Tulane, and one of his assistants, Greg Gary saw Singleton win a slam dunk competition and invited him to visit the Crescent City school.

"They flew me down there to see the campus," he noted. "But I didn't have the grades so they placed me at Pearl River Community College."

In his first year at the Poplarville, Miss. school Singleton tore his ACL. And, it would take months of painful rehabilitation before he was able to play again.

"My father got me a membership at Bally's (Bally Total Fitness) in Chicago and I spent hours just working on my legs," he said. "I went to the beach and ran in the water at Lake Michigan and I played ball at the YMCA. Once I started playing again I didn't feel any plain because of the adrenaline. But, at night it would really hurt. My mom was really worried about me."

After his knee injury, Tulane backed off. Singleton says they wouldn't even speak to him when their coaches came to Pearl River to see another player.

"They just waved," he recalled.

But, other schools quickly became interested.

"I had schools calling me all the time," he said. "It was driving me crazy. Louisiana – Monroe was pressuring me to sign. But my coach told me not to sign until I talked to Coach T. He called and asked me when I'd like to visit and I said, 'Today.' He asked if I was serious but I just wanted to get it all over with."

Singleton credits Anderson's willingness to allow him to fully utilize his talents as one of the primary reasons he signed with Murray State.

"When I came for my visit he knew that I could do a lot of things and he told me he'd let me do what I can do," Singleton said. "I really thought I fit in at

Murray State. I got along well with the players. And, its halfway between Chicago and Mississippi where I also had family."

Singleton had been planning to sign with Texas Tech before head coach James Dickey was fired. The day after he signed with the Racers he got a call from the Red Raiders new coach.

"Bobby Knight called me the day after I signed with Murray State," he said with a grin. "He said it was Coach Knight and I said, 'Quit playing.' But, it really was him. He said the previous coach told him I was a good player. But, I told him I'd already signed with Murray State."

Anderson points to Singleton's attitude and explosiveness as things that impressed him early on and prompted him to offer a scholarship to the kid from Chicago.

"I really liked his demeanor as a person," Anderson said. "He was very confident and he wanted to be a good player. I knew he needed to put on some weight and add strength. But, he had good feet and he was a good leaper. I was really impressed with his explosiveness."

After arriving at MSU in the fall of 2001, Singleton surprised even Anderson with how quickly he adjusted to Division I basketball.

"I was pleasantly surprised by how quickly he was able to play at the Division I level," Anderson noted. "He only played one year in junior college because he was injured his first year. So, it was only his second year of playing above the high school level."

"It really wasn't that hard," Singleton said. "The players are basically the same in junior college as they are in Division I. Before I got to MSU I didn't have any solid post moves though. The coaches at Murray State helped me a lot. Particularly coach (Anthony) Boone. I hear he was a monster when he was in college. I tried to get with him as much as I could."

It didn't take Singleton long to become a crowd favorite. His constant hustle and rim rattling dunks quickly won him a legion of fans who roared with approval whenever he entered a game. And, he enjoyed dunking as much as the fans enjoyed watching him do it.

"I loved getting out on the fast break and seeing an opponent who thought he could jump with me," he said. "I would slow down like I was just going to lay it up, then I would just dunk on him."

Singleton served notice that he would have a major impact as a junior in the season opener against West Florida as he scored eight points and grabbed 10 rebounds in 22 minutes of action.

Then, with Murray State trailing UAB by as many as 19 points in the fifth game of the season he was a vital element in a stunning 74-69 come from behind victory that Racer fans still recall. For the game Singleton had 15 points and 12 rebounds and during MSU's startling 38-13 run in the second half he had six points, seven rebounds and four blocked shots.

A 12 point, seven rebound effort against Indiana State followed and after that Anderson decided he needed Singleton in the game from the outset. So he became a fixture in the starting lineup. He registered his second double-double of the year against Louisville with 21 points and 11 rebounds. That performance helped earn him OVC Newcomer of the Week honors.

The Racers struggled at times but they hit their stride in February, winning seven straight and 10 out of 12 games down the stretch. Singleton flourished too as he reached double figures in points in each of those games and in 10 of them he posted a double-double.

In the first round of the OVC tournament the Racers played Eastern Illinois. They had split with the Panthers during the regular season, losing 88-86 at home in mid January and winning 77-76 on the road a month later. So everyone expected a close, hard fought game.

Everyone was wrong. James Singleton scored 25 points and pulled down 18 rebounds as the Racers crushed EIU 103-56.

"The coaches pretty well told us they expected a little more out of us if we wanted to make it through the tournament," Singleton told reporters after the game. "We know we have time to make it to the NCAA tournament. If we can play like we did tonight, we think we can do it."

Murray State went on to beat Morehead 89-75 in the semifinal game before edging Tennessee Tech to earn that trip to the Big Dance. Singleton wound up averaging a double-double, 12.2 points and 10.1 rebounds. And he was a second team All-OVC selection.

Expectations were high for his senior season but both he and the Racers tended to run hot and cold. And oddly enough, when Singleton posted big numbers MSU often came up short.

He had 22 points and 11 rebounds against Southeast Missouri but the Racers lost by 10. The next game he went for 20 and 17 against Morehead but MSU lost by seven. And he had 28 and 14 in a losing effort at Austin Peay.

But on February 13, 2003 against Eastern Illinois he had what might be the best game anyone wearing a Racer uniform has ever had – 37 points and 18 rebounds while hitting 14-of-16 shots from the floor. He also hit 8-of-8 three-point attempts, setting an OVC and school record. And MSU won 96-77.

It took EIU by complete surprise. Singleton had won the three-point contest at Fan Jam back in October. But he had only attempted 13 shots from beyond the arc during the regular season, of which he had hit five.

"Lucky us," the Panthers's head coach Rick Samuels said. "He destroyed us on the boards, he was defending, and he was intimidating us too. If you take Singleton's effort out of tonight's game, it is very competitive."

Anderson said Singleton's three-point bombardment was part of his game plan.

"I decided to let him shoot the three-point shot," he told the press. "That was my decision. I've probably been a pretty dumb coach for not letting him shoot it earlier on. I said let it all hang out, go out and shoot it, try it. If it works, continue. If it doesn't work, we will pull your coattails back."

"I told him I was feeling it," Singleton said at the time. "We've been falling behind early in games, and I was getting sick and tired of it. I know how teams play me now. Everyone plays me for post play. No one in the OVC knows what I am capable of doing."

You might expect that after a performance like that Singleton would start letting it fly from the outside in every game. He didn't though. Over the next seven games he took just 12 more three-pointers, hitting two. But on that night in February, James Singleton was truly "feeling it."

He again averaged a double-double as he finished the 2002-03 season at 14.9 points and 11.0 rebounds per game. And this time he was a first team All-OVC selection.

Following his career at Murray State, Singleton played pro basketball in Europe. He went on to play in the NBA for the Los Angeles Clippers, Dallas Mavericks, and Washington Wizards. And he currently plays for the Xinjiang Flying Tigers of the Chinese Basketball Association.

Mick Cronin

by Steve Parker

On March 17, 2006, the Murray State Racers were playing NCAA Tournament game No. 14. This time it was in Dayton, Ohio against North Carolina in the first round. As usual, those with Murray State ties – alums, students, fans – were either in Dayton Arena or watching it on television. So when Shawn Witherspoon left the floor with eight minutes to play in the first half and the Racers right in the game with the Tar Heels, all eyes of the "Racer Nation" saw the team's unquestioned leader limp to the end of the bench.

They all saw Witherspoon with his right shoe off and his foot being examined by team physicians and athletic trainers. All eyes except two.

"We're winning the game about eight minutes in and 'Spoon motions to me that he needs to come out. I figure he's tired because he hasn't been subbed out yet," recalled Mick Cronin, the head coach of the Racers on this night. "A couple of minutes later I tell my staff to get 'Spoon back in, but he never goes to the scorer's table. I'm screaming at my staff, Where's Spoon? But nobody would answer me.

"Then, (MSU athletic trainer) Eric Frederick comes up to me with tears in his eyes and he tells me that Spoon broke his foot. I said, What? He just came out to get some water."

Such was the focus of Mick Cronin. An entire arena could empty out in the middle of one of his games and all he might say in the post-game press conference is, "I thought it seemed a little quieter."

That focus served him well during his brief, but meteoric, coaching career at Murray State. Hired by MSU at the age of 31 in 2003, Cronin had only worked for Bob Huggins at Cincinnati and Rick Pitino at Louisville. There were no graduate assistant jobs at "Little Southern College" on Cronin's resume. He came to Murray having worked only in the big-time and having lived only in metropolitan areas.

"Going to Murray I was scared to death, if you want to know the truth. I didn't know anyone there, and it was such a different lifestyle than I was used to," Cronin said in the fall of 2011, six years after he left MSU to coach at Cincinnati. "I was an eat-out guy before I came to Murray, but there were so few restaurants I just stayed home and grilled. I became the grill king while I was at Murray."

If it took a while to adjust to the pace of life in Murray, Cronin hit the ground running when it came to coaching the Racers. Taking over a veteran squad in 2003-04, Cronin guided the Racers to a 28-6 record and an OVC Tournament championship. Along the way, the Racers won at Western Kentucky and TCU and pummeled Conference USA member Southern Miss by 40 points at home. That Cronin proved in his first season that he could handle his first head coaching job should have surprised no one because he was practically raised to coach basketball.

Mick Cronin

Cronin grew up in Cincinnati, Ohio as the son of a legendary high school basketball coach, Hep Cronin. "I grew up in a gym. When I was 12 years old I could draw up a late-game out-of-bounds play," he joked.

When Mick's high school basketball career ended with a knee injury, he adjusted his aim and targeted coaching as a way to stay in the game. When not attending classes at the University of Cincinnati, Cronin was at his alma mater, Woodward High School, coaching basketball. At age 19, he was an assistant varsity basketball coach/head junior varsity coach.

From 1991-96, he spent his winters coaching at Woodward and his summers coaching various summer camps. Whether it was Huggins' UC camps or Pitino's University of Kentucky camps, Cronin was working. When he got the urge to move on from Woodward in 1996, he called Huggins to get his advice on a couple of prospective jobs. Huggins suggestion? Come work for him.

"(Huggins) created a spot for me. I was the first-ever fourth (assistant) at Cincinnati," remembered Cronin, who noted the he was paid $800 per month to coordinate the program's video. "The next year, two assistants left and I went from being the fourth guy to the first guy."

Cronin attacked the job, learning the ins and outs of recruiting. According to him, he lived on the phone, "An early night for me was leaving the office at 9 o'clock. Usually, I worked until 11." It paid off, however, as Cronin earned a reputation as a talented recruiter. He was being offered six-figure jobs elsewhere, but he stayed with Huggins, until one call came that he had to answer.

First-year Louisville coach Rick Pitino had earned a reputation as a head coach developer, so when he called Cronin and asked him to join his first staff at U of L, Cronin had to consider it. "I was coaching at the highest level under Coach Huggins, but I had never been away from home," said Cronin, who went to the NCAA Tournament in each of his five seasons at Cincy. "I felt like I need to do that to mature as a coach and as a man."

Moving from Cincinnati to Louisville meant more money, but it was a gut-wrenching decision. "The hardest thing I've ever done is leave home and Coach Huggins," admitted Cronin. "It was not an easy thing to do. It was a harder path to choose, but it was important for career building."

He soaked up all he could from Pitino, handling recruiting, on-court instruction, and scouting opponents. In the 2001-02 season, one of the Cardinals' opponents was Murray State.

"We played them in Freedom Hall and I was thoroughly impressed," said Cronin. "I thought we might lose that one to be honest. When you see a team with that kind of talent you don't expect the job to open up."

A year later, when Racer head coach Tevester Anderson was let go, then-MSU athletic director E.W. Dennison contacted Cronin. Though other offers were sure to come, the Racers intrigued him.

"If Murray State was in bad shape, or I thought it would take a while to turn around, I might have waited," Cronin said. "Coach Pitino didn't want me to leave, and I was taking a pay cut, but I thought we could win right away."

On April 5, 2000, Cronin was introduced as Murray State's 13th head coach, and he was taking over a veteran-laden team that had slumped to a 17-12 record the year before. Chris Shumate, Cuthbert Victor and Andi Hornig formed the nucleus of Cronin's first team. After their appeals for a fourth year were upheld by the NCAA, Cronin added veterans Antione Whelchel and Kevin Paschel back to the roster.

"I really challenged those guys," Cronin said of his first team. "My message to them early on was that we were going to be the hardest working team in America. At our first team meeting I told them that I would see them at six the next morning for conditioning."

If there was an adjustment period between the 31-year-old head coach and his first team, it didn't show on the court. Newcomers Adam Chiles and Kelvin Brown meshed well with the returning players and the Racers got off to an 8-0 start with wins over TCU, Southern Miss (by 40 points) and Western Kentucky. In the win over WKU, the Racers erased a 12-point deficit in the second half. "When we left Bowling Green that night I knew we had a good team," Cronin said.

Murray State's first loss of the season came on Dec. 20 at Pittsburgh, but the next loss was an emotional one for Cronin. On Jan. 3, the Racers traveled to Louisville to face the Cardinals. Cronin's Racers battled galliantly but lost 91-69.

As the OVC season kicked off it was obvious that the championship would be between the Racers and long-time rival Austin Peay. Even with Murray State dropping a home game to league newcomer Samford at home, the Racers' game at Austin Peay on Feb. 14 was a quasi championship game. A near capacity crowd assembled at the Dunn Center in Clarksville, Tenn., to watch to Governors and Racers. As expected, the game was back and forth throughout and when MSU's Chiles left the game in the second half with a separated shoulder, the Govs took control.

Despite the 63-56 loss, Cronin and company felt good about the rest of the season, especially any re-match with the Govs. "They were really good, obviously, but I was confident we had a deeper team and a little more talent."

Sure enough, when the two teams met on March 6 in Nashville's Municipal Auditorium, the Racers had just enough to pull out a 66-60 victory and sew up the berth in the Big Dance.

Having coached at Cincinnati and Louisville previously, Cronin was very familiar with the NCAA Tournament, having settled for the NIT instead of the Big Dance just once his previous eight seasons. But his first as a head coach had the Racers seeded No. 12 taking on No. 5-seed Illinois in Columbus, Ohio. Trailing by just seven at half-time, the Racers watched the Illini pull away in the second half behind its trio of stars: Dee Brown, Deron Williams and Luther Head.

"The best game we played all year was against Illinois, but we just couldn't get a rebound," lamented Cronin. "And, they had three NBA players."

MSU finished the season with a 28-6 record, which meant Cronin had the fifth-best season of any first-year coach in NCAA history. Murray State was losing most of its roster, saying goodbye to mainstays such as Shumate, Whelchel, Victor, Paschel and Rick Jones.

As the 2004-05 season loomed, Cronin was optimistic because even though his team lacked the veterans of the previous team, he was adding explosive firepower. Chief among the new faces were guards Trey Pearson and Keith Jenifer, who sat out 2003-04 season after transferring from Ole Miss and Virginia, respectively. They were joined by newcomers Issian Redding, Charles Johnson and Pearson Griffith among others. Though his second team was bigger, quicker, more athletic, and deeper than his inaugural team, Cronin's Racers never could turn their talent into success.

"I learned as a young coach that there's nothing like experience," he said. "Our first year, ten times we came back from double-digit deficits – seven on the road – and won. I quickly learned the value of experience."

Though the Racers never managed to put together a long winning streak, they still managed to finish 11-5 in league play, just one game out of first. Overall, the team finished 17-12, but Cronin knew "what could

happen if all those guys came back" the following season.

An undefeated trip to Canada in the preseason confirmed to Cronin that his third team was on the same page and that the 2005-06 season could be special. Adding Tyler Holloway gave them another perimeter shooter, so the roster was set. MSU overcame early losses to Cincinnati and Tennessee to head into the OVC portion of the schedule as the team to beat. Though Samford knocked off the Racers in December in Birmingham, Murray State got revenge in late January to propel them to the conference championship.

In the 2006 OVC Tournament, the Racers dispatched UT Martin and Jacksonville State to set up a rubber match against pesky Samford. For all of Cronin's tenure at MSU, the Bulldogs' Princeton-style approach flustered the Racers. He lost his first three meetings with them until the 2006 win in Murray. Simply put, the Racers had hard time defending the Bulldogs – until the victory in Murray when Cronin employed a 2-3 zone to notch a 21-point victory.

Using 6-foot-10 Pearson Griffith in the middle to swat away layup attempts, Cronin pressured the Bulldog shooters and guided the Racers to a 75-57 championship game triumph. He was named OVC Coach of the Year after leading the Racers to both the regular season and tournament titles. But there was work left to be done for the third-year head coach.

"When I got the job the boosters told me to get them to the NCAA Tournament. I said, You don't need me for that, you're already doing that," recalled Cronin. "I really wanted to win a game and advance for all those fans."

Despite a favorable matchup – a young North Carolina team – the Racers couldn't pull off the first upset since 1988, falling 69-65 in Dayton. Witherspoon's broken foot was a difficult blow to overcome. Recalled Cronin, "We go in at halftime tied and I've got Spoon crying in the corner and half my team in tears."

And, like a traditional parting shot – or punch to the gut – to Racer fans each time they fell in first round of the NCAAs, their coach was being mentioned for another job. This time it was Cincinnati, which was staggering after a public divorce with long-time leader Huggins. It seemed like Cronin was a logical choice.

Cronin said years later that it was far from a done deal.

"I swear I thought I was the last guy they would consider," stated Cronin. "I was a Huggins guy and there were a lot of negatives associated with that. I did not dream I would be a candidate."

But, eventually, he did get a call from the Bearcats, and he rightly accepted the job. After all, he'd left home, become a better coach, and was ready to go back to his alma mater.

He wrapped up his tenure at Murray State with a 69-23 record for a .742 winning percentage, best among MSU coaches with at least three years on the job. He reached great heights during his stay, leading the Racers to two NCAA Tournaments. But he also had one low.

On March 1, 2005 in the Regional Special Events Center, MSU lost 61-58 to Southeast Missouri in the first round of the OVC tournament, the first time a Racer team failed to make the semifinals since 1987. Fans who count on making the trip to Nashville each spring to watch their Racers sat in stunned silence as SEMO celebrated. Though he had only been at MSU for two seasons, Cronin knew what the OVC Tournament in Nashville means to Racer fans. "It was hard to get out of bed the next day," he said, looking back years later. "So many people are part of your program, you feel like you're responsible for the whole town."

That passion is also what Cronin loved about coaching at Murray State. "The support is equal to the expectations, which is all a coach wants. You get that at Murray State. They demand that you win big, but they also support you."

As for the big-time coach who had never lived in a city smaller than Louisville when he arrived in 2003, Cronin learned to love Murray. If he was scared to come to Murray then, he was singing its praises when he left in 2006. "I tell my friends when they ask me what it was like, 'I see why people in Murray wouldn't want to leave."

In seven years at Cincinnati, Cronin is 135-99 with three straight 20-win seasons. In 2012 he led the Bearcats to the Sweet Sixteen of the NCAA tournament.

CUTHBERT VICTOR

by Will Aubrey

No one ever accused Cuthbert "Cuffy" Victor of being chatty. He was as quiet off the court as he was active on it.

Off the court Victor was direct and to the point in interviews, answering precisely any question put to him without elaboration. On the court, he was in the middle of the action. If there was a loose ball you could bet he either deflected it or would come up with it. And despite being generously listed at 6-5 he was a terror on the boards.

"Cuffy was as good on the grab and putback as I have ever seen," longtime MSU radio announcer Neal Bradley declared. "Although he was undersized for his position, he played with heart and a will to win, reminiscent of Vincent Rainey, who also got the most out of his size. As far as heart goes, he took a backseat to no one.

"I don't recall the game, but it was at the Regional Special Events Center. An opponent was running a fastbreak and Cuffy was on the wing when an opposing player tried a bounce pass to the corner. Cuffy pinned the ball to the floor, picked it up and triggered a fast break, finishing at the other end. Amazing! It was one of the best plays I have ever seen by anybody at any level."

Victor grew up in the United States Virgin Islands and his brother introduced him to the game of basketball when he was about six years old. By the time he was 10 he was playing youth league and it was readily apparent that he had a gift for the game.

"They called it Biddy Basketball," he recalled. "It was a lot of fun because I was kind of tall. I scored a lot and got a lot of rebounds. The first year I played I won seven trophies."

He progressed rapidly and was dunking by the time he was a high school freshman.

"I was 13 or 14 at the time," he noted. "It was a big deal because in junior high all I could do was touch the rim. Then one day I was trying it and I ended up dunking the ball and I said, 'Huh? What did I do?' I surprised myself when it happened."

As a freshman Victor played for Complex High School. But he transferred to St. Joseph when he was a sophomore. In one particular game against Complex, Victor scored 40 points despite facing a box-and-one defense most of the game.

Murray State's head coach at the time, Tevester Anderson, also coached the Virgin Islands' national team. And Victor quickly caught his eye.

"I first noticed that he was going to be a good basketball player when he was a sophomore and we were playing the Puerto Rican national team," Anderson said.

Cuthbert Victor

"He was a young kid and we had other players who were veterans of international ball and had gone to college and played pro ball overseas.

"But Cuthbert got some key rebounds and made some strong plays. We were getting beaten up pretty bad and he was the one bright spot. He kind of took over the game as a sophomore against much older guys. I knew then that he had a chance to be a good basketball player."

Victor was twice named Most Valuable Player at the World Youth Games held in Chicago. And as a senior, he was named the St. Croix

Athlete of the Year and the top basketball player in the Virgin Islands.

With honors like that it should come as no surprise that he received scholarship offers from several major Division I schools. But, his relationship with Anderson led him to choose Murray State over suitors like DePaul, Georgia Southern, Louisville, Indiana, and Purdue.

"I liked the coaching staff at Murray State," Victor explained. "They were all really nice. Coach T was a very nice guy and he stood up for his players. He made sure everyone was treated fairly. I love Coach T very much. He knew how hard it was for me to be away from my mother and he took care of me."

Anderson certainly holds Victor in high regard.

"Cuffy was one of the top players to come through the program during my time there," he said. "He just did so many things. He was a good player and a good person. And he was easy to coach. He would do whatever you asked him to.

"He was mentally tough. Although he smiled a lot, underneath that was a mental toughness a lot of players don't have. And he could adjust to almost any situation."

Victor broke into the starting lineup midway through his freshman year. And, although his 6.2 points and 4.3 rebounds per game may not have been impressive, his per 40 minute averages of 15.2 points and 10.6 rebounds were, especially considering how raw he was.

Indeed, when you consider how little experience he had coming in, his development was phenomenal. High school teams in the Virgin Islands only played about 12 games each year. Stateside schools played twice as many or more. And when he did play in high school he was in the low post. His only experience on the perimeter was in international competition. And he was just 17 when he donned a Racer uniform for the first time.

"I can't really explain what it felt like to play in the RSEC," Victor recalled. "I remember the first game I played there. All the fans were cheering and acting crazy. It was a whole new experience for me. I was so nervous that I was hoping and praying the coach wouldn't put me in the game. But after I got used to playing in front of that crowd it was the best feeling I ever had."

Making the leap from high school to college was definitely a challenge for him.

"It was hard to adjust at first," he admitted. "The biggest difference was defense, though. We played zone most of the time in high school, but in college it was almost all man-to-man. And, I missed my family and friends. But, I got used to it.

"I still remember the game against Tennessee State on my birthday when I was a freshman. I scored 27 points and was 10-for-10 from the field and 7-for-7 on free throws. I was really ready to play because it was my birthday. When they told me I had a perfect game I couldn't believe it."

As a sophomore Victor started 28 of 32 games and averaged 11.7 points and 7.3 rebounds. He led the Ohio Valley Conference in offensive rebounds. He also shot 54.7 percent from the field, blocked 44 shots, and had six double-doubles.

He was even better down the stretch as he averaged 15.8 points over the last 10 games, scoring 23 in an NCAA tournament tilt against Georgia.

As a junior Victor led the Racers in scoring with 15.3 points per game while averaging eight rebounds and shooting 59.6 percent from the field. He was among the top-10 in the OVC in seven different categories.

Unfortunately, Murray State staggered to a

disappointing 17-12 record and was eliminated in the semifinals of the OVC tournament. At the end of the year Anderson was encouraged to retire and Mick Cronin was chosen to replace him.

Cronin had coached under Rick Pitino at Louisville and in his first year he installed Pitino's press-and-run attack. After a brief period of adjustment, Victor flourished in the new style of play.

"The press was difficult to learn," he explained. "I had never been on the ball in the press before. I was always a safety. So it was hard for me to adjust to."

After he adjusted he proved to be more effective than his new coach could have ever expected.

"Cuthbert Victor has been a big surprise to me," Cronin said midway through the 2003-04 season. "I had no idea he was as good as he is either from film or individual instruction. He didn't display at any time that he was a dominant player. I'd like to think we've pushed him to another level. We've definitely tried to challenge him."

As a senior, Victor led the team in scoring (14.6 ppg) and rebounding (10.2 rpg) while shooting an amazing 62.9 percent from the field and a career high 32.1 percent from three-point range.

He put on a show in the Racers' 100-95 victory at Western Kentucky with 26 points and 20 rebounds. He had 35 points and eight rebounds against Chicago State.

Following the win over Chicago State, Cronin said: "Cuthbert played like he had Superman's cape on, and he finished so strong. As his coach, I can tell you that I really believe he's making his case as the best player in the nation at this point in the season."

The Racers pushed their record to 6-0 in the next game as they erased a 13 point halftime deficit to beat Southern Illinois 68-64. Victor once again led the way with 19 points and 15 rebounds.

"At halftime, Coach Cronin just told us to pick it up defensively and do a better job of rebounding," Victor told reporters after the game. "We weren't getting enough ball-pressure in the first half, and he told us that if we'd do a better job of rebounding and put more pressure on them defensively, we'd win. And that's what happened.

"In the first half, we were a little bit sloppy with the ball, but we were able to get things going in the second half the way we knew we were capable of and we got a big victory."

Victor finished the season with 13 double-doubles. He led the OVC in rebounding and field goal percentage. In fact, he was ninth in the entire nation in field goal percentage. He was second in the league in blocked shots and he was in the top-10 in both scoring and steals. Not surprisingly, he was voted the Most Valuable Player for both the regular season and the OVC tournament.

The Racers finished the regular season 15-1 in conference play with the only loss coming at Austin Peay. But a quirk in the schedule allowed Peay to win the regular season title with a 16-0 mark without having to play in Murray.

MSU beat the Govs 66-60 in the OVC tournament championship game though. And they went on to play Illinois in the first round of the NCAA tournament as they finished the season with a 28-6 record.

Following graduation, Victor played professional basketball in Europe. Over the last nine years he has played for eight different teams and was a candidate for his league's MVP award in 2009. He currently plays in the French league for Le Mans.

"Playing in Europe is very challenging," Victor noted. "They practice a lot more and the games are very intense because there are so many good players. I still follow the Racers the best way I can but it is difficult to watch the games because of the time difference."

SHAWN WITHERSPOON

by Will Aubrey

It's not often that Murray State beats the University of Kentucky for a recruit. But when Shawn Witherspoon selected the Racers he spurned the Wildcats, Florida State, Kansas State, Louisville, and Auburn.

"Murray State recruited me from the very beginning," Witherspoon noted. "Some big schools came in at the end but Murray State was with me the whole way. I just figured the big schools didn't get who they wanted so that's why they started recruiting me. But I felt like I was at the top of Murray State's list."

Witherspoon came for an official visit in March of 2002 and attended the Racers NCAA Selection Show party.

"I wasn't completely sure when I came to visit on Selection Sunday," he said. "But the atmosphere really got me, to have that many people for a selection show was terrific.

"And the other players were kind of like big brothers telling me what I needed to know.

Everybody was just so close. Everyone's a big family here. Everyone sits together for everything."

The 6-foot-5, 210-pound forward from Oviedo High School near Orlando, Fla. was named first-team all-state as a junior and senior. Following his junior year, Witherspoon earned the Sunshine State's top honor when he was named Florida 6A Player of the Year.

Although he was recruited by Tevester Anderson, Witherspoon was redshirted as a freshman. So the first MSU coach he actually suited up for was Mick Cronin.

As a freshman, 'Spoon, as he was known to the fans, averaged 5.3 points while playing a little over 14 minutes a game. He only made two of his first 19 3-point attempts but he kept working on his shot and it paid off as he made 5-of-7 over the final six games of the season. In fact, the biggest shot he hit all year was a 3-pointer that gave the racers a 29-27 lead late in the first half of the OVC Tournament final against Austin Peay.

When he was a sophomre Witherspoon led the team in rebounding despite being just 6-5. And he scored 33 points against Morehead on 13-of-17 shooting.

Witherspoon really came into his own as a junior, leading the team in scoring at 10.6 points per game and finishing second on the team in assists with 95.

"'Spoon is very consistent and he's a tough matchup because we're playing him like a point-forward," Cronin noted midway through the season. "It's tough for a bigger guy to defend him because he can shoot the ball so well. And that's a credit to how hard he's worked. He's gotten better every day. He's stronger, his understanding is better and he has better balance. We run a lot of our offense through him because he can do so many things."

At the end of the year Witherspoon was a first team All-OVC selection and led the Racers into the NCAA tournament where they

Shawn Witherspoon

threw a scare into North Carolina. Unfortunately, he broke his foot in that game and MSU came up just short, losing to the Tar Heels 69-65.

"Before the game a reporter had asked one of their players about us and he started talking about someone who wasn't even on our team," he recalled. "They didn't even know our personnel.

"That really upset us. We could tell you who their players were, how they shot the ball, what hand they used – and they didn't even know who was on our team."

Then Cronin left to take the head job at Cincinnati and when Billy Kennedy took over Witherspoon had his third coach in five years.

He approached the 2006-07 season with optimism. Unfortunately, his foot never healed properly.

"We know he has heart and we have to have him on the floor," Kennedy said midway through the season. "You can't say that about all of our guys. We're going to go with him until he can't play and hopefully that won't happen."

It didn't happen. Witherspoon gutted it out and played anyway as he averaged 10.3 points and 5.5 rebounds. Murray State struggled to a 16-14 record and "Spoon" was conspicuously absent from the OVC's all-conference teams.

Witherspoon may not have been flashiest player to ever wear the Blue and Gold. But he was a warrior. And a fan favorite. Cast your mind back in time and you can almost hear the fans scream "Spooooooon!"

BILLY KENNEDY

by Will Aubrey

It has been said that college basketball is a coach's game. And many college basketball coaches certainly act like they think it's all about them, with their outsized personalities and on-court histrionics.

Off the court they act like rock stars and on it they act like professional wrestlers.

But many of the great ones weren't like that at all. They worked quietly and gave their players the credit. Hall of Famers like John Wooden and Dean Smith – they didn't throw chairs and they didn't crave the spotlight.

And those are the coaches Billy Kennedy tried to pattern himself after.

"I have a great deal of respect for those men and the way they handled themselves," Kennedy said. "Hank Iba, John Wooden, Pete Newell, and Dean Smith got it right. You prepare your team in practice and the games are like exams.

"You practice to play and you let the players play the games. You shouldn't have to make a lot of adjustments during games if you do your job in practice. If you have good kids and they're playing hard for you there may still be times when you have to get on them. But if you have to do that very often then you aren't going to be very good.

"You can't get too high or too low either. You have to stay on an even keel. It's all about balance, balance in your life, balance on the court and balance off the court."

And underlying all of that is faith.

Billy Kennedy

"Faith is very important to me," he continued. "I feel like coaching is a ministry for me. I'm here to train and develop young men. We talk about training them physically, mentally and spiritually."

Kennedy grew up in Metairie, La., a suburb of New Orleans.

"I went to Holy Cross High School to play football," he recalled. "That was my favorite sport at the time. I became interested in basketball because Holy Cross was a powerhouse.

Don Maestri was the basketball coach there and he's the head coach at Troy State now.

"They had packed gyms and they played for state championships. I just fell in love with it and jumped on the bandwagon. I got cut my freshman year but I asked coach Maestri if I could be the manager. He gave me the opportunity to do that and then I made the team as a sophomore and started for the next three years."

Kennedy earned all-district honors but by his own admission he wasn't a great player.

"I was basically just a defensive player," he said. "I could shoot a little bit, but I just played hard all the time. Coach Maestri left before I graduated and I ended up playing for Kevin Trower who took me under his wing and nurtured me. He married my mom so he's my stepdad now.

"Coach Maestri had a big influence on my career. He was the head coach at Troy State for a long time. We're from the same neighborhood and we've remained close over the years. His passion and his love for basketball are what I admire the most. And he cares about people.

"My stepfather was the same way. And he was a great teacher of the game. I learned a lot of X's and O's from him. He's a brilliant man. He's written Latin books. He's an attorney and a high school coaching legend. He's in the Hall of Fame in the state of Louisiana. What we do today is based more on my high school experience than my college experience."

After high school, Kennedy went to Southeast Louisiana as a preferred walk-on. He didn't get to play much so he transferred to Delgado Community College. After one year, a broken nose and a broken wrist he decided to give up playing and focus on getting his degree. So he transferred back to Southeast.

"While I was working on my degree I started coaching AAU and I refereed some," he recalled. "I wanted to be like my stepfather because he had an interest in me and he was close with his players. I wanted to influence people the way he influenced me. So I decided to get into coaching.

"I coached some really good AAU players – Robert Pack who played in the NBA, Jaren Jackson who played in the NBA, Tim Singleton who played at Notre Dame and Randy Livingston who played at LSU. And I made connections in the college game because college coaches recruited my players."

The staff at Southeast wanted Kennedy to help them get AAU players so they hired him as a student assistant.

"One of the regular assistants got in a car wreck and he couldn't work so I kind of took over his position," Kennedy said. "So I was working as an assistant coach and scouting teams when I was just 22 years old."

From there, Kennedy went to work for Benny Dees at the University of New Orleans. The Privateers made it to the NCAA tournament where they defeated Brigham Young. Dees left to become the head coach at Wyoming and Kennedy went with him.

"Coach Dees was a great recruiter and a great defensive coach," Kennedy noted. "He was probably the best recruiter that I've been around and he took good care of me. He was just great with people. He taught me how to recruit and how important recruiting was."

After a year at Wyoming coaching future NBA players Eric Leckner and Fennis Dembo, Kennedy took a job as an assistant at Northwestern State in Natchitoches, La.

"It was my first full time job and I made $8,000 a year," he recalled. "It was a tough life. I was married and I had a little boy. I rode a bicycle to work every day because we only had one car. From there I went to Tulane as the third assistant making $15,000 a year so I almost doubled my pay. My strength was recruiting. That's what people hired me for.

"Then I went to Texas A & M with Kermit Davis and doubled my salary again so I finally had a real job. I was there a year and then I went to Creighton for two years."

In 1993 Todd Bozeman, who had been on the staff at Tulane, got the head job at California. One of his first moves was to hire Kennedy as his top assistant.

"That was a breakthrough job for me," Kennedy noted. "I was associate head coach at an early age and we had the #1 recruiting class in the country. We were in the top-10 for three years in a row so we had some really good teams.

"After Bozeman resigned I was the interim head coach. Coach Newell and a number of people wanted me to get the job but it didn't work out. And knowing what I know now, I wasn't ready to be the head coach at Cal at 31 years old."

California hired Ben Braun away from Eastern Michigan to replace Bozeman and Kennedy worked under him for another year. Then he left to take the head coaching job at Centenary even though it meant taking a 50 percent pay cut.

"Coach Braun wasn't comfortable with me being at Cal because a lot of people had wanted me to get the head job instead of him," Kennedy explained. "And then I was trying to move my family back toward Louisiana. It was head coaching experience and it was really good for me.

"At the time Centenary was the smallest Division I school in the country and they only won six games the year before I got there. I was 31 and Billy Donovan and I were the youngest head coaches in the nation.

"We turned the program around really quick and we beat Southeast Louisiana. Then when that job came open they contacted me about coming back to my alma mater. It was special for me to coach at the place where I went to school. They were trying to make basketball work and the university president was really good to work with."

Kennedy took Centenary from six wins to 14 in just two seasons. And he rebuilt a moribund Southeast Louisiana, leading them to consecutive Southland Conference championships and a trip to the NCAA tournament in 2005. He was the National Association of Basketball Coaches District 8 Coach of the Year in 2004 and 2005.

But after six years in Hammond, La. he left to take an assistant's job at the University of Miami (Fla.).

"It was a good move for me financially," he noted. "I felt like I had done all I could at Southeast and I felt like God wanted me to get uncomfortable again. Jumping to the ACC and working for a good friend in Frank Haith was very attractive to me."

After a single season in south Florida, Kennedy got the call that brought him to Murray.

"I wasn't looking for a job but I got a call from Darren Boatright (MSU's former assistant athletic director) while I was on the road recruiting in Baton Rouge," he noted. "I knew Darren and he asked me if I would be interested in this job. I wasn't very familiar with Murray State other than I knew they had always been good. When he explained how committed the people here are to winning championships that impressed me. That's what attracted me.

"I didn't know what I was walking into though. I didn't know I was going to have to build a team from scratch. I did that at Centenary and Southeast Louisiana and I didn't want to have to do that again. I knew it was a great school with great tradition, and great support. And I looked at the roster and it looked like a good team coming back. I didn't know about the problems and that was my fault. But I think God was protecting me from seeing that because if I had known everything I wouldn't have taken the job."

Kennedy had to scramble just to field a team in his first season. Only four players returned from the previous year. And of those four, one had a broken foot, two had played limited minutes, and the other had redshirted.

Even so, Kennedy held it together and led Murray State to a 16-14 record and a second place finish in the Ohio Valley Conference. He followed that with two more second place finishes as he went about recruiting the kind of players he needed to run his system.

Then in 2010 he led the Racers to a 31-5 record, an OVC championship, an OVC tournament championship, and a first round NCAA tournament victory over Vanderbilt. Not surprisingly, he also won the OVC Coach of the Year award

MSU just missed the Sweet Sixteen as they lost to Butler 54-52 in the second round. Butler went on to finish second, losing in the final to Duke by just two points.

"That team is what I envisioned from the start," Kennedy said. "And for it to work out the way it did was a blessing. We played defense the way I want to and on offense we played fast like I want to. We did it with good kids too. Earlier I mentioned the importance of balance. That team was balanced in every way.

"But I couldn't have imagined everything going as well as it did. The attitude our guys had, the team chemistry, the toughness, not having any injuries, winning the close games... Everything seemed to go right. It was more than I could have imagined."

Kennedy led the Racers to a 23-9 record and a second consecutive OVC championship in his fifth year. After the season he left to take over the program at Texas A & M.

"I could have stayed at Murray a lot longer than five years because of the support we had, the love for the community my wife and I had, and how good people were to us," Kennedy said. "I just felt like it was a special place and I built relationships there that will last a lifetime. It took a special situation to pull me away.

"The community support was outstanding, even outside of Murray. Whether it was Princeton, Paducah, or Benton the community support made it special. And the school's commitment to being successful in basketball separates it from the rest of the schools in the OVC and most of the schools in the country."

DANERO THOMAS

by Will Aubrey

Danero Thomas will be remembered for two things – the smile and the shot.

Thomas was, without a doubt, one of the most affable players to ever wear a Racer uniform. The easy going young man from New Orleans always had a smile on his face and joy in his heart. And he always had time for fans whether that meant signing autographs or just talking hoops.

Ironically, the road he traveled to get to Murray State was anything but easy.

"It was kind of rough growing up," he said. "There were seven of us and only four bedrooms. I went to a public school in elementary, middle and high school."

Now it may sound odd that he would emphasize having gone to public school. But private and parochial schools were numerous in New Orleans before Hurricane Katrina. Few people went to public school unless they had no other choice.

Thomas grew up playing football and thought he was going to be a star quarterback.

"I really enjoyed it," he recalled. "It was my first organized sport and I had trophies and everything. I played quarterback and strong safety and I won awards for Most Valuable Player, Defensive Player of the Year and things like that.

"Then my freshman year of high school I was the backup quarterback and the first string quarterback got a concussion. He came to the sideline and had his water bottle and started squirting water in his ear while he was trying to drink with his mouth. He was out of it and I decided right then that football was not for me."

Thomas started playing basketball when he was in middle school.

"When I was in the eighth grade we won the national championship," he said. "Miss Gay was our coach and I loved her to death. It was kind of odd though, being coached by a woman, because she tried to be really rough on us. But she couldn't because she was a lady.

"She knew what she was doing though. She called me Big D. When I graduated she gave me this big picture of me and her, I still have it today."

When he was a high school freshman Thomas expected to play for the junior varsity. And he did, for two games.

"I scored like 40 points in each of those games so they moved me up to the varsity," he recalled. "My coach, Brian Simmons, said I was too advanced to play J.V.

Danero Thomas

"He was the best coach I've ever been around. He was out there cheering us on every day. He would get on you, but he really just wanted you to be the best you could be. And he emphasized defense. That's probably why I am the way I am now. On the defensive end I'm really active with my hands and I learned all that from him.

"My freshman year we made it to the state championship, but we lost. My 10th grade year we went back to the championship and we won. Then my junior year we lost in the third round."

Following his junior year

Simmons recommended that Thomas consider prep school.

"I was going to be the only senior playing with a bunch of freshmen and sophomores and he thought Mount Zion prep school would be good for me," Thomas said. "But he left it up to me and when I decided to go it made a lot of people mad.

"I think it was good for me though because when I was in New Orleans I didn't have many schools recruiting me, just Louisiana Tech, Mississippi State, Tulane and New Orleans

But when I went to prep school, my first year I averaged like 17 points. I was the second leading scorer, behind Brandon Rush. I could have signed with Georgia Tech my first year there. Paul Hewitt told my coach – 'I want him to sign now.' But I wasn't really sure about it so I just wanted to wait until my senior year to make a decision like that."

Between his first and second year of prep school Thomas would have to endure more hardship. While he was home for the summer Hurricane Katrina almost wiped New Orleans off the map.

"It was like a nightmare," he recalled. "My mom had planned on taking us to a hotel to ride out the storm. But as it got closer she said she had a bad feeling about it. And so we left. We just packed like we were going to be gone for a weekend though. I think I took two pair of jeans. The roads were jammed with cars and it was so hot. It was very uncomfortable but we made it to Atlanta where we could stay with family.

"My mom went back a couple of months later and she said there was a ring on the walls where you could see how high the water got. The beds were split in half and there were snakes and dead fish in the house. It was a mess."

During his final year of prep school Thomas averaged 14 points, six rebounds and four assists. And Mount Zion was ranked in the top five in the nation. He also set a school record by hitting nine three-pointers in a game against Gulf Shores High School.

At the end of the season he had offers from Virginia Tech, LSU, Illinois, and Miami (Fla.).

"I was going to Miami because of Coach (Billy) Kennedy," Thomas said. "Then he called me and said he got the head coaching job here. I had never heard of

Murray State before. And I didn't even take a visit up here because I signed late. But I knew I wanted to play for Coach Kennedy."

"I had friends at bigger schools who wound up sitting on the bench. I didn't want to do that. I wanted to play right away."

Having no idea what Murray State was like Thomas relied on Kennedy, who was in his first year at MSU, not to steer him wrong.

"Because I didn't visit the campus before I signed, when I got here I didn't know any of the other players," he noted. "But really almost all of us were strangers. It was tough to get us all on the same page. But Coach Kennedy was always breaking us up into different groups and changing room assignments on the road to help us get to know each other. And we eventually pulled it together.

"Shawn Witherspoon, one of the seniors, was a great role model for me. And he stayed on my case man. I was just trying to figure out why he was so hard on me. But he was a great person and a great player."

As a freshman Thomas played in 28 games during the 2006-07 season and started eight times as he averaged 5.1 points. He scored in double figures five times and had a season best 19 points in the BracketBuster game against Rider. But the Racers finished the year with a 16-14 record and lost at home to Samford in the first round of the Ohio Valley Conference tournament.

"I was so confused I didn't know what was going on at the end of that game," Thomas admitted. "But with seven seconds left I saw the seniors start tearing up and I thought – 'Man this is really serious.' I certainly didn't want to lose like that again."

As a sophomore, Thomas became a fixture in the starting lineup as he averaged 12.3 points and 4.9 rebounds. He shot 44.9 percent from the field and 38.8 percent from three-point range. He scored 20 points at Jacksonville State and 19 at Tennessee-Martin.

He also became a defensive stopper as he led the team in steals with 45. And despite being just 6-5, he was tied for second in blocked shots with 19.

The Racers improved to 18-13 overall and made it to the semifinals of the OVC tournament where they lost to Tennessee State 83-75.

"We were determined to get to Nashville and we did that," Thomas said. "So we accomplished what we set out to do. But we were disappointed with the loss to TSU."

During the summer between his sophomore and junior years Thomas toured Africa with an Athletes in Action team that visited Senegal, Mali, and Guinea.

"I saw some children who didn't have much," he said. "Your heart just goes out to them, and you want to help them all you can. I left the USA with so much stuff, but the plan was to give it all away."

Thomas said he gave away everything that he took on the trip including shoes, clothing, t-shirts, socks, toiletries and towels.

It was expected that he would take another step forward as a junior and become one of the top players in the conference. He was a first team preseason All-OVC selection. But he struggled, shooting just 42.2 percent from the field and 29.5 percent from behind the arc. He did average a team best 12.5 points to go with 4.3 rebounds per game. He scored 22 points at Indiana State and 30 at Austin Peay and he led the team in both steals and blocked shots.

At season's end he was a second team all-conference selection. The Racers finished 19-12 as they again lost in the semifinals of the OVC tournament. This time they were blown out by arch-rival Austin Peay 67-50.

"That was embarrassing," Thomas recalled with a grimace. "But it was one of those nights when we just couldn't buy a basket."

And the shooting slump? The three-point line was moved back a foot after Thomas' sophomore year. Could that be the reason why he struggled? He doesn't think so.

"You know what I think it was?" he asked rhetorically. "I just stopped working, man. I guess I got overconfident. I had to get back in the gym and work on my shot to bounce back."

And that's exactly what he did.

"My senior year I started coming to practice 45 minutes to an hour early," he explained. "I worked specifically on 3's from each side of the court on both ends. I took about 200 extra shots a day."

As a senior Thomas shot 42.1 percent from the field and 32.5 percent from three-point range while averaging 10.1 points and 4.3 rebounds. He scored 23 points against Austin Peay and was once again a second team All-OVC selection.

The Racers had a magical season as they finished 31-6, the first 30 win season in school history. And they won their first OVC tournament title since 2006 so they were off to San Jose, Calif. to play Vanderbilt in a first round NCAA tournament game.

With 4.2 seconds left Murray State trailed the Commodores by a single point. Head coach Billy Kennedy called timeout and Thomas told assistant coach Amir Abdur-Rahim that he wanted the ball. Kennedy, knowing that Vandy would have scouted the Racers' out of bounds plays, drew up a new one.

"He called a play for Isacc Miles to get the ball and either get to the rim or get somebody open," Thomas recalled. "When we took it out I set a screen for Isacc so he could get the ball. But as soon as he got it they double-teamed him. So he kicked it to me with a little over two seconds left. I just wanted to get separation. I could see the hand of the defender on my right though so I had to shoot a fall-away but It felt good when I let it go. I knew it was going in.

"And then when it did go in I felt like I had won a million dollars. It was the best feeling in the world. Every day, everywhere I go, someone asks me about that shot."

That 66-65 victory gave the Racers their first win in the NCAA tournament since 1988. Unfortunately they lost to Butler in the second round 54-52, the closest game the Bulldogs would play before losing to Duke in the national title game.

"If you look at his track record, academically and off the court he was a good student and representative of our school," Kennedy said of Thomas. "He was always solid and he was one of our best defenders because he could guard a 2,3, or 4. He had size and quick hands which allowed him to get deflections and steals on the perimeter. And although he wasn't a prolific scorer he could explode for a big game at any time."

THREE SENIORS

by Ricky Martin

Donte Poole walked onto the court with both arms raised towards the roof of Louisville's KFC Yum! Center.

The lanky guard walked across the floor and embraced fellow seniors Ivan Aska and Jewuan Long. Then the three walked together into Murray State's locker room.

It was Murray State's second NCAA Tournament victory in three years, but even more than that, it was the last time Aska, Long and Poole – the most successful senior class in Racer history – would earn a win together.

While the March 15, 2012 victory over Colorado State was the final time the three seniors from the 2011-2012 Racer basketball team would walk off the floor as winners, it was far from their final contributions to the Murray State basketball program.

"Those three guys embody what it means to play basketball at Murray State," head coach Steve Prohm said. "You take their character, their toughness and their leadership, and you have not only what it takes to be a successful basketball player, but to be a successful person.

"Those guys represent what it is to play Murray State basketball."

Aska, a former Ohio Valley Conference Freshman of the Year, graduated from Murray State as one of only six players in Racer basketball's 87-year history to accumulate over 1,000 career points and over 600 career rebounds.

That, coupled with his maturation during his four years in the blue and gold, made Aska the bona fide leader of Murray State's most successful men's basketball team in history.

Just ask his former roommate Poole.

"Everyone on the team called Ivan 'big bro,'" Poole said. "He was the guy that we knew we could go to for anything, and he was always just so consistent in what he did. Everyday in practice or in games, we knew what we were getting from Ivan.

"When he got to Murray State as a freshman he was already such a great player, but after playing for four years under coach (Billy) Kennedy and coach Prohm, he grew into a great leader and an even better person."

Prohm said Aska's emotional growth during his four years at Murray State was even more impactful, perhaps than his physical contributions.

"There's no doubt about the type of player Ivan was, a physical and imposing guy, but very athletic as well," Prohm said. "But the biggest thing I think I saw out of Ivan, was his development into a leader of the team.

"Every single guy in that locker room looked up to Ivan, and that's just a testament to his character, not as a player, but as a man."

Aska and Poole began living together during their freshman year, and the two quickly became close.

One of the more iconic images of their careers came in San Jose, Calif., when the No. 13 seeded Racers defeated No. 4 seed Vanderbilt in the first round of the 2010 NCAA Tournament.

Moments after Danero Thomas hit the most famous shot in Murray State history at the buzzer, Aska hoisted Poole up onto his shoulders, and the two paraded around the HP Pavilion floor in celebration.

It was an image captured and shown on Murray State's RacerVision during the three seniors final home game on Feb. 18, a 65-51 victory over nationally ranked St. Mary's.

After the win, Prohm spent several minutes addressing the sell-out crowd in honor of Aska, Long and Poole.

Poole, who played sparingly during his first three seasons with Murray State, became the scorer many thought he could be during the 2011-2012 season.

After averaging just under five points per game through both his sophomore and junior seasons, Poole exploded onto the scene in a big-time way during his senior campaign.

The Las Vegas native averaged 14.0 points per game in 2011-2012, and pitched in a career-high 28 points in a Feb. 14 home sell-out against Tennessee Tech.

Not only was Poole invaluable to the Racer offense as a secondary scorer to All-American Isaiah Canaan, he was also an integral part to what Murray State was able to do defensively.

Poole notched a team-high 63 steals during his senior season.

"Donte was a scorer, we know that," Prohm said. "His offensive abilities go without saying, but what he did for us on the defensive end with his length and his ability to get into the passing lanes and create deflections was crucial to what we did.

"He could get in there and knock a ball away, then next thing you know we are out in transition, and we were a very tough team to stop in transition. You saw that."

While Poole – who was named to the Ohio Valley Conference's First-Team in 2012 – was as good defensively as anyone, it was Long who earned the OVC's Defensive Player of the Year award.

Long, who like Poole played sparingly in his first three seasons, was paramount to the Racers success in 2011-2012, guarding the likes of Tennessee Tech's Kevin Murphy, Tennessee State's Robert Covington and St. Mary's Matthew Dellavedova.

Long was also pressed with defending Colorado State's Wes Eikmeier and Marquette's Darius Johnson-Odom in the 2012 NCAA Tournament.

The Jackson, Tenn. native not only played well defensively for the Racers, but he was the man whose right-handed floater with 4.4 seconds remaining won the OVC Tournament title for the Racers over Tennessee State.

Moments like that, Aska said, made Long the type of player that every Racer loved to play with.

"He isn't a guy that was known for his scoring, but he could when he needed to," Aska said. "His defensive abilities were big to what we were able to do, but Jewuan was just so good about not forcing the issue and taking his shots.

"Every time Jewaun stepped on the floor, he was ready to check the other team's best player, and that was important to us, to know we had a guy out there that could get the job done defensively."

ED DANIEL

by Will Aubrey

Ed Daniel might have been the most athletic player to ever run the floor for the Racers. He could jump out of the gym; he had very quick hands; and he was one of the quickest post players the Ohio Valley Conference has ever seen.

But that's not what makes him unique. Daniel is unique because he was also one of the smartest players on the floor.

"Ed had a great basketball I.Q.," MSU head coach Steve Prohm said. "He helped everyone defensively by blocking shots and taking charges. And he realized what we wanted to do on both ends of the floor at all times."

And yet, if he'd had his way, Daniel might have been chasing down quarterbacks instead of blocking shots.

"I started playing Pee-Wee football when I was about eight years old and that was my favorite sport," he explained. "I didn't start playing basketball until seventh grade. I liked football better and that's what I wanted to play. But I just kept growing so I thought my best bet would be basketball.

"I used to play in the gym and the middle school coach asked me to come out for the team. So I gave it a try and I ended up making it. I started playing AAU a year or two after that."

Daniel played for three years at Hayes High School in Birmingham, Ala. Then when the school was closed he played his senior year at Woodlawn.

Ed Daniel

While at Hayes, Daniel played alongside the highly regarded Eric Bledsoe. Bledsoe went on to star at Kentucky and currently plays for the Phoenix Suns.

"Eric and I put on a show," Daniel said with a grin. "Everybody came to watch us play."

During the summer between his junior and senior year, Daniel played in the Adidas Top-150 camp. To his surprise he was named "Most Athletic."

"Just playing there was a great experience," he said. "I tried to play my game and I was determined not to be intimidated just because someone was being recruited by a big name school. But I was surprised they picked me because there were a lot of great players there."

He averaged 15.8 points, 11 rebounds and 3.5 blocked shots as a senior. He was named to the regional finals all-tournament team and the Birmingham News 2009 class of Super Seniors. He also won the Class 5-A slam dunk contest.

He was recruited by Alabama, South Alabama, Tennessee State, Chattanooga and Murray State.

"I chose MSU because it was the only school that stayed on top of things and made sure I was getting all my work done," he explained. "They called me more than anyone else to check on me and see how my family was doing. A lot of the time we didn't even talk about basketball. They were more concerned about my grades than anything else."

Daniel played in all 36 games as a freshman at Murray State, although he saw limited action. He averaged just 3.0 points and 2.7 rebounds as the Racers went 31-5 and beat Vanderbilt in the first round of the NCAA tournament.

"I didn't play as much as I expected to," he admitted. "But I knew what my role was supposed to be. And I tried to do what was expected of me. It was hard to wait my turn but I understood that I was playing behind two or three upperclassmen."

While some people were stunned by the Racers' success, Daniel says he expected it.

"I expected us to have a great season because we were really tight as a team," he said. "We were more like a family and we knew each other and cared about each other more than a lot of teams do.

Murray State was rarely challenged, winning 14 games by 20 or more points.

"That was a lot of fun, the way we beat teams so badly," Daniel said with a smile. "Of course it meant that I got to play more than I would have otherwise.

"It was a learning process for me though and Tony Easley stuck behind me the whole way. He told me what I needed to focus on. And he worked with me on my post moves."

And despite being matched up against highly regarded Vanderbilt in the NCAA tournament, Daniel says that nerves weren't a factor.

"We just wanted to stay focused and make sure we were on top of our game," he said. "We took it like they were just another team.

"There were a lot of people cheering us on that didn't really have anything to do with Murray State and that made us feel special. And playing in the tournament as a freshman was really special.

"We went to the locker room after the game and everyone was screaming and yelling. It was the most exciting thing that I had ever been a part of."

Heading into Daniel's sophomore year Murray State was the focus of a lot of media attention. But that quickly evaporated as the Racers won just four of their first eight games.

"In a way all the attention we got was a good thing," he said. "But I think all the hype messed us up. We let it get into our heads and I think that's why our season turned out the way it did. We tried to do too much at times instead of sticking to the routine that worked for us the year before."

After coming off the bench the first eight games, Daniel suddenly found himself in the starting lineup.

"Coach Kennedy came to me after practice one day and told me I was going to start," he recalled. "I saw it as a reward for all the hard work I had put in. And that made me keep working hard."

Murray State went 19-5 the rest of the way and Daniel finished the season averaging 6.3 points and 4.3 rebounds. He finished second on the team in shooting percentage at .548 and he led the team in offensive rebounds. He scored a career high 21 points and grabbed 14 rebounds against Tennessee State.

The Racers won the regular season OVC championship but they stumbled in the semifinals of the conference tournament, losing to Tennessee Tech 64-59.

So at the beginning of the 2011-12 season, there was no hype. The Racers were picked third in the OVC's preseason poll and one publication picked them fifth.

"We expected to do well," Daniel said. "They picked us third and we took that as an insult. But that just made us work harder to prove everybody wrong.

"When we won the Great Alaska Shootout that made us think that we could be one of the best teams in Murray State history."

As they headed to Memphis to play the Tigers in December, Murray State was unbeaten and playing for a spot in the Top-25. That's heady stuff. But the Racers were more than up to the challenge as they came away with a 76-72 victory.

"We didn't feel any pressure at all, playing at Memphis," Daniel said. "We treated it just like any other game. We wanted to prove a point and show everybody what we could do."

Then senior Ivan Aska got hurt and Daniel scored 16, 19, and 11 points in the first three games Aska missed.

"When Ivan got hurt I knew I had to step up," he said. "I had to step up and play even smarter, not commit crazy-dumb fouls. I guess I needed to score a little more. But I really didn't even think about that. I just tried to play smart and play defense."

The Racers kept winning. In fact, they were the last unbeaten team in the nation, finishing with a 31-2 record and beating Colorado State in the NCAA tournament.

"For us to go almost undefeated, as a mid-major, only losing two games in the entire season was amazing," Daniel said. "It was hard to beat anybody because we got everyone's best effort. They played their hardest against us. So to only lose two games? That was really special."

Along the way, Daniel caught the imagination of fans old and young alike by wearing his hair in a 70's style afro. Fans often wore wigs to emulate him.

"I thought it was kind of funny," he said. "But it was a sign of respect. They didn't do that just because of my hair. They did it because they knew I was a good player. My hair is just what stood out.

During the summer between his junior and senior years Daniel played in a couple of NBA skills camps and drew rave reviews from the scouts in attendance.

Then as a senior he averaged 13.2 points and 10.0 rebounds, earning first team All-OVC honors as the Racers made it all the way to the finals of the conference tournament before ending the season with a 21-10 record.

"It was fun playing with Isaiah (Canaan) for four years, meeting new guys, traveling to different places," he said. "We won a lot. Everybody loves each other here and they all love the Racers."

At the end of his senior season Daniel signed a free agent contract with the Atlanta Hawks.

ISAIAH CANAAN

by Will Aubrey

There are great players and then there are stars. Stars command your attention and their popularity transcends what they do on the court. Isaiah Canaan has always been a star.

"I started playing city league basketball when I was five," he recalled. "The team I played on was always #1 and everybody wanted to be on my team because I was the center of everything."

Canaan has always played the game with a flair for the dramatic whether he's dunking the ball on a fast break despite being the smallest player on the floor, rising in the air to block a much taller player's shot, or hitting a half court shot from his knees with just a flick of his wrists.

The 6-1 phenom honed his skills on the playgrounds of Biloxi, Miss.

"Biloxi is at the very bottom of Mississippi," he said. "It's as far south as you can go. If you go any further you'll end up in the Gulf of Mexico. It's a good place to go for vacation. They have plenty of casinos and condos. And they also have a man-made beach. When I was a kid I spent a lot of time on the beach with my daddy fishing."

Canaan was just 14 when Hurricane Katrina slammed into Biloxi on August 29, 2005.

"My grandma and I had spent the night in my church on the second floor and when I woke up it was windy and rainy," he recalled. "But then the wind picked up and the rain got heavier. I heard a loud noise and ran to look and I saw the front door had given way and a lot of water was rushing in. I went upstairs and looked out the window and all the houses around us were under water up to the rooftops.

Isaiah Canaan

"The second floor of our church was pretty high but the water got up to our ankles. And the wind was so strong that the building was moving from side to side. We were afraid it was going to collapse. We climbed into the attic of the church because we didn't know how high the water was going to get.

"All we had was the clothes that we took with us, my PlayStation, and a couple of pairs of shoes. That was the worst day of my life. I was really scared. My grandma stayed after the storm to get everything taken care of, insurance and things like that. I went with my momma to Atlanta for a little while and went to school up there so I wouldn't get behind."

After three or four months Canaan wanted to go home and see what the city looked like. And his coaches back in Biloxi were just as eager for him to return.

"It was right at the beginning of basketball season, the coaches were calling me saying that the schools were open," he recalled. "So I went back and finished out my freshman year and my high school career in Biloxi."

"I lived in a FEMA trailer for a couple of years. We had the house we lived in before the storm gutted it and we were going to fix it up but it caught on fire. So we had to tear that down and our church gave us a house that they owned."

Canaan's coach at Biloxi High School was Seber Windham.

"Coach Windham was a good guy," he said. "He was always pushing us like we were his sons. He goes to my church and he was always

there for us when we needed him. He would get on you but he was calm and laid back. When he had to say something he would though."

As a junior Canaan averaged 20 points and seven assists and was an all-state selection. As a senior he averaged 24 points and seven assists, led Biloxi to the 5A state championship, and was a Mr. Basketball finalist. He was also voted Most Valuable Player of the Mississippi Sate Tournament and was a Gatorade Player of the Year finalist.

Following his senior season he played in the Mississippi-Alabama All-Star game and was named MVP for the Mississippi squad after leading his team with 18 points.

He began attracting the attention of college recruiters during his junior year and he thought picking among them would be an easy task.

"I thought I was going to go to LSU, Mississippi State or Ole Miss," he said. "But they didn't offer me early. So I had to rethink things and I decided to come to Murray State. Then after we won the state championship those other schools started contacting me. But I came here anyway because I believed in the coaches and they had a great group of guys coming back."

Canaan was thrown into the fray in the 2009-10 opener at California. Even though he was just a freshman he logged 17 minutes. And when he was on the floor he often guarded Cal's All-American, Jerome Randle. He gave the senior fits though, picking him clean on a couple of occasions.

"I'm not scared of anyone except my momma and my grandma," he said with a laugh. "So, I wasn't worried about guarding him. I'm too competitive for that. I don't back down from anybody. It was just another game to me."

Canaan finished the season as the Racers' second leading scorer at 10.4 points per game. And he shot the ball extremely well, hitting 49.8 percent of his shots overall and a league leading 48.2 percent of his three-point attempts. He was the Ohio Valley Conference Freshman of the Year and MVP of the OVC tournament. CollegeInsider.com named him to their Freshman All-America team.

"With my ability I knew I was going to play but I didn't know I would have as big an impact as I did," he admitted. "I knew I could play. I just didn't expect to play as much as I did.

"The individual awards show that all the hard work I put in paid off and that other people took notice of my talent. That meant a lot to me."

But statistics and awards aside, he got more attention for a single shot he hit against Southeast Missouri than anything else. With the shot clock running down he lost control of the ball near midcourt. He managed to recover it but had to just flick it at the basket from his knees as time ran out. And to his surprise it went in.

The shot was replayed for days on ESPN and he was interviewed on ESPN2's First Take program. A YouTube video of the play has over 2.2 million hits.

"That was crazy," he said. "Everyone asked me about that shot for a month. I was stuck. I didn't have anything else to do so I just tried shooting it. I was either going to miss it and get taken out of the game or I was going to make it and something good was going to happen."

The Racers finished 31-5, setting a school record for wins in a season and breaking the record for consecutive victories. Then they beat Vanderbilt in the NCAA tournament. It was a dream season.

"When you're winning it seems like nothing else matters," Canaan said. "We won a whole lot of games so it was a lot of fun. We were solid and everyone knew what they had to do. And nothing beats the feeling we got from beating Vandy in the NCAA tournament."

The media spent the next eight months fawning

over the Racers. ESPN's Andy Katz said they might make it all the way to the Elite Eight. Almost every preseason publication had them ranked in the top-50 and a few had them in the top-25. But from the outset head coach Billy Kennedy said the hype was unwarranted. And as much fun as it was for the fans; it may not have been good for the team.

"Everyone had high expectations," Canaan said. "And I don't blame them. But I think at times we played not to lose instead of playing to win."

The result was a 23-9 record and a loss in the semifinals of the OVC tournament. Canaan averaged a team best 11.7 points despite starting just 20 of the team's 32 games. And he was a first team all-conference selection.

The hype that swirled around the Racers at the beginning of 2010-11 season had evaporated by the time Canaan's junior year got underway. The Racers had lost three starters and head coach Billy Kennedy. So it wasn't surprising that they were picked to finish third in the OVC.

The surprise was that they were the last undefeated team in the nation as they climbed as high seventh in the polls. They finished 31-2, won a game in the NCAA tournament and Canaan had a season for the ages. He averaged 19 points while making 45.6 percent of his three-point attempts.

And many of those three-point shots were well beyond the line. More than one national reporter dispatched to cover the Racers was heard to exclaim, "Oh my!" at the press table as Canaan buried shots so deep most players wouldn't have considered taking them.

After Canaan scored 32 points in an 81-73 victory over Southeast Missouri, the Redhawks' Corey Wilford said, "I thought I did a pretty good job on Canaan in the first half. Then he started pulling from halfcourt in the second half. There wasn't anything I could do about that."

At the end of the season Canaan was named OVC Player of the Year and was a first team All-American.

"The Player of the Year award meant a lot to me after all the hard work I put in," he said. "A lot of people talked about it before the season started but I didn't focus on it, I just wanted to go out and do whatever I could to help my team win. I knew if I did that everything else would take care of itself. And I give a lot of credit to my teammates for pushing me every day in practice."

Canaan's senior year was kind of a mirror image of his sophomore season. The hype surrounding the team at the beginning of the year was unprecedented. Fans talked openly about making a deep run in the NCAA tournament. But the Racers struggled to play up to those outsized expectations, in part due to the absence of two players who were expected to be in the starting lineup – Zay Jackson and Latreze Mushatt.

Their absence forced Canaan to shoulder even more of the burden to carry the team than he had in the past. Without Jackson he didn't get many catch and shoot opportunities. He generally had to create his own shot while playing an astounding 36.5 minutes a game, even after he sprained his foot at midseason.

Despite all that, he averaged a career best 21.8 points and was again named OVC Player of the Year.

"I hated to see it come to an end," he said. "It seems like yesterday I was a freshman. Now here we are as seniors. But it's been fun. We've played against a lot of good teams and won a lot of games, kept the tradition going."

With his career at Murray State over, Canaan was taken by the Houston Rockets with the 34th pick in the 2013 NBA Draft. But he will always be a Racer.

"I'll always remember the people and the way the whole town rallied around the team," he said. "They made us feel like family. Murray will always have a place in my heart."

Steve Prohm

by Will Aubrey

Some coaches motivate their players through intimidation. They yell and scream, berate players, throw clipboards – whatever they have to do to bully their players into playing hard.

That approach can work, and work well. Look at the success Bobby Knight had at Indiana.

But that's not Steve Prohm's way.

You often hear coaches say, "That kid would run through a brick wall for me." But if you talk to Prohm's players they'll tell you that *he* would run through a brick wall for *them*.

"If he could put on a jersey he would get out there and play with us," Isaiah Canaan said of Prohm in 2012. "He'll do anything he can for us. He loves us like we were all his sons."

Prohm will tell you that's the foundation of all he does.

"Coaching is about relationships, relationships with my players, my staff, and people on campus and in the community," he said. "I want our program to be like a family. I want my players to know I care about them and that's of the utmost importance to me. That's why I'm in this business."

Although his approach to coaching is uniquely his own; Prohm's philosophy was shaped by the years he spent working under former Murray State head coach Billy Kennedy.

He grew up in rural Georgia where he played basketball at Northwest Whitfield High School. He started college at Oglethorpe University where he played Division III basketball. But he decided to follow his passion for coaching and transferred to the University of Alabama where he worked as a student assistant under head coach Dave Hobbs.

"You could tell then that he was a real gym rat in a lot of ways," Hobbs said. "He just loved being in the gym and would do anything he could to help a player out. He would always be coaching up the players and you could see his aptitude and attitude early on. He's a real student of the game and relates well to the players.

"I think he is a guy that will very likely be a superstar. He is kind of understated in ways. He is not the big flamboyant guy, but he is a guy that will roll up his sleeves. He is a guy who knows where he came from."

After five years at Alabama, Prohm went to work as a volunteer assistant for Kennedy at Centenary College where he lived in the basement of a dormitory and ate at the cafeteria. He followed Kennedy to Southeastern Louisiana where he spent five seasons. After that he spent one year at Tulane before joining Kennedy at Murray State in 2006.

Steve Prohm

"He's made an impact on my life," Prohm said of his mentor. "And I'm not just talking about basketball. He showed me how to understand what's important and how to have a balance in my life. He showed me how important faith and family are and taught me to rely on and trust in those things.

"I had known about Murray forever. We had a kid at Alabama, M.C. Mazique, who had actually been enrolled here. This is a special

place to me. When you're in a community that truly embraces the basketball program, truly embraces the coaches and the players, and you know how much it means to them... Well, that's something very special."

When Kennedy left MSU for Texas A & M in 2011 the Racers hired Prohm to take his place. What happened next was like something out of a dream.

After being picked third in the Ohio Valley Conference at the beginning of the season, Prohm led the Racers to 23 straight victories as Murray State was the last unbeaten team in the nation. At one point they were ranked 7th in the ESPN/USA Today coaches poll. They went into the NCAA tournament with a 30-1 record, ranked 10th by the coaches and 11th by the Associated Press. They were ranked for 14 consecutive weeks.

Murray State finished the season with the most road wins of any team in the country and they were 3-0 against the top 35 teams in the RPI during the regular season. At the end of the year Prohm was named national Coach of the Year by Basketball Times.

So, how did he do it?

Well, his assistants were all new to the program and he had five new players coming in. So he scheduled an August trip to Canada to help the players and coaches get to know each other.

He retained Kennedy's emphasis on defense. But he tweaked the offense a little. He emphasized scoring in transition even if that meant taking an open three-pointer. He also used more ball screens and called more plays in the flow of the game.

Those changes paid immediate dividends as the Racers started 4-0, scoring 80 points twice in that span. The fourth victory came at UAB where they won 62-55 after trailing by 12 points with 10 minutes to play.

"I called timeout and I told them they could either get beat by 20 or they could make it a game," Prohm recalled. "Then we started to play defense, started to make some shots and before you knew it we were back in the game."

The Racers broke into the top-25 after beating #21 Memphis on the road. A 73-40 victory at Eastern Illinois pushed their record to 14-0 but starting center Ivan Aska broke his hand in that game and would miss the next six games. Surprisingly, Murray State didn't miss a beat.

"When Ivan got hurt we had to change things a little," Prohm said. "We had been playing with two posts and we went to one post with four out and one ball-screener. And our players adapted and made it work."

After Aska came back Murray State just kept winning. They won the OVC regular season title with a 15-1 record and then they won the OVC tournament. They finished the season at 31-2 and beat Colorado State in the first round of the NCAA tournament.

Prohm's second season posed even stiffer challenges. He had to replace three starters. On top of that, Zay Jackson, who had been expected to start at one of the guard spots, was suspended for the entire season. And Latreze Mushatt, who had been expected to start on the front line, tore his Achilles tendon.

The Racers got off to a great start anyway as they beat Auburn and St. John's in the Charleston Classic. And despite more injuries along the way, Prohm guided his team to a 21-10 record and an OVC West Division championship. Then they came within a whisker of winning the OVC tournament as they lost in the final to Belmont 70-68.

Two years into his head coaching career Prohm is 52-12 overall, the best record of any coach in MSU history through his first two seasons.

But numbers aside, if you want to know what makes Steve Prohm a success, listen to Donte Poole, "He's honest, loyal, and emotional. He'll tell you how he feels and he means it. If he's mad about something he's going to let you know. But he also lets you know when you've done something good. And if he wants to cry he's going to cry. But he would do anything in the world for his players."

That kind of devotion is a powerful thing.

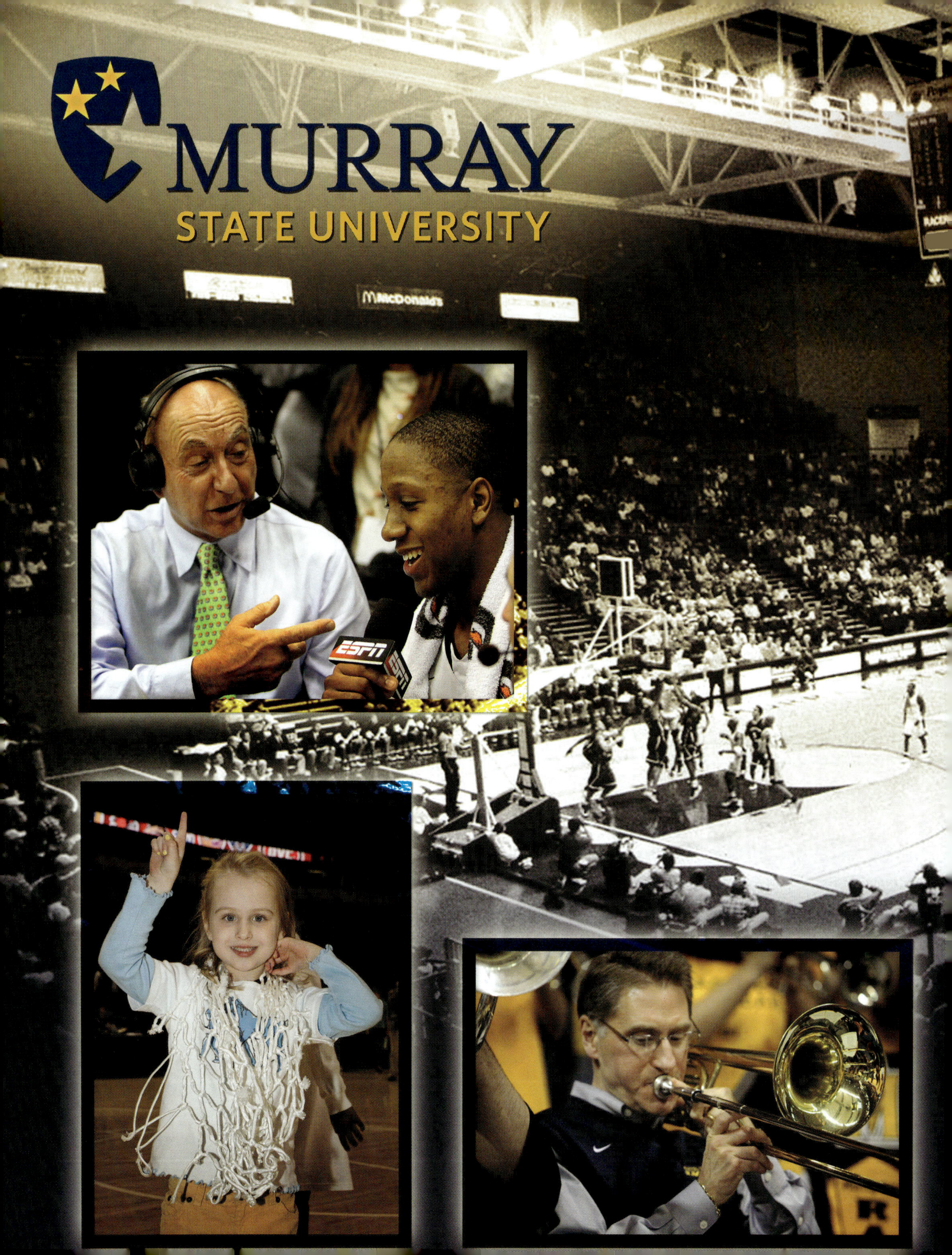
MURRAY
STATE UNIVERSITY
McDonald's
ESPN

Racer Basketball is BIG Stuff!

Racer Basketball is BIG Stuff

by Duane Bolin

Beginning on January 17, 1926, when team captain Ty Holland led Murray State Normal School onto the court against Will Mayfield College, Racer basketball has been big stuff. First in the small but vibrant hamlet of Murray, where students, cheerleaders and faculty gathered on campus in a Wilson Hall second floor balcony to cheer the home team, then later throughout the Jackson Purchase, and later still throughout the Commonwealth of Kentucky, the United States and the world.

That's no exaggeration. It is not uncommon for Racer sportswear to be seen in China on the streets of Beijing, or in Germany in the historic city of Regensburg. You might meet a Racer basketball fan in Belize, or South Korea. The Murray State athletics brand is international in scope. After two students wrote and produced "The Murray State Anthem" in early 2012, a video of the rap song quickly had over 130,000 hits on YouTube.

I learned that Murray State basketball is big stuff in a more traditional way. My high school basketball coaches, Eddie Ford and Gene Pendleton, played for Cal Luther's Racers in the 1960s and took our Webster County High School teams to see what big-time college basketball was all about in the 1970s. We traveled in a caravan on two-lane back roads through Fredonia and Eddyville and when we got to Murray we had access to the Murray State dressing rooms in Racer Arena, one of the truly great venues to watch or to participate in a college basketball game. As a starry-eyed high school freshman, I thought I had entered basketball heaven as we sat in the first three rows on the baseline and saw Les Taylor play defense for the Racers like only Cal Luther could teach it. Taylor was one of my basketball heroes. He was an offensive machine, but it made quite an impression on me that he spent a great deal of energy and effort on defense as well.

Racer Arena was always packed and electricity filled the building. When Taylor and his teammates slapped the floor on the defensive end of the court, Racer fans knew the other team was in for a fight. All this was big stuff to me. This was basketball the way it was meant to be played.

During the 16-year Cal Luther coaching era, Racer basketball grew in popularity beyond Calloway County, beyond the Jackson Purchase of West Kentucky. Racer Mania engulfed the Western Coal Field and the Pennyroyal, and the Murray State and Western Kentucky rivalry was big stuff across the Commonwealth. I remember MSU/WKU games in Racer Arena where fans stood seven deep at the top of the bleachers and the chair back seats. Another person could not have squeezed into the arena, not even if the fire marshal had gone home and the doors leading into the building had been reopened.

Of course, the reputation, exposure and expectation of Racer basketball have grown over the years. From the time when Murray State's "Jumping Joe" Fulks perfected his newfangled jump shot in the early 1940s and became professional basketball's first true superstar, to the days when some of the nation's most promising coaches had remarkable runs while mentoring the Racer players. National recognition came to Murray State in 1978 when Ron Greene, the Southeastern Conference Coach-of-the-Year, was hired away from Mississippi State. Winning seasons, Ohio Valley Conference championships and trips to the NCAA Tournament are now the norm. And with All-American guard Isaiah Canaan returning from last season's remarkable 31-2 team, coach Steve Prohm's 2012-13 Racers seem poised to excite Racer Nation once again.

As you will read in the following essays, Racer basketball is indeed big stuff: to Murray State University and the OVC; to the fans and to Dick Vitale, perhaps the biggest fan of the college game; to those who tell the Murray State story on the radio, in front of the TV camera and in the print media; and to those who disseminate the information to the press.

IN FRONT OF THE TV CAMERA

by Dave Winder

Just like the times in which we live, Murray State Basketball has been affected by the world of media and especially television.

Since 1979, fans have been able keep up with the Racers by tuning into the weekly television show. From its birth at WPSD TV in Paducah, Ky., the Murray State coaches TV show has been largely heavy on highlights and head coach comments. The show has given Racer Basketball something that few if any had in the Ohio Valley Conference. Over its 33 years, the weekly television offering of MSU Basketball morphed from a once-a-week airing to a program that can be viewed anytime on YouTube and GoRacers.com. Various cable outlets now carry the show in multiple weekly showings.

The TV show has also featured MSU Football during the same time period.

As the author of this chapter and host of the show off and on since 1993, I have been honored to sit down with the Racers' coach each week and review highlights of the games and talk about the program. If a person is not a fan of MSU Basketball, then it's probably not their cup of tea. But for those who follow the Racers, this is real must-see TV. Having been involved with the show for so long, I feel the need to keep it going for as long as I can and someday I'll hand it off to the next host.

When the season rolls around, we start our shows usually the week after Thanksgiving and continue to end of the season. For many seasons, the show was recorded in a studio, but recently, the show has gone mobile and is regularly produced in the field and sometimes on the road wherever the Racers might be playing.

The MSU Basketball coaches' television show has featured eight different head coaches and a long list of hosts. I'm privileged to be the current keeper of this special program.

The first host was Frank Murock, sports director and anchor for WPSD TV-6 in Paducah, Ky., who started the show with MSU Basketball Coach Ron Greene in 1979.

There have been many memorable moments in show history, but none bigger than when the Racers recorded their first win in the NCAA Tournament, in Lincoln, Neb., over North Carolina State in 1988. Host Paul Brown, who also worked at WPSD, was front and center at the biggest win in Racer history.

"I remember WPSD flew us out to Lincoln in Fred Paxton's (WPSD owner) plane," said Brown, who is a columnist for the Ladue News in St. Louis, Mo. "My colleagues Joe Wilson and Paul Donohue were on the flight. When it became apparent that Murray State was going to win, we couldn't hold back and celebrated on press row in Lincoln, even though we weren't supposed to."

"This was on a Friday and we taped part of show with Coach Newton immediately after the game at the arena because we had to get back to Paducah to throw something together for the Sunday night show," Brown said. "So I wasn't there for the second game against KU."

The Racers narrowly missed a trip to the Sweet 16 against Kansas in a 61-58 loss.

Brown vividly remembers putting together a music video for the final show of the season that used the song "The Time of our Lives" from the movie Dirty Dancing.

"It really was the time of my life," Brown said. "It was something special for me to be part of. Working on that Murray State coaches show was so great for me. Coach Newton and the team always made me feel like I was part of the team."

Brown believes the initial days of the Racer TV show, before cable television and the internet, helped recruit what is now a loyal local fan base and some talented players.

"Even though the show aired once on Sunday nights, the show did get into the four-state area," Brown said. "Maybe guys like Don Mann from Dyersburg,

Tenn., or Popeye Jones of Dresden knew about MSU because of that TV show. It had to have a recruiting impact during the time."

Another amazing moment was witnessed by host Mark Miller at the 1999 OVC Tournament championship game at then Gaylord Entertainment Center in Nashville, Tenn. Aubrey Reese's buzzer beater against Southeast Missouri State sent the Racers to their third straight NCAA appearance with a 62-61 victory.

"I remember thinking this is going to be a tough post-game because the MSU people are going to be very disappointed," said Miller, who is now the communications director at Drury University in Springfield, Mo. "When Reese hit the shot, it was absolute bedlam. My cameraman Chad Darnell was following Reese as the celebration spilled on to the court. At that point it felt like the Racers had a team that had some destiny behind it."

"The show aired on WPSD on Saturdays at that time, so there wasn't a scramble to get the show on for a Sunday night," Miller said. "We taped on Wednesday's, so it was more relaxed. I do remember we started the show that next Wednesday with Coach T with an entire segment on that shot. It was an amazing time."

Miller also remembers other big moments. In the

1997-98 season, Mark Gottfried's Racers were 29-4 and earned a No. 9 seed in the NCAA Tournament and the Racers recorded that legendary 47-game home court win streak that spanned the end of Racer Arena and the beginning of the Regional Special Events Center.

"Coach Gottfried was about my age so it was great to get to know him and he made me feel like I was part of the team," Miller said. "Coach Anderson was a father-type figure for me and I learned a lot about life from him. The value of hosting the coaches show was the relationships you had with the coaches and players, I really enjoyed it."

So what is a weekly television show for a basketball program supposed to look like?

For starters, you have to have a name for the show and it always involves the name of the current head coach. For years the program was called Murray State Basketball with…(head coach name). Starting in 2009, the program's name changed to The Racer Report, and still includes the name of the coach.

The show has never had huge numbers in viewership, but has enjoyed a loyal group of fans that rarely miss a show. These days most catch it on GoRacers.com. The program at its core is about the games. Fans want to see extended highlights of Racer games and comments from the head coach, more than the 30-seconds that might be shown on the local news.

As those epic moments have occurred, the Racer TV show has documented them. When the Racers won the 1995 Ohio Valley Conference Tournament at Municipal Auditorium in Nashville, Tenn., I watched Head Coach Scott Edgar get a Gatorade bath from his team after the big win over Austin Peay and he did the show soaking wet. In 2006, Mick Cronin's Racers nearly beat North Carolina in Dayton, Ohio and I pulled an all-nighter to get the highlights edited so we could record the show early the next morning at an old Holiday Inn we stayed in.

Through the years, I've sat down with the Racers' coach for their final show before they left MSU. Most times, I wasn't aware of this because the decision to leave hadn't been made yet. I must admit though, there were times when I had a strong feeling that this was his last. For the host and the head coach, the television show can become a little awkward when the team isn't playing well and winning. Fortunately, this is rare. Since the show's birth in 1979, the Racers have posted 692 victories and 28 combined OVC regular season and tournament championships through the 2011-12 season. During the amazing run in Steve Prohm's rookie season, he and I laughed each week that we hadn't yet had to talk about a loss as the Racers' streak eventually went to 23-0.

The list of known hosts for Murray State coaches' television show includes: Murock, Joe Amato, Larry McIntosh, Paul Brown, Mark Miller, Darren Boatright, Josh Perigo and myself; most of them worked at one time or another at WPSD, including me. Although many years have passed since the program last aired on WPSD, the leaders of the station are to be thanked for agreeing to do the show in first place. A lot of that had to do with Coach Greene who took the idea to WPSD. Thanks also go out to the numerous behind the scenes staff that have had a part in airing the show. These talented people include: photographers, studio staff, directors and producers.

Dick Vitale

by Ricky Martin

On Feb. 18, 2012, the hype surrounding nationally ranked Murray State and its men's basketball team reached its crescendo.

After a grassroots movement through various social networking sites such as Twitter and Facebook, ESPN college basketball analyst and sports icon Dick Vitale arrived in Murray for the network's national broadcast between the Racers and nationally ranked St. Mary's.

It was the first time in the program's 87-year history that the Racers were pitted against a fellow, top-25 ranked team, and the first time a top-25 ranked team visited the CFSB Center.

For Vitale, the opportunity to visit Murray was something he longed for, knowing the rich tradition and pride that runs deep within Racer Country.

"I told my bosses that it was a game I wanted to do, but of course that doesn't always mean I'll get to do it," Vitale said. "It's so important to me, the game of basketball is so important to me, that I absolutely love being in environments that absorb the tradition of college basketball the way Murray State does.

"It was something I was hoping to get to do."

Vitale originally expressed interest in visiting Murray during a Jan. 16, 2012 national broadcast of a game between Kansas and Baylor.

Vitale said he would love to get a chance to call a Murray State game, in large part due to the success of the Racers to that point in the season.

Murray State opened the season with 23-straight wins, going unbeaten until Feb. 9, 2012, when they fell 72-68 to visiting Tennessee State.

Despite the small blemish on an otherwise perfect record, Murray State was given its deserved respect with the release of the Sears BracketBuster schedule, which was revealed just days before the Racers were set to host the game of their life.

Murray State was guaranteed a home game in the event, which pits mid-major programs against one another in hopes of bolstering some of the top tier team's tournament resumes.

It wasn't guaranteed, however, that Murray State would host one of the premier mid-major teams in the nation.

With announcement that the nationally-ranked Gaels would travel to Murray, so to was the announcement that Vitale was Murray-bound as well.

With that, came plenty of excitement from the 2008 Naismith Basketball Hall of Fame inductee.

"It's exciting for me to get the chance to go to a place where the people are so passionate about college basketball and the game as a whole," Vitale said. "It's incredible, some of the places and environments I've been in, and there's nothing like being in a place where for a few hours, college basketball is the most important thing."

Vitale wasn't the only one excited about his visit, however.

Hundreds of Murray State fans reached out to the Hall-of-Famer on his Twitter feed, eager for their chance to meet Vitale and possibly get his name inked to some Racer memorabilia.

Hours before the event, hundreds of students and fans lined up around the CFSB Center for their chance to get inside for the perhaps the biggest event in the building's history.

Murray State sports information director Dave Winder said even the requests for media credentials increased with

the hype surrounding Murray State's game with St. Mary's.

"I would say media requests up until mid-February were probably double what they normally were," he said. "After that it went triple what I'd normally have.

"That St. Mary's game, that was probably the biggest event that's ever been in the building."

Couple that with Vitale's presence on press row, and it's a recipe for one historic night.

As Vitale arrived at the CFSB Center after flying into Calloway County's Kyle-Oakley Field, Vitale circled the building, meeting and greeting hundreds of Racer faithful, including a select few who camped out over night to claim their front-row seats for the day's event.

Hundreds of painted faces and clever signs littered the sidewalks, and that was just on the outside.

Once inside, Vitale causally walked onto the court, where then senior Donte Poole was beginning to do some pre-warm-up workouts.

Poole, who grew up watching Vitale's broadcasts, couldn't help but flash his signature smile when Vitale came onto the floor, took the basketball from Poole, and began to take several of his patented hook-shots.

Vitale made just one, then pretended to play some defense on the All-Ohio Valley Conference guard, before taking his place on the Racers bench for a chance to speak with rookie coaching sensation Steve Prohm.

"That was an absolute thrill," Prohm said of his pre-game visit with Vitale. "That guy right there, he is college basketball. To have a chance to coach a game that he is a part of is a tremendous honor.

"I have so much respect for him and his work, not only in basketball, but in life, and his character and demeanor is something that I will always respect."

Behind 23 points from junior guard Isaiah Cannan, the Racers defeated the Gaels by a final score of 65-51 on senior day.

Afterwards, Vitale had only praise for his experience in Murray, in what may have been the biggest regular-season game in history.

"I just want to thank coach Prohm and everyone in Racer Nation who came out," Vitale said. "The atmosphere was electric, and it was a truly special night."

SHARING STORIES, SHARING EXPERIENCES

by Dusty Luthy Shull

The byline is one of a writer's most prized possessions. Seeing it in print almost daily covering sports for *The Paducah Sun* gives me an immense amount of pride, and is something that keeps me yearning to get better at my craft.

But as a journalist, there are times when the byline just isn't fair.

These aren't my stories I'm writing that appear in the newspaper. They belong to the players, the coaches and the fans – the people who are changed and affected by the way the ball bounces on a hardwood court, the way a football zips through the air, or the way a bat cracks on a diamond.

Covering Murray State basketball since I began working at the *Sun* in 2007 has given me access to an immense amount of stories.

Some have been easy to tell, some have been fun, some have been a struggle and some have been downright hard.

Telling the story of Isacc Miles and his mother, who died of breast cancer not long after the Racers' 2009 NCAA Tournament appearance, I cried for days as I wrote it, empathizing with Miles as my own mother has survived breast cancer.

I tear up at the season-ending games. B.J. Jenkins' visible torture at losing early in the Ohio Valley Conference tournament in 2011 was heart-wrenching. I've not run across many student-athletes who have expressed their hatred of losing quite like Jenkins did.

Ed Daniel's revelation during his junior season (2011- 2012) that his mother believes he has split personalities – based on his June 13 birth date and Gemini Zodiac – much like his split hairstyles that season of braided cornrows and an afro.

One of my favorite interviews of all time was with Racer junior college transfer Ray George. A senior for the 2007-2008 season, George was easily one of the most gifted athletes on the team. He just hadn't learned how to harness his energies within then-coach Billy Kennedy's system.

The game he yanked his chewing gum out of his mouth and flung it in frustration across the court at the CFSB Center was one of the most fascinating responses to an emotion I've ever seen on the court.

I always thought George was misunderstood. His tattoos, his supreme athleticism, especially in the dunking arena, were sometimes hard to get beyond.

But chatting with him one day for a story, I learned a lot about his past life. It was hard. It was filled with disappointments. And all he wanted to do was make Kennedy happy and Racer fans proud.

George ended his career in a fairly unmemorable way. He didn't set records; didn't hit buzzer beaters. But by the end of his two-year career as a Racer, he found his place at the table and his story remains as one I can't forget.

An in-depth interview with Kennedy himself? It was most challenging tale I've told in five years. I wrote

a feature story on the Louisiana native before the 2009 NCAA Tournament, and had to write it three times before I was remotely happy with it. How do you tell the tale of a quiet man with immense faith in God and his vocation as a basketball coach in just a few column inches? I couldn't do it justice. But Kennedy lives the story every day.

How do you tell the tale of an improbable hero in Danero Thomas, cementing his name in the Racer books of lore with a simple jump shot in San Jose, Calif.? He told it himself.

How can you adequately prophesy about a freshman named Isaiah Canaan who would become Murray State's first All-American in nearly a decade? Try telling your readers about a rookie head coach who sets the college basketball world on fire when his team was the last in the nation to suffer a loss.

These are stories that live beyond the yellowing pages of a newspaper or an outdated link on a website.

My offering to Racer history has been telling the tale of the present. I'm not a western Kentucky native, rather I'm a transplant from Missouri. My history with the Racers spans just six short years: the Billy Kennedy regime and the Steve Prohm era. But in order to tell the tales of the present, you have to be able to learn from the stories of the past.

I remember driving down from Paducah to Murray in 2007 with my sports editor, where we met Dave Winder, associate athletic director for media relations at Murray State, and took a tour of the campus and learned a little bit about the history of the school I would cover for the foreseeable future.

I was fresh out of the Missouri School of Journalism and I had happily accepted the job to cover the Racers, among other things at the *Sun*. I don't know what I expected, but I didn't expect to be covering a program with such a rich basketball history and a fan base as hungry for stories on the Racers as it was and still is.

We toured Roy Stewart Stadium and the then-named Regional Special Events Center. We also drove by the former baseball field, where I was informed

38 BASKETBALL TIMES

College Report

The Little Empire

During the last four decades there has been no more successful mid-major program in the nation than Murray State University. Coaches and players have come and gone, but the winning has never stopped. Yet in the aftermath of their succeses here, the architects have found failure

By Larry Donald

MURRAY, Ky. – As the game's final 15 seconds ticked off the clock Murray State guard Marlon Towns stood just in front of the Racers' bench palming the basketball in his large right hand and no Eastern Illinois defender even made an effort to come and take it from him. Perhaps this lack of a challenge was simply a mature response to the insurmountable difference on the scoreboard and, then again, maybe there are just a lot of history students on the Panthers roster.

It was another night and another win, not really so different than it has been here for the last four plus decades. At Murray State success has been, to give it Lombardian script, not just a sometimes thing, but a nearly always thing. Numerically it probably could be successfully argued that in the entirety of college basketball no mid-major program has done better what with 34 winning seasons in the last 41 attempts – and, remember, five of those seven losing campaigns came from 1974 to 1979, the dark days of the Fred Overton years. Since 1979 there's been just one sub .500 season, in 1987, and none are in sight.

Murray State coach Tevester Anderson

All this comes at a level of college basketball where, typically, good teams are developed over a period time by growing youth, reaping a reward at the end of their time before turning to walk back to the end of the line where the process begins anew. At Murray State that has not happened. There are no special advantages apparent, certainly none that regularly accompany dynasty-like operations at a higher level – television appearances, nearby talent, etc. Murray State enjoys none of that. Yet it has thrived, impressively so.

In its own world of the Ohio Valley Conference, a league populated by what former North Carolina State coach Jim Valvano would call "directional" schools, Murray State is the unchallenged giant, especially in the past two decades. Where once Western Kentucky reigned, now Murray State has taken over, shattering all of the Hilltoppers marks for regular season and postseason championships. There have been 18 league titles, either regular or post season here, including 11 in the past 12 years and the last six consecutively. Nationally, Murray State ranks No. 16 for the decade in winning percentage and is tied with Coppin State for the most league championships in the 1990s. It is unquestionably a great tragedy for the OVC that WKU moved away to the SunBelt for the lure of money instead of staying around to create a backyard rivalry with Murray State (the schools are located about

Murray State's run

CAL LUTHER	
1959	10-15
1960	12-11
1961	13-10
1962	13-12
1963	13-9
1964	16-9
1965	19-7
1966	13-12
1967	14-9
1968	16-8
1969	22-6
1970	17-9
1971	19-5
1972	15-11
1973	17-8
1974	12-13
FRED OVERTON	
1975	10-15
1976	9-17
1977	17-10
1978	8-17
RON GREENE	
1979	4-22
1980	23-8
1981	17-10
1982	20-8
1983	21-8
1984	15-13
1985	19-9
STEVE NEWTON	
1986	17-12
1987	13-15
1988	22-9
1989	19-11
1990	21-9
1991	24-9
SCOTT EDGAR	
1992	17-13
1993	18-12
1994	23-6
1995	21-9
MARK GOTTFRIED	
1996	19-10
1997	20-10
1998	29-4
TEVESTER ANDERSON	
1999	27-6

OVC TITLES
1964, 1969, 1980, 1982, 1983, 1988, 1989, 1990, 1991, 1992, 1994, 1995, 1996, 1997, 1998, 1999

NCAA APPEARANCES
1964, 1969, 1988, 1990, 1991, 1992, 1995, 1997, 1998 AND 1999.

NIT APPEARANCES
1982, 1983, 1989, 1994, 1996,

Little Empire Story about Racer basketball that appeared in The Basketball Times.

Front cover of the first Racer Insider.

Winder had hit the last home run at the old field. I was impressed then, and still now, even though I've heard the story at least five times since.

I remember looking up at all the banners in the arena, noting the championships and reading the names of the retired jerseys. Jeff Martin, Howie Crittenden, Bennie Purcell. The letters read as strangers' names to me then, but I've since had the opportunity to meet many of the legendary Racers and learn of their stories.

The newspaper archives and media guides have offered one version of Murray State history. Another one lives in the in the hearts and minds of those who love Racers athletics.

I've cherished the storytelling I've absorbed from the best of fans and media folks. Neal Bradley, the radio voice of the Racers, has been one of the best witnesses to Murray State basketball history and he recounts each game-winner and buzzer-beater exactly like it happened. Media lunches with colleagues provide tale after tale of behind-the-scenes actions that enshrine past characters like Aubrey Reese, Mark Gottfried, Scott Edgar, Popeye Jones, Marcus Brown, Tevester Anderson and others.

Lindy Suiter's inside knowledge and narratives add at least another 20 years to my ever-growing memory bank, and meeting the spark plug known as Bennie Purcell, well, he's a gold mine waiting to be panned. Covering the Racers next to MSU alums at the Murray Ledger and Times and the Murray State News has also provided great context and a unique perspective to the program. Then there are the stories from the streets that captivate you. A fan's first game at Racer Arena. A fan's last game at Racer Arena.

I count myself as just one of many who have been privileged to share the stories of the Racers. Archives at *The Paducah Sun* show the Racers have been news and newsworthy for decades. And as long as the stories continue, the Racers will continue to live out Murray State history.

Voices of the Racers

by Will Aubrey

The first Racer basketball game to be broadcast in some fashion appears to have been the 1936 Southern Intercollegiate Athletic Association tournament final against Western Kentucky in Bowling Green, a game Murray State won 28-26. There was no radio station in Murray at the time, so the game was broadcast over telephone lines to a crowd gathered in Lovett Auditorium.

WNBS began broadcasting in the 1940's and Troy Glidewell became the first voice of Murray State athletics.

"I remember Troy," longtime Racer fan Gearl Suiter said. "I was just a kid at the time but we listened to the games on the radio when we couldn't go and I always thought he was a good announcer. Of course he was Murray State all the way but we liked that and there was no TV back then so we depended on the radio. He did a heck of a job."

Then in 1957 Chuck Shuffett took over the play-by-play duties after he purchased WNBS.

Shuffett had gotten his start at a station in Glasgow, Ky.

"I auditioned for a job as an announcer and when they hired me they told me that I would also be calling ballgames, which was something I had never done," he said. "A month or so later they told me I had a game on Friday night. Well, I thought that was peculiar because most places don't start basketball in early September.

"It turned out that I was supposed to do a football game. I had never even seen a football game. So I called the first football game I ever saw and I went on to do basketball, too."

Rex Alexander was the head coach at MSU when Shuffett took over as the Voice of the Racers. But Alexander was replaced by Cal Luther in 1958.

"In my opinion Cal was the best coach we ever had," he declared. "He had less to work with than modern coaches. And of course he got paid a lot less.

"He was extremely fiery on the sideline, at practice, and after games if we lost. There were times I had to walk him down after games the way you would a race horse and we became very good friends."

Anyone who does play-by-play will tell you the biggest downside of the job is travel. But no matter how bad announcers have it now, it was far worse in Shuffett's day.

In 1963 the Racers played defending national champion Loyola of Chicago in a first round NCAA tournament game in Evanston, Ill. But they almost didn't make it to the arena.

"We were going to go up there on a train but there was a flood and the train couldn't get across the river at Wickliffe," Shuffett recalled. "We finally managed to get some kind of transportation to Carbondale and we rode the train from there.

"We jumped out ahead of Loyola 22-8 and a broadcaster from Mutual Radio the following day said 'Murray State was beating Loyola handily until the referees took charge.' And I agreed with that. Most people who ever heard me do a ball game knew I thought I was a better official than I was a broadcaster."

The names of players from those days roll off of Shuffett's tongue with ease – Skeeter Sullens, Scott Schlosser, Jim Jennings, Hector Blondette…

"I remember Hector very well," Shuffett said. "He was a great passer. He never gave away what he was going to do with his eyes. We went to play Eastern Kentucky and he stayed out beyond curfew so the morning of the game Cal told me to take Hector to the bus station and buy him a ticket home. And he said not to give him any money. I thought that would be the last we ever saw of Hector but he played in the next game."

There were, of course, lighthearted moments along the way.

"We were down at Middle Tennessee one year and the guy who did play-by-play for Middle sent an exotic dancer to grab me by the neck during the game," Shuffett said smiling. "She was a lady of considerable physical endowment and it was kind of embarrassing."

Shuffett stopped doing the games in 1975 and several people did play-by-play over the next few years. Then Darrell Gibson took over in 1981.

"I was a Kentucky Wildcat fan when I was a kid," Gibson admitted. "I listened to Cawood Ledford and Ralph Hacker, and every once in a while there would be a college basketball game on television.

"When I moved to this area I started listening to Chuck Shuffett and Bob Swisher do the Racer games. I listened to a Murray-Western game when Western had Jim McDaniels and I thought, 'I've got to go watch these guys play.' And once I had been to Racer Arena I was hooked. No arena I've ever been in could match it for atmosphere. And after that I bled Blue and Gold and I didn't care anything about the Wildcats."

Gibson did color on Calloway County basketball games when he was in high school. And then he worked at WCBL in Benton calling Marshall County baseball and basketball.

"Sam Parker started a new station here in Murray – WSJP," Gibson said. "And although WNBS did the Murray State games they didn't have exclusive rights. So Sam asked me if I'd come to work for him and do the games. And I said, 'When do we start?'"

Gibson took over the play-by-play duties shortly after Ron Greene replaced Fred Overton as head basketball coach at Murray State. Overton had suffered through two losing seasons in his three-year tenure and the Racers were 8-17 in his final year.

"Ron's signature was the four-to-score," Gibson said. "At first people didn't like it and then we started winning and it become the grandest thing. We'd spread it out and the fans would go wild.

"He never seemed comfortable with a lead until the game was over though. One time after a game I was interviewing him and I said, 'Well, it wasn't pretty but it was a win.' And he replied gruffly: 'I remember when it didn't have to be pretty.' I never said that again."

Greene turned the Racers into a winner again in fairly short order with players like Lamont Sleets and Tony Slaughter.

"I remember Sleets going up for a slam dunk on an alley-oop," Gibson said. "He was listed at 5-10 but he wasn't that tall. On that play though he was looking down at the basket.

"Tony Slaughter was very tall and had long arms. He didn't usually start but one night after a game Ron and I were talking and I told him the game had seemed very sluggish and he said, 'That's why I put Tony in. I know when I put him in the game something is going to happen. I never know what. I don't know whether it's going to be really good or really bad but I know the game is going to change.

"I think Ron really brought class back to Racer basketball and I don't think I've ever seen a coach who hated losing any more than he did."

Like Shuffett, Gibson was occasionally on the receiving end of a prank.

"Danny Roberts used to do TV work for Murray State and he'd sometimes do color with me," Gibson recalled. "One time I had a really bad sore throat. So he disappeared for a few minutes and when he came back he told me he had something to help my throat. So he set something wrapped in a paper towel down in front of me. It was one of those urinal deodorizers. I hit the air laughing and it took me a while to recover."

One player who consistently victimized the Racers in those days was Akron's Joe Jacubick.

"He was the most unusual ballplayer I ever saw," Gibson said. "The first time I saw Akron warm up I thought he was somebody that they just allowed to dress out. He looked as uncoordinated as anyone I had ever seen. And he would light us up for 40+ points and double digit assists every time we played."

In addition to Roberts, Chad Stewart, Bob Swisher, Larry Crouse, and Randy Herndon did color with Gibson.

"I don't think there was a better technical guy in the field than Randy," Gibson said. "When he did color with me he made my job so much easier. And when he took over the play-by-play job he was great at that as well.

"I miss doing play-by-play but I still do it in my head when I watch a game. I don't miss the travel though. I really don't miss being the first one there down on my hands and knees looking for telephone line and power outlets. And I really, really don't miss being the last one to leave.

Herndon took over the play-by-play duties in the fall of 1986.

"I did some high school games in the early 80's, some for Murray and some for Calloway," he said. "I worked at the radio station and had an interest in sports so I just kind of stumbled into it. It seemed like a fun thing to do.

Herndon's tenure paralleled that of MSU head coach Steve Newton.

"He wasn't animated on the sideline like some coaches are," Herndon recalled. "Some coaches wear their feelings on their sleeves but he wasn't like that. He could be stern with his players when he needed to though."

The signature moment of Herndon's career was calling the victory over North Carolina State in the 1988 NCAA tournament

"That was one of the most memorable events in my entire life," he said. "No one knew who Murray State was and the players felt like they were being overlooked. The other teams stayed in nice hotels and they put us in dorm rooms on campus.

"I was nervous before the game because I didn't want to sound like an idiot. But it's hard to separate your emotional ties to the team from your description of the action. Of course, you aren't supposed to be an objective voice. You're the *Voice of the Racers*, not a CBS announcer. And it's far more interesting to listen to an announcer who lets his emotion show than one who doesn't.

"It was pandemonium when they won and honestly I had to choke back tears to talk through that. They hadn't been there in so long and getting a win over Jimmy Valvano's team? He had become a coaching legend. I got to record a pregame interview with him and I thought just doing that was pretty cool."

The Racers followed that victory with a three point loss to eventual national champion Kansas.

"We gave them the closest game they had in the tournament although at the time no one expected Kansas to win it all," Herndon said. "But a few weeks later you look back and say: 'Wow!' That team found ways to win all year long even when it looked hopeless. They were down 16 points against Eastern Kentucky late in the second half and came back and won it. They did that several times. They just found ways to win.

"When I think about all the excitement I miss it," he said. "I think Neal Bradley does an excellent job

though. He's much better than anything I ever did and better than a lot of the guys at bigger schools."

Bradley took over for Herndon in 1991 but like Gibson he started life as a Kentucky fan.

"All my friends were UK fans and I was too," he said. "And then when I was about 12 a friend of mine had tickets to a Murray State game and asked if I wanted to go."

It just happened to be the same Murray-Western game that provided Gibson with his introduction to Racer basketball.

"Western was nationally ranked and it was an absolute zoo that night," Bradley said. "We had to wait about an hour to get into the building. It was one of the greatest games ever played in Racer Arena and I don't think I've cared about UK ever since.

"I could barely get WNBS where I lived so I listened to Chuck Shuffett whenever I could. I thought he did a great job. He painted a great picture and I became a Racer fan by listening to him. I never thought I'd be doing something like that myself."

Bradley took over play-by-play duties the same year that Scott Edgar took over as head coach.

"I got one year of Popeye Jones, his senior year," Bradley said. "Edgar was the new coach and he wanted to press and run. He wasn't going to feature Popeye but they started 3-9 so he decided maybe they should give the ball to the big guy and we wound up going to the NCAA tournament.

"Of all the teams over the years my favorite was the team that played Duke in the NCAA because they achieved more than I ever thought they could. In retrospect they may have just been better players than anyone thought at the start of the year."

No one gave the Racers a chance in that 1997 match-up with the powerful Blue Devils.

"Everyone expected annihilation, but Vincent Rainey just missed a mid-court shot at the end that would have sent it into overtime," Bradley said. "At one point in that game a Duke player ran by me and called out to a teammate, 'You've got to help me! I can't guard that guy!' He was talking about Rainey."

As *Voice of the Racers,* Bradley got to see a side of the players and coaches that most fans never see.

"When Marcus Brown was a senior he got on a hot streak and it started after he had come to talk to us before a game," he recalled. "So he started to come and visit with us before each game. And of course he was on the post game show a lot so we got to know him pretty well.

"I remember after one game he asked us to make it brief because he had to study for a test. So I asked him what subject it was in and told me it was a swimming test. I asked him if he could swim and when he said he could I told him he shouldn't have any trouble passing it."

There have been times when even *The Voice* had to keep his mouth shut though.

"Mick Cronin's first year we had a chance to break into the Top-25 and we went up to Eastern Illinois and lost," Bradley said. "Well, a couple of players were laughing in the back of the bus after the game. So Mick walks back there and asks what's so funny. Of course they didn't have an answer.

"He was really angry and he told them they had just lost to the worst team in Division I college basketball and he couldn't imagine what could be so funny. Well, I had looked at the Sagarin ratings earlier that day and Morehead was actually below EIU in the rankings but I didn't think that was a good time to point it out."

Bradley has been doing play by play for Murray State for such a long time that he's become an institution. To Racer fans he's a legend, ever bit the equal of Cawood Ledford. It's a status he had no thought of attaining at the outset.

"Oh gosh no!" he exclaimed. "I had no idea I'd be doing this for 20 years. I thought if I could do it for four or five years it would be amazing."

Now people even have some of his famous calls on their cell phones as ring tones.

"It's a little odd hearing that," he admitted. "But it's flattering that anyone would want my voice as their ring tone."

Shuffett, Gibson, Herndon and Bradley – the *Voices of the Racers* – are as big a part of the Racer Nation as any player or coach. Their voices still echo through our minds and make our pulse quicken.

"Jumper for the win. Good! It's good! It's good! The Racers win on the jumper by Danero Thomas. A dogpile in the end zone! We're dancing and extending the stay in San Jose!"

Cheerleaders

Ginger Adams

by Will Aubrey

On Saturday, March 17, 1995 the Murray State Racers played North Carolina in a first round NCAA tournament game in Tallahassee, Fla. They threw a scare into the Tarheels, but came up just a little short in the end, losing 80-70.

The next day tragedy struck the Racer family when a van carrying a group of cheerleaders back to Murray crashed on I-24, near Cadiz. Press reports indicated that the crash occurred after the tread on the drivers' side rear tire separated, causing the driver to lose control of the vehicle. The van rolled over several times before it came to rest in an upright position.

All 12 cheerleaders and their sponsor were treated at area hospitals. Eight of the 13 had been released by Monday. Eventually all but one would recover. Junior Ginger Adams died on March 24th at Vanderbilt University Medical Center.

Adams was a local girl, a graduate of Calloway County High School where she had been co-captain of the cheerleading squad. She was the daughter of Hank and Joanna Adams and the sister of Scott Adams.

CCHS principal Jerry Ainley told the *Ledger and Times*, "She was a very vibrant, outgoing girl. She had a light in her eyes – an All-American girl that any parent would be proud to have as a daughter."

The *Ledger* went on to quote former Calloway County basketball player Monica Evans Hodges, "My senior year when I played basketball the cheerleaders made individual scrapbooks for each of us. Ginger made mine for me and covered it with material and lace.

"It had clippings from every game that we had and she took the time to cut them all out. She really took a lot of time to do this for me."

Adams graduated in the top-10 of her class at CCHS and continued to excel in her studies at Murray State. She had a 4.0 grade point average at the time of the wreck and she was third runner-up in the Miss Murray State pageant.

"She was a typical cheerleader," her brother recalled. "She was always bubbly, and excited and jumping around. She wanted to be an English teacher and go back to Calloway and teach."

A scholarship in Adams name has been established at Murray State for sophomores, juniors, or seniors majoring in education.

A Hilltopper's Look at MSU

by Gary P. West

The phone rang in my Bowling Green home back in 1973. It was Dr. Dino Curris, the relatively new president at Murray State.

"Our Sports Information Director, Joe Tom Ervin is taking a leave of absence and I am wondering if you would like to come down and fill in for him for a few months?" Dino asked.

I had been a fraternity brother of Dino's at the University of Kentucky so he was well aware of my interest in sports writing, and being a smart man he probably figured I couldn't mess things up too much in two or three months.

Of course I accepted his offer and it was indeed a life altering experience, especially when it came to new friends.

Now keep in mind that although I had graduated from U.K., I began my college career at Western. I was a Hilltopper through and through. However, the Murray experience gave me a new "my team."

Eastern vs. Western. Forget it. "Game On" was when Western and Murray played in anything, and I'll give you an example.

In the early 1960's Coach Bill Ferguson's cross-country team was a dominating force in the OVC, But Western's new, brash, cocky track coach Tom Ecker had his sights on dethroning the Racer runners. Ecker had been my track coach at Elizabethtown High School, and because of our relationship, when he saw me on campus one day he asked me if I wanted to have some fun. Hey, I was all about fun, still am. He asked me if a couple of my high school buddies had gone to school at Murray. I told him they had, and with that here's the scheme he laid out:

"Have them send a telegram from Murray saying they are going to run our butts in the ground at the conference meet, and sign it Bill Ferguson and the Murray cross-country team," Ecker told me.

I made the call to them from his office. They thought it was funny and agreed to do it. The next day I was in the team's locker-room when Ecker walked in and in a cool, calculating way paced around the room mumbling to himself, occasionally allowing the words arrogance, audacity, and superior to be easily heard. Some of the Western runners fell into Ecker's web by asking what was wrong.

"I don't want to even tell you, but if you really want to know, here it is," he said while showing them the telegram."

It worked. The Western runners were incensed and the record will show that Western pulled off the upset.

Years later after Coach Ferguson and I became friends while I was at Murray, I told him of Ecker's scheme.

"I knew something funny had to happen, he said, shaking his head." There's no way they should have beaten us."

There's the often told story of Coach Diddle's radio interview the day before a Murray game. He was very concerned about the rebounding of 6'10" All-American Dick Cunningham.

Keep in mind that Diddle had his own way of talking, often getting first and last names mixed up. When the interviewer asked him what Western needed to do to win against Murray, Diddle matter-of-factly said, "We've got to stop the big Dick boy if we want to have a chance."

I'll never forget a call I got from Racer basketball coach Fred Overton after I was no longer at Murray. He was recruiting Warren East all-stater Jerry Lee Britt, brother of Hilltopper great Johnny Britt.

"Western is not recruiting him," Fred told me. A quick call to Western's coach Jim Richards, verified that, so I made a couple of calls to Jerry's home and set up an appointment for Fred and I to meet with his mother. When we arrived, Jerry and his mom invited us in. By the time Fred got through laying it out, and then with a couple of halleluiah's thrown in for good measure, heck, I wanted to play.

"You're my man, you'll run the show, the only time you'll come out of the game is when you tell me you

one of them quickly picked up a local paper searching for more exotic entertainment than might be found in west Kentucky. He found it. Excitedly, he told his friends that Sally Rand, then the nation's famous burlesque queen, was performing. It didn't take much coaxing for all of them to agree that since Murray was the overwhelming favorite to win the first game, they would all go to see Sally. Their hasty decision was not a good one. Murray was upset that night, so the chagrined boys returned home vowing to never tell anyone about what they had done. Like most such vows, that one was quickly broken, and as the years passed the story grew with each telling.

Barker loved to tell the story, and said, "You never saw an old man move as fast as Bradburn did when he thought Diddle was coming after him."

When recalling devoted fans, who can pass up Pete Waldrop, who was born just a few blocks from the Murray State campus?

Pete, Hal Houston, and Bennie Purcell for many years drove together for almost all away games. One day, after an exciting practice, Pete returned to his home on Olive Street. Bennie stopped by his house to see him and said to Pete, "I believe you like Murray State Basketball more than I do." Pete shot right back, "You're right. I'm just eat up with it."

Another story involved Bill Barker directly. Murray was playing Evansville and Cal Luther was coaching. His assistant, Bennie Purcell, was off on a recruiting trip, so there was no assistant on the bench. Cal got after the officials rather heavily that night, and in the last quarter was ejected from the game. As Luther was leaving he motioned for Bill Barker to take over. Bill came out of the stands and coached the remainder of the game.

Sometimes fans get so excited with the condiments of following the Racers, they fail to devour the main course. Greg McKeel recalls a time in 1951 when several local Murray men, whose names will not be called, all piled in a car and headed for the NIAA tournament in Kansas City.

When the Murray boys arrived in Kansas City,

An entirely new set of fans is quickly evolving as the internet becomes intertwined with Murray State basketball. No longer does distance separate the true fan from his or her passion for the Racers. Thai Racer, Moline Racer, Barnsley Racer, Cowboy Racer, Racer Power, and Smidge, to name a few, join a loyal internet fan crew on a message board constantly discussing Racer hoops. Thai Racer, whose real name is Kitt Chu, lives around the world in Thailand and is an avid follower of the Racers. He is an incredible researcher, and shares many fascinating obscure facts with the Racer cyberspace faithful.

We could never forget those auto dealers in west Kentucky who have provided cars for coaches, nor can we forget those who advertise year after year to support the team. To name one would not be fair to the others. Fan support is most evident in those large numbers of fans who make annual donations and buy season tickets year after year.

The beauty of the Murray State fans is that they seem to just keep on coming. Some of the younger fans, who no doubt someday will rewrite this history and include other chapters about legendary coaches, future retired jerseys, and championships yet to come, will continue the tradition.

There are also those fans who are either Murray State alumni or who adopted the Racers early in life as "their team" but now view the team from afar, who never ever lost their affection for "their team." Those moments of memory are more poignant when great victories occur. One such moment was beating Vanderbilt in the first round of the NCAA Tournament in March of 2010.

Don Easley, a portfolio manager for T.Rowe Price mutual funds in Baltimore, memorializes the feelings of those who viewed the Racers from afar on that special day in 2010.

"Twenty years ago this fall, I left Murray, Kentucky for a small liberal arts college just outside of Philadelphia. Since then, I've lived in New York, Boston, Chicago, and now, Baltimore. I've endured the good-hearted ribbing and downright provincial ignorance of those with condescending attitudes towards small towns, towards Kentucky, and towards the South in general.

With time, my reaction has morphed from one of anger to one of pride. What I have come to realize is that my whole life has been shaped by Murray, Kentucky. To deny it or to ridicule it is to deny or to ridicule myself. I see the world through the eyes of a little town nestled neatly in the crib of the Jackson Purchase. And for that, I am grateful, indebted, and proud.

For me, Murray State basketball has become my connection to home. The Racer fight song is a cavalry call for a group of core fans whose loyalty knows no bounds. When the blue and the gold come through that tunnel, it means something. It's tradition of a school that expects to win, that expects excellence. For those who really care, it seeps deep into their being to the point that it becomes part of who they are as a person.

For better or for worse, Racer basketball has its own heartbeat that powers a whole town, puts it on its back, and gallops forward. In the whirlwind of the past few days, Racer fans have been taken on a joyride; the sheer, unadulterated ebullience of a last second victory over an SEC powerhouse. I danced on the couch like a little kid. My wife looked at me quizzically and said,

'I've never seen you show so much emotion.' My reply, 'Honey, you just don't understand.'

Danero Thomas, you will forever have a safe place in the spacious house of Racer legends. No matter what happens in your life and well into your old age, you will always have the memory of 'The Shot,' a time when the eyes of America were on you. So few will ever have that experience. I acknowledge that there are many fans much more loyal to the team than myself. Distance brings with it a cruel objectivity. I've cursed them, criticized them, and blamed them, but I never left them. In the end, this tight-knit group of warriors can raise their heads in triumph. To the players, from a fan who has derived so much joy from your exploits, I love you guys."

We have been able to mention only a few as representative of the thousands of fans who have contributed to the rich history of Murray State Basketball. They bought tickets, made contributions to the Foundation, gave their time, and unselfishly contributed their money for countless projects that support the program. Then there were those who simply showed up and added a smiling face and a dose of optimism to those who slave in the trenches to make this program what it has become.

There are so many that quietly go on their way, but when the doors are open they are there to cheer on the Racers. They buy seats, drink in the excitement of the game, and go back to their homes or places of work or play with stories of the game, pride in their players and coaches, and pride in their college that makes all of this dream in their midst possible.

The quieter ones remind us of a passage from the famous English statesman, Edmund Burke, who said, "Because half a dozen grasshoppers under a fern make the field ring with their importunate chink, whilst thousands of great cattle, reposed beneath the shadow of the British Oak, chew the cud and are silent, pray do not imagine that those who make the noise are the only inhabitants of the field." So it is with Racer fans. A few of us make the noise, but the thousands of quieter fans who show up at every game and event supporting their Racers are the real power of our brilliant fan base.

Gearl Suiter

Gearl Suiter

by Will Aubrey

A few select fans are so closely identified with a particular team that they become iconic themselves. When you see Jack Nicholson you think of the Los Angeles Lakers. You can't see Spike Lee without thinking of the New York Knicks. And at the college level, any time you saw Bill Keightley you thought of the Kentucky Wildcats.

Gearl Suiter was as iconic a symbol of Murray State basketball as Dunker himself. When you saw Gearl your mind immediately turned to Racer basketball. And he was always more than happy to discuss it with you.

Gearl summarized his devotion to Racer basketball during a 2010 interview, "My family was always all about Racer basketball. When we got together at Thanksgiving and Christmas that's what we talked about. It has been a big part of my life. Family, church, and then Racer basketball."

Unfortunately, Gearl passed away on June 8, 2013. But his memory lives on.

"My grandad, Elroy Suiter, was a big Murray State fan and he took my dad to the games when he was a kid," Gearl's son Lindy Suiter said. "Then my dad took me and my brother Larry to the games. He went to almost all the games, home and away, until his health began to fail him. And he went to a lot of the practices too.

"He was always loyal to the players and coaches. If you said anything bad about one of the players or the coaches you'd have to answer to him. He was a father figure to many of the players and he was good friends with many of the coaches, especially Cal Luther, Scott Edgar and Tevester Anderson."

Remembering Gearl Suiter...

"He put as much care, concern and passion into our program as anybody. He took every win or loss the way a coach would. I remember after one loss he took it worse than I did," Scott Edgar said with a laugh. "He was the heart and soul of the Racer Nation."

"Gearl was Mr. Murray State," Tevester Anderson said. "He was like a father to some of our kids. He did whatever he could to promote Murray State. And he did it the right way, under the rules. He was a special person."

"It was like all of Murray State's jerseys said Suiter on the back," MSU radio announcer Neal Bradley said. "Those were his boys out there, whether they had a good game or not. He was behind them 100 percent."

"I'll always remember watching a scrimmage with Gearl back when Tevester Anderson was the head coach," Racer Insider head writer Will Aubrey said. "Gearl was yelling at the officials and one of them came over and asked why he was doing that at a scrimmage. And he said, 'I've got to get in practice too!"

"He's been a basketball fan of Murray State since at least when I was here," the Racers' "living legend" Bennie Purcell said. "And that was way back in 1948. His dad took him and his brothers to all of the games, and I really remember them coming to the away games.

"When you think of Murray State basketball, you definitely think of Gearl Suiter and how he supported this program. It's tough to lose Gearl."

Banner Years Patrons

Proud To Be A Racer Publications and Acclaim Press would like to thank the following patrons whose generous financial contributions made this book possible.

Gold Level Patrons

Dean & Nona Akridge
Dr. Richard Blalock
Mike & Caroline Cappock
Bob & Jennifer Cornelison
Harold G. & Kelly Doran Jr.
Don Easley
Sid & Melissa Easley
Jim & Norma Frank
Gary & Van Haverstock
Charles & Anne Hoke
Drs. Hal & Tara Houston
Chuck & Sarah Jones
Ricky & Adam Lamkin
Greg McKeel – McKeel Equipment
Bill & Irene Morgan
Steve & Kathy Newton
Steve & Lori Parker
Bennie Purcell
Alice Rouse – *Murray Ledger & Times*
W. Hunt & Jennye Smock
Larry & Susan Suiter
Lindy & Lisa Suiter
C. Dwain Taylor – Dwain Taylor Chevrolet-Buick-GMC-Cadillac
David Taylor – Taylor Bus Sales, Taylor Chrysler Dodge Jeep Ram
Dr. Randy Taylor – Taylor Family Dental
Dick & Jan Weaver
Jimmy & Joanna Wilder
J.D. & Debbie Williams
Dr. William & Sharon Green Wilson

Silver Level Patrons

Bill Beasley
Stephen C. Bell
Phil & Amberly Billington
Tommy Blair
Billy Chumbler
Howie & Meg Crittenden
Howie Crittenden Jr.
Terry Darnall
Dr. Melvin W. Deweese
Mike & Marilyn Dill
Jerry B. Duncan – Murray Mold & Dye
Dr. Steve & Janet Farmer
Frank Fazi
Dr. Scott Foster – Calloway County Chiropractic
Marty & Amy Futrell – A&F Warehousing
Bob Hargrove – The Murray Bank
Ronnie Hesselrode
James R. Kevil
Bill & Kathy Kopperud – Kopperud Realty
Cal Luther
Len & Willine Mahony
Bobby & Shirley Martin
Dr. Jerry W. Mayes
Herb McPherson
Dr. Dan & Laura Miller
Ronnie Moore
Kevin & Indya Newell
Robert & Marie Norsworthy
Tim Perkins – Perkins MotorPlex
Gene W. & Taffen Ray
Jack & Janice Rose
Kenny & Beverly Roth
Heath & Heather Scott
Scott & Pat Seiber
Chad & Betty Stewart
Gearl & Jeanette Suiter
Peggy Taylor
Zak & Alysha Taylor
James H. Thomas & Elizabeth Williams
David & Vickie Travis
Jack L. & Edna Vaughn
Mark & Jennifer Waldrop
Pete & Joy Waldrop
Randy & JoAnn Wilder
Dale H. Willis – Willis Insurance

Bronze Level Patrons

Sue Adams
Tom Adams
Chip & Shannan Adkins
Clyde & Marilyn Adkins
Russ & Fran Adkins
Stuart Alexander – Kentucky Farm Bureau
Frank Allen
Lance Allison
Steve Andrus
Henry Armstrong
Will & Marilyn Aubrey
Dr. Ronald & Jane Babb
Art & Anna Bailey
Brad & Deann Barnett
Joe & Jane Barnett
Ralph & Kathy Barnwell Jr.
Steve Barrett
Matt Bartholomy – Matt B's Main Street Pizza
Jim & Phyllis Baurer
Evan & Allison Beck
George Bell
Don & Jean Bennett
Hughes & Hilda Bennett
Claire Benton
Mark Bernsen
Bob Berry – B&C Farms
Bob & Jeannie Billington
Mason & Wilma Billington
Robert Billington Jr.
Dr. Michael L. & Sharon Bobo
Howard & Tony Boone – Boone's Cleaners
Curtis & Connie Boyd Jr.
Max & Barbara – Brandon
Tony & Lisa Brannon
Tab Brockman
John A. & Marilyn Brooks
Marcus Brown
David Buckingham
Andy & Ginny Buhler
Ed & Emily Burge
Jordan Burge
Andrew & Tanya Cain
Mike Calhoun
David & Donna Carr
Michael & Emily Carr
Adam & Lisa Carver – Sirloin Stockade
Jim & Sue Cash
James Cass
Mike Cathey
Skip Chambers – Big Apple Café
Joe Chaney
Don Cherry
Dr. Cathy Christopher
Ronald & Ann Churchill
Chad Cochran – State Farm Insurance
Howard & Joann Coy
Arvin & Martha Crafton
Everett L. Craig
Don & Berniece Crawford
Casey & Dr. Nikki Crosser
Stephen Crouch
Billy Dan Crouse – Billy D. Crouse Auto Brokers
Justin & Heidi Crouse
T. Christian Crouse
Terry Curtis
Jeff Curtsinger
Joe & Amy Darnall
R.C. Davidson
Walt Davis
Willis & Ella Deitz
Joe & Linda Dick
Shawn & Jennifer Dunnaway
Brian & Amy Edwards
Don Edwards
Charles L. & Kate Eldridge
Dr. James & Kay Ellis
Otis H. & Barbara Erwin
John H. Espey
Danny & Norma Evitts
Jimmy & Rhonda Felts
Terry Fergason
James A. Fischer
Derrick Flowers
Dr. H.W. & Beverly Ford
Ron & Lashlee Foster
Billy Fryer
Gregg & Cathy Garland
Don Gibbs
Darrell & Dianne Gibson
Ronnie Gibson
Johnnny Gingles

Ron Gladden – Zax/Murray Banquet Center
Benny Goheen
Glen Green
Jim & Patsy Buchanan Green
Leo Green Jr.
Ron & Aileen Greene
Kenney Hammonds
Karol Hardison – University Store
Lee & Laci Hargis
Bob & Kathy Hargrove
James L. Harmon
Rabon & Joyce Harper
Virgil & Anna Roth Harris
Lochie Hart
Doug Hawthorne
Larry Heflin
Woody & Donna Herndon
Bill & Angela Higdon
Tom Higgins
David & Janet Higgs
J. Carol Hill
Tyler Holloway
Dr. Bill & Sandy Holman
Ricky & Vicky Hood
Gary Hooker
David & Marilyn Hornback
Jerry Howard
Carroll Hubbard
Dr. J. Jeffrey Hughes
Chuck & Paula Hulick
Eddie & Lanette Hunt
Michael W. Hunt
Derek Hunter
Harold & Kathey Hurt
Dr. Richard & Mary Hurt
Karl & Sarah Hussung
Cindy Hutson
Ron Hutson
John & Shannon Imes
Kenny Imes – Imes-Miller Funeral Home, Heritage Family Funeral Home
Robert L. Jackson
Joe Pat James
Danny Jarrett
Jim Jennings
Barry & Mary Gail Johnson
Dr. Conrad H. Jones
Darren & Danette Jones
Donald E. & Bonnie Jones
Popeye Jones
Brett & Jennifer Justice
Jim & Joetta Kelly
David Kimbell
David R. & Cindy King
Brandon Kirkham
Richard & Annie Knight
Dr. David W. & Peggy Koelsch
Roger Korte
David & Dottie Kraemer
Kevin Kroeper
Dean Lampkins
Jeremy & Lauralee Latimer
Pat Latimer
Eddie Lewis
Tim & Sandra Lusk
Jeff Majors
John P. Mancuso
Don & Brenda Mann
Joe Manning
Bourke Mantle
Jeff Martin
Hugh Graves Massey
Tom S. Maddox Jr.
Paul Matthia
Terry & Janice McClard
Michael & Donna McClure
Don & Betty McCord
Jerry McCoy – Jerry's Custom Cabinets
Lila McCuiston
Marilyn McCuiston
Bobby McDowell
Robert H. McGaughey III
Greg McNutt
Lauraine McPherson
Peggy L. Meriedeth
Mike & Betsy Miller
Darrell & Peggy Mitchell
David Moore
David Morgan
Mike & Jeanie Morgan
David Moss
Col. Harv & Becky Newton
Jay & La Shay Newton
Royce & Julie Newton
Judge Christopher Shea Nickell
Rickie & Annette Nimmo
Billy Rue & Janice Nix
James & Brenda Nix
Wade & Bib Northington
Dr. George & Patsy Oakley
Ronald Orr
Charles & Mary Outland
Fred Overton
Aaron Page
Tony Page
Clint D. & Carla Parish
Dan & Mitzi Parker
Barry & Melissa Paschall
Dr. William Nall Pasco
Deon Payne
Marc & Belinda Peebles
Gene Pendleton
Eric & Regina Penniston
Ken & Wanda Peterson
Dr. James B. & Terri Pickens
Steve Pierson
Bud Poat
Ronnie & Caroline Pool
Stuart & Donna Poston
Denny Potts
Jamie Potts
James Preston
Harold & Rosemary Prow
Del Purcell
Ken Purcell
Mel Purcell
Johnny Quertermous
Paul & Rosanne Radke
David & Camela Ramey
Allen & Becky Rayburn
Bill & Jan Rayburn
J.D. & Mary Lou Rayburn
Johnny & Carolyn Reagan
Dave & Kate Reeves
Jason C. Riley
Steve Riley
Charles Ripley
William E. & Ann Robinson
David F. Rogers
Glenn & Sandra Rogers
Bill Rouse
Lita Rushing
Frank R. Saul
Roger & Adelaide Schoenfeldt
Scott & Kathleen Schossler
John & Beth Sharpe
Peggy Shoemaker
Ed & Janis Shultz
Chris Shumate
Bert & Sharon Siebold
Raymond Sims
Scott & Catherine Sivills
Dewayne & Becky Smith
Beverly Solomon
Ray & Nancy Solomon
David & Jane Spahr
Don W. & Carolyn Lowe Sparks
Don & Norma Stephenson
Brian Stewart
Jim Story
Alan & Doris Stout
Mike & Martha Strickland
Joseph Suiter
Quitman Sullins
Steve Swain
Tim Swain
Todd Swain – Hungry Bear Restaurant & Fun Center
Shea & Brenda Sykes
Dan T. Taylor
Greg Taylor
Judge Jeff S. & Betty Taylor
Shirley Thomas
Tony Thompson
Bob & Teresa Thurman
Barney & Ann Thweatt
Jim & Anita Totten
Joel & Rhonda Tracy
Martin B. Tracy
Tim Tucker
Mike Turner
Sam & Susan Underwood
Dennis Utley
Dr. Glen & Joy Van Loon
Howard Dale Voss
Bo Walden
Mike & Kristen Wasielewski
John Weatherly
Bill & Cheryl Whitaker
Mark Whittington
Russ Whittington
Bart & Amy Wilder
Donnie & Gina Winchester
Dave & Janice Winder
Donna Witherspoon
Deborah Woolfolk
Ken Wray
Tony Wretlund
Mike & Cole Wyatt
John Yates
Keith York – York Funeral Home
Jimmy Young

Afterword

by Lindy Suiter

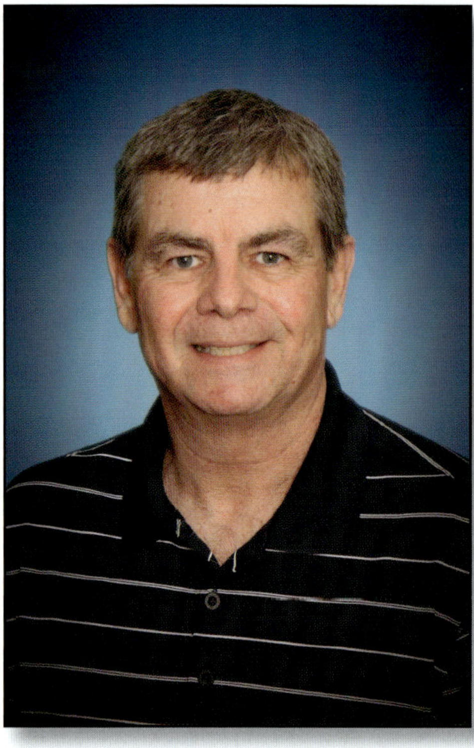

Murray State basketball has been part of the fabric of my life for as long as I can remember. I can recall sitting in our living room when I was in the first grade, listening to the radio as the Racers played Loyola of Chicago in the first NCAA Tournament in 1964.

My dad took me to Carbondale, Ill., in 1969 to watch Murray State play Marquette in the NCAA Tournament.

In my mind's eye I can still see Jimmy Young, Hector Blondet and Claude Virden run the floor at old Racer Arena.

I can still remember standing in line to get into Racer Arena to watch Murray State play Western Kentucky one night in 1971. I got to the arena at about 4:30 in the afternoon, and the line stretched all the way to Woods Hall. When the doors opened, it was a mad dash as everyone tried to get a seat.

I was in Lincoln, Neb., in 1988 when Murray State beat North Carolina State in the NCAA Tournament. What an unbelievable feeling that was.

It seems to me that it was yesterday when Aubrey Reese's heroic shot beat Southeast Missouri and sent the Racers to the NCAA Tournament in 1999. I'll never forget the jump shot Danero Thomas made to beat Vanderbilt in the NCAA Tournament in 2010.

Then, there was the thrill of the Racers being ranked the nation's No. 7 team in the 2011-12 season. And what can I say about last February's Murray State win against Saint Mary's in a BracketBusters game televised on ESPN? Dick Vitale was courtside at a packed CFSB Center, Racer fans were decked out in all kinds of costumes, and the atmosphere was electric.

What makes Racer basketball unique is the way the teams and the community become one big family. It's not just coaches coaching and players playing. It also involves people who care deeply about the Racer program.

When Murray State wins, we share in the joy with the coaches and the players. When Murray State loses, we feel their pain. Both emotions stay with us for a long time.

BANNER YEARS gives readers the opportunity to relive the many magical moments of Racer basketball – and the disappointments. And to feel Murray State legends like Bennie Purcell, Howie Crittenden, Cal Luther, Jeff Martin, Popeye Jones, Steve Newton and Marcus Brown are a part of their lives.

The book represents a labor of love for those who worked on it over a three-year period. My desire is that Racer fans enjoy the stories, the photos and the memorabilia you now have access to. It's your financial support that paved the way for *BANNER YEARS* to come to fruition.

Go Racers!

Authors

Will Aubrey

Will Aubrey has been the senior writer for the *Racer Insider* for 14 years and is the radio voice of the Calloway County Lakers. He spent two years as the radio voice of the Murray State University women's basketball team and has written free-lance articles for a variety of publications. He attended Murray State from 1976-1981. While attending MSU he wrote for the *Murray State News* and was an award-winning member of the Murray State Speech and Debate team. He was a national finalist in Extemporaneous Speaking. He met his wife Marilyn while both were Murray State students and they have been Racer fans ever since.

Sid Easley

Sid Easley is an attorney in Murray. He served as President of the Murray State Alumni Association and as Chairman of the Murray State Board of Regents for 12 years. Presently he is a member of the Murray State Foundation. He is married to the former Melissa Henry, an alumnus of MSU, and they have two sons, Eric and Don Easley. Sid was briefly a walk-on candidate for the Racer basketball team when Cal Luther was the head coach and Bennie Purcell was an assistant coach. Today, Sid and Bennie enjoy talking about Racer basketball and sometimes traveling to away games together.

Steve Parker

From student to alumnus to employee, Steve Parker has had a nearly three-decade relationship with Murray State. Through it all, he was, is and will always be a Racer basketball fan. Parker's association with Murray State began in 1985 when he enrolled as a freshman from St. Louis, Mo. Following graduation, he began covering the Racers as a sportswriter at the *Benton Tribune-Courier* and the *Murray Ledger & Times*. After a stint as sports editor at the *Ledger & Times*, Parker joined the MSU athletic department in 1996 as sports information director. He left the university in 2003 to pursue a career in private business. Parker now works for The Kingdom Trust Company and resides in Murray with his wife, Lori, and their daughter, Brooke. Lori and Brooke are, of course, fans of Racer basketball.

Kim Trevathan

A native of Murray and a Racer basketball fan since the late 1960s, Kim Trevathan is the author of three books: "Paddling the Tennessee River: A Voyage on Easy Water" (2001), Coldhearted River: A Canoe Odyssey Down the Cumberland" (2006), and "Liminal Zones: Where Lakes End and Rivers Begin" (2013). He got his MFA in creative writing from the University of Alabama, his MA in journalism from the University of Wyoming and his MA in English from the University of Illinois. He teaches writing at Maryville College in Maryville, Tenn. Trevathan says he has learned much about tennis and life from Murray State Hall of Fame honoree Bennie Purcell, who remains a mentor and inspiration.

Jimmy Wilder

Jimmy Wilder is a former sportswriter and Murray State sports information director who "retired" from his position as director of athletic development at UNC Asheville in the summer of 2004 and moved with his wife Joanna back to her hometown of Murray. Since their return to Kentucky, the Wilders have once again enjoyed being fans of Racer athletics and supporters of the university. "Banner Years" represents Wilder's first involvement with a nationally circulated book that he has been responsible for helping pull together, but it is not his first association with a book. While living in Asheville, N.C., he authored and edited former Southern Conference commissioner Dave Hart's biography titled "Dynamite Dave." Wilder is an alumnus of Arkansas State University with a BS degree in Journalism.

Index

The "Banner Years Patrons" on pages 362 and 363 do not appear in the index since they are in alphabetical order in their section.

CFSB CENTER
RACERS
Concessions
WOODCRAFTERS